FI
N

Sir
he
ing
Use the following tools to
information you need:

- The **Brief Contents** here lists all the parts and chapters in the handbook.

- The **Detailed Contents** inside the back cover shows the chapter sections as well as chapters and parts.

- The **Index** lists all handbook topics covered in alphabetic order. Find your topic, note the page number, and then turn to that page to locate your information quickly.

- **Quick Boxes** throughout the book give you an easy way to skim and access the most common and important issues that will come up as you write.

- The **Terms Glossary** at the end of the book defines important terms related to writing and grammar. Every word printed in SMALL CAPITAL LETTERS is defined in the glossary.

- **Proofreading Marks** and **Response Symbols** that your instructor may use to mark your writing appear on the last page of the book. Refer to these lists to find the section of the handbook that will help you edit and proofread your work.

- The **eText version** of the handbook provides many links to additional resources. For example,

  👁 Video tutorials show key concepts in writing, grammar, and research.

  〽● Audio podcasts explain common grammar and punctuation issues.

  ⚙ Exercises offer opportunities for online practice.

  🔍 Model documents provide examples of different kinds of writing.

Simon & Schuster
Handbook for Writers

Why Do You Need This New Edition?

Here are seven features that you'll find only in the new edition of the *Simon & Schuster Handbook for Writers:*

1. Eight new chapters provide advice on writing commonly assigned papers—personal essays, informative writing, process analysis, cause and effect analysis, textual analysis, arguments, proposal and solution essays, and evaluations. Each chapter helps you identify your audience and purpose, gives you a Frame chart to organize your paper, provides Sentence and Paragraph Guides to help you develop common writing moves, and presents an annotated model paper (Part 2).

2. A new chapter on evaluating sources provides five key questions to ask about each of your research sources so that you use only credible, reliable sources in your papers. Each question includes a chart that contrasts characteristics of reliable versus questionable sources as well as examples (Ch. 23).

3. An expanded chapter on using sources in a research paper helps you decide what to do when your sources agree, partly agree, or disagree with one another. Sentence and Paragraph Guides demonstrate common moves you can make to transition among different sources while building your own argument (Ch. 18).

4. A new chapter "Ten Troublesome Mistakes Writers Make" highlights the most common grammar and punctuation errors and examples and exercises help you identify and correct these errors in your own writing (Ch. 2).

5. A new chapter, "Writing About Readings," covers summary, response, analysis/interpretation, and synthesis essays, emphasizing how often assignments, not just in formal research papers, require writing about texts (Ch. 20).

6. Completely updated MLA, APA, CM, and CSE documentation styles show you how to document and cite your sources. Examples for electronic sources like e-readers, wikis, and tweets help you accurately cite increasingly common types of new sources (Chs. 25–27).

7. Media-rich eText versions of the handbook provide videos, animations, model documents, and exercises to create a rich, interactive learning experience. You can access additional resources online to help you write effectively and correctly.

PEARSON

Simon & Schuster
Handbook for Writers

TENTH EDITION

LYNN QUITMAN TROYKA

DOUGLAS HESSE

PEARSON

Boston Columbus Indianapolis New York San Francisco Upper Saddle River
Amsterdam Cape Town Dubai London Madrid Milan Munich Paris Montreal Toronto
Delhi Mexico City Sao Paulo Sydney Hong Kong Seoul Singapore Taipei Tokyo

Senior Acquisitions Editor: Lauren A. Finn
Senior Development Editor: Marion B. Castellucci
Editorial Assistant: Shannon Kobran
Executive Marketing Manager: Thomas DeMarco
Senior Supplements Editor: Donna Campion
Executive Digital Producer: Stefanie A. Snajder
Digital Manager: Janell Lantana
Digital Editor: Sara Gordus
Production Manager: Savoula Amanatidis
Project Coordination, Text Design, and Electronic Page Makeup: Laserwords

Cover Designer/Manager: John Callahan
Cover Image: *Enclosed Field with Rising Sun, Saint-Remy 1889* Vincent van Gogh (1853–1890/Dutch) Oil on canvas Private Collection, © SuperStock/SuperStock
Photo Researcher: Integra–New York
Senior Manufacturing Buyer: Dennis J. Para
Printer and Binder: R. R. Donnelley and Sons Company–Crawfordsville
Cover Printer: Lehigh-Phoenix Color Corporation–Hagerstown

For permission to use copyrighted material, grateful acknowledgment is made to the copyright holders on pp. C-1–C-2, which are hereby made part of this copyright page.

Library of Congress Cataloging-in-Publication Data
Troyka, Lynn Quitman
  Simon & Schuster handbook for writers / Lynn Quitman Troyka, Douglas Hesse. — 10th ed.
    p.cm.
  Includes index.
  ISBN 978-0-205-90360-3 (student ed.) — ISBN 0-205-90360-6 (student ed.)
  1. English language—Rhetoric—Handbooks, manuals, etc. 2. English language—Grammar—Handbooks, manuals, etc. 3. Report writing—Handbooks, manuals, etc. I. Hesse, Douglas Dean. II. Title. III. Title: Simon and Schuster handbook for writers. IV. Title: Handbook for writers.
    PE1408.T696 2012
    808'.042—dc23
                                                                                      2012030985

10 9 8 7 6 5 4 3 2 1— DOC —15 14 13 12

Student Edition
ISBN-10: 0-205-90360-6
ISBN-13: 978-0-205-90360-3

Instructor's Review Copy
ISBN-10: 0-321-84660-5
ISBN-13: 978-0-321-84660-0

PEARSON

www.pearsonhighered.com

In memory of David Troyka,
my sweetheart and
husband of 47 years

LYNN QUITMAN TROYKA

To Don and Coral Hesse

DOUG HESSE

FINDING WHAT YOU NEED ON A PAGE

The runninghead shows the last section on the current page.

Chapter and section

5G What works in writing a first draft?

Section heading indicates new section of a chapter.

Drafting means getting ideas onto paper or into the computer, in sentences and paragraphs. A draft is a version of the paper; experienced writers produce several drafts. The early ones focus on generating ideas, whereas later versions focus on developing and polishing ideas. But you can't polish something that doesn't exist, so your goal on the first draft is just producing words. Don't expect perfection; the pressure to "get it right the first time" can paralyze you.

Words in bold or SMALL CAPITAL LETTERS are discussed in various places in the book and are defined in the Terms Glossary.

Quick Boxes highlight key information.

Quick Box 4.6

Questions for analyzing genre

- What is the PURPOSE of the writing?
- Who is the apparent AUDIENCE?
- Are there clearly identified parts of individual works? Are there headings, for example?

NO **Approaching the island, a mountainous rock wall** was terrifying.

This sentence suggests that the mountainous wall was approaching the island.

YES Approaching the island, **we** saw a terrifying mountainous rock wall.

Examples show how to apply a rule.

ESOL Tip: If the cultural background of your readers differs from yours, you might find it difficult to estimate how much your readers know about your topic. To get a better idea of your readers' backgrounds, you might browse for information on the Internet or discuss your topic with people who might know more than you do about your readers' backgrounds. ●

ESOL icons call out information of particular use for multilingual students.

13. Article in a Newspaper with Print Version: Database

Hesse, Monica. "Falling in Love with St. Andrews, Scotland." *Washington Post* 24 Apr. 2011. *LexisNexis Academic.* Web. 3 Oct. 2011.

14. Article in a Newspaper with Print Version: Direct Online Access

Hesse, Monica. "Falling in Love with St. Andrews, Scotland." *Washington Post.* Washington Post, 22 Apr. 2011. Web. 3 Oct. 2011.

Citation examples are color-coded for clarity.

The runninghead shows the last section on the current page.

Chapter and section

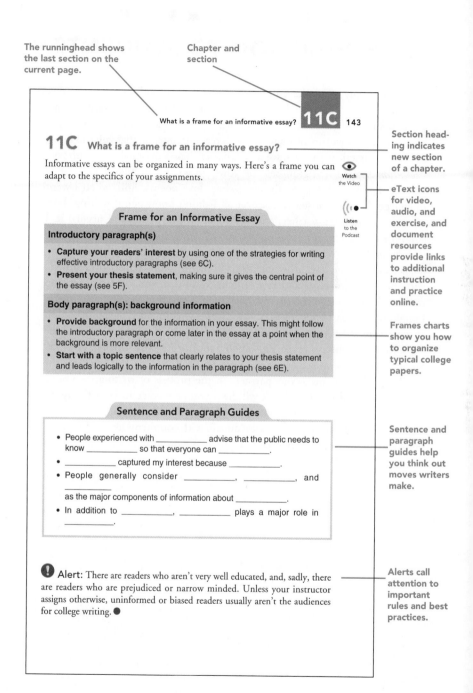

11C What is a frame for an informative essay?

Informative essays can be organized in many ways. Here's a frame you can adapt to the specifics of your assignments.

Watch the Video

Listen to the Podcast

Section heading indicates new section of a chapter.

eText icons for video, audio, and exercise, and document resources provide links to additional instruction and practice online.

Frame for an Informative Essay

Introductory paragraph(s)

- **Capture your readers' interest** by using one of the strategies for writing effective introductory paragraphs (see 6C).
- **Present your thesis statement**, making sure it gives the central point of the essay (see 5F).

Body paragraph(s): background information

- **Provide background** for the information in your essay. This might follow the introductory paragraph or come later in the essay at a point when the background is more relevant.
- **Start with a topic sentence** that clearly relates to your thesis statement and leads logically to the information in the paragraph (see 6E).

Frames charts show you how to organize typical college papers.

Sentence and Paragraph Guides

- People experienced with _____ advise that the public needs to know _____ so that everyone can _____.
- _____ captured my interest because _____.
- People generally consider _____, _____, and _____ as the major components of information about _____.
- In addition to _____, _____ plays a major role in _____.

Sentence and paragraph guides help you think out moves writers make.

Alert: There are readers who aren't very well educated, and, sadly, there are readers who are prejudiced or narrow minded. Unless your instructor assigns otherwise, uninformed or biased readers usually aren't the audiences for college writing. ●

Alerts call attention to important rules and best practices.

INTRODUCTION TO STUDENTS

As writers, many of you have much in common with both of us. Sure, we've been at it longer, so we've had more practice, and most rules have become cemented in our heads. However, we share with you a common goal: to put ideas into words worthy of someone else's reading time. So that you can know us better as practicing writers, we'd each like to share a personal story with you.

From Doug: I first glimpsed the power of writing in high school, when I wrote sappy—but apparently successful—love poems. Still, when I went to college, I was surprised to discover all I didn't know about writing. Fortunately, I had good teachers and developed lots of patience. I needed it. I continue to learn from my colleagues, my students, and my coauthor, Lynn.

From Lynn: When I was an undergraduate, questions about writing nagged at me. One day, browsing in the library, I found a dust-covered book with the words *handbook* and *writing* in its title. Such books weren't common in those days, so I read it hungrily. Back then, I never imagined that someday I might write such a book myself. Now that we've completed the tenth edition of the *Simon & Schuster Handbook for Writers*, I'm amazed that I ever had the nerve to begin. This proves to me—and I hope to you—that anyone can write. Students don't always believe that. I hope you will.

We welcome you as our partners in the process of writing. We hope that the pages of this handbook will help you give voice to your thoughts, in school and in life. Please know that you're welcome always to write us at 2LTROYKA@gmail.com or dhesse@du.edu with comments about this handbook and about your experiences as a writer. We promise to answer.

Lynn Quitman Troyka

Doug Hesse

PREFACE

This tenth edition of the *Simon & Schuster Handbook for Writers* provides all the information students need about writing, from writing college papers to using and documenting sources, from writing online to writing using visuals, and from mastering grammar to using correct punctuation. We designed the *Simon & Schuster Handbook* for easy use and speedy entrée into all topics, welcoming students into a conversation about becoming better writers.

WHAT'S NEW IN THE TENTH EDITION?

- **Eight new chapters, "Frames for College Writing,"** advise students on commonly assigned papers. They offer guidance on the personal essay, informative writing, process analysis, cause and effect analysis, textual analysis, argument, proposal and solution, and evaluation. They include a discussion of audience and purpose, a frames chart illustrating a typical organization, sentence/paragraph guides that help develop common writing moves, and an annotated sample student paper (Part 2).

- **A new chapter on evaluating sources** emphasizes five critical thinking questions for students. For each question, a chart contrasts the characteristics of reliable versus questionable sources while illustrations of sample sources show those qualities in practice (Ch. 23).

- **New sections on synthesizing researched sources** in a paper helps students decide what to do when multiple sources agree, partly agree, or disagree. Sentence and paragraph guides demonstrate common moves writers make to transition among different sources while building their arguments (sections 18F–18L).

- **A new chapter "Ten Troublesome Mistakes Writers Make" with interactive online resources** highlights for students the most common grammar and punctuation mistakes, alerting them to key areas that they might otherwise overlook in what can seem a sea of grammar rules. This overview of common mistakes provides additional examples to help students identify and correct these errors in their own writing (Ch. 2). In the e-textbook, online videos provide interactive instruction, practice, and remediation of the ten troublesome mistakes.

- **A new chapter, "Writing About Readings,"** covers the summary essay, response essay, and synthesis essay, emphasizing the importance of writing about readings in many college assignments, not just in formal research papers (Ch. 20).

- **A new chapter "Ten Top Tips for College Writers"** suggests ten fundamental writing practices and encourages students to keep basic rhetorical principles at the forefront of their writing, to record source information immediately during research, and more (Ch. 1).

- **MLA, APA, CM, and CSE documentation examples** have been completely updated, and examples of electronic sources like e-readers and wikis help students accurately cite increasingly common types of new sources (Chs. 25–27). All citation examples are color coded for clarity.

- **More than 40 new exercises** support students with opportunities to apply what they've learned about grammar and punctuation as well as thinking and writing strategies.

- **New media enhancements in the e-textbook** link students to videos, animations, model documents, and exercises to create a rich, interactive learning experience. Resources that reinforce and extend the instructional content in the *Simon & Schuster Handbook* let students access additional help and assessment as needed and support students who have different learning styles. See E-textbook Resources on page xi for more information.

OTHER FEATURES OF THE HANDBOOK

- **Authoritative advice about grammar, punctuation, and mechanics** provides comprehensive and clear explanations with plentiful examples of correct usage.

- **Quick Boxes** highlight and summarize key content throughout the text, providing quick access to important strategies, suggestions, and examples to improve student writing.

- **Extensive samples of student writing** include 18 full academic essays and complete workplace documents to illustrate key elements of various types of writing and help students apply them in their own writing.

- **Annotated source illustrations** show students how to identify citation information in a range of typical sources—journal articles, web pages, and books—and how to arrange that information into correct MLA and APA citations.

- **Support for multilingual writers** includes seven stand alone chapters devoted to areas of special concern, as well as ESOL Tips integrated throughout the handbook and embedded within specific grammar, research, and writing topics.

- **Contemporary emphasis on visual and media literacy** includes coverage of reading visuals critically (Ch. 3), using photos and graphics to support a verbal text (Ch. 7), searching for images (Ch. 20), using multimedia in presentations (Ch. 61), and writing in online environments such as blogs and wikis (Ch. 62).

- **Thoughtful, up-to-date documentation** coverage includes more MLA, APA, and CMS example citations than most other comparable titles.
- **The Terms Glossary** provides a convenient cross-referencing system: key terms are boldfaced and defined where they first appear in this book, and are thereafter presented in small capital letters—providing visual cues to readers when more complete definitions can be found in the Terms Glossary.

PRINT AND ELECTRONIC FORMATS

The tenth edition of the *Simon & Schuster Handbook* is available both in print and as an e-textbook in the following formats:

Pearson eText. An interactive online version of the *Simon & Schuster Handbook* is available in MyWritingLab. This eText brings together the many resources of MyWritingLab with the instruction and content of this successful handbook to create an enriched, interactive learning experience for students. See below for more on the eText resources.

CourseSmart e-textbook. Students can subscribe to the *Simon & Schuster Handbook* at CourseSmart.com. The format of the eText allows students to search the text, bookmark passages, save their own notes, and print reading assignments that incorporate lecture notes.

Android and iPad e-textbooks. Android and iPad versions of the text provide the complete handbook and the electronic resources described below.

E-textbook resources
Marginal icons in the handbook's eText, CourseSmart, iPad, Android, and print versions link to a wealth of electronic resources in MyWritingLab:

- Exercises from the handbook as well as additional exercises in MyWritingLab offer ample opportunities to help students sharpen their writing, grammar, and research skills.
- Video tutorials illustrate key concepts, offering tips and guidance on critical reading, evaluating sources, avoiding plagiarism, and many other topics.
- Audio podcasts discuss common questions about grammar, usage, punctuation, and mechanics.
- Sample documents illustrate the range of writing students do in composition classes, their other courses, the workplace, and the community.

MYWRITINGLAB

MyWritingLab empowers student writers to improve their writing, grammar, research, and documentation skills by uniquely integrating an e-text of the *Simon & Schuster Handbook for Writers* and book-specific resources with market-leading instruction, multimedia tutorials, exercises, and assessment.

Students can use MyWritingLab on their own, benefiting from self-paced diagnostics and a personal learning path that recommends the instruction and practice each student needs to improve his or her writing skills. Instructors can use MyWritingLab in ways that best complement their courses and teaching styles. They can recommend it to students for self-study, track student progress, or leverage the power of administrative features to be more effective and save time. The assignment builder and commenting tools, developed specifically for writing instruction, bring instructors closer to their student writers, make managing assignments more efficient, and put powerful assessment within reach. To learn more, visit MyWritingLab online or ask your Pearson representative.

SUPPLEMENTS

- **Instructor's Manual.** *Instructor's Resource Manual to accompany the Simon & Schuster Handbook for Writers, Tenth Edition* offers practical, hands-on advice for new and experienced composition instructors for organizing their syllabi, planning, and teaching.
- **The *Simon & Schuster Handbook* Exercise Answer Key.** Contains answers to the many exercises and activities in the *Simon & Schuster Handbook*.
- **Student Workbook.** *Workbook for Writers* has additional instruction and exercises for the writing, research, and grammar sections.

If you would like additional information about supplements for your composition course(s), please contact your Pearson sales representative.

ACKNOWLEDGMENTS

With this tenth edition of the *Simon & Schuster Handbook for Writers*, we heartily thank all those students who, to our great luck, have landed in our writing courses. We yearly learn from them how to stay up to date with students' needs and concerns as writers. We greatly admire how they strive to write skillfully, think critically, and communicate successfully. We especially thank the individual students who have given us permission to make them "published authors" by including their exemplary writing in this handbook.

We also are grateful to our many colleagues who have helped us with their criticisms, suggestions, and encouragement. In particular, we thank: Kaye Brown, Owensboro Community and Technical College; Anita P. Chirco, Keuka

College; Linda De Roche, Wesley College; Jason DePolo, North Carolina A&T State University; Christopher Ervin, Western Kentucky University; Joshua W. Everett, Central Texas College; Eric Fish, Northeast State Community College; Gary Heba, Bowling Green State University; Rebecca Heintz, Polk State College; Tina Hultgren, Kishwaukee College; Shanie Latham, Jefferson College; Nancy McGee, Macomb Community College; Joan Reeves, Northeast Alabama Community College; and Marcella Remund, University of South Dakota.

A project as complicated as the *Simon & Schuster Handbook* cannot be completed without the expertise and dedication of many professionals. We thank all the exceptional people at Pearson who facilitated this new edition. We're especially endebted to Marion Castellucci, Senior Development Editor, for her splendid vision and disciplined leadership; we thank also Paul Sarkis, Development Editor, Lauren Finn, Senior Acquisitions Editor, and Joe Opiela, Senior Vice President and Editorial Director for English. We appreciate the several contributions of Geoff Stacks. We wish to call special attention to the admirable work of Michael Montagna, a fellow faculty member, for reviewing, clarifying, and streamlining our grammar sections.

Doug values Lynn Troyka's vast knowledge, skill, dedication to teaching, and patience. He appreciates the support of all his colleagues in the writing program at the University of Denver, the knowledge and dedication embodied in the memberships of CCCC, TYCA, and WPA, and the hardworking team at Pearson. He further states, "My children, Monica, Andrew, and Paige, amaze me with their creativity, as does the very best writer I know: Becky Bradway, my wife."

Lynn wishes first to pay tribute to David Troyka, her beloved husband of 47 years, who inspired her to enjoy teaching and writing along with their amazing adventures in barely explored parts of the world. She thanks also her coauthor Doug Hesse for his gentle friendship and wisdom while writing the new 7th edition of *Quick Access Reference for Writers* and this newest edition of the *Simon & Schuster Handbook for Writers.* For their energetic, clever thoughts on logos, ethos, and pathos, she thanks Lynn Reid and Elisa Ham. For their unwavering support and love, Lynn also thanks Ida Morea, her steadfast friend and Administrative Assistant for 18 years; Kristen and Dan Black, her amazing daughter and son-in-law, and their superb children, Lindsey and Ryan; Bernice Joseph, her "adopted" sister and anchor of an amazing family: Mauricia Joseph, and Rachael and Eric Thomas, and their gifted children Nickyla, Nicholas, and Nehemiah; Michael Burns and his wife, Janelle James; and her grand pals Alice, Melanie, Avery, Jimmy, Gitam, Ian, Gavin, Hy Cohen, Doug Young, Andrene, Tzila, Susan, Rose, and Amanda.

Lynn Quitman Troyka
Doug Hesse

ABOUT THE AUTHORS

Paulette Martin

Lynn Quitman Troyka

Lynn Quitman Troyka, Adjunct Professor of English in the MA Program in Language and Literature at the City College (CCNY) of the City University of New York (CUNY), taught freshman English and basic writing for many years at Queensborough Community College. Dr. Troyka is a past chair of the Conference on College Composition and Communication (CCCC); the College Section of the National Council of Teachers of English (NCTE); and the Writing Division of the Modern Language Association (MLA). She has won many awards for teaching, scholarship, and service, and has conducted hundreds of faculty workshops about teaching writing and its relation to college-level reading.

"This information," says Dr. Troyka, "tells what I've done, not who I am. I am a teacher. Teaching is my life's work, and I love it."

Doug Hesse

Douglas Hesse is Professor of English and Executive Director of Writing at the University of Denver, one of only thirty writing programs to receive the CCCC Certificate of Excellence. Dr. Hesse is a past chair of the CCCC, the nation's largest association of college writing instructors. A past president, as well, of the Council of Writing Program Administrators (WPA), Dr. Hesse edited *WPA: Writing Program Administration*. He has served on the NCTE executive committee, chaired the MLA Division on Teaching as a Profession, and served on the MLA Committee on Contingent Labor. Author of nearly sixty articles and book chapters, he has been named University Distinguished Scholar at the University of Denver.

"Of various awards I've received," says Dr. Hesse, "the one that matters most is Distinguished Humanities Teacher. That one came from my students and suggests that, in however small a way, I've mattered in their education and lives."

Simon & Schuster
Handbook for Writers

PART

1

Writing Situations and Processes

Ten Top Tips
for College Writers

1 ■ ■ ■ ■ ■ ■ ■ ■ ■ ■

Quick Points   You will learn to

➤ Focus on ten elements to improve your college writing.

Lynn, having taught writing and teachers of writing for over 30 years, has always surveyed her students at the close of each term by asking, "What tips for writers that you've learned this term have proved most helpful?" She has seen approximately 7,200 responses. After considering the most frequent advice Doug has given thousands of writers, he found his students had a lot in common with Lynn's. Our combined results are shown in Quick Box 1.1, starting with the top favorite tip.

Quick Box 1.1   ■ ■ ■ ■ ■ ■ ■ ■ ■ ■ ■

Ten top tips for college writers

1. Be specific by thinking of RENNS: **R**easons, **E**xamples, **N**ames, **N**umbers, and the five **S**enses (see 6F).

2. Create a personal system to record writing ideas that pop into your head.

3. Use essay frames and sentence and paragraph guides as aids to writing (see Chapters 10–17).

4. Stay focused on the concepts of "purpose" and "audience" throughout your writing process (see 4B and 4C).

5. Weave *logos* (logic), *ethos* (credibility), and *pathos* (emotion) into your writing (see 3B).

6. Engage your readers by presenting and then complicating a topic.

7. Play the "believing game" and the "doubting game" (see page 8).

8. Record source information the very first time you find a source, even if you're not sure you will use it (see Chapters 21–22).

9. Welcome feedback about your writing (see Chapter 9).

10. Avoid slipping into "textspeak" in your writing.

■ TIP 1. Be specific: use RENNS.

Successful college writing moves back and forth between main ideas, usually stated in TOPIC SENTENCES,* and specific details. The letters "RENNS" start words that lead to specific details: **R**easons, **E**xamples, **N**ames, **N**umbers, and the five **S**enses (sight, sound, smell, taste, and touch). You might include emotions along with the five senses when they fit your topic. Only some RENNS need to appear as specific details in a piece of writing. For more on RENNS with additional examples, see 6F.

Here's a paragraph that uses specific details to describe an environmental disaster.

On April 20, 2010, an oil drilling rig in the Gulf of Mexico exploded, killing 11 workers and causing a huge oil spill that leaked 340,000 gallons a day of crude oil into the waters 40 miles southeast of the Louisiana coast. Because the rig, called The Deepwater Horizon, sat half submerged so that it could extract more oil per day than a surface rig, the spilled oil went into deeper water than ever in the history of oil spills. The devastation of life below, on, and above the water was unusually widespread because the Gulf's strong currents spread the oil over large areas. Coral beds that live in darker waters far below the surface died quickly as oil fell onto their fragile formations. Fish such as flounder and monkfish that normally live in deep water were quickly suffocated by the oil entering their gills. On the surface, microorganisms such as algae and krill, vital to oxygen in the water and food for

Numbers
Names

Reasons

Examples

---

* Words printed in SMALL CAPITAL LETTERS are discussed elsewhere in the text and are defined in the Terms Glossary at the back of the book.

many types of whales, were wiped out. Sea life closer to shore, such as dolphins, turtles, and seals, died slowly, coated in the thick oil that seeped into their mouths and skin. Sea grasses and kelp, near-shore nesting sites for many species, wilted and died in the oil. And who can forget photographs of oil-coated pelicans, guillemots, and other sea birds held by human hands rushing against time to wash off the thick, sticky crude oil from feathers, bills, and feet? Or the videos of people weeping silently, angry at the sight of the dead birds and turtles that could not be saved? The oil poured out of the explosion site for over a month, creating the second worst environmental disaster in the United States.

Senses and emotions

■ TIP 2. Create a personal system to record writing ideas that pop into your head.

Writers often find that ideas pop into their heads while they're thinking of something else. You might be doing your laundry, driving your car or riding on a bus, or waking up in the middle of the night. Those ideas can slip through your fingers like snowflakes if you don't save them right away. We urge you to devise a recording system that suits your lifestyle. It might be a paper pad and a pencil, a cell phone, a small recording device, or a combination of these.

From time to time, check what you've saved because one idea might lead you to expanded or new thoughts. And while you're writing each of your assignments, consider whether some of what you've saved might fit in well with the current project. For more on brainstorming a topic and other techniques to help you plan your writing, see 5E.

■ TIP 3. If you're unsure how to approach a writing assignment, check Part 2, "Frames for College Writing."

The eight essay frames in Part 2 of this handbook introduce you to different types of college writing assignments and immerse you in a variety of practical techniques to help you think clearly and write effectively. Our purpose is to give you sufficient general guidance so that you can concentrate on your own concerns: building a good THESIS STATEMENT, writing paragraphs that relate to your thesis statement and topic sentences, and making sure that you're staying on topic. For lots of information about eight different essay types, see Chapters 10–17. Also, for frame information to help you write research papers, see Chapter 24.

■ TIP 4. Stay focused on the concepts of "purpose" and "audience" throughout your writing process.

All human communication starts with a PURPOSE: to explain something, to describe an experience, to mount an argument that you hope will persuade, or to inspire someone to take action or think in new ways. Your AUDIENCE is the person or people you're reaching out to with your words. To write successfully in college, begin thinking about your topic—whether assigned by an instructor or chosen on your own—by consciously deciding from the start

- What is your purpose?
- Who is your audience?

Develop this habit until it flows naturally each time you start a writing assignment. One excellent way to check yourself is to participate in class-sponsored peer review sessions, so that other students read your writing and tell you whether they can discern the purpose of your writing and your intended audience. For more about the concepts of purpose and audience, see sections 4B and 4C.

In the following excerpt, the author's *purpose* is to give helpful advice; her *audience* is people who want to write.

If you dream of writing the screenplay for next summer's blockbuster movie, keep in mind one thing: writing is work. Oh, it can be enjoyable and immensely satisfying work, but you have to put in the time, often when you'd rather be doing something else. You'll need to put your butt in a chair, your hands on the keyboard, and crank out words—not just now and then, but pretty regularly, at least several minutes most days of the week, for weeks, months, even years. You see, it's that constant practice over time that gets you to the level of experts. Of course, you can learn some strategies and techniques that can help you be competent with specific kinds of writing. But for really good writing, the paragraphs of professional prose that win book contracts and screen credits, you'll need to work at it, just like all the rest of us.

—Kiri Irvin, "You Just Can't Toss This Stuff Off"

■ TIP 5. Weave logical, ethical, and emotional appeals into your writing.

The advice that Greek philosopher Aristotle gave 2,300 years ago to people who wanted to persuade others is still excellent guidance for writers today. Aristotle taught that all effective communication needs three qualities:

- **Logical appeal (in Greek, *logos*).** Writers need to make statements that are logical so that the audience can accept and believe them.
- **Ethical appeal (*ethos*).** Writers need to choose words that communicate good character and integrity so their readers feel confident they're reading the ideas of someone who can be trusted and is not trying to manipulate them.
- **Emotional appeal (*pathos*).** Writers need to use words to establish an emotional connection with the audience.

Without these three qualities, readers will not easily accept the message being offered by the writer. Weaving all three qualities into your writing takes practice. You need to dig into yourself to make sure you're being honest, refraining from distorting information, showing personal humility, and exhibiting an understanding of the human condition. For more about the logical, ethical, and emotional appeals, see section 4B.

The following paragraph uses only a few words to communicate a logical position (*logos*), engages in a bit of self-mockery that conveys humility (*pathos*), and shows that the writer is honest and forthright in accepting her position in relation to others (*ethos*).

Wearing a canvas jumpsuit zipped up to my neck, I must have looked as though I was stepping onto the set of *ET: The Extra Terrestrial*, but my actual destination was Madison Avenue, home to some of the fanciest boutiques in New York City. The bright blue jumpsuit I wore was far from high fashion; it was sized for a full-grown man, and it ballooned about my slender frame. My blonde hair was pulled back in a pony tail, and the only label I displayed was the bold-lettered logo on my back: Ready, Willing, & Able. I was suited up to collect trash from the sidewalks of New York.

Logical appeal. The author states the facts logically.

Ethical appeal. The author describes herself honestly; she isn't concerned about appearing unattractive.

Emotional appeal. The author has become a street cleaner, which many people consider undignified.

—Zoe Shewer, "Ready, Willing, and Able"

■ TIP 6. Engage your readers by presenting and then complicating a topic.

One way to capture and hold readers' attention is to present and then complicate a topic. A simple procession of details to support the **generalization** in a topic sentence can bore readers. When you introduce a complication into your ideas, you lure your readers to think more deeply about a topic, a habit of mind that greatly enhances the pleasure people get from reading. If you can't resolve the complication, you can close your discussion by acknowledging that the complication remains, and, by implication, you can invite your readers to think more about it on their own.

Here's a paragraph that contains a topic sentence as its generalization and specific details to support it. The complicating sentence is shown in boldface. By the end of the essay, the author doesn't smooth over the stark differences in worldviews that he presents, but he acknowledges them and suggests readers will see future evidence of their impact.

> The world can be divided in many ways—rich and poor, democratic and authoritarian—but one of the most striking is the divide between societies with an individualistic mentality and the ones with a collectivist mentality. **This divide goes deeper than economics into the way people perceive the world**. If you show an American an image of a fish tank, the American will usually describe the biggest fish in the tank and what it is doing. If you ask a Chinese person to describe a fish tank, the Chinese will usually describe the context in which the fish swim. These experiments have been done over and over again, and the results reveal the same underlying pattern. Americans usually see individuals; Chinese and other Asians see contexts.
>
> —David Brooks, "Harmony and the Dream"

■ TIP 7. Play the "believing game" and the "doubting game."

The "believing game" comes in handy when you're brainstorming and drafting your writing. If you suddenly feel you have nothing to say, or you think your ideas aren't smart enough or your writing isn't good enough, turn on your ability to believe. Push yourself to become confident that you have something worth saying and the right to say it. Write boldly. Believing can propel you to get enough on paper to start your revising processes.

The "doubting game" is the flip side of the believing game. It's invaluable when you really don't want to bother doing any more with an essay—even though you know there's room for improvement. At these times, the doubting game can jump-start your revision process by turning up the volume of that quiet little voice, the one you'd like to ignore, that whispers maybe you had better look over your work one last time before you hand it in—perhaps you need more specific details or maybe you've cited one of your sources incorrectly. If you're like most professional writers, chances are you'll find holes that need filling or flaws you want to fix.

■ TIP 8. Record source information the very first time you find a source, even if you're not sure you will use it.

At the very moment you access a source, take an extra few minutes to record publication information so that you won't need to retrace your steps later on. Retracking down sources can take days, meaning wasted time and destructive stress. Use a master checklist of the publication details you'll need for the DOCUMENTATION STYLE you'll be using. Record that information every time. Never put it off. Even if a source seems irrelevant to the focus of your topic, force yourself to note its publication information. You never know! One day as you're writing you might suddenly realize you do indeed want to use that source.

Another important reason for recording publication information from the start is it helps you avoid unintentional PLAGIARISM. With the exact source information, you can always go back to it to make sure that you're not claiming an author's words as your own, or that your summary or paraphrase uses too many of the author's own words. For more about what publication information to record, see section 21M.

■ TIP 9. Welcome feedback about your writing.

Feedback about your writing from your instructor, your classmates, and other trusted readers can be invaluable when you want to improve your writing. Avoid reacting defensively or becoming resentful when you hear constructive criticism. If this is hard for you to tolerate or if it frightens you at first,

discipline yourself to listen to the comments and consider the points made. You might see possibilities you didn't notice on your own. Similarly, you can help others see their writing with new eyes.

Of course, always remember that you are the author, the one to make the final choice about whether to use each suggestion. (Please note that because some instructors require students refrain from asking for feedback about their writing before handing it in, be sure to check the teacher's policy in each of your writing classes.) For more about receiving feedback on your writing and giving feedback to others about their writing, see sections 9C–9D.

■ TIP 10. Avoid slipping into "textspeak" in your writing.

Textspeak is a coined term for shortening words, mostly by omitting vowels, in informally written text and chat messages. It's quicker to type "2morrow" or "cu soon." Of course, people who text know that texting forms aren't acceptable in ACADEMIC WRITING. Yet after a while for many people,

textspeak starts to look normal, and it creeps without notice into their formal writing. Students particularly seem to allow textspeak to slip into their writing in blogged entries for class. Professors expect blogs for class to be written with serious, formal intent. Little will annoy your instructors and peer readers as much as assignments written in textspeak, so monitor your college writing carefully.

2 Ten Troublesome Mistakes Writers Make

■ ■ ■ ■ ■ ■ ■ ■ ■ ■

Quick Points   You will learn to

➤ Recognize and correct ten common errors in writing.

Ten troublesome mistakes tend to pop up frequently in college students' writing because students often forget what they learned years before. Most stand out more in written than in spoken English. We urge you to work through the quick review in this chapter to check whether any of these ten errors gives you trouble. If you see any, put aside some time right away to learn to recognize and eliminate them. You'll also find a full chapter on each error in this handbook (the chapter numbers are in parentheses in Quick Box 2.1).

Quick Box 2.1   ■ ■ ■ ■ ■ ■ ■ ■ ■ ■ ■

Ten troublesome mistakes in writing

1. Sentence fragments instead of complete sentences (see Chapter 33)
2. Comma-spliced sentences and run-on sentences (see Chapter 34)
3. Subject–verb disagreement (see Chapter 31)
4. Pronoun–antecedent disagreement (see Chapter 31, sections 31O–31T)
5. Pronouns unclear in what they refer to (see Chapter 30, sections 30L–30N)
6. Illogical sentence shifts (see Chapter 36)
7. Modifiers placed incorrectly (see Chapter 35)
8. Homonyms misused (see Chapter 49, section 49F)
9. Commas misused (see Chapter 42)
10. Apostrophes misused (see Chapter 45)

■ 1. Sentence fragments

👁
Watch
the Video

A **sentence fragment** is a written mistake that looks like a sentence but isn't one. Even though it starts with a capital letter and ends with a period, it's not a sentence. It's only a group of words. Sentence fragments are written errors created by three types of incomplete word groups. Chapter 33 lists the types and shows how to turn them into complete sentences.

NO **When** companies show employees respect.

The fragment starts with *when*, a SUBORDINATING CONJUNCTION, and is only a group of words.

YES **When** companies show employees respect, the best workers rarely quit.

The fragment is joined with a complete sentence.

NO A positive working atmosphere most employees productive and happy.

The fragment lacks a VERB and is only a group of words.

YES A positive working atmosphere **keeps** most employees productive and happy.

Keeps, a verb, completes the sentence.

■ 2. Comma splices and run-on sentences

Comma splices and run-on sentences are written mistakes that look almost alike. A **comma-spliced sentence** uses only a comma between two complete sentences. A **run-on sentence** uses no punctuation between two complete sentences. These errors disappear with any one of three fixes: placing a period or semicolon between the two sentences; writing a CONJUNCTION with needed punctuation between the two sentences; or turning one of the sentences into a DEPENDENT CLAUSE. Chapter 34 describes the types of comma splices and run-on sentences and explains how to revise them correctly.

Watch the Video

COMMA SPLICES

NO Bad bosses quickly stand out in workplaces, they scream impatiently at everyone.

YES Bad bosses quickly stand out in workplaces. They scream impatiently at everyone.

A period replaces the comma, which corrects the error. A semicolon also works.

YES Bad bosses quickly stand out in workplaces, **for** they scream impatiently at everyone.

Inserting the COORDINATING CONJUNCTION *for* corrects the error.

YES Bad bosses quickly stand out in workplaces **because** they scream impatiently at everyone.

The SUBORDINATING CONJUNCTION *because* turns the second sentence into a dependent clause, which corrects the error. The comma is dropped.

YES **Because** they scream impatiently at everyone, bad bosses quickly stand out in workplaces.

The SUBORDINATING CONJUNCTION *because* turns the second sentence into a dependent clause, which corrects the error. Now the dependent clause comes before the complete sentence, so the comma is retained.

RUN-ON SENTENCES

NO Bad bosses quickly stand out in workplaces they scream impatiently at everyone.

YES Bad bosses quickly stand out in workplaces. They scream impatiently at everyone.

A period or semicolon between the two sentences corrects the error.

YES Bad bosses quickly stand out in workplaces, **for** they scream impatiently at everyone.

A comma and the COORDINATING CONJUNCTION *for* correct the error.

YES Bad bosses quickly stand out in workplaces **because** they scream impatiently at everyone.

The SUBORDINATING CONJUNCTION *because* turns the second sentence into a dependent clause, which corrects the error.

YES **Because** they scream impatiently at everyone, bad bosses quickly stand out in workplaces.

The SUBORDINATING CONJUNCTION *because* turns the second sentence into a dependent clause, which corrects the error. Now the dependent clause comes before the complete sentence and is followed by a comma.

■ **3. Mistakes in subject–verb agreement**

Watch
the Video

A mistake in subject–verb agreement occurs when a VERB and its SUBJECT are mismatched, often within one sentence. This error, in written as well as spoken English, often occurs when singulars and plurals are mixed incorrectly. Chapter 31 explains all the ways subject–verb agreement errors occur and shows how to correct them.

NO **Effective leaders** in business **knows** how to motivate people to excel.

YES **Effective leaders** in business **know** how to motivate people to excel.

The plural subject *Effective leaders* matches the plural verb *know*.

YES **An effective leader** in business **knows** how to motivate people to excel.

The singular subject *Effective leader* matches the singular verb *knows*.

■ 4. Mistakes in pronoun–antecedent agreement

Pronoun–antecedent agreement errors occur when a PRONOUN and its ANTECED-
ENT are mismatched. A pronoun—such as *it, its, they,* and *their*—takes the place
of a NOUN; an antecedent is the specific noun that a pronoun replaces in the
same sentence or a nearby sentence. Errors in pronoun–antecedent agreement,
in written as well as spoken English, often occur when singulars and plurals are
mixed incorrectly. Chapter 31, sections 31O–31T, explains all the ways mistakes
in pronoun–antecedent agreement occur and shows how to correct them.

Watch
the Video

> **NO**   My office partner admired my new computer **monitors** for **its** sleek design.
>
> **YES**   My office partner admired my new computer **monitors** for **their** sleek design.
>
> The plural antecedent ***monitors*** matches the plural pronoun ***their.***
>
> **YES**   My office partner admired my new computer **monitor** for **its** sleek design.
>
> The singular subject ***monitor*** matches the singular pronoun ***its.***

■ 5. Unclear pronoun reference

Unclear pronoun reference, in written as well as spoken English, is a mistake
that happens when the noun to which a pronoun—often *it, they, them*—refers
is not obvious. Chapter 30, sections 30L–30N, describes the sentence structures that often have unclear pronoun reference problems and explains how
to revise them correctly.

Watch
the Video

> **NO**   The construction supervisors paid little attention to the bricklayers when
> **they** were distracted.
>
> ***They*** is an unclear pronoun reference. Who is distracted, the ***construction
> supervisors*** or the ***bricklayers?***
>
> **YES**   When the construction supervisors were distracted, ***they*** paid little atten-
> tion to the bricklayers.
>
> ***They*** clearly refers to the ***construction supervisors.***
>
> **NO**   Experienced bricklayers waste little motion to preserve their energy so that
> they can finish an entire section of wall without taking a break. **This** creates
> a sturdy wall.
>
> ***This*** is an unclear pronoun reference. Is the wall sturdy because the brick-
> layers wasted little motion to preserve their energy or because the bricklayers
> finished an entire section without taking a break?
>
> **YES**   So that the wall they build is sturdy, experienced bricklayers waste little
> motion to preserve their energy so that they can finish an entire wall sec-
> tion without taking a break.
>
> ***This*** is eliminated when the revised sentence makes clear how bricklayers
> can create a sturdy wall.

■ 6. Illogical shifts within sentences

👁 **Watch the Video**

Illogical shifts within sentences are mistakes, in written as well as spoken English, that occur midsentence when a category of word, such as the verb, changes form for no reason. In addition to verb tenses, other categories of words need to remain consistent within sentences as well as in groups of sentences. Chapter 36 shows how shifts create unclear writing and how they can be avoided.

NO   Our union representative **explained** the new salary schedule and then **allows** time for questions.

YES   Our union representative **explained** the new salary schedule and then **allowed** time for questions.

YES   Our union representative **explains** the new salary schedule and then **allows** time for questions.

> In the correct sentences, both verbs are in same tense, either PAST TENSE or PRESENT TENSE.

■ 7. Mistakes with modifiers

👁 **Watch the Video**

Mistakes with MODIFIERS are more obvious in written than spoken English. Such errors happen when a modifier is placed in the wrong spot in a sentence, thereby muddling the meaning. Misplaced modifiers and dangling modifiers are two of the four types of incorrect placements for modifiers. Chapter 35 explains all four and how to correct them.

MISPLACED MODIFIER

NO   The consultant who observed our meeting **only** took notes with a pen.

YES   The consultant who observed our meeting took notes **only** with a pen.

> Modifier *only* belongs with *pen* to clarify that nothing else was used to take notes.

NO   The consultant took notes with a pen **sporting a large handlebar mustache**.

YES   The consultant **sporting a large handlebar mustache** took notes with a pen.

> The mustache belongs to the consultant, not the pen.

DANGLING MODIFIER

NO   Studying our company's budget projection, the numbers predicted bankruptcy.

> *Numbers* after the comma says that numbers can study.

YES   Studying our company's budget projection, I saw that the numbers predicted bankruptcy.

> *I saw* after the comma says that a person is studying.

■ 8. Mistakes with homonyms

Mistakes with HOMONYMS are obvious in written English more than in spoken English. Homonyms are words that sound alike, but they have different meanings and spellings. We advise you to compile your own personal list of the homonyms that you habitually mix up. Then set aside time to master the correct usage of each word. Although an almost overwhelming number of homonym sets turn up in any Internet search, you need be concerned only with those that give you trouble. Chapter 49, section 49F, lists the homonym sets most frequently confused.

Watch the Video

> **NO**   **Its** important **too** lock **you're** office door and **right** a note **four** the guards if you have **all ready** turned off the heat.
>
> Simply to illustrate common homonym errors, we exaggerate how many show up in one sentence.
>
> **YES**   **It's** important **to** lock **your** office door and **write** a note **for** the guards if you have **already** turned off the heat.

■ 9. Comma errors

Comma errors are written, not spoken, mistakes. Commas clarify meaning for readers, especially when a sentence contains both major and minor information. Currently, commas turn up in published writing far less frequently than they did only 20 years ago. As a writer, beware of the suggestion to insert a comma whenever you pause because everyone speaks and thinks at different rates. This fact is particularly noticeable when people gather from different parts of the United States and Canada, or when a person's native language isn't English.

Watch the Video

We suggest that you copy and carry with you the major rules for using commas, listed in Quick Box 42.1 on pages 620–621. The more you check this list of rules, the more quickly you'll know it by heart. Chapter 42 presents and explains all rules for comma use in written English.

To help you start, here's a list you'll probably master quite quickly—the five spots where a comma *never* belongs.

- Never after *such as*, but before it, it's fine: *Our office staff enjoyed perks*, *such as free coffee, tea, and hot chocolate.*
- Never before *than* in a comparison: *That company's truck was safer **than** ours.*
- Never between a subject and verb written close together: ***Our firm's maternity leave program** is **enlightened**.*
- Never immediately after a subordinating conjunction, and only after a clause that starts with one: ***Because** I developed a nasty cold, I left work early.*
- Never before an opening parenthesis, but after a closing parenthesis, it's fine: *When an office's intercom system works by public announcements **(people tend to ignore alerts by telephone)**, everyone's concentration suffers.*

■ 10. Apostrophe errors

Watch
the Video

Apostrophe errors are written, not spoken, mistakes. Apostrophes serve only two purposes: they indicate possession (the president's car; the president's schedule), and they indicate missing letters in contractions (isn't). For complete information about apostrophes, see Chapter 45.

> **NO** The main **office's** are closed for the evening.
>
> **YES** The main **offices** are closed for the evening.
>
> Apostrophes never create plural words.

> **NO** The security guard **patrol's** the building every hour.
>
> **YES** The security guard **patrols** the building every hour.
>
> Apostrophes are never involved with verbs.

> **NO** The security guards **do'nt** need dogs to help them.
>
> **YES** The security guards **don't** need dogs to help them.
>
> If you write a contraction, place an apostrophe only where a letter is omitted.

3

Thinking, Reading, and Analyzing Images Critically

■ ■ ■ ■ ■ ■ ■ ■ ■ ■ ■

Quick Points You will learn to

> ➤ Use critical thinking when examining ideas (see 3A).
> ➤ Recognize and use the logical, ethical, and emotional appeals (see 3B).
> ➤ Reason inductively and deductively (see 3H).
> ➤ Recognize logical fallacies (see 3I).

3A What is critical thinking?

Watch
the Video

Thinking isn't something people choose to do, any more than fish choose to live in water. But although thinking may come naturally, critical thinking demands more. **Critical thinking** means thoroughly examining ideas, readings, or images. It means identifying weaknesses, strengths, connections, and implications.

For example, consider the claim, "Because climate change is natural, we shouldn't worry about it." It's true that the earth's climate has varied over the millennia, but critical readers won't immediately accept the claim without further thought. They might ask, for example, whether the conditions that caused climate change in the past are the same ones causing it today. It could prove true that we shouldn't worry about climate change (though scientists almost universally agree we should), so a critical reader might ultimately accept the original claim—but not without careful analysis.

The word *critical* here has a neutral meaning. It doesn't mean taking a negative view or finding fault. Quick Box 3.1 lists questions that critical thinkers ask themselves.

Quick Box 3.1

Questions critical thinkers ask themselves

- Do I insist on examining an idea from all sides?
- Do I resist easy solutions that are being pushed at me?
- Do I face up to uncomfortable truths?
- Do I insist on factual accuracy?
- Do I remain open to ideas that don't fit with what I'm used to believing?
- Do I insist on clarity?
- Do I insist on hearing "the whole story," not just one point of view?
- Do I resist being hurried to make up my mind?

3B How can understanding rhetorical principles help critical thinking?

Rhetoric is the art and skill of speaking and writing effectively. If you understand three central principles of rhetoric—the **persuasive appeals**—you can greatly enhance your ability to think critically. Often the three are called by their Greek names: *logos*, meaning logic; *ethos*, meaning credibility; and *pathos*, meaning empathy or compassion. These appeals turn up in most material you read, see, hear, or run into every day. To recognize them in action, see Quick Box 3.2 (page 18).

Watch the Video

Quick Box 3.2 ■ ■ ■ ■ ■ ■ ■ ■ ■ ■ ■

Three central principles of rhetoric: the persuasive appeals

- **Logical appeals** (*logos*) evoke a rational response. People use them when they
  - Demonstrate sound reasoning.
  - Define terms.
  - Give accurate facts and statistics.
  - Use relevant quotations from experts and authorities.
  - Use deductive and inductive reasoning well (see 3I).
  - Use effective evidence (see 6F).

- **Ethical appeals** (*ethos*) evoke confidence in the writer's reliability and trustworthiness. People use them when they
  - Show respect by using appropriate language and tone.
  - Are fair-minded.
  - Are well informed and sincere.
  - Are open to a variety of perspectives.
  - Use reliable sources (see Chapter 23).

- **Emotional appeals** (*pathos*) stir emotions, passion, or compassion. People use them when they
  - Reflect values that call upon one's "better self."
  - Use concrete details and descriptive or figurative language to create mental pictures.
  - Add a sense of humanity and reality.
  - Appeal to hearts more than minds, but never manipulate with biased or slanted language.

Figure 3.1 is an example of these principles in action. It is an excerpt from the Web site of Doctors Without Borders, an organization dedicated to providing medical and humanitarian help. Perhaps most obvious are the emotional appeals, with the descriptions of malnourished children. For logical appeals the writer includes very specific information about medical processes (the "MUAC test") and treatments (the use of "ORS [oral rehydration salts] and zinc sulphate"). The medical terminology enhances the writer's ethical appeals, strengthening his

Figure 3.1 Three rhetorical appeals in action.

South Sudan: "These People Tell Us That They Are Desperate"

DECEMBER 9, 2011

Some of the thousands of refugees in Doro.

South Sudan © Jean-Marc Jacobs

Robert Mungai Maina, from Kenya, has eight years of professional experience as a clinical officer. He has worked with Doctors Without Borders/Médecins Sans Frontières (MSF) in South Sudan for the past five months, and was assigned to the emergency team working in the Doro refugee camp last week. Here, he describes what he has seen.

"Many of the patients that we see in our clinic have respiratory diseases. This is because most of the refugees are sleeping outside without anything to cover themselves. . . .

We are also seeing malnourished children, some with moderate and some with severe malnutrition. They don't come with any particular complaint. You have to spot them. The child might come with diarrhea or a cough but the mother will not say to you, "this child is malnourished." So we do the MUAC test, the criterion that we use for detecting malnutrition in children. We measure their middle upper left arm using a measuring tape with a colored scale.

Yesterday I did a consultation with a mother who had one-year-old twins, both coughing and with fever. They both had severe malnutrition. She is still breastfeeding but doesn't have enough milk because she's not feeding herself well. She is just eating sorghum mixed with hot water to make a porridge, which is carbohydrates, nothing else. . . . We started both of the twins on specially formulated therapeutic food and one of them, who has frequent diarrhea, we started on ORS (oral rehydration salts) and zinc sulphate. . . .

I try my level best to do what I can do for them. Those who are sick, we take care of them and do the follow-up to make sure they get the right treatment. I tell them to come back any time they have a medical problem. That's what we are here to do."

credibility as someone who can characterize the problem accurately. The writer's credentials and his careful, quiet tone also build his ethical appeals.

3C How can I break down the critical thinking process?

Quick Box 3.3 describes the general steps of critical thinking. Expect sometimes to combine them, reverse their order, and return to parts of the process you thought you had completed.

Quick Box 3.3   ■ ■ ■ ■ ■ ■ ■ ■ ■ ■ ■

Steps in the critical thinking process

1. **Summarize.** Comprehend the **literal meaning**: the "plain" meaning on the surface of the material. Be able to extract and restate the main message or central point or to accurately and objectively describe an image, event, or situation. Add nothing. Read "on the lines" (see 3D).

2. **Analyze.** Break ideas component parts. Figure out how each idea contributes to the overall meaning. Read "between the lines" for INFERENCES; look to see what's implied by the ideas, even if not stated (see 3E).

3. **Synthesize.** Connect what you've summarized and analyzed with your prior knowledge or experiences, with other ideas or perspectives, or with other readings (see 3F).

4. **Evaluate.** Read "beyond the lines." Judge the quality of the material or form your own informed opinion about it. Answer such questions as, "Is it reasonable? Fair? Accurate? Convincing? Ethical? Useful? Comprehensive? Important?" (see 3G).

3D How do I summarize or comprehend?

To summarize or comprehend, first, try to understand the basic, literal meaning of an idea, argument, or reading. The following activities can help.

3D.1 Read closely and actively

Reading is an active process, an interaction between the page or screen and your brain. The secret to reading closely and actively is to **annotate**. Annotating means writing notes to yourself in a book or article's margins, inserting comments electronically, or keeping a separate file or notebook about your reading. **Close reading** means annotating for content. You might, for

Figure 3.2 Example of close reading (blue) and active reading (black).

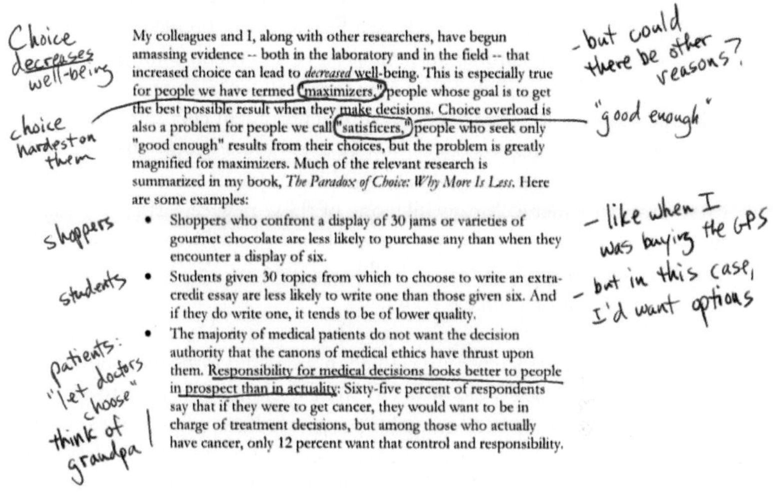

example, use the margin to number steps in a process or summarize major points. **Active reading** means annotating to make connections between the material and your own knowledge or experiences. This is your chance to converse on paper with the writer.

Figure 3.2 is an example of one kind of annotated reading, a section from "The Tyranny of Choice," an essay printed in Exercise 3-1. The student has written notes in the margin in two colors of ink. The blue ink shows close reading, and the black ink shows active reading.

Figure 3.3 (page 22) is another kind of annotation, using a double entry method. In the left column the student put close reading or content notes. The right column has active reading or synthesis notes.

● **EXERCISE 3-1**   Annotate the following essay. Depending on your instructor's directions, either follow the annotation example in Figure 3.2, the double-entry example in Figure 3.3, or try both.

"THE TYRANNY OF CHOICE"
Barry Schwartz

Does increased affluence and increased choice mean we have more happy people? Not at all. Three recently published books—by the psychologist David Myers, the political scientist Robert E. Lane, and the journalist Gregg Easterbrook—point out how the growth of material affluence has not brought with it an increase in subjective well-being. Indeed, they argue that we are actually experiencing a *decrease* in well-being.

Why are people increasingly unhappy even as they experience greater material abundance and freedom of choice? Recent psychological research suggests that increased choice may itself be part of the problem.

It may seem implausible that there can be too much choice. As a matter of logic, it would appear that adding options will make no one worse off and is bound to make someone better off. If you're content choosing among three different kinds of breakfast cereal, or six television stations, you can simply ignore the dozens or hundreds that get added to your supermarket shelves or cable provider's menu. Meanwhile, one of those new cereals or TV stations may be just what some other person was hoping for. Given the indisputable fact that choice is good for human well-being, it seems only logical that if some choice is good, more choice is better.

Logically true, yes. Psychologically true, no. My colleagues and I, along with other researchers, have begun amassing evidence—both in the laboratory and in the field—that increased choice can lead to *decreased* well-being. This is especially true for people we have termed "maximizers," people whose goal is to get the best possible result when they make decisions. Choice overload is also a problem for people we call "satisficers," people who seek only "good enough" results from their choices, but the problem is greatly magnified for maximizers. Much of the relevant research

Figure 3.3   Double entry notebook example.

Content Notes	Synthesis Notes
--increased wealth and choice hasn't made people happier	
--14 million people fewer than in 1974 report being "very happy"	I wonder if people define happiness different today than they did 30-40 years ago
--depression and suicide has increased, especially among young people	Scary. There could be lots of causes, and I wonder if wealth and choice are the most important
--demand for counseling has increased at colleges	Could it be that more students seek counseling? Maybe need was there before but people didn't act.

is summarized in my book, *The Paradox of Choice: Why More Is Less*. Here are some examples:

- Shoppers who confront a display of 30 jams or varieties of gourmet chocolate are less likely to purchase *any* than when they encounter a display of six.

- Students given 30 topics from which to choose to write an extra-credit essay are less likely to write one than those given six. And if they do write one, it tends to be of lower quality.

- The majority of medical patients do not want the decision authority that the canons of medical ethics have thrust upon them. Responsibility for medical decisions looks better to people in prospect than in actuality: Sixty-five percent of respondents say that if they were to get cancer, they would want to be in charge of treatment decisions, but among those who actually have cancer, only 12 percent want that control and responsibility.

- Maximizing college seniors send out more résumés, investigate more different fields, go on more job interviews, and get better, higher paying jobs than satisficers. But they are less satisfied with the jobs, and are much more stressed, anxious, frustrated, and unhappy with the process.

These examples paint a common picture: Increasing options does not increase well-being, especially for maximizers, even when it enables choosers to do better by some objective standard. We have identified several processes that help explain why increased choice decreases satisfaction. Greater choice:

- Increases the burden of gathering information to make a wise decision.

- Increases the likelihood that people will regret the decisions they make.

- Increases the likelihood that people will *anticipate* regretting the decision they make, with the result that they can't make a decision at all.

- Increases the feeling of missed opportunities, as people encounter the attractive features of one option after another that they are rejecting. ●

3D.2 Read systematically

Reading systematically helps you pay attention. It's tempting to read quickly and carelessly, especially when you run up against long or complicated readings. Here's a three-part plan to help you read systematically.

1. **Preview:** Before you begin reading, start making **predictions** and jot down your questions.

   - For books, first look at the table of contents. What topics are included? What seems to be the main emphasis? If there's an introduction or preface, skim it.

- For chapters, or Web sites, first read all the headings, both large and small. Look for call-outs (quotations or excerpts in boxes or in the margins) and for figures, tables, and boxes.

- Check for introductory notes. Is there an abstract (a summary of the entire piece)? A note about the author? Other information?

- Jot a few questions that you expect—or hope—the reading will answer.

2. **Read:** Read the material closely and actively (see 3D.1). Identify the main points and start thinking about how the writer supports them. Annotate as you read.

3. **Review:** Go back to questions you jotted during previewing. Did the reading answer them? If not, either your predictions could have been wrong, or you didn't read carefully; reread to determine which.

Quick Box 3.4 lists more ways to help your reading comprehension.

🛈 **Alert:** The speed at which you read depends on your purpose. When you're hunting for a particular fact, you might skim the page until you find what you want. When you read about a subject you know well, you might read somewhat rapidly, slowing down only when you come to new material. When you're unfamiliar with the subject, you need to work slowly to give your mind time to absorb the new material. ●

Quick Box 3.4   ■ ■ ■ ■ ■ ■ ■ ■ ■ ■ ■

More ways to help reading comprehension

- **Make associations.** Link new material to what you already know. You may even find it helpful to read an encyclopedia article or an easier book or article on the subject first to build your knowledge base.

- **Simplify tough sentences.** If the author's writing style is complex, break long sentences into several shorter ones or reword them into a simpler style.

- **Make it easy for you to focus.** Do whatever it takes to concentrate.

- **Allot the time you need.** We know it's tough to balance classes, work, and social or family activities, but allow sufficient time to read, reflect, reread, and study.

- **Master the vocabulary.** As you encounter new words, try to figure out their meanings from context clues. See if definitions (called a *glossary*) are at the end of the reading. Have a good dictionary at hand or access an online dictionary site like dictionary.com.

3E How do I analyze readings?

To analyze something is to break it into parts, just as a chemist does, for example, to figure out the compounds in a particular mixture. Quick Box 3.5 explains how.

Quick Box 3.5 ■ ■ ■ ■ ■ ■ ■ ■ ■ ■ ■

Strategies for analysis

1. Identify the key assertions or claims (see 3E.1).
2. Separate facts from opinions (see 3E.2).
3. Identify rhetorical appeals (see 3B and 3E.3).
4. Identify the evidence (see 3E.4).
5. Identify cause and effect (see 3E.5).
6. Describe the tone, and look for bias (see 3E.6).
7. Identify inferences and assumptions (see 3E.7).
8. Identify implications (see 3E.8).

3E.1 Identify the key assertions or claims

Most writings are a combination of main ideas and the evidence, examples, or illustrations provided to support them. The most important idea is the writing's THESIS STATEMENT, which states the main idea for the whole piece. Identifying main ideas is crucial to evaluating how well the writer supports them.

3E.2 Separate facts from opinions

Distinguish **fact** from **opinion**.

- Facts are statements that can be checked objectively by observation, experiment, or research.

EXAMPLE:

Abraham Lincoln was the sixteenth president of the United States.

- Opinions are statements open to debate.

EXAMPLE:

Abraham Lincoln is the greatest U.S. president who ever lived.

Most statements are not so easy to discern as the ones given here about Abraham Lincoln. For example, is the statement, "All people desire a steady income," a fact or an opinion? If read without reflection, it can seem a fact. However, critical readers realize that although it's common for people to equate success with a constant stream of money, some individuals prefer a more freewheeling approach to life. They may work hard, save money, and then travel for months, not working at all. Thus the statement is an opinion because although it's accurate for most people, it isn't true for all.

Problems arise when a writer blurs the distinction between fact and opinion. Critical readers recognize the difference.

● **EXERCISE 3-2**   Working individually or with a collaborative group, decide which of the following statements are facts and which are opinions. When the author and source are provided, explain how that information influenced your judgment.

1. The life of people on earth is better now than it has ever been—certainly much better than it was 500 years ago.

> —Peggy Noonan, "Why Are We So Unhappy
> When We Have It So Good?"

2. The fast food industry pays the minimum wage to a higher proportion of its workers than any other American industry.

> —Eric Schlosser, *Fast Food Nation*

3. Grief, when it comes, is nothing we expect it to be.

> —Joan Didion, *The Year of Living Dangerously*

4. History is the branch of knowledge that deals systematically with the past.

> —*Webster's New World College Dictionary*, Fourth Edition

5. In 1927, F. E. Tylcote, an English physician, reported in the medical journal *Lancet* that in almost every case of lung cancer he had seen or known about, the patient smoked.

> —William Ecenbarger, "The Strange History of Tobacco"

6. Trucks that must travel on frozen highways in Alaska for most of the year now sometimes get stuck in the mud as the permafrost thaws.

> —Al Gore, *An Inconvenient Truth*

7. You change laws by changing lawmakers.

—Sissy Farenthold, political activist, *Bakersfield Californian*

8. A critical task for all of the world's religions and spiritual traditions is to enrich the vision—and the reality—of the sense of community among us.

—Joel D. Beversluis, *A Sourcebook for Earth's Community of Religions* ●

3E.3 Identify rhetorical appeals

As we explained in 3B, writers use logical, ethical, and emotional appeals to persuade readers. Identifying how each of these appear in a reading is a key step to evaluating whether material is reasonable or fair.

3E.4 Identify the evidence

Evidence consists of facts, examples, the results of formal studies, and the opinions of experts. A helpful step in analysis is to identify the kind of evidence used for any claims or opinions—or where evidence is missing.

You might especially look for how the writer uses primary or secondary sources. **Primary sources** are firsthand evidence based on your own or someone else's original work or direct observation. Primary sources can take the form of experiments, surveys, interviews, memoirs, observations (such as in ETHNOGRAPHIES), original creative works (for example, poems, novels, paintings and other visual art, plays, films, or musical compositions). **Secondary sources** report, describe, comment on, or analyze the experiences or work of others. Quick Box 3.6 (page 28) illustrates the difference.

Secondary sources sometimes don't represent original material accurately, whether intentionally or by accident. For example, suppose a primary source concluded, "It would be a mistake to assume that people's poverty level reflects their intelligence," while a secondary source represents this as, "People's poverty level reflects their intelligence." Problem! This is a distortion. Examining the quality of sources is so important that we devote all of Chapter 23 to this topic.

● **EXERCISE 3-3** Individually or with a group, choose one of the following thesis statements and list the kinds of primary and secondary sources you might consult to support the thesis (you can guess intelligently, rather than checking to make sure that the sources exist). Then, decide which sources in your list would be primary and which secondary.

THESIS STATEMENT 1:

People who regularly perform volunteer work lead happier lives than those who don't.

THESIS STATEMENT 2:

Whether someone regularly performs volunteer work or not ultimately has no effect on their happiness. ●

Quick Box 3.6

■ ■ ■ ■ ■ ■ ■ ■ ■ ■ ■

Examples of differences between primary and secondary sources

Primary Source	Secondary Source
Professor Fassi interviews thirty single parents and reports his findings in a journal article.	*Time* magazine summarizes Professor Fassi's study in a longer article on single parents.
Medical researcher Molly Cameron publishes the results of her experiments with a new cancer drug in the *New England Journal of Medicine*.	*The Washington Post* runs an article that summarizes findings from Cameron's study.
The National Assessment of Educational Progress publishes test results on the reading abilities of ninth graders.	National Public Radio refers to the NAEP study in a story on reading in America.
A team of researchers at Bowling Green State University survey 2,259 Ohio citizens about their voting patterns and write an article explaining their findings.	Scholar Maya Dai conducts a study of politics in Colorado; in her review of literature section of her study, she summarizes the Bowling Green study, along with studies in four other states.
Rosa Rodriguez writes a memoir about life as a migrant worker.	Writer Phil Gronowski discusses Rodriguez's memoir in his daily blog.
Gerhard Richter exhibits his paintings at the Art Institute of Chicago.	The *Chicago Tribune* publishes a review of Richter's exhibition.

Once you've identified the evidence used to support claims, you can evaluate it by asking the questions in Quick Box 3.7.

Quick Box 3.7

Questions for analyzing evidence

- **Is the evidence sufficient?** A claim with no support should alert you to a possible problem. As a further rule, the more evidence, the better. Readers have more confidence in the results of a survey that draws on a hundred respondents rather than on ten.

- **Is the evidence representative?** Evidence is representative if it is typical. For example, a pollster surveying national political views would not get representative evidence by interviewing people only in Austin, Texas, because that group doesn't represent the regional, racial, political, and ethnic makeup of the entire U.S. electorate.

- **Is the evidence relevant?** Relevant evidence is directly related to the conclusion you're drawing. Suppose you read that one hundred high school students who watched television for more than two hours a day earned significantly lower scores on a college entrance exam than one hundred students who didn't. Can you conclude that all students who watch less television are more successful after college? Not necessarily.

- **Is the evidence accurate?** Accurate evidence is correct and complete. To be accurate, evidence must come from a reliable source. If someone includes a figure (for example, "The average new college graduate earns $78,000 per year"), ask yourself where that figure comes from. (NOTE: We just made up that $78,000 figure; we wish it were true! According to the *New York Times*, the median salary for new college grads in 2010 was $27,000.)

- **Is the evidence qualified?** Reasonable evidence doesn't make extreme claims. Claims that use words such as *all, always, never*, and *certainly* are disqualified if even one exception is found. Conclusions are more sensible and believable when they are qualified with words such as *some, many, may, possibly, often*, and *usually*.

3E.5 Identify cause and effect

Cause and effect describes the relationship between one event (cause) and another event that happens as a result (effect). The relationship also works in reverse: One event (effect) results from another event (cause).

Quick Box 3.8 (page 30) gives brief advice for assessing claims of cause and effect.

> **Quick Box 3.8**   ■ ■ ■ ■ ■ ■ ■ ■ ■ ■ ■
>
> ## Assessing cause and effect
>
> - **Is there a clear relationship between events?** Imagine this sequence: First the wind blows; then a door slams; then a pane of glass in the door breaks. You conclude that the wind caused the glass to break. But CHRONOLOGICAL ORDER merely implies a cause-and-effect relationship. Perhaps it was windy, but actually someone slammed the door or threw a baseball through the glass. The fact that B happened after A doesn't prove that A caused B.
>
> - **Is there a pattern of repetition?** To establish that A causes B, every time A is present, B must occur. The need for repetition explains why the U.S. Food and Drug Administration (FDA) runs thousands of clinical trials before approving a new medicine.
>
> - **Are there multiple causes and/or effects?** Avoid oversimplification. Multiple causes and/or effects are typical of real life. For example, it would be oversimplification to state that high unemployment is strictly due to poor schools.

● **EXERCISE 3-4**   For each of the following sentences, explain how the effect might not be a result of the cause given.

EXAMPLE

The number of shoppers downtown increased because the city planted more trees there.

Explanation: Of course, planting trees might have made the downtown more attractive and drawn more shoppers. However, perhaps there are other reasons: new stores opening, more parking, a suburban mall closed down, and so on.

1. Attendance at baseball games declined because the team raised prices.
2. Test scores improved because the school instituted a dress code.
3. Amy Williams got elected to Congress because she was the smartest candidate. ●

3E.6 Describe tone, bias, and point of view

Tone emerges from a writer's use of words and ways of presenting ideas. Just as our voices emit certain tones when we're happy, bored, sad, or excited, so do our words. Tone can be serious, respectful, friendly, humorous, slanted, sarcastic, or angry. Consider the difference between, "Would you please refrain from doing that?" and "Knock it off right now!"

When their tone is extreme, writers may be seeking to manipulate readers rather than to have them think logically.

> **NO** Urban renewal must be stopped. Greedy politicians are ruining this country, and money-hungry capitalists are robbing law-abiding citizens.

> **YES** Urban renewal may revitalize our cities, but it can also cause serious problems. When developers wish to revitalize decaying neighborhoods, they must also remember that they're displacing people who don't want to leave familiar homes.

In addition, you'll want to detect **bias**, also known as prejudice. When writing is distorted by hatred or distrust of individuals, groups of people, or ideas, critical readers want to suspect the accuracy and fairness of the material.

Considering the writer's **point of view**, the situation from which he or she is writing, can open up new perspectives. For example, consider the statement, "Freedom isn't the ability to do what you want but rather the ability to do what you should." If you were told this statement was made by a third-world dictator, you would interpret it differently than if you were told it was made by a leader of the American Legion (which it actually was).

Although considering point of view can help you draw inferences, take care that you don't fall prey to the LOGICAL FALLACY of personal attack (see 3H). Just because a position was stated by someone you don't like doesn't mean that the position is wrong.

● **EXERCISE 3-5** Identify any bias and prejudice in the following paragraph. Then, rewrite the paragraph so that it presents the same basic point of view but with a more reasonable tone.

> Once again we see the consequences of babying college students. Now these spoiled kids want the library to be open later at night. They claim it's for homework, but anyone who's not a fool know they really just want to hang out and hit on each other while pretending to study. Hey, I have an idea. They should drag their lazy carcasses out of bed at a decent hour and get to the library first thing in the morning. Of course, that will never happen as long as they continue to party, watch television, and play games all night. ●

3E.7 Identify inferences and assumptions

When you read for **inferences**, you're trying to understand what's suggested or implied but not explicitly stated. Here's an example.

The band finally appeared an hour after the concert was scheduled to start. The lead singer spent the first two songs staring at the stage and mumbling into his microphone, before finally looking at the audience and saying, "It's great to be here in Portland." The only problem was that they were playing in Denver. At that point the crowd was too stunned even to boo. I started texting some friends to see if they had better options for the evening.

—Jenny Shi, student

Literally, this paragraph describes what happened at a concert. But there's clearly more going on. Among the inferential meanings are that (1) the band wasn't very enthusiastic about this concert; and (2) this wasn't a very pleasant experience for Jenny.

👁
Watch
the Video

An **assumption** is a statement or idea that writers expect readers to accept as true without proof. For example, in writing this handbook, we assume that students are open to advice about how to write successfully. (You are, aren't you?) Critical readers need to take time to uncover and examine **unstated assumptions**.

3E.8   Identify implications

An implication takes the form, "If this is true (or if this happens), then that might also be true (or that might be the consequence.)" One way to consider implications, especially for readings that contain a proposal, is to ask, "Who might benefit from an action, and who might lose?" For example, consider the following short argument.

> Because parking downtown is so limited, we should require anyone putting up a new building to construct a parking lot or contribute to parking garages.

It doesn't take much to infer who might benefit: people who are looking for places to park. Who might lose? More room for parking means less room for building, so the downtown could sprawl into neighborhoods. More parking can encourage more driving, which contributes to congestion and pollution.

● **EXERCISE 3-6**   Consider the implications of the following short argument, focusing on who might gain and lose from the following proposal: "In an effort to cut tuition costs, Machiavelli College will increase its enrollment from 5,000 students to 10,000 over the next four years by reducing the admissions requirements and increasing the number of students who don't require financial aid and can pay full price." ●

● **EXERCISE 3-7**   Read the following passage, then (1) list all literal information, and (2) list all assumptions and implications.

EXAMPLE

The study found many complaints against the lawyers were not investigated, seemingly out of a "desire to avoid difficult cases."

—Norman F. Dacey

Literal information: Few complaints against lawyers are investigated.

Assumptions or implications: The term *difficult cases* implies a cover-up: Lawyers, or others in power, hesitate to criticize lawyers for fear of being sued or for fear of a public outcry if the truth about abuses and errors were revealed.

[T]he sexual balance of power in the world is changing, slowly but surely. New evidence can be found in the 2007 World Development Indicators from the World Bank. It is something to celebrate.

The most obvious changes are in education. In 2004 girls outnumbered boys at secondary schools in almost half the countries of the world (84 of 171). The number of countries in which the gap between the sexes has more or less disappeared has risen by a fifth since 1991. At university level, girls do better still, outnumbering boys in 83 of 141 countries. They do so not only in the rich world, which is perhaps not surprising, but also in countries such as Mongolia and Guyana where university education for anyone is not common.

—*The Economist*, "A Man's World?" ●

3F How do I synthesize?

To **synthesize** is to put things together. It happens when you connect the ideas you generate through analysis with things you know from readings or experience. We discuss synthesis at great length in Chapter 20.

Watch
the Video

3G How do I evaluate?

The final step in critical thinking is evaluation. **Evaluation** requires an overall assessment of the the writer's reasoning, evidence, and fairness. Quick Box 3.9 (page 34) lists questions to help you evaluate ideas generated by analysis.

Watch
the Video

3H How do I use inductive and deductive reasoning?

Two thought patterns, inductive reasoning and deductive reasoning, can help you think critically.

Watch
the Video

Quick Box 3.9

■ ■ ■ ■ ■ ■ ■ ■ ■ ■ ■

Questions to move from analysis and synthesis to evaluation

- How does the argument connect to other ideas, readings, or experiences? Do they support, complicate, or contradict each other (see 3F)?

- Does the argument use rhetorical appeals effectively and fairly? In particular, does it rely too much on emotional appeals (see 3E.3)?

- Is the evidence provided sufficent, representative, relevant, accurate, and qualified (see Quick Box 3.7)?

- Are any claims about cause and effect reasonable (see 3E.5)?

- Is the tone reasonable? Is the argument free from bias (see 3E.6)?

- Are the inferences and assumptions reasonable (see 3E.7)?

- Are the implications of the argument reasonable and desirable (see 3E.8)?

- Does the argument use inductive or deductive reasoning effectively (see 3H)?

- Is the argument free of logical fallacies (see 3I)?

3H.1 Inductive reasoning

Inductive reasoning moves from specific, explicit facts or instances to broad general principles. For example, suppose you go to the Registry of Motor Vehicles closest to your home to renew your driver's license, and you stand in line for two hours. A few months later, you return to the same location to get new license plates and again stand in a two-hour line. Your friends have had similar experiences. You conclude, therefore, that all offices of the Registry of Motor Vehicles are inefficient. Your conclusion is based on inductive reasoning, from your specific experiences to your general judgment.

As a critical thinker, you might ask whether the conclusion is an absolute truth. It is not. The conclusion is only a statement of probability. After all, perhaps another Registry of Motor Vehicles office is so well run that no one ever stands in line for more than ten minutes. Quick Box 3.10 lists the characteristics of inductive reasoning.

3H.2 Deductive reasoning

Deductive reasoning moves from general claims, called **premises**, to a specific conclusion. The three-part structure of two premises and a conclusion is known as a **syllogism**.

Quick Box 3.10

■ ■ ■ ■ ■ ■ ■ ■ ■ ■ ■ ■

Features of inductive reasoning

- Inductive reasoning begins with specific evidence—facts, observations, or experiences—and moves to a general conclusion.

- Inductive reasoning is based on a sampling of facts, not on the whole universe of related facts.

- The conclusions in inductive reasoning are considered reliable or unreliable, but never true or false.

- The advantage of inductive reasoning is that you can speculate on the unknown based on what's known.

PREMISE 1	Students who don't study fail Professor Sanchez's exams.
PREMISE 2	My friend didn't study.
CONCLUSION	My friend failed Professor Sanchez's exams.

Premises in syllogism can be facts or ASSUMPTIONS. Assumptions need close scrutiny. Because some assumptions are based on incorrect information, a critical thinker needs to evaluate each premise—that is, each assumption— carefully. When the conclusion logically follows from premises, a deductive argument is **valid** or acceptable. When the conclusion doesn't logically follow from the premises, a deductive argument is invalid.

VALID—DEDUCTIVE REASONING EXAMPLE 1

PREMISE 1	When it snows, the streets get wet. [fact]
PREMISE 2	It is snowing. [fact]
CONCLUSION	Therefore, the streets are getting wet. [valid]

INVALID—DEDUCTIVE REASONING EXAMPLE 2

PREMISE 1	When it snows, the streets get wet. [fact]
PREMISE 2	The streets are getting wet. [fact]
CONCLUSION	Therefore, it is snowing. [invalid]

Deductive argument 2 is invalid because even though the two premises are facts, the conclusion is wrong. After all, the streets can be wet for many reasons other than snow: from rain, from street-cleaning trucks that spray water, or from people washing their cars.

INVALID—DEDUCTIVE REASONING EXAMPLE 3

PREMISE 1   Learning a new language takes hard work.

PREMISE 2   Nicholas has learned to speak Spanish.

CONCLUSION   Nicholas worked hard to learn Spanish.

Deductive argument 3 is invalid because it rests on a wrong assumption: not everyone has to work hard to learn a new language; some people—for example, young children—learn new languages easily. Therefore, Nicholas might have learned Spanish effortlessly.

As a critical thinker, whenever you encounter an assumption, either stated or unstated, you need to check whether it's true. If it isn't, the reasoning is flawed. Quick Box 3.11 lists the characteristics of deductive reasoning.

Quick Box 3.11

Features of deductive reasoning

- Deductive reasoning moves from the general to the specific. Its three-part structure, called a syllogism, consists of two premises and a conclusion drawn from them.

- Deductive reasoning is valid if its conclusion follows logically from its premises.

- In deductive reasoning, if one or both premises state an assumption, the truth of the assumption needs to be proven before the truth of the reasoning can be established.

- The conclusion in deductive reasoning can be judged true or false.

  - If both premises are true, and the conclusion follows logically from them, the conclusion is true.

  - If either premise is false, the conclusion is false.

- Deductive reasoning can build stronger arguments than inductive reasoning as long as any assumptions in the premises can be proven to be true.

● **EXERCISE 3-8**   Working individually or with a peer-response group, determine whether each conclusion listed is valid or invalid. Be ready to explain your answers. For help, consult section 3H.

1. Faddish clothes are expensive.

   This shirt is expensive.

   This shirt must be part of a fad.

2. When a storm is threatening, the Coast Guard issues small-craft warnings.

   A storm is threatening.

   The Coast Guard will issue small-craft warnings.

3. The Pulitzer Prize is awarded to outstanding literary works.

   The Great Gatsby never won a Pulitzer Prize.

   The Great Gatsby isn't an outstanding literary work.

4. All states send representatives to the U.S. Congress.

   Puerto Rico sends a representative to the U.S. Congress.

   Puerto Rico is a state.

5. Finding a good job requires patience.

   Sherrill is patient.

   Sherrill will find a good job. ●

31 What are logical fallacies?

Logical fallacies are statements with defective reasoning based on irrational ideas. For example, suppose you see a teenager driving dangerously over the speed limit on a crowded highway. You would be irrational if you decided that all teens drive dangerously. The label for this type of flawed statement is *hasty generalization*, which is one of the most common logical fallacies.

Critical thinking calls for making sure arguments aren't based on logical fallacies. To avoid falling prey to manipulation, study the following list of the most common logical fallacies.

- **Hasty generalization** occurs when someone draws a conclusion based on inadequate evidence. Stereotyping is a common example of hasty generalization. For example, it is faulty to come to the conclusion that *all college students leave bad tips at restaurants* based on a few experiences with some students who have.

- The **either-or fallacy**, also called the *false dilemma*, limits the choices to only two alternatives when more exist. For example, *Either stop criticizing the president or move to another country* falsely implies that completely supporting elected officials is a prerequisite for living in America, to the exclusion of other options.

- A **false analogy** claims that two items are alike when actually they are more different than similar. The statement *If we can put a man on the moon, we should be able to find a cure for cancer* is faulty because space science is very different from biological science.

Watch
the Video

- A **false cause** asserts that one event leads to another when in fact the two events may be only loosely or coincidentally related. A common type of false cause is called *post hoc, ergo propter hoc*, which is Latin for "after this, therefore because of this." For example, *Ever since we opened that new city park, the crime rate has increased* suggests that the new park caused a change in criminal activity. There are many more likely causes.

- **Slippery slope** arguments suggest that an event will cause a "domino effect," a series of uncontrollable consequences. Some argue that the anti–gun control and pro-choice movements use the slippery slope fallacy when they say that *any* limitation of individual rights will inevitably lead to the removal of other civil rights.

- A **personal attack**, also known as an *ad hominem attack*, criticizes a person's appearance, personal habits, or character instead of dealing with the merits of the individual's argument. The following example is faulty because the writer attacks the person rather than the person's argument: *If Senator Williams had children of her own, we could take seriously her argument against permanently jailing all child abusers.*

- The **bandwagon** effect, also known as an *ad populum appeal*, implies that something is right because everyone else is doing it. An example is a teenager asking, "Why can't I go to the concert next week? All my friends are going."

- **False authority** means citing the opinion of an "expert" who has no claim to expertise about the subject at hand. Using celebrities to advertise products unrelated to their careers is a common example of this tactic.

- An **irrelevant argument** is also called a *non sequitur*, which is Latin for "it does not follow." This flaw occurs when a conclusion does not follow from the premise: *Ms. Chu is a forceful speaker, so she will be an outstanding mayor.* Ms. Chu's speaking style does not entirely reflect her administrative abilities.

- A **red herring** is a fallacy of distraction. Sidetracking an issue by bringing up totally unrelated issues can distract people from the truth. The following question diverts attention from the issue of homelessness rather than arguing about it: *Why worry about the homeless situation when we should really be concerned with global warming?*

- **Begging the question** is also called *circular reasoning*. The supporting reasons only restate the claim. For example, in the statement *We shouldn't* *increase our workers' salaries because then our payroll would be larger,* the idea of *increased salaries* and a *larger payroll* essentially state the same outcome; the reason simply restates the claim rather than supporting it.

- **Emotional appeals**, such as appeals to fear, tradition, or pity, substitute emotions for logical reasoning. These appeals attempt to manipulate readers by reaching their hearts rather than their heads. The following statement attempts to appeal to readers' pity rather than their logic: *This woman has lived in poverty all her life; she is ill and has four children at home to care for, so she should not be punished for her crimes.*

- **Slanted language** involves biasing the reader by using word choices that have strong positive or negative connotations. Calling a group of people involved in a political rally a *mob* elicits a negative response from readers, whereas referring to the group as *concerned citizens* receives a positive response.

● **EXERCISE 3-9** Following are comments posted to a newspaper Web site. Working alone or with a peer-response group, do a critical analysis of each, paying special attention to logical fallacies.

1. I oppose the plan to convert the abandoned railroad tracks into a bicycle trail. Everyone knows that the only reason the mayor wants to do this is so that she and her wealthy friends can have a new place to play. No one I know likes this plan, and if they did, it would probably be because they're part of the wine and cheese set, too. The next thing you know, the mayor will be proposing that we turn the schools into art museums or the park into a golf course. If you're working hard to support a family, you don't have time for this bike trail nonsense. And if you're not working hard, I don't have time for you.

—Mike1218

2. I encourage everyone to support the bicycle trail project. Good recreation facilities are the key to the success of any community. Since the bike trail will add more recreation opportunities, it will guarantee the success of our town. Remember that several years ago our neighbors over in Springfield decided not to build a new park, and look what happened to their economy, especially that city's high unemployment rate. We can't afford to let the same thing happen to us. People who oppose this plan are narrow-minded, selfish, and almost unpatriotic. As that great patriot John Paul Jones said, "I have not yet begun to fight."

—Bikerdude ●

3J How can I view images with a critical eye?

Watch
the Video

You can view images critically in the same way that you can read texts critically by using summary, analysis, synthesis, and evaluation (Quick Box 3.3). For example, look at Figure 3.4 with a critical eye.

View
the Model
Document

- *Summarizing* the picture, as well as viewing it literally, you can see—at a minimum—a park with some men playing football, with some geese in the front.

View
the Model
Document

- *Analyzing* the picture, as well as viewing it inferentially, you can "read between the lines" to see that it's fairly rich with layers of meaning. For example, you can tell from the leaves on the ground and the color in some trees, the bareness of others, that it's fall. You can tell the football game is probably happening in a park, not a football field because there are no goal posts or stands. The fact that at least three people are wearing football jerseys indicates that this game was planned, not something that just happened spontaneously. The fact that the geese are milling around on the field suggests either that the game hasn't yet started or that it's been a pretty quiet affair. In fact, the relationship between the geese and players is the most interesting part of the photograph. Notice how the clump of four geese on the right, with a fifth separated to the left mirrors the group of players on the right, with a separate player on

Figure 3.4 An image for critical viewing.

the left. Notice how a couple players have their heads down, as do three of the geese. Now ask yourself, "Why might the photographer have chosen to frame the picture this way, with the geese in front, players in back? What message (perhaps a humorous one) might the photographer have been trying to convey about football—or about geese?"

- *Synthesizing* the picture, you can connect what you've analyzed and inferred to your previous knowledge and experiences, readings, or even other images.

- *Evaluating* the picture is the last step in viewing it critically. You can speak of how the visual "struck" you at first glance; how it did or didn't gain depth of meaning as you analyzed it; and how it lent itself to synthesis within the realms of your personal experience and education.

See Quick Box 3.12.

Quick Box 3.12

Some helpful questions for analyzing visual images

- What does the image show?

- What are its parts? Do the parts belong together (like a lake, trees, and mountains), or do they contrast with one another (such as a woman in a fancy dress sitting on a tractor)? What might be the significance of the relationships among the parts?

- If there is a foreground and a background in the image, what is in each, and why?

- If the image is a scene, what seems to be going on? What might be its message? If the image seems to be part of a story, what might have happened before or after?

- How do the people, if any, seem to be related?

- If the image has a variety of shadings, colorings, and focuses, what's sharply in focus, blurry, bright, in shadows, colorful, or drab? How do such differences call attention to various parts of the image?

- Can you think of any connections between the image and things you've experienced or learned from school, work, reading, or other aspects of your life?

- What is your evaluation of the image?

Figure 3.5 Photo of barrels in a natural setting.

3K How can images persuade?

Because they convey lots of information in a small space, and because they can generate powerful emotional responses, images play a strong role in persuasion. (Just think about advertising!) Sometimes persuasion comes through a single well-chosen image: a picture of a bruised child's face demonstrates the cruelty of child abuse; a picture of a grateful civilian hugging a soldier seeks to show that a military action is just and good.

Figure 3.5 is a photograph of a pile of rusted barrels in a beautiful natural setting. The contrast between the barrels and the snow-covered mountains in the background, the lake, and the blue sky is stark and alarming. The barrels stand between viewers and the stunning scenery; they can't be ignored. The photographer has created this juxtaposition to persuade you—but to what purpose? Perhaps this photo makes an argument against pollution. Perhaps it's a statement against industrial development. Perhaps it emphasizes that people can act carelessly. Images can't state what they mean, although they can move viewers in certain fairly predictable directions.

● **EXERCISE 3-10** Working individually or with a peer-response group, use critical thinking and the questions in Quick Box 3.10 to consider one or both of the following photographs: Figure 3.6 and Figure 3.7. Write either informal notes or a miniessay, according to what your instructor requires.

Figure 3.6 Photo of houses against a city skyline.

Figure 3.7 Photo of students at a university gate.

Figure 3.8 An advertisement about texting while driving.

3L How can I analyze words combined with images?

Many texts—from Web pages to advertisements, posters, brochures, and so on—are **multimodal** in that they combine words and images. (See Chapters 7 and 63.) These texts can take advantage of logical and ethical appeals, in addition to the emotional appeals readily created by pictures alone. Critically analyzing multimodal texts means considering the images (see Quick Box 3.12) and the words separately, and then analyzing how the two elements combine to create a single effect. Figure 3.8 shows a simple example.

A critical thinker asks, "What is the relationship between the words and the image(s)?" and "Why did the writer choose this particular image for these particular words?"

- Sometimes words and images reinforce one another. A poster with several sentences about poverty, for example, may have a picture of an obviously malnourished person.

- Other times, words and images contrast with one another for effect. Think of a picture of a belching smokestack accompanied by a caption that says, "Everyone deserves fresh air."

- Occasionally, a text might contain images simply to add visual interest. A little decoration is sometimes fine, but always be wary of images that seem simply to be thrown in for the sake of including an image.

● **EXERCISE 3-11** Working individually or with a peer-response group, use critical thinking to analyze one of the visual arguments that follow in Figures 3.9 and 3.10. Write either informal notes or a miniessay, according to what your instructor requires.

Complete the Chapter Exercises

Figure 3.9 An advertisement about college preparation.

Figure 3.10 An advertisement about saving money.

4 Understanding College and Other Writing Situations
■ ■ ■ ■ ■ ■ ■ ■ ■ ■

Quick Points   You will learn to

> ➤ Use "purpose" and "audience" in your writing (see 4B).
> ➤ Use "role" and "genre" in your writing (see 4C–4D).

4A   What is a writing situation?

Consider two situations: (1) you're texting a message to a friend or (2) you're completing a research paper for a history class. In both cases, you're writing, but if you're going to be successful, the results need to be very different. A history paper in the short, casual style of a text message definitely won't impress a professor. Similarly, texting friends in long paragraphs followed by a works cited page would make them impatient (and likely wonder who's stolen your phone). For each task they encounter, effective writers analyze the **writing situation**: a combination of several elements, most importantly your purpose (see 4B) and audience (see 4C). Then they adjust their writing to fit that situation. Quick Box 4.1 lists elements of writing situations.

Understanding a writing situation guides your WRITING PROCESS and shapes your final draft. For example, consider the following task: "In a five-page paper for a political science course, describe government restrictions on

---

Quick Box 4.1   ■ ■ ■ ■ ■ ■ ■ ■ ■ ■

Elements of writing situations

- **Topic:** What will be the subject of your writing (see 5C)?
- **Purpose:** What should the writing accomplish (see 4B)?
- **Audience:** Who are your main readers (see 4C)?
- **Role:** How do you want your audience to perceive you (see 4D)?
- **Genre:** What form or type of writing do readers expect (see 4E)?
- **Context and Special Requirements:** When and how will your writing be read? Do you have requirements such as length, format, or due dates (see 4F)?

giving to political campaigns." Your INFORMATIVE purpose would require careful research and an objective, serious style, complete with a list of works cited or references, in a paper that explains without judging or arguing. In contrast, imagine the following assignment: "Write a 300-word newspaper editorial arguing that people should (or shouldn't) be allowed to give as much money as they want to a political candidate." As a short editorial, your writing would reflect your PERSUASIVE purpose for a public audience. It would state and explain a position quickly, probably have an energetic style, and include no list of references. The rest of this chapter discusses the other elements of writing situations.

● **EXERCISE 4-1** Either in a class discussion or in a short paper, explain how these different situations would result in different kinds of writing: a résumé and cover letter; a research paper for a sociology course; an e-mail to a friend about that sociology paper; a poster for an upcoming concert; a newspaper editorial; a newspaper news article; an essay exam; a movie review. ●

4B What does "purpose" mean for writing?

A writer's **purpose** is the reason he or she is writing. It's the general result that he or she wants the writing to achieve. Quick Box 4.2 lists five major purposes for writing.

Quick Box 4.2 ■ ■ ■ ■ ■ ■ ■ ■ ■ ■

Purposes for writing

- To express yourself (see 4B.1)
- To build connections (see 4B.2)
- To entertain readers (see 4B.3)
- To inform readers (see 4B.4)
- To persuade readers (see 4B.5)

The purpose of most college writing is to **inform** and to **persuade**.

4B.1 What is expressive writing?

Expressive writing is writing to convey your thoughts, experiences, feelings, or opinions. Some expressive writing is for your eyes only, as in diaries, personal journals, or exploratory drafts. Some expressive writing just blows off

Figure 4.1 A blog written for friends.

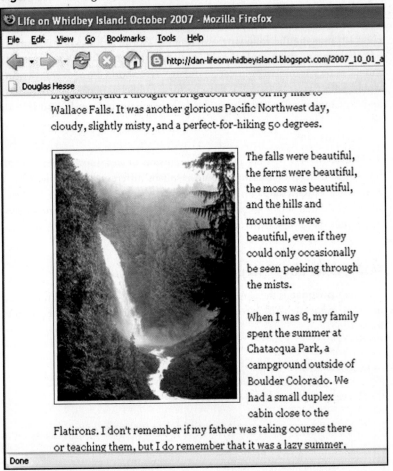

steam. For example, writing that "Congressman Jameson is a total idiot" might make an author feel good, but simply expressing that belief won't change many minds. At best, it lets people know where you stand. Finally, some expressive writing has the purpose of engaging or entertaining readers. We say more about this kind of writing in section 4B.3.

4B.2 What is writing to connect?

In our connected digital world, people do a lot of writing simply to connect to others. They tweet messages, put status updates on social networking sites, comment on others' postings, and share notes, photos, and videos.

Why? Mostly to maintain friendships or relationships. Digital communication has enlivened, this purpose, which is as old as writing personal letters or sticking a child's finger painting on a refrigerator door. Yes, channels like Facebook and Twitter, often do impart information and do try to persuade others. However, their main purpose is to establish and deepen human contact. For example, Figure 4.1 is part of a blog kept by Doug's friend, Dan.

4B.3 What is writing to entertain and engage?

Why do people write novels, movie scripts, comic strips, or jokes? For many reasons, perhaps, but the most important is to entertain. And why do people read sports pages, romances, or horror novels? Mainly for enjoyment. Much writing happens to entertain, and much reading occurs not because people *have* to do it but because they *want* to. Of course, there is "light" entertainment and "serious" entertainment; after all, for all the messages in *Romeo and Juliet*, Shakespeare wrote it for an audience who bought theatre tickets.

Personal essays are a form of expressive writing written for wider readership. Chapter 10 provides advice on writing them.

4B.4 What is writing to inform?

The essential goal of informative writing is to educate your readers about observations, ideas, facts, scientific data, and statistics. Like all good educators, therefore, you want to present your information clearly, accurately, completely, and fairly. Quick Box 4.3 (page 50) gives you a checklist to assess your informative writing. But first, here's a paragraph written to inform.

> "Diamonds in the rough" are usually round and greasy looking. But diamond miners are in no need of dark glasses to shield them from the dazzling brilliance of the mines for quite another reason: even in a diamond pipe, there is only one part diamond per 14 million parts of worthless rock. Approximately 46,000 pounds of earth must be mined and sifted to produce the half-carat gem you might be wearing. No wonder diamonds are expensive!
>
> —Richard B. Manchester, "Diamonds"

As informative writing, this paragraph works because it focuses clearly on its TOPIC (diamonds in the rough), presents facts that can be verified (who, what, when, where), and is written in a reasonable tone.

Informative writing comes in many types and varieties. Chapter 11, for example, provides general advice for writing informative essays. Chapter 12 discusses process essays, Chapter 13 cause and effect analysis, and Chapter 14 textual analysis.

> ### Quick Box 4.3
>
> ### Questions important to informative writing
>
> - Is its information clear?
> - Does it present facts, ideas, and observations that can be verified?
> - Does its information seem complete and accurate?
> - Does it explain ideas or concepts clearly and effectively?
> - Is the writer's TONE reasonable and free of distortions (see 3E.6)?

4B.5 What is writing to persuade?

Persuasive writing, also called *argumentative* writing, seeks to persuade readers to support a particular opinion. When you write to persuade, you deal with debatable topics—those that people can consider from more than one point of view. Your goal is to change your readers' minds—or at least to bring their opinions closer to yours. You want your audience to think beyond their present position (for example, reasoning why national security should—or shouldn't—limit individual rights) or to take action (for example, register to vote). Examples of persuasive writing include newspaper editorials, letters to the editor, opinion essays in magazines, reviews, sermons, advertising, fund-raising letters, books that argue a point of view, business proposals, and so on.

Argument is a frequent purpose for college writing. We discuss common types of argument in three chapters: Chapter 15: Argument Essays (covering general principles, strategies, and examples), Chapter 16: Proposal and Solution Essays, and Chapter 17: Evaluation Essays.

In general, persuasive writing means you need to move beyond merely stating your opinion. You need to support your opinion by using specific, illustrative details to back up your claims and assertions, as you can see in the following short passage:

> Our nation's economic and democratic future depends on preparing more students to succeed in college, work and life. We must engage all students in meaningful and rigorous academic work in high school and prepare more of them to succeed in college.
>
> Connecting studies to real-world issues through learning communities is a proven way to get students engaged and motivated. But there is a difference between providing students with good learning environments that include fellow students with similar interests and narrowing students' options

by tracking especially less-advantaged students into career-oriented paths in high school.

The fact is that many of the well-paying jobs that today's ninth graders might have 10 years from now do not yet exist—and the technical demands of all jobs are changing so rapidly that narrowing one's academic focus too early won't prepare one well for college and will diminish rather than enhance one's employability over the long term.

The key to success in the global economy is having the broad capacities and knowledge developed by a solid liberal education. In an economy fueled by innovation, these capabilities have, in fact, become America's most valuable economic asset.

—Debra Humphreys, "Give Students Broad Education,
Not Narrow Vocational Tracks"

As persuasive writing, this passage works because it provides factual information on school and work; it expresses a point of view that resides in sound reasoning; it offers a logical line of reasoning; and it tries to get the reader to agree with the point of view. Quick Box 4.4 lists questions to assess persuasive writing.

Quick Box 4.4

■ ■ ■ ■ ■ ■ ■ ■ ■ ■ ■

Persuasive writing

- Does it present a point of view about which opinions vary?
- Does it support its point of view with specifics?
- Does it provide sound reasoning and logic?
- Are the parts of its argument clear?
- Does it intend to evoke a reaction from the reader?

● **EXERCISE 4-2** For each paragraph, decide what the dominant purpose is for each of the following paragraphs. Use the information in section 4B to explain your answers.

A.   Trees are living archives, carrying within their structure a record not only of their age but also of precipitation and temperature for each year in which a ring was formed. The record might also include the marks of forest fires, early frosts and, incorporated into the wood itself, chemical elements the tree removed from its environment. Thus, if we only knew how to unlock its secrets, a tree could tell us a great deal about what was happening in its neighborhood from the time of its beginning. Trees can tell us what was happening before written records became available. They also have a great deal to tell us about our future. The records of past climate that they contain can help us to understand the natural forces that produce our weather, and this, in turn, can help us plan.

—James S. Trefil, "Concentric Clues from Growth Rings Unlock the Past"

B. Actual physical location threatens to evaporate everywhere we look. Information, we are everywhere taught, has annihilated distances. Surgeons can cut you open from a thousand miles away. Facsimile Las Vegas casinos deliver Rome and New York on the same daily walk. You don't have to go to the office to go to the office. You can shop in your kitchen and go to school in your living room. And, sadly enough, when you actually do go out shopping, one mall seems much like another. For what actually matters, physicality doesn't matter anymore. Even with money; now, we are told, information about money is more important than the actual green.

—Richard Lanham, *The Economics of Attention*

C. I've had it with hipsters. I've had it with their skinny jeans and their plastic glasses. I've had it with their smug superiority over everyone else—at least as they see it. They pay stupid amounts of money drinking cheap beer just because it's trendy. They decide a restaurant is popular and cram it like sheep until the poor regulars no longer feel welcome. I wish they'd all decide to stick to one neighborhood, concentrating the idiocy there.

—Rod Bateman, student

D. Soybeans. The smell hangs thick over Decatur, like a lollipop left to melt on a heat register—sweet and sticky and almost nauseating. Locals are used to this: the scent of money, Archer Daniels Midland, jobs. Midwestern and rural as corn, soybeans are fillers in ice cream and gasoline.

—Becky Bradway, *Pink Houses and Family Taverns* ●

● **EXERCISE 4-3** Consulting section 4B, write on each of these topics twice, once to inform and once to persuade your reader: reality television, part-time jobs, a current movie. Your instructor can tell you if you should write paragraphs or short papers. Be prepared to discuss how your two treatments of each topic differ. ●

4C What does "audience" mean for writing?

Your **audience** consists of everyone who will read your writing, but it especially refers to **readers** to whom you're most directly aiming your words.
For example, anyone can try to read an issue of *The New England Journal of
Medicine*, but that publication is aimed at doctors and medical researchers. An
article about how to treat a certain illness would be written very differently if,
instead of doctors, the audience consisted of parents whose children had that
illness. The article would be even more different if it were written for children
themselves. Effective writers know they need to adjust their writing for different audiences. The questions in Quick Box 4.5 (page 54) will help you analyze
your audience for a particular writing situation.

Watch
the Video

There are four general kinds of audiences:

- General educated audiences (see 4C.1)
- Specialist audiences (see 4C.2)
- Your instructor (who represents your general or specialized readers)
  (see 4C.3)
- Your peers (classmates, coworkers, friends, or others like yourself) (see 9A)

4C.1 What is a general educated audience?

A general educated audience is composed of experienced readers who regularly read newspapers, magazines, and books, whether in print or on the
screen. They read not just because they have to but because they want to
be an informed citizen. These readers typically have a basic knowledge of
many subjects and are likely to understand something about your topic. If
your writing contains too many technical details or unusual references, your
writing may confuse and alienate them. Consequently, for general educated
readers you need to avoid using uncommon terms without plainly defining
or explaining them.

General educated readers usually approach a piece of writing expecting to become interested in it, to learn something, or to see a subject
from a perspective other than their own. As a writer, work to fulfill those
expectations.

🛈 **Alert:** There are readers who aren't very well educated, and, sadly, there
are readers who are prejudiced or narrow minded. Unless your instructor
assigns otherwise, uninformed or biased readers usually aren't the audiences
for college writing. ●

Quick Box 4.5

■ ■ ■ ■ ■ ■ ■ ■ ■ ■ ■

Ways to analyze your audience

IN WHAT SETTING ARE THEY READING?

- Academic setting? Specifically, what subject?
- Workplace setting? Specifically, what business area?
- Public setting? Specifically, what form of communication? (newspaper? blog? poster?)

WHO ARE THEY?

- Age, gender, economic situation
- Ethnic backgrounds, political philosophies, religious beliefs
- Roles (student, parent, voter, wage earner, property owner, veteran, and others)
- Interests, hobbies

WHAT DO THEY KNOW?

- General level of education
- Specific level of knowledge about topic: Do they know less than you about the subject? As much as you about the subject? More than you about the subject?
- Beliefs: Is the audience likely to agree with your point of view? Disagree with your point of view? Have no opinion about the topic?
- Interests: Is the audience eager to read about the topic? Open to the topic? Resistant to or not interested in the topic?

WHAT IS THEIR RELATIONSHIP TO YOU?

- Distance and formality: Do you know your audience personally or not?
- Authority: Does your reader have the authority to judge or evaluate you (a supervisor at work, a teacher)? Do you have the authority to evaluate your reader, or does this not apply?

4C.2 What is a specialist audience?

A specialist audience is composed of readers who have a thorough knowledge of specific subjects or who are particularly committed to certain interests or viewpoints. Many people are experts in their occupational fields, and some become experts in areas that simply interest them, such as astronomy or raising orchids.

Specialist readers may also share certain assumptions and beliefs. For example, suppose you're writing for an audience of immigrants to the United States who feel strongly about keeping their cultural traditions alive. You can surely assume your readers know those traditions well, so you won't need to describe and explain the basics. Similarly, if you intend to argue that immigrants should abandon their cultural traditions in favor of U.S. practices, you'll want to write respectfully about their beliefs. Examples of specialized audiences include

- Members of specific academic disciplines, such as chemistry, political science, art history;
- People in specific professions, such as finance, education, engineering;
- People with common interests or hobbies, such as fans of certain television shows, of cooking, of NASCAR;
- People with common political beliefs (conservatives, liberals, independents) or views (on health care, the environment, immigration);
- People with common experiences, such as veterans, single parents, athletes.

ESOL Tips: (1) If you do not share a cultural background with your readers, it may be difficult for you to estimate how much your readers know about your topic. Discussing your topic with friends or classmates might help you decide what background information you need to include in your paper.

(2) As someone from a non–U.S. culture, you might be surprised— even offended—by the directness with which people speak and write in the United States. If so, we hope you'll read our open letter—it introduces Part 8 of this handbook—to multilingual students about honoring their cultures. U.S. writers and readers expect language and style that are very direct, straightforward, and without embellishment (as compared with the styles of many other cultures). U.S. college instructors expect essays in academic writing to contain a thesis statement (usually at the end of the introductory paragraph). They further expect your writing to contain an organized presentation of information that moves tightly from one paragraph to the next, with generalizations that you always back up with strong supporting details, and with an ending paragraph that presents a logical conclusion to your discussion. Also, for writing in the United States, you need to use so-called edited American English. This means following the

rules used by educated speakers. In reality, the United States has a rich mixture of grammar systems, but academic writing nevertheless requires edited American English. ●

4C.3   What is my instructor's role as audience?

As your audience, your instructor functions in three ways. First, your instructor assumes the role of your target audience by reading and responding to your writing as though he or she is one of your intended general or specific readers. Second, your instructor acts as a coach who is dedicated to helping improve your writing. Third, your instructor evaluates your final drafts.

Although instructors know that few students are experienced writers or experts on the subjects they write about, they expect your writing to reflect that you've taken the time to learn something worthwhile about a topic and then to write about it clearly. Don't assume that your instructor can mentally fill in what you leave out of your writing. Indeed, you might think that it's wrong, even insulting to your instructor, if you explain things in depth. However, instructors—indeed, all readers—can't be mind readers, and they expect students' writing to fully explore their chosen topic.

4D   What is role in writing?

It may surprise you to learn that you can take on different **roles** (personalities or identities) for different writing situations. For example, suppose you're trying to persuade readers to save energy.

- You might emphasize your role as a prospective parent who is personally worried about energy for your future children.
- You might present yourself as a conservationist concerned about the environment.
- You might present yourself as someone giving budget advice to consumers.

The point is that the role your readers see can affect how they react to your argument. For example, some readers unfortunately dismiss students as young or naive. So, you might want to emphasize your role as a voter or a taxpayer on some issue, not your role as a student. Both of us (Lynn and Doug) have found that sometimes it's useful if readers know that we're professors, but other times it's not. Some readers are intimidated by professors, whereas some other readers think professors are "impractical" or lack the ability to identify with them. We hope neither are true.

4E What is genre in writing?

To say that a writing fits in a particular **genre** means that it can be grouped with others in a category of writings that share features in common. You might be most familiar with the genres of and distinctions between poetry, fiction, and drama. However, there are many other genres of writing. Consider the following list:

A term or research paper

A resume

A lab report

A personal essay

A newspaper editorial

A job application letter

A movie review

A Web site

A reader encountering each genre would expects to see certain characteristics. For example, imagine that you turned in a lab report that began, "It was a warm, sunny April afternoon as I walked into the chemistry lab, shivering with gleeful anticipation at the prospect of titrating beakers full of colorful substances, arrayed on the lab bench like dancers in a Broadway musical." Your chemistry instructor would almost certainly give you a low grade for failing to write something that fit the objective and precise genre of a lab report.

The best way to understand the type of writing that you've been assigned is to look at some examples. The main reason we've put in so many examples of actual writing, especially in Chapters 10 to 17 but also throughout the book, is that students learn best from seeing what real writers actually do. Quick Box 4.6 (page 58) lists questions that help you analyze pieces that represent a genre.

 Alert: Terms that describe different types of writing are often used interchangeably. Most instructors attach specific meanings to each one; we've listed several terms. If your instructor's use of terms isn't clear, ask for clarification. For example, the words *essay*, *theme*, and *composition* usually—but not always—refer to written works of about 500 to 1,500 words. *Essay* is probably the most common. Similarly, the word *paper* can mean anything from a few paragraphs to a complex research project; it often refers to longer works. Finally, the general term *piece of writing* can refer to all types of writing. ●

Quick Box 4.6

■ ■ ■ ■ ■ ■ ■ ■ ■ ■ ■

Questions for analyzing genre

- What is the PURPOSE of the writing?
- Who is the apparent AUDIENCE?
- Are there clearly identified parts of individual works? Are there headings, for example?
- What kind of evidence or sources seem to count in this genre? Readings? Author's experiences? Measurements or data? Observations?
- What is the TONE or style of works in the genre? Formal? Informal? Friendly? Stuffy? Cautious? Energetic?
- What seems to be the writer's role? For example, is he or she an impartial observer who keeps in the background or a center of attention whose experience and personality are on display?
- What DOCUMENTATION STYLE, if any, does it use?

For centuries, formal writing has consisted of essays and reports containing paragraphs of connected words. These texts will always remain essential, and you need to master them. However, computers have enabled different kinds of genres, and we list some of them in Quick Box 4.7. Don't worry if your knowledge about producing any of these types of writing is limited. Instructors who require such projects can tell you how to proceed.

4F What are context and special requirements in writing?

Context refers to the circumstances in which your readers will encounter your writing. For example, persuading people to buy fuel-efficient cars when gas costs $2 per gallon is very different than when it costs over $4. Arguing that we should have a military draft is different in a time of war than in a time of peace.

Special requirements are practical matters such as how much time you're given to complete an assignment, the required length of your writing, the format of your final draft, and so on. For example, your audience expects more from an assignment that you had a week to complete than from one written in class. In the second case, your readers realize you had to write in relative haste, though no one ever accepts sloppy or careless work. Make sure you know—and follow—all special requirements.

Quick Box 4.7

■ ▪ ▪ ▪ ▪ ▪ ▪ ■ ▪ ▪ ▪

Some digital genres

Complete the Chapter Exercises

BLOGS   Short for We**b logs**, the term refers to messages that writers post in sites that anyone can read on the Internet. Blogs can be personal, such as daily reflections written for an audience of friends and family, or they can be on cultural, political, social, scientific or other topics and intended general educated or specialized audiences.

WIKIS   A Web site that allows multiple readers to change its content. We explain how to write in wikis in section 63C.

PRESENTATION SLIDES   Visuals created with software such as PowerPoint to be projected or viewed on screens. They can incorporate both words and images. Chapter 62 provides advice on creating presentations.

PODCASTS   Sound files that can be shared over the Internet. Many podcasts are miniature essays or commentaries that their writers have carefully polished and then read, as a script.

VIDEOS   Digital cameras or smartphones allow people to convey ideas or information through short movies on sites like YouTube and elsewhere. Similar to podcasts, effective videos are often built around carefully written and narrated scripts and often contain titles or captions. We discuss composing in digital environments in Chapter 63.

PORTFOLIOS   A collection of several of your own texts that you've chosen to represent the range of your skills and abilities. They can appear on paper or in digital form. See Chapter 8.

5 Essential Processes for Writing

■ ■ ■ ■ ■ ■ ■ ■ ■

Quick Points   You will learn to

➤ Adapt the writing processes to your own needs (see 5A).
➤ Think like a writer, especially about your purpose and audience (see 5B).
➤ Use different strategies to develop ideas (see 5C–5D).
➤ Write an effective thesis statement (see 5E).
➤ Use outlines to help you write (see 5F).

5A   What are writing processes?

Many people assume that a real writer can magically write a finished product, word by perfect word. Experienced writers know that writing is a process, a series of activities that starts the moment they begin thinking about a topic and ends when they complete a final draft. In addition, experienced writers are aware that good writing is actually rewriting—again and yet again. Their drafts contain additions, deletions, rewordings, and rearrangements. Figure 5.1 shows how we drafted and revised the first few sentences of this chapter.

Figure 5.1   Draft and revision of the first paragraph in Chapter 5.

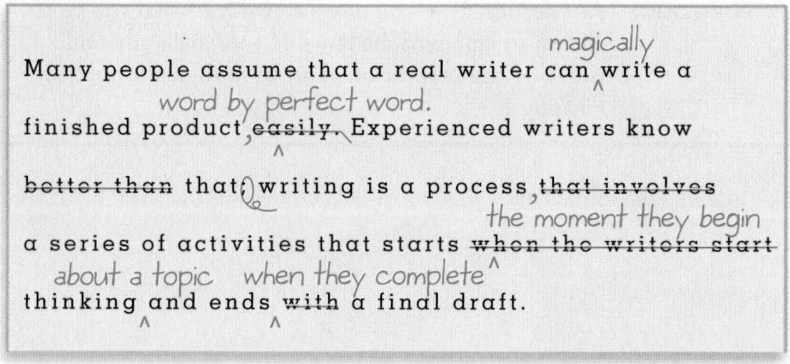

60

Quick Box 5.1

Steps in the writing process

- **Planning** means you think like a writer (see 5B); select a topic (see 5C); determine your purpose and audience (see 4B and 4C); develop ideas about your topic (see 5D); compose a tentative thesis statement (see 5E); and consider using an outline (see 5F).

- **Drafting** means you compose your ideas into sentences and paragraphs (see 5G).

- **Revising** means rewriting your drafts, often more than once (see 5I).

- **Editing** means you check for the correctness of your surface-level features, including grammar, spelling, punctuation, and mechanics (see 5J).

- **Proofreading** means you carefully scrutinize your final draft to fix errors (see 5K).

All writers adapt their **writing processes** to suit their personalities as well as specific WRITING SITUATIONS. For typical steps in the writing process, see Quick Box 5.1. Although these steps are listed separately, few writers in the real world work in lockstep order. They know that the steps overlap and double back on themselves, as the circles and arrows in Figure 5.2 show.

What is the major difference between weak writers and successful ones? The good ones refuse to give up. Good writing takes time. As you discover your personal preferences for your writing process, be patient with yourself. Remember that experienced writers sometimes struggle with ideas that are difficult to express, sentences that won't take shape, and words that aren't precise. When that becomes frustrating, they put their writing aside for a while and return later with the "new eyes" that only distance makes available.

Figure 5.2 Visualizing the writing process.

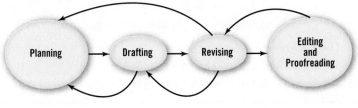

5B How do I think like a writer?

Watch the Video

Quick Box 5.2 summarizes effective writers' habits of mind and practices.

Quick Box 5.2   ■ ■ ■ ■ ■ ■ ■ ■ ■ ■ ■

How to think like a writer

Think *by engaging in writers' habits of mind*

- Realize that writing takes time.
- Know that writing requires focused attention free of distractions.
- Recognize that all writing involves rewriting, often many times (see 5L).
- Believe that the physical act of writing helps ideas spring to mind (see 5D).
- Think critically (see Chapter 3).

Think *by completely understanding the task at hand*

- Read writing assignments completely. Then reread them.
- Estimate how long you'll need for
  - Planning (see 5C–5H)
  - Drafting (see 5G)
  - Revising (see 5I)
  - Editing (see 5J)
  - Proofreading (see 5K)
- Calculate and set aside the total time you'll need to complete the assignment.

Think *by analyzing the writing task*

- Think about your topic (see 5C).
- Consider multiple ways to develop your topic (see 5D).
- Think carefully about your thesis statement (see 5E).
- Consider outlining (see 5F).
- Consider all elements of the writing situation (see Quick Box 4.1).

Think *of writing as an ongoing process*

- Use revising opportunities to their fullest.
- Expect to edit and proofread your work carefully.

5C How do I begin planning?

Begin every writing assignment by carefully analyzing the writing situation you're given. Some assignments are very specific. For example, here's an assignment that leaves no room for choice: "In a 500-word article for an audience of seventh graders, explain how oxygen is absorbed in the lungs." More often, however, writing-class assignments aren't nearly as specific as that one.

5C.1 Selecting your own topic or purpose

If you have to choose a **topic**, take time to think through your ideas. Avoid getting so deeply committed to one topic that you cannot change to a more suitable topic in the time allotted.

Beware of topics so broad that they lead to well-meaning but vague generalizations (for example, "Education is necessary for success"). Also, beware of topics so narrow that they lead nowhere after a few sentences.

GENERAL TOPIC	Marriage
TOO BROAD	What makes a successful marriage?
TOO NARROW	Couples can go to a municipal hall to get married.
APPROPRIATE	Compromise is vital for a happy marriage.

Suppose your assignment doesn't indicate a writing purpose—for example, "Write an essay on exercising." Here, you're expected to choose a purpose. Will you try to explain to a general educated audience why some people exercise regularly and others don't? Will you try to persuade a specialized audience of nonexercising college students to start? Will you summarize the current literature on exercise to inform an audience of school nurses? Considering different audiences and purposes can help you find a topic angle that engages you.

5C.2 Broadening a narrow topic

You know a topic is too narrow when you realize there's little to say after a few sentences. When faced with a too-narrow topic, think about underlying concepts. For example, suppose you want to write about the television show *American Idol*. If you chose "*American Idol* debuted in 2002," you'd be working with a single fact rather than a topic. To expand beyond such a narrow thought, you could think about a general area that your fact fits into—say, the impact of television shows on popular culture. Although that is too broad to be useful, you're headed in the right direction. You might arrive at a suitable topic like, "What impact has *American Idol* had on popular music since it began broadcasting in 2002?" Depending on your WRITING SITUATION (4A), you might need to narrow your idea further by focusing on one aspect, such as how the appearances and behaviors of performers affected what people expect on stage.

5C.3 Narrowing a broad topic

Narrowing a broad topic calls for you to break the topic down into subtopics. For example, if you're assigned "relationships" as the topic for a 1,000-word essay, you'd be too broad if you chose "What kinds of relationships are there?" You'd be too narrow if you came up with "Alexandra and Gavin have dated for two years." You'd probably be on target with a subtopic such as "In successful relationships, people learn to accept each other's faults." Here are two more examples.

SUBJECT	*music*
WRITING SITUATION	freshman composition class
	informative purpose
	instructor as audience
	500 words; one week
POSSIBLE TOPICS	"How music affects moods"
	"The main characteristics of country music"
	"The types of songs in Disney animations"
SUBJECT	*cities*
WRITING SITUATION	sociology course
	persuasive purpose
	peers and then instructor as audience
	950 to 1,000 words; ten days
POSSIBLE TOPICS	"The importance of public transportation"
	"Discomforts of city living"
	"How open spaces enhance the quality of city life"

5D How can I develop ideas about my topic?

When you're looking for ideas to develop your topics, try the strategies in Quick Box 5.3. Experiment to find out which strategies you find most helpful, adapting to your PURPOSE and AUDIENCE for each new writing assignment.

Quick Box 5.3

Strategies for developing ideas

- Freewriting and focused freewriting (see 5D.1)
- Brainstorming (see 5D.2)
- Asking and answering structured questions (see 5D.3)
- Clustering, also called "mapping" (see 5D.4)
- Writing in a journal or a blog (see 5D.5)
- Chatting with other people (see 5D.6)
- Read, browse, or search (see 5D.7)

5D.1 Freewriting

Freewriting is writing nonstop. You write down whatever comes into your mind without stopping to wonder whether the ideas are good or the spelling is correct. When you freewrite, don't interrupt the flow. Don't censor any thoughts. Don't delete.

Watch the Video

The physical act of writing triggers ideas, memories, and insights. Freewriting works best if you set a goal—perhaps writing for fifteen minutes or filling one or two pages. Keep going until you reach that goal, even if you have to write one word repeatedly until a new word comes to mind. Sometimes your writing might seem mindless, but often interesting ideas will startle or delight you.

In **focused freewriting**, you write from a specific starting point—a sentence from your general freewriting, an idea, a quotation, or anything else you choose. Except for this initial focal point, focused freewriting is the same as regular freewriting. See where your thoughts take you. Just keep moving forward.

5D.2 Brainstorming

Brainstorming means listing everything that comes to mind about your topic. Don't censor your thoughts. Let your mind roam, and jot down all ideas that flow logically or that simply pop into your head. After you've brainstormed for a while, look over your lists for patterns. If you don't have enough to work with, choose one item in your list and brainstorm from there. Next, move the items, even if loosely related, into groups. Discard items that don't fit into any group.

Here's some brainstorming by student Carol Moreno, whose essay about the benefits for women of learning to lift weights appears in Chapter 11. Carol grouped the items marked here with an asterisk and used them in her second paragraph.

*women don't want masculine-looking muscles

how much weight is safe for a woman to lift?

how long does it take?

*women's muscles grow long, not bulky

how to bend down for lifting?

*firm muscles are attractive

free weights or machines?

*exercise type—anaerobic

*exercise type—aerobic exercise

injuries

*toning the body

● **EXERCISE 5-1** Here's a list brainstormed for a writing assignment. The topic was "Ways to promote a new movie." Working individually or in a peer-response group, look over the list and group the ideas. You'll find that some ideas don't fit into a group. Then, add any other ideas you have to the list.

previews in theaters	book the movie was based on	topical subject
TV ads		special effects
provocative	locations	dialogue
movie reviews	Internet trailers	excitement
how movie was made	adventure	photography
sneak previews	newspaper ads	Facebook page ●
word of mouth	stars	
suspense	director	

5D.3 Asking and answering structured questions

Asking and answering structured questions can stimulate you to think of ideas for developing your topic. One popular question set consists of those journalists use: *Who? What? Where? When? Why? How?*

Here's how Alex Garcia used the journalists' questions to start him writing about why organic foods are worth the cost, shown in Chapter 15:

Who are the people who care about the benefits of eating organic foods?

What are typical foods people prefer to be organically grown?

Where did the idea of organic foods originate?

When did organic foods become popular?

Why do organic foods cost more than nonorganic foods?

How are organic foods processed?

Another generative question set was developed years ago by rhetorician Richard Young and his colleagues.

- What are the major characteristics of the topic?
- What's the topic's history? How has the topic changed recently? How might the topic change in the future?
- To what categories does the topic belong? How does the topic fit into a larger context?
- How does the topic relate to other aspects of culture or ideas? How is the topic similar or different?

Some of these questions, in addition to the journalists' questions, helped Alex Garcia develop his essay about organic foods in Chapter 15:

What are the major characteristics of organic foods?

What's the history of growing organic food, and how has the process changed?

How might it change in the future?

What are larger contexts for organically grown food, such as being related to overall health issues?

How does interest in organically grown food connect to other aspects of our culture?

5D.4 Clustering

Clustering, also called *mapping*, is a visual form of brainstorming. Write your topic in the middle of a sheet and then circle it. Next, move out from the middle circle by drawing lines with circles at the end of each line. Put in each circle a subtopic or detail related to the main topic. If a subtopic or detail in a given circle has further subtopics, draw lines and circles fanning out from that circle. Continue using this method as far as it can take you.

Watch
the Video

Though you might not include in your essay all the subtopics and details in your map, chances are that some the material might come in handy. For example, here's the map that Miguel Sanz drew to help him think of ideas for the second paragraph of his essay about auditioning to be in a musical.

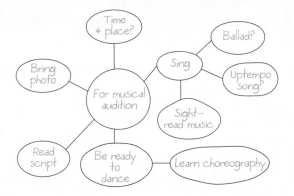

5D.5 Writing in a journal or blog

Watch
the Video

Writing in a journal or blog every day for 5 to 10 minutes is like having a conversation with yourself. The habit of regular writing makes getting started easier and gets you used to expressing yourself through words.

Draw on your thoughts, experiences, observations, dreams, reactions to your course work, or responses to something you've read recently. Use a paper notebook or a computer, depending on what's most handy and pleasurable for you. One good use for your journal or blog is to serve as a source of topics for essays as well as related supporting specifics.

5D.6 Chatting

Chatting with others means talking with them—but with a targeted purpose. Talk about your topic, and toss around ideas. Keep paper, or your journal or computer, at hand so that you'll be sure to jot down the ideas as they emerge. Little is as frustrating as remembering you'd had a good idea—but you've now forgotten it. Chatting today has come to mean more than only talking. You can chat online through texting, messaging, e-mail, and other electronic forums. Digital chats not only stimulate your thinking but also put ideas into words.

5D.7   Reading or browsing

Reading newspapers, magazines, or books, whether in print or online, provides a constant source of ideas. Experienced writers do this all the time. Check out online versions of newspapers or magazines every day, especially national papers like the *New York Times* or *Washington Post*. Follow blogs on topics you find interesting. Spend time in the PERIODICALS or new books section of a library or browse a bookstore; just looking at covers, images, or contents can generate fresh ideas.

● **EXERCISE 5-2**   Try each structured technique for discovering and compiling ideas discussed in 5D. Use your own topics or select from the suggestions here.

1. Professions and job prospects
2. An important personal decision
3. Professional sports
4. Advertisements on television
5. What you want in a life partner ●

5E   How can a thesis statement help me plan?

A **thesis statement** serves as the central, controlling point for most college writing assignments. A thesis statement gives readers a general preview of what they can expect to read about. The basic requirements of a thesis statement are listed in Quick Box 5.4 (page 70), but just as a complete essay doesn't appear in full bloom in a first draft, so too the first draft of a thesis statement is tentative. As you revise your essay, continually check your thesis statement to make sure that it goes well with the content of your essay. If you find a mismatch, revise one or the other—or perhaps both.

Watch the Video

In writing "Women Can Pump Iron Too," shown in Chapter 11, student Carol Moreno describes how with the right training woman can become strong by lifting free weights. She uses the idiom "pumping iron," a commonly used term in gyms. Her thesis statement evolved from a thin assertion to a full one that makes her message clear.

> **NO**   I think women can pump iron like men.
>
> This has too little information.

> **NO**   If trained, any woman can get strong.
>
> The concept of lifting weights is gone; "any" is too broad.

Quick Box 5.4

Basic requirements for a thesis statement

1. It states the essay's subject—the topic of the writing.

2. It states the essay's **assertion** or **claim**, putting forward the central message or point.

3. It leads to the essay's TOPIC SENTENCES (see 6E) that start the essay's BODY PARAGRAPHS (see 6D).

4. It usually comes at the end of the INTRODUCTORY PARAGRAPH (see 6C).

5. It uses clear, straightforward language without IRONY or SARCASM.

6. It might lay out the major subdivisions of a topic, but a more graceful technique is to imply them rather than stating them outright.

7. It avoids common mistakes in writing a thesis statement:

   a. Don't use it to give a fact that leads nowhere.
   b. Don't say you're not an expert in your topic; your readers expect you to have learned enough about it to write your essay.
   c. Don't announce your essay's PURPOSE with words such as "The purpose of this essay is . . . "
   d. Don't refer back to your essay's title using words such as "This is an important issue . . ." or "My essay is called 'XYZ' because . . ."

NO   In spite of thinking only men can "pump iron," women can also do it with the right training.

> This repeats the essay's title rather than give its central message.

YES   With the right training, women can "pump iron" to build strength.

> Captures the central message of Moreno's essay, meets the thesis statement requirements, and avoids the pitfalls listed in in Quick Box 5.7.

Following are three other examples.

TOPIC   *Reality television*

NO   There are many kinds of reality television shows.

YES   A common feature of reality television shows is a villain, a contestant that viewers love to hate.

TOPIC   *Public transportation*

NO   Public transportation has many advantages.

YES   Investing in public transportation pays strong benefits in environmental quality, economic development, and social interactions.

TOPIC   *Deceptive advertising*

NO   Deceptive advertising can cause many problems for consumers.

YES   Deceptive advertising costs consumers not only their money but also their health.

● **EXERCISE 5-3**   Each set of sentences offers several versions of a thesis statement. Within each set, the thesis statements progress from weak to strong. Work individually or with a group to explain why the first three choices in each set are weak and the last is best.

A. 1. Advertising is complex.
   2. Magazine advertisements appeal to readers.
   3. Magazine advertisements must be creative and appealing to all readers.
   4. To appeal to readers, magazine advertisements must skillfully use language, color, and design.
B. 1. Soccer is a widely played sport.
   2. Playing soccer is fun.
   3. Soccer requires various skills.
   4. Playing soccer for fun and exercise requires agility, stamina, and teamwork.
C. 1. We should pay attention to the environment.
   2. We should worry about air pollution.
   3. Automobile emissions cause air pollution.
   4. Congress should raise emissions standards for passenger cars and SUVs.
D. 1. Cell phones are popular.
   2. People use cell phones in many situations.
   3. The increased use of cell phones causes problems.
   4. Using cell phones while driving should be illegal. ●

5F   How can outlining help me plan?

An **outline** is a structured, sequential list of the contents of a text. Some instructors require an outline with assignments, but others don't. Always ask. When given a choice, some students never outline, whereas others find that outlining helps them write. Figure out what works best for you by experimenting.

Watch the Video

For example, you might like to use outlines for some, but not all, types of writing assignments (see Chapters 10–17). Also, you might find that outlining helps at different stages of your writing process: perhaps before DRAFTING to help you flesh out, pull together, and arrange material; or perhaps during REVISION to help you check your flow of thought or make sure you haven't gone off the topic.

An **informal outline** does not follow the numbering and lettering conventions of a formal outline. It often looks like a BRAINSTORMING list, with ideas jotted down in a somewhat random order. Here's an informal outline for the second paragraph of student Yanggu Cui's argument essay, "A Proposal to Improve Fan Behavior at Children's Games" (see Chapter 16).

Sample Informal Outline

little league games

parents on sidelines

softball, baseball, soccer

parents yell at officials

insult opposing team

A **formal outline** follows long-established conventions for using numbers and letters to show relationships among ideas. No one outline format is endorsed for MLA STYLE, but instructors generally prefer the format used in Quick Box 5.5. Outlines usually don't show the content of introductory

---

Quick Box 5.5   ■ ■ ■ ■ ■ ■ ■ ■ ■ ■

Outline formats

FORMAT OF TRADITIONAL FORMAL OUTLINE

Thesis statement: Present the entire thesis statement.

I. First main idea

    A. First subordinate idea

        1. First reason or example

        2. Second reason or example

           a. First supporting detail

           b. Second supporting detail

    B. Second subordinate idea

II. Second main idea

continued >>

Quick Box 5.5 (continued)

EXAMPLE: FORMAL SENTENCE OUTLINE
This outline goes with the second paragraph of student Yanggu Cui's argument essay, "A Proposal to Improve Fan Behavior at Children's Games" (see Chapter 16).

Thesis statement: The league organizers need to bring an end to this kind of abuse, and the best way to do so is by requiring parents to sign a code of good behavior.

I. For decades, parents have proudly watched their sons and daughters play little league softball, baseball, soccer, and other sports.

   A. In recent years, the parents who attend little league games have become more vocal on sidelines.

   B. Parents who used to shout encouragement and congratulations to their children and the teams are now rude.

      1. They scream protests about the coaches' decisions.

      2. They yell insults at the opposing team.

      3. They hurl threats at officials, many of whom are young.

EXAMPLE: FORMAL TOPIC OUTLINE
This outline goes with the second paragraph of Yanghgu Cui's argument essay, "A Proposal to Improve Fan Behavior at Children's Games" (see Chapter 16).

Thesis Statement: The league organizers need to bring an end to this kind of abuse, and the best way to do so is by requiring parents to sign a code of good behavior.

I. Parents at little league softball, baseball, soccer, and other sports.

   A. Parents vocal on sidelines.

   B. Parents not encouraging but rude.

      1. Protesting coaches' decisions.

      2. Insulting the opposing team.

      3. Threatening officials.

and concluding paragraphs, but some instructors want them included, so always ask.

To compose a formal outline, always use at least two subdivisions at each level—no I without a II, no A without a B, etc. If a level has only one subdivision, either integrate it into the higher level or expand it into two subdivisions.

In addition, all subdivisions need to be at the same level of generality: don't pair a main idea with a subordinate idea or a subordinate idea with a supporting detail. In format, use PARALLELISM so that each outline item starts with the same PART OF SPEECH.

A formal outline can be a **sentence outline**, of only complete sentences, or a **topic outline**, of only words and PHRASES. Be careful never to mix the two styles in one outline. Quick Box 5.5 shows both types.

● **EXERCISE 5-4** Here is one section of a sentence outline. Individually or with your peer-response group, revise it into a topic outline. Then, be ready to explain why you prefer using a topic outline or a sentence outline as a guide to writing.

Thesis statement: Taxpayers should demand more investment in public transportation.

  I. The current level of public transportation is inadequate everywhere.
     A. Cities need the ability to move lots of residents.
        1. Increased population in large cities causes transportation pressures.
        2. Some cities have responded well.
        3. Most cities have responded poorly.
     B. People need to move easily and cheaply between cities and towns.
        1. Cars are the only way to reach many cities and towns.
        2. It is easier and less expensive to travel in Europe.
 II. The lack of public transportation causes many problems.
     A. Driving individual cars increases pollution.
     B. Space for building new roads and highways is limited.
     C. Congestion on city streets limits productivity.
     D. Many people aren't able to drive themselves.
        1. Young or elderly people may not drive.
        2. Many people cannot afford cars.
III. Improving public transportation is possible.
     A. Cities can expand bus services and light rail services.
     B. The United States can develop a wider national rail service.
     C. Although improvements are costly, we can afford them.
        1. We can reallocate money from building new roads.
        2. Building and running transportation creates jobs and adds to our tax base.
        3. Individual savings will offset any tax increases. ●

5G What works in writing a first draft?

Drafting means getting ideas onto paper or into the computer, in sentences and paragraphs. A draft is a version of the paper; experienced writers produce several drafts. The early ones focus on generating ideas, whereas later versions focus on developing and polishing ideas. But you can't polish something that doesn't exist, so your goal on the first draft is just producing words. Don't expect perfection; the pressure to "get it right the first time" can paralyze you. On the other hand, remember that a first draft isn't a final draft, even if it looks like it's finished. Rather, it's the basis for REVISING, EDITING, and PROOFREADING, as shown in Figure 5.3.

Here are three alternatives for writing a first draft.

- Write a discovery draft. Put aside any planning notes and use FOCUSED FREEWRITING about your topic. When you finish the first draft, you can consult your notes.

- Write a structured draft. Consult your planning notes or an OUTLINE as you write, but don't allow yourself to stall at a part you don't like. Signal you want to return to it, and keep on going.

- Combine using a DISCOVERY DRAFT and a STRUCTURED DRAFT. Start with a discovery draft, and when stalled, switch to a structured draft. Or do the reverse.

The direction of drafting is forward. Keep pressing ahead. If a spelling, a word choice, or a sentence bothers you, use a signal that says you want to check it later—underline it, highlight it in a color, or switch it to capital letters. Type a note to yourself in brackets, [like this], but charge onward. Research proves that the physical act of writing without pausing makes ideas and connections among them "pop into people's heads unbidden."

Figure 5.3 Using a first draft for later revising, editing, and proofreading.

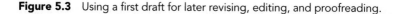

Here are some drafting problems and possible solutions.

MY DRAFTING PROBLEM: I open a blank document, write a few words, don't like them, delete them, and start again, repeatedly.

SOLUTION: Open a new document, darken your computer screen, and type without stopping. When you think you have a complete first draft, save it. Then lighten your computer screen to see what you've written.

MY DRAFTING PROBLEM: I start out well, but soon I see that I'm going off the topic.

SOLUTION: Mark the spot with a highlighter or a large arrow showing a direction change (↝). Consult your notes or outline and get right back onto the topic.

MY DRAFTING PROBLEM: I'm writing only general statements and no specifics, but I can't think of any supporting examples or details as I go along.

SOLUTION: Keep on writing. When you revise, you can concentrate on supplying the supporting details.

5H How do I get over writer's block?

Watch the Video

If you're afraid or otherwise feel unable to start writing, perhaps you're being stopped by **writer's block**. You want to get started but somehow can't. Often, writer's block occurs because the writer harbors a fear of being wrong. But the only thing "wrong" about a first draft is if the page or screen is empty, so don't worry! If you get blocked, try the suggestions in Quick Box 5.6.

5I How does revision work?

Watch the Video

REVISING is rewriting. The word *revision* breaks down into *re-vision*, literally, "again vision": to see again with fresh eyes. During DRAFTING you suspended judgment of your writing, but for revision, you switch to evaluating the writing you've done so far. How well does it meet the assignment? How well does it address your audience and purpose? What are ways that you can make it better? As you revise, keep all your drafts and notes. You might want to go back to an earlier revision and use part of it. Quick Box 5.7 (page 78) shows the major types of revision, and the levels you can apply them in your paper.

Quick Box 5.6

Ways to overcome writer's block

- **Start in the middle.** Rather than start at the beginning of your essay, start with the body paragraph you feel will be easiest or most interesting for you to write.

- **Visualize yourself writing, moving your fingers across the keyboard.** Top athletes always use visualizing, imagining themselves mechanically going though each motion involved in their sport. Visualize yourself writing easily.

- **Write an e-mail about your topic to a friend, even if you don't send it.** Write informally. Be playful with your language or ideas. Loosen up.

- **Write a draft to a different, "easier" audience.** If it feels scary to write to your instructor or an academic audience, imagine you're writing for someone much younger or someone who knows nothing about the topic. You can revise that writing later.

- **Call a friend or relative to chat about your topic.** Ask if they'll give you a few minutes to chat with you about your topic, inviting them to disagree or argue with you.

- **Play the role of someone else, and write to yourself about your topic.** Take on someone else's identity—an expert or teacher or friend—and pretend "they" are explaining the topic to you.

- **Imagine a scene or sound that relates to your topic.** Start to write by describing what you see or hear. Allow yourself to sink into the environment of that scene or sound.

In revising you work on the overarching elements of your essay. Save the last two steps—editing and proofreading—until after you've finished revising the draft. This tactic is important: "premature editing" distracts writers too soon from the content of their material.

51.1 Using your thesis statement or title to guide revision

To use your THESIS STATEMENT as a guide your revision, ask at the end of every body paragraph, "Does the topic sentence and content of this paragraph relate to my thesis statement?" If they do not, revise the thesis statement, your paragraph, or both.

Watch the Video

Quick Box 5.7   ■ ■ ■ ■ ■ ■ ■ ■ ■ ■ ■

Types and levels of revision

Type \ Level	Word	Sentence	Paragraph	Idea
Add Insert words, sentences, paragraphs ideas.				
Subtract Cut whatever goes off the topic or is repetitive.				
Replace Substitute more effective words or ideas for less effective ones				
Move Change the order of things, from sentences to paragraphs, to find the most effective arrangement.				

Your essay **title** is an important part of revising, so create a working title during your first draft. Use it consistently as a checkpoint as your essay evolves. A **direct title** tells exactly what the essay will be about: for example, "Why We're Going Less Often to the Movies." An **indirect title** hints at an essay's topic: "Can We Really Afford It?" Such an indirect title can capture a reader's interest as long as the connection is not too obscure. For example, this indirect title would not work: "Too Much and Getting Worse." Never tack on a title at the last minute.

🛇 **Alert:** A title stands alone. Don't open an essay with a reaction to the title or with an opening sentence that is a continuation of the title. For example, the following would be an inappropriate first sentence in student Cheryl Cusack's essay "Why We're Going Less Often to the Movies" in Chapter 13: "It's too expensive these days." Such an opening sentence is improper because it leans on the essay's title, and "It" is an unclear PRONOUN REFERENCE. ●

5I.2 Considering style and tone to guide revision

As you revise your writing, you want to consider *how* you say something as well as *what* you're saying. You create the STYLE of your writing by how you shape sentence structures and how you choose to address readers. TONE involves using the right words to deliver your meaning.

Chapters 37 to 40 cover style and tone in greater detail.

5I.3 Other revision aids

Probably the best source of ideas for revision is feedback that your instructor or a careful peer reviewer provides on a draft. Keep in mind that any comments your instructor makes are designed to help you get better. Take them seriously, and recognize this feedback as a gift. Revision checklists, like the one in Quick Box 5.8 (page 80), can also focus your attention as you revise your writing.

Here's a section of the earliest draft of the fifth paragraph in student Cheryl Cusack's essay "Why We're Going Less Often to the Movies" in Chapter 13.

> Ticket prices are very high, with the national average at $8.00. Throw in purchasing refreshments, and a night at the movies for a couple can reach $40.00. What about a family of four? Given the recent troubles in our economy, movies are out of reach for many.

If you compare this earliest draft with Cheryl's final draft, you see that in her revision (a) she's inserted a topic sentence to start the paragraph to tie into the essay's other topic sentences and its thesis statement; (b) she's more specific about the average price; (c) she's more specific by converting her question into a sentence so that she can use a number: "twice that"; (d) she's expanded her last sentence. In section 5L we provide a complete early draft of Cheryl's essay.

5J How does editing work?

Editing comes after you've revised the content and organization of your paper to your critical satisfaction. Some people use the terms *editing* and *revising* interchangeably, but these terms refer to very different steps. Revising refers to making changes that affect the content, meaning, and organization of a paper. In contrast, editing means finding and fixing errors you've made in grammar, spelling, punctuation, capitals, numbers, italics, and abbreviations. Some instructors call these *surface-level features*. When do you know you've finished revising and are ready to edit? Ask yourself, "Is there anything else I can do to improve the content, organization, and development of this draft?" If the answer is no, you're ready to edit.

Watch the Video

Quick Box 5.8

■ ■ ■ ■ ■ ■ ■ ■ ■ ■ ■ ■

Revision checklist

Your goal is to answer *yes* to each question on the following list. If you answer *no*, you need to revise your writing accordingly. The section numbers in parentheses tell you where to look in this handbook for help.

1. Is your essay topic suitable and sufficiently narrow (see 5C)?

2. Does your thesis statement effectively focus on your topic and purpose (see Quick Box 5.4)?

3. Does your essay show that you are aware of your audience (see Quick Box 4.5)?

4. Have you checked for places where your reader would be confused or need more information?

5. Have you checked for places where a skeptical reader would not be convinced?

6. Is your essay arranged effectively?

7. Have you checked for material that strays off the topic?

8. Does your introduction prepare your reader for the rest of the essay (see 6C)?

9. Do your body paragraphs express main ideas in topic sentences as needed (see 6E)? Are your main ideas clearly related to your thesis statement?

10. Do you provide specific, concrete support for each main idea (see 6F)?

11. Do you use transitions and other techniques to connect ideas within and between paragraphs (see 6G and 6I)?

12. Does your conclusion give your essay a sense of completion?

Slapdash editing distracts and annoys your reader; lowers that reader's opinion of you and what you say in your essay; and, in a college assignment, usually earns a lower grade. The best editors work slowly and methodically. Whenever you question your use of a rule or a writing technique, look it up in this handbook. Use the Index at the back of this handbook to find the page for the exact rule or technique you want to check.

Using an editing checklist—either one provided by your instructor or one based on Quick Box 5.9—can help you find errors by moving through editing systematically.

You may also want to ask friends, classmates, or colleagues with a good "editing eye" to read your papers and circle anything they think you need to check for correctness.

Quick Box 5.9

■ ■ ■ ■ ■ ■ ■ ■ ■ ■ ■

Editing

Your goal is to answer *yes* to each of the following questions. If you answer *no*, you need to edit. The numbers in parentheses tell you which chapters in this handbook to go to for more information.

1. Are your sentences concise (see Chapter 40)?

2. Are your sentences interesting? Do you use parallelism, variety, and emphasis correctly and to increase the impact of your writing (see Chapters 38–39)?

3. Have you used exact words (see 37F)?

4. Is your usage correct and your language appropriate (see Chapter 37)?

5. Have you avoided sexist or stereotypical language (see 37I)?

6. Is your grammar correct (see Chapters 28–36)?

7. Is your spelling correct (see Chapter 49)?

8. Have you used commas correctly (see Chapter 42)?

9. Have you used all other punctuation correctly (see Chapters 41 and 43–47)?

10. Have you used capital letters, italics, abbreviations, and numbers correctly (see Chapter 48)?

11. Have you used the appropriate citation and documentation formats (see Chapters 25–27)?

🛈 **Alert:** Be careful relying on the editing features in word processing programs or apps. Many of them are wrong or outdated. For example, some versions of Microsoft Word flag correct contractions when your choice is correct. When in doubt, consult this handbook.

Watch the Video

Spell-check programs can both help and hinder. They help when they spot a misspelled or mistyped word (for example, if you type "abot" for "about"). However, they don't spot a wrong word (for example, if you type "form" but mean "from"), so if you rely only on them, your paper can still have mistakes.

Thesaurus programs give you **synonyms** for words. You need to select the ones that fit well into your particular sentences. Many offered synonyms have slightly different meanings than what you intend, so never use one that's unfamiliar or that you know only vaguely. Always first look it up in your dictionary. Misused words make readers assume you don't know what you are saying or that you're trying to show off. ●

5K What strategies can I use to proofread?

👁
Watch
the Video

Proofreading is a careful, line-by-line reading of a final, clean version of your writing. Always proofread for errors and correct them before you hand in a paper. If you find errors during proofreading, always print a fresh, clean copy of your work.

Almost all writers proofread more effectively on a printed page rather than on a screen, so print your pages whenever possible for proofreading purposes. If you cannot help working onscreen, try highlighting a small section of your writing at a time so that you are visually separating it from the rest of the screen.

Here are effective proofreading strategies that are popular with many writers.

- Proofread with a ruler held just under the line you are reading so that you can focus on one line at a time.
- Start at the end of a paragraph or the end of your essay and read each sentence in reverse order or word by word, to avoid being distracted by the content.
- Read your final draft aloud so that you see and/or hear errors.
- Look especially carefully for omitted letters and words.
- Watch out for repeated words (*the* or *and* are common repeats).
- Keep lists of spelling, punctuation, or grammar errors that you often make. For example, you may know you have trouble keeping *to, too,* and *two* straight. Consult those lists before you revise, edit, and proofread so that you look specifically for those personal troublemakers.

5L A student's draft essay with revision notes

Cheryl Cusack received the following assignment: "Write an essay for a general educated audience in which you analyze the cause of a current situation or behavior in our society. Your essay should be 500–1000 words." After freewriting and brainstorming, Cheryl decided to write on the topic of movie attendance and why it is falling. We've included Cheryl's first draft here, and we've included her final draft in Chapter 13. When you look carefully at these drafts, you'll see that she did substantial revisions between them. We've included some of her revision notes.

Cheryl's First Draft

Cheryl Cusack

The Problem with Movies Today

The other day I heard that total movie attendance keeps going down. This surprised me because there seem to be more movies showing now than ever. There's certainly more movie advertising, and the popularity of the Oscars and other awards suggests that people are interested in the movies. Movie stars show up all the time on the news and on entertainment programs. So, it's surprising that people aren't going to movies. The purpose of this paper will be to explain what people aren't going to the movies.

One reason is that ticket prices are very high, with the national average at $8.00. Throw in purchasing refreshments, and a night at the movies for a couple can reach $40.00. What about a family of four? Given the recent troubles in our economy, movies are out of reach for many.

Another reason is that the movies are bad. I recently saw *Tinker, Tailor, Soldier, Spy*, and I haven't been so bored in all my life. There was almost no action in the movie, just a lot of slow talking. Of course, at the other end of the spectrum, having a lot of action doesn't necessarily make a good movie, either. At Christmas I saw the sequel to *Sherlock Holmes*, and there was scarcely a minute when Robert Downey Jr. or Jude Law weren't punching someone in the face or escaping some calamity. The problem in Sherlock Holmes was that the plot didn't make much sense. It was just an excuse for fights and explosions. Even though there are lots of movies out there, not many of them are very good.

Better title?

Need to check attendance figures

Improve thesis. This one will do for a start.

My taste might not be shared by others. Drop this?

But there were good movies, too.

continued >>

Needs more details.   A third reason is that going to the movies is no longer a special experience. People behave rudely in movie theaters. In addition to watching previews, which are actually OK, people now have to watch endless commercials. You can get that experience at home.

Can I expand?   A fourth reason is that there are new forms of entertainment. There are hundreds of channels on cable TV these days, with many of them running movies. Plus, you can rent movies, so if you just wait a couple of months, you can see a film in the privacy of your own home and for a fraction of the cost. Movies just can't compete with that.

Not a very interesting conclusion   As you can see, there are four reasons why people are going less often to movies: cost, quality, lack of a special experience, and competition for other forms of entertainment. Unless movie makers can address each of these four problems, it won't be long until movie theaters close down.

Complete the Chapter Exercises

—Put the best idea last. Maybe that's the experience?

Writing Paragraphs, Shaping Essays

6 ■ ■ ■ ■ ■ ■ ■ ■ ■ ■

Quick Points   You will learn to

➤ Write effective paragraphs (see 6C–6K).
➤ Use topic sentences (see 6E).
➤ Use rhetorical patterns to help you write paragraphs (see 6H).

6A How do I shape essays?

A good essay has an effective beginning, middle, and end. The key word is *effective*. Beginnings interest your reader and create expectations for the rest of the essay, usually through a THESIS STATEMENT. Middles explain or provide arguments for the thesis, usually through a series of statements and supporting details or evidence. Endings provide closure. They make readers feel that the writing achieved its purpose and that the writer had a skilled sense of the audience to the very end.

6B How do paragraphs work?

A **paragraph** is a group of sentences that work together to develop a unit of thought. Paragraphing permits writers to divide material into manageable parts, and it cues your readers about shifts in ideas. Paragraphs function differently in different types of writing. In many college papers, each paragraph is a logical unit that develops a single idea, often expressed as a topic sentence (see 6E), with each topic sentence contributing to the paper's thesis. In writings that tell a story or explain a process, there are often few topic sentences. In newspaper or journalistic writings, paragraph breaks frequently occur more for dramatic effect than for logic.

Watch
the Video

6C How can I write effective introductory paragraphs?

An **introductory paragraph** leads the reader to sense what's ahead. It also, if possible, attempts to arouse a reader's interest in the topic.

Watch
the Video

A THESIS STATEMENT is an important component in most introductions. Many instructors require students to place the thesis statement at the end of the opening paragraph. Doing so disciplines students to state early the central point of the essay. Professional writers don't necessarily include a thesis statement in their introductory paragraphs. Most have the skill to maintain a line of thought without overtly stating a main idea.

Be careful not to tack on a sloppy introduction at the last minute. That doesn't mean you have to write an introduction first; you might put down ideas and a thesis to start, then return during the revision process to write a full, polished introduction. Quick Box 6.1 (page 86) lists strategies to use and pitfalls to avoid for introductory paragraphs.

Quick Box 6.1   ■ ■ ■ ■ ■ ■ ■ ■ ■ ■ ■

Introductory paragraphs

STRATEGIES TO USE

- Provide relevant background information.
- Relate a brief interesting story or anecdote.
- Give one or more pertinent—perhaps surprising—statistics.
- Ask one or more provocative questions.
- Use an appropriate quotation.
- Define a KEY TERM.
- Present one or more brief examples.
- Draw an ANALOGY.

STRATEGIES TO AVOID

- Writing statements about your purpose, such as "I am going to discuss the causes of falling oil prices."
- Apologizing, as in "I am not sure this is right, but this is my opinion."
- Using overworked expressions, such as "Haste makes waste, as I recently discovered" or "According to Webster's dictionary."

Here's an introductory paragraph that uses two brief examples to lead into the thesis statement at the end of the paragraph.

1   On seeing another child fall and hurt himself, Hope, just nine months old, stared, tears welling up in her eyes, and crawled to her mother to be comforted—as though she had been hurt, not her friend. When 15-month-old Michael saw his friend Paul crying, Michael fetched his own teddy bear and offered it to Paul; when that didn't stop Paul's tears, Michael brought Paul's security blanket from another room. Such small acts of sympathy and caring, observed in   **Thesis** scientific studies, are leading researchers to trace the roots of empathy—the ability to share another's emotions—to infancy, contradicting a long-standing assumption that infants and toddlers were incapable of these feelings.

—Daniel Goleman, "Researchers Trace Empathy's Roots to Infancy"

Paragraph 2 opens with an interesting fact and image (the brain as oatmeal).

2   Arguably the greatest mysteries in the universe lie in the three-pound mass of cells, approximately the consistency of oatmeal, that reside in the skull of each of us. It has even been suggested that the brain is so complex that our species is smart enough to fathom everything except what makes us so smart; that is, the brain is so cunningly designed for intelligence that it is too stupid to understand itself. We now know that is not true. The mind is at last yielding its secrets to persistent scientific investigation. We have learned more about how the mind works in the last twenty-five years than we did in the previous twenty-five hundred.

    Thesis

    —Daniel T. Willingham, *Why Don't Students Like School?*

In paragraph 3, the writer asks a direct question and next puts the reader in a dramatic situation to arouse interest in the topic.

3   What should you do? You're out riding your bike, playing golf, or in the middle of a long run when you look up and suddenly see a jagged streak of light shoot across the sky, followed by a deafening clap of thunder. Unfortunately, most outdoor exercisers don't know whether to stay put or make a dash for shelter when a thunderstorm approaches, and sometimes the consequences are tragic.

    —Gerald Secor Couzens, "If Lightning Strikes"

● **EXERCISE 6-1** Write an introduction for each of the three essays informally outlined here. Then, for more practice, write one alternative introduction for each. For help, see section 6C.

1. Play at school

   Thesis statement: School recesses today differ tremendously from recess a generation ago.

   Body paragraph 1: types of recess activities thirty years ago

   Body paragraph 2: types of games now, including ultimate frisbee

   Body paragraph 3: other activities, including climbing walls and free running

2. Cell phones

   Thesis statement: Cell phones have changed how some people behave in public.

   Body paragraph 1: driving

   Body paragraph 2: restaurants

   Body paragraph 3: movies and concerts

   Body paragraph 4: sidewalks, parks, and other casual spaces

3. Identity theft

Thesis statement: Taking some simple precautions can reduce the danger of identity theft.

Body paragraph 1: discarding junk mail

Body paragraph 2: watching store purchases

Body paragraph 3: Internet security ●

6D   What are body paragraphs?

In most **academic writing**, each **body paragraph**, the several paragraphs between an introductory paragraph (see 6C) and a concluding paragraph (see 6K), consists of a main idea and support for that idea. What separates most good writing from bad is the writer's ability to move back and forth between main ideas and specific details. To be effective, a body paragraph needs development and coherence. Development consists of detailed and sufficient support for the paragraph's main idea (see 6F). Coherence means that all the ideas in the paragraph connect to each other and that the sentences progress smoothly (see 6G). Paragraph 4 is an example of an effective body paragraph.

4   The Miss Plastic Surgery contest, trumpeted by Chinese promoters as "the world's first pageant for artificial beauties," shows the power of cosmetic surgery in a country that has swung from one extreme to another when it comes to the feminine ideal. In the 10th century, Emperor Li Yu ordered his consort to bind her feet; women practiced the painful ritual for more than 900 years in the belief that small feet were more alluring. In contrast, at the height of the Cultural Revolution in the 1960s and 1970s, Maoist officials condemned any form of personal grooming or beautification as "unrevolutionary" and regularly beat women for owning hairbrushes, wearing blush, or painting their nails.

—Abigail Haworth, "Nothing about These Women Is Real"

The main idea stated in the TOPIC SENTENCE (see 6E) is developed with detailed examples. The content of every sentence ties into the content of the other sentences, and the paragraph *coheres*—sticks together—because of the use of transitional phrases ("In the 10th century" and "In contrast," for example).

6E   What are topic sentences?

A **topic sentence** contains the main idea of a paragraph and controls its content. Often, the topic sentence comes at the beginning of a paragraph, though not always. Professional writers, because they have the skill to carry the reader along without explicit signposts, sometimes decide not to use topic sentences. However, instructors often require students to use topic sentences to help them stay focused and coherent.

TOPIC SENTENCE STARTING A PARAGRAPH

When paragraphs begin with a topic sentence, readers know immediately what to expect, as in paragraph 5.

5   Music patronage was at a turning point when Mozart went to Vienna in the last part of the eighteenth century. **Topic sentence** Many patrons of music continued to be wealthy aristocrats. Haydn's entire career was funded by a rich prince. Mozart's father and, for a time, Mozart himself were in the employ of another prince. But when Mozart went to Vienna in 1781, he contrived to make a living from a variety of sources. In addition to performances at aristocratic houses and commissions for particular works, Mozart gave piano and composition lessons, put on operas, and gave many public concerts of his own music.

—Jeremy Yudkin, "Composers and Patrons in the Classic Era"

TOPIC SENTENCE ENDING A PARAGRAPH

When a topic sentence ends a body paragraph, the sentences need to lead up to it clearly.

6   The third most popular language in America—after English and Spanish—is American Sign Language (ASL). It is a visual-gestural language composed of a collection of coded gestures based on a system developed in France in the eighteenth century. It was brought to the United States by Thomas Hopkins Gallaudet, a young Congregational minister from Connecticut. After traveling to France and learning about this system of signing, Gallaudet returned to the United States, bringing a young French deaf-signing teacher, Laurent Clerc, with him. Together they developed sign language system that blended French signs with American signs. As a legacy, today deaf people in both **Topic sentence** France and the United States can recognize similarities in the signs they use.

—Roger E. Axtell, *Gestures: The Do's and Taboos of Body Language around the World*

TOPIC SENTENCE IMPLIED, NOT STATED

Some paragraphs work even without a topic sentence. Yet, most readers can catch the main idea anyway. The implied topic sentence of paragraph 7 might be stated something like, "Filmmakers tend to care more about characters and action than about facts."

7   It is easy to identify with the quest for a secret document, somewhat harder to do so with a heroine whose goal is identifying and understanding the element radium, which is why in dramatic biography writers and directors end up reverting to fiction. To be effective, the dramatic elements must, and finally will, take precedence over any "real" biographical facts. We viewers do not care—if we wanted to know about the element radium, we would read a book on the element radium. When we go to the movies to see *The Story of Marie Curie* we want to find out how her little dog Skipper died.

—David Mamet, *Three Uses of the Knife: On the Nature and Purpose of Drama*

● **EXERCISE 6-2** Working individually or with a group, identify the topic sentences in the following paragraphs. If the topic sentence is implied, write the point the paragraph conveys. For help, consult section 6E.

A.   A good college program should stress the development of high-level reading, writing, and mathematical skills and should provide you with a broad historical, social, and cultural perspective, no matter what subject you choose as your major. The program should teach you not only the most current knowledge in your field but also—just as important—prepare you to keep learning throughout your life. After all, you'll probably change jobs, and possibly even careers, at least six times, and you'll have other responsibilities, too—perhaps as a spouse and as a parent and certainly as a member of a community whose bounds extend beyond the workplace.

8

—Frank T. Rhodes, "Let the Student Decide"

B.   The once majestic oak tree crashes to the ground amid the destructive flames, as its panic-stricken inhabitants attempt to flee the fiery tomb. Undergrowth that formerly flourished smolders in ashes. A family of deer darts furiously from one wall of flame to the other, without an emergency exit. On the outskirts of the inferno, firefighters try desperately to stop the destruction. Somewhere at the source of this chaos lies a former campsite containing the cause of this destruction—an untended campfire. This scene is one of many that illustrate how human apathy and carelessness destroy nature.

9

—Anne Bryson, student

C.   Rudeness isn't a distinctive quality of our own time. People today would be shocked by how rudely our ancestors behaved. In the colonial period, a French traveler marveled that "Virginians don't use napkins, but they wear silk cravats, and instead of carrying white handkerchiefs, they blow their noses either with their fingers or with a silk handker-

10   chief that also serves as a cravat, a napkin, and so on." In the 19th century, up to about the 1830s, even very distinguished people routinely put their knives in their mouths. And when people went to the theater, they would not just applaud politely—they would chant, jeer, and shout. So, the notion that there's been a downhill slide in manners ever since time began is just not so.

—"Horizons," *U.S. News & World Report* ●

6F   How can I develop my body paragraphs?

You develop a BODY PARAGRAPH by supplying detailed support for the main idea communicated by your TOPIC SENTENCE (6E), whether stated or implied. **Paragraph development** is not merely repeating the main idea using other words. When this happens, you're merely going around in circles.

To check whether you are providing sufficient detail in a body paragraph, use the **RENNS** Test. Each letter in the made-up word *RENNS* cues you to remember a different kind of supporting detail at your disposal, as listed in Quick Box 6.2 (page 92). Of course, not every paragraph needs all five kinds of RENNS details, nor do the supporting details need to occur in the order of the letters in *RENNS*. Paragraph 11 contains three of the five types of RENNS details. Identify the topic sentence and as many RENNS as you can before reading the analysis that follows the paragraph.

Between 1910 and 1920, "The Rubber Capital of the World" was the fastest-growing city in the nation, thanks to a booming automobile industry. Akron, Ohio, had a few crucial features that helped it thrive as a hub. It was not only located close to auto makers, it also had water power and cheap coal

11 to draw on. During the peak years, more than 300 rubber companies called the city home, but most died off in the fierce pricing competition. Then, in the 1970s, French manufacturer Michelin introduced the longer-lasting radial tire. In Akron, profits slipped and plants closed. Goodyear Tire & Rubber Co. is now the only major tire company that still has headquarters in Akron.

—Wall Street Journal research "Akron, Ohio"

In paragraph 11, the first sentence serves as the topic sentence. Supporting details for that main idea include reasons, examples, numbers, and names.

Quick Box 6.2

■ ■ ■ ■ ■ ■ ■ ■ ■ ■ ■

The RENNS test: checking for supporting details

R = Reasons provide support.

- Jules Verne, a nineteenth-century writer of science fiction, amazes readers today **because he imagined inventions impossible to develop until recent years**.

E = Examples provide support.

- **For example**, he predicted submarines and moon rockets.

N = Names provide support.

- He forecast that the moon rockets would take off from an area in the **state of Florida**.

N = Numbers provide support.

- Specifically, he declared as the point of departure **27 degrees North Latitude and 5 degrees West Longitude**.

S = Senses—sight, sound, smell, taste, touch—provide support.

- Today, space vehicles are **heard blasting off** from Cape Kennedy, only eighty miles from the site Verne chose.

The writer provides reasons for growth (there was a booming auto industry; Akron was close to auto makers; there was water power and cheap coal) and examples (Michelin introducing the radial tire). The writer also provides numbers (300 rubber companies) and names (Rubber Capital of the World; Akron, Ohio; Goodyear Tire & Rubber Co.).

● **EXERCISE 6-3** Working individually or with a peer-response group, look again at the paragraphs in Exercise 6-2. Identify the RENNS in each paragraph. For help, consult 6F. ●

6G How can I create coherence in paragraphs?

Watch
the Video

A paragraph is coherent when its sentences connect in content and relate to each other in form and language. To show you broken **coherence**, in paragraph 12 we've deliberately inserted two sentences (the fourth and the next to last) that go off the topic and ruin a perfectly good paragraph, shown as paragraph 13. (Neither a personal complaint about stress nor hormones produced by men and women during exercise belong in a paragraph defining different kinds of stress.)

NO Stress has long been the subject of psychological and physiological speculation. In fact, more often than not, the word itself is ill defined and overused, meaning different things to different people. Emotional stress, for example, can come about as the result of a family argument or the death of a loved one. Everyone says, "Don't get stressed," but I have no idea how to do that. Environmental stress, such as exposure to excessive heat or cold, is an entirely different phenomenon. Physiologic stress has been described as the outpouring of the steroid hormones from the adrenal glands. During exercise, such as weightlifting, males and females produce different hormones. Whatever its guise, a lack of a firm definition of stress has seriously impeded past research.

12

YES Stress has long been the subject of psychological and physiological speculation. In fact, more often than not, the word itself is ill defined and overused, meaning different things to different people. Emotional stress, for example, can come about as the result of a family argument or the death of a loved one. Environmental stress, such as exposure to excessive heat or cold, is an entirely different phenomenon. Physiologic stress has been described as the outpouring of the steroid hormones from the adrenal glands. Whatever its guise, a lack of a firm definition of stress has seriously impeded past research.

13

—Herbert Benson, MD, *The Relaxation Response*

Techniques for achieving coherence are listed in Quick Box 6.3.

Quick Box 6.3 ■ ■ ■ ■ ■ ■ ■ ■ ■ ■ ■

Techniques for achieving coherence

- Using appropriate transitional expressions (see 6G.1)
- Using pronouns when possible (see 6G.2)
- Using **deliberate repetition** of a key word (see 6G.3)
- Using parallel structures (see 6G.4)
- Using coherence techniques to create connections among paragraphs (see 6G.5)

6G.1 Using transitional expressions for coherence

Transitional expressions are words and phrases that express connections among ideas, both within and between paragraphs. Common transitional expressions are listed in Quick Box 6.4 (page 94).

Quick Box 6.4

Transitional expressions and the relationships they signal

ADDITION	also, in addition, too, moreover, and, besides, furthermore, equally important, then, finally
EXAMPLE	for example, for instance, thus, as an illustration, namely, specifically
CONTRAST	but, yet, however, nevertheless, nonetheless, conversely, in contrast, still, at the same time, on the one hand, on the other hand
COMPARISON	similarly, likewise, in the same way
CONCESSION	of course, to be sure, certainly, granted
RESULT	therefore, thus, as a result, so, accordingly, consequently
SUMMARY	hence, in short, in brief, in summary, in conclusion, finally
TIME	first, second, third, next, then, finally, afterward, before, soon, later, meanwhile, subsequently, immediately, eventually, currently
PLACE	in the front, in the foreground, in the back, in the background, at the side, adjacent, nearby, in the distance, here, there

- Vary your choices of transitional words. For example, instead of always using *for example*, try *for instance*.
- When choosing a transitional word, make sure it correctly says what you mean. For instance, don't use *however* in the sense of *on the other hand* if you mean *therefore* in the sense of *as a result*

Alert: In ACADEMIC WRITING, set off a transitional expression with a comma, unless the expression is one short word (see 42C). ●

Paragraph 14 demonstrates how transitional expressions (shown in **bold**) enhance a paragraph's COHERENCE. The TOPIC SENTENCE is the final sentence.

14   Before the days of television, people were entertained by exciting radio shows such as *Superman, Batman,* and "War of the Worlds." **Of course**, the listener was required to pay careful attention to the story if all details were to be comprehended. **Better yet**, while listening to the stories, listeners would form their own images of the actions taking place. When the broadcaster would give brief descriptions of the Martian space ships invading earth, **for example**, every

member of the audience would imagine a different space ship. **In contrast**, television's version of "War of the Worlds" will not stir the imagination at all, for everyone can clearly see the actions taking place. All viewers see the same space ship with the same features. Each aspect is clearly defined, and **therefore**, no one will imagine anything different from what is seen. **Thus**, television can't be considered an effective tool for stimulating the imagination.

—Tom Paradis, "A Child's Other World"

6G.2 Using pronouns for coherence

PRONOUNS—words that refer to nouns or other pronouns—allow readers to follow your train of thought from one sentence to the next without boring repetition. For example, this sentence uses no pronouns and therefore has boring repetition: *After Gary Hanson, now 56, got laid off from **Gary Hanson's** corporate position in 2003, **Gary Hanson, Gary Hanson's** wife, Susan, and **Gary Hanson's** son, John, now 54 and 27, respectively, wanted to do a spot of cleaning.* Paragraph 15 illustrates how pronouns (shown in **bold**) contribute to COHERENCE.

15 After Gary Hanson, now 56, got laid off from **his** corporate position in 2003, **he, his** wife, Susan, and **his** son, John, now 54 and 27, respectively, wanted to do a spot of cleaning. Though **they** are hard at work, **they** are not scrubbing floors or washing windows. **They** are running **their** very own house-cleaning franchise, *The Maids Home Services*, which **they** opened in February.

—Sara Wilson, "Clean House: Getting Laid Off from His Corporate Job Gave This Franchisee a Fresh Start"

6G.3 Using deliberate repetition for coherence

Repetition of key words or phrases is a useful way to achieve COHERENCE in a paragraph. The word or phrase usually appears first in the paragraph's TOPIC SENTENCE and then again throughout the paragraph. Use this technique sparingly to avoid being monotonous. Paragraph 16 contains repeated words and phrases (shown in **bold**).

16 **Anthropology**, broadly defined, is the study of **humanity**, from its evolutionary origins millions of years ago to its present great numbers and worldwide diversity. Many other disciplines, of course, share with **anthropology** a focus on one aspect or another of **humanity**. **Like** sociology, economics, political science, psychology, and other behavioral and social sciences, **anthropology** is concerned with the way people organize their lives and relate to one another in interacting, interconnected groups—societies—that share basic beliefs and practices. **Like** economists, **anthropologists are interested in** society's material foundations—in how people produce and distribute food and other valued goods. **Like** sociologists, **anthropologists are interested in** the way people structure their relations in society—in families, at work, in institutions. **Like** political scientists, **anthropologists are interested in** power and authority: who has them and how they are allocated. And, **like** psychologists, **anthropologists are interested in** individual development and the interaction between society and individual people.

—Nancy Bonvillain, "The Study of Humanity"

6G.4 Using parallel structures for coherence

Parallel structures are created when grammatically equivalent forms are used in series, usually of three or more items, but sometimes only two (see Chapter 39). The repeated parallel structures reinforce connections among ideas, and they add both tempo and sound to the sentence.

In paragraph 17, the author uses several parallel structures (shown in **bold**):

Our skin is what stands between us and the world. If you think about it, no other part of us makes contact with something not us, but the skin. It imprisons us, but it also **gives us** individual shape, **protects us** from invaders, **cools us down** or **heats us up** as need be, **produces** vitamin D, **holds** in our
17 body fluids. Most amazing, perhaps, is that it can mend itself when necessary, and it is constantly renewing itself. Weighing from six to ten pounds, it's **the largest organ of the body**, and **the key organ of sexual attraction**. Skin can take a startling variety of shapes: claws, spines, hooves, feathers, scales, hair. It's waterproof, washable, and elastic.

—Diane Ackerman, *A Natural History of the Senses*

● **EXERCISE 6-4** Working individually or with a peer-response group, locate the coherence techniques in each paragraph. Look for transitional expressions, pronouns, deliberate repetition, and parallel structures. For help, consult 6G.

A.   Kathy sat with her legs dangling over the edge of the side of the hood. The band of her earphones held back strands of straight copper hair that had come loose from two thick braids that hung down her back. She swayed with the music that only she could hear. Her shoulders raised, making
18   circles in the warm air. Her arms reached out to her side; her open hands reached for the air; her closed hands brought the air back to her. Her arms reached over her head; her opened hands reached for a cloud; her closed hands brought the cloud back to her. Her head moved from side to side; her eyes opened and closed to the tempo of the tunes. Kathy was motion.

—Claire Burke, student

B. Newton's law may have wider application than just the physical world. In the social world, racism, once set into motion, will remain in motion unless acted upon by an outside force. The collective "we" must be the outside force. We must fight racism through education. We must make sure every school **19** has the resources to do its job. We must present to our children a culturally diverse curriculum that reflects our pluralistic society. This can help students understand that prejudice is learned through contact with prejudiced people, rather than with the people toward whom the prejudice is directed.

—Randolph H. Manning, "Fighting Racism with Inclusion" ●

● **EXERCISE 6-5** Working individually or with a peer-response group, use RENNS (see 6F) and techniques for achieving coherence (see 6G) to develop three of the following topic sentences into paragraphs. When finished, list the RENNS and the coherence techniques you used in each paragraph.

1. Video games reflect current concerns in our culture.
2. The content of trash in the United States says a great deal about U.S. culture.
3. Reality shows on television tend to have several common elements.
4. In many respects, our culture is very wasteful.
5. College students face several true challenges. ●

6H How can rhetorical patterns help me write paragraphs?

Rhetorical patterns (sometimes called *rhetorical strategies*) are techniques for presenting ideas clearly and effectively in academic and other situations. Quick Box 6.5 (page 98) lists the common rhetorical strategies at your disposal.

NARRATIVE

Narrative writing tells a story. A *narration* relates what is happening or what has happened. Paragraph 20 is an example.

Watch the Video

Gordon Parks speculates that he might have spent his life as a waiter on the North Coast Limited train if he hadn't strolled into one particular movie house during a stopover in Chicago. It was shortly before World War II began, and on the screen was a hair-raising newsreel of Japanese planes attacking a gunboat. When it was over the camera operator came out on stage and the audience **20** cheered. From that moment on Parks was determined to become a photographer. During his next stopover, in Seattle, he went into a pawnshop and purchased his first camera for $7.50. With that small sum, Parks later proclaimed, "I had bought what was to become my weapon against poverty and racism." Eleven years later, he became the first black photographer at *Life* magazine.

—Susan Howard, "Depth of Field"

> **Quick Box 6.5**
>
> **Common rhetorical patterns of thought (strategies) for paragraphs**
>
> - Narrative
> - Description
> - Process
> - Examples
> - Definition
> - Analysis
> - Classification
> - Comparison and contrast
> - Analogy
> - Cause-and-effect analysis

DESCRIPTION

Watch
the Video

Writing a **description** is a rhetorical strategy that appeals to a reader's senses—sight, sound, smell, taste, and touch. *Descriptive writing* paints a picture in words. Paragraph 21 is an example.

21 Walking to the ranch house from the shed, we saw the Northern Lights. They looked like talcum powder fallen from a woman's face. Rouge and blue eye shadow streaked the spires of a white light which exploded, then pulsated, shaking the colors down—like lives—until they faded from sight.

—Gretel Ehrlich, "Other Lives"

PROCESS

Writing about a **process** reports a sequence of actions or pattern by which something is done or made. A process usually proceeds in **chronological order**—first do this, then do that. A process's complexity dictates the level of detail in the writing. For example, paragraph 22 provides an overview of a complicated process.

22 Making chocolate isn't as simple as grinding a bag of beans. The machinery in a chocolate factory towers over you, rumbling and whirring. A huge cleaner first blows the beans away from their accompanying debris—sticks and stones, coins and even bullets can fall among cocoa beans being bagged. Then they go into another machine for roasting. Next comes separation in a winnower, shells sliding out one side, beans falling from the other. Grinding follows, resulting in chocolate liquor. Fermentation, roasting, and "conching" all influence the flavor of chocolate. Chocolate is "conched"—rolled over and over against itself like pebbles in the sea—in enormous circular machines named conches for the shells they once resembled. Climbing a flight of steps to peer into this huge, slow-moving glacier, I was expecting something like molten mud but found myself forced to conclude it resembled nothing so much as chocolate.

—Ruth Mehrtens Galvin, "Sybaritic to Some, Sinful to Others"

EXAMPLES

A paragraph developed by **examples** presents particular instances of a larger category. Paragraph 23 is an example of this strategy. On the other hand, sometimes one extended example, often called an **illustration**, is useful. Paragraph 24 is an example of this technique.

Watch the Video

23 Certain numbers have magical properties. E, pi and the Fibonacci series come quickly to mind—if you are a mathematician, that is. For the rest of us, the magic numbers are the familiar ones that have something to do with the way we keep track of time (7, say, and 24) or something to do with the way we count (namely, on 10 fingers). The "time numbers" and the "10 numbers" hold remarkable sway over our lives. We think in these numbers (if you ask people to produce a random number between one and a hundred, their guesses will cluster around the handful that end in zero or five) and we talk in these numbers (we say we will be there in five or ten minutes, not six or 11).

—Daniel Gilbert, "Magic By Numbers"

24 He was one of the greatest scientists the world has ever known, yet if I had to convey the essence of Albert Einstein in a single word, I would choose *simplicity*. Perhaps an anecdote will help. Once, caught in a downpour, he took off his hat and held it under his coat. Asked why, he explained, with admirable logic, that the rain would damage the hat, but his hair would be none the worse for its wetting. This knack of going instinctively to the heart of the matter was the secret of his major scientific discoveries—this and his extraordinary feeling for beauty.

—Banesh Hoffman, "My Friend, Albert Einstein"

DEFINITION

When you define something, you give its meaning. **Definition** is often used together with other rhetorical strategies. If, for example, you were explaining how to build a picture frame (process), you'd probably want to define *mitre box*, a tool needed for the project. You can also develop an entire paragraph by using definition, called an extended definition. An extended definition

Watch the Video

discusses the meaning of a word or concept in more detail than a dictionary definition. Sometimes a definition tells what something is not, as well as what it is.

> 25 When it comes to soft skills, most people think they are all about those warm-and-fuzzy people skills. Yes, it's true that people skills are a part of the equation, but that's just for starters. While hard skills refer to the technical ability and the factual knowledge needed to do the job, soft skills allow you to more effectively use your technical abilities and knowledge. Soft skills encompass personal, social, communication, and self-management behaviors. They cover a wide spectrum of abilities and traits: being self-aware, trustworthiness, conscientiousness, adaptability, critical thinking, attitude, initiative, empathy, confidence, integrity, self-control, organizational awareness, likeability, influence, risk taking, problem solving, leadership, time management, and then some. Quite a mouthful, eh? These so-called soft skills complement the hard ones and are essential for success in the rough-and-tumble workplace.
>
> —Peggy Klaus, *The Hard Truth about Soft Skills*

ANALYSIS

Analysis, sometimes called *division*, divides things up into their parts. It usually starts, often in its topic sentence, by identifying one subject and continues by explaining the subject's distinct parts, as in paragraph 26.

> 26 Jazz is by its very nature inexact, and thus difficult to define with much precision: humble in its roots, yet an avenue to wealth and fame for its stars; improvised anew with each performance, but following a handful of tried-and-true formulas; done by everybody but mastered by an elite few; made by African Americans, but made the definition of its age by white bands—and predominantly white audiences. Jazz is primarily an instrumental idiom, but nearly all jazz is based on songs with words, and there are great jazz singers. "If you have to ask what jazz is," said Louis Armstrong, "you'll never know."
>
> —D. Kern Holoman, "Jazz"

CLASSIFICATION

👁 **Classification** groups items according to an underlying, shared characteristic.
Watch
the Video
Paragraph 27 groups—classifies—interior violations of building-safety codes.

> 27 A public health student, Marian Glaser, did a detailed analysis of 180 cases of building code violation. Each case represented a single building, almost all of which were multiple-unit dwellings. In these 180 buildings, there were an incredible total of 1,244 different recorded violations—about seven per building. What did the violations consist of? First of all, over one-third of the violations were exterior defects: broken doors and stairways, holes in the walls, sagging roofs, broken chimneys, damaged porches, and so on. Another one-third were

interior violations that could scarcely be attributed to the most ingeniously destructive rural southern migrant in America. There were, for example, a total of 160 instances of defective wiring or other electrical hazards, a very common cause of the excessive number of fires and needless tragic deaths in the slums. There were 125 instances of inadequate, defective, or inoperable plumbing or heating. There were 34 instances of serious infestation by rats and roaches.

—William Ryan, "Blaming the Victim"

COMPARISON AND CONTRAST

A paragraph developed by *comparison* deals with similarities; a paragraph developed by *contrast* deals with differences. **Comparison and contrast** writing is usually organized one of two ways: You can use *point-by-point organization*, which moves back and forth between the items being compared; or you can use *block organization*, which discusses one item completely before discussing the other. Quick Box 6.6 lays out the two patterns visually.

Watch
the Video

Quick Box 6.6

■ ■ ■ ■ ■ ■ ■ ■ ■ ■ ■

Comparison and contrast

POINT-BY-POINT STRUCTURE

Student body: college A, college B
Curriculum: college A, college B
Location: college A, college B

BLOCK STRUCTURE

College A: student body, curriculum, location
College B: student body, curriculum, location

Paragraph 28 is structured point by point.

28   The world can be divided in many ways—rich and poor, democratic and authoritarian—but one of the most striking is the divide between the societies with an **individualist mentality** and the ones with a **collective mentality**. This is a divide that goes deeper than economics into the way people perceive the world. If you show an **American** an image of a fish tank, the **American** will usually describe the biggest fish in the tank and what it is doing. If you ask a **Chinese** person to describe a fish tank, the **Chinese** will usually describe the context in which the fish swim. These sorts of experiments have been done over and over again, and the results reveal the same underlying pattern. **Americans** usually see individuals; **Chinese** and other Asians see contexts.

—David Brooks "Harmony and the Dream"

Paragraph 29 uses the block pattern for comparison and contrast. The writer first discusses games and then business (each key word is in **boldface**).

Games are of limited duration, take place on or in fixed and finite sites, and are governed by openly promulgated rules that are enforced on the spot by neutral professionals. Moreover, they're performed by relatively evenly matched teams that are counseled and led through every move by seasoned hands. Scores are kept, and at the end of the game, a winner is declared.

29 **Business** is usually a little different. In fact, if there is anyone out there who can say that the business is of limited duration, takes place on a fixed site, is governed by openly promulgated rules that are enforced on the spot by neutral professionals, competes only on relatively even terms, and performs in a way that can be measured in runs or points, then that person is either extraordinarily lucky or seriously deluded.

—Warren Bennis, "Time to Hang Up the Old Sports Clichés"

ANALOGY

An **analogy** is an extended comparison between objects or ideas that aren't normally associated. Analogy is particularly effective in explaining new concepts because readers can compare to what is familiar.

30 Casual dress, like casual speech, tends to be loose, relaxed, and colorful. It often contains what might be called "slang words": blue jeans, sneakers, baseball caps, aprons, flowered cotton housedresses, and the like. These garments could not be worn on a formal occasion without causing disapproval, but in ordinary circumstances, they pass without remark. "Vulgar words" in dress, on the other hand, give emphasis and get immediate attention in almost any circumstances, just as they do in speech. Only the skillful can employ them without some loss of face, and even then, they must be used in the right way. A torn, unbuttoned shirt or wildly uncombed hair can signify strong emotions: passion, grief, rage, despair. They're most effective if people already think of you as being neatly dressed, just as the curses of well-spoken persons count for more than those of the customarily foul-mouthed do.

—Alison Lurie, *The Language of Clothes*

CAUSE-AND-EFFECT ANALYSIS

👁
Watch
the Video

Causes lead to an event or an effect, and effects result from causes. Paragraph 31 discusses the causes of economic collapses.

31 Many collapses of the past appear to have been triggered, at least in part, by ecological problems: people inadvertently destroyed their environmental resources. But societies are not doomed to collapse because of environmental damage. Some societies have coped with their problems, whereas others have not. But I know of no case in which a society's collapse can be attributed simply to environmental damage; there are always complicating factors. Among them are climate change, the role of neighbors (who can be friendly or hostile), and most important, the ways people respond to their environmental problems.

—Jared Diamond, "Collapse: Ecological Lessons in Survival"

● **EXERCISE 6-6** Working individually or with a peer-response group, decide what rhetorical strategies are used in each of paragraphs 32–35. Choose from any one or a combination of narrative, description, process, example, definition, analysis, classification, comparison and contrast, analogy, and cause and effect. For help, consult 6H.

A.   Another way to think about metamessages is that they frame a conversation, much as a picture frame provides a context for the images in the picture. Metamessages let you know how to interpret what someone
32   is saying by identifying the activity that is going on. Is this an argument or a chat? Is it helping, advising, or scolding? At the same time, they let you know what position the speaker is assuming in the activity, and what position you are being assigned.

—Deborah Tannen, *You Just Don't Understand*

B.   I retain only one confused impression from my earliest years: it's all red, and black, and warm. Our apartment was red: the upholstery was of red moquette, the Renaissance dining-room was red, the figured silk hangings over the stained-glass doors were red, and the velvet curtains in Papa's study
33   were red too. The furniture in this awful sanctum was made of black pear wood; I used to creep into the kneehole under the desk and envelop myself in its dusty glooms; it was dark and warm, and the red of the carpet rejoiced my eyes. That is how I seem to have passed the early days of infancy. Safely ensconced, I watched, I touched, I took stock of the world.

—Simone de Beauvoir, *Memoirs of a Dutiful Daughter*

C.   In the case of wool, very hot water can actually cause some structural changes within the fiber, but the resulting shrinkage is minor. The fundamental cause of shrinkage in wool is felting, in which the fibers scrunch
34   together in a tighter bunch, and the yarn, fabric, and garment follow suit. Wool fibers are curly and rough-surfaced, and when squished together under the lubricating influence of water, the fibers wind around each other, like two springs interlocking. Because of their rough surfaces, they stick together and can't be pulled apart.

—James Gorman, "Gadgets"

D.   Lacking access to a year-round supermarket, the many species—from ants to wolves—that in the course of evolution have learned the advantages of hoarding must devote a lot of energy and ingenuity to protecting their stashes from marauders. Creatures like beavers and honeybees, for example, hoard food to get them through cold winters. Others, like desert rodents that face food scarcities throughout the year, must take advantage of the short-lived harvests that follow occasional rains. For animals like burying beetles that dine on mice hundreds of times their size, a habit of biting off more than they can chew at the moment forces them to store their leftovers. Still others, like the male MacGregor's bowerbird, stockpile goodies during mating season so they can concentrate on wooing females and defending their arena d'amour.

35

—Jane Brody, "A Hoarder's Life: Filling the Cache—and Finding It" ●

6I What is a transitional paragraph?

Transitional paragraphs form a bridge between one long discussion on a single topic that requires a number of paragraphs and another discussion, usually lengthy, of another topic. Paragraph 36 is an example of a transitional paragraph that allows the writer to move from a long discussion of anger to a long discussion of possible remedies.

So is there any hope for you and your anger? Is there any reason to believe that you will be able to survive the afternoon commute without screaming or tailgating or displaying choice fingers?

36

—Andrew Santella, "All the Rage"

6J What are effective concluding paragraphs?

● Watch the Video

A **concluding paragraph** ends the discussion smoothly by following logically from the essay's introductory paragraph (see 6C) and the essay's body paragraphs (see 6D). A conclusion that is hurriedly tacked on is a missed opportunity to provide a sense of completion and a finishing touch that adds to the whole essay. Quick Box 6.7 lists strategies for concluding your essay as well as strategies to avoid.

The same writers who wait to write their introductory paragraph until they've drafted their body paragraphs often also wait to write their concluding paragraph until they've drafted their introduction. They do this to coordinate the beginning and end so that they can make sure they don't repeat the same strategy in both places.

Paragraph 37 is a concluding paragraph that summarizes the main points of an essay.

Quick Box 6.7

Strategies for concluding paragraphs

STRATEGIES TO TRY

- Adapt a strategy from those used for introductory paragraphs (see 6C)— but be careful to choose a different strategy for your introduction and conclusion.
- Relate a brief concluding interesting story or anecdote.
- Give one or more pertinent—perhaps surprising—concluding statistics.
- Ask one or more provocative questions for further thought.
- Use an appropriate quotation to sum up the THESIS STATEMENT.
- Redefine a key term for emphasis.
- Use an ANALOGY that summarizes the thesis statement.
- Use a SUMMARY of the main points, but only if the piece of writing is longer than three to four pages.
- Use a statement that urges awareness by the readers.
- Use a statement that looks ahead to the future.
- Use a call to readers.

STRATEGIES TO AVOID

- Introducing new ideas or facts that belong in the body of the essay
- Rewording your introduction
- Announcing what you've discussed, as in "In this paper, I have explained why oil prices have dropped."
- Making absolute claims, as in "I have proved that oil prices don't affect gasoline prices."
- Apologizing, as in "Even though I'm not an expert, I feel my position is correct."

37 Now the equivalent to molecule fingerprints, DNA profiles have indeed proven to be valuable investigative tools. As the FBI Laboratory continues to develop innovative technologies and share its expertise with criminal justice professionals worldwide, it takes great strides in bringing offenders to swift and sure justice, while clearing innocent individuals and protecting crime victims.

—"DNA Profiling Advancement: The Use of DNA Profiles in Solving Crimes," *The FBI Law Enforcement Bulletin*

Paragraph 38 is a concluding paragraph from an essay on the potential collapse of public schools. It looks ahead to the future and calls for action that involves taking control of them.

38 Our schools provide a key to the future of society. We must take control of them, watch over them, and nurture them if they are to be set right again. To do less is to invite disaster upon ourselves, our children, and our nation.

—John C. Sawhill, "The Collapse of Public Schools"

● **EXERCISE 6-7** Working individually or in a group, return to Exercise 6-1, in which you wrote introductory paragraphs for three informally outlined essays. Now, write a concluding paragraph for each. ●

Complete the Chapter Exercises

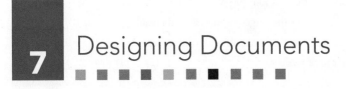

7 Designing Documents

Quick Points You will learn to

> Identify the elements of good document design (see 7A–7C).
> Use text and headings effectively (see 7D).
> Use photographs and other visuals for a purpose (see 7E–7F).
> Lay out the pages of a document (see 7G).

7A What is document design?

Watch the Video

Document design refers to the physical appearance of your writing. Design focuses on how a document looks rather than on what it says, although how we present information affects how others understand and respond to it. Quick Box 7.1 lists the elements of document design.

🛇 **Alert:** Most instructors are very particular about the design and format of papers for their courses. They want certain margins, spacing, fonts, headings, and so on. It's disrespectful not to follow their directions—and it can also harm your grade! ●

Quick Box 7.1

Elements of document design

Text—Fonts, type sizes, and highlighting (see 7C)

Headings—(see 7D)

Images—Photographs or illustrations (see 7E)

Visuals—Tables or charts as well as features like lines, arrows, or boxes (see 7F)

White Space—Empty areas for emphasis (see 7G)

Layout—The relationships among the previous elements (see 7G)

7B What are basic principles of design?

The basic principles of design are unity, variety, balance, and emphasis. Quick Box 7.2 describes how to check for these principles.

Quick Box 7.2

Checklist for document design

- **Unity:** Do all elements in my document work together visually with effective consistency?

- **Variety:** Have I introduced design elements, where appropriate, that break up monotony and add interest, such as headings or illustrations?

- **Balance:** Are the parts of my document in proportion to one another?

- **Emphasis:** Does my document design draw attention to key information?

The flyer that a student produced for the environmental group Sustain! in Figure 7.1 (page 108) reflects the four design principles.

7C How do I design with text?

Text consists of letters and words. You need to decide which font you'll use. Also called typefaces, fonts fall into two major categories. **Serif** fonts have little "feet" or finishing lines at the top and bottom of each letter; **sans serif** fonts (*sans* is French for "without") don't. Times New Roman is serif; Arial is sans serif.

Figure 7.1 Flyer that has unity, variety, balance, and emphasis.

Fonts come in different sizes that are measured in "points." There are 72 points in an inch. For body text in longer documents, use 10- to 12-point serif typefaces. Avoid using playful fonts (**Comic Sans MS**) or simulated handwriting fonts (*Monotype Corsiva*) in academic and business writing. Twelve-point Times New Roman usually is best for academic writing.

8 point   12 point   16 point   24 point

7C.1 Highlighting text

Highlighting draws attention to key words or elements of a document. You can highlight in various ways, but the one guideline that applies in all cases is this: Use moderation.

BOLDFACE, ITALICS, AND UNDERLINING

Italics and underlining—they serve the same purpose—have special functions in writing (for example, to indicate titles of certain works), but they're also useful for emphasis and for headings. **Boldface** is reserved for heavy emphasis.

BULLETED AND NUMBERED LISTS

Bulleted and numbered lists are useful when you discuss a series of items or steps in a complicated process or when you want to summarize key points or guidelines. Bullets are small dots or marks in front of each entry.

COLOR

You can change the color of text for emphasis or you can highlight a text segment. Take time, however, to judge whether color helps accomplish your purpose. Use color sparingly for variety and emphasis. For college writing, use black text.

7C.2 Justifying text

When you make your text lines even in relation to the left or right margin, you **justify** them. There are four kinds of justification, or ways to line up text lines on margins: left, right, centered, and full, as shown here. Most academic and business documents are left-justified.

Left-justified text (text aligns on the left)

Right-justified text (text aligns on the right)

Center-justified text (text aligns in the center)

Full-justified text (both left and right justified to full length, or measure, of the line of type)

7C.3 Indentation

When you move text in from the left margin, you are indenting. Using the ruler line in your word processing program to control indentations makes it easier to make global changes in your indentation. The top arrow of the bar sets the paragraph indentation, and the bottom arrow sets the indentation for everything else in the paragraph.

7D How do I use headings?

Headings clarify how you've organized your material and tell your readers what to expect in each section. Longer documents, including handbooks (like this one), reports, brochures, and Web pages, use headings to break content into chunks that are easier to read and understand. In ACADEMIC WRITING, APA STYLE favors headings, and MLA STYLE tends to discourage them. Following are some guidelines for writing and formatting headings.

- **Create headings in a slightly larger type than the type size in the body of your text.** You can use the same or a contrasting typeface, as long as it coordinates visually and is easy to read.

- **Keep headings brief and informative.**

- **Change the format for headings of different levels.** Think of levels in headings the way you think of items in an OUTLINE. First-level headings show main divisions. Second-level headings divide material that appears under first-level headings, and so on.

- **Use parallel structure.** All headings at the same level should be grammatically similar. For example, you might make all first-level headings questions and all second-level headings noun phrases. Quick Box 7.3 presents common types of headings.

7E How can I incorporate photographs?

Watch
the Video Digital cameras and the Internet have made it cheap and easy to take photographs and circulate them. As a result, pictures can sometimes enhance a variety of documents.

7E.1 Finding photographs

Every Internet browser has a way to search for images, which you can then copy and paste into a document. However, there are three crucial considerations.

Quick Box 7.3

■ ■ ■ ■ ■ ■ ■ ■ ■ ■

Common types of headings

- **Noun phrases can cover a variety of topics.**
  - Executive Branch of Government
- **Questions can evoke reader interest.**
  - When and How Does the President Use the Veto Power?
- **Gerunds and -*ing* phrases can explain instructions or solve problems.**
  - Submitting the Congressional Budget
- **Imperative sentences can give advice or directions.**
  - Identify a Problem

- **Copyright and permissions.** Just because you find something on the Web doesn't mean you can do whatever you want with it. Getting permission from its owner or maker is important. Generally, you're okay to use an image one time for a class project that will not appear anywhere else, especially online. But to be extra careful—and often to find better images—consider using online "stock photo" sites (such as istockphoto .com or gettyimages.com) that have hundreds of thousands of images available for small fees or even free.

- **Quality.** Many images you find through a browser search are low resolution or poor quality. They may look fine online, but if you print them in a document they're often fuzzy. That's another reason to use stock photos.

- **Documentation.** Regardless of how you've found an image, you must document it in your Works Cited or References page. (See Chapters 25 to 27.)

7E.2 Taking photographs

Sometimes it's easier and more effective just to take a picture yourself. Consider your camera as a drafting tool. Take multiple pictures of each subject, using different camera settings and zooms so that you can choose the best one. Your main subject should fill most of the image; a common mistake is having people get lost against a background that's too large.

7E.3 Adjusting photographs

It's fine to adjust an image by making it lighter or darker, fixing colors, and making other changes. A very useful adjustment is cropping, which means removing some parts of the image. Figure 7.2 presents two versions of the same image, creating two different meanings.

Figure 7.2 Original and cropped versions of a photograph.

PLACING PHOTOGRAPHS

How you place photographs in relation to text is an important part of layout. Unless an image is the width of the page itself, it's generally more effective to wrap the text around it. (Look for "picture tools" or formatting commands in your word processing program.) Figure 7.3 shows a picture centered by itself, whereas Figure 7.4 shows a more effective version in which that same

Figure 7.3 Photograph simply inserted and centered

Without a doubt, the best pitcher in baseball in 2011 was Justin Verlander of the Detroit Tigers. Verlander won the American League Cy Young and the Most Valuable Player Awards, something that almost never had happened previously. He had 250 strikeouts, won 24 games, with only five losses, and had an earned run average of 2.40.

Figure 7.4 Photograph wrapped by text

Without a doubt, the best pitcher in baseball in 2011 was Justin Verlander of the Detroit Tigers. Verlander won the American League Cy Young and the Most Valuable Player Awards, something that almost  never had happened previously. He had 250 strikeouts, won 24 games, with only five losses, and had an earned run average of 2.40.

Figure 7.5 Photograph with text superimposed on it.

picture is wrapped by text. Of course, digital technologies offer a third possibility, useful in posters, brochures, etc.: placing words over the picture, as Figure 7.5 shows.

7F How can I incorporate other visuals?

Visuals, also called graphics, often can condense, compare, and display information more effectively than words.

7F.1 Charts, graphs, and tables

- **Bar graphs** compare values, such as the number of different majors at a college, as shown in the graph at right.

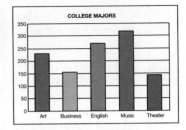

- **Line graphs** indicate changes over time. For example, advertising revenue is shown over an eight-month period in the graph at left.

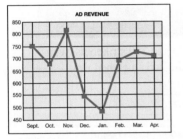

- **Pie charts** show the relationship of each part to a whole, such as a typical budget for a college student, as shown in the chart at right.

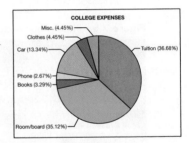

- **Tables** present data in list form, as shown here, allowing readers to grasp a lot of information at a glance.

TABLE 1   STUDENT RATINGS OF SUSTAINABILITY, BY TERM

Semester	Students rating sustainability as important	Percentage of All Students
Fall 2011	2,321	65.8%
Spring 2012	2,892	72.3%
Fall 2012	3,425	78.1%

Number figures and tables, if there are more than one, and number them sequentially. Quick Box 7.4 offers guidelines for using visuals in your documents.

Quick Box 7.4

Guidelines for using visuals

- **Design all visuals to be simple and uncluttered.**
- **Include a heading or caption for each visual.**
- **Never use unnecessary visuals.** Visuals should clearly enhance your purpose, not simply decorate your document.
- **Consider your audience and their sensibilities.** You don't want to offend or confuse your readers.
- **Credit your source if an image or visual isn't your own.** Always avoid PLAGIARISM by crediting your SOURCE. If you plan to use a visual for anything other than a class project, you need to obtain written permission from the copyright holder.

7G What is page layout?

Layout is the arrangement of text, visuals, color, and space on a page. You'll want to arrange these elements so that you follow the basic principles of design (see 7B). White space, the part of your document that has neither text nor visuals, allows readers to read your document more easily. Quick Box 7.5

Quick Box 7.5

Guidelines for positioning text and visuals

- Consider the size of visuals in placing them so they don't cluster at the top or the bottom of a page. In other words, avoid creating a page that's top heavy or bottom heavy.
- To create balance in a document, imagine it as divided into halves, quarters, or eighths. As you position text or images in the spaces, see which look full, which look empty, and whether the effect seems visually balanced.
- Avoid splitting a chart or table between one page and the next, if at all possible. If it runs slightly more than a page, look for ways to adjust spacing or reduce wording. If you have no choice but to continue a chart or table, then on the second page repeat the title and add the word *continued* at the top.
- Create various layouts, and look at their strengths and weaknesses. Ask others to tell you what they like best and least about each.

explains how to position text and visuals. (Also see Figures 7.3, 7.4, and 7.5 for some options.)

● EXERCISE 7-1   Figure 7.6 shows a very poorly designed poster advertising events for The Civic Society. Working alone or in a small group, explain all the design problems you see with this poster, and suggest improvements. You might even draw a rough sketch of how the improved poster might look.

Complete
the
Chapter
Exercises

Figure 7.6   A poorly designed poster for The Civic Society.

8 Creating a Writing Portfolio

Quick Points   You will learn to

➤ Plan a writing portfolio that shows your writing skill (see 8A–8B).
➤ Write a self-reflective essay or letter to introduce a portfolio (see 8C).
➤ Present a paper or digital portfolio (see 8D).

8A What is a writing portfolio?

A **writing portfolio** is a collection of your writing (see Quick Box 8.1). It is often a required final project in a writing course, so you need to keep track of all writing from the first day of class. Carefully date everything you write: all drafts of every paper, project, and exam. Preserve all your computer files, clearly labeled for future reference, and keep backups.

Quick Box 8.1

What's in a writing portfolio?

- Some or all of your writings completed for a course, according to your instructor's requirements (see 8B)
- An essay or letter of self-reflection to discuss what you've learned about yourself as a writer and your writing (see 8C)
- A list of all items in the portfolio
- An appealing format, whether paper-based (see 8D) or digital (see 8E)

8B What writing do I include in a portfolio?

Read your portfolio assignment carefully to understand the purpose your instructor has in mind. Three types of portfolio are most common.

- **Portfolios that demonstrate your general writing ability** Consider this kind of assignment: "Present three works that best display your strengths as a writer." You'll want, of course, to choose what you consider is your best writing; however, if the course called for you to demonstrate the range of your abilities, you might want to include an example of a risk you took to stretch as a writer.

- **Portfolios that demonstrate your range of responses** Consider another kind of situation: "Create a portfolio of three works that demonstrates how you're able to write for different AUDIENCES and PURPOSES." Here, you want to choose examples that respond to more than one WRITING SITUATION and one FRAME.

- **Portfolios that demonstrate your improvement as a writer** Consider a third kind of portfolio: "Select four examples of your writing from this semester that demonstrate how your writing has developed." In this case, your instructor wants to see your improvement. You might choose writings from the beginning, middle, and end of the course; or, you might choose both early and revised drafts from the same paper.

8C How do I write my self reflection?

Quick Box 8.2 explains how to structure a self-reflection.

Quick Box 8.2   ■ ■ ■ ■ ■ ■ ■ ■ ■ ■ ■

Structure of a self-reflective essay or letter

1. Opening paragraph introduces yourself as a writer and makes a generalization about the writing in your portfolio.

2. A paragraph, either here or after the set of BODY PARAGRAPHS described in item 3, discusses how you have evolved, or have not evolved, as a writer during the course. Specific examples refer to discussions with peers, your instructor, or other teachers.

3. A set of body paragraphs, each referring to a separate piece of writing in your portfolio and explaining why you chose to include it. If you do this systematically, your reader knows precisely which piece of writing you're discussing in each paragraph.

4. Concluding paragraph wraps up your self-reflection. You might mention the goals you've set for yourself as a writer in your future.

EXCERPT FROM A STUDENT'S REFLECTIVE ESSAY

Following is the opening section of a student's reflective essay for his portfolio. Here is the assignment he received: "Create a portfolio in which you select three papers from the course that best demonstrate your abilities and your development as a writer in this course. Please write a reflective essay of two to three pages in which you explain and analyze the papers you've chosen and what they reveal about your writing."

View
the Model
Document

During the 2013 fall semester, I completed five papers in English 101, revising each of them several times based on responses from my peers and feedback from my instructor. In the beginning, I was very frustrated. I was getting low grades, but I had been told in high school my writing was excellent. After a few weeks in this class, I came to realize my critical thinking about our topics was too superficial and my peers didn't always understand what I thought was clear in my writing. I'm leaving this course with a different kind of confidence as a writer, based on the strengths the three papers in this portfolio demonstrate.

One quality apparent in these papers is my ability to adjust writings for different audiences, both academic and general. For example, "Analyzing the Merits of Organic Produce" addresses an academic readership, specifically members of the scientific community reading a review of the literature. This can be seen in my consistent use of APA citation style and a scholarly tone suitable for experts, as in my opening sentence, "Research on the health values of organic produce over nonorganic reveals that this issue remains unresolved" (Johnson, 2006; Akule, 2007). The paper begins bluntly and directly because I decided scholars would require little orientation and would value my getting right to the point. Stressing that "research . . . reveals" emphasizes my ethos as a careful scholar, a quality reinforced by my including two citations. Academic readers will value this ethos more than they would an opinionated or informal one. The objective and cautious tone of "remains unresolved" differs from a more casual phrase like "is messy." In contrast, my paper "Is That Organic Apple Really Worth It?" is aimed at a more general audience, such as readers of a weekly news magazine. That paper uses scenes and examples designed to engage readers with a friendly tone. On pages seven and eight, for example, I include an interview with organic grower Jane Treadway in which I describe the setting. . . .

Marginal annotations:

Opening introduces writer and writings in portfolio

Generalization

Specific example

Quotation

Explanation of specific example

Another specific example

8D How do I format a writing portfolio?

8D.1 Paper portfolios

Paper portfolios can come in several formats, from a set of papers stapled or clipped together to writings collected in a folder or a binder. Add page numbers and a list of contents so that readers can locate your writings. Follow any further specific directions from your instructor. For an example of a cover page that includes contents, see Figure 8.1.

Figure 8.1 Print portfolio cover page, with contents.

"Paths to Progress"

Portfolio by

Alba Carmen

WRIT 1133: Writing and Research

Casey Sampson, Instructor

May 30, 2012

Contents

Figure 8.2 Opening screen of a student's digital portfolio.

8D.2 Digital portfolios

A **digital portfolio** is a collection of several texts in electronic format. Unlike paper portfolios, digital versions contain links between—and within—individual texts; they can be modified and shared easily and cheaply; and they can be put online for public reading. Figure 8.2 shows the opening screen of one student's digital portfolio for a first semester writing course. Note that all the titles function as links to the papers themselves.

9 Writing with Others

Quick Points   You will learn to

> Collaborate with other writers (see 9A–9B).
> Give useful feedback to others (see 9C).
> Benefit from others' help (see 9D).
> Participate effectively in online discussions (see 9E).

9A What is writing with others?

Although writing may often seem like a lonely act, a surprising amount of it depends on people working together. Any time you ask someone else to give you feedback for revision, you're working with others. The other person could be a friend, a classmate, a campus writing center tutor, or an instructor.

A more direct kind of writing with others happens when two or more people **collaborate** (work together) to complete a single project. This handbook is a prime example. Lynn wrote some sections, then Doug revised them—and vice versa. We planned the book over e-mail, in telephone calls, and in person. Drafts flew back and forth over the Internet. We also worked with editors who suggested—and sometimes required—revisions. Each of us brought different knowledge, experience, and talents.

Collaborative writing projects are common in the professional world. Often, the size or complexity of a project means that only a team of people can accomplish it in the given amount of time.

Collaborative writing assignments are also popular in college courses; small groups are commonly asked to brainstorm a topic together before individual writing tasks, to discuss various sides of a debatable topic, to share reactions to a reading, or so on. Collaborative experience you gain in college is a skill that employers value.

Alert: Some instructors and students use the terms *peer-response group* and *collaborative writing* to mean the same thing. In this handbook, we assign the terms to two different situations. We use *collaborative writing* (see 9B) for students writing a paper together in a group. We use *peer-response group* (see 9C) for students getting together in small groups to help one another write and revise. ●

9B How can I collaborate with other writers?

Three qualities are essential to collaborative writing.

Watch the Video

1. **Careful planning.** Your group needs to decide when and how it will meet (in person, in a telephone call, in an online discussion); what steps it will follow and what the due dates will be; what technology you'll use; and who will be responsible for what. You'll also probably find it useful to assign people basic roles such as leader (or facilitator) and recorder (or secretary).

2. **Clear communication.** Open and honest communication is vital, and people need to build a productive and trusting atmosphere. Keep

notes for every meeting. If people disagree over the group's decisions, the group should resolve that disagreement before moving on. You'll also find it effective to ask for regular brief reports from each group member.

3. **A fair division of labor.** Almost nothing causes bad feelings more quickly than when some group members feel like they're doing more than their share. There are two basic ways to divide tasks:

Watch the Video

A. Divide according to the different steps in the writing process. One or more people can be in charge of generating ideas or conducting research; one or more can be in charge of writing the first draft; one or more can be in charge of revising; and one or more may be in charge of editing, proofreading, and formatting the final draft. It's hard to separate these tasks cleanly, however, and we warn that writing the first draft usually requires more effort than any other element.

B. Assign part of the project to each person. Many projects can be broken into sections, and using an outline (see 5G) can help you see what those sections are. Each person can then plan, write, revise, and edit a section, and the other members can serve as a built-in peer-response group to make suggestions for revision. This approach can have the advantage of distributing the work more cleanly at the outset, but it often takes a lot of work at the end to stitch the parts together.

See Quick Box 9.1 (pp. 124–125) for some guidelines for collaborative writing.

● **EXERCISE 9-1** Working in a small group, plan how your group might proceed on one or more of the following collaborative projects, satisfying each of the three essential criteria for group work. (*Note:* You don't actually have to complete the project; the purpose of this exercise is to develop your planning skills.)

- A report for a public audience in which you explain trends in social media
- A research project in which you analyze the religious views of students on your campus
- A persuasive paper in which you argue whether the United States should pass laws to make it harder for American companies to move jobs to other countries

Be prepared to explain your planning to your instructor or to class members in a way that shows your group has been thoughtful and thorough. ●

Quick Box 9.1

Guidelines for collaborative writing

STARTING

1. Learn each other's names and exchange contact information.

2. Participate actively. During discussions, help set a tone that encourages everyone to participate. Conversely, help the group set limits if someone dominates the discussions or makes all the decisions.

3. As a group, assign everyone work to be done between meetings. Distribute the responsibilities as fairly as possible. Also, decide whether to choose one discussion leader or to rotate leadership.

4. Make decisions regarding the technology you'll use. Make sure everyone can access all word processing documents. Decide if you'll share materials via e-mail attachments, flash drives, a shared document like GoogleDocs, or even through a WIKI (see 62C). Help any group members who are unfamiliar with these processes.

5. Set a timeline and deadlines. Agree on what to do if someone misses a deadline.

PLANNING

6. After discussing the project, brainstorm as a group or use structured techniques for discovering ideas. Agree on the ideas that seem best. Repeat the process, if needed.

7. As a group, divide the project into parts and distribute assignments fairly.

8. As a group, OUTLINE or otherwise sketch a preliminary overview of the project.

9. As you work on your part of the project, prepare progress reports for your group.

DRAFTING

10. Draft a THESIS STATEMENT. Each member of the group can draft a possible thesis statement, but the group needs early to agree on one version. Your group might revise the thesis statement after the whole paper has been drafted, but using a preliminary version starts everyone in the same direction.

11. Draft the paper using one of the strategies described above for dividing tasks. Share draft materials among all group members. For most group meetings, it will be important to have copies for everyone.

___ continued >> ___

| Quick Box 9.1 | (continued) |

REVISING

12. Read over the drafts. Are all the important points included?

13. Use the revision checklist (see Quick Box 5.8), and work either as a group or by assigning portions to subgroups. If different people have drafted different sections, COHERENCE should receive special attention in revision, as should the introduction and the conclusion.

14. Agree on a final version. Either work as a group, or assign someone to prepare the final draft and make sure every group member has a copy.

EDITING AND PROOFREADING

15. Use the editing checklist (see Quick Box 5.9) to double-check for errors. No matter how well the group has performed, a sloppy final version reflects negatively on the entire group.

16. As a group, review printouts of the final draft. Use everyone's eyes for proofreading.

17. If your instructor asks, be prepared to describe your personal contribution to the project and to describe or evaluate the contributions of others.

9C How can I give useful feedback to others?

There are two main ways to give feedback to other writers. One is in a small group of three to five people (usually), who together discuss each group member's draft out loud. Another way is to work in pairs, providing oral or written comments for each other.

9C.1 Working in peer-response groups

A peer is an "equal": another writer like you. Participating in a **peer-response group** makes you part of a respected tradition of colleagues helping colleagues. Professional writers often seek comments from other writers to improve their rough drafts. As a member of a peer-response group, you're not expected to be a writing expert. Rather, you're expected to offer responses as a practiced reader and as a fellow student writer who understands what writers go through.

🛈 **Alert:** Some instructors use the term *workshopping* for peer response. The term comes from creative-writing programs, sometimes called "Writers' Workshops." ●

Peer-response groups are set up in different ways.

1. Students pass around and read one another's drafts silently, writing down reactions or questions in the margins or on a response form created by the instructor. Figure 9.1 shows an example of a response form.

2. Students read drafts aloud, and then others respond orally or in writing.

Figure 9.1 A peer-response group form.

Peer Response Questions and Directions

Reviewer's name: _____

Writer's name: _____

*Directions to **Writer**: Please choose three questions you'd like the reviewer to address. Circle them. After you receive feedback, write a half-page synthesis and plan for revision.*

*Directions to **Reviewer**: Please read the work and provide clear and detailed answers to each of the THREE questions to which the writer has asked you to respond. Continue on the back, if needed.*

1. How can this writer make the central argument of this essay stronger, clearer, or more easily accessible to readers?

2. Identify any paragraphs whose purpose is unclear or that seem to be working at cross purposes, and explain how the writer can revise them to make the purpose clear.

3. Does the sequence of the argument build successfully? If not, suggest a way to reorder it and identify transitions that may need clarifying.

4. Writers can offer their readers guidance in a number of ways, such as clearly defining their terms, explaining exactly how the evidence supports their claims, etc. **Identify places in this essay where these forms of guidance could be stronger, and explain specifically how the writer can strengthen them.**

5. Are there places in which you feel the textures or structures of language are serving the writer's purpose effectively? Are there places in which the language could be modified?

3. In yet another arrangement, students provide focused responses to only one or two features of each draft (perhaps each member's thesis statement, or topic sentences and supporting details, for example).

If your instructor gives you directions, follow them carefully. The guidelines in Quick Box 9.2 will also help you.

Quick Box 9.2

Guidelines for participating in peer-response groups

Always take an upbeat, constructive attitude, whether you're responding to someone else's writing or receiving responses from others.

Watch
the Video

Watch
the Video

- Think of yourself as a coach, not a judge.

- Consider all writing by your peers as "works in progress."

- After hearing or reading a peer's writing, summarize it briefly to check that both of you are clear about what the peer actually wrote. (It's useful to know when you thought you were saying one thing but people thought you meant something else.)

- Start with what you think is well done. No one likes to hear only negative comments.

- Be honest in your suggestions for improvement.

- Base your responses on an understanding of the writing process, and remember that you're reading drafts, not finished products. All writing can be revised.

- Give concrete and specific responses. General comments such as "This is good" or "This is weak" don't offer much help. Describe specifically what is good or weak.

- Follow your instructor's system for recording your comments so that your peer can recall what you said. For example, one group member might take notes from the discussion; the group should take care that they're accurate.

9C.2 Giving peer response as an individual

Often an instructor will have two people exchange drafts and provide responses and suggestions to each other. All the general guidelines for peer response in groups apply to situations when you're the only person giving feedback, especially being helpful, specific, and polite.

You might find it useful to play a role if you feel awkward about giving reactions or suggestions to a classmate—especially if you think that some critical comments will help revision. For example, instead of responding as yourself, pretend that you're a skeptical member of the writer's target audience. Respond as that person would, even in his or her voice. However, you should still aim to be constructive. Of course, you could also take the opposite role, responding as someone who agrees with the writer; that role can be particularly helpful if you personally disagree with a draft's position. If you're playing a role as you respond, you should make that clear to the writer.

As with peer response, your instructor may have you use a response form or follow a set of questions. (See Figure 9.1.) Here are some specific questions you might find useful for giving peer feedback:

- What part of the paper was most interesting or effective?
- If you had to remove one paragraph, which would you sacrifice, and why?
- If you had to rearrange two parts of the paper, which would you change, and why?
- What is one additional fact, argument, or piece of information that might improve the paper?

Another good strategy is for the writer to generate a couple of questions that he or she would particularly like the reviewer to answer. Avoid questions that require only a *yes* or *no* response. For example:

Watch
the Video

| NOT HELPFUL | Is paragraph two on page three effective? |
| HELPFUL | How can I improve paragraph two on page three? |

Watch
the Video

| NOT HELPFUL | Do you like my tone in the paper? |
| HELPFUL | How would you describe my tone in this paper? |

Instead of answering specific questions, the instructor might ask you simply to write to the author about the strengths and weaknesses of the draft. Such responses can take the form of a letter to the author, as in Figure 9.2. Our students usually find that if they're thoughtful while writing open responses to others, they get useful responses in return.

● EXERCISE 9-2

1. Choose a paper that you're writing (or have written). Create a set of questions that you would ask a peer reviewer to answer about that paper.
2. Show your questions to someone else in your class. Ask them to comment on how well those questions might generate constructive comments; ask them to suggest additional questions. ●

Figure 9.2 An example of one student's peer response.

Directions. I'll pair you up with another student. Your task is to write a letter in which you play the role of someone who disagrees with the author of the paper; explain as carefully as you can why you disagree. State your own arguments and explain why they lead to a different conclusion. Now, I want you to be polite about this; don't indulge in the extreme language we looked at earlier in the course. However, to be helpful to the author you should be as persuasive as possible—even if you're playing a role that you actually disagree with. Send this letter by e-mail, with a copy to me (dhesse@du.edu).

Dear Leslie,

   To begin with I thought your paper was very thorough and well thought out. It was lengthy and covered all the important things you needed to. But as I've been asked to take the role of someone who disagrees, then offer constructive criticism, there are some things that I think would help clarify and convince your readers who are on the fence about your position.

   Your argument is that sex education in schools needs to be complete and that "abstinence only" education is inadequate. You use a lot of statistics and surveys. This is good, it added credibility and "scientific reasoning," but when I see these, I wonder where you found these studies and whether they are themselves factual? You reiterated multiple times that abstinence-only educators use statistics that are untrue or slanted to favor their position. How does the reader know that you haven't made your own facts up or slanted them in your favor? My suggestion would be to label your studies and discuss where they came from and why they're credible. If one of them is from a government agency, you can include the address so if the reader wanted to they could verify the facts. I'm not accusing you of doing this, but it would only make your paper more believable.

   Because I am a strong believer in no sex before marriage, I worry about giving students too much information. I think that sex before marriage causes more problems than it solves. I do believe that giving out specific advice about contraception can encourage people to engage in sex before they are ready. Instead we should encourage students to wait. Can you prove to me that having information doesn't lead to early sexual activity?

   You stated on page two that a study found that consensual sex between two teenagers had no mental health effects on them. I disagree with this finding. Regardless of age and relationship status of the two parties involved, someone often gets hurt by casual sex. If there was a relationship before, it has the potential to be destroyed due to the new baggage. If one of the parties involved uses it as a one night stand and the other person really liked the other, he or she suffers emotional distress that could be extreme. Actually, I'm not sure this point belongs in your paper; because it's contoversial, I wonder if your paper would be stronger without it.

                                                      Sincerely,
                                                      Stephen

9D How can I benefit from others' help?

Watch the Video

We offer you three pieces of advice from our own experiences.

1. Keep in mind that most students don't like to criticize their peers. They worry about being impolite or inaccurate, or losing someone's friendship. Try, therefore, to cultivate an attitude that encourages your peers to respond as freely and as helpfully as possible. It's particularly important to show that you can listen without getting upset or defensive.

2. Realize that most people can be a little defensive about even the best-intentioned and most tactful criticism. Of course, if a comment is purposely mean, you and all the others in your peer-response group have every right to say so.

3. Listen and resist any urge to interrupt during a comment or to jump in to react. A common rule in many writing workshops is that the paper's author must remain silent until the group has finished its responses and discussion.

4. Ask for clarification if a comment isn't clear or is too general.

Finally, no matter what anyone says about your writing, you keep ownership of your writing always, and you don't have to make every suggested change. Use only the comments that you think can move you closer to reaching your intended AUDIENCE and PURPOSE. Of course, if a comment from your instructor points out a definite problem, and if you choose to ignore it, that could affect your grade.

ESOL Tip: International students might feel especially uncomfortable about responding to peers. Please know, however, that peer-response groups are fairly common in U.S. schools and at jobs because people usually think that "two heads are better than one." Sharing and questioning others' ideas—as well as how they are expressed in writing—is an honorable tradition in North American colleges, so please feel free to participate fully and politely. In fact, some instructors grade students on their participation in such activities. ●

9E How can I participate effectively in online discussions?

You might take a course that happens entirely online, where discussion takes place through e-mail, a class blog, or a course management system like Blackboard. However, even traditional courses often have an online component.

There are two kinds of online discussions. In synchronous discussions, all the participants are online at the same time. The discussions are scheduled in advance, and everyone meets online in "real time" for a specific amount of time. In asynchronous discussions, participants are online at different times. The discussion is usually open for hours or days, and there may be long periods of time between individual messages. Quick Box 9.3 contains some additional guidelines about online discussions.

Quick Box 9.3

Guidelines for online discussions

Complete the Chapter Exercises

- Follow your instructor's directions about the content, length, and timing of your post.

- Write in complete sentences and paragraphs, unless specifically instructed to do otherwise. Academic discussions are more formal than messages between friends.

- Provide a context for your remarks. You might begin by summarizing a point from a reading before giving your opinion. Your contribution should be able to stand on its own, or it should clearly connect to the rest of the conversation.

- Respond to other writers. Discussions work better when people are actually discussing. If someone makes a particularly good point, say so—and explain why. If you disagree with someone, politely explain why you disagree, and be sure to support your reasoning.

- Be polite and work for the good of the discussion. When people aren't meeting face-to-face, they can be rude—even when they don't mean to be. You need to work extra hard to make sure that your TONE is constructive and helpful.

PART

2

Frames for College Writing

Frames for College Writing

Essay **frames** are guides that suggest how to develop and structure an effective college essay. We offer frames for eight types of essays, the ones most frequently assigned in college writing courses. Each frame lays out how the elements of essays can combine to create the greatest possible unity, clarity, and impact. Each frame is followed by a complete student essay, with annotations to show how the essay works, along with the writer's thinking that includes integrating the three persuasive appeals of logical reasoning (*logos*), ethical credibility (*ethos*), and compassionate emotions (*pathos*).

Before each frame, we thoroughly explain how the writing process works for that type of essay. First, we discuss that type's PURPOSE* and probable AUDIENCE and then list specific strategies for planning and revising it. Following each frame is a collection of sentence and paragraph guides that offer hands-on experience with the language moves expected in ACADEMIC WRITING.

In using the frames and guides, you must adapt them to the specifics of each of your writing assignments. Although we place the eight essay types in separate chapters, we hope you use them flexibly and creatively.

10 Personal Essays

Quick Points   You will learn to

- ➤ Describe key elements of a personal essay (see section 10A).
- ➤ Apply the writing process to a personal essay (see 10B).
- ➤ Adapt frames and guides for a personal essay to your own needs (see 10C).

10A What is a personal essay?

👁 Watch the Video

Personal essays narrate one or more true experiences to reveal something worth knowing about their writers' lives or ideas. Personal essays often use stories and explain what they mean. The trick in writing a personal essay for audiences

---

* Words printed in SMALL CAPITAL LETTERS are discussed elsewhere in the text and are defined in the Terms Glossary at the back of the book.

wider than your family and friends is to narrate your experiences so that readers care about not only what happened but also what you thought of it.

What makes a personal essay effective are specific details and an engaging STYLE and TONE (see 37A). Consider the following example.

> **NO** I can remember my father driving our car into a filling station at the edge of Birmingham. Two miles after we passed a particular motel, he would turn onto Callahan drive, which was a gravel road.

> **YES** After lunch, our father would fold up his map and tuck it in the felt visor until we pulled into the filling station on the outskirts of Birmingham. Are we there yet? We had arrived when we saw the Moon Winx Motel sign—a heart-stopping piece of American road art, a double-sided neon extravaganza; a big taxicab-yellow crescent with a man-in-the-moon on each side, a sly smile, a blue eye that winked, and that blatant misspelling that "x" that made us so happy.

> —Emily Hiestand, *Angela the Upside-Down Girl*

10A.1 Purpose

Personal essays mainly have an expressive or literary purpose that's designed to engage and enlighten readers. The best personal essays have a message or point that they reveal artistically. (For more about purposes for writing, see 4B.)

10A.2 Audience

People tend to read personal essays for "serious pleasure." They want to be entertained by true stories, especially by the way the writer tells them, but they also want to encounter thoughts and ideas. Work for a mixture of scene, in which you explain the action or setting in detail, and SUMMARY, in which you cover events quickly so that you can get to the interesting stuff. (For more about audience, see 4C.)

10B How do I plan and revise personal essays?

Generating ideas

- Concentrate on getting the basic story down. Perhaps imagine you're writing to a friend who's interested in your story.
- Try creating detailed scenes. Work on describing the physical setting in detail and perhaps use some dialogue so that readers can get a sense of being there. In descriptive words, recreate the place, time, and people who were involved, to allow readers to form their opinion of the scene.

Revising

- Does your story and its details convey your impression of the experience? Be sure to "show, not tell."
- Do you need more specific details (see "RENNS" 6F)?
- Would your essay benefit if you included some dialogue?

10C What is a frame for a personal essay?

The basic shape of a personal essay is a story, but it will also probably have some commentary or reflection (when you "step back" and explain what it all means). Here is a possible frame for a personal essay to adapt to the specifics of your assignment.

Frame for a Personal Essay

Introductory paragraph(s): Dramatic scene from the story

- **Capture your readers' attention** with an event or significant detail.
- (1) **Describe a specific scene or action** at the start of your story; (2) begin with the end of the story, OR (3) begin at a dramatic point in the middle of the story. Each way creates a different kind of suspense.
- **Use your THESIS STATEMENT** to give readers a preview of the central point of your narrative.

Background

- **Explain the background** of the story, the general setting, the time and place it happened.
- **Include here, if you wish, some reflection** or the point of your experience.

Rest of the story

- **Tell what happened** in several paragraphs.
- **Keep your story going** if you started at its beginning. However, if you started at the middle or end, be sure to return to the beginning so that you tell the whole story. Use a mixture of SUMMARY (covering time in a few sentences) and scene (slowing down and including details and dialogue).

(continued)

Personal Essay Frame (cont.)

Reflection or analysis

- **Explain what readers can learn** from this event—about you, about other people or human nature, about situations, ideas, institutions, etc.

Optional: Include related experience or event

- **Include a second experience** or story that relates to your main one, or an event in the news, someone else's story, or an historical situation.
- **Include your reflection or analysis** of the related material.
- **Connect any related material** to your main story.

Conclusion

- **Include a final detail, a final observation**, a restatement of the main message of your story, or relate what happened after your story ended as long as it flows smoothly with the rest of your paragraph.

10D What sentence and paragraph guides can help generate ideas?

Adapt these sentence and paragraph guides to your PURPOSE and AUDIENCE.

Sentence and Paragraph Guides

- One day [incident, event, experience, etc.] in particular stands out because _____.
- The experience of _____ ultimately taught me [helped me realize, illustrated how] _____.
- At first, this event might have seemed _____, but on deeper reflection it was _____.
- The most interesting [strangest, disturbing, humorous, perplexing, etc.] thing about the experience was _____. That was because _____. Furthermore, _____.

10E A student's personal essay

Neuchterlein 1

Samantha Neuchterlein

WRIT 1622

Dr. Hesse

2 Feb. 2012

Dramatic opening starts in the middle of the story, making readers wonder how the writer got there and what will happen. Embeds an emotional appeal (*pathos*).

Ethical appeal (*ethos*) hints at the character and human side of the writer.

Paragraph of reflection and analysis with point at the end.

Paragraph explains context, introducing the people and setting the background.

Saved by Technology—or Distracted by It?

In the late afternoon of a cold January day, Kurt and I were struggling through deep snow. We had slung our skis over our shoulders and had spent the past hour hiking up the face of a mountain, searching for familiar territory. It would be getting dark soon, and we were lost.

I have often exaggerated that my smartphone has "saved my life." Usually these perilous moments happen when, for example, a calendar notice pops up to remind me that I have a meeting with a teacher in fifteen minutes that I had totally forgotten. Recently though, my friend and his iPhone actually saved my life. Well, maybe that's a little extreme but the phone certainly helped. In the process, however, I had a disturbing realization about the way technology has infiltrated our lives.

A few Saturdays ago, I joined two friends, Kurt and Carter, for a day of skiing. We left our dorms at the University of Denver before dawn to drive two hours west, to the Arapahoe Basin ski area. The sun came up as we neared the Continental Divide, bathing the high peaks in pink and gold light. It was a spectacular cloudless morning with temperatures in the teens, and the brilliant skies promised a great day on the slopes.

continued >>

Neuchterlein 2

By early afternoon we had completed several runs and had just taken the lift up to the top of the mountain. Standing at 12,000 feet, we stared at the backside, considering several options in the Montezuma Bowl. One was the tempting area out of bounds, the unpatrolled and unofficial slopes where signs warned us of dangers, including death. Most skiers have a love affair with untouched powder, fluffy snow with no tracks that surrounds you in a shimmering white cocoon as you swoosh through it. Any powder had long since been packed down on Arapahoe's ski runs, but out of bounds everything was still clean and pure. So, naturally (and foolishly) the three of us ducked under the ropes and hurtled down uncharted territory.

At first it was terrific. The fresh snow squeaked with each turn that sent up white sparkling waves, as we dodged boulders and looked for a path down. We called to each other in delight. But after about fifteen turns, things changed. Carter got split off from Kurt and me, and suddenly the untouched terrain became unskiable, over sixty degrees steep, with cliffs and drop-offs. Although we had started above tree line, our path was now blocked with lodgepole pines. Going further would have been even more suicidal, so we stopped.

"What's our plan?" Kurt asked.

"Our best hope is hiking up."

So we took off our skis and began trudging back up toward the edge of the boundary. Ski boots, deep snow, and thin air are a bad combination, especially when you're trying to climb a thousand feet and it's getting late. After nearly an hour

Writer summarizes most of the day so that she can focus on the most dramatic events. In this paragraph and the next, she slows down to provide details.

Logical explanation (logos) of the situation.

Writer combines logical appeal (logos) with ethical and emotional appeals (ethos and pathos).

Details give a clear picture of the situation.

continued >>

Neuchterlein 3

and a half, we were exhausted. It was around five o'clock, well after the lifts had closed, dusk was falling, and it was getting colder. Suddenly, Kurt's cell phone rang. He quickly ripped off his gloves thinking it was Carter. However, it was the ski patrol. Kurt told them that we had climbed back to the edge of bounds and would be back at the bottom momentarily. Two ski patrollers met us near the lift, which they started to get us out of the back bowl. One said, "We got your phone numbers from your friend. He's OK. He's skiing down with other patrollers."

Dialogue creates immediacy. Writer maintains emotional (pathos) and ethical (ethos) appeals.

Forty-five minutes later, when we finally all met at the car, Carter explained more or less how he and his iPhone had saved us from a cold night in the middle of the woods. When he had realized that he was lost and much too far away from the resort, he took out his iPhone to check if there was 3G. There was. The first thing he Googled was when the sun would set at his location. 5:30. He had about an hour and a half of sunlight left. He then Googled the phone number for Arapahoe Basin ski patrol, called them, and said he was in the middle of the woods, split from his friends. He gave them our phone numbers, emailed his coordinates, and sat down waiting. "So I was sitting in the snow in the middle of the woods, waiting for them, going through my iTunes library trying to decide which song I'd like to die listening to." The three of us got a laugh out of this, but later I got thinking.

Writer shows the logic of the situation (logos).

Dialogue shows Carter's character, rather than telling us about it.

Carter's comment is the epitome of how technology has infiltrated our daily life. At all times, even a situation where someone is contemplating his "pre-death ritual," technology affects our decisions. Rather than thinking of his family or his

continued >>

Neuchterlein 4

life's accomplishments, Carter was caught between Dr. Dre and Eminem's "Forgot About Dre" and the classic by Kanye West, "Higher." Our unique thoughts and experiences are overshadowed by a small rectangle of plastic and metal. Even in an extreme moment, we're not entirely in that moment. Although this technology certainly holds the power to take us out of danger, as that day on the mountain showed, it also can distract us from our very lives.

> This paragraph begins the writer's reflection of thinking back on her friend's comment and what it might signify.

That night on the dark drive back to Denver, we listened to music. We told each other the story of that afternoon over and over, remembering details, sharing thoughts. We knew that our irresponsibility in going out of bounds had cost others trouble and effort, but we also knew we got a great story out of it. It was a story we would tell with some guilt, but we would happily tell it anyway. Beyond that, I knew that I had seen two sides of our reliance on technology, which can both save us and distract us from ourselves.

> Concluding paragraph includes both the end of the story and more reflection. It ends with a powerful sentence, a logical statement (*logos*).

11 Informative Essays
■ ■ ■ ■ ■ ■ ■ ■

Quick Points   You will learn to

➤ Describe key elements of informative essays (see 11A).
➤ Apply the writing process to an informative essay (see 11B).
➤ Adapt frames and guides for an informative essay to your own needs (see 11C).

11A What are informative essays?

Watch the Video

When you write an informative essay, you play the role of an expert on the topic you're assigned or you choose.

11A.1 Purpose

Your PURPOSE in writing an informative essay is solely to give your readers information about your topic in a logical sequence, written clearly and engagingly. If the assignment asks only for information, don't add an argument.

Although assignments might not include the word *informative*, you can usually figure out the purpose from the wording. (For more about purposes for writing, see 4B.)

11A.2 Audience

To give information, you want to consider whether your readers might be specialists on your topic. If you can't know this, you're safest in assuming that your audience consists of nonspecialists, which means you need to present full information for people who have no background in your topic. Your readers hope to learn not only the basics of your topic but also sufficient, interesting specifics to hold their interest. (For more about audience, see 4C.)

11B How do I plan and revise informative essays?

Generating ideas

- Do some reading or talk to people knowledgeable about your topic.
- Find published sources (see Chapter 22) that have useful, interesting information about your topic, remembering to use only reliable, credible sources, quote them carefully, and avoid PLAGIARISM (see Chapters 18 and 19).

Revising

- Have you included the right amount of information if your audience members are specialists in your topic? Conversely, if your audience members aren't specialists on your topic, have you provided sufficient information?
- Have you answered "Why is this information important or significant?"
- Have you used specific details to make your information come alive (for example, see 6F)?

11C What is a frame for an informative essay?

Informative essays can be organized in many ways. Here's a frame you can adapt to the specifics of your assignments.

Frame for an Informative Essay

Introductory paragraph(s)

- **Capture your readers' interest** by using one of the strategies for writing effective introductory paragraphs (see 6C).
- **Present your THESIS STATEMENT,** making sure it gives the central point of the essay (see 5F).

Body paragraph(s): background information

- **Provide background** for the information in your essay. This might follow the introductory paragraph or come later in the essay at a point when the background is more relevant.
- **Start with a TOPIC SENTENCE** that clearly relates to your thesis statement and leads logically to the information in the paragraph (see 6E).

Body paragraph(s)

- **Present sections of information,** divided into logical groups, generally one to a paragraph.
- **Start each paragraph with a topic sentence** that clearly relates to the essay's thesis statement and leads logically to the information in the paragraph (see 6E).
- **Support each topic sentence with specific details**—use RENNS (see 6F).

Conclusion

- **Bring the essay to a logical conclusion,** using one of the strategies for writing effective concluding paragraphs (see 6G).

11D What are sentence and paragraph guides for an informative essay?

Adapt the sentence and paragraph guides on page 144 to your PURPOSE and AUDIENCE.

Sentence and Paragraph Guides

- People experienced with _____ advise that the public needs to know _____ so that everyone can _____.
- _____ captured my interest because _____.
- People generally consider _____, _____, and _____ as the major components of information about _____.
- In addition to _____, _____ plays a major role in _____.
- For many people, the most compelling information about _____ is _____. However, they often overlook _____. That aspect is important because _____.
- Other important information about _____ is _____.
- In conclusion, _____.
- After considering all the information available about _____, we can conclude that _____.

11E A student's informative essay

Carol Moreno

English 1122

Professor Fleming

12 Feb. 2012

Introductory paragraph uses ethical and emotional appeals (*ethos* and *logos*, telling an anecdote to set the stage for the essay's information.

Weight Lifting for Women

Last summer, after my grandmother fell and broke her hip, I wanted to help care for her. Because she was bedridden, she needed to be lifted at times. I was shocked to discover that I could not lift her fragile frame of 90 pounds without my brother's help. At least I could tend to her in other ways,

continued >>

Moreno 2

especially by reading aloud to her, which she loved. Still, my
pride was hurt, so I signed up for a Physical Education class at
the local community college in weight lifting for women. The
course brochure captured my interest immediately because it
said that women can indeed "pump iron" as long as they learn
how to do so properly.

What excited me the most about the weight lifting
course for women was that my career goal was to be a nurse.
Once my two children were old enough to go to school all day,
I intended to start my studies. Nursing care for the elderly had
always appealed to me. My experience with my grandmother
proved how important physical strength would be in nursing.
Although in the United States the elderly usually are not
revered as much as they are in Asian countries, I had great
respect for my grandparents. They all lived nearby, and I
would seek them out to tell me their life stories. For example,
my grandmother who had broken her hip had lived in Nairobi,
Kenya, for ten years as a U.S. Trade Representative to various
African countries. She had to have been a strong, resourceful
woman. Not being able to lift her when she was ill really
upset me.

The first fact that I learned in my course for women
lifting weights was we can rely on our biology to protect us
from developing masculine-looking muscle mass. Women's
bodies produce only small amounts of the hormones that
enlarge muscles in men. If women want to be bodybuilders and
compete for titles such as Ms. Olympia and Ms. International,
they need to take supplements to alter their chemistry so

Thesis
statement
presents
writer's point
of view about
the topic.

Topic sentence ties
into the
thesis statement and the
information
in this paragraph about
the writer's
career goal.

Background
body paragraph tells
how the writer's career
goal fits with
her experience with her
grandmother.

Specific
details name
a location
and job.

Topic
sentence ties
into thesis
statement
and leads into
information
about biology.

Specific
details name
two titles.

continued >>

Moreno 3

that their muscles become bulkier rather than longer. The students in my class did not want that look. We wanted smooth, firm muscles, not massive bulges. Aside from gaining nicer looking muscles, some students said from the start that they expected the course to help them lose weight. Our teacher had disappointing news for them. Muscles actually weigh more than fat. The good news was that when our flab turned into muscle, we would lose inches from our limbs and waist. Those students might not weigh less, but they would look slimmer.

Striving for strength can end in injury unless weight lifters learn the safe use of free weights and weight machines. Free weights are barbells, the metal bars that round metal weights can be attached to at each end. To be safe, no matter how little the weight, lifters must never raise a barbell by bending at the waist. Instead, they should squat, grasp the barbell, and then use their leg muscles to straighten into a standing position. To avoid a twist that can lead to serious injury, lifters must use this posture: head erect and facing forward, back and neck aligned. The big advantage of weight machines, which use weighted handles and bars hooked to wires and pulleys, is that lifters must use them sitting down. Therefore, machines like the Nautilus and Universal actually force lifters to keep their bodies properly aligned, which drastically reduces the chance of injury.

Once a weight lifter understands how to lift safely, she needs a regimen personalized to her physical needs. Because benefits come from "resistance," which is the stress that lifting weight puts on a muscle, no one has to be strong to get

Specific details give factual information.

Writer uses logical appeal (logos).

continued >>

Moreno 4

started. A well-planned, progressive weight-training program begins with whatever weight a person can lift comfortably and gradually adds to the base weight as she gets stronger. What builds muscle strength is the number of repetitions, or "reps," the lifter does, not necessarily the addition of weight. Our instructor helped the women, who ranged from 18 to 43, scrawny to pudgy, and couch potato to superstar, to develop a program that was right for our individual weight, age, and overall level of conditioning. Everyone's program differed in how much weight to start out with and how many reps to do for each exercise. Our instructor urged us to not try more weight or reps than our programs called for, even if our first workouts seemed too easy. This turned out to be good advice because those of us who did not listen woke up the next day feeling as though evil forces had twisted our bodies.

In addition to fitting a program to her physical capabilities, a female weight lifter needs to design an individual routine to fit her personal goals. Most students in my class wanted to improve their upper body strength, so we focused on exercises to strengthen our arms, shoulders, abdomens, and chests. Each student worked on specifically tailored exercises to isolate certain muscle groups. Because muscles toughen up and grow when they are rested after a workout, our instructor taught us to alternate muscle groups on different days. For example, a student might work on her arms and abdomen one day and then her shoulders and chest the next day. Because I had had such trouble lifting my grandmother, I added exercises to strengthen my legs

Writer uses specific details for an emotional appeal (pathos).

Writer uses humor for ethical appeal (ethos).

Topic sentence ties back to the essay's thesis statement and uses transition "in addition."

Specific details give factual information about biology.

Writer uses ethical appeal (ethos).

continued >>

Moreno 5

and back. Another student had hurt her neck in a car crash, so she added exercises that focused exclusively on her neck and upper shoulders. Someone else who was planning to be a physical therapist added finger and hand-strengthening routines. By the middle of the term, we each had our specific, personal routine to use during class and continue once the term ended.

At the end of our 10 weeks of weight training, we had to evaluate our progress. Was I impressed! I felt ready to lift the world. If my grandmother were still bedridden, I could lift her with ease. When I started, I could not lift 10 pounds over my head twice. Midterm, I could lift that much only for four repetitions. By the end of the course, I could lift 10 pounds over my head for 15 repetitions, and I could lift 18 pounds for two repetitions. Also, I could swim laps for 20 sustained minutes instead of the five I had barely managed at first. In conclusion, I am so proud of my accomplishments that I still work out three or four times a week. I am proof that any woman can benefit from "pumping iron." After all, there isn't anything to lose— except some flab.

Closing sentence sums up the discussion and leads into the concluding paragraph.

Opening sentence starts drawing the essay to a logical end.

Specific detail ties into the introductory paragraph.

Specific details wrap up the student's experience.

Concluding sentences tie back to the essay's thesis statement and end with a humor.

12 Process Essays

■ ■ ■ ■ ■ ■ ■ ■ ■

Quick Points You will learn to

➤ Describe key elements of a process essay (see 12A).
➤ Apply the writing process to a process essay (see 12B).
➤ Adapt frames and guides for a process essay to your own needs (see 12C).

12A What is a process essay?

Process essays explain how to do or understand things that involve an ordered sequence of steps. Indeed, some process writing takes the form of simple lists. However, your instructors expect an essay with complete sentences, not lists. For example, these topics require a human touch that only sentences can deliver: "how to buy a used car," "how to comfort a friend who has lost a loved one," or "how to decorate an apartment when you have little money."

12A.1 Purpose

The PURPOSE (see 4B) of most process essays is INFORMATIVE (see 4B.4); they tell readers how to do something. Clarity is vital. When a process can be done more than one way, a secondary purpose is to persuade the reader that your approach is superior to others. In such cases, you not only explain steps, but you also give reasons why your strategy is best.

12A.2 Audience

What does your AUDIENCE (see 4C) already know about the information in your essay? That's the most important question as you're writing process essays. If your readers don't know what an Allen wrench is, you'll have to explain that basic tool before telling readers how to use it. On the other hand, if you go into great detail telling a chemist what it means to "titrate 50 mL of aqueous solution," you'll both use unnecessary words and insult her.

12B How do I plan and revise process essays?

Generating Ideas

- Break the process you're explaining into the best possible order of steps. You can try different sequences on yourself until you find the one that makes most sense, or ask some friends to try to follow your directions and comment.

- Pay close attention to what your readers already know—or don't know. Check always for terms you need to define.

- Anticipate common mistakes or problems that people might encounter, and explain what to look for, or what to do, in those situations.

Revising

- Are the steps in the best order, or do they require more detailed explanations? Be sure to provide enough discussion so that your material makes sense.

- Do you have too much explanation or detail in some sections of your essay and not enough in others?

- Might pictures, drawings, or other graphics help your readers?

- Would using numbers or headings for the sections in your essay help your readers?

- Is your final THESIS STATEMENT a concise preview of the process you explain in your essay?

12C What is a frame for a process essay?

Process essays are usually organized in time order. Here's a process essay frame you can adapt to the specifics of your assignment.

Frame for a Process Essay

Introductory paragraph(s)

- **Lead into your topic** by engaging your readers' attention (see 6C).
- **Explain your topic**, and give an overview of the process, what the results will be, and any benefits of this process. (If appropriate, state the number of steps involved.)
- **Use your THESIS STATEMENT** to note the outcome of the process, which can be the payoff to the reader of the essay.

(continued)

Process Essay Frame (cont.)

Body paragraphs

- **Give each step its own paragraph**, unless the step is very short.
- **Use a TOPIC SENTENCE** as the first sentence of each paragraph to introduce the step.
- **Follow the topic sentence** with sentences that offer clarifications, anticipate difficulties, provide reasons for doing this step, and so on.

Conclusion

- **Explain the outcome** of the process, perhaps how the readers will know whether they're successful in following the process to its conclusion.
- **Mention other ways of executing** the process, if appropriate, and give reasons why the process you have described is the preferable one.

12D What are sentence and paragraph guides for process essays?

Sentences and paragraphs in process essays signal the order of events, explain steps, or offer solutions or outcomes. Adapt these sentence and paragraph guides to your PURPOSE and AUDIENCE.

Sentence and Paragraph Guides

- The first (second, third, etc.) step is _____.
- Next, you _____.
- Finally, _____.
- The most important thing to keep in mind at this step is _____.
- An alternative at this point is to _____. The advantage of that alternative is _____. However, the disadvantage is _____.
- A problem that might arise is _____. One solution is _____. Another solution is _____. For example, you might _____.
- One indication that you have been successful is _____. Another is _____. However, the most important is _____.

12E A student's process essay

Sanz 1

Miguel Sanz

Professor Taczak

English A

11 Feb. 2012

Opens with an attention-getting sentence. Appeals to the readers emotions (*pathos*).

Auditioning for a Musical

If you've always had a secret desire to perform on Broadway with Neil Patrick Harris or Sutton Foster, you'll need to get started somewhere. Musical productions at your college or, even better, your local community theater offer your best opportunity. Knowing how the audition process works will help you get ready and calm your nerves. The process has two phases: one before the audition, the other the day of the audition itself.

The last sentence is a thesis that forecasts the general shape of the essay.

Headings quickly show the parts of the process.

Before the Audition

Paragraph begins with a step clearly labeled first. The following sentences elaborate what requirements might exist.

First, you need to learn the specific requirements for your audition. Knowing the time and place is obvious, of course. But will you need to prepare a song or two? If so, should it be an up-tempo song, a ballad, or both? You might also have to sight-read from the score. You'll almost certainly need to read part of a scene from a script, and you'll likely have to learn a little choreography for a dance audition. Sometimes you'll need to bring a headshot (a shoulders-up photograph) of yourself. In any case, be clear about everything you'll need to do; you won't be as nervous.

Writer shows he's a credible source about the process, which is an ethical appeal (*ethos*).

"Next" signals the second step. The writer provides specific illustrations for choosing the right kind of song.

Next, well in advance, choose a song for your audition. Find one that fits the musical; in most cases, it's best not to choose a song from the musical itself, unless you're specifically asked to do so. Generally, this means that if the show is a

continued >>

Sanz 2

"classic" one being revived, like *South Pacific*, *Guys and Dolls*, or *The Sound of Music*, you'll want a song from that era. If it's a more contemporary show, like *Rent* or *Avenue Q*, you'll want a more modern tune. The song should showcase the best qualities of your voice. Once you choose a song, be sure to rehearse with a pianist because you need to be comfortable singing with the accompanist at the audition.

About the same time, if you may need a headshot, which is a picture of your face only, arrange to have it taken. Dozens of people will probably audition, and the people casting the show find it helpful to associate a face with their notes on each person. They may want people of a certain age or look for each part, and pictures provide good records. You can pay a professional photographer quite a bit of money for a quality studio session, and if you're a professional actor, that's a good investment. However, for most college or community theaters, a friend who is good with a camera can take an effective portrait. Just choose a fairly plain background and make sure that your face is well lit on all sides.

Next, familiarize yourself with the script, if you know the name of the show. If you don't know the show well, get a sense of the characters in it, their relation to other characters, and the plot. Why? You'll likely be asked to read a scene, so it will help you "get in character" if you aren't reading the scene cold in front of the director. You may even be able to figure out which scenes are the best candidates for auditions. See if you can find a score so you can get familiar with songs you might have to sight-read. Of course, if the show is an original one for which you can get no script, see if you can tactfully find out the type

> The writer again states the step in a clear topic sentence, then provides details and explanations.
>
> Writer shows sensitivity to the actor's finances, which again shows he's a credible person.
>
> Because readers might wonder why the step is important, the writer answers this question directly.
>
> The writer uses a logical appeal (*logos*) concerning how to handle not having a script.

continued >>

Sanz 3

of musical and look over existing scripts of that type. Whatever you can do to prepare yourself will help you be comfortable at the audition.

On the Day of the Audition

On the day of the audition itself, a few preparations will help. Most important, dress appropriately. You want to look your best, of course, but you also need to be ready to move. Overly tight or revealing clothing won't do you much good. The most important thing is wearing proper shoes. Neither stiletto heels nor tennis shoes are useful for the dance part of the audition. The bottoms of your shoes should allow you to slide without their being slippery. Sexism prevails on stage; men almost always need to be taller than women with whom they're partnered. Sorry.

Show up on time or a little early. Bring a copy of your audition music. You'll need to sign in, which usually consists of filling out a data sheet about yourself. That includes name, address, and contact information, of course, but you'll also be asked your height and weight (for both costuming and casting purposes). Resist the urge to lie. The information sheet will also ask you about your previous acting or performing experiences. Don't panic if you don't have much to put down, especially if you're trying out for a community production. High school productions, dance or music lessons, choirs you've sung with: all of these are reasonable to list.

Now comes the audition itself. Usually, everyone who is auditioning will sit together in the theater. (You've seen this on *American Idol*, for example.) The casting team will be there, too. This always includes the director, the music director, and

The heading and following paragraph signal shift to the second phase.

Practical information, along with a little humor, reveals the writer's awareness of his possible emotional impact of his advice (*pathos*) and helps establish his credibility (*ethos*).

By giving specific information, the writer uses a personal touch to anticipate the fears or anxieties the reader might have, which is an emotional appeal (*pathos*).

Giving a popular analogy can help people understand the situation better.

continued >>

Sanz 4

the choreographer, but there might be others. Someone will call people up one at a time. Generally, you'll be asked to sing first, but this can vary. Quite often you'll only sing 16 bars of your song, so expect to be interrupted. Say thank you and return to your seat. Most theater people are quite friendly, even if they have to give disappointing news. Try not to be nervous; of course, that's much easier said than done! After everyone has sung, different combinations of actors will be called to the stage to read scenes. After everyone has read, the choreographer may teach the group a few simple steps, let them practice, and then have small groups perform the routine. Especially in community theaters, remember that very few people have dance training. In such situations, you aren't expected to be a professional.

The process is almost finished. After the audition, the casting team will announce the results, but almost never does that happen the same day. It can be the next day or even longer. Most productions include a round of call-backs, which are just what they sound like. The director asks a few people to return for a second round of auditioning so that he or she can gather more information and make tough decisions.

If you get cast, congratulations! Your efforts have paid off, and you're on your way to Broadway—or at least to a lot of fun. But if you don't get chosen, it's not the end of the world. You've gained some valuable experience, and you've almost certainly met some interesting and friendly people who share some of your passions. Look for the next audition call!

Here is another place where the writer tries to be personal and reassuring.

This sentence cues readers that they're nearing the end. The essay has used chrono-logical order throughout.

Concluding paragraph explains the outcome of a success-ful process but also addresses a failure. Tone shows ethical and emotional appeals (*ethos* and *pathos*) in action.

13 Essays Analyzing Cause or Effect

Quick Points   You will learn to

➤ Describe key elements of a cause or effect essay (see 13A).
➤ Apply the writing process to a cause or effect essay (see 13B).
➤ Adapt frames and guides for a cause or effect essay to your own needs (see 13C).

13A   What is an essay analyzing cause or effect?

An essay that analyzes **cause** explains why a particular event or situation happened. Why did a certain candidate lose the election? Why has a certain musician become popular?

An essay that analyzes **effect** explains what happened or might happen as a result of a particular action or idea. If we increase or decrease taxes, what will happen to the economy? If I study nursing, what will my life be like?

13A.1   Purpose

Essays that focus on cause or effect can be either

- Mainly INFORMATIVE, providing information and ideas to help readers understand a situation or idea (see 4B.4). Mainly informative essays have an element of argument. Many events have several possible causes, and you need to show readers why the ones you've identified are the best. The same is true for effects. After all, predicting the future is usually open to debate.

- Mainly PERSUASIVE, convincing readers that your explanation of causes or effects is reasonable (see 4B.5).

In writing both kinds of essays, you need to identify good reasons and support them.

13A.2   Audience

Three important questions will help you write for your AUDIENCE (see 4C):

- **How much do your readers know about the topic?** Decide how much background information or explanation you need to provide.

- **What do your readers already believe about the topic?** If your audience already accepts some causes or effects as true, then you know you face certain challenges if you want to propose different ones.

- **How interested are your readers in the topic?** For some readers, questions on their minds like, "Who cares?" or "So what?" are significant, so you'll want to find ways to create interest in your topic.

13B How do I plan and revise essays that analyze cause or effect?

Generating Ideas

- **Brainstorm as many causes or effects as possible**. Some ideas might end up being silly, but get them down first before you pass judgment.

- **Look for possible causes by exploring various categories:** events; attitudes or beliefs; popular culture; social developments or behaviors; economic conditions; and so on.

- **Look for possible effects in related situations**. Did something like this happen in the past? How is the present situation like (and not like) the previous one? What might be the possible social, legal, economic, or personal effects?

- **Develop as many reasons, illustrations, or examples as you can for each cause or effect**. Decide if you need to do research to find facts, gather information, or seek expert perspectives.

- **Choose the one cause or effect** that looks most promising for your essay.

- See section 3E.5 for more advice on analyzing cause and effect.

Revising

- **Consider your audience.** Is the information or ideas that your readers will need to know clear? (In contrast, do your readers already know some of your content, so that you need to trim?)

- **Play the doubting game.** Imagine someone saying, "Sure, that's a possible cause, (or effect) but the real cause (or effect) is _____." How would you answer?

- **Ask, "So what?"** Ask youself what's important or interesting about knowing that X caused Y, or that if Y happens, then Z is likely to follow? Make that clear in your essay.

- **Examine the order in which you presented your material.** What is your reason for putting them in the order you did? Is it the best order?

- Is your final THESIS STATEMENT a concise preview of your essay?

13C What are frames for essays that analyze cause or effect?

The frame we offer here suggests not only how you might use these structures to organize your essay but also how you can generate ideas.

Frame for a Cause or Effect Essay

Introductory paragraph(s)

- **Explain the event, situation, idea**, etc., that you're analyzing.
- **Explain why understanding** its cause(s)/effect(s) is important or interesting.
- **Give your main point or** THESIS STATEMENT, explaining why the cause or effect in your essay is significant.

Background or context
(Optional if your topic can be explained in introduction)

- **Use a** TOPIC SENTENCE to start each major body paragraph.
- **Provide further information** that readers need to understand the topic.
- **Include history, facts, or circumstances**, if appropriate.

Your main cause(s)/effect(s)

In each paragraph:
- **State the cause(s)/effect(s)** you identify as the strongest or most interesting
- **Use RENNS** to generate support for your reasons (see 6F).
- **Use a** TOPIC SENTENCE to start each major body paragraph.

Possible alternative causes/effects; place this before or after your main cause(s) or effect(s)

- **Discuss some possible explanations/outcomes** that you don't think are the best ones.
- **Comment on their strengths** but make sure to show their weaknesses.

Or

- **If there are multiple causes or effects**, discuss the less important ones, giving reasons why they're reasonable.
- **Use a** TOPIC SENTENCE to start each major body paragraph.
- **Generally devote one paragraph** to all your alternative or secondary causes or effects. However, if they are complicated, you might write a paragraph on each one.

(continued)

Frame for a Cause or Effect Essay (cont.)

Conclusion

- **Summarize the cause/effect** you've identified as strongest.

Or

- **If you explained multiple causes and effects**, explain how they relate to or combine with one another.
- **Explain insights or advantages** that readers get from understanding this cause or effect, or explain what might be the consequences of this knowledge.

13D What are sentence and paragraph guides for essays that analyze cause or effect?

Adapt these guides to your PURPOSE and AUDIENCE.

Sentence and Paragraph Guides

- Of three [or however many] possible causes [or effects], the most important one is ____.
- Although it might appear that the causes [or effects] of ____ were ____ or even ____, the most significant cause [effect] was actually ____.
- Recognizing that the most likely effect of ____ will be ____ should lead to us to ____.
- Two [or however many] primary reasons that _____ is the most likely cause [effect] of ____ are ____ and ____.
- One possible cause [effect] is ____. This cause is reasonable because ____. For example, it helps explain ____. However, the cause is weak/ has limitations because ____. Still, it's worth considering because ____.
- The most important result of this action [or decision or belief] will be ____. One reason is ____. Noted scholar ____ points out that ____. A second reason is ____. After all, this situation is closely related to ____ , and in that case the result was _____. Some people will argue that ____ can't happen because of ____. However, their argument is weak because ____.
- Someone people contend that ____ is the main cause [will be the actual effect] of ____. They argue that ____. However, they fail to take into account ____. Furthermore, they ignore such evidence as ____. There- fore, although _____ has some attractive [promising, credible] aspects, we should reject it as a satisfactory [convincing, accurate] cause.

13E A student's essay analyzing cause

Cusack 1

Cheryl Cusack

Writing 100

Professor Leake

24 Feb. 2012

Why We're Going Less Often to the Movies

Introduction. Explains topic and creates interest.

On December 31, 2010, when someone purchased the last ticket for the last showing of a movie (perhaps *Little Fockers*), that year's annual box office results were complete. They

Good use of RENNS (see 6F) for specific details.

showed that 5.2% fewer Americans attended movies in 2010 than did in 2009 ("Yearly"). What accounts for that significant decline in attendance? After all, the number of movies released increased in 2010. The films were heavily advertised, and they featured the kinds of stars that moviegoers have long flocked to see. Among the possible causes of the attendance decline are the types of films released, the cost, and the existence of other forms of entertainment. However, the most significant cause is

Thesis statement

actually the poor quality of the movie theater experience itself.

Writer presents information logically (logos), which carries an ethical appeal (ethos).

Movies have been a mainstay of American entertainment for over a century. According to figures gathered by Box Office Mojo, an industry group based in Burbank, California, we spend nearly $10 billion buying tickets each year, not to mention billions more on popcorn and snacks. Audiences have

Writer gives specific details using RENNS (see 6F), and in so doing appeals to logic (logos).

generally increased in the past thirty years, from about a billion tickets sold in 1980 to about 1.3 billion in 2010. However, even this number is down from the peak of 1.6 billion tickets sold in 2002.

One possible reason is that the quality and variety of movies themselves has declined. Quality is a subjective thing, of

continued >>

Cusack 2

course. Still, the movies released in 2010 seem to have a wide range of appeals. Consider that year's top ten films: *Toy Story 3, Alice in Wonderland; Iron Man 2; The Twilight Saga: Eclipse; Harry Potter and the Deathly Hallows Part 1; Inception; Despicable Me; Shrek Forever After; How to Train Your Dragon;* and *Tangled.* Together they show a range from action adventure to family features, including some popular series and franchises. Lack of quality and variety don't seem to have been a problem.

> Paragraph introducing possible cause and explaining why it's not satisfactory.

Cost might be a better reason. Ticket prices have continued to increase, to a national average of $8.00 and, of course, much higher many places. Throw in modest refreshments and travel costs, and a night at the movies for a couple can easily be $40. A family of four can spend almost twice that. Given recent troubles in our economy, movies may have priced themselves out of reach for many. However, at other times of financial stress, including the Great Depression of the 1930s, people still went to movies. Cost can account for some, but not all of the decline.

> Paragraph introducing second possible cause and explaining its strengths and weaknesses.

> Once again, writer uses RENNS (see 6F) to give specific details that support her topic sentence and the essay's thesis statement.

More plausible is the rise of alternative forms of entertainment, especially at home. Video sales and rentals have gone from tapes and DVDs at stores like Blockbuster, to mail distribution through services like Netflix, to today's instant online access. Not only is the cost cheaper (for much less than the price of one night at the theater, people can have unlimited access to a month of movies), but also the number of titles available far exceeds what's playing at the local multiplex. Even with that, people would likely pay for a quality and kind of movie experience superior to the one they can get at home. That leads to the most important reason movie attendance is declining.

> Paragraph introducing third possible cause and explaining its strengths and weaknesses.

continued >>

Cusack 3

Paragraph introducing the cause that the student thinks is most important and provides a reason and support.

The quality of the movie theater experience these days is terrible. Consider, first, the advertising. While previews have been around for a long time and have even been welcome entertainments in their own right, they are now joined by ads for everything from body sprays, to new cars, to joining the U.S. Army. Some commercials that you see on television you also

A particularly accurate statement that appeals to the emotions (*pathos*).

see on the big screen. The combination of ads and previews now creates a gauntlet of twenty or more minutes before you even see the first frame of Brad Pitt or Gwyneth Paltrow. Unlike at home, you can't fast forward.

Paragraph provides a second reason and support.

Equally distracting is the behavior of others in the theater. Listening to cell phone conversations or watching the bright screens of people texting, networking, or whatever is standard. Some people talk to companions as if they were sitting in a basement or backyard, not in a place where others have paid eight bucks—and not to listen to them. Being

The writer is pleasantly blunt about her feelings.

annoyed is one thing, but paying to be annoyed is another thing altogether.

Conclusion. Suggests who should care about this analysis and why.

Unless the movie industry can restore some of the atmosphere of being in the theater, the combination of cost, quality, and alternatives will continue to feed the decline of attendance. Perhaps this is no one's concern except the theater owners' themselves, along with the people who work for them.

A clear statement of the writer's opinion using appeals of logic, ethics, and emotions (*logos, ethos,* and *pathos*).

However, it would be sad to see a vital part of American public life disappear just because we aren't willing to keep some things special, some things part of what used to be the magic of the movies.

continued >>

Cusack 4

Work Cited

"Yearly Box Office." *Box Office Mojo*. IMDB.com, 15 Feb. 2012. Web. 17 Feb. 2012.

14 Essays Analyzing a Text

Quick Points You will learn to

➤ Describe key elements of textual analysis essays (see 14A).

➤ Apply the writing process to your textual analysis (see 14B).

➤ Adapt frames and guides for a textual analysis to your own needs (see 14C).

14A What is textual analysis?

A **textual analysis** essay is either (a) a content analysis that explains the meaning of a text, such as an article, a book, a Web site, a poem, a script, a song, or so on; or (b) a rhetorical analysis that explains how a text works to achieve a certain purpose or effect. Some textual analyses combine the two. Examples of textual analysis are papers that explain, for example, how women are portrayed in popular songs; what biases are evident in a politician's speech; or how characters, themes, imagery, or word choices develop meaning in a short story. To analyze a text, use this four-step process.

Watch the Video

1. **Make sure you understand the text** by reading or viewing it carefully and critically (see Chapter 3) and perhaps doing research to understand its context.

2. **Identify the text's separate elements or features**, such as ideas, words, figures of speech, evidence, and references. Pay attention to patterns or connections between elements.

3. **Explain the meaning of the elements** you've identified. What INFER-ENCES can you make from them?

4. **Explain the meaning that you've identified** by providing evidence and using sound reasoning.

14A.1 Purpose

Textual analyses can have two purposes. Descriptive analyses explain some features or patterns, what they mean, and how they function. Evaluative analyses to describe features as well as judge them. (For more about purposes for writing, see 4B.)

14A.2 Audience

Many audiences of textual analysis are academic: your instructors, other students, people who read scholarly journals, and so on. At times, textual analysis can also have a broader public audience, such as for book and movie reviews.

Whether your audience is academic or popular, take care to explain the text that's your focus, using SUMMARY or DESCRIPTION. Remember always that your readers will probably not have the text you're discussing in front of them nor will they be as familiar with the text as you are. Still, one major pitfall in writing a textual analysis is offering almost exclusively only SUMMARY and sacrificing analysis and evaluation. (For more about audience, see 4C.)

14B How do I generate ideas for a rhetorical or content analysis?

👁 Watch the Video

Usually, your instructors will assign a text to analyze, but sometimes you need to choose the specific text from a broad category, such as an advertisement, a newspaper editorial, or a Web site. If so, choose a text with enough features and elements to support a suitable analysis.

14B.1 Generating ideas for a rhetorical analysis

A basic **rhetorical analysis** explains how the writer tries to influence his or her readers. It focuses on the three major rhetorical principles, also called the three persuasive appeals (see 3B): logic (*logos*), ethical credibility (*ethos*), and compassion and empathy (*pathos*).

14B.2 Generating ideas for a content analysis

A **content analysis** focuses on the "what" of a text—its ideas or meanings—rather than on the "how." It can answer questions such as how images or ideas in the text relate to each other, and if there are repetitions of images or phrases, why is this done? what evidence does the writer use or exclude?

14B.3 Revising

- Do you use QUOTATION, SUMMARY, PARAPHRASE, or DESCRIPTION to explain the elements of the text you've identified?
- Do you discuss why you've identified those elements or how they tie to your THESIS STATEMENT?
- Is your analysis structured effectively? (See 14C.)
- Have you used appropriate CITATIONS? Do you have an appropriate WORKS CITED or REFERENCES page (see Chapters 25–27)?

14C What is a frame for a textual analysis?

Essays of textual analysis can be organized in many ways. Here's a possible frame you can adapt to the specifics of your assignments.

Frame for a Textual Analysis

Introductory paragraph

- **Capture your readers' interest** by using one of the strategies for writing effective introductory paragraphs (see 6C).
- **Present your THESIS STATEMENT**, making sure it states the point of your analysis and offers your readers a concise preview of your essay (see 5F).

Paragraph(s) summarizing the text

- **Characterize the text you're analyzing.** Provide information that readers will need to understand the text you're analyzing.
- **Summarize the source** and, if appropriate, information about its context: where it was published, what its purpose and audience was, etc.

Body paragraphs analyzing the text

- **Start each paragraph with a TOPIC SENTENCE** that makes a point about the text you're discussing.
- **Support each topic sentence** with specific information from the text, using quotations, summaries, or paraphrases.
- **Include discussion or explanation** that makes clear why you included the example and how it supports your topic sentence.

(continued)

Textual Analysis Frame (cont.)

Evaluative paragraphs (if your assignment requires you to evaluate)

- **Start each paragraph with a topic sentence.** The topic sentence should judge the success or quality of an element you've analyzed.
- **Support topic sentences with reasons.** Include reasons and explanations that convince readers your judgment is acceptable.

Conclusion

- **Wrap up the essay.** Readers should finish the essay clearly understanding the points you've made. Most important, make clear why your analysis matters.

Works Cited or References

- **Include a Works Cited or References page.** Because you're analyzing a text, your readers will need clear information on how to find it. Follow the required style: MLA, APA, or Chicago.

14D What are some sentence and paragraph guides for textual analysis?

Adapt these guides to your PURPOSE and AUDIENCE.

Sentence and Paragraph Guides

- The writer attempts to _____ primarily by using the strategy of _____.
- The most significant feature (interesting aspect/important quality/etc.) of this text is _____ because _____.
- The writer uses emotional [or logical or ethical] appeals to create a sense of _____ in readers. Consider for example the statement that "_____" or the statement that "_____." The language of these passages suggests _____ because _____. Consider, for example, how different the emotional appeals would be if the wording had been _____.
- A noteworthy pattern in the text is _____. For example, at one point the writer states _____. At another she asserts _____. At a third, she claims _____. This pattern is significant because _____.
- Reading this text through _____'s theory that _____ reveals a key meaning.

14E A student's textual analysis

Gotlin-Sheehan 1

Matt Gotlin-Sheehan

Professor Hesse

WRIT 1622

17 Nov. 2011

Rhetorical Strategies in Two Airport Security Web Sites

Is the current level of security screening at American airports a patriotic way to safeguard travelers, or is it a ruthless assault by power-crazed bureaucrats? Most people are somewhere between these two positions; they might be annoyed by things they have to do to board a plane, but they find the experience reasonable and serving a good purpose. Other people, though, hold an extreme view. For example, the group We Won't Fly protests, "We will not be treated like criminals," while the federal government's Transportation Security Administration (TSA), soothes, "Your safety is our priority." Analyzing the web sites of these two groups reveals not only contrasting messages but also quite different rhetorical strategies for delivering them.

Airport security measures changed drastically following the September 11, 2001, attacks. Previously, private companies performed airport security and passenger screenings. However, in November 2001 the Transportation Security Administration (TSA) was created to standardize security practices and promote safer travel. In the decade that followed, a few incidents and threats persuaded the TSA to enhance their measures, culminating in full-body scanners and passenger pat downs. These practices have been the subject of intense scrutiny, criticism, and ridicule, especially over the Internet.

> Opening sentence captures attention by stating two options.

> Thesis statement sets up promise to discuss both the content and the strategies of two different texts.

> Paragraph of background information orients readers.

continued >>

Gotlin-Sheehan 2

Topic sentence tells readers this paragraph will give arguments against the current level of airport security.

Wewontfly.com voices anger over airport security. The ultimate point of the site is to convince visitors that the TSA security procedures are invasive. Adorned with aggressive imagery, such as mock scanner images underneath a foreboding red "no" symbol, the site has bold headlines: "Act Now. Travel With Dignity" and "Stop Flying Until the Scanners and Gropers are Gone." Characterizing the screening agents as "gropers" associates them with sex offenders and criminals, not faithful public servants, and it casts travelers as innocent victims. This strong language is reinforced by the "distressed" fonts used for the headlines on the page, as seen in Figure 1.

Writer appeals to logic (*logos*) with information and emotions (*pathos*) by quoting inflammatory language.

Emotional appeals (*pathos*) are focus of this paragraph.

The main rhetorical strategy is to arouse readers' emotions. The page calls the TSA "ineffective and dangerous" as well as a "health risk." The site claims that security scanners may cause radiation poisoning, and that screeners don't change gloves between pat-downs, increasing the chance of spreading harmful contagion like lice. The emotional appeals are heightened by passenger stories reported on the site's blog. In one of them, a passenger named Elizabeth narrates in detail how she was "a victim of a government

Inserting a screen capture of the Web site provides a helpful visual. It also confirms the writers' credibility (*ethos*) by showing a concrete example.

Figure 1   Heading from the home page for http://wewontfly .com.

continued >>

Gotlin-Sheehan 3

sanctioned sexual assault." Another anonymous poster explains that she had once been raped, so that being touched against her will, as during a search, was traumatic. Because physical modesty is a strong cultural value and people regard sexual assault as a particularly offensive crime, these stories might upset people. They imply that, if disturbing things can happen in such graphic detail to others, they can also happen to me, my friends, or family.

Two specific examples arouse readers' sense of compassion, an aspect of an emotional appeal (pathos).

In general, the site uses examples and stories rather than statistics or other kinds of evidence to support its claims. As a result, logical appeals are minimal. Consider the following argument:

> Al-Qaeda is an agile, networked organization. It's peer-to-peer. The TSA is a top-down, lumbering bureaucracy. Al-Qaeda operatives are passionate and motivated. TSA employees are order-takers. There is simply no contest between these two types of organizational structures. It's like David and Goliath, the Viet Cong vs the US Army, Luke vs the Death Star. The TSA is structurally incapable of defending against this threat, just as the US Army was structurally incapable of defeating the Viet Cong.

To make the point most clearly, the writer includes an extended block quotation.

Many readers will probably find the analogies between the TSA and Goliath, the American army in Vietnam, and the Death Star clever, perhaps even convincing. However, the site provides no evidence to support these claims. The TSA may or may not be a "lumbering bureaucracy," but there aren't enough facts or evidence in this paragraph to make an informed judgment about the truth of this claim.

Writer explains and analyzes. Thus, the writer uses a logical appeal (logos).

continued >>

Gotlin-Sheehan 4

Transitional sentence to the next text also serves as a topic sentence for the paragraph.

The TSA (www.tsa.gov) site also uses emotional and ethical appeals, but to a very different effect. Featuring smooth, clean lines, soothing shades of blue, and calming photos of empty airports, the site implies "It's all cool. Relax!" The site's banner features the slogan "Your Safety Is Our Priority," and information for travelers and the media, along with explanations of "Our Approach" suggest that the TSA has nothing to hide. The site is easy to navigate, looks clean, and presents visitors with extensive information, in a systematic manner. Figure 2 shows a page from the site.

Topic sentence announces the theme of the paragraph, which goes on to provide examples, using quotations and discussion.

The TSA tries to project a personality of friendship and common purpose. It identifies employees as "your neighbors, friends, and relatives" who work hard so that "you and your family can travel safely." Rather than being distant or harsh bureaucrats, TSA workers are presented as just like us, sharing our values and interested in our safety. The site portrays them as hard working. They "look for bombs," "inspect rail cars," and "patrol subways." A worker "saves a life" or "helps a stranded motorist," suggesting that the TSA goes beyond faithfully performing assigned duties to help people in need. These techniques are designed to provide comfort to, and instill confidence in, the TSA.

The writer saves the most important rhetorical strategy, logic (*logos*), for this paragraph, introducing it with a clear topic sentence.

However, the most striking rhetorical strategy on the TSA site is the extensive use of logical appeals. The information available ranges from poll results and surveys to news articles and television reports from credible sources like *USA Today*. An entire tab is devoted to "Research," which is divided into three main headings and fourteen subheadings, each of which lists numerous facts. "Screening Statistics," for example, notes that,

continued >>

Gotlin-Sheehan 5

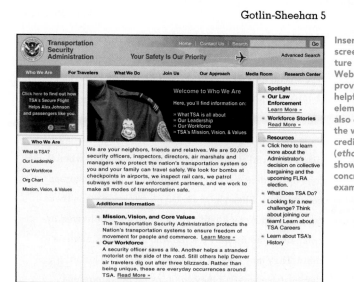

Inserting a screen capture of the Web site provides a helpful visual element. It also confirms the writers' credibility (*ethos*) by showing a concrete example.

Figure 2   Page from TSA Web site: www.tsa.gov/who_we_are/index.shtm.

"We screened 708,400,522. The average wait time was 3.79 minutes and the average peak wait time was 11.76 minutes." Clearly, then, the TSA site puts a strong emphasis on knowledge. Suggesting that airline passengers understand TSA security policies *before* they arrive at the airport seems designed to make people less upset by surprise procedures. "What to know before you go" explains various traveling scenarios, and a search bar tells passengers whether they can take particular items through a checkpoint. The strategy seems to be one of overwhelming travelers with mountains of information so that TSA looks like it's thorough, open, and cooperative, and that travelers have nothing to fear.

Writer uses RENNS (see 6F) to give readers specific details to bring the material alive.

The two Web sites will succeed with different types of visitors. Chances are that an anti-government activist will

continued >>

Gotlin-Sheehan 6

Once again, the writer goes beyond simply summarizing to include discussion of its meaning.

distrust the extensive information on the TSA site. Likewise, a staunch supporter of U.S. security measures after 9/11 would likely scoff at *We Won't Fly's* emotional outbursts. The two sites employ rhetorical strategies that reinforce their audience's biases. Sites like www.wewontfly.com succeed when they make readers feel threatened, uncomfortable, and angry by using powerful slogans and anecdotes. They fail when they lack the evidence of just how legitimate and widespread

A balanced conclusion that uses a logical appeal (*logos*) and shows the that writer is fair minded, an emotional appeal (*ethos*).

concerns are. Sites like www.tsa.gov succeed when they reassure readers with information and facts delivered by competent and friendly people who have their interests in mind. They may be less successful when they fail to demonstrate whether they can prevent the dangerous situations they're trying to prevent.

Gotlin-Sheehan 7

Works Cited appears alone on the next page in the actual paper.

Works Cited

Transportation Security Administration. "Who We Are." *Transportation Security Administration*, 2011. Web. 15 Nov. 2011.

Wewontfly.com. 2011. Web. 15 Nov. 2011.

15 Argument Essays

■ ■ ■ ■ ■ ■ ■ ■ ■ ■

Quick Points   You will learn to

➤ Describe key elements of arguments (see 15A).
➤ Apply the writing process to an argument (see 15B).
➤ Adapt frames and guides for an argument to your own needs (see 15C).

15A   What is an argument?

A written ARGUMENT consists of

- A THESIS STATEMENT (also called a *claim*) that clearly presents the topic to be debated in the essay and sets forth the writer's opinion regarding that topic

- **Support** for the writer's position on the debatable topic, consisting of reasons, with EVIDENCE, EXAMPLES, and logical explanations to back them up

If you were to judge the nature of arguments only by the popular media, you might think arguments are simply name-calling or fighting. For college-level writing, however, arguments need to demonstrate CRITICAL THINKING and sound reasoning (see Chapter 3).

15A.1   Purpose

The goal of your argument essay is try to convince readers to believe or do something. In some instances, you can't reasonably expect to change a person's mind, especially on highly controversial issues like capital punishment or a woman's right to choose. In those cases, your purpose is to demonstrate that your position is thoughtful and reasoned.

Sometimes instructors assign students a position to argue. In such cases, even if you personally disagree with it, you need to reason logically and effectively.

If instructors tell you to select your own topic, choose one suitable for college writing. For example, "Should public libraries block certain Web sites?" is worthy of a college-level essay. In contrast, "Which color is best for baseball caps?" is not. (For more about purposes for writing, see 4B.)

Arguments fall into four general categories, as explained in Quick Box 15.1.

Quick Box 15.1

Purposes and types of arguments

- **Definition arguments** persuade readers to interpret a term or concept in a particular way. Is something a "work of art," or is it "obscene"? Is assisted suicide "murder" or "a medical procedure" or an "act of kindness"? What characteristics must a film have to be called a romantic comedy?

- **Evaluation arguments** persuade readers that something is good or bad, worthwhile or a waste of time, or better or worse than other things like it. We explain evaluation arguments further in Chapter 17.

- **Cause and effect arguments** take two different forms. One argues that a situation results from a particular cause. For example, you might argue that certain causes are responsible for homelessness. Another argues that an action will have a specific effect. For example, you might argue that building more nuclear power plants would reduce global warming.

- **Proposal or solution arguments** convince readers that a particular solution to a problem or a particular way of addressing a need is best. For more about proposal and solution arguments, see Chapter 16.

15A.2 Audience

More than any other kind of writing, arguments require being sensitive to readers' interests and needs. What are their values, viewpoints, and assumptions? As you present your argument, you want to demonstrate your command of CRITICAL THINKING, especially how you carefully avoid LOGICAL FALLACIES. The approach most commonly used for such arguments is known as **classical argument**. Section 15C offers you a frame for it.

Some readers hold extreme or one-sided opinions. Your arguments can rarely change the minds of such people. Still, you're expected to demonstrate that you can use sound reasoning and avoid logical fallacies. If you think that your audience is likely to read your point of view with hostility, you might consider using the approach to argument known as **Rogerian argument**. It's based on psychologist Carl Rogers's communication principles, which suggest that even hostile readers can respect your position, if you show that you understand their viewpoint and treat it with respect. Section 15C offers you a frame for a Rogerian argument. For more about audience, see 4C.

15B How do I plan and revise arguments?

Generating ideas

- Make sure your topic is open to debate. For example, "We will eventually run out of fossil fuels" is not a debatable topic. "We should require car makers to increase mileage by 50 percent" is.

  👁 Watch the Video

- Check that your topic is open to debate by testing whether it answers a question that could receive more than one possible answer.

TOPIC	Students at Mitchler College must study a foreign language.
DEBATABLE QUESTION	Should Mitchler College require students to study a foreign language?
FIRST ANSWER	Mitchler College should not require students to study a foreign language.
SECOND ANSWER	Mitchler College should require students to study a foreign language.
THIRD ANSWER	Mitchler College should require all business majors to study a foreign language.
	All answers show that the topic is open to debate.

Alex Garcia, the biology major who wrote the argument essay that appears in section 15E, was interested in whether organic food was really better. Here's how Alex progressed from topic to claim to thesis statement.

DEBATABLE QUESTION	Are organic foods better than regular foods?
MY POSITION	I think people should buy organic foods when they can.
THESIS STATEMENT (FIRST DRAFT)	It is good for people to buy organic foods. This is a preliminary thesis statement. It clearly states the writer's position, but the word *good* is vague.
THESIS STATEMENT (SECOND DRAFT)	To achieve health benefits and improve the quality of the environment, organic foods should be purchased by consumers. This revised thesis statement is better because it states the writer's claim as well as a reason for the claim. However, it suffers from a lack of conciseness and from the unnecessary passive construction "should be purchased."
THESIS STATEMENT (FINAL DRAFT)	Research shows that the health and environmental benefits of organic foods outweigh their extra costs. This final version works well because it states the writer's claim clearly and concisely, with verbs all in the active voice. This thesis statement is suitable for the time and length given in the assignment. It also meets the requirements for a thesis statement given in Quick Box 5.4.

- Use the three persuasive appeals, explained in 3B: logical appeal (*logos*), ethical appeal (*ethos*), and emotional appeal (*pathos*).
- Use CRITICAL THINKING techniques. One strategy for generating and analyzing logical appeals was developed by philosopher Stephen Toulmin and is explained in Quick Box 15.2.
- Ask yourself *why* you take the position you do on your debatable topic. When you respond, "Because . . . ," you're ready to offer reasons. Arrange your possible reasons in logical order, which might suitably become TOPIC SENTENCES of your paragraphs.
- List the pros (in favor) and cons (against) your position.
- Consider evidence that could be useful: facts, statistics, expert testimony, personal experience, analogies, and so on.
- Decide whether support for your position involves research. (See Chapters 21–23.)

Revising

- Does your essay take a clear position on your debatable topic?
- Do your reasons and evidence support your argument?
- Is your evidence sufficient, representative, relevant, and accurate (see 23D)?
- Do you use logical, emotional, and ethical appeals (*logos, pathos,* and *ethos*) appropriately to convince your audience (see 3B)?
- Have you avoided logical fallacies (see 3I)?

Quick Box 15.2   ■ ■ ■ ■ ■ ■ ■ ■ ■ ■

Toulmin model for analyzing arguments

1. **Look for CLAIMS.** Identify all the main assertions in an argument.
2. **Identify and evaluate data (support).** The term *data* refers to evidence or support. Claims are unsupported if they have no data or if the data are weak.
3. **Identify warrants.** WARRANTS are the assumptions, often unstated, that connect data or reasons to claims. For example, in "We should not elect Daniels as mayor because she is divorced," the warrant (which is unstated) is, "Divorced people shouldn't be elected." Certainly that is open to debate. On the other hand, in "We should elect Daniels as mayor because she served in the Military," the warrant (which is stated) is "Military service is good preparation for public office."

- Have you anticipated objections or counterarguments that others might have?
- Is your tone reasonable, thoughtful, and fair?

15C What are frames for arguments?

Successful arguments can take many forms. We present here two possible frames—one for classical argument and one for Rogerian argument—to adapt to the specifics of your assignments.

Frame for a Classical Argument

Introductory paragraph(s)

- **Capture your readers' interest** by using one of the strategies for writing effective introductory paragraphs (see 6C).
- **Present your THESIS STATEMENT**, making sure it makes the central point that you will argue.

Body paragraph(s): background information

- **Provide background** for the information in your essay. This might follow the introductory paragraph or come later in the essay at a point when the background is more relevant.
- **Start with a TOPIC SENTENCE** that clearly relates to your thesis statement and leads logically to the information in the paragraph.

Body paragraphs: Reasons to support your claim

- **Present reasons for your argument**, one to a paragraph. If a reason is very complicated, use two paragraphs divided at a logical point.
- **Start each paragraph with a topic sentence** that states your reason.
- **Support each topic sentence** with evidence, examples, and reasoning (see RENNS, 6F).

Body Paragraphs: Rebuttal

- **Present objections and answer them.** State reasons that someone might give against your position. Answer these criticisms by explaining why your position is stronger.
- **Start each paragraph with a topic sentence** that helps your readers follow your line of reasoning.

Conclusion

- **Wrap up the essay**, often with a summary of the argument.
- **Present an elaboration of the argument's significance**, or a call to action for the readers or use one of the strategies for an effective concluding paragraph listed in Quick Box 6.8.

Frame for a Rogerian Argument

Introductory paragraph(s)

- **Capture your readers' interest** by using one of the strategies for writing effective introductory paragraphs (see 6C).
- **Present your thesis statement**, making sure it makes the central point that you will argue.

Body paragraph(s): Establish common ground with readers

- **Explain the issue**, acknowledging that some readers probably don't agree with you.
- **Explain the points of agreement** you and your readers probably share concerning underlying problems or issues.
- **Summarize opposing positions** and even acknowledge ways that some of them may be desirable. This may take one paragraph or several, depending on the complexity of the issue.
- **Start each paragraph with a** TOPIC SENTENCE that ties into your thesis statement and previews the content of the paragraph.

Body paragraphs: Reasons to support your claim

- **Present reasons for your claim**, one to a paragraph.
- **Start each paragraph with a topic sentence** that states your reason.
- **Support each topic sentence** with evidence, examples, and reasoning.

Conclusion

- **Use an engaging strategy** for a concluding paragraph (see 6J).
- **Summarize why your position is preferable** to your opponent's. Use a reasonable tone.

15D What are some sentence and paragraph guides for arguments?

Adapt these guides to your PURPOSE and AUDIENCE.

Sentence and Paragraph Guides

- The main reason [the most compelling argument] is _____.
  Recent statistics show that _____. These statistics are important because _____.

| Argument Guides (cont.) |

- Many experts support this position. For example, _____, who is _____, has argued "_____." _____ makes a similar point by explaining _____. The significance of this quotation is _____.

- I understand that my opponents believe _____. I respect their reasoning that _____ and also that _____. In fact, one thing we have in common is _____.

- Some people might oppose my position by arguing that _____. They might explain that _____, and they might point to support such as _____. However, this argument fails to take into account _____. Furthermore, other evidence suggests a different conclusion, namely _____. Ultimately, this opposing argument is unconvincing because _____.

15E A student's argument essay

Garcia 1

View the Model Document

Alex Garcia

Professor Brosnahan

WRIT 1122

4 Oct. 2012

Why Organic Foods Are Worth the Cost

Judging from cable television, many Americans apparently like talking about or watching food being made almost as much as eating it. A mainstay of these cooking programs and competitions, from *Top Chef* to *Iron Chef*, is an emphasis on fine ingredients. Beyond the caviar, truffles, and lobster, however, one small quality gets big attention: organic. Increasingly, that word matters not only on the Food Network but also in supermarkets, where displays of similar fruits and vegetables differ by cost and a tiny sticker reading "organic."

Writer uses a popular reference to get readers' attention and introduces a key debatable question.

continued >>

Garcia 2

Are organics worth the extra money, especially when budgets are tight? Have American consumers simply fallen victim, yet again, to peer pressure and advertising? After all, even the United States Department of Agriculture (USDA) "makes no claims that organically produced food is safer or more nutritious than conventionally produced food." Despite all the confusion, current research shows that the health and environmental benefits of organic foods outweigh their extra costs.

Thesis statement

Organic foods are produced without using most chemical pesticides, without artificial fertilizers, without genetic engineering, and without radiation (USDA). In the case of organic meat, poultry, eggs, and dairy products, the animals are raised without antibiotics or growth hormones. As a result, people sometimes use the term "natural" instead of "organic," but "natural" is less precise. Before 2002, people could never be quite sure what they were getting when they bought supposedly organic food, unless they bought it directly from a farmer they knew personally. In 2002, the USDA established standards that food must meet in order to be labeled and sold as organic.

Writer provides background information, making sure that readers understand what "organic" means.

Organic foods do tend to cost more than nonorganic, even up to 50% more (Zelman), mainly because they are currently more difficult to mass-produce. Farmers who apply pesticides often get larger crops from the same amount of land because there is less insect damage. Artificial fertilizers tend to increase the yield, size, and uniformity of fruits and vegetables, and herbicides kill weeds that compete with desirable crops for

A second paragraph of background information. Because cost is a key issue, this entire paragraph explains why organic foods are expensive.

continued >>

Garcia 3

sun, nutrients, and moisture. Animals that routinely receive antibiotics and growth hormones tend to grow more quickly and produce more milk and eggs. In contrast, organic farmers have lower yields and, therefore, higher costs. These get passed along as higher prices to consumers.

Still, the extra cost is certainly worthwhile in terms of health benefits. Numerous studies have shown the dangers of pesticides for humans. An extensive review of research by the Ontario College of Family Physicians concludes that "Exposure to all the commonly used pesticides . . . has shown positive associations with adverse health effects" (Sanborn et al. 173). The risks include cancer, psychiatric effects, difficulties becoming pregnant, miscarriages, and dermatitis. Carefully washing fruits and vegetables can remove some of these dangerous chemicals, but according to the prestigious journal *Nature*, even this does not remove all of them (Giles 797). An extensive review of research by medical professor Denis Lairon found that "the vast majority (94–100%) of organic food does not contain any pesticide residues (38). Certainly, if there's a way to prevent these poisons from entering our bodies, we should take advantage of it. The few cents saved on cheaper food can quickly disappear in doctors' bills needed to treat conditions caused or worsened by chemicals.

Organic meat, poultry, and dairy products can address another health concern: the diminishing effectiveness of antibiotics. In the past decades, many kinds of bacteria have become resistant to drugs, making it extremely difficult to treat some kinds of tuberculosis, pneumonia, staphylococcus

Topic sentence introduces health benefits.

Writer uses an emotional appeal (pathos) and gives the first main reason in support of the thesis. Details explain the dangers of pesticides in foods, and three expert studies provide support.

A second reason in favor of organic foods. The writer uses careful reasoning to explain.

continued >>

Garcia 4

infections, and less serious diseases ("Dangerous" 1). True, this has happened mainly because doctors have over-prescribed antibiotics to patients who expect a pill for every illness. However, routinely giving antibiotics to all cows and chickens means that these drugs enter our food chain early, giving

Writer uses logical, ethical, and emotional appeals (*logos, ethos,* and *pathos*).

bacteria lots of chances to develop resistance. A person who switches to organic meats won't suddenly experience better results from antibiotics; the benefit is a more gradual one for society as a whole. However, if we want to be able to fight infections with effective drugs, we need to reserve antibiotics for true cases of need and discourage their routine use in animals raised for food. Buying organic is a way to persuade more farmers to adopt this practice.

Writer explains a third reason, again using an expert source in support.

Another benefit of organic foods is also a societal one: Organic farming is better for the environment. In his review of several studies, Colin Macilwain concluded that organic farms nurture more and diverse plants and animals than regular farms (797). Organic farms also don't release pesticides and herbicides that can harm wildlife and run into our water supply, with implications for people's health, too. Macilwain notes that those farms also can generate less carbon dioxide, which will help with global warming; also, many scientists believe that organic farming is more sustainable because it

By arousing the "better self" of readers, the writer uses an ethical appeal (*ethos*).

results in better soil quality (798). Once again, these benefits are not ones that you will personally experience right away. However, a better natural environment means a better quality of living for everyone and for future generations.

Some critics point out that organic products aren't more nutritious than regular ones. Four years ago, media star and

continued >>

Garcia 5

physician Sanjay Gupta, for example, found the medical evidence for nutritional advantages is "thin" (60), and the *Tufts University Health and Nutrition Letter* reported that the research on nutritional benefits is mixed, ("Is Organic" 8). However, other studies differ. For example, research shows that organically raised tomatoes have higher levels of flavonoids, nutrients that have many health benefits (Mitchell et al.). More recently, both Denis Lairon and Walter J. Crinnion found higher levels of several nutrients in organic found. Nutritional value, which includes qualities such as vitamins and other beneficial substances, is a different measure than food safety. Even if the nutritional evidence is uncertain, food safety from avoiding chemicals and environmental quality remain convincing reasons to purchase organic food.

One point has to be conceded. Claims that organic foods taste better are probably groundless. Researchers at Cornell University gave people identical chips, yogurt, and cookies but labeled some of them "organic" and others "regular." People rated the organic ones as better tasting even though there was no difference ("Even Organic"). Labels clearly shape our perceptions.

Despite considerable benefits for purchasing organic products, consumers have to make individual purchasing decisions. There are no simple ways to measure that spending fifty cents more on a cantaloupe will improve my quality of life by fifty cents. However, there is a position between all organics and none. The nonprofit Environmental Working Group identifies a dozen types of organic produce (including apples, strawberries, and spinach) as safer and worth the extra cost,

Writer acknowledges an objection and even cites expert opinions that contradict his argument. However, he counters those objections and concludes with a strong comment in support of organic foods.

*Writer uses logical appeal (*logos*) to try to convince his readers.*

*Writer concedes a possible objection. This builds an ethical case (*ethos*) by showing writer is open-minded.*

Concluding paragraph returns to issues of cost in the thesis statement, summarizes the reasons the paper has provided, and ends with a strong call for action.

continued >>

Garcia 6

but they conclude another dozen are not, including bananas, pineapples, and onions (Zelman). The bottom line is that countless people are rightly concerned these days about our personal health and the health of the world in which we live. It's nearly impossible to put a value on a sustainable, diverse natural environment and having the physical health to enjoy it. The long-term benefits of buying organic, for anyone who can reasonably afford to, far outweigh the short-term savings in the checkout line.

The writer ends by appealing to logic, ethics, and emotions (logos, ethos, and pathos).

Garcia 7

Works Cited

In an actual paper, the Works Cited appears alone on a new page.

"Dangerous Bacterial Infections Are on the Rise." *Consumer Reports on Health* (Nov. 2007): 1–4. Print.

Crinnion, Walter J. "Organic Foods Contain Higher Levels of Certain Nutrients, Lower Levels of Pesticides, and May Provide Health Benefits for the Consumer." *Alternative Medicine Review* 15.1 (Apr. 2010): 4–12. Web. 14 Sept. 2011.

"Even Organic Cookies and Chips Enjoy Health 'Halo'." *Tufts University Health and Nutrition Letter* 29.5 (July 2011): 3. Web. 12 Sept. 2011.

Giles, Jim. "Is Organic Food Better for Us?" *Nature* 428.6985 (2004): 796–97. Print.

continued >>

Garcia 8

Gupta, Sanjay, and Shahreen Abedin. "Rethinking Organics."
Time (20 Aug. 2007): 60. Print.

"Is Organic Food Really More Nutritious?" *Tufts University
Health and Nutrition Letter* (Sept. 2007): 8. Web. 25 Sept.
2011.

Lairon, Denis. "Nutritional Quality and Safety of Organic Food.
A Review." *Agronomy for Sustainable Development* 30
(2010): 33–41. Web. 14 Sept. 2011.

Macilwain, Colin. "Is Organic Farming Better for the
Environment?" *Nature* 428.6985 (2004): 797–98. Print.

Mitchell, Alyson E., et al. "Ten-Year Comparison of
the Influence of Organic and Conventional Crop
Management Practices on the Content of Flavonoids in
Tomatoes." *Journal of Agricultural Food Chemistry* 55.15
(2007): 6154–59. Web. 30 Sept. 2011.

United States. Dept. of Agriculture. "Organic Food Labels and
Standards: The Facts." National Organic Program. Jan.
2007. Web. 26 Sept. 2011.

Sanborn, Margaret, et al. *Pesticides Literature Review:
Systematic Review of Pesticide Human Health Effects.*
Toronto: Ontario College of Family Physicians, 2004. Web.
28 Sept. 2011.

Zelman, Kathleen M. "Organic Food—Is 'Natural' Worth the
Extra Cost?" *WebMD*. 2007. Web. 17 Sept. 2011.

16 Proposal or Solution Essays
■ ■ ■ ■ ■ ■ ■ ■ ■ ■

Quick Points You will learn to

➤ Describe key elements of a proposal or solution essay (see 16A).
➤ Apply the writing process to a proposal or solution essay (see 16B).
➤ Adapt frames and guides for a proposal or solution essay to your own needs (see 16C).

16A What are proposal or solution essays?

Watch the Video

Proposal or solution essays are specific types of ARGUMENTS (see Chapter 15) that require you to do three things:

1. Convince readers that a particular problem or opportunity exists and requires action.

2. Propose a specific solution or course of action and offer reasons for proposing it.

3. Defend your solution or proposal as better than others.

16A.1 Purpose

Proposal or solution essays seek to persuade readers to act on a solution. In your essay, you need to address the problem you want to write about, your proposed solution(s), and the beliefs your readers hold about them. Here are two examples:

A. Problem: Students can't get the classes they need to graduate on time.

Solution 1: The college should offer more courses by either (a) hiring more faculty, or (b) having faculty teach more students.

Solution 2: The college should increase its number of popular or required courses by cutting unpopular or elective courses.

Solution 3: The college should change graduation requirements.

B. Problem: Unemployment is high.

> Solution 1: The government should hire unemployed people to build roads, bridges, parks, and other public projects.

> Solution 2: The government should reward businesses that hire people to work in this country or penalize businesses that send jobs overseas.

> Solution 3: Workers should be less choosey about the jobs they will accept, or they should start their own businesses.

The preceding examples list several possible solutions, but no doubt you can think of others. Which solution would be best? Why? (For more about purposes for writing, see 4B.)

16A.2 Audience

Consult Quick Box 16.1 for four considerations of audience specifically for problem or solution essays. For more about audience, see 4C.

Quick Box 16.1 ■ ■ ■ ■ ■ ■ ■ ■ ■ ■ ■

Four aspects of audience for problem or solution essays

1. **The audience doesn't know or agree that a problem exists.** Here explaining the problem is your most important task. You want to increase public awareness so that the desperate need for solutions becomes obvious, but your solution isn't your central concern.

2. **The audience generally agrees on a problem—but not on a solution.** Here you explain the problem briefly and spend your time and energy on writing about the value of your solution.

3. **The audience believes there's a problem, but it favors a different solution.** Here you emphasize why your solution is better (for instance, more practical, easier to achieve, less expensive) than theirs.

4. **The audience is in a direct position to act versus an indirect position.** Here you target your argument to the audience that has direct power to act or indirect power to influence.

16B How do I plan and revise proposal or solution arguments?

Consult section 15B for advice useful for generating arguments and their support, or use these questions for proposal or solution essays.

- **What caused the problem?** Complex problems usually have many possible causes so take time to brainstorm a list.

- **What are possible solutions?** Because each cause might have a different solution, don't rush into settling on one of them. Allow yourself time to be creative.

- **Why is your solution effective?** Who needs to be involved? What do they need to do? When? How? Why?

- **Why is your solution feasible?** A solution is feasible when it is practical and affordable. For example, we could solve poverty by giving every poor person $50,000 a year, but that's not feasible.

- **What are drawbacks of other solutions?** Apply questions of effectiveness and feasibility to all solutions to reveal weaknesses in alternative proposals. Also, you might consider unintended effects or results.

- **What will happen if people don't act?** This question can generate an effective conclusion and be a good source of emotional appeals (*pathos*).

Revising

- Have you established that there's a problem that needs a solution?
- Is your solution effective, feasible, and better than others?
- Have you used evidence that is sufficient, representative, relevant, and accurate (see Quick Box 3.7)?
- Have you used appropriate logical, emotional, and ethical appeals (*logos, pathos,* and *ethos;* see 3B)?
- Is your TONE reasonable, thoughtful, and fair?

16C What is a frame for a proposal or solution essay?

Here is a possible proposal/solution essay frame to adapt to the specifics of your assignments.

Frame for a Proposal or Solution Essay

Introductory paragraph(s)

- **Capture your readers' interest** in your topic by using one of the strategies for writing effective introductory paragraphs (see 6C).
- **Introduce** a problem or opportunity.
- **Present your THESIS STATEMENT**, making sure it proposes an action or solution (see 5F).

Body paragraph(s): Background information

- **Provide background information.** Note: If the background isn't complicated, your essay might move directly to persuading readers that a problem exists.
- **Start each paragraph with a TOPIC SENTENCE** that clearly relates to your thesis statement and leads logically to the information in the paragraph (see 6E).

Body paragraphs: Persuade readers that a problem exists

- **Explain the problem that exists**, grouping the parts of the problem effectively within separate paragraphs.
- **Start each paragraph with a TOPIC SENTENCE** that makes clear what you will explain in the paragraph.
- **Support each topic sentence** with evidence, examples, and reasoning.
- **If your emphasis is on the solution** because the problem is well known, keep this section short.

Solution paragraph(s)

- **Explain why your solution will be effective and feasible**.
- **Divide parts of your solution** into sensible paragraphs, starting each one with a topic sentence that leads into the point you are making.
- **If your emphasis is on the problem**, keep this section short.

Rebuttal paragraph(s): Place here or immediately before your solution

- **Present alternative solutions and refute them.** State other possible solutions and explain why they aren't as good as yours. Answer possible criticisms.
- **Again, if your emphasis is on the problem**, keep this section short.

Conclusion

- **Wrap up the essay** with one of the strategies for concluding paragraphs in 6J.
- **Summarize** your problem or solution.
- **Make a call to action** or portray the negative consequences of not acting or the clear benefits of adopting your solution.

16D What are some sentence and paragraph guides for proposal/solution essays?

Adapt these guides to your PURPOSE and AUDIENCE.

Sentence and Paragraph Guides

- The best way to solve the problem of _____ is by _____.
- To address the problem of _____, _____ (we, you, the city council, the board, parking services, etc.) should _____.
- There are _____ reasons the current situation is a problem. The first is _____. The second is _____. However, the most important is _____.
- The most effective and practical solution to this problem is _____. One result of implementing this solution would be _____. That's because _____. Another outcome would be _____. A potential difficulty of this solution is _____. However, we can overcome that difficulty by _____.
- Some other possible solutions would be to _____ or to _____. The first is problematic because _____. The second is impractical because _____. My solution is preferable to both alternatives because _____.
- Failing to take this action will have several negative consequences. First, _____. Furthermore, _____.

16E A student's solution essay

View the Model Document

Cui 1

Yanggu Cui

Professor Leade

Writing 102

10 Dec. 2012

Quotations get readers' attention and lead to the introduction.

A Proposal to Improve Fan Behavior at Children's Games

"Ref, you're an idiot!"

"You're blind as a bat and twice as stupid!"

continued >>

Cui 2

"Get a life, ref!"

"I'll see you after the game!"

Those were just a few yells I heard from the sidelines of a soccer game last Saturday. I wasn't watching a professional match or even a high school one. Instead, it was my eight year old cousin's game in the Arapahoe Recreation League. The referee wasn't a 30 year old professional but, rather, a skinny high school girl who seemed to be fifteen or sixteen. The people yelling weren't drunken guys in sweatshirts or even coaches with red faces and bulging neck veins; instead, they were moms and dads drinking lattes. The league organizers need to bring an end to this kind of abuse, and the best way to do so is by requiring all parents to sign a code of good behavior.

Parents for decades have proudly watched their sons and daughters play little league softball, baseball, soccer, and other sports. In recent years, these sports have gotten more competitive, with more games, longer seasons, more practices, and greater expectations for winning. One result is that parents have gotten more vocal on the sidelines, not only yelling encouragement for Julio and Jenny but also screaming protests at coaches, the opposing team, and officials. Almost every call against their team is greeted by a loud disbelief, at best, and insults or threats, at worst.

The current level of fan abuse is troubling for at least four reasons. First, it discourages officials, especially younger ones who are just learning the job themselves. No one fears making a wrong call more than someone who is just gaining experience as a referee. If parents make the job so unpleasant

---

Margin annotations:

Details create emotional appeals (*pathos*) by giving a picture of the events.

Introductory paragraph sets up the problem. In the thesis sentence at the end of the paragraph, the writer presents a solution.

By invoking parents with children, the writer appeals to emotions (*pathos*) and provides context on the issue.

Topic sentence announces four reasons for convincing readers that a problem exists and is a logical appeal (*logos*).

continued >>

Cui 3

that kids making minimum wage stop doing it, the games will come to a halt. Second, it makes what should be a fun recreational experience for all into an ordeal. Rather than paying attention to the game, players and spectators alike get distracted by the drama on the sidelines, even getting nervous that a physical confrontation or fight might occur. Third, it embarrasses the kids themselves. Parents might feel like their kids appreciate and value someone sticking up for them, but the truth of the matter is that most children would rather not have that particular kind of attention.

Each reason receives a brief explanation. Numbering them creates clarity.

The writer keeps the most important reason for last and devotes an entire paragraph to explaining it in detail.

The fourth, and most distressing, problem is that fan abuse warps the nature of the game itself. At a time when participating, having fun, and learning new skills should be primary, young players get the clear message that only winning matters, winning at all costs. Rather than assuming that officials and others are trying their best to be impartial and fair, kids are being taught that people are incompetent and malicious. Rather than assuming that sometimes in life we make mistakes that get penalized, but life goes on, kids learn that they are rarely, if ever at fault. Rather than accepting adversity, even if sometimes it's wrong, kids learn to dwell on every hardship. The result is that, instead of learning lessons valuable for a happy life, kids learn to be intolerant and bitter, and they learn it from their parents.

*Writer uses ethical and emotional appeals (*ethos* and *pathos*) by showing the negative influence on children.*

*Writer introduces the solution and provides an explanation using a logical appeal (*logos*).*

It would be nice to assume that merely talking to parents would control the situation, but the situation actually requires a more active solution. The Arapahoe Recreational League should adopt a code of conduct for all parents, in the form of an agreement they must sign. This code should indicate

continued >>

Cui 4

fan behaviors that are approved and encouraged; these would include yelling encouragement or congratulations for all players. The code would also specify behaviors that are banned; these would include taunting or criticizing players, coaches, and officials. Children whose parents refuse to sign would not be allowed to participate.

Granted, merely signing a code of conduct will not prevent all abuse. However, it gives a clear mechanism to end it once it happens. If there's a violation, officials can stop the game, and ask the coach of the team with offending parents to remind them of the code they signed. If extreme behavior continues, the official can stop the game for an extended period, and if it still persists, he or she can declare a forfeit and end the game. This series of events puts responsibility on the parents, who cannot claim they didn't understand the consequences, and it puts a clear end to the abuse.

> Writer strengthens her ethical appeal (*ethos*) by recognizing some limitations. She goes on to explain how the solution would be effective.

Other solutions have been proposed in different leagues. The most extreme is to ban spectators from even attending games. While a ban would surely prevent fan abuse, it would unfairly penalize those many parents who are good sports and supportive spectators. Plus, who wants to deprive people from seeing an important part of their children, grandchildren, and friends' childhood? Another solution has been to require spectators to be absolutely silent during games. This solution, while also potentially successful, deprives players and parents alike of the joys of praise and encouragement.

> Topic sentence acknowledges other possible solutions and explains their shortcomings.

I urge you, then, to adopt my solution. Having a code of conduct will reduce fan abuse, restore some of the fun to

continued >>

Cui 5

The essay concludes with a call to action that has a logical appeal (*logos*). It shows the benefits of the solution and portrays the consequences of not adopting it. our games, and keep them in perspective as fun, not battles. Failing to take this action would worsen the attitude that winning is everything and leave children even less prepared for the inevitable disappointments and struggles of life. Ultimately, it might eventually result in empty fields with no one willing to endure threats and insults from spectators who lack the discipline and perspective to behave in ways that their own children deserve.

17 Evaluation Essays

Quick Points   You will learn to

➤ Describe key elements of an evaluation (see 17A).
➤ Apply the writing process to an evaluation (see 17B).
➤ Adapt frames and guides for an evaluation to your own needs (see 17C).

17A   What are evaluation essays?

Watch the Video

EVALUATION essays judge the quality of a text, object, individual, or event by providing reasons and support. Here are typical categories of evaluations:

- **Reviews.** Movie, concert, book, theater, television, architecture, restaurant, product, or art reviews are all evaluations. They answer questions such as: Is that play worth seeing? Will certain readers like that book? Is the current season of this television series as good as last year's?

- **Recommendations or performance reviews.** Letters of recommendation and/or reviews of performances evaluate peoples' qualifications for a particular job or how well they've done it.
- **Critical analyses.** A critical analysis judges ideas, recommendations, or proposals. It assesses whether an argument is sound or whether an informative text is accurate or useful. It answers questions such as, "Do the facts support the writer's claims? Is the writer fair and reasonable? Is the recommended action practical and more effective than other actions?"

17A.1 Purpose

Evaluations have mainly an argumentative purpose although they also inform readers about what is being evaluated. (For more about purpose, see 4B.)

17A.2 Audience

Audiences for evaluations can be as small as a single person (such as an employee's annual job evaluation) or as large as the general public who reads a magazine or blog. (For more about audience, see 4C). If your audience is general, the questions below will help you.

- **What will readers already know about your subject?** Are they familiar with the text, object, individual, or event being evaluated? Do you need to explain your subject in detail, or is a brief explanation sufficient?
- **What might readers already believe about your subject?** Most people think fondly of *The Wizard of Oz*, so if you argue that Judy Garland played Dorothy poorly, be aware that readers might disagree with you.
- **What are the circumstances in which your readers will read your evaluation?** For an academic audience, including scholars like your instructor, you need to be scholarly and your TONE relatively formal. You might need research to support your position. On the other hand, for a popular blog, your tone can be more informal, but you still need sound reasons for your position.

17B How do I plan and revise evaluation essays?

Several questions can generate ideas for evaluations. Although we've arranged them here according to types, they can be mixed in the order you find most effective.

Generating ideas for reviews

- What seems to be the main purpose of the author, director, artist, etc.? How well was it achieved? Is that purpose worthwhile?
- Was the plot plausible? Interesting? Original?
- Were characters interesting and effective? In other words, if you infer that viewers are supposed to like, hate, or sympathize with them, can they?
- How well did the setting work, including what it looked like, its lighting, sounds, any music, etc.? (These questions apply to restaurants, galleries, or other settings, too.)
- What other works does this particular one resemble? Does it compare well? Why or why not?

Generating ideas for performance evaluations

- What specific qualities are needed to perform a particular job? Does the individual have those qualities? How can you tell?
- What are examples of the person's main strengths? Main weaknesses?
- How does this person compare with others in similar positions?
- What advice do you have for this person or anyone working with him or her?

Generating ideas for critical analyses

- Is the support the writer gives for his or her claims reasonable? Sufficient?
- Are there missing facts, viewpoints, or interpretations?
- Who would agree and who would disagree with the text? On what basis? How right would people be who disagree?
- If the text proposes an action, would it work? Is it practical? Is it the best one available?

Revising

- Does your THESIS STATEMENT present a clear judgment of the text, object, person, or event you're evaluating?
- Will your readers have a clear understanding of the text, object, person, or event you're summarizing? Have you given enough detail but not too much?
- Do you give and support reasons for your evaluation?

- Do you take into account your audience's knowledge, belief, and expectations?

- If your evaluation is mostly negative, have you tried to acknowledge possible strengths? If your evaluation is mostly positive, have you tried to acknowledge possible critiques?

- Do you need to include a WORKS CITED or REFERENCES page? If so, is it formatted correctly, with proper in-text citations (see Chapters 25–27)?

17C   What is a frame for an evaluation essay?

Here is a possible frame for an evaluation essay to adapt to your assignments.

Frame for an Evaluation Essay

Introductory paragraph(s)

- **Capture your readers' interest** in your topic by using one of the strategies for writing effective introductory paragraphs (see 6C).
- **Present your THESIS STATEMENT**, making sure it states your overall evaluation (see 5F).

Background paragraph(s):

- **Clearly explain what you're evaluating.** Give a brief objective overview by providing a brief plot summary if you're evaluating a book, play, movie, etc.; providing a description of an event or object; introducing the person if you're writing a recommendation.

Body paragraphs: Stating evaluations

- **Start each paragraph with a TOPIC SENTENCE** that states a reason that ties in logically to your thesis statement.
- **Support each topic sentence** with examples, evidence, and reasoning (including SUMMARIES or QUOTATIONS, if appropriate).
- **Include as many paragraphs as there are reasons** for your evaluation. If a reason is especially complicated, or if you have extensive examples or explanations, you might divide it into two or more paragraphs.
- **Save your most important evaluation for last.** Building toward your most powerful judgment will leave readers with the best reason for believing you.

(continued)

Evaluation Frame (cont.)

Rebuttal or "conceding" paragraph(s): Place either after your evaluating paragraphs, as in this frame; or immediately after your background paragraph(s) above.

- **Present alternative evaluations and refute them.** If it seems practical, state some reasons why others might disagree with your evaluations, and explain why your evaluation is still strong.
- **[optional] Concede some points.** To concede a point means to admit that it's valid. If it seems practical and honest, and you think it will make your readers more receptive to your evaluation, concede a positive point or two (if your overall evaluation is negative) or concede a negative point or two (if you're positive). Still, explain why your overall evaluation is reasonable.

Conclusion

- **Wrap up the essay with an engaging strategy** for concluding paragraphs (see 6J).
- **Summarize your point of view.**
- **Give your readers a recommendation,** such as buy this, don't attend that, hire this person, don't accept this argument, etc.

17D What are some sentence and paragraph guides for evaluations?

Adapt these guides to your PURPOSE and AUDIENCE.

Sentence and Paragraph Guides

- Despite a few redeeming qualities, this _____ (book, movie, CD, etc.) is ultimately _____ (disappointing, frustrating, etc.).
- Four qualities are especially strong. First, _____. Second, _____. Third, _____. Most important, however, is _____.
- Admittedly, _____ has a couple of strong features. For example, _____. In addition, _____. However, even taking these into consideration, the total effect is not enough to overcome an overall weakness. That is primarily because _____.

Evaluation Guides (cont.)

- The author's strongest point is _____. The idea is effective because _____. For example, she _____, as is clear from the statement that "_____."

- _____'s most impressive quality is her [or his] ability to _____. That quality came through most clearly when _____. Although other employees might have _____, _____ instead chose to _____.

17E A student's evaluation essay

Pietruszynski 1

View the Model Document

Kelly Pietruszynski

Communications 100

Professor Moeller

12 Nov. 2012

The Worthy Rise of the Planet of the Apes

In the famous scene at the end of the 1968 movie *The Planet of the Apes*, Charlton Heston rides along a desolate beach until he comes across the top of the Statue of Liberty buried in the sand. At that moment, he and the movie's audience realize that the planet on which he's been stranded, where apes rule humans, is actually Earth in the future. That successful original movie led to sequels and even a remake in 2001, starring Mark Wahlberg. But not until the 2011 film *Rise of the Planet of the Apes* did we get any explanation of how the strange future came to be. The result is a satisfying film well worth seeing.

Rise of the Planet of the Apes is set in contemporary San Francisco. Will Rodman (played by James Franco) is a scientist

> Opening paragraph stirs interest by giving some background, ending with a thesis sentence that states the evaluation the writer will support.

continued >>

Pietruszynski 2

who develops a drug meant to grow new brain cells and, as a result, cure diseases like Alzheimer's. Through a series of events, Rodman adopts and raises an ape exposed to that drug. Caesar (the ape) demonstrates human-like intelligence that eventually gets him in trouble, resulting in his being imprisoned with a number of apes, gorillas, and orangutans in a medical testing facility. After being exposed to another drug, the entire colony of apes develops intelligence and escapes, led by Caesar.

> *The writer summarizes the movie's plot so that readers have a clear context for the writer's arguments.*

One impressive quality of this movie is the plot. Admittedly, any attempt to explain how apes become intelligent and humans stupid is finally going to stretch credibility. However, *Rise of the Planet of the Apes* is fairly plausible. Because finding a cure for Alzheimer's and related diseases is such a strong interest in our society, we can easily imagine extensive research and animal testing. To the plot's credit, the ape's intelligence breakthrough isn't sudden and miraculous. Even after Caesar is exposed to the drug, years pass while he lives with Will, allowing him to accumulate human experiences and intelligence. We see conflict development in Caesar between the world of nature and the world of human society, and his mistreatment at the hands of cruel humans, especially a keeper named Dodge explains why the apes eventually turn against humans.

> *Topic sentence gives one reason for the evaluation. The rest of this paragraph supports the topic sentence.*

> *An appeal to logic as well as ethics (logos and ethos).*

This plot benefits from exceptional camera work and special effects. There are powerfully breathtaking scenes. For example, when Will takes Caesar to play in a redwood forest, the size and scope of the trees as Caesar climbs through them is stunning. When the apes later escape, we see them swarm through the trees on San Francisco streets; or, rather, we see

> *Topic sentence gives a second reason for the evaluation. Note the transitional connection to the previous paragraph.*

continued >>

Pietruszynski 3

the trees shuddering, as the apes are invisible among them, which is a more suggestive effect. The final battle takes place with dramatic fury on Golden Gate Bridge. But some of the best camera work depicts quiet scenes, not energetic ones. In one profound scene, Caesar is alone in the attic. Through a small window, he watches children play on the street far below, and the camera angle and distance creates a powerful sense of isolation and loneliness.

> The writer uses an emotional appeal here (*pathos*)

The best special effect is Caesar himself. While the original movie had actors wearing masks and makeup that won an Academy Award in 1969, *Rise of the Planet of the Apes* uses motion capture computer graphics. Andy Serkis (who played Gollum in *Lord of the Rings*) wore multiple computer sensors while acting the role of Caesar. The results were translated by skilled technicians and powerful computers into extraordinarily realistic images. The apes look like real animals, not actors in costumes. Most impressive are the emotions conveyed. At various times, Caesar looks happy, sad, confused, scheming, and so on. The effects alone are worth seeing.

> Topic sentence ties back to the previous paragraph and explains one effect in detail.

> Writer uses an emotional appeal (*pathos*) to urge readers to see the movie.

The movie's most impressive quality, however, is the way it establishes relationships between its characters. Will lives with his father, played by John Lithgow, who has Alzheimer's, and you can see not only the loving relationship between the two of them, but also Lithgow and Caesar. Indeed, Caesar gets into trouble at one point because he comes to the ailing man's defense. The most important relationship, of course, is between Will and Caesar, which develops fairly convincingly as identical to one between father and son. The relationship is

> Topic sentence states the third reason in support of the thesis. Note that the writer saved what she thought was the best reason for last.

continued >>

Pietruszynski 4

complete with struggles for autonomy that characterize human families, as children move through adolescence and parents try to find the right combination of discipline and independence. As a result, we identify with and care about Will and Caesar. Instead of just being an action flick, *Rise* has emotional depth.

There are silly relationships, too. It's hard to imagine what Will's love interest, an attractive veterinarian played by Frieda Pinto, sees in him. He's so obsessed with his work and his family situation, that I can't see her putting up with him through the several years in which the movie unfolds.

This is just one of several negative elements of the film. Critics can accurately point out that the villains in the film are just too extreme, from the evil animal keepers, to an angry neighbor, to the ultimate bad guy, the director of Will's lab who pursues profits at any cost. Also, the final battle scenes clash a little with the rest of the movie. The director seems to trade subtle relationships and characterizations for chases and explosions.

Rise of the Planet of the Apes, then, is hardly a perfect movie. However, it is an entertaining and thoughtful one. It provides a plausible origin story for the entire series of films, delivering a solid plot, great special effects, and engaging relationships. As with any science fiction, viewers have to go along with certain premises. Because this movie makes you willing to do so, it's well worth seeing.

PART

3

Source-Based Writing

18 Quoting, Paraphrasing, and Summarizing

■ ■ ■ ■ ■ ■ ■ ■ ■ ■

Quick Points   You will learn to

> ➤ Use quotations effectively (see 18B).
> ➤ Integrate sources using paraphrasing and summarizing (see 18C–18D).
> ➤ Synthesize two or more sources (see 18F–18L).

18A   How can I integrate sources into my writing?

You integrate sources into your writing when you combine information or ideas from other writers with your own. To integrate sources well, you use three techniques: QUOTATION (see 18B), PARAPHRASE (see 18C), and SUMMARY (see 18D). The techniques are essential for SYNTHESIZING sources (see 18F to 18L). Mastering them allows you to write smooth, effective papers that avoid PLAGIARISM: stealing or representing someone else's words or ideas as your own (see Chapter 19).

18B   How can I use quotations effectively?

👁
Watch the Video

A **quotation** is the exact words of a source enclosed in quotation marks (see Chapter 46). Well-chosen quotations can lend a note of authority and enliven a document with someone else's voice.

Avoid adding too many quotations, however. If more than a quarter of your paper consists of quotations, you make readers suspect that you haven't bothered to develop your own thinking. Quick Box 18.1 provides guidelines for using quotations. All examples are in MLA documentation style.

18B.1   Making quotations fit smoothly with your sentences

When you use quotations, the greatest risk you take is that you'll end up with incoherent, choppy sentences. You can avoid this problem by making the words you quote fit smoothly with three aspects of your writing: grammar, style, and logic. Here are some examples of sentences that don't mesh well with quotations, followed by a revised version.

Quick Box 18.1

Guidelines for using quotations

- Use quotations from authorities on your subject to support or refute what you've written.
- Never use a quotation to present your THESIS STATEMENT or a TOPIC SENTENCE.
- Choose a quotation only for the following reasons.

  Its language is particularly appropriate or distinctive.

  Its idea is particularly hard to paraphrase accurately.

  Its authority comes from a source that is especially important for support.

  Its words are open to interpretation.
- Never allow quotations to make up a quarter or more of your paper. Instead, rely on PARAPHRASE (see 18C) and SUMMARY (see 18D).
- Quote accurately. Always check a quotation against the original source—and then recheck it.
- Integrate quotations smoothly into your writing (see 18B.1–18B.4).
- Document quotations carefully.
- Avoid plagiarism (see Chapter 19).

SOURCE

Turkle, Sherry. *Alone Together: Why We Expect More from Technology and Less from Each Other.* New York: Basic Books, 2011. Print.

ORIGINAL (TURKLE'S EXACT WORDS)

Digital connections and the sociable robot may offer the illusion of companionship without the demands of friendship. Our networked life allows us to hide from each other, even as we are tethered to each other.   [from page 1]

GRAMMAR PROBLEM

Turkle explains how relying on network communication "illusion of companionship without the demands of friendship" (1).

STYLE PROBLEM

Turkle explains that digital connections and the lives of robots "offer the illusion of companionship without the demands of friendship" (1).

LOGIC PROBLEM

Turkle explains networked connections "without the demands of friendship" (1).

ACCEPTABLE SMOOTH USE OF QUOTATION

Turkle explains that networked connections "may offer the illusion of companionship without the demands of friendship" (1).

18B.2 Using brackets to add words

One way to fit a quotation smoothly into your writing is to add a word or very brief phrase to the quotation by placing it in brackets—[ ]—so that it fits seamlessly with the rest of your sentence.

ORIGINAL (TURKLE'S EXACT WORDS)

If we divest ourselves of such things, we risk being coarsened, reduced.   [from page 292]

QUOTATION WITH EXPLANATORY BRACKETS

"If we divest ourselves of such things [as caring for the sick], we risk being coarsened, reduced" (Turkle 292).

18B.3 Using ellipses to delete words

Another way to fit a quotation smoothly into your sentence is to use ellipses. Delete the part of the quotation that is causing the problem, and mark the omission by using ELLIPSIS POINTS. When you use ellipses to delete troublesome words, make sure that the remaining words accurately reflect the source's meaning and that your sentence still flows smoothly.

ORIGINAL (TURKLE'S EXACT WORDS)

The idea of addiction, with its one solution that we know we won't take, makes us feel hopeless.   [from page 294]

QUOTATION USING ELLIPSIS

Turkle notes that "the idea of addiction . . . makes us feel hopeless" (294).

18B.4 Integrating author names, source titles, and other information

A huge complaint instructors have about student papers is that quotations sometimes are simply stuck in, for no apparent reason. Without context-setting information, the reader can't tell exactly why the writer included a particular quotation. Also, always be sure your readers can tell who said each group of quoted words in your writing.

SOURCE

Wright, Karen. "Times of Our Lives." *Scientific American* Sept. 2002: 58-66.
    Print.

ORIGINAL (WRIGHT'S EXACT WORDS)

In human bodies, biological clocks keep track of seconds, minutes, days, months and years.   [from page 66]

PROBLEM: DISCONNECTED QUOTATION

The human body has many subconscious processes. People don't have to make their hearts beat or remind themselves to breathe. "In human bodies, biological clocks keep track of seconds, minutes, days, months and years" (Wright 66).

ACCEPTABLY CONNECTED QUOTATION

The human body has many subconscious processes. People don't have to make their hearts beat or remind themselves to breathe. However, other processes are less obvious and perhaps more surprising. Karen Wright observes, for example, "In human bodies, biological clocks keep track of seconds, minutes, days, months and years" (66).

Quick Box 18.2 lists other strategies for working quotations smoothly into your paper by integrating the author's name, the source title, or other information into your writing.

Quick Box 18.2   ■ ■ ■ ■ ■ ■ ■ ■ ■ ■ ■

Strategies for smoothly fitting quotations into your sentences

- Mention in your sentence (before or after the quotation) the name of the author you're quoting.
- Mention in your sentence the title of the work you're quoting from.
- If the author of a quotation is a noteworthy figure, mention the author's credentials.
- Add your own introductory analysis to the quotation.
- Combine any of the previous four strategies.

Applying strategies from Quick Box 18.2, here are some examples, using a quotation from Karen Wright.

AUTHOR'S NAME

Karen Wright explains that "in human bodies, biological clocks keep track of seconds, minutes, days, months and years" (66).

AUTHOR'S NAME AND SOURCE TITLE

Karen Wright explains in "Times of Our Lives" that "in human bodies, biological clocks keep track of seconds, minutes, days, months and years" (66).

AUTHOR'S NAME AND CREDENTIALS

Karen Wright, an award-winning science journalist, explains that "in human bodies, biological clocks keep track of seconds, minutes, days, months and years" (66).

AUTHOR'S NAME WITH STUDENT'S INTRODUCTORY ANALYSIS

Karen Wright reviews evidence of surprising subconscious processes, explaining that "in human bodies, biological clocks keep track of seconds, minutes, days, months and years" (66).

● **EXERCISE 18-1** Working individually or with a group, read the following original material, from page 295 of *Deep Water: The Gulf Oil Disaster and the Future of Offshore Drilling*, published in 2011 by the National Commission on the BP Deepwater Horizon Oil Spill and Offshore Drilling. Then, read items 1 through 4 and explain why each is an incorrect use of a quotation. Next, revise each numbered sentence so that it correctly uses a quotation. End each quotation with this MLA-STYLE parenthetical reference: (National 295).

Yet growing demand for oil around the world, particularly in the huge and rapidly developing economies of Asia, ensures heightened competition for supplies, putting upward pressure on oil prices. That poses a long-term challenge for the United States, which is not and cannot be self-sufficient in oil supply.

UNACCEPTABLE USES OF QUOTATIONS

1. Demand for oil is increasing globally. "That poses a long-term challenge for the United States, which is not and cannot be self-sufficient in oil supply" (National 295).
2. One obvious cause is that "the huge economies of Asia are putting upward pressure on prices" (National 295).

3. A difficult situation, "that poses a long-term challenge for the United States" (National 295).

4. In the 1990s, "that poses a long-term challenge for the United States" (National 295). ●

● **EXERCISE 18-2** Integrate each of the following quotations into a sentence using one of the strategies in Quick Box 18.2. Use at least two different strategies as you complete the exercise; you may use only part of the quotation if doing so fits your strategy. The author of all the quotations is Thomas Larson. Larson is a journalist who has lectured across America about the classical music composer Samuel Barber. The citation for the source is

> Larson, Thomas. *The Saddest Music Ever Written: The Story of Samuel Barber's* Adagio for Strings. New York, Pegasus, 2010. Print.

EXAMPLE

Original: "Sad music must be seductive enough to induce the state of sorrow" (226).

Integrated quotation 1: As Thomas Larson points out, "Sad music must be seductive enough to induce the state of sorrow" (226).

Integrated quotation 2: An expert on the composer Samuel Barber notes that "Sad music must be seductive enough to induce the state of sorrow" (Larson 226).

1. "'Gloomy Sunday,' written in 1933 and recorded by Billie Holiday in 1941, is quite sad" (218).

2. "The Internet Movie Database lists thirty films and TV shows in which the *Adagio* has appeared" (204).

3. "Higher art has a higher calling" (227).

4. "Like the book before and the TV and computer after it, the radio . . . changed the way our grandparents experienced the world" (22).

5. "The *Adagio* is a sound shrine to music's power to evoke emotion" (7). ●

18C How can I write good paraphrases?

A **paraphrase** precisely restates in your own words the written or spoken words of someone else. Paraphrase only passages that carry ideas you need to reproduce in detail to explain a point or support an argument. Avoid trying to paraphrase more than a paragraph or two; for longer passages, use summary (see 18D). Quick Box 18.3 (page 210) offers advice for paraphrasing.

Watch the Video

Here is an example of an unacceptable paraphrase and an acceptable one. The first paraphrase is unacceptable because the highlighted words have been plagiarized. The second paraphrase is acceptable. It captures the meaning of the original in the student's own words.

Quick Box 18.3

■ ■ ■ ■ ■ ■ ■ ■ ■ ■ ■

Guidelines for writing paraphrases

- Never use a paraphrase to present your THESIS STATEMENT or a TOPIC SENTENCE.
- Say what the source says, but no more.
- Reproduce the source's sequence of ideas and emphases.
- Use your own words, phrasing, and sentence structure to restate the material. If some technical words in the original have only awkward synonyms, quote the original words—but do so sparingly.
- Read your sentences over to make sure they don't distort the source's meaning.
- Expect your material to be as long as the original or even slightly longer.
- Integrate your paraphrase into your writing so that it fits smoothly.
- Avoid PLAGIARISM (see Chapter 19).
- Document your paraphrase carefully.

SOURCE

Hulbert, Ann. "Post-Teenage Wasteland?" *New York Times Magazine*
    9 Oct. 2005: 11–12. Print.

ORIGINAL (HULBERT'S EXACT WORDS)

[T]he available data suggest that the road to maturity hasn't become as drastically different as people think—or as drawn out, either. It's true that the median age of marriage rose to 25 for women and almost 27 for men in 2000, from 20 and 23, respectively, in 1960. Yet those midcentury figures were record lows (earnestly analyzed in their time). Moreover, Americans of all ages have ceased to view starting a family as the major benchmark of grown-up status. When asked to rank the importance of traditional milestones in defining the arrival of adulthood, poll respondents place completing school, finding full-time employment, achieving financial independence and being able to support a family far above actually wedding a spouse or having kids. The new perspective isn't merely an immature swerve into selfishness; postponing those last two steps is good for the future of the whole family.   [from page 11]

UNACCEPTABLE PARAPHRASE (HIGHLIGHTED WORDS ARE PLAGIARIZED)

Data suggest that the road to maturity hasn't changed as much as people think. True, the median age of marriage was 25 for women and 27 for men in 2000, up from 20 and 23 in 1960. Yet those 1960 figures were record lows. Furthermore, Americans have stopped regarding beginning a family as the signpost of grown-up status. When they were asked to rank the importance of traditional benchmarks for deciding the arrival of adulthood, people rated graduating from school, finding a full-time job, gaining financial status, and being a breadwinner far above marrying or having kids. This new belief isn't merely immature selfishness; delaying those last two steps is good for the future of the whole family (Hulbert 11).

ACCEPTABLE PARAPHRASE

According to Ann Hulbert, statistics show that people are wrong when they believe our society is delaying maturity. She acknowledges that between 1960 and 2000, the median age at which women married rose from 20 to 25 (for men it went from 23 to 27), but points out that the early figures were extreme lows. Hulbert finds that Americans no longer equate adulthood with starting a family. Polls show that people rank several other "milestones" above marriage and children as signaling adulthood. These include finishing school, securing a full-time job, and earning enough to be independent and to support a family. Hulbert concludes that we should regard postponing marriage and children not as being selfish or immature but as investing in the family's future (11).

● **EXERCISE 18-3** Working individually or with your peer-response group, read the original material given here, a paragraph from page 34 of *What Technology Wants* by Kevin Kelly (New York: Viking, 2010. Print). Then, read the unacceptable paraphrase, and point out each example of plagiarism. Finally, write your own paraphrase, starting it with a phrase naming Kelly and ending it with this parenthetical reference: (34).

ORIGINAL (KELLY'S EXACT WORDS)

Most hunter-gatherers clustered into family clans that averaged about 25 related people. Clans would gather in larger tribes of several hundred at seasonal feasts or camping groups. One function of the tribes was to keep genes moving through intermarriage. Population was spread thinly. The average density of a tribe was less than .01 person per square kilometer in cooler climes.

The 200 to 300 folk in your greater tribe would be the total number of people you'd meet in your lifetime. (34)

UNACCEPTABLE PARAPHRASE

Kevin Kelly says that most hunter-gatherers lived in groups that averaged about 25 related people. Clans would gather tribes of several hundred at seasonal feasts or gatherings. The larger tribes allowed intermarriage, which meant more diversity in the gene pool. Population was spread thinly. Fewer than .01 person lived per square kilometer in cooler climates. The 200 to 300 people in your tribe would be the complete number of individuals you'd meet in your lifetime (34). ●

18D How can I summarize?

Watch the Video

A **summary** differs from a paraphrase (see 18C) in an important way: Whereas a paraphrase restates the original material in its entirety, a summary states only the main points of the original source in a much briefer fashion. A summary doesn't include supporting evidence or details. As a result, a summary is much shorter than a paraphrase. Summarizing is the technique you'll probably use most frequently to integrate sources. Quick Box 18.4 explains how to summarize effectively.

Here's an example of an unacceptable summary and an acceptable one.

SOURCE

Tanenbaum, Leora. *Catfight: Women and Competition*. New York: Seven Stories, 2002. Print.

ORIGINAL (TANENBAUM'S EXACT WORDS)

Until recently, most Americans disapproved of cosmetic surgery, but today the stigma is disappearing. Average Americans are lining up for procedures—two-thirds of patients report family incomes of less than $50,000 a year—and many of them return for more. Younger women undergo "maintenance" surgeries in a futile attempt to halt time. The latest fad is Botox, a purified and diluted form of botulinum toxin that is injected between the eyebrows to eliminate frown lines. Although the procedure costs between $300 and $1000 and must be repeated every few months, roughly 850,000 patients have had it performed on them. That number will undoubtedly shoot up now that the FDA has approved Botox for cosmetic use. Even teenagers are making appointments with plastic surgeons. More than 14,000 adolescents had plastic

Quick Box 18.4

■ ■ ■ ■ ■ ■ ■ ■ ■ ■ ■

Guidelines for summarizing

- Identify the main points, and take care not to alter the meaning of the original source.
- Don't be tempted to include your opinions; they don't belong in a summary.
- Never use a summary to present your THESIS STATEMENT or a TOPIC SENTENCE.
- Keep your summary as short as possible to accomplish your purpose.
- Integrate summarized material smoothly into your writing.
- Use your own words. If you need to use key terms or phrases from the source, include them in quotation marks, but otherwise put everything into your own words.
- Document the original source accurately.
- Avoid PLAGIARISM (see Chapter 19).

surgery in 1996, and many of them are choosing controversial procedures such as breast implants, liposuction, and tummy tucks, rather than the rhinoplasties of previous generations.   [from pages 117–118]

UNACCEPTABLE SUMMARY (HIGHLIGHTED WORDS ARE PLAGIARIZED)

Average Americans are lining up for surgical procedures. The latest fad is Botox, a toxin injected to eliminate frown lines. This is an insanely foolish waste of money. Even teenagers are making appointments with plastic surgeons, many of them for controversial procedures such as breast implants, liposuction, and tummy tucks (Tanenbaum 117–18).

ACCEPTABLE SUMMARY

Tanenbaum explains that plastic surgery is becoming widely acceptable, even for Americans with modest incomes and for younger women. Most popular is injecting the toxin Botox to smooth wrinkles. She notes that thousands of adolescents are even requesting controversial surgeries (117–18).

The unacceptable summary has several major problems: It doesn't isolate the main point. It plagiarizes by taking much of its language directly from the source and it includes the writer's interpretation. The acceptable summary concisely isolates the main point, puts the source into the writer's own words, calls attention to the author by including her name in the summary, and remains objective throughout.

DEGREES OF SUMMARY

The degree to which your summary compresses the original source depends on your situation and assignment. For example, you can summarize an entire 500-page book in a single sentence, in a single page, or in five or six pages. Following are two different levels of summary based on the same source.

SOURCE

[Note: We included the text of this article in section 3D, on pages 21–23]

Schwartz, Barry. "The Tyranny of Choice." *Chronicle of Higher Education.* Chronicle of Higher Education, 23 Jan. 2004. Web. 3 Apr. 2011.

SUMMARY IN A SINGLE SENTENCE

Research finds that people with large numbers of choices are actually less happy than people with fewer choices (Schwartz).

SUMMARY IN 50 TO 100 WORDS

Research finds that people with large numbers of choices are actually less happy than people with fewer choices. Although the amount of wealth and number of choices have increased during the past thirty years, fewer Americans report themselves as being happy, and depression, suicide, and mental health problems have increased. While some choice is good, having too many choices hinders decision making, especially among "maximizers," who try to make the best possible choices. Research in shopping, education, and medical settings shows that even when people eventually decide, they experience regret, worrying that the options they didn't choose might have been better (Schwartz).

Notice that the longer summary begins with the same sentence as the short one; leading a summary with the reading's main idea is effective. One decision to make in summary writing is whether to refer to the author or to leave him or her out, as in the earlier examples. Check if your instructor has a preference. The previous example could be rewritten as follows:

SUMMARY THAT INCLUDES THE AUTHOR'S NAME

In "The Tyranny of Research," Barry Schwartz explains that people with large numbers of choices are actually less happy than people with fewer choices. Although the amount of wealth and number of choices have increased during the past thirty years, Schwartz notes that fewer Americans report themselves as being happy, and depression, suicide, and mental health problems have increased.

Instructors sometimes assign a paper that consists entirely of writing a summary. We discuss that kind of assignment in section 20B.

● **EXERCISE 18-4** Working individually or with your peer-response group, read the following original material from pages 23–24 of *Quiet: The Power of Introverts in a World that Can't Stop Talking* by Susan Cain (New York: Crown, 2012. Print). Then, read the unacceptable summary. Point out each example of plagiarism. Finally, write your own summary, starting it with a phrase mentioning Cain and ending it with this parenthetical reference: (4).

ORIGINAL (CAIN'S EXACT WORDS)

It makes sense that so many introverts hide from themselves. We live with a value system that I call the Extrovert Ideal—the omnipresent belief that the ideal self is gregarious, alpha, and comfortable in the spotlight. The archetypal extrovert prefers action to contemplation, risk-taking to heed-taking, certainty to doubt. He favors quick decisions, even at the risk of being wrong. She works well in teams and socializes in groups. We like to think that we value individuality, but all too often we admire one *type* of individual—the kind who's comfortable "putting himself out there."   [from page 4]

UNACCEPTABLE, PLAGIARIZED SUMMARY

The Extrovert Ideal is the omnipresent belief that the ideal self is gregarious, favoring action, risks, and decisions. Extroverts work well in teams and socialize in groups. People too often admire one *type* of person despite thinking they value individuality. (4) ●

18E Which verbs can help me weave source material into my sentences?

Use the verbs in Quick Box 18.5 appropriately according to their meanings in your sentences.

Quick Box 18.5

■■■■■■■■■■■

Useful verbs for integrating quotations, paraphrases, and summaries

acknowledges	contrasts	illustrates	recommends
agrees	declares	implies	refutes
analyzes	demonstrates	indicates	rejects
argues	denies	insists	remarks
asserts	describes	introduces	reports
begins	develops	maintains	reveals
believes	discusses	means	says
claims	distinguishes	notes	shows
comments	between	notices	specifies
compares	among	observes	speculates
complains	emphasizes	offers	states
concedes	establishes	points out	suggests
concludes	explains	prepares	supports
confirms	expresses	promises	supposes
considers	finds	proves	wishes
contends	focuses on	questions	writes
contradicts	grants	recognizes	

18F   What is synthesizing sources?

Watch the Video

When you SYNTHESIZE sources, you connect them to one another and to your own thinking, in an original paper. The resulting text needs to be more than just a succession of summaries. Your CRITICAL THINKING (see Chapter 3) skills help you synthesize, as do QUOTING, SUMMARIZING, and PARAPHRASING (see 18B–18D).

The following example shows how student Devon Petersen synthesized two sources. Read source 1 and source 2 to familiarize yourself with the information he read.

SOURCE 1

Shishmaref is melting into the ocean. Over the past 30 years, the Inupiaq Eskimo village, perched on a slender barrier island 625 miles north of Anchorage, has lost 100 ft. to 300 ft. of coastline—half of it since 1997. As Alaska's climate warms, the permafrost beneath the beaches is thawing and the sea ice is thinning, leaving its 600 residents increasingly vulnerable to violent storms. One house has collapsed, and 18 others had to be moved to higher ground, along with the town's bulk-fuel tanks.

—Margot Roosevelt, "Vanishing Alaska"

SOURCE 2

Since 2000 more than 6.5 million acres have perished in the U.S., turning forests into meadows in almost a dozen states. The culprit: the pine beetle, a fingernail-size bug that's become more voracious as the planet warms. Once a balanced part of forest life, the tree-eating insect now usually survives the winter, starts feeding earlier in the spring, and continues to plunder late into the fall.

—Jim Robbins, "Global Warming Kills Forests in Colorado"

Now read Devon's synthesis. Notice that he used summary (see 18B) and paraphrase (see 18C). Also look at how the first sentence in his synthesis weaves the sources together with a new concept.

EXAMPLE OF A SYNTHESIS OF TWO SOURCES

Global warming is affecting both the natural and artificial worlds. Rising temperatures have allowed pine beetles to survive winters and thrive, killing over 6.5 millions of forests (Robbins 8). Climate change has also altered life for residents of Arctic regions. For example, eighteen families in Shishmaref, Alaska, had to move their houses away from the coast because the permafrost under the beaches had thawed (Roosevelt 68).

Watch
the Video

—Devon Petersen, student

In his synthesis, Devon also used in-text citations (in MLA STYLE). In the Works Cited list at the end of his paper, Devon listed full source information for both sources. To learn how to document your sources, see Chapters 25 through 27.

SOURCES LISTED ON DEVON'S WORKS CITED PAGE

Robbins, Jim. "Global Warming Kills Forests in Colorado." *Newsweek* 19 Apr. 2010: 8. Print.

Roosevelt, Margot. "Vanishing Alaska." *Time* 4 Oct. 2004: 68–70. Print.

● **EXERCISE 18-5** Write a one-paragraph synthesis of the passage by Barry Schwartz published in section 3D, pages 21–23, and the following opening to a short article by Ronni Sandroff, editor of *Consumer Reports on Health:*

Last time I dropped by my pharmacy in search of a decongestant, I was stopped cold by the wall-sized display of remedies. The brands I had used in the past had multiplied into extended families of products. Yes, I saw *Contac, Excedrin, Tylenol,* and *Vicks,* but each brand came in multiple versions. Products for severe colds, coughs and colds, and headache and flu abounded, and there were further choices: gels, tablets, capsules, extended release, extra strength. I was eager to just grab a product and go, but to find the right one I had to dig out my reading glasses and examine the fine print.

—Ronni Sandroff, "Too Many Choices" ●

18G What are possible relationships between sources?

Knowing five relationships between sources can help you go beyond simply listing or summarizing your sources. Those relationships are

- **Different Subtopic:** Sources are on same broad subject but about different subtopics.
- **Agreement:** Two sources make the same basic point, though perhaps in different words.
- **Part Agreement:** Two sources mostly agree but differ a little bit.
- **Disagreement:** Two sources disagree.
- **General and Specific:** One source offers specific information that either supports or contradicts a more general point in a second source.

In the next five sections of this chapter, we explain each relationship. We present quotations from two different readings on a common topic, and we follow them with CONTENT NOTES (21P) that a student took on each reading. Next, we suggest a sentence or paragraph guide that shows how you might synthesize the readings. Finally, we give an example of a paragraph that shows this synthesis.

18H What can I do when sources are about different subtopics?

You will likely find sources that present different subtopics of the same broad subject. For example, as you research career options, one source might discuss salaries, another might discuss workplace environments, and a third might discuss expectations for job openings. When student Matthew Yan was researching how the Internet has affected the way we get information (you'll see part of his paper in Chapter 24), among the sources he found were these.

Source A	Source B
"While new technology eases connections between people, it also, paradoxically, facilitates a closeted view of the world, keeping us coiled tightly with those who share our ideas. In a world that lacks real gatekeepers and authority figures . . . conspiracy theories, myths, and outright lies may get the better of many of us." (17–18)	"CNN used to be a twenty-four-hour news outlet shown only on TV. The *New York Times* and the *Wall Street Journal* were simply newspapers. But on the Internet today, they are surprisingly similar. . . . Online, the lines between television and newspapers have blurred—and soon the same will be said about books, movies, TV shows, and more." (14)
Manjoo, Farhad. *True Enough: Learning to Live in a Post-Fact Society.* Hoboken, NJ: Wiley. 2008. Print.	Bilton, Nick. *I Live in the Future & Here's How It Works.* New York: Crown Business, 2010. Print.
Content Note	Content Note
Manjoo 17–18 —although technology can connect us to others, it can also allow us to communicate only with people that agree with us; we might be susceptible to lies [paraphrase]	Bilton 14 —TV network and newspaper sites have become similar on the Internet. Examples: CNN and *NY Times*, *WSJ* [summary]

Following each source, you can see the content note that Matthew wrote. Notice how he included the kind of note he took in brackets (see 47C).

One possible sentence/paragraph guide for sources on different subtopics

There are (one, two, or however many) important considerations for (aspects of, reasons for, etc.) _____. One is _____ [from Source A]_____. A second is _____ [from Source B]_____.

EXAMPLE

There are two important developments in the way we receive news online. One is that, even though it is easier to connect to information, we tend to seek people with whom we already agree (Manjoo 17–18). A second, as Nick Bilton notes, is that distinctions between types of news sources on the Internet are disappearing (14).

181 What can I do when sources agree?

Sources agree when they present similar information or make the same point. Of course, if sources are truly repetitious, you might use only one. Sometimes, however, including multiple similar sources strengthens your point. Here is an example.

Source A	Source B
"Our study confirmed the well-known gender gap in gaming, verifying that this overall trend also occurs among college students. Seventy percent of male undergraduates had played a digital game the week of the survey, compared to only one quarter of the females. The majority of women fell in the category of non-gamers, those who had not played a game in over 6 months, or never." (Winn 10)	"Women proportionally were more likely than men to only play an hour or less per week. . . . Twenty-one percent of the women and 68% of the men played two or more hours per week." (Ogletree 539)
Winn, Jillian, and Carrie Heeter. "Gaming, Gender, and Time: Who Makes Time to Play?" *Sex Roles* 61 (2009): 1–13. Web. 9 May 2011.	Ogletree, Shirley Matile, and Ryan Drake. "College Students' Video Game Participation and Perceptions: Gender Differences and Implications." *Sex Roles* 56 (2007): 537–42. Web. 9 May 2011.
Content Notes	Content Notes
Winn 10 —70% of male students played video games; 25% of female [summary]	Ogletree —68% of men and 21% of women played 2 or more hour per week [summary]

One possible sentence/paragraph guide for synthesizing sources that agree

A and B reach the same conclusion (provide similar information, argue the same point, reach the same conclusion etc.) about _____.
A explains that _____. B found that _____.

EXAMPLE

Researchers Winn and Heeter and researchers Ogletree and Drake reached the same conclusion that men play video games more extensively than women. Winn and Heeter found that 70% of male students but only 25% of females regularly play games (10). In a study of how many hour per week students play, Ogletree and Drake learned that 68% of men and only 21% of women play two or more hours per week (539).

A REVISION (TO MAKE THIS MORE EFFECTIVE)

Two studies show that men play video games more extensively than women. Winn and Heeter found that 70% of male students but only 25% of females regularly play games (10). In a study of how many hour per week students play, Ogletree learned that 68% of men and only 21% of women play two or more hours per week (539).

18J What can I do when sources partly agree?

Often sources generally agree with each other but cite different evidence or emphasize slightly different conclusions. Here is an example.

Source A	Source B
"[M]ore males reportedly developed leadership skills as a result of playing video games as opposed to females. More males also reported that playing video games helped them develop skills that will help them in the workplace, such as the ability to work as a team member, to collaborate with others and the ability to provide directions to others." (Thirunarayanan, 324)	"Games make it easy to build stronger social bonds with our friends and family. Studies show that we like and trust someone better after we play a game with them—even if they beat us. And we're more likely to help someone in real life after we've helped them in an online game." (McGonigal)
Thirunarayanan, M. O., Manuel Vilchez, Liala Abreu, Cyntianna Ledesma, and Sandra Lopez. "A Survey of Video Game Players in a Public, Urban Research University." *Educational Media International* 47.4 (2009): 311–27. Web. 9 May 2011.	McGonigal, Jane. "Be a Gamer, Save the World." *Wall Street Journal*. Dow Jones, 22 Jan. 2011. Web. 9 May 2011.
Content Note	Content Note
Thirunarayanan, 324 —more men said they learn leadership and team member skills than women said they did [summary]	McGonigal —games build social connections like trust and willingness to help others [summary]

> **One possible sentence or paragraph guide to use when sources partly agree**
>
> Scholars generally agree (conclude, share the opinion, or demonstrate, etc.) that _____. However, a difference between them is _____. A emphasizes (asserts, believes, etc.) _____. B, on the other hand, emphasizes _____.

EXAMPLE

Scholars generally agree that playing video games can have some positive social effects. However, they differ as to who benefits most. Jane McGonigal asserts that games build social connections such as trust and the willingness to help others, suggesting this is true for all players. Thirunarayanan et al., on the other hand, found that men believe they learn leadership and team member skills more than women say they do (324).

18K What can I do when sources disagree?

Because people can disagree on everything from whether certain laws should be passed to whether certain movies are any good, it's no surprise that sources can disagree, too. Here is an example.

Source A	Source B
"Imagine that everything stays 99 percent the same, that people continue to consume 99 percent of the television they used to, but 1 percent of that time gets carved out for producing and sharing. The connected population still watches well over a trillion hours of TV a year; 1 percent of that is more than one hundred Wikipedias' worth of participation per year." (Shirky 23)	"With hundreds of thousands of visitors a day, Wikipedia has become the third most visited site for information and current events; a more trusted source for news than the CNN or BBC Web sites, even though Wikipedia has no reporters, no editorial staff, and no experience in news-gathering. It's the blind leading the blind—infinite monkeys providing infinite information for infinite readers, perpetuating the cycle of misinformation and ignorance." (Keen 4)
Shirky, Clay. *Cognitive Surplus, Creativity and Generosity in a Connected Age.* New York: Penguin, 2010. Print.	Keen, Andrew. *The Cult of the Amateur.* New York: Doubleday, 2007. Print.

Content Note	Content Note
Shirky 23	Keen 4
—If people used even 1% of time they spend watching TV instead to produce content for the Web they'd create "one hundred Wikipedia's worth" each year [paraphrase and quotation]	—Wikipedia used more for information and current events than CNN or the BBC —no professionals writing for W. —writers are "infinite monkeys" who create "misinformation and ignorance" [summary and quotation]

One possible sentence/paragraph guide to use for sources that disagree

There are two different perspectives (positions, interpretations, or opinions, etc.) about _____. A says _____. B, on the other hand, says _____.

However, your writing will be stronger if you go a step further and use critical thinking to understand the nature of the disagreement. For example:

- Writers might disagree because they use different facts or information (or no information at all!).
- Writers might disagree when they use the same information but interpret it differently.
- Writers might operate with different assumptions or perspectives.

A stronger sentence/paragraph guide for sources that disagree

There are two different perspectives (positions, interpretations, or opinions, etc.) about _____. A says _____. B, on the other hand, says _____. They disagree mainly because they cite different facts (interpret information differently, operate with different assumptions). A points to _____, while B _____. On this point, B's [or A's] perspective is more convincing because _____.

EXAMPLE

There are two different opinions about Wikipedia. Clay Shirky is enthusiastic and notes that if people diverted just 1% of their TV watching time to writing for the Web, they could generate "one hundred Wikipedia's worth" of content each year (23). Andrew Keen, on the other hand, sees Wikipedia writers as "infinite monkeys" who only spread "misinformation and ignorance" (4). They disagree mainly because they have different assumptions about the quality of Wikipedia entries. Shirky believes it is generally fine, while Keen sees almost nothing of value.

REVISED VERSION, WITH MORE EFFECTIVE WORDING

Some writers find Wikipedia a reason for celebration, while others declare it a cause for despair. Clay Shirky hopes people will divert just 1% of their TV watching time to writing for the Web, which could generate "one hundred Wikipedia's worth" of content each year (23). That possibility would trouble Andrew Keen, who characterizes those writers as "infinite monkeys" who only spread "misinformation and ignorance" (4). Shirky and Keen assume quite different things about quality of knowledge on Wikipedia. Keen has considerably less faith in the ability of people to write accurate information.

18L What can I do when one source is more specific than the other one?

1. **When a specific source supports a more general idea in another source.** Sometimes a source provides examples, illustrations, or evidence that support a more general point in another. Here is an example:

Source A	Source B
"Old media is facing extinction." (Keen 9)	"In 2008, paid newspaper circulation in the United States fell to 49.1 million, the lowest number since the late 1960s and well below the peak of 60 million reached in the 1990s, when the internet was just starting to come into its own." (Bilton 6)
Keen, Andrew. *The Cult of the Amateur*. New York: Doubleday, 2007. Print.	Bilton, Nick. *I Live in the Future & Here's How It Works*. New York: Crown Business, 2010. Print.
Content Note	Content Note
Keen 9	Bilton 6
"Old media is facing extinction" [quotation]	—newspaper circulation was 60 million in the 1990s, 49.1 million in 2008 [summary]

> ## Two useful sentence/paragraph guides when a specific source supports a general one
>
> A observes (claims, argues, concludes, etc.) that _____. B provides an example (a set of data, some information, etc.) to support this observation. B states that _____.
> *or*
> According to B, _____. This illustrates A's concept (point, claim, conclusion) that _____.

EXAMPLE

According to Nick Bilton, newspaper circulation declined over ten million between the 1990s and 2008, from 60 million to 49.1 million subscribers (6). His figures illustrate Andrew Keen's observation that "Old media is facing extinction" (9).

2. **When a specific source contradicts a more general idea in another source.** As we've noted, sources can disagree with each other at the level of ideas or claims. Sometimes, however, specific information in one source can contradict a more general point made in another. This can happen when writers make a claim but offer no proof or when they offer partial or different evidence. Here's an example:

Source A	Source B
"But college students are, in fact, getting lazier. 'Aggregate time spent studying by full-time college students declined from about 24 hours per week in 1961 to about 14 hours per week in 2004,' Babcock writes, citing his own research." (de Vise)	"Nationally, approximately 80 percent of community college students work, and they work an average of 32 hours per week. Research indicates that working a few hours each week is actually beneficial to students' persistence and success, provided that they are in school full time and attending consistently. However, to succeed academically, experts suggest working no more than 15–20 hours per week." (Zomer 2)
de Vise, Daniel. "Grade Inflation is Making Students Lazier." *washingtonpost.com/college-inc.* Washington Post, 22 July 2010. Web. 9 May 2011.	Zomer, Saffron. *Working Too Hard to Make the Grade.* Sacramento, CA: California Public Interest Research Group, 2009. Web. 9 May 2011.

(continued)

Content Note	Content Note
de Vise	Zomer 2
—college students getting "lazier;" they studied 7 hours a week less in 2004 than in 1961 [summary]	—80% of CC students work average of 32 hours/week —some work is good, but should be no more than 15–20 hours [summary]

One useful sentence/paragraph guide when specific information contradicts a general claim

Evidence suggests (proves, demonstrates, etc.) that A's claim that _____ is wrong (incomplete, overstated, etc.) B shows that _____.

EXAMPLE

Complete the Chapter Exercises

Daniel de Vise's claim that college students are getting lazier fails to recognize complete information. De Vise points to students studying seven hours per week less in 2004 than in 1961. However, he fails to take into account how much students are now working. For example, 80% of community college students now work an average of 32 hours per week, even though experts recommend working no more than 20 hours per week (Zomer 2). Far from being lazy, college students are working hard, perhaps with less time for studying.

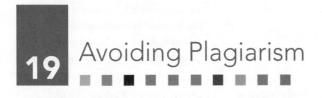

19 Avoiding Plagiarism

Quick Points   You will learn to

➤ Identify plagiarism (see 19A).
➤ Use techniques to avoid the different types of plagiarism (see 19B).

19A What is plagiarism?

To use SOURCES well, you need to learn how to incorporate others' words and ideas into your own papers accurately, effectively, and honestly. This last skill is especially important, so that you avoid **plagiarism**, which is presenting another person's words, ideas, or visual images as if they were your own. Plagiarizing, like stealing, is a form of academic dishonesty or cheating. It's a serious offense that can be grounds for a failing grade or expulsion from a college. Beyond that, you're hurting yourself. If you're plagiarizing, you're not learning.

Watch the Video

Plagiarism isn't just something that college instructors get fussy about. In the workplace, it can get you fired. Plagiarism at work also has legal implications; using someone else's intellectual property without permission or credit is a form of theft that may land you in court. Furthermore, plagiarism in any setting—academic, business, or civic—hurts your credibility and reputation. Quick Box 19.1 lists the major types of plagiarism.

Quick Box 19.1

Types of plagiarism

You're plagiarizing if you . . .

- Buy a paper from an Internet site, another student or writer, or any other source.

- Turn in any paper that someone else has written, whether the person has given it to you, you've downloaded it from the Internet, or you've copied it from any other source.

- Change selected parts of an existing paper and claim the paper as your own.

- Neglect to put quotation marks around words that you quote directly from a source, even if you list the source in your Works Cited or References.

- Type or paste into your paper any key terms, phrases, sentences, or longer passages from another source without using documentation to tell precisely where the material came from.

- Use ideas or reasoning from a source without correctly citing and documenting that source, even if you put the ideas into your own words. (See 19E.)

- Combine ideas from many sources and pass them off as your own without correctly citing and documenting the sources.

- Use photographs, charts, figures, or other visual images from anyone (colleagues, organizations, Web sites, and so on) without crediting and documenting them.

Never assume that your instructor won't detect plagiarism. Instructors have a keen eye for writing styles that differ from the ones students generally produce and from your own style in particular. Instructors can check your work against online paper providers or materials, look up sources, or check with their colleagues.

ESOL Tip: Perhaps you come from a country or culture that considers it acceptable for students to copy the writing of experts and authorities. Some cultures, in fact, believe that using another's words, even without citing them, is a sign of respect or learning. However, this practice is unacceptable in American colleges.

19B How do I avoid plagiarism?

Watch
the Video

The first step in avoiding plagiarism is to learn the techniques of quoting (see 18B), paraphrasing (see 18C), and summarizing (see 18D) source materials. The second step is to document sources correctly. A third step is to take advantage

---

Quick Box 19.2

Strategies for avoiding plagiarism

- Acknowledge and document when you're using the ideas, words, or images of others.

- Become thoroughly familiar with the documentation style your instructor requires you to use (see Chs. 25–27).

- Follow a consistent notetaking system. Use different colors, or some other coding system, to distinguish three different types of material.

  1. **Quotations** from a source; write clear, even oversized quotation marks so you can't miss them later (documentation required)

  2. **Material you have paraphrased, summarized**, or otherwise drawn from a source (documentation required)

  3. **Your own thoughts**, triggered by what you have read or experienced (no documentation required; see 20D)

- Immediately when you quote, paraphrase, or summarize in your draft, include the appropriate in-text citation, and add the source to your Works Cited or References. Don't wait to do this later.

- As part of editing and proofreading, look carefully at your paper for any places that might need documentation.

- Consult your instructor if you're unsure about any aspect of the documentation process.

of the learning opportunities your instructor may build into assignments. Many instructors require students to hand in a WORKING BIBLIOGRAPHY or ANNOTATED BIBLIOGRAPHY, a research log, working notes, a copy of the sources, or a draft (see 21G). Quick Box 19.2 suggests some practical steps you can take to avoid plagiarism.

19C How do I avoid plagiarism when using Internet sources?

You might be tempted to download a paper from the Internet. Don't. That kind of intellectual dishonesty can get you into real trouble. We've been dismayed to hear that some students believe if they buy a paper or hire someone else to write it, the paper is "theirs." No. It's not. This is clearly plagiarism.

⊙ Watch the Video

Even if you have absolutely no intention of plagiarizing, being careless can easily lead to trouble. Quick Box 19.3 suggests some ways you can avoid plagiarism when you're working on the Internet.

Quick Box 19.3 ■ ■ ■ ■ ■ ■ ■ ■ ■ ■ ■

Guidelines for avoiding plagiarism when using Internet sources

- Never copy material from an online source and paste it directly into your paper without taking great care. You can too easily lose track of which language is your own and which comes from a source. If you have to copy and paste a direct quotation or visual, immediately place quotation marks around the material. Be sure to document the source at the same time, or you may forget to do it later or do it incorrectly.

- Keep downloaded or printed material separate from your own writing, even if you intend to quote, summarize, or paraphrase the material. Use another color or a much larger font as a visual reminder that this isn't your work.

- Summarize or paraphrase materials *before* you include them in your paper. Document the sources of summarized passages at the same time.

- Use an Internet service to check a passage you're not sure about. If you're concerned that you may have plagiarized by mistake, use Google to search one or two sentences that concern you. To make this work, always place quotation marks around the sentences you want to check when you type them into the search window.

19D What don't I have to document?

You don't have to document common knowledge or your own thinking. Common knowledge is information that most educated people know, although they might need to remind themselves of certain facts by looking them up in a reference book. For example, you would not need to document statements like these:

- George W. Bush was the U.S. president before Barack Obama.
- Mercury is the planet closest to the sun.
- Water boils at 212°F.
- All the oceans on our planet contain saltwater.

A very important component of a paper that doesn't need documentation is *your own thinking*. It consists of your ANALYSIS, SYNTHESIS, and evaluation of new material as you read or observe it.

19E How do I document ideas?

You need to document everything that you learn from a source, including ideas or reasoning. Expressing others' ideas in your own words doesn't release you from the obligation to tell exactly where you got them. Consider the following example.

SOURCE

Silberman, Steve. "The Placebo Problem." *The Best American Science Writing 2010.* Ed. Jerome Groopman and Jesse Cohen. New York: Ecco, 2010. 31–44. Print.

ORIGINAL (SILBERMAN'S EXACT WORDS)

The fact that an increasing number of medications are unable to beat sugar pills has thrown the industry into crisis. The stakes could hardly be higher. In today's economy, the fate of a long-established company can hang on the outcome of a handful of tests. (33)

PLAGIARISM EXAMPLE

The fact that more and more drugs are unable to beat sugar pills has caused problems. Much is at stake. Currently, the future of established companies can depend on the outcome of a handful of tests.

Even though the student changed some wording in the preceding example, the ideas aren't original to her. The highlighted phrases are especially problematic examples of plagiarism because they're Silberman's exact wording. To avoid plagiarism the student needs both to document the source and to use quotation marks to show Silberman's wording.

1. CORRECT EXAMPLE USING QUOTATION, PARAPHRASE, AND DOCUMENTATION

Steve Silberman claims that the increasing success of placebos "has thrown the [drug] industry into crisis." The market is so competitive that even "a handful of tests" can determine whether a company survives (33).

2. CORRECT EXAMPLES USING SUMMARY AND DOCUMENTATION

A. Steve Silberman argues that the success of placebos challenges drug company profits (33).

B. The success of placebos challenges drug company profits (Silberman 33).

In correct example 1, the writer has properly integrated Silberman's ideas through quotation and paraphrase, and she has included an in-text citation that points to her Works Cited page. In correct example 2A, the writer summarizes the idea, including the author's name in the sentence and a parenthetical citation. In correct example 2B, she also summarizes, but here she includes the author's name as part of the parenthetical citation.

● **EXERCISE 19-1** Following the quoted passage here are three passages. Each passage is plagiarized. For each one (1) explain why it is plagiarism, and (2) revise the passage so that it no longer is plagiarized.

ORIGINAL (SARAH NASSAUER'S EXACT WORDS)

How the check is brought to the table can make diners grumble. Some guests want the check without asking, some feel rushed if a check is placed on the table before they ask. When researchers asked customers which restaurant service mistake is worst in terms of overall satisfaction, they said not promptly settling the check when the guest is ready to leave, or problems with the check amount. (This complaint was second only to messing up the food order.) The research, which surveyed 491 people who had dined at a table-service restaurant within the past month, was published in the *Cornell Hospitality Quarterly* in 2010.

Nassauer, Sarah. "How Waiters Read Your Table." *Wall Street Journal.* Dow Jones, 22 Feb. 2012. Web. 9 April 2012.

PLAGIARIZED PASSAGES

1. If a waiter brings a check too soon, some guests are upset. However, other guests don't feel they should have to ask for the check.
2. When researchers asked customers which restaurant serve mistake is worst in terms of overall satisfaction, they said not promptly settling the check when the guest is ready to leave (Nassauer).
3. Restaurant customers reported being most bothered by waiters "not promptly settling the check" at the end of the meal. ●

20 Writing About Readings

■ ■ ■ ■ ■ ■ ■ ■ ■ ■

Quick Points   You will learn to

➤ Write summary and response essays (see 20B–20C).
➤ Write analysis essays (see 20D).
➤ Write essays that apply readings (see 20E).

20A What are typical assignments for writing about readings?

Although much college writing requires using techniques for integrating sources (QUOTATION, PARAPHRASE, SUMMARY, and SYNTHESIS, which we explain in Chapter 18), some assignments focus entirely on writing about reading. Some common types of papers are summary essays (see 20B), response essays (see 20C), analysis essays (see 20D), and essays that apply readings (see 20E). Research paper assignments require finding and synthesizing multiple sources. Chapters 21 to 24 give extensive advice about RESEARCH writing.

20B How do I write a summary essay?

Watch
the Video

Your instructors may assign papers that consist entirely of summary. Although some students may consider writing summaries as simple or obvious, we've found it takes practice and skill to do them well.

Here is specific advice for writing a summary paper.

1. **Generating ideas**

   - Identify TOPIC SENTENCES or main ideas, separating them from examples or illustrations. You want to focus on the main ideas.

   - Take notes in your own words, then put the source away. Write from your notes, going back to check the original only after you've written a first draft.

2. **Shaping and drafting**

   - Begin with a sentence that summarizes the entire reading, unless you're writing a particularly long summary.

   - Follow the order of the original.

   - Summarize proportionally. Longer and more important aspects of the original source need to get more space and attention in your summary.

   - Include a Works Cited (see Chapter 25) or References (see Chapter 26) page, depending on the required DOCUMENTATION STYLE.

3. **Revising your summary**

   - Have I maintained objectivity throughout?

   - Have I put ideas into my own words?

   - Is the summary proportional?

   - Is documentation accurate?

   - Can I make any statements more CONCISE (see Chapter 40)?

A STUDENT'S SUMMARY ESSAY

Brian Jirak received the assignment to write a 200-word summary of an article.

Jirak 1

Brian Jirak

Economics 101

Professor Connolly

15 Jan. 2012

continued >>

Jirak 2

Summary of "Living by Default"

In "Living by Default," James Surowiecki argues that there is a double standard regarding defaulting on loans. When corporations like American Airlines do so, analysts call them "very smart" (44). However, when homeowners don't pay mortgages, they are called deadbeats.

Surowiecki notes that millions of American homeowners owe far more than their homes are worth, so that paying the mortgage is "like setting a pile of money on fire every month" (44). Still, most people keep doing so. Why? Although one reason is worry about damaging their credit ratings, the more important reason is that people feel ashamed not to pay.

While Surowieki generally agrees that people should pay debts, he believes that if we consider it reasonable for corporations to walk away from loans, we should think the same for homeowners. Of course, banks and corporations could help by changing loans or modifying debts, but they choose not to. Surowieki calls them hypocritical for scolding homeowners when they have done worse. In the end, he suggests it might make sense for people just to stop paying on bad mortgages, because it may force banks to change their ways.

Jirak 3

Work Cited

Surowiecki, James. "Living by Default." *The New Yorker*. 19 and 26 Dec. 2011. 44. Print.

20C How do I write a response essay?

A **response** essay has two missions: to provide a SUMMARY of a source and to make statements—supported by reasons—about the source's ideas or quality. Responses may

⊙
Watch
the Video

1. Comment on a work's accuracy, logic, or conclusions. ("Is this history of hip-hop music accurate?" "Is this argument about requiring military service convincing?")

2. Present the writer's reaction to a source. ("I found the ideas in the reading shocking/intriguing/confusing/promising, etc.")

3. Focus on a work's form, or genre ("How well does this poem satisfy the requirements of a sonnet?").

4. Explain a reading's relation to other works ("Is this novel better than that novel?") or to the "real" world ("To what extent does this article accurately portray student life?").

Quick Box 20.1 explains elements of effective response essays.

Quick Box 20.1　■ ■ ■ ■ ■ ■ ■ ■ ■ ■ ■

Effective response essays

- Include a clear and concise summary of the source.
- State agreements, disagreements, or qualified agreements. (In a qualified agreement, you accept some points but not others.)
- Provide reasons and evidence for your statements.

Try the following processes for writing responses.

1. **Generating ideas**
   - Use ACTIVE READING and CRITICAL READING (see 3D) to identify the main points and generate reactions to the source.
   - Use techniques for ANALYZING (see 3E), drawing INFERENCES (see 3G), and assessing reasoning processes (see 3G–3I).
   - Discuss or debate the source with another person. Discussions and debates can get your mind moving. If in your writing you use that other person's ideas, be sure to give the person credit as a source.

2. Shaping and drafting

- Write a SUMMARY of the material's main idea or central point.
- Write a thesis statement that provides a smooth TRANSITION between the summary and your response. Your thesis clearly signals the beginning of your response.
- Respond based on your prior knowledge, experience, reading, or research.

3. Revising your response

Respond to the following questions as you consider revisions.

- Have I combined summary and response? Have I explained my response in a way that readers will find thoughtful and convincing?
- Have I fulfilled all DOCUMENTATION requirements? See Chapters 25–27 for coverage of four DOCUMENTATION STYLES (MLA, APA, CM, and CSE). Ask your instructor which style to use.

A STUDENT EXAMPLE

Here is student Kristin Boshoven's short response to Barry Schwartz's essay, "The Tyranny of Choice." We printed Schwartz's essay in section 3D, on pages 21–23, and we included Kristin's summary of that essay in 18D, on page 214. Note that Kristin incorporates the summary before using her own experience and her general knowledge to respond.

Boshoven 1

Kristin Boshoven

English 101

Professor Lequire

12 Apr. 2011

Too Much Choice: Disturbing but Not Destructive

Barry Schwartz argues that people with large numbers of choices are actually less happy than people with fewer

---

continued >>

choices. Although the amount of wealth and choice has increased during the past thirty years, studies show that fewer Americans report themselves as being happy. Depression, suicide, and mental health problems have increased. While some choice is good, too many choices hinder decision making, especially among people who Schwartz calls "maximizers," people who try to make the best possible choices. Research in shopping, education, and medical settings shows that even when people eventually decide, they experience regret, worrying that the options they didn't choose might have been better.

Although Schwartz cites convincing evidence for his claims, he ultimately goes too far in his conclusions. Excessive choice does seem to make life harder, not easier, but it alone can't be blamed for whatever unhappiness exists in our society.

My own experience supports Schwartz's finding that people who have thirty choices of jam as opposed to six often don't purchase any. A week ago I decided to buy a new smart phone. When we went to the store, we were confronted with twenty different models, and even though a helpful salesperson explained the various features, I couldn't make up my mind. I decided to do more research, which was a mistake. After reading reviews in everything from *Consumer Reports* to the *New York Times*, I am close to making a decision. However, I have a sinking feeling that as soon as I buy a phone, I'll learn that another choice would have been better, or mine will drop $50 in price. I could relate similar experiences trying to choose

continued >>

which movie to see, which dentist to visit, and so on. I suspect others could, too, which is why I find Schwartz's argument convincing at this level.

However, when he suggests that the increase of choice is a source of things like depression and suicide, he goes too far. Our society has undergone tremendous changes in the past forty or fifty years, and many of those changes are more likely to cause problems than the existence of too much choice. For example, workers in the 1950s through the 1970s could generally count on holding jobs with one company as long as they wanted, even through retirement. A 1950s autoworker, for example, might not have been thrilled with his job (and these were jobs held almost exclusively by men), but at least he could count on it, and it paid enough to buy a house and education for his family. The economic uncertainties of the past decade have meant that workers— and now women as well as men—do not have the same job stability they once did.

Although I agree that too many choices can lead to anxiety and even unhappiness, there are larger factors. If Americans report more depression and suicide than previously, a more likely candidate is economic and social uncertainty, not having too many kinds of cereal on the grocery store shelves.

continued >>

> Boshoven 4
>
> Work Cited
>
> Schwartz, Barry. "The Tyranny of Choice." *Chronicle of Higher Education*. Chronicle of Higher Education, 23 Jan. 2004. Web. 3 Apr. 2011.

20D What are analysis or interpretation essays?

Analysis and interpretation are TEXTUAL ANALYSIS. An analysis identifies elements or parts of a source and explains how those elements work. An interpretation explains a reading's possible meaning by stating and defending an idea that perhaps isn't obvious. Textual analyses are so important in college writing that we devote an entire chapter to writing them (see Chapter 14). Literature instructors may assign you to write a literary interpretation. Chapter 58 can help you with that kind of writing. Meanwhile, Quick Box 20.2 reviews features of effective analyses or interpretation.

Quick Box 20.2 ■ ■ ■ ■ ■ ■ ■ ■ ■ ■ ■

Effective analyses or interpretations

- Have a thesis that states the main idea of the analysis or interpretation.
- Refer to specific elements (sentences, examples, ideas, etc.) of the source, using quotation, paraphrase, or summary.
- Explain the meaning of the elements identified.

20D.1 Essays that report quantitative information

Some essays that analyze readings require writers to translate quantitative date into words and to explain what they mean. Quantitative information comes in the form of numbers. These essays require two activities: reporting and analyzing.

When reporting data, you need clearly and objectively to translate numbers into words. To illustrate this kind of writing, we've included part of a paper here, in which student Marcus Kapuranis reports information from the National Survey of Student Engagement.

SAMPLE STUDENT REPORT OF QUANTITATIVE DATA

Kapuranis 1

Marcus Kapuranis

English 1122

Professor Bateman

24 May 2012

Diversity of Student Experiences Reported in the National
Survey of Student Engagement

Part of the 2007 National Survey of Student Engagement
(NSSE) asked college freshmen and seniors to report on their
experiences with people different from themselves. These
differences included racial and ethnic backgrounds as well
as attitudes and beliefs, and the final report provides not
only totals for each group of students but also a breakdown
of responses according to types of college. Responses to three
questions, shown in Figure 1, provide a clear picture of the
national situation.

When asked how often they had serious conversations
with students whose religious beliefs, personal opinions,
or values differed from their own, 12% of first year students

Figure 1   Student experiences with difference.

First-Year Students Seniors (in percentages)		DRU-VH		DRU-H		DRU		Master's-L		Bac-DIV		Top 10%		NSSE 2007	
Had serious conversations with students who are very different from you in terms of their religious beliefs, political opinions, or personal values	Never	10	8	12	10	12	10	13	11	15	11	8	6	12	10
	Sometimes	33	33	33	35	34	35	34	35	37	38	29	30	34	35
	Often	31	31	30	30	29	28	29	29	28	28	30	33	29	30
	Very often	27	27	26	26	25	27	24	25	21	23	33	32	25	26
Had serious conversations with students of a different race or ethnicity than your own	Never	14	11	15	12	15	12	18	14	19	15	11	8	16	12
	Sometimes	34	34	34	35	35	33	34	34	37	38	31	32	34	35
	Often	28	29	27	28	27	28	26	27	24	26	28	28	27	28
	Very often	24	27	24	26	23	26	22	25	20	21	31	32	23	25
Institutional emphasis: Encouraging contact among students from different economic, social, and racial or ethnic backgrounds	Very little	12	21	14	20	14	18	14	18	15	19	11	17	13	19
	Some	33	36	34	36	32	34	32	35	33	36	29	35	33	35
	Quite a bit	33	27	32	28	32	29	33	29	32	37	33	28	32	28
	Very much	22	16	21	16	22	19	21	18	21	18	27	20	22	17

continued >>

Kapuranis 2

reported "never," 34% said "sometimes," 29% said "often," and 25% said "very often." In response to the same question, seniors reported similarly. 10% said "never," 35% said "sometimes," 30% said "often," and 26% said "very often."

The NSSE study also broke the responses down according to type of institution. There are three categories of "Doctoral Research University" (DRU): those that have "very high" (VH) research levels, those that have "high" (H), and others. There are three categories of "Master's Universities," Large, Medium, and Small (L, M, S), and two categories of "Baccalaureate Colleges," traditional liberal arts and sciences colleges (AS) and those that have a broader range of course and programs (DIV). (This particular study didn't survey two-year colleges, although the *Two-Year College Survey of Student Engagement* does.) The findings across the institutional types were fairly comparable, with the largest differences between traditional liberal arts colleges and medium-size master's universities. The liberal arts colleges had the fewest students (8%) reporting "never" talking to diverse students and most students (30%) reporting "very often" doing so. In contrast the medium-sized master's colleges had the most students (16%) reporting "never" talking to diverse students and the second fewest (22%) reporting "very often."

A second question asked students to report how frequently they had serious conversations with someone of a different race or ethnicity . . .

continued >>

Kapuranis 3

Work Cited

NSSE: National Survey of Student Engagement. *Experiences That Matter: Enhancing Student Learning and Success Annual Report 2007*. Center for Postsecondary Research, Indiana University, 2007. Web. 14 May 2012.

In his report, Marcus opens with a brief overview of the study. When he starts summarizing its findings, he moves from the big picture to the more detailed, and he takes care to explain information (such as the institutional types) that would be unclear to his audience. He selects the most important information, which takes some judgment. Most important for this type of writing, he remains objective.

Important Elements of Reporting Data

- Clear and accurate translations of numbers into language.
- Judicious selection and summary of data to report.
- Objective reporting, unless your task is to go a step further to analyze or interpret.

Advice on Process

1. **Generating**
   - Ask yourself what readers most need to see or recognize in the data.
   - If you're stuck, begin by trying to put everything into sentences. You probably won't want to keep all these sentences in your final draft because it would get boring; however, you should start writing rather than stare at a blank page.

2. **Shaping and drafting**
   - In the first paragraph, provide a summary or overview of the data you're reporting. Tell its source, how it was gathered, and its purpose. Your thesis will generally forecast the kind of information that follows.

- Group pieces of related information. Each grouping will potentially become a paragraph.
- Create or reproduce any charts or tables that would be too wordy to translate into language.

3. **Revising**
   - Do your words accurately report the main information?
   - Will your readers better understand the information through your language?
   - Have you made the writing as interesting as you can, given the limitations of maintaining objectivity?
   - Have you documented the source(s) accurately?

20D.2 Essays that analyze quantitative information

Most essays go beyond reporting information to analyzing and interpreting it: drawing conclusions about what the information means. Marcus Kapuranis's paper reports how frequently first-year students and seniors had serious conversations with people different from them. Here is what a paragraph analyzing that data might say:

> In terms of how often they had serious conversations with students whose religious beliefs, personal opinions, or values differ from their own, first-year students and seniors were disappointingly similar. For example, 34% of first years said "sometimes," almost identical to the 35% of seniors, and 25% of first years said "very often," almost identical to 26% of seniors. The reason this is disappointing is that four years in college seem to have had little effect on students in this dimension. If one of the purposes of college is to have students learn from new knowledge and experiences, one would expect an increase in the frequency of serious encounters with different types of people. Apparently, this isn't happening.

Notice that the analysis emphasizes why the results are disappointing and provides reasons for that interpretation.

Important Elements of Quantitative Information Analyses
- A clear report of the data
- Statements that make interpretations, inferences, or evaluations of the data
- Reasoning and support that convince readers that your statements are justified

Advice on Process

1. **Generating**
   - Follow strategies for generating reports of data.
   - Use techniques for analysis and making inferences (see 3E).
   - Brainstorm. For example, try to write five different statements about what the information means or what its implications might be. Many of them will be silly or invalid, but don't let that stop you. At least one or two will probably be worthwhile.

2. **Shaping and drafting**
   - Your basic organization will be a summary of the data (report) followed by analysis. However, you don't want to summarize everything up front—just the most important materials. During your analysis, you'll want to quote or cite some of the data, and it becomes boring to see the information twice.

3. **Revising**
   - Have you been fair and accurate in presenting the information?
   - Have you considered alternative interpretations?
   - Have you provided clear and convincing explanations for any analytic, interpretive, or evaluative comments?
   - Have you documented your paper appropriately?

● **EXERCISE 20-1** Following are two tables of data from the General Social Survey. Table A reports responses from the 1970s and Table B from the 2000s. Write a 100- to 300-word analysis of the findings.

Figure 20.2 Data tables from the general social survey.

"Men are better suited for politics than are women"

A. 1970's results, by two age groups, by percent

	18-40	41-89	TOTAL
AGREE	38.3	55.9	47.5
DISAGREE	61.7	44.1	52.5
Total Percent	100.0	100.0	100.0
(Total N)	(2,418)	(2,612)	(5,030)

B. 2000's results, by two age groups, by percent

	18-40	41-89	TOTAL
AGREE	20.7	25.5	23.4
DISAGREE	79.3	74.5	76.6
Total Percent	100.0	100.0	100.0
(Total N)	(1,480)	(1,915)	(3,395)

SDA: Survey Documentation and Analysis. "General Social Survey Quick Tables." <http://sda.berkeley.edu/archive.htm>

20E How do I write essays that apply readings?

Some assignments require you to apply ideas or concepts from one reading to another source. Four example assignments will make this clearer.

1. How does Smith's theory of social deviance explain the behaviors of the criminals who are portrayed in Jones's book?

2. Based on your own experiences, are Beaudoin's categories of high school cliques accurate and sufficient?

3. Which symptoms of depression, as explained by Kho, does the narrator of *The Bell Jar* seem to display? Which does she not?

4. Kevin Sarkis argues that baseball pitchers have progressed further than batters in the past fifty years. Analyze statistics in *The Baseball Abstract* to either confirm or disprove his claim.

Instructors assign essays of application for three reasons.

1. To test how well you grasp concepts; being able to apply an idea to a new situation demonstrates your deeper understanding of it.

2. To help you analyze information in a way you might not have considered. For example, suppose you're asked to apply an article that theorizes gender determines the roles assumed by children at play to your own observations. You would pay attention to that situation differently if asked to apply a different theory—for example, that physical size determines play roles.

3. To have you test a theory or explanation to see if it fits a situation.

The following advice will help you write essays that apply readings.

1. **Generating ideas**
   - Brainstorm a list of all the possible ways your target information or situation illustrates or "fits" the ideas from your reading.
   - Brainstorm a list of ways your information or situation disproves or complicates the ideas from your reading.

2. **Shaping and drafting**
   - Begin your essay by introducing your topic, the reading, and the source to which you're applying the reading.
   - Write a thesis that states how reading helps interpret your other target source or how your source illustrates, supports, or contradicts the reading.
   - Summarize the reading briefly.

- Summarize your target source.
- Include paragraphs to support your thesis, giving reasons for your assertion.

3. **Revising your essay**
   - Have you explained your sources accurately and efficiently?
   - Have you written a strong thesis and provided reasons and support?

AN EXAMPLE OF A STUDENT ESSAY APPLYING A READING

Carlotta Torres received the following assignment.

> Choose a recent movie, television show, or book that has a female action hero. Analyze that character using ideas from Gladys Knight's book *Female Action Heroes.* Your purpose, in a paper of 500 to 750 words, is to explain how well Knight's ideas describe the character in the source you're analyzing.

Carlotta chose to focus on the movie *X-Men: First Class.*

Torres 1

Carlotta Torres

English 101

Professor Parrish

22 October 2011

The Complicated Character of Raven in *X-Men: First Class*

For most of the twentieth century, heroes and superheroes in action movies were mostly men, from Superman and Batman to Spiderman and Wolverine, joined by only a few characters like Wonder Woman. However, from the last part of the century to the present, women superheroes have become more frequent. In *Female Action Heroes*, Gladys L. Knight explains the qualities of contemporary women characters, especially as they developed in the past three decades. The recent movie *X-Men: First Class* includes both a female villain, the character

---

continued >>

Torres 2

Emma Frost, and a female hero, Raven. Raven complicates the qualities that Knight has identified.

Knight describes the transition of women in films from being "weak, unintelligent, and needing to be rescued" at the turn of the twentieth century (xvi) to being tough, smart and independent by the end, including in action films, where they have emerged as heroes. The character Ellen Ripley in the *Alien* film series shows this change most clearly. In defeating alien monsters, Ripley represents "second wave feminism," Knight claims. Ripley is tough, unemotional, and stronger than her male companions in space (xx). Knight contends that female heroes in the 1990's to the present are different, with many of them characterized less by masculine toughness than by "youthfulness, girliness, and combativeness" (xxi). She points to Buffy the Vampire Slayer and Lara Croft as examples. Even as female heroes become more athletic and powerful, they continue having "all-impossible beautiful and svelte figure[s]," and they reflect "third-wave feminism, with its advocacy of looking good and being powerful" (xxi).

X-Men: First Class explains the origins in the early 1960's of the popular team of superheroes, the X-Men, whose mutations give them special powers. The group's leader, a telepath named Charles Xavier, identifies and recruits people with mutant powers, including characters named Banshee, whose impossibly loud voice can destroy buildings, and Beast, who has hands instead of feet and who possesses tremendous agility and strength. However, the first mutant that Xavier

continued >>

Torres 3

meets is a girl named Raven. Raven is a shape shifter; she can assume the exact appearance, manners, and voice of anyone else.

Although Raven matches some of Gladys Knight's description of modern heroes, she doesn't fit them all. Raven is certainly beautiful, even if in an odd way. Her natural form is as a dark blue woman whose skin has elaborate patterns of ridges and swirls. When she appears in this form, she is nude; although her skin color and texture camouflage specific bodily details, her figure is clearly curvy and sexy. Raven is smart and powerful, too. At a crucial point in the movie, for example, she imitates the lead villain, which confuses a situation long enough to let the X-Men escape. However, Raven lacks the confidence of modern female heroes as Knight depicts them. Although she is the main female hero of the movie, she is secondary to Xavier and the other male hero, Magneto. Most important, she alternates between being proud of her natural form and being ashamed of it; she even considers taking a drug that promises to make her "normal." In the end, she embraces who she is, but this decision brings a powerful change: she turns from good to evil, changing her name to Mystique in the process.

The character Raven may signal another stage of development in female action movie heroes. Instead of being purely beautiful, powerful, and in control, Raven has doubts. Her unconventional beauty causes problems, and in the end she decides to use her powers against society. In this way, Raven resembles problematic male film superheroes like

continued >>

Torres 4

Batman, who is a dark outsider whose powers don't necessarily bring him happiness. Perhaps Gladys Knight will have to write a new chapter for female action heroes like Raven.

Torres 5

Works Cited

Knight, Gladys L. *Female Action Heroes: A Guide to Women in Comics, Video Games, Film, and Television.* Santa Barbara, CA: Greenwood, 2010. Google eBook, 2010. Web. 14 Oct. 2011.

X-Men: First Class. Dir. Matthew Vaughn. Twentieth Century Fox, 2011. Film.

Complete the Chapter Exercises

PART

4

Research and Documentation

21 Starting and Planning Research Projects

■ ■ ■ ■ ■ ■ ■ ■ ■ ■

Quick Points   You will learn to

➤ Understand purposes of research (see 21A–21C).
➤ Plan the steps of a research project (see 21D).
➤ Choose a research topic and refine a research question (see 21E–21H).
➤ Identify two main types of research papers (see 21I–21J).
➤ Develop a search strategy (see 21K).
➤ Understand field research (see 21L).
➤ Create a bibliography, an annotated bibliography, and content notes (see 21M–21O).

21A   What is research?

Research is a systematic process of gathering information to answer a question. You're doing research when you're trying to decide which college to attend or which smartphone to buy.

How much research you will do for a writing assignment can vary, depending on your AUDIENCE*, PURPOSE, and type of writing (see Ch. 5; Chs. 10–17). However, any writing might benefit from a little research. Consider these original and revised statements.

ORIGINAL   Most people own a cell phone these days.

RESEARCHED   According to the Pew Research Center, 84% of American adults owned a cell phone in 2011 (Purcell 2).

WORK CITED

Purcell, Kristen, Lee Rainie, Tom Rosenstiel, and Amy Mitchell.
   "How Mobile Devices are Changing Community Information
   Environments." *Pew Internet Project*. Pew Research Center, 14 Mar.
   2011. Web. 20 Apr. 2011.

---

* Words printed in small capital letters are discussed elsewhere in the text and are defined in the Terms Glossary at the back of the book.

In the second version, the writer uses research to answer the question, "How many people own cell phones?" See Quick Box 21.1.

Quick Box 21.1   ■ ■ ■ ■ ■ ■ ■ ■ ■ ■ ■

Reasons for doing research

- **To find a single fact.** Sometimes you simply need to answer a direct question of "How much?" or "When?" or "Where?" or "Who?"

    ● How does the cost of college today compare to the cost twenty years ago?

- **To understand an issue or situation more broadly.** Sometimes you need to learn basic information as well as the range of viewpoints or opinions on a particular topic.

    ● What are the effects of globalization?

- **To gather current information.** You may need to bring together the most current information. A **review of the literature** is a comprehensive synthesis of the latest knowledge on a particular topic.

    ● What treatments are possible for diabetes?

- **To identify a specific opinion or point of view.** You might want to find out what the people who disagree with you believe—and why. You can then defend your position. Of course, you might also look for experts who support your view.

    ● What are the arguments for colleges restricting student Internet downloads?

- **To create new knowledge.** Researchers make new knowledge as well as find existing knowledge. Chemists and biologists as well as psychologists, sociologists, journalists, and others do this kind of research. They conduct experiments, surveys, interviews, and observations. For instance, if you were writing a guide to coffee houses in a certain area for a sociology course, you'd need to visit all of them, take notes, and present your findings to readers.

● **EXERCISE 21-1** The following paragraph has a number of general statements. Generate a list of all the possible research questions you might pursue to strengthen the paragraph.

EXAMPLE

"If we fail to act on climate change, our coastal cities will be damaged by rising ocean levels."

POSSIBLE QUESTIONS How will climate change affect oceans? How much will oceans rise? Which cities will be affected? How?

> In a troubling reversal of roles, boys are now considerably more at risk in school than are girls. Girls used to be denied many opportunities in schools and colleges, as boys enjoyed several unfair advantages. Now, however, girls are graduating from high schools at much higher rates. They are performing better on standardized tests and entering colleges and universities at much higher levels, to the extent that several colleges now have programs specifically targeted to attract and admit more male students. Women substantially outnumber men in admission to medical and law schools. A number of factors is responsible, but unless we take actions to ensure academic quality and success for both boys and girls, we will need to create affirmative action programs for men. ●

21B What is a source?

Watch the Video

A **source** is any form of information that provides ideas, examples, or evidence. One broad category is PUBLISHED SOURCES: books, articles, Web sites, and so on. You find published sources by searching library and other databases; we explain how in Chapter 22, and we explain how to judge the quality of published sources in Chapter 23. A second broad category of sources is FIELD RESEARCH, studies that you carry out directly yourself through experiments, observations, interviews, or surveys as we explain in section 21C.

Sources are either primary or secondary, as we explain in Quick Box 3.6, on page 28.

Suppose you are researching student attitudes toward American policy in the Middle East. Surveying several students would be primary research. Consulting scholars' books and articles about student attitudes toward the Middle East would be secondary research. Your decision to use primary or secondary sources depends on your research question or the requirements of your assignment. For her paper in Chapter 26, Leslie Palm conducted primary research by analyzing several video games and secondary research by reading scholarly articles.

21C What is a research paper?

A **research paper** (sometimes called a *term paper*) is a specific kind of researched writing common in many college courses. It most commonly requires the SYNTHESIS of published sources (see Chapter 22). See Quick Box 21.2.

Quick Box 21.2

Steps in most research projects

1. **Develop a research question.** What is the question that you need to answer by conducting research? Some questions might be very specific, such as when you're looking for a piece of data; for example, "How much methane is produced by dairy cattle in the United States?" Other questions are broad and complex; for example, or "How might the depiction of schools on television influence people's decisions to become teachers?" See section 21F for more about effective research questions.

2. **Decide what kinds of sources will best answer your question.** Will you need PUBLISHED SOURCES, or the results of field research (see 21L)?

3. **Develop a search strategy.** Develop a plan for finding the sources you need (see 21K).

4. **Gather and evaluate sources.** Try to accumulate more than enough materials so that you feel confident you can answer your research question (see Chapter 22). As you do so, it's crucial to use good and credible sources (see Chapter 23).

5. **Take notes on your source materials.** Take CONTENT NOTES about your sources, using summary, quotation, and paraphrase (see 21P).

6. **Draft, revise, edit, and proofread your paper.** Chapter 24 explains how to apply the general writing processes presented in Chapter 5 specifically to writing research papers.

21D How do I plan a research project?

If you feel overwhelmed by the prospect of writing an extended research project, you're not alone. Dividing your project into steps makes the process less intimidating. Giving yourself target deadlines along the way keeps you on track. Quick Box 21.3 (pages 256–257) shows how you can plan a research project.

🛈 **Alert:** While the steps in Quick Box 21.3 are generally true for writing research papers, the process doesn't always occur in a straight line. For example, during the drafting process, writers often discover the need to go back and find some additional sources, or even to revise their thesis statement. Being flexible will help your research process go better. ●

Quick Box 21.3

Sample schedule for a research project

Assignment received _____
Assignment due date _____

PLANNING   **FINISH BY (DATE)**

1. Choose a topic suitable for research (see 21E). _____

2. Draft my research question (see 21F). _____

3. Start my research log (see 21G). _____

4. Understand my writing situation (see 21H) _____
   and type of research paper (see 21I).

5. Determine what documentation style I need _____
   to use (see 21J).

RESEARCHING

6. Plan my SEARCH STRATEGY, and modify as _____
   necessary (see 21K).

7. Decide if I need or am required to conduct _____
   field research; if so, plan those tasks (see 21M).

8. Locate and evaluate published sources _____
   (see Chs. 22 and 23).

9. Compile a working bibliography (see 21M) _____
   or annotated bibliography (see 21O).

10. Determine whether online software can be _____
    useful for me to track sources (see 21N).

11. Take content notes from sources I find _____
    useful (see 21P).

WRITING

12. Draft my thesis statement (see 24B). _____

13. Review my content notes and determine _____
    relations between sources (see 21P).

14. Create an outline, as required or useful _____
    (see 24C) or use a research paper frame (see 24E).

15. Draft my paper (see 24D). _____

16. Use correct in-text citations (see 25B–C, _____
    26B–C, 27A, 35A).

continued >>

Quick Box 21.3   (continued)

17. Compile my final bibliography (Works Cited or _____ References), using the documentation style required (see 25A–B, 26A–B, 27).

18. Revise my paper (see 24G).   _____

19. Edit and proofread paper for content, lack of _____ plagiarism, in-text citations, bibliography, and format (see 24H).

21E How do I choose a research topic?

Sometimes college instructors assign specific topics; other times you get to choose. When you need to select your own research topic:

Watch
the Video

- Select a topic that interests you. It will be your companion for quite a while, perhaps most of a term.

- Choose a sufficiently narrow topic that will allow you to be successful within the time and length given by the assignment. Avoid topics that are too broad.

  NO   Emotions

  YES   How people respond to anger in others.

  NO   Social networking

  YES   The effect of Facebook on physical relationships

- Choose a topic that your readers will perceive as significant. Avoid trivial topics that prevent you from investigating ideas, analyzing them critically, or synthesizing complex concepts.

  NO   Kinds of fast food

  YES   The relation between fast food and obesity

The freedom to choose any topic you want can sometimes lead to research topic block. Don't panic. Instead, use some of the following strategies for generating ideas.

- **Talk with others.** Ask instructors or other experts in your area of interest what issues currently seem hot to them. Ask them to recommend readings or the names of authorities on those issues.

- **Browse the Internet.** Browse SUBJECT DIRECTORIES found in some Web search engines (see 23E).

- **Pay attention to news and current events.** Regularly browse newspapers or magazines (print or online), blogs, or social network channels.

- **Browse textbooks in your area of interest.** Read the table of contents and major headings. As you narrow your focus, note the names of important books and experts, often mentioned in reference lists at the end of chapters or at the back of the book.

- **Read encyclopedia articles** about your area of interest, its subcategories, and possible ideas for real investigation. Even Wikipedia can be useful as a starting place—but only as a starting place—be sure to read the Alert in section 22H. Never, however, stop with the encyclopedia—it is too basic for college-level research.

- **Browse the library or a good bookstore.** Look at books and popular magazines to find subjects that interest you. Also, skim academic journals in fields that interest you.

21F What is a research question?

A **research question** provides a clear focus for your research and a goal for your WRITING PROCESS. For example, you can more successfully research the question "How do people become homeless?" than you can research the broad topic of "homelessness." Some questions can lead to a final, definitive answer (for example, "How does penicillin destroy bacteria?"). Others can't (for example, "Is softball a better sport than volleyball?").

You may often find that you need to refine your question, as in the following example.

1. What is the current situation regarding homelessness?

2. What are the causes of homelessness in the United States?

3. Are the reasons for homelessness today the same reasons that existed twenty-five years ago?

Compared to the first broad question, the third is more focused. Because the third question is more complicated, it provides a better focus for your research writing.

The answer to your research question usually, but not always, appears in your THESIS STATEMENT (see Ch. 5). Sometimes, however, your thesis statement simply suggests or hints at your answer, especially when the answer is long or complicated.

21G What is a research log?

A **research log**, which is a diary of your research process, can be useful for keeping yourself organized and on track. Research logs can also show instructors and others how carefully and thoroughly you've worked. To set one up, follow these steps:

Figure 21.1 A selection from the research log of Andrei Gurov, who wrote the paper in 25G.

November 17: Finished reading Brown's book, The Déjà Vu Experience. Great source. I wonder if he's published anything more recently. Will meet with reference librarian this afternoon to identify sources.

November 18: Followed librarian's suggestion and searched the PsycINFO database for more recent articles. Found a chapter by Brown in a 2010 book that looks promising.

- Create a "Research Log" file or folder on your computer or use a separate notebook.

- Record each step in your search for information. Enter the date; your search strategies; the gist of the information you discovered; the details of exactly where you found it; and exactly where you filed your detailed notes. This step is crucial if you ever, which you often will, need to retrace your steps.

- Write down the next step you think you should take when you return to your research.

- Decide when you're ready to move away from gathering material to organizing it or to writing about it.

- Write down your thoughts and insights as you move through the research and writing processes.

Although much of what you write in your research log will never find its way into your paper, it will greatly increase your efficiency. Figure 21.1 shows a page from Andrei Gurov's research log for his paper in Chapter 25.

21H How does the writing situation shape my research paper?

Your TOPIC, PURPOSE, AUDIENCE, ROLE, and special considerations (see 4A) all influence your research paper. If you receive an assignment to argue for a position but instead you inform readers about possible positions, your paper will fall short. The same would happen if you were assigned to write a ten-page paper, in MLA style, for an audience of people knowledgeable on a certain topic and instead you wrote fifteen pages in APA style, for a very general audience. When you receive a research paper assignment, make sure to understand the required writing situation.

AUDIENCES for research papers can vary. Your instructor, of course, is always an audience. However, in most cases he or she will read as a representative of other, larger audiences, and you'll want to meet their expectations. For example, if you're writing about the topic of déjà vu for a specialized audience (see 4C) that knows psychology and expects your paper to have the characteristics of writing in that field, your research paper will differ slightly from one on the very same topic but for a general educated audience (see 4C).

21I What are two main types of research papers?

Most research papers are either informative or argumentative. Informative research papers explain a topic by SYNTHESIZING several sources (see 20E). Your goal is to gather and clarify information for your readers. Informative research papers answer questions like, "What is the current state of knowledge about X?" or "What are the current controversies or positions about Y?"

Argumentative research papers go a step further. In these papers, you choose a topic on which intelligent people have different positions, identify and analyze sources, and argue the position that appears best. You back up your reasons with support. Argumentative research papers answer questions like, "What is the best course of action regarding X?" or "Why should I believe Y?" Section 24E presents two FRAMES for research papers to guide you.

21J What documentation style should I use?

A **documentation style** is a system for providing information about each source you use. Documentation styles vary from one academic discipline to another. The types are

MLA (Modern Language Association) STYLE (see Ch. 25): Humanities

APA (American Psychological Association) STYLE (see Ch. 26): Social sciences

CM (*Chicago Manual*) STYLE (see Ch. 27): Various disciplines, generally in the humanities

CSE (Council of Science Editors) STYLE (see Ch. 27): Many natural sciences

If you don't know which style to use, ask your instructor. Use only one documentation style in each piece of writing.

At the start determine the required documentation style. This helps you write down the exact details you need to document your sources. You'll need to document all sources. If you're doing field research, your instructor may have special requirements for documentation, such as asking you to submit your research notes or results from observations, questionnaires, surveys, interviews, or anything else that has produced your primary data.

21K What is a search strategy?

A **search strategy** is an organized procedure for locating and gathering sources to answer your research question. Using a search strategy helps you work more systematically and quickly. If you are doing FIELD RESEARCH, see 21L. Here are three frequently used search strategies for PUBLISHED SOURCES. You can switch or combine these strategies or even create your own.

QUESTIONING METHOD	Useful when you have a topic. Brainstorm to break your overall research question into several smaller questions, then find sources to answer each of them. This method has the advantage of allowing you to see if your sources cover all the areas important to your research question. Generating a list of questions like this can give your search a direction and purpose.
EXPERT METHOD	Useful when your topic is specific and narrow. Start with articles or books by an expert in the field. You might want to interview an expert on the topic.
CHAINING METHOD	Useful when your topic is a general one. Start with reference books and bibliographies in current articles or WEB SITES; use them to link to additional sources. Keep following the links until you reach increasingly expert sources. Alternatively, talk with people who have some general knowledge of your topic and ask them to refer you to experts they might know.

Start and complete your search as soon as possible after you get your assignment. Early in your process you may discover sources that take time to obtain (for example, through an interlibrary loan).

One more piece of advice: Evaluate your topic before getting too far along in your search. Rather than spend endless hours simply gathering sources, take time to read and analyze some of your materials to make sure your topic will work. Your research log (see 21G) can be useful for this purpose.

21L What is field research?

Field research involves going into real-life situations to observe, survey, interview, or participate in some activity firsthand. As a field researcher, you might go to a factory, a lecture, a day-care center, or a mall—anywhere that people engage in everyday activities. You might also interview experts and other relevant individuals. Finally, you might observe and describe objects, such as paintings or buildings, or performances and events, such as concerts or television shows.

21L.1 Surveying

Watch
the Video

Surveys use questions to gather information about peoples' experiences, situations, or opinions. Multiple-choice or true/false questions are easy for people to complete and for researchers to summarize and report. Open-ended questions, in which people are asked to write responses, require more effort. However, they sometimes provide more complete or accurate information. For advice, see Quick Box 21.4.

When you report findings from a survey, keep within your limitations. For example, if the only people who answer your survey are students at a particular campus, you can't claim they represent "all college students."

Quick Box 21.4 ■ ■ ■ ■ ■ ■ ■ ■ ■ ■

Guidelines for developing a survey

1. Define what you want to learn.
2. Identify the appropriate types and numbers of people to answer your survey so that you get the information you need.
3. Write questions to elicit the information.
4. Phrase questions so that they are easy to understand.

   NO   Recognizing several complex variables, what age generally do you perceive as most advantageous for matrimony?

   YES   What do you think is the ideal age for getting married?

5. Make sure that your wording does not imply what you want to hear.

   NO   Do irresponsible and lazy deadbeats deserve support from hardworking and honest taxpayers?

   YES   Should we provide benefits to unemployed people?

6. Decide whether to include open-ended questions that allow people to write their own answers.
7. Test a draft of the questionnaire on a small group of people. If any question is misinterpreted or difficult to understand, revise and retest it.

🚫 **Alert:** Online tools can help you distribute and analyze surveys easily. Two popular free services for small surveys are Zoomerang and SurveyMonkey. You go to the service's site, enter your survey questions, and then receive a URL to send participants. After you receive responses, you can go back to the site to download the results or do some analysis. ●

21L.2 Interviewing

Instead of surveying, you might interview people to gather data or opinions. You might also interview experts, who can offer valuable information and viewpoints. Probably the best place to start is with the faculty at your college, who may also suggest additional sources. Corporations, institutions, or professional organizations often have public relations offices that can answer questions or make referrals.

👁 Watch the Video

Make every attempt to conduct interviews in person so that you can observe body language and facial expressions. However, if distance is a problem, you can conduct interviews over the phone or online. Quick Box 21.5 provides suggestions for conducting interviews.

Quick Box 21.5 ■ ■ ■ ■ ■ ■ ■ ■ ■ ■ ■

Conducting research interviews

- Arrange the interview well in advance, do background research, prepare specific questions, and show up on time.

- Rehearse how to ask your questions without reading them (perhaps highlight the key words). Looking your interviewee in the eye as you ask questions establishes ease and trust. If you're interviewing on the telephone, be organized and precise.

- Take careful notes, listening especially for key names, books, Web sites, or other sources.

- Create a shortcut symbol or letter for key terms you expect to hear during the interview. This cuts down on the time needed to look away from your interviewee.

- Use standard paper so that you have room to write. (Many people are annoyed when others type while they're talking.)

- Bring extra pens or pencils.

- Never depend on recording an interview. People have become reluctant to permit such recording.

21L.3 Observing people and situations

Anthropologists, education or marketing researchers, sociologists, and other scholars conduct research by observing people and situations. For observations of behavior (for example, fans at a game or tourists at a museum), take notes during the activity. Try to remain objective so that you can see things clearly. One strategy is to take notes in a two-column format. On the left, record only objective observations; on the right, record comments or possible interpretations. Figure 21.2 is an example of a double-column note strategy.

21L.4 Gathering data about things or practices

Some kinds of field research involve looking at objects, artifacts, or practices, describing or counting what you observe, and reporting what you find. Consider these two sample research questions:

1. How are women portrayed on the covers of fashion magazines?

2. Are characters with foreign-sounding names or accents in current movies more likely to be heroes or villains?

Figure 21.2 A double-column set of notes.

Notes	Comment/Analyses
Small conference room; round table covered with papers	
JP suggests fundraising plan	JP seems nervous. Her normal behavior, or is it this situation?
AR and CT lean forward; SM leans back	
SM interrupts JP's plan, asks for more; CT silent	The fact that JP and AR are women might explain SM's response. Or is it that he's more senior?
JP continues proposal	
SM looks out window, taps pencil	Seems to have made up his mind. A power move?

You might be able to answer these questions by finding published sources, interviewing experts, or using existing means. However, it is more likely that you'd need to collect this information yourself, by directly and systematically looking at examples. For sample question one above, you'd need to examine dozens of magazine covers. For sample question two above, you'd need to view several movies. Quick Box 21.6 summarizes steps for this kind of research.

Quick Box 21.6 ■ ■ ■ ■ ■ ■ ■ ■ ■ ■ ■

Research using direct observations

1. Identify your research question.
2. Identify the sample (the group of individual examples) that you're going to examine, count, describe, or analyze.
3. Develop a system for recording your observations.
4. Look for patterns, make conclusions, or draw inferences after recording all observations.
5. Explore questions such as "Why are things as I found them?" or "What might be the implications of my findings?"

● **EXERCISE 21-2**   For each of the research questions, what kinds of research would be appropriate? If more than one type would work, explain all that apply.

1. What types of television programs most appeal to college students?
2. Do men and women behave differently in fast-food restaurants?
3. What factors led to the genocide in Rwanda in the 1990s?
4. What are the working conditions in a job that interests me?
5. How do clothing displays in upscale stores differ from clothing displays in discount stores? ●

21M   What is a working bibliography?

A **working bibliography** is a preliminary list of the sources you gather in your research. It contains information about each source and where others might find it. Here's a list of basic elements to include (for more detailed information about documenting specific types of sources, see Chapters 25–27).

ELEMENTS OF A CITATION TO RECORD

Books	Periodical Articles	Online Sources
Author(s)	Author(s)	Author(s) (if available)
Title of book	Title of article; digital object identifier (doi), if any	Title of document
Publisher and place of publication	Name of periodical, volume number, issue number	Name of Web site or database; editor or sponsor of site
Year of publication	Date of issue	Date of electronic publication
Call number	Page numbers of article	Electronic address (URL)
Print or Web version?	Print or Web version?	Date you accessed the source

Begin your working bibliography as soon as you start identifying sources. If your search turns up very few sources, you may want to change your topic. If it reveals a vast number, you'll want to narrow your topic or choose a different one. Expect to add and drop sources throughout the research process. As a rough estimate, your working bibliography needs to be about twice as long as the list of sources you end up using.

You can record your working bibliography on note cards or on a computer. On the one hand, note cards are easy to sift through and rearrange. At the end of your WRITING PROCESS, you can easily alphabetize them to prepare your final bibliography. Write only one source on each card (see Figure 21.3).

On the other hand, putting your working bibliography on a computer saves having to type your list of sources later. Clearly separate one entry from another. You can organize the list alphabetically, by author, or by subtopics.

Whichever method you use, when you come across a potential source, immediately record the information exactly as you need it to fulfill the requirements of the DOCUMENTATION STYLE your assignment requires. Spending a few extra moments at this stage can save you hours of retracing your steps and frustration later on.

Figure 21.3 Bibliographic entry in MLA format.

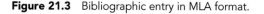

> Brown, Alan S. and Elizabeth J. Marsh. "Digging into Déjà Vu:
> Recent Research on Possible Mechanisms." The Psychology of
> Learning and Motivation: Advances in Research and Theory.
> Ed. Brian H. Ross. Burlington: Academic P, 2010, 33–62. Web.
> 20 Nov. 2011.

21N How might online software help me create bibliographies or organize sources?

Several software programs allow you to store bibliographic information about your sources. You can then access this information and organize it in many ways. For example, a program like NoodleBib or RefWorks lets you type in information (author, title, publisher, and so on) about each source you find. Then, with a click of a button, you can generate an MLA-style "Works Cited" page, an APA-style "References" page, or a bibliography in other formats. You can export the bibliography into the paper you're writing, without having to retype. Of course, you're still responsible for the accuracy of any bibliography you generate with this software.

Furthermore, these programs allow you to import citations directly from many databases. That means you never have to type them. Check to see if your library gives you access to bibliographic software, or use an application like NoodleBib (Figure 21.4.)

Other online tools can help you collect, store, access, and organize materials you find on the Web. For example, Diigo (http://www.diigo .com/) allows you to store URLs or even copies of Web pages so you always have access to them from any device that connects to the Internet (see Figure 21.5). You can tag each entry (add descriptive words so you can search for particular topics later), and you can highlight or add notes. You can share your bibliographies with others, which can be helpful for group projects. We have one caution. Because this software makes it so easy to gather materials, it can be tempting to avoid analysis. Analysis, however, is vital to making sources your own (see Chs. 4 and 14).

Figure 21.4 Page showing the start of a project in NoodleBib

NoodleBib

Projects | Dashboard | Bibliography | Notecards

NoodleTools

My Projects > Create a New Project

Welcome, pearsonas Sign Out My Account Help

Create a New Project

Select the bibliographic style (MLA, APA, or Chicago/Turabian) you wish to use and enter a short description of your topic.

Projects style:

○ **MLA Advanced**
  ▪ follows the *MLA Handbook*, 7th ed.

○ **APA Advanced**
  ▪ follows the *APA Publication Manual*, 6th ed.

○ **Chicago/Turabian Advanced**
  ▪ bibliography/notes formatting
  ▪ follows *The Chicago Manual of Style*, 16th ed.

Description: Deja vu project

For example, "History 101 report on George Washington"

Cancel | Create Project

Copyright © NoodleTools Inc. Privacy Policy Terms of Service Legal

Figure 21.5 Example of a source management system.

210 What is an annotated bibliography?

View the Model Document

An **annotated bibliography** includes not only publishing information about your sources but also a brief summary and perhaps a commentary. We suggest you include three types of information:

1. the thesis or a one-sentence summary;
2. the main claims or arguments in support of the thesis;

Figure 21.6 Section from an annotated bibliography in MLA style.

Brown, Alan S. and Elizabeth J. Marsh. "Digging into Déjà Vu: Recent
Research on Possible Mechanisms." *The Psychology of Learning
and Motivation: Advances in Research and Theory.* Ed. Brian
H. Ross. Burlington: Academic P, 2010, 33-62. Web. 20 Nov. 2011.

   This chapter summarizes laboratory research that tried
   to explain déjà vu. The authors discuss three theories.
   "Split perception" refers to people seeing part of a scene
   before seeing the whole. "Implicit memory" refers to people
   having had a previous experience that, however, is stored in
   their memories imprecisely, so they remember only the
   sensation and not the scene. "Gestalt familiarity" refers to
   having experienced something very familiar to the present
   setting.

Carey, Benedict. "Déjà Vu: If It All Seems Familiar, There May Be
a Reason." *New York Times* 14 Sept. 2004: F1+. *LexisNexis.*
Web. 11 Nov. 2011.

   Scientific research shows that déjà vu is a common and real
   phenomenon, even if its causes are unclear. Perhaps the
   best explanation is that people have had a similar previous
   experience that they have since forgotten.

3. the kind of evidence used in the source. For example, does the source
   report facts or results from formal studies? Are these PRIMARY SOURCES or
   SECONDARY SOURCES?

Instructors sometimes require annotated bibliographies as a step in research
projects, or they sometimes assign them as separate projects in their own right.
Whether it's assigned or not, you may find making an annotated bibliography
helps you better understand sources. Figure 21.6 shows part of an annotated
bibliography using MLA-style documentation.

21P How do I take content notes?

When you write **content notes**, you record information from your sources.
Writing content notes is a crucial bridge between finding and evaluating sources
(see Chs. 22 and 23) and moving on to drafting your paper. Understanding

some basic strategies and procedures will make taking content notes more efficient and effective. On each index card or computer document

- Put a heading (title and author) that gives a precise link to one of your bibliography items.

- Keep careful track of what ideas came from each source if you use a computer document. Create a document called "Research Project Notes" and then create a heading for each source you use. Always include the author and page at the beginning or end of each note you type into a document.

- Include the page numbers from which you're taking notes unless an online source has no page numbers.

- Do one of three things for every note: (1) copy the exact words from a source, enclosing them in quotation marks; (2) write a paraphrase; or (3) write a summary. To avoid PLAGIARISM keep track of the kind of note you're taking. You might use the code *Q* for QUOTATION, *P* for PARAPHRASE, and *S* for SUMMARY.

- Record your own reactions and ideas separately. Use critical thinking skills (see Chapter 3). Record what might be useful from the source. Does it provide an example? An idea? A fact? Take care to differentiate your ideas from those in your sources. If you don't, you risk plagiarizing. You might write your own thoughts in a different color ink (note card) or font (computer).

Figure 21.7 shows one of Andrei Gurov's note cards for his research paper in section 25G.

Complete
the
Chapter
Exercises

Figure 21.7 Bibliographic entry in MLA format.

Brown, Alan S. "The Déjà Vu Illusion." *Current Directions in Psychological Science* 13.6 (2004): 256–59. Print.

Summary: Recent advances in neurology and the study of cognitive illusions reveal that two seemingly separate perceptual events are indeed one.

Comment: This is the part that grabs my attention. How could this be?

22 Finding Published Sources

■ ■ ■ ■ ■ ■ ■ ■ ■

Quick Points You will learn to

➤ Identify the different types of published sources (see 22A).

➤ Locate sources using libraries, databases, and online tools (see 22B–22J).

22A What kinds of published sources are there?

Published sources refer to books, articles, documents, and other writings that appear online or in print. Because most college research writing relies on published sources, we've written this chapter to explain how to find them. The sheer number and types of published sources today can be confusing. However, you can clarify things by asking two questions: Is the source "scholarly" or "popular"? Quick Box 22.1 (page 272) helps you decide. Is the source "edited" or "unedited"? Quick Box 22.2 (page 273) explains the differences.

Popular sources can be high quality, especially if they're edited and from serious publishers or periodicals (such as *The New York Times* or *The Atlantic Monthly*). Unedited sources can be useful, too, but because no editor has selected or reviewed them, you should judge them carefully. Chapter 23 explains how to evaluate all your sources.

22B How can libraries help me?

In an age when the Web contains billions of pages of information, it might seem almost prehistoric to talk about libraries. After all, so much is now available online. Still, many sources, especially scholarly ones, are available only through the library. Notice that we've said "through" the library, not necessarily "in" it. That's because many library sources and services are available through the Internet to students or registered users.

⊙ **Watch** the Video

In many respects, the function that a library performs is even more important than the physical building. Librarians and scholars have systematically gathered and organized sources so you can find the best ones efficiently and reliably. You can access and search electronic catalogs, **indexes,** and databases

Quick Box 22.1

Scholarly sources versus popular sources

Scholarly Sources	Popular Sources
Examples: Journal articles; books published by university presses; professional organization Web sites	**Examples:** Newspapers and magazines; general Web sites and blogs
Audience: Scholars, experts, researchers, students	**Audience:** General readers; people who may be interested but don't necessarily have specific knowledge or expertise
Purpose: To provide cutting-edge ideas and information supported by research	**Purpose:** To entertain; to translate expert information for general readers; to persuade
Authors: Researchers; professors; content experts; professionals	**Authors:** Journalists or freelance writers; hobbyists or enthusiasts; people from all walks of life
Characteristics: Citations and bibliographies show sources of ideas; sources explain research methods and limitations of conclusions	**Characteristics:** Rarely include citations or bibliographies; may refer to people or sources in the body of the work
Where published: Appear in scholarly books and periodicals or on Web sites maintained by professional organizations	**Where published:** Appear in popular books and periodicals; blogs; personal or informal Web sites
How you find them: Mainly through DATABASES	**How you find them:** Sometimes through databases; often through SEARCH ENGINES

from computers with the library itself or, in many cases, by connecting to the library via the Internet. If you have remote access, you'll probably have to log in with an ID and password. Our point is that you might be able use library-based sources without ever setting foot in the building.

Still, the building itself continues to be a vital place for all research. One key advantage of going to the library is your chance to consult with librarians face-to-face. Helping is their profession. Never hesitate to ask how to proceed or where to find a resource. Quick Box 22.3 lists ten useful questions.

Quick Box 22.2

■ ■ ■ ■ ■ ■ ■ ■ ■ ■ ■

Edited versus unedited sources

Edited	Unedited
Examples: Periodicals; books from a publisher; organizational or professional Web site	**Examples:** Personal blogs and Web sites; online comments or discussion postings; self-published books
Selection: An editor or other professional has evaluated and chosen the work to publish	**Selection:** The individual publishes the work him or herself (for example, in a blog)
Accuracy/Quality: Reviewed by an editor or expert readers	**Accuracy/Quality:** Not reviewed by others before publication.
Publisher: A periodical, book publisher, or professional organization	**Publisher:** The author him- or herself (as in blogs or discussion posts) or perhaps a special-interest group
How you find them: Mainly through databases or catalogs	**How you find them:** Mainly through search engines; unedited works almost never appear in databases

Quick Box 22.3

■ ■ ■ ■ ■ ■ ■ ■ ■ ■ ■

Top ten questions to ask a librarian

1. Do I need to log in to use the library's computer system? If so, how?
2. Can I access the library's computer system from home or off campus?
3. How do I search the library's catalog?
4. Can I find books directly on the shelves, or do I have to request them? How do I check out materials?
5. How can I use an electronic version of a book, if the library has one?
6. What databases would you recommend when I'm looking for scholarly sources on topic X?
7. What might be the best keywords or search strategy when I'm searching databases for sources on topic X?
8. How can I keep track of sources I find? E-mail them to myself? Print a list of citations? Use source management software?
9. How do I get copies of articles or other sources I've found?
10. Is there a way for me to access or order a copy if our library doesn't own a source I need?

22C What are search engines and databases?

Using search engines and using databases are two related, but different, ways to find published sources.

22C.1 Search engines

Watch
the Video

Search engines are programs designed to hunt the Web for sources on specific topics by using KEYWORDS (see 22D) or subject directories (see 22E). Once you use a **browser** (a program like Internet Explorer, Firefox, or Safari) to get on the Web, you can use a search engine like Google (www.google. com) or Yahoo! (www.yahoo.com). Of course, if you know a specific Web address—called a **URL**, for Universal (or Uniform) Resource Locator—you can type it directly in a search box. Quick Box 22.4 offers tips for using search engines.

Because anyone can put anything on the Web, the Web is a rich source of information. However, it also makes finding what you need difficult, and it opens the possibility of encountering inaccurate or biased materials. In addition, many articles and documents, especially those published in scholarly journals or some edited periodicals, can't be found on the Web through search engines. To find them, you need to use databases, as explained next.

Quick Box 22.4 ■ ■ ■ ■ ■ ■ ■ ■ ■ ■ ■

Tips on using Web search engines

- Use keyword combinations or BOOLEAN EXPRESSIONS (see Quick Box 22.5).

- Try using more than one search engine because different search engines will provide different results for the same search.

- Go to the toolbar at the top of the screen and click on "Bookmark" and then click on "Add" when you find a useful site. This will make it easy for you to return to a good source. Or use social networking software (see 21N) to gather your sources.

- Use the "History" function on your browser to revisit sites.

- Sources on the Web come in various formats. Most common are Web pages in html (Hypertext Markup Language) format. However, you may also encounter Word or Excel documents, PowerPoint slides, or PDF (portable document format) files.

22C.2 Databases

Databases are collections of sources that experts or librarians have gathered. You find databases mostly in libraries or through library **Web sites,** and you search them mainly by using keywords. We explain how in section 22D. Sources that you identify through databases are usually more reliable and appropriate than sources you find by simply browsing the Web. Therefore, we recommend that you search a database as part of any college research project.

Watch the Video

Alert: Google Scholar is a site within Google that does pretty much what it announces: lists scholarly sources, including books and articles, that are on the Web. It functions somewhat like a database. ●

Most college libraries subscribe to one or more database services, such as EBSCO, ProQuest, and FirstSearch. Your library's Web site will show the resources it has available. Because the college pays for these services, you don't have to, but you'll need an ID or password to use them. Commonly, your student number serves as your ID, but check with a librarian to see what's required at your college. Figure 22.1 shows a college library Web site.

Figure 22.1 College library Web site.

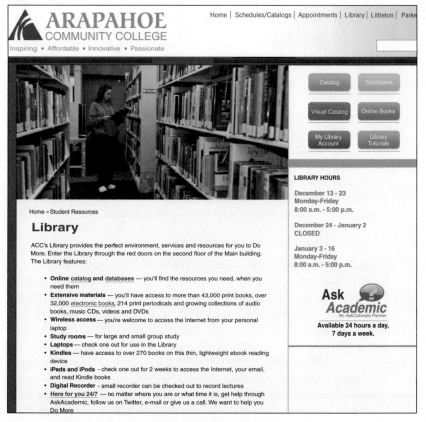

General databases include sources from a broad range of periodicals and books, both popular and scholarly. General databases are suitable for academic research projects. Just take care to focus on scholarly sources and well-regarded popular publications. Large libraries have many general databases. A common one is *Academic Search Premier.*

Specialized databases focus on specific subject areas or disciplines. They list books and articles published by and for expert readers. Some examples include *Art Abstracts, MLA International Bibliography, PsycINFO,* and *Business Abstracts.*

Each source in a DATABASE contains bibliographic information, including a title, author, date of publication, and publisher (in the case of books or reports) or periodical (in the case of articles). The entry might also provide a summary or a list of contents.

● **EXERCISE 22-1** Working either individually or as part of a group, access your library's Web site. List all the types of information available. In particular, list the indexes and databases you can search and the subject areas each one covers. Note whether any of the databases have full-text versions of articles. ●

22D How do I use search engines and databases?

Watch
the Video

Keywords (also called descriptors or identifiers) are your pathways to finding sources in databases, catalogs, and Web sites. Keywords are the main words in a source's title or words that an author or editor has identified as most important to its topic and content. Figure 22.2 shows three screens from a keyword search of *PsycINFO* on *déjà vu.* Andrei Gurov consulted this source while working on the paper that appears in section 25G.

You can search with a single keyword, but often that will generate far toow many or far too few hits. Combinations of keywords can solve both problems. You can use BOOLEAN EXPRESSIONS or ADVANCED SEARCHES.

22D.1 Using Boolean expressions

Using **Boolean expressions** means that you search a database or search engine by typing keyword combinations that narrow and refine your search. To combine keywords, use the words *AND, OR*, and *NOT* (or symbols that represent those words). Quick Box 22.5 (page 278) explains how to search with keywords more effectively.

22D.2 Using advanced searches

Advanced searches (sometimes called guided searches) allow you to search by entering information in a form. A typical search involves selecting a range of dates of publication (for example, after 2010 or between 1990 and 1995)

Figure 22.2 Keyword search of *déjà vu* in a database.

Keyword

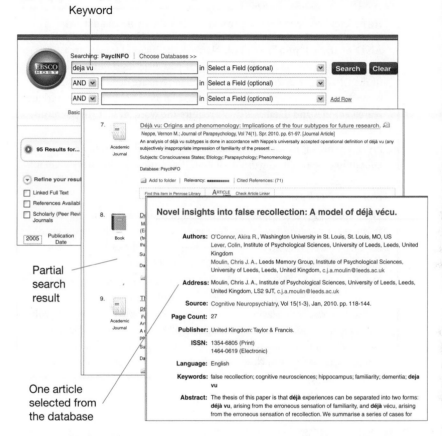

Partial
search
result

One article
selected from
the database

and specifying only a certain language (such as English) or format (such as books). Figure 22.3 (page 278) shows a search for sources that have *déjà vu* in their titles and use *false memory* as another keyword but are not about *crime*.

22E How do I use subject directories?

Subject directories provide an alternative to keyword searches. These directories are lists of topics (education, computing, entertainment, and so on) or resources and services (shopping, travel, and so on), with links to sources on them. Most search engines, and some library catalogs or databases, have one or more subject directories. In addition, there are independent subject directories. Some examples are *Educator's Reference Desk* (http://www.eduref.org), *Library of Congress* (http://www.loc.gov), and *Refdesk.com* (http://www.refdesk.com).

Quick Box 22.5

■ ■ ■ ■ ■ ■ ■ ■ ■ ■ ■

Refining keyword searches with Boolean expressions

AND or the + ("plus") symbol: Narrows the focus of your search because both keywords must be found. If you were researching the topic of the APA paper in 26I (how women characters are depicted in video games), try the expression *video games AND women AND characters*. Many search engines and databases don't require the word *AND* between terms. Figure 22.4 illustrates the results.

NOT or the – ("minus") symbol: Narrows a search by excluding texts containing the specified word or phrase. If you want to eliminate women playing games from your search, type *video games AND women AND characters NOT players*.

Or: Expands a search's boundaries by including more than one keyword. If you want to expand your search to include sources about women characters who are either heroes or villains in game, try the expression *video games AND women AND characters OR heroes OR villains*.

Quotation marks (" "): Direct the search to match your exact word order. For example, a search for *"role playing games"* will find sources that contain the exact phrase "role playing games." Also, if you search for *James Joyce* without using quotation marks, search engines will return all pages containing the words *James* and *Joyce* anywhere in the document; however, a search using "James Joyce" brings you closer to finding Web sites about the Irish writer.

Figure 22.3 Advanced keyword search.

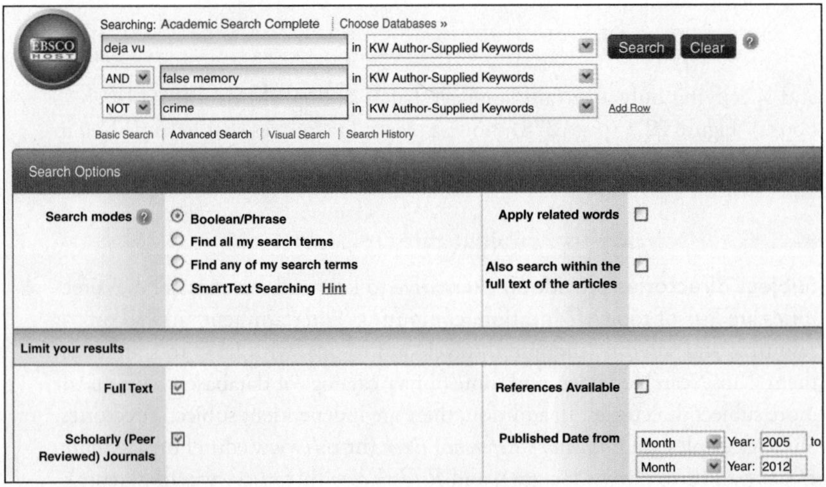

Figure 22.4 A Venn diagram showing overlaps among video games, women, and characters.

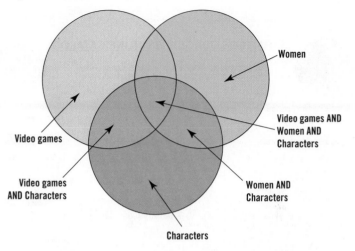

Clicking on a general category in a subject directory will take you to lists of increasingly specific categories. Eventually, you'll get a list of Web pages on the most specific subtopic you select.

22F How do I find books?

A library's **catalog**, which lists its holdings (its entire collection), exists as a computer database in almost every modern library. To find a book, you can search by author, by title, by subject, or by keyword. Figure 22.5 shows the home page for a typical **book catalog**, this one at the Library of Congress. Note that it allows you to search by title, author, subject, CALL NUMBER, or keyword; to search particular indexes; or to search using Boolean expressions.

Suppose a source recommends that you find a book by the author, Tim Wu, but you don't know its title. A screen on your library's computer will have a place for you to type *Wu, Tim* in a space for "author." (Usually, you enter last name, then first name, but first check which system your library uses.) If your library owns any books by Tim Wu, the computer will display their titles and other bibliographic information, such as the library call number. Then you can use the call number to request the book or to find it yourself. Figure 22.6 shows results from search for books by author Tim Wu.

Among the books you might find when searching for "Wu, Tim" is *The Master Switch: The Rise and Fall of Information Empires* (New York: Knopf, 2010. Print.). Suppose you know that book's title but not its author and want to see if your library owns a copy. Find the place to type in the title. In some

Figure 22.5 Library of Congress online catalog.

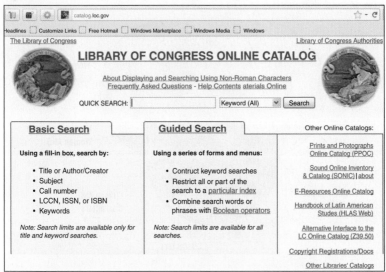

Figure 22.6 Results of an author search for Tim Wu.

systems, you don't type articles (*a, an, the*), so then you would type in only *"Master Switch Rise Fall Information Empires."*

Suppose, however, you don't know an author's name or a book title. You have only a research topic. In this case, you need to search by subject, using the terms listed in the *Library of Congress Subject Headings (LCSH)*. The *LCSH* is a multivolume catalog available in the reference section of every library. A version of the information in the *LCSH* is online at http://authorities.loc.gov.

Finally, you may wish to search by keyword in your library's holdings. You could find Wu's book using the keywords *information, media, technology*, and so on. A sample book catalog keyword search is shown in Figure 22.7.

Scan the results to identify promising sources. When you select a record (usually by clicking on it or on a box next to it), you encounter detailed information about the source, as we illustrate in Figure 22.8 (page 282).

Some libraries allow you to print out this information, send it to your e-mail account, download it, or use online software (see 21N). Whether you choose one of these options or copy the information directly into your WORKING BIBLIOGRAPHY, it's crucial to record the **call number** exactly as it appears, with all numbers, letters, and decimal points. The call number tells where the book is located in the library's stacks (storage shelves). If you're researching in

Figure 22.7 A catalog search using keywords.

	Keyword ⌄	(information) and (media) and (tec	Penro

Limited to: Year after 2009 *5 results found. sorted*

Save Marked Records   **Save All On Page**

Keywords (1-5 of 5)

1 Government secrecy [electronic resource] / edited by Susan Maret.
Government secrecy

Save ☐
Bingley, U.K. : Emerald. 2011.
1 online resource (xxx, 434 p.) : multiple formats, ill.
▸ Website

LOCATION	CALL #	STATUS
Internet	JF1525.S4 G68 2011eb	ONLINE

2 The Routledge Companion to Literature and Science [electronic resource].
The Routeledge Companion to Literature and Science

Save ☐
Clarke, Bruce.
Hoboken : Taylor & Francis, 2010
1 online resource (569 p.)
▸ Website

LOCATION	CALL #	STATUS
Internet	PN55.R68 2010eb	ONLINE

3 The master switch : the rise and fall of information empires / Tim Wu.
The master switch : the rise and fall of information empires

Save ☐
Wu, Tim.
New York : Alfred A. Knopf, 2010.
x, 366 p. : ill. ; 25 cm.

Figure 22.8 Detailed book record in a library catalog.

Start Over	Request It	Export	MARC Display	Return to Browse	Limit This

Author	Wu, Tim	Penrose/Music

Record 2 of 4
Record: Prev Next

Author	Wu, Tim.
Title	The master switch : the rise and fall of information empires / Tim Wu.
Publ Info	New York : Alfred A. Knopf, 2010.
Edition	[1st ed.]

LOCATION	CALL #	STATUS
Books Upper Level	HE7631 .W8 2010	DUE 06-21-11

Description	x, 366 p. : ill. ; 25 cm.
Note(s)	"This is a Borzoi book" --T.p. verso.
	Includes bibliographical references (p. [323]-354) and index.
Contents	The rise. The disruptive founder ; Radio dreams ; Mr. Vail is a big man ; The time is not ripe for feature films ; Centralize all radio activities ; The Paramount ideal -- Beneath the All-seeing Eye. The foreign attachment ; The legion of decency ; FM radio ; We now add sight to sound -- The rebels, the challengers, and the fall. The right kind of breakup ; The radicalism of the Internet revolution ; Nixon's cable ; Broken Bell ; Esperanto for machines -- Reborn without a soul. Turner does television ; Mass production of the spirit ; The return of AT&T -- The Internet against everyone. A surprising wreck ; Father and son ; The separations principle.
Summary	As Wu's sweeping history shows, each of the new media of the twentieth century- radio, telephone, television, and film- was born free and open. Each invited unrestricted use and enterprising experiment until some would-be mogul battled his way to total domination. Explaining how invention begets industry and industry begets empire- a progress often blessed by government, typically with stifling consequences for free expression and technical innovation alike- Wu identifies a time-honored pattern in the maneuvers of today's great information powers
Subject(s)	Telecommunication -- History.
	Show similar items
	Information technology -- History.
	Show similar items
	Mass media -- History.
	Show similar items
ISBN	9780307269935
	0307269930

This book is on the library's upper level, at the call number listed. However, the book is currently checked out.

a library with open stacks (shelves that are accessible without special permission), the call number leads you to the area in the library where all books on the same subject can be found.

A CALL NUMBER is especially crucial in a library or special collection with closed stacks, a library where you hand in a slip in at the call desk (or submit a request online) and wait for the book to arrive. Such libraries don't permit you to browse the stacks, so you have to rely entirely on the book catalog.

22F.1 Electronic books

You're probably familiar with electronic books, tablets, and readers like the Kindle, Nook, or iPad. Many books have electronic versions that you can access—and without paying, if you go through a library. Figure 22.9 shows one book found in a library catalog that's available only in an electronic format. Students at this school can log in to read the book online.

Google has scanned many books and put them on the Web, where you find them by searching Google Books. Even if you find a book you want online,

Figure 22.9 Book available only online.

Author	Clarke, Bruce.
Title	**The Routledge Companion to Literature and Science [electronic resource].**
Publ Info	Hoboken : Taylor & Francis, 2010.

The links below are for electronic versions of this publication:
Access online: Individual login with EBL required

LOCATION	CALL #	STATUS
Internet	PN55.R68 2010eb	ONLINE

Description	1 online resource (569 p.)
Series	Routledge Literature Companions.
	Routledge Literature Companions.
	Routledge Literature Companions.
Note	Book preview interface supplies PDF, image or read-aloud access. Adobe Digital Editions software required for book downloads.
	Mode of access: World Wide Web.
Note(S)	Description based upon print version of record.
Contents	BOOK COVER; TITLE; COPYRIGHT; CONTENTS; FIGURES; CONTRIBUTORS; PREFAE; PART I: LITERATURES AND SCIENCES; 1 AI AND ALIFE; 2 ALCHEMY; 3 BIOLOGY; 4 CHAOS AND COMPLEXITY THEORY; 5 CHEMISTRY; 6 CLIMATE SCIENCE; 7 COGNITIVE SCIENCE; 8 CYBERNETICS; 9 ECOLOGY; 10 EVOLUTION; 11 GENETICS; 12 GEOLOGY; 13 **INFORMATION** THEORY; 14 MATHEMATICS; 15 MEDICINE; 16 NANOTECHNOLOGY; 17 PHYSICS; 18 PSYCHOANALYSIS; 19 SYSTEMS THEORY; 20 THERMODYNAMICS; PART II: DISCIPLINARY AND THEORETICAL APPROACHES; 21 AGRICULTURAL STUDIES; 22 ANIMAL STUDES; 23 ART CONNECTIONS; 24 CULTURAL SCIENCE STUDIES; 25 DECONSTRUCTION

unless it's very old, only a portion of it will be available. If you're lucky, it will be the part you want; otherwise, you'll need to find the entire book through other means. Figure 22.10 shows the Google Books contents for *The Master Switch*.

Figure 22.10 Google Books contents for *The Master Switch*.

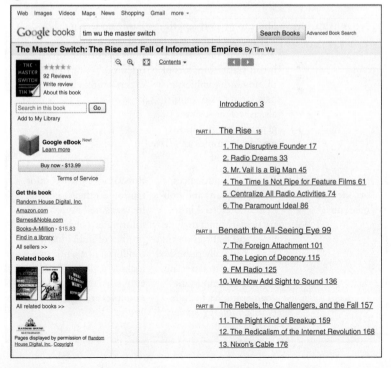

22G How do I find periodicals?

Periodicals are edited magazines, journals, and newspapers published periodically, that is, at set intervals. Periodicals used to appear only in print, but many now publish electronic versions or appear only online. You find periodicals by searching DATABASES (see 22C, 22D). Quick Box 22.6 describes several types of periodicals.

Quick Box 22.6

Types of periodicals

Type	Characteristics	Useful for
Journal	Scholarly articles written by experts for other experts; usually focus on one academic discipline; published relatively infrequently; examples are *College Composition and Communication* and *American Journal of Public Health*.	The most reliable expert research on a particular subject; detailed articles and extensive bibliographies that can point to other sources or experts; may also have book reviews
News magazines	Short to modest-length articles on current events or topics of interest to a broad readership; lots of photos and graphics; may have opinions or editorials, as well as reviews; generally are published weekly; examples are *Time* and *Newsweek*	Easily understandable and timely introductions to current topics; often can point to more expert sources, topics, and keywords
Special-interest or "lifestyle" magazines	Written for audiences (including fans and hobbyists) interested in a particular topic; include news and features on that topic; generally published monthly, with entertainment as an important goal; examples include *Outside, Rolling Stone, Wired*	Providing "how-to" information on their topics of focus, as well as technical information or in-depth profiles of individuals, products, or events; many include reviews related to emphasis; the more serious examples are well written and reliable

continued >>

Quick Box 22.6 (continued)

Type	Characteristics	Useful for
"Intellectual" or literary magazines	Publish relatively longer articles that provide in-depth analysis of issues, events, or people; may include creative work as well as nonfiction; aimed at a general, well-educated audience; usually published monthly; examples include *The Atlantic, Harper's, The New Yorker*	Learning about a topic in depth but in a way more accessible than scholarly journals; becoming aware of major controversies and positions; learning who experts are and what books or other sources have been published; reading arguments on topics
Trade magazines	Focus on particular businesses, industries, and trade groups; discuss new products, legislation, or events that will influence individuals or businesses in that area; examples include *National Hog Farmer, Sound and Video Contractor*	Specialized information focusing on applying information or research in particular settings; seeing how specific audiences or interest groups may respond to a particular position
Newspapers	Publish articles about current news, sports, and cultural events; contain several sections, including opinions and editorials, lifestyle, sports; most appear daily; examples are *The Washington Post, The DeWitt, Iowa, Observer*	Very current information; national newspapers (such as *The New York Times*) cover world events and frequently have analysis and commentary; local newspapers cover small happenings you likely won't find elsewhere; opinion sections and reviews are sources of ideas and positions

22G.1 Locating articles themselves

Databases help you find information about sources, but the important question is how do you get your hands on the source itself? Often you can find an online full-text version of the article to read, download, or print. A full-text version may be either in HTML format or PDF; the listing will tell you which one. If you have a choice, we recommend using the PDF version, which is easier to cite because it has the layout of a print article, including page numbers.

Sometimes, however, you need to find a printed copy of the periodical. Often the listing in the database will say whether your library owns a copy and what its call number is. Otherwise, you'll need to check if the periodical is listed in the library's CATALOG; search for the periodical name you want (for example, *American Literature* or *The Economist*).

Use the periodical's call number to find it in the library. To find the specific article you want, look for the issue in which the article you need appears. For advice on locating sources that you library doesn't own, see the Alert on page 289.

● **EXERCISE 22-2** Use two databases that are available through your library to conduct two searches for one or more of the following terms. (Alternatively, your instructor may suggest a different term or have you pursue a topic of your own choosing.)

Suggested terms for searching (with type of specialized database to consult in parentheses): memory (psychology); globalization (business, economics, sociology); cloning (biology); climate change (geology, geography, political science); obesity (medicine, psychology).

If possible, choose one general and one specialized database. Compile a brief report that compares the sources you generate. You might address questions like these: How many sources did each search turn up? Is there any overlap? What kinds of periodicals are represented in each database? What access does your library provide to the several sources you find most interesting in each search? ●

🛈 **Alert:** If you're generating lots of hits, restrict your search to the past year or two. ●

22H How do I use reference works?

Reference works include encyclopedias, almanacs, yearbooks, fact books, atlases, dictionaries, biographical reference works, and bibliographies. Reference works are the starting point for many college researchers—but they're no more than a starting point. *General* reference works provide information on a vast number of subjects, but without much depth. *Specialized* reference works provide information on selected topics, often for more expert or professional audiences.

22H.1 General reference works

General reference works help researchers identify useful keywords for subject headings and online catalog searches. In addition, they are excellent sources for finding examples and verifying facts.

Most widely used reference works are available in electronic versions. Check your library's Web site to see what's available online through a subscription the library has purchased. For example, you may find a subscription to the *Gale Virtual Reference Library*, which allows libraries to make up to 1,000 reference books available to users online. Alternatively, search the Web (for example, *Encyclopaedia Britannica* is at http://www.britannica.com). Be aware that often you have to pay a fee for works you don't access through the library.

GENERAL ENCYCLOPEDIAS

Articles in general scholarly encyclopedias, such as the *Encyclopaedia Britannica*, can give you helpful background information, the names of major experts in the field, and, often, a brief BIBLIOGRAPHY on the subject.

🔵 **Alert:** A Note on *Wikipedia*. *Wikipedia* is an unedited source that almost anyone can modify. The accuracy and quality of information it contains, therefore, must always be investigated further. Still, *Wikipedia* is often a possible starting place for some quick information on a topic. For example, Doug, like many professionals and even professors, will occasionally check *Wikipedia* to learn names, concepts, or basic information on a particular topic. But *Wikipedia* is only a starting place, a way to get oriented. You need to find other sources that serve you better for college-level research. As important, your ETHOS is weak when you use *Wikipedia* extensively. Your readers will suspect you haven't taken the time or responsibility to find more scholarly sources. You surely want to avoid that suspicion. We strongly recommend, then, that you use *Wikipedia* only to get some first impressions of a research topic, then find and use other, better recognized sources. ●

ALMANACS, YEARBOOKS, AND FACT BOOKS

Often available both in print and online, almanacs, yearbooks, and fact books are huge compilations of facts and figures. Examples include the *World Almanac, Facts on File*, and the annual *Statistical Abstract of the United States* (accessed online through http://www.census.gov).

ATLASES AND GAZETTEERS

Atlases (such as the *Times Atlas of the World*) contain maps of our planet's continents, seas, and skies. Gazetteers (such as the *Columbia Gazetteer of the World*) provide comprehensive geographical information on topography, climates, populations, migrations, natural resources, and so on.

DICTIONARIES

Dictionaries define words and terms. In addition to general dictionaries, specialized dictionaries exist in many academic disciplines.

BIOGRAPHICAL REFERENCE WORKS

Biographical reference books give brief factual information about famous people—their accomplishments along with pertinent events and dates in their lives. Biographical references include the *Who's Who* series and the *Dictionary of American Biography*.

BIBLIOGRAPHIES

Bibliographies are guides to sources on particular topics. They list books, articles, documents, films, and other resources and provide publication information so that you can find those sources. Annotated or critical bibliographies describe and evaluate the works that they list.

22H.2 Specialized reference works

Specialized reference works provide authoritative and specific information on selected topics, often for more expert researchers. These works are usually appropriate for college-level research because the information is more advanced and detailed.

Here are a few examples of specialized references:

Dictionary of American Biography

Encyclopedia of Banking and Finance

Encyclopedia of Chemistry

Encyclopedia of Religion

Encyclopedia of the Biological Sciences

International Encyclopedia of Film

New Grove Dictionary of Music and Musicians

Oxford Companion to the Theatre

22I How can I find images?

If you need or want to include images in a research paper, you have three options. A keyword search through the "Images" menu on Google or Yahoo! will generate links to images as they appear in sites and documents across the Internet. However, there are ethical and, sometimes, even legal concerns in using what you find this way (see 7E.1).

A good alternative to general Internet searches is to use a "stock photo" Web site. These are services like iStockphoto.com or GettyImages.com that have gathered thousands, even millions, of photographs, which you can browse by category or keyword. For a small fee you can purchase the use of an image from these sites. (There are a few "free" sites, too.)

Finally, your library may provide access to image archives or databases. Ask a librarian.

22J How do I find government documents?

Government publications are available in astounding variety. You can find information on laws and legal decisions, regulations, population, weather patterns, agriculture, national parks, education, and health, to name just a few topics. Most government documents are available online.

- The Government Printing Office maintains its searchable *Catalog of U.S. Government Publications* at http://www.gpoaccess.gov/index.html.

- THOMAS, a service of the Library of Congress, offers information about legislation at http://thomas.loc.gov/.

- A directory of all federal government sites that provide statistical information is at http://www.fedstats.gov.

- The LexisNexis database service provides access to a huge number of other governmental reports and documents. For example, the Congressional Information Service indexes all papers produced by congressional panels and committees.

🛈 **Alert:** Almost no library will contain every source that you need. However, many libraries are connected electronically to other libraries' book catalogs, giving you access to additional holdings. Often you or a librarian can request materials from other libraries through interlibrary loan (generally free of charge). ●

Complete the Chapter Exercises

23 Evaluating Sources

■ ■ ■ ■ ■ ■ ■ ■ ■ ■

Quick Points   You will learn to

➤ Evaluate sources (see Ch. 23).
➤ Find useful sources (see 23A–23F).

👁
Watch
the Video

Not all sources are created equal. We don't just mean the differences explained in Chapter 22 between books, PERIODICALS, and Web sites, or between scholarly and popular sources. Sources also differ in quality. Some present information that has been carefully gathered and checked. Others report information, even rumor, that is second- or third-hand and, worse, perhaps not even based in fact.

Some sources make claims that are accompanied by strong evidence and reasoning. Others make claims based only on opinion, or they use information illogically. Some are written by experts wanting to advance knowledge. Others are produced by people wanting to promote special interests however they can, even if it means ignoring data, oversimplifying issues, or overpromising results. Some sources have been reviewed by experts and published only after passing standards. Others appear without anyone judging their quality.

You don't want to conduct research and organize it for writing, only to have weak sources hurt your ETHOS and weaken your paper. Therefore, you want to evaluate each source you find by asking the questions in Quick Box 23.1.

Quick Box 23.1

■ ■ ■ ■ ■ ■ ■ ■ ■ ■ ■

Five questions for evaluating sources

1. How did you find the source? (See 23A.)
2. Is the publisher authoritative? (See 23B.)
3. Is the author qualified to write about the topic? (See 23C.)
4. Does the source have sufficient and credible evidence? (See 23D.)
5. Does the source pass other critical thinking tests? (See 23E.)

23A How did you find the source?

Sources that you find through DATABASES, especially databases you access through a library Web site (see 22B), are more likely to be good than sources found through a general Google search. If a source is in a database, it has passed a level of review. It comes from a book or periodical that has been edited and checked for quality. Certainly you can find useful sources through a general search, but you'll have to work harder to sort strong ones from weak.

For example, suppose you want to research the safety of vaccines. (We illustrate the range of options in Figure 23.1 (pages 292–293), where a student has done four different searches.) A Google search will produce thousands of sources. Some of them will be reliable; many will not. If, instead, you search a library database like Academic Search Premier, you'll still find hundreds of sources, but these will mainly be of higher quality. The most authoritative sources will come from a college library's CATALOG or a scholarly database that specializes in a specific field, such as Medlines, which is created for physicians, researchers, and other medical professionals.

23B Is the publisher authoritative?

The publisher is the company or group ultimately responsible for a book, periodical, or Web site. Authoritative publishers produce journals, respected magazines and newspapers, and books from university and other major presses. Professional organizations sponsor authoritative Web sites.

Figure 23.1 Four searches with less to more reliable results.

A. Least Reliable:
A general Google search

A site that expresses the strong opinion that doctors cause autism. You'd have to check this one carefully.

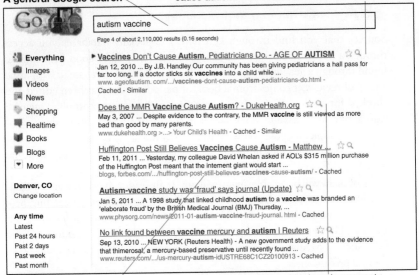

Blogs can have opinions unsupported by facts. Check carefully.

The name and the .org domain suggests that it might be associated with Duke University.

B. More Reliable:
A Google Scholar Search

Sources on this page come from journals in the field, which are edited and written by experts.

Full text versions show that these are articles, not Web sites.

The sources are somewhat old, however, for medical research.

C. Also Reliable: A search using a common college library database

Database includes popular sources like newspaper articles, which will be easier to understand.

Database also includes scholarly sources like journal articles. These PRIMARY SOURCES will have most authoritative research but can sometimes be difficult.

D. Expert: A search using a database designed for experts in a field

Short descriptions provide some information about article contents.

All articles in this database come from scholarly journals, and many report research.

Is the publisher authoritative?

Reliable sources are . . .	Questionable sources are . . .
• **From reputable publishers.** Generally, encyclopedias, textbooks, and academic journals (*Journal of Counseling and Development*) are authoritative. Books from university and other established presses are authoritative. Reliable sources are published in major newspapers (*The Washington Post*); in general-readership magazines (*Time, Harpers*); and by textbook publishers such as Pearson. See Figure 23.2.	• **From special-interest groups.** Some groups exist only to advance a narrow interest or political viewpoint. Examples would be a group existing only to legalize marijuana or one to stop all immigration. Special-interest groups might publish useful sources, but you'll want to check their facts and reasoning. Ask, "Why does the group exist?" Be sure to question its motives, especially if it asks you to take a specific action, such as donate money. See if materials published by the group are included in scholarly databases, and apply other tests listed in this chapter.
• **Web sites from educational, not-for-profit, or government organizations.** One sign is an Internet address ending in *.edu, .gov*, or a country abbreviation such as *.ca* or *.uk*. Web sites from professional associations (such as the National Council of Teachers of English or The American Medical Association) are reliable. If you don't recognize an organization, you'll want to investigate how long it has existed, whether it is not-for-profit, who its members and leaders are, and so on.	• **Web sites from commercial enterprises** that end in *.com*. These sites may or may not provide evidence or list sources for claims they make. If they fail to do so, or if the evidence and sources seem weak, don't use them. Be sure the Web site is not only a front for some money-making enterprise. See Figure 23.3.
• **Direct online versions of authoritative print sources.** Many journals, newspapers, and book publishers release online versions of print publications. Online versions of authoritative publications are reliable.	• **Secondhand excerpts, quotations, and references.** Quoted or summarized materials may have been edited in a biased or inaccurate manner. Check the original. Figure 23.4 illustrates a problem that can occur with secondhand materials.

Figure 23.2 A commercial (nonscholarly) book and a scholarly book.

Commercial Book

A self-help book that gives diet and relationship advice and promises results. The publisher also sponsors a commercial Web site focusing on spin-off products. This is not a scholarly source.

McIntire, Marilyn. *Love Yourself Thin!* Ankeny, IA: Maddie, 2012. Print.

Scholarly Book

A scholarly book that reports findings from a research study of body image and relationships among young college graduates. The publisher is a university press.

Neufeld, Sarah. *Body Image, Relationships, and the Influence of Popular Culture.* Evergreen, CO: Evans UP, 2012. Print.

Figure 23.3 An authoritative Web site and a questionable Web site.

An authoritative Web site

A .gov URL signals government sponsorship.

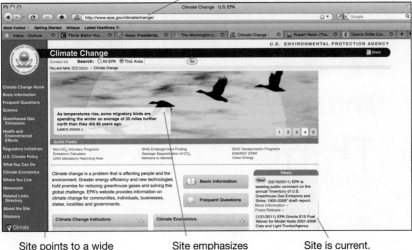

Site points to a wide range of information.

Site emphasizes facts.

Site is current.

A questionable Web site

A .com URL means you should check the nature and motives of the group.

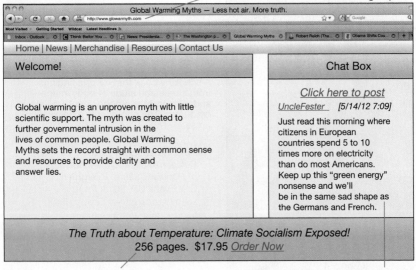

Advertising.

Chat box will contain information that hasn't been reviewed.

Note: Site might have worthy information, but it needs checking.

Figure 23.4 A section from an original article and a misused quotation from that article.

THURSDAY, MARCH 10, 2011   SEARCH OUR SITE

the *Atlantic*

POLITICS | BUSINESS | CULTURE | INTERNATIONAL |

APRIL 2011 ATLANTIC MAGAZINE

At an individual level, I think the "distracted Americans" scare will pass. Either people who manage to unplug, focus, and fully direct their attention will have an advantage over those constantly checking Facebook and their smart phone, in which case they'll earn more money, get into better colleges, start more successful companies, and win more Nobel Prizes. Or they won't, in which case distraction will be a trait of modern life but not necessarily a defect. At the level of national politics, America is badly distracted, but that problem long predates Facebook and requires more than a media solution.

Fallows, James. "Learning to Love the (Shallow, Divisive, Unreliable) New Media." *The Atlantic,* April 2011. Web. 10 Mar. 2011.

Comment on original: In the original full article from *The Atlantic*, a serious magazine for general readers, James Fallows agrees that Americans are distracted when it comes to politics, but he does not blame the Internet for that situation.

CIVILIZATION
The Truth about Our Declining World
About / Links / Campaigns / Donations

James Fallows complains about the effects of the internet on democracy when he says that, "At the level of national politics, America is badly distracted."

Comment on misused quotation: The Civilization Web site misrepresents Fallows. By using only part of his quotation, it makes him express exactly the opposite of what he actually wrote. It would be a serious mistake to quote this site.

23C   Is the author qualified to write about the topic?

Anyone can express an opinion or argue a course of action, but writers worth quoting or summarizing have knowledge and expertise about their topics. Often, their credentials appear in an introduction, at the bottom of the first page, or at the end of an article. Look for an "About the Author" statement in a book; a short biography on a Web site; or a "Contributors" note (see Figure 23.5). Sometimes, however, you might need to do a little investigating to learn about the author.

ESOL Tip: The definition of "authority" can differ across cultures. However, in the United States, a source must meet specific criteria to be considered authoritative. It must appear in a scholarly book or journal; its author must have a degree, title, or license; or other authorities must seek his or her knowledge. A source is not reliable simply because the author or speaker is an influential or well-known member of the community, claims to have knowledge about a topic, or publishes material in print or online.

Figure 23.5 An author with scholarly credentials and an author without.

Start Loving Life!

Hi! I'm **Marilyn McIntire**, motivational speaker, fitness guru, relationship coach, and author. My life has been an astonishing adventure, and yours can be, too. Let's walk this journey together! Check me out whenever you need inspiration, advice, and a good laugh. —Rainbow joys, Marilyn

If you were writing an academic paper on dieting and evaluating the two books in Figure 23.2 (page 295), the credentials of Sarah Neufeld would be much more credible. (Marilyn McIntire's credentials would be suitable for other purposes, perhaps, but not for an academic paper.)

Sarah Neufeld

Psychology Department Chair

Dr. Sarah Neufeld, Professor of Psychology at Evans University, was named chair of the department in 2011. She joined the faculty after receiving her Ph.D. from New York University in 1998 and has published over 35 articles in her area of research: the effects of popular culture on self-esteem and interpersonal behavior.

Is the author qualified to write about the topic?

Reliable sources are . . .	Questionable sources are . . .
• **From expert authors.** Experts have degrees or credentials in their field. Biographical material in the source may list these credentials. If in doubt, look up the author in a biographical dictionary, search online for a resume or bio, or search a database. Check if the author's name appears in other reliable sources; do others cite him or her? Check whether there is contact information for questions or comments.	• **From authors with fuzzy credentials.** A warning sign should flash when you can't identify who has produced a source. Discussion threads, anonymous blogs, and similar online postings are questionable when they don't give qualifying information. Check that listed credentials fit the topic. Just because someone has a graduate degree in history, for example, doesn't qualify him or her to give medical advice.

23D Does the source have sufficient and accurate evidence?

If an author expresses a point of view but offers little evidence to back up that position, reject the source. See Figure 23.6 for an example of how sources use evidence.

Figure 23.6 Source that cites evidence and source that does not.

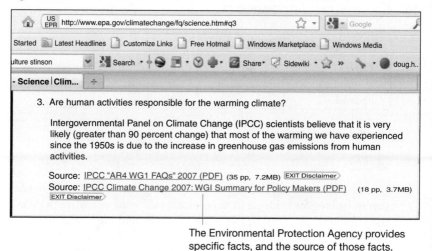

3. Are human activities responsible for the warming climate?

Intergovernmental Panel on Climate Change (IPCC) scientists believe that it is very likely (greater than 90 percent change) that most of the warming we have experienced since the 1950s is due to the increase in greenhouse gas emissions from human activities.

Source: IPCC "AR4 WG1 FAQs" 2007 (PDF) (35 pp, 7.2MB) EXIT Disclaimer
Source: IPCC Climate Change 2007: WGI Summary for Policy Makers (PDF) (18 pp, 3.7MB)
EXIT Disclaimer

The Environmental Protection Agency provides specific facts, and the source of those facts.

RedDawn [6/13/2012]
So it's been hot and the global warming clones are screaming again. Big deal. many scientists show that theres no proof we're making the world warmer, just google it if you want to know the truth. If the temperatures increasing, its because of natural causes not pollution, smoke, etc. Politicians wont give money to real scientists to prove it. Common sense, people!

This posting, from a blog, makes claims but provides no evidence, simply telling readers to "just google it."

The source has some proofreading errors, substitutes name-calling for reasoning, and has other logical fallacies.

Does the source have sufficient and accurate evidence?

Reliable sources are . . .	Questionable sources are . . .
• **Well supported with evidence.** The writer cites clear and plentiful facts and reasons to support assertions.	• **Unsupported or biased.** They carry assertions that have little or no supporting evidence.
• **Factually accurate**. Listed are the sources for statistics, quotations, and other information. You (or anyone else) could look them up to check their accuracy.	• **Factually questionable.** Although they may include statistics or other information, they fail to identify who generated them or how. You have no way to check facts because the writer failed to provide this information.

(*continued*)

Reliable sources are . . .	Questionable sources are . . .
• **Current.** Information is recent or, in the case of Web sites, regularly updated.	• **Outdated.** You don't want to cite 20-year-old medical advice, for example.

23E Does the source pass other critical thinking tests?

Use CRITICAL THINKING skills when you evaluate a source (see Ch. 3). In addition to looking for evidence in the source, you'll want to analyze the TONE, check for BIAS, and consider the ASSUMPTIONS behind the source. You'll certainly want to check for LOGICAL FALLACIES (see Ch. 3). Figure 23.7 shows a Web site with a fairly balanced tone and one that is more biased.

Figure 23.7 A source with balanced tone and a source with biased tone.

Balanced tone

The writer acknowledges there is a difference of opinion.

The writer summarizes the point of view with which he or she disagrees.

There is a slight element of bias in saying that people have an ideology.

Biased tone

The writer relies on name-calling rather than acknowledging others.

The comparison to "vampires avoid silver bullets" gets readers' attention, but it's hardly respectful.

At least the writer promises to send readers to a "rigorous but accessible" informational site. You would have to evaluate that site to be sure.

Does the source pass other critical thinking tests?

Reliable sources are . . .	Questionable sources are . . .
• **Balanced in tone.** The author is respectful of others and creates a sense of fairness.	• **Biased in tone.** Some warning signs of biased tone are name-calling, sarcasm, stereotyping, or absolute assertions about matters that are open to interpretation.
• **Balanced in treatment.** Even if they advocate a particular position, credible sources acknowledge different viewpoints. For example, they summarize contradictory evidence.	• **One-sided.** Sources that omit any mention or fair summary of competing views or information may be unreliable, especially if they openly ridicule competing positions.
• **Logical.** The source draws fair conclusions from evidence. The reasoning is clear.	• **Full of logical fallacies.** See section 31.
• **Well-edited.** The source has been proofread and is free of grammatical errors.	• **Marked by errors.** Beware if the source has typos or sloppy errors.

23F How do strategies for evaluating sources work together?

The most important quality of any reliable source is to be based on facts, evidence, and clear reasoning. If you're using sources that you find through library databases, from authoritative publishers or groups, and from expert writers, then the sources are likely to be reliable. You still need to think critically about them. On the other hand, if you're using sources that you find through general searches, from questionable publishers or organizations, or from writers with unclear expertise, then you have to work hard. You have to make sure that the facts, evidence, and reasoning are all solid.

24 Drafting and Revising a Research Paper

■ ■ ■ ■ ■ ■ ■ ■ ■

Quick Points   You will learn to

➤ Write and revise a research paper (see following sections).

24A How does the writing process apply to research papers?

DRAFTING and REVISING a research paper is like drafting and revising any piece of writing (see Ch. 5). However, you need extra time to write a research paper because you need to demonstrate that:

- You've followed the steps of the research process (see Chs. 21–22).
- You've evaluated your SOURCES (see Ch. 23).
- You haven't PLAGIARIZED (see Ch. 19).
- You've correctly employed QUOTATIONS, PARAPHRASES, and SUMMARIES (see Ch. 18).
- You've moved beyond summary to SYNTHESIS so that your sources are interwoven with each other and with your own thinking, not merely listed one by one (see 18F–18L).
- You've used DOCUMENTATION accurately. (For MLA STYLE, see Chapter 25; for APA STYLE, see Chapter 26; for other documentation styles, see Chapter 27.)

24B How do I draft a thesis statement for a research paper?

A THESIS STATEMENT in a research paper sets out the central theme, which you need to sustain throughout the paper. As with any piece of writing, your research paper must fulfill the promise of its thesis statement. Remember that a good thesis statement makes an assertion that conveys your point of view about your topic and foreshadows the content of your paper.

One way to start your thesis statement is to try to convert your RESEARCH QUESTION into a preliminary thesis statement. Another way is to ask yourself whether the material you've gathered from sources can effectively support your thesis statement. If your answer is "no," you want to revise your thesis statement, conduct further research, or do both.

Here are examples of subjects narrowed to topics, focused into research questions, and then cast as thesis statements.

SUBJECT	***nonverbal communication***
TOPIC	Personal space
RESEARCH QUESTION	How do standards for personal space differ among cultures?
INFORMATIVE THESIS STATEMENT	Everyone has expectations concerning the use of personal space, but accepted distances for that space are determined by each person's culture.
PERSUASIVE THESIS STATEMENT	To prevent intercultural misunderstandings, people must be aware of cultural differences in standards for personal space.
SUBJECT	***computers***
TOPIC	artificial intelligence
RESEARCH QUESTION	How close are researchers to developing artificial intelligence in computers?
INFORMATIVE THESIS STATEMENT	Scientists disagree about whether computers need emotions to have artificial intelligence.
PERSUASIVE THESIS STATEMENT	Because emotions play a strong role in human intelligence, computers must have emotions before they can truly have artificial intelligence.

Andrei Gurov (whose research paper appears in section 25G) revised his preliminary thesis statement twice before he felt that it expressed the point he wanted to make. Andrei also took the key step of checking that he would be able to support it sufficiently.

FIRST PRELIMINARY THESIS STATEMENT

Déjà vu can be explained by a variety of scientific theories.

Andrei realized that this draft thesis would lead to a paper that would merely list, paragraph by paragraph, each theory, and that the paper would lack synthesis.

SECOND PRELIMINARY THESIS STATEMENT

Many people believe feelings of déjà vu have mysterious origins, but science has shown this is not true.

Andrei liked this statement better because it began to get at the complexity of the topic, but he wanted to work on it more because he felt the second part was too general.

FINAL THESIS STATEMENT

Although a few people today still prefer to believe that feelings of déjà vu have mysterious or supernatural origins, recent research in cognitive psychology and the neurosciences has shed much rational light on the phenomenon.

24C How do I outline a research paper?

Some, though not all, instructors require an OUTLINE of your research paper, either before you hand in the paper or along with the paper (see 5G). In such cases, your instructor is probably expecting you to be working from an outline as you write your drafts. Your research log can come in handy when you group ideas in an outline, especially for a first draft of your paper. To see a topic outline of Andrei Gurov's research paper, turn to section 25G.

24D How do I draft a research paper?

Watch the Video

You need to expect to write several drafts of your research paper. The first draft is a chance to discover new insights and fresh connections. Then use your first draft to revise into more developed and polished further drafts. Here are some ways to write your first draft.

- **Some researchers work from a source map.** They organize their notes into topics and determine the relationship between sources.

- **Some researchers work with their notes at hand.** They organize CONTENT NOTES into broad categories by creating a separate group for each topic. Each category then becomes a section of the first draft. This method often reveals any gaps in information that call for additional research. Also, you may discover that some of your research doesn't fit your topic or thesis statement. If so, put it aside; it might be useful in a later draft.

- **Some writers generate a list of questions that their paper needs to address.** Then they answer each question, one at a time, looking for the content notes that will help them. For example, writing on the topic of déjà vu, some possible questions might be, "What is déjà vu? What are possible explanations for it? Are there any benefits or dangers of déjà vu?" Generating and answering questions can be a very useful way of turning a mass of information into manageable groupings.

- **Some researchers stop at various points and use FREEWRITING to get their ideas into words.** Researchers who use this method say that it helps them to recognize when they need to adjust their research question or change their search. After a number of rounds of researching and freewriting, these researchers find that they can write their complete first draft relatively easily.

- **Some researchers review their sources and create an OUTLINE before drafting (see 5G).** Some find a FORMAL OUTLINE helpful, whereas others use a less formal approach.
- **Some researchers use a frame to guide their drafting (see 24E).**

24E What are frames for research papers?

Although all research papers seek to answer a question, some are mainly informative, others are mainly persuasive, and still others are a mix. We offer two possible frames for research papers in this section.

Frame for an Informative Research Paper

Introductory paragraph(s)

- **Establish why your topic is important or interesting.** Consider, "Why does this matter? To whom does this matter? What might happen if we resolve this issue one way versus another?"
- **Your THESIS STATEMENT needs to make clear** how you will answer your research question.

Body paragraph(s): background information

- **Provide the history or background of your topic.** Why is it a problem or concern at this time?

Body paragraphs: Explanations of topics

- **Discuss the main subtopics** of your general topic in a paragraph with a clear TOPIC SENTENCE.
- **If a subtopic is lengthy**, it may require more than one paragraph.

Body Paragraphs: Complications

- **Discuss what is controversial or in dispute.** What do people disagree about? Why? Do they dispute facts? Interpretations? Causes? Effects or implications? Solutions?

Watch the Video

Conclusion

- **Wrap up your topic.** What questions or issues remain? What are areas for further research or investigation? What might readers do with this information?

Works Cited or References

- **If you are using MLA STYLE,** include a list of Works Cited (see Ch. 25); if you are using APA style, include a References list (see Ch. 26).

For an example of an informative research paper, see the MLA STYLE research paper in section 25G.

Frame for an Argumentative Research Paper

Introductory paragraph(s)

- **Establish why your topic is important or interesting.** Consider, "Why does this matter? To whom does this matter? What might happen if we resolve this issue one way versus another?"
- **Your THESIS STATEMENT needs to make clear** how you will answer your research question.

Body paragraph(s): background information

- **Provide the history or background of your topic.** Why is it a problem or concern at this time?

Body paragraph(s): Agreement among sources

- **Discuss points of agreement.** What is uncontroversial or widely accepted?
- **Depending on the size or nature of the topic,** this may be one or several paragraphs.

Body paragraph(s): Complications

- **Discuss what is controversial or in dispute.** What do people disagree about? Why? Do they dispute facts? Interpretations? Causes? Effects or implications? Solutions?

Body paragraph(s): Arguments

- **Present your arguments.** What reasons do you have for your position or proposed action? State each reason as a TOPIC SENTENCE, and provide evidence and support in the paragraph.
- **If you have extensive support** for a particular reason, you might need more than one paragraph.

Conclusion

- **Wrap up your argument.** Why is your position or proposal best? What actions should follow?

Works Cited or References

- **If you are using MLA STYLE,** include a list of Works Cited (see Ch. 25); if you are using APA style, include a References list (see Ch. 26).

For an example of an argumentative research paper in MLA STYLE, see Chapter 15. For an example of an argumentative research paper in APA STYLE, see section 26I.

24F How do I revise a research paper?

To revise your research paper, before you write each new draft, read your previous draft with a sharp eye. Assess all of the features listed in Quick Box 24.1. For best results, take a break for a few days (or at least a few hours) before beginning this process. Consider asking a few people you respect to read and react to a draft (see 9D).

Quick Box 24.1 ■ ■ ■ ■ ■ ■ ■ ■ ■ ■

Revision checklist for a research paper

If the answer to a question in this checklist is no, you need to revise. The section numbers in parentheses tell you where to find helpful information.

WRITING

✓ Does your introductory paragraph lead effectively into the material (see 6C)?

✓ Have you met the basic requirements for a written thesis statement (see 5F)?

✓ Do your thesis statement and the content of your paper address your research question(s) (see 24B)?

✓ Have you developed effective body paragraphs (see 6F)?

✓ Do your ideas follow sensibly and logically within each paragraph and from one paragraph to the next (see 6G)?

✓ Does the concluding paragraph end your paper effectively (see 6J)?

✓ Does your paper satisfy a critical thinker (see Ch. 3)?

RESEARCH

✓ Have you fully answered your research question (see 21F)?

✓ Have you evaluated the quality of your sources? Do you have the kinds of sources that are appropriate for academic writing (see Ch. 23)?

✓ Have you used quotations, paraphrases, and summaries well (see Ch. 19)?

✓ Have you integrated your source material well without plagiarizing (see Chs. 18 and 20)?

One key to revising any research paper is to examine carefully the evidence you've included. **Evidence** consists of facts, statistics, expert studies and opinions, examples, and stories. Use RENNS (see 6F) to develop paragraphs more fully. Identify each of the points you have made in your paper, including your THESIS STATEMENT and all your subpoints. Then ask the following questions.

- **Is the evidence sufficient?** To be sufficient, evidence can't be thin or trivial. As a rule, the more evidence you present, the more convincing your thesis will be to readers.

- **Is the evidence representative?** Representative evidence is customary and normal, not based on exceptions.

- **Is the evidence relevant?** Relevant evidence relates directly to your thesis or topic sentence. It never introduces unrelated material.

- **Is the evidence accurate?** Accurate evidence is correct, complete, and up to date. It comes from a reliable source. Equally important, you present it honestly, without distorting or misrepresenting it.

- **Is the evidence reasonable?** Reasonable evidence is not phrased in extreme language and avoids sweeping generalizations. Reasonable evidence is free of LOGICAL FALLACIES (see 3I).

24G How do I edit and format a research paper?

View the Model Document

As with every paper, you'll want to make sure that there are no errors in grammar, punctuation, or mechanics. You'll want to check your style and tone. Research papers have additional requirements in documentation, citation, and format. Quick Box 24.2 lists questions to ask.

Quick Box 24.2   ■ ■ ■ ■ ■ ■ ■ ■ ■ ■

Editing and formatting checklist for a research paper

✓ Is the paper free of errors in grammar, punctuation, and mechanics?

✓ Are your style and tone effective?

✓ Have you used the correct format in your parenthetical references (see 25A or 26A)?

✓ Does each of your parenthetical references tie into an item in your Works Cited list (MLA STYLE) or References list (APA STYLE) at the end of your paper or follow CM or CSE styles (see Ch. 25, 26, or 27)?

✓ Does the paper exactly match the format you've been assigned to follow? Check margins, spacing, title, headings, page numbers, font, and so on (see 25F or 26F).

MLA Documentation with Case Study

■ ■ ■ ■ ■ ■ ■ ■ ■

Quick Points You will learn to

➤ Use MLA in-text parenthetical documentation (see 25B and 25C).
➤ Create an MLA Works Cited page (see 25D and 25E).
➤ Format your paper according to MLA guidelines (see 25F).

25A What is MLA documentation style?

A DOCUMENTATION STYLE* is a standard format that writers use to tell readers what SOURCES they used and how readers can locate them. Different disciplines follow different documentation styles. The one most frequently used in the humanities is from the Modern Language Association (MLA).

MLA style requires writers to document their sources in two connected, equally important ways.

1. Within the body of the paper, you need to use parenthetical documentation, as described in sections 25B and 25C.

2. At the end of the paper, you need to provide a list of the sources you used in your paper. This list is called "Works Cited," as described in 25D and 25E.

The guidelines and examples in this chapter are based on the Seventh Edition of *The MLA Handbook for Writers of Research Papers* (2009), which is the most current edition. If you need more information regarding MLA STYLE updates, check http://www.mla.org. See Quick Box 25.1 on pages 317–320 for more guidance on following these requirements.

25B What is MLA in-text parenthetical documentation?

MLA-style **parenthetical documentation** (also called **in-text citations**) places source information in parentheses within the sentences of your research papers. This information—given each time you SUMMARIZE, PARAPHRASE, or

---

* Words printed in SMALL CAPITAL LETTERS are discussed elsewhere in the text and are defined in the Terms Glossary at the back of the book.

use a QUOTATION from source materials—signals materials used from sources and enables readers to find the originals. (See Chapter 18 for information on how to quote, paraphrase, and summarize.)

Author name cited in text; page number cited in parentheses If you include an author's name (or, if none, the title of the work) in the sentence to introduce your source material, you include in parentheses only the page number where you found the material:

> According to Brent Staples, IQ tests give scientists little insight into intelligence (293).

For readability and good writing technique, try to introduce the names of authors (or titles of sources) in your own sentences.

Author name and page number cited in parentheses If you don't include the author's name in your sentence, you need to insert it in the parentheses, before the page number. Use no punctuation between the author's name and the page number:

> IQ tests give scientists little insight into intelligence (Staples 293).

25B.1 Placement of parenthetical reference

When possible, position a parenthetical reference at the end of the quotation, summary, or paraphrase it refers to. The best position is at the end of a sentence, unless that would place it too far from the source's material. When you do place the parenthetical reference at the end of a sentence, insert it before the sentence-ending period.

When you cite a quotation enclosed in quotation marks, place the parenthetical information after the closing quotation mark but before sentence-ending punctuation.

> Coleman summarizes research that shows that "the number, rate, and direction of time-zone changes are the critical factors in determining the extent and degree of jet lag symptoms" (67).

25B.2 Block quotations: longer than four lines

The one exception to the rule of putting parenthetical information before sentence-ending punctuation concerns quotations that you set off in block style, meaning one inch from the left margin. (MLA requires that quotations longer than four typed lines be handled this way.) For block quotations, put the parenthetical reference after the period.

Bruce Sterling worries that people are pursuing less conventional medical treatments, and not always for good reasons:

> Medical tourism is already in full swing. Thailand is the golden shore for wealthy, sickly Asians and Australians. Fashionable Europeans head to South Africa for embarrassing plastic surgery. Crowds of scrip-waving Americans buy prescription drugs in Canada and Mexico. (92)

If you're quoting part of a paragraph or one complete paragraph, don't indent the first line of quoted words any extra space beyond the one inch of the entire block. But if you quote more than one paragraph, indent the first line of each paragraph—including the first if it's a complete paragraph from the source—an additional quarter inch.

25C What are examples of MLA parenthetical citations?

The directory at the beginning of this tab corresponds to the numbered examples in this section. Most of these examples show the author's name or the title included in the parenthetical citation, but remember that it's usually more effective to include that information in your sentence.

1. One Author

Give an author's name as it appears on the source: for a book, on the title page; for an article, directly below the title or at the end of the article.

> IQ tests give scientists little insight into intelligence (Staples 293).

2. Two or Three Authors

Give the names in the same order as in the source. Spell out *and*. For three authors, use commas to separate the authors' names.

> As children get older, they begin to express several different kinds of intelligence (Todd and Taylor 23).

> Another measure of emotional intelligence is the success of inter- and intrapersonal relationships (Voigt, Dees, and Prigoff 14).

3. More Than Three Authors

If your source has more than three authors, you can name them all or use the first author's name only, followed by *et al.*, either in a parenthetical reference or in your sentence. *Et al.* is an abbreviation of the Latin *et alii*, meaning "and others." Don't underline or italicize *et al.* Note that no period follows *et*, but one follows *al.*

> Emotional security varies, depending on the circumstances of the social interaction (Carter et al. 158).

4. More Than One Source by an Author

When you use two or more sources by the same author, include the title of the individual source in each citation. In parenthetical citations, you can use a shortened version of the title. (The Works Cited listing requires the whole title.) For example, in a paper using two of Howard Gardner's works, *Frames of Mind: The Theory of Multiple Intelligences* and "Reflections on Multiple Intelligences: Myths and Messages," use *Frames* and "Reflections," respectively. In shortening titles be sure they aren't ambiguous to readers, and always start with the word by which the work is alphabetized in your WORKS CITED list. Separate the author's name and the title with a comma, but don't use punctuation between the title and page number.

> Although it seems straightforward to think of multiple intelligences as multiple approaches to learning (Gardner, *Frames* 60–61), an intelligence is not a learning style (Gardner, "Reflections" 202–03).

When you incorporate the title into your own sentences, use the full title, though you can omit a subtitle. After the first mention, you can shorten the title.

5. Two or More Authors with the Same Last Name

Use each author's first initial and full last name in each parenthetical citation. If both authors have the same first initial, use the full first name in all instances.

> According to Anne Cates, psychologists can predict how empathetic an adult will be from his or her behavior at age two (41), but other researchers disagree (T. Cates 171).

6. Group or Corporate Author

When a corporation or other group is named as the author of a source you want to cite, use the corporate name the same way you would an author's name.

> A five-year study shows that these tests are usually unreliable (Boston Women's Health Collective 11).

7. Work Cited by Title

If no author is named, use only the title. If the title is long, shorten it. Here's an in-text citation for an article titled "Are You a Day or Night Person?"

> The "morning lark" and "night owl" descriptions typically are used to categorize the human extremes ("Are You" 11).

8. Multivolume Work

If you use more than one volume of a multivolume work, include the relevant volume number in each citation. Separate the volume number and page number with a colon followed by a space.

Although Amazon forest dwellers had been exposed to these viruses by 1900 (Rand 3: 202), Borneo forest dwellers escaped them until the 1960s (Rand 1: 543).

9. Novel, Play, Short Story, or Poem

Literary works frequently appear in different editions. When you cite material from literary works, provide the part, chapter, act, scene, canto, stanza, or line numbers. This usually helps readers locate what you're referring to more easily than do page numbers alone. Unless your instructor tells you not to, use arabic numerals for these references, even if the literary work uses roman numerals. For novels that use part and/or chapter numbers, include them after page numbers. Use a semicolon after the page number but a comma to separate a part from a chapter.

> Flannery O'Connor describes one character in *The Violent Bear It Away* as "divided in two—a violent and a rational self" (139; pt. 2, ch. 6).

For plays that use them, give act, scene, and line numbers. Use periods between these numbers. For short stories, use page numbers.

> Among the most quoted of Shakespeare's lines is Hamlet's soliloquy beginning "To be, or not to be: that is the question" (3.1.56).

> The old man in John Collier's "The Chaser" says about his potions, "I don't deal in laxatives and teething mixtures . . ." (79).

For poems and songs, give canto, stanza, and/or line numbers. Use periods between these numbers.

> In "To Autumn," Keats's most melancholy image occurs in the lines "Then in a wailful choir the small gnats mourn / Among the river swallows" (3.27–28).

10. Bible or Sacred Text

Give the title of the edition you're using, the book (in the case of the Bible), and the chapter and verse. Spell out the names of books in sentences, but use abbreviations in parenthetical references.

> He would certainly benefit from the advice in Ephesians to "get rid of all bitterness, rage, and anger" (*New International Version Bible*, 4.31).

> He would certainly benefit from the advice to "get rid of all bitterness, rage, and anger" (*New International Version Bible*, Eph. 4.31).

11. Work in an Anthology or Other Collection

You may want to cite a work you have read in a book that contains many works by various authors and that was compiled or edited by someone other than the person you're citing. Your in-text citation should include the author of the selection you're citing and the page number. For example, suppose you want to cite the poem "Several Things" by Martha Collins, in a literature text edited by Pamela Annas and Robert Rosen. Use Collins's name and the title of her work in the sentence and the line numbers (see item 9) in a parenthetical citation.

> In "Several Things," Martha Collins enumerates what could take place in the lines of her poem: "Plums could appear, on a pewter plate / A dead red hare, hung by one foot. / A vase of flowers. Three shallots" (2–4).

12. Indirect Source

When you want to quote words that you found quoted in someone else's work, put the name of the person whose words you're quoting into your own sentence. Give the work where you found the quotation either in your sentence or in a parenthetical citation beginning with *qtd. in*.

> Martin Scorsese acknowledges the link between himself and his films: "I realize that all my life, I've been an outsider. I splatter bits of myself all over the screen" (qtd. in Giannetti and Eyman 397).

13. Two or More Sources in One Reference

If more than one source has contributed to an idea, opinion, or fact in your paper, cite them all. An efficient way to credit all is to include them in a single parenthetical citation, with a semicolon separating each source.

> Once researchers agreed that multiple intelligences existed, their next step was to try to measure or define them (West 17; Arturi 477; Gibbs 68).

14. An Entire Work

References to an entire work usually fit best into your own sentences.

> In *Convergence Culture*, Henry Jenkins explores how new digital media create a culture of active participation rather than passive reception.

15. Electronic Source with Page Numbers

The principles that govern in-text citations of electronic sources are exactly the same as the ones that apply to books, articles, or other sources. When an electronically accessed source identifies its author, use the author's name for parenthetical references. If no author is named, use the title of the source. When an electronic source has page numbers, use them exactly as you would the page numbers of a print source.

> Learning happens best when teachers truly care about their students' complete well-being (Anderson 7).

16. Electronic Source without Page Numbers

Many online sources don't number pages. In such cases, simply refer to those works in their entirety. Try to include the name of the author in your sentence.

> In "What Is Artificial Intelligence?" John McCarthy notes that the science of artificial intelligence includes efforts beyond trying to simulate human intelligence.

25D What are MLA guidelines for a Works Cited list?

In MLA-style DOCUMENTATION, the **Works Cited** list gives complete bibliographic information for each SOURCE used in your paper. Include all—but only—the sources from which you quote, paraphrase, or summarize. Quick Box 25.1 gives general information about the Works Cited list. The rest of this chapter gives models of many specific kinds of Works Cited entries.

Watch the Video

Quick Box 25.1 ■ ■ ■ ■ ■ ■ ■ ■ ■ ■

Guidelines for an MLA-style Works Cited list

See 25G for a sample student Works Cited list.

TITLE
Use "Works Cited" (without quotation marks), centered, as the title.

PLACEMENT OF LIST
Start a new page numbered sequentially with the rest of the paper, following the Notes pages, if any.

CONTENT AND FORMAT
Include all sources quoted from, paraphrased, or summarized in your paper. Start each entry on a new line and at the regular left margin. If the entry uses more than one line, indent the second and all following lines one-half inch from the left margin. Double-space all lines.

SPACING AFTER PUNCTUATION
Use one space after a period, unless your instructor asks you to use two. Always put only one space after a comma or a colon.

ARRANGEMENT OF ENTRIES
Alphabetize by author's last name. If no author is named, alphabetize by the title's first significant word (ignore *A*, *An*, and *The*).

continued >>

Quick Box 25.1 (continued)

AUTHORS' NAMES

Use first names and middle names or middle initials, if any, as given in the source. Don't reduce to initials any name that is given in full. For one author or the first-named author in multiauthor works, give the last name first. Use the word *and* with two or more authors. List multiple authors in the order given in the source. Use a comma between the first author's last and first names and after each complete author name except the last, which ends with a period: Fein, Ethel Andrea, Bert Griggs, and Delaware Rogash.

Include *Jr., Sr., II,* or *III* but no other titles or degrees before or after a name. For example, an entry for a work by Edward Meep III, MD, and Sir Richard Bolton would start like this: Meep, Edward, III, and Richard Bolton.

CAPITALIZATION OF TITLES

Capitalize all major words and the first and last words of all titles and sub-titles. Don't capitalize ARTICLES (*a, an, the*), PREPOSITIONS, COORDINATING CONJUNCTIONS, or *to* in INFINITIVES in the middle of a title. These rules also apply to the titles of your own papers.

SPECIAL TREATMENT OF TITLES

Use quotation marks around titles of shorter works (poems, short stories, essays, articles). Use italics for the titles of longer works (books, periodicals, plays).

When a book title includes the title of another work that is usually in italics (such as a novel, play, or long poem), the preferred MLA style is not to italicize the incorporated title: *Decoding* Jane Eyre.

If the incorporated title is usually enclosed in quotation marks (such as a short story or short poem), keep the quotation marks and italicize the complete title of the book: *Theme and Form in "I Shall Laugh Purely": A Brief Study.*

Drop *A, An,* or *The* as the first word of a periodical title.

PLACE OF PUBLICATION

If several cities are listed for the place of publication, give only the first. MLA doesn't require US state names, so give only the city name. For an unfamiliar city outside the United States, include an abbreviated name of the country or Canadian province. If there is no place of publication, use "N.p."

PUBLISHER

Use shortened names for publishers as long as they're clear: *Random* for *Random House.* For companies named for more than one person, name only the first: *Prentice* for *Prentice Hall.* For university presses, use the capital letters

continued >>

Quick Box 25.1 (continued)

U and *P* (without periods) instead of the words *University* and *Press:* Oxford UP, U of Chicago P

PUBLICATION MONTH ABBREVIATIONS

Abbreviate all publication months except *May, June,* and *July.* Use the first three letters followed by a period (*Dec., Feb.*) except for September (*Sept.*).

PAGE RANGES

Give the page range—the starting page number and the ending page number, connected by a hyphen—of any paginated electronic source and any paginated print source that is part of a longer work (for example, a chapter in a book, an article in a journal). The range indicates that the cited work is on those pages and all pages in between. If that is not the case, use the style shown next for discontinuous pages (see below). In either case, use numerals only, without the word *page* or *pages* or the abbreviation *p.* or *pp.*

Use the full second number in a range through 99. Above that, use only the last two digits for the second number unless it would be unclear: 103–04 is clear, but 567–02 is not, so use the full numbers 567–602.

DISCONTINUOUS PAGES

A source has discontinuous pages when the source is interrupted by material that's not part of the sections of the source you're using (for example, an article beginning on page 32 but continued on page 54). Use the starting page number followed by a plus sign (+): 32+.

MEDIUM OF PUBLICATION

Include the medium (the type) of publication for each Works Cited entry. For example, every entry for a print source must include "Print" at the end, followed by a period. Every source from the World Wide Web must include *Web* at the end, followed by a period and the date of access. The medium of publication can be broadcast sources (*Television, Radio*), sound recordings (*CD, LP, Audiocassette*), as well as films, DVDs, live performances, musical scores and works of visual art, and so on. If required, certain supplementary bibliographic information like translation information, name of a book series, or the total number of volumes in a set should follow the medium of publication.

ISSUE AND VOLUME NUMBERS FOR SCHOLARLY JOURNALS

Include both an issue and volume number for each Works Cited entry for scholarly journals. This applies both to journals that are continuously paginated and those that are not.

continued >>

Quick Box 25.1   (continued)

URLs IN ELECTRONIC SOURCES

Entries for online citations should include the URL only when the reader probably could not locate the source without it. If the entry does require a URL, enclose it in angle brackets <like this>. Put the URL before the access date and end it with a period. If your computer automatically creates a hyperlink when you type a URL, format the URL to look the same as the rest of the entry. In applications like Microsoft Word, you can use the command "remove hyperlink," which you can find on the "Insert" menu or by right-clicking on the hyperlink. If a URL must be divided between two lines, only break the URL after a slash even if a line runs short. Do not use a hyphen.

25E What are MLA examples for sources in a Works Cited list?

The directory at the beginning of this chapter corresponds to the numbered examples in this section. Not every possible documentation model is here. You may find that you have to combine features of models to document a particular source. You will also find more information in the *MLA Handbook for Writers of Research Papers*. Figure 25.1 provides another tool to help you find the Works Cited model you need: a decision-making flowchart.

PERIODICALS

You can read periodical articles in four different formats. Some articles appear in all print and electronic versions; others are published in only one or two formats.

1. **Print.**

2. **Digital version in a database.** You most commonly access these sources through a DATABASE such as EBSCO or Academic Search Premier, which your library purchases.

3. **Digital version with direct online access.** Without going through a database, you access these sources directly on the Web, either by entering a specific URL or clicking on links provided by a search. (Of course, many other Web sources are not from periodicals; we explain them in examples 76–88.)

4. **Digital version on a digital reader.** Many devices allow you to access online content. These include e-readers like Kindle or Nook, computers or tablet computers (like iPads), or smart phones (like Android).

Figure 25.1 Decision-making flowchart for finding the right MLA citation format.

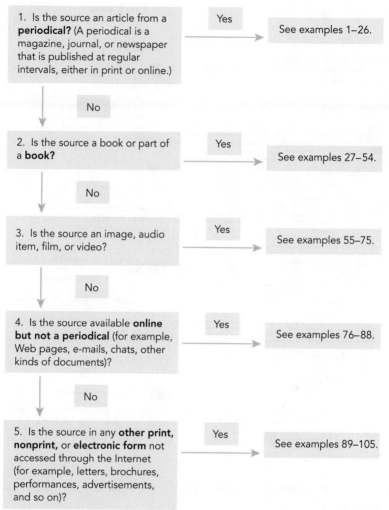

1. Is the source an article from a **periodical?** (A periodical is a magazine, journal, or newspaper that is published at regular intervals, either in print or online.) — Yes → See examples 1–26.

No ↓

2. Is the source a book or part of a **book?** — Yes → See examples 27–54.

No ↓

3. Is the source an image, audio item, film, or video? — Yes → See examples 55–75.

No ↓

4. Is the source available **online but not a periodical** (for example, Web pages, e-mails, chats, other kinds of documents)? — Yes → See examples 76–88.

No ↓

5. Is the source in any **other print, nonprint,** or **electronic form** not accessed through the Internet (for example, letters, brochures, performances, advertisements, and so on)? — Yes → See examples 89–105.

Citations for periodical articles contain three major parts: author, title of article, and publication information. The publication information differs according to not only the type of source (such as an editorial or a cartoon; see 16, below) but also how you access it (print, Web, and so on). If you access a source on the Web, you must include your date of access.

Figure 25.2 shows how to cite a print article from a scholarly journal.

MLA

322

25E

Key: **Author. Title. Type of source. Publication information.**

MLA DOCUMENTATION WITH CASE STUDY

Figure 25.2 Print article from a scholarly journal.

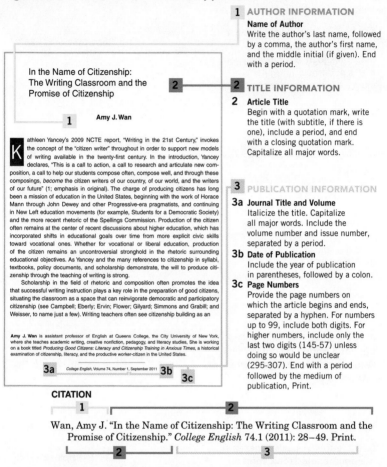

1 AUTHOR INFORMATION

Name of Author
Write the author's last name, followed by a comma, the author's first name, and the middle initial (if given). End with a period.

2 TITLE INFORMATION

2 Article Title
Begin with a quotation mark, write the title (with subtitle, if there is one), include a period, and end with a closing quotation mark. Capitalize all major words.

3 PUBLICATION INFORMATION

3a Journal Title and Volume
Italicize the title. Capitalize all major words. Include the volume number and issue number, separated by a period.

3b Date of Publication
Include the year of publication in parentheses, followed by a colon.

3c Page Numbers
Provide the page numbers on which the article begins and ends, separated by a hyphen. For numbers up to 99, include both digits. For higher numbers, include only the last two digits (145-57) unless doing so would be unclear (295-307). End with a period followed by the medium of publication, Print.

Figure 25.3 shows how to cite an article from a scholarly journal that was accessed in a database.

Figure 25.4 (page 324) shows how to cite an article from a periodical that appears on the Web.

1. Article in a Scholarly Journal: Print

Williams, Bronwyn T. "Seeking New Worlds: The Study of Writing beyond Our Classrooms." *College Composition and Communication* 62.1 (2010): 127–46. Print.

Provide both volume and issue number, if available.

Figure 25.3 Article from a scholarly journal accessed in a database.

1 AUTHOR INFORMATION

Name of Author
Write the author's last name, followed by a comma, the author's first name, and the middle initial (if given). End with a period.

2 TITLE INFORMATION

Article Title
State the full title of the article, enclosed in quotation marks. Use a period before the closing quotation mark.

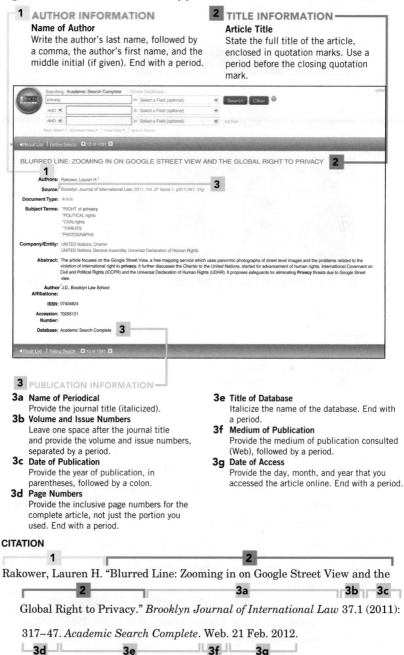

3 PUBLICATION INFORMATION

3a Name of Periodical
Provide the journal title (italicized).

3b Volume and Issue Numbers
Leave one space after the journal title and provide the volume and issue numbers, separated by a period.

3c Date of Publication
Provide the year of publication, in parentheses, followed by a colon.

3d Page Numbers
Provide the inclusive page numbers for the complete article, not just the portion you used. End with a period.

3e Title of Database
Italicize the name of the database. End with a period.

3f Medium of Publication
Provide the medium of publication consulted (Web), followed by a period.

3g Date of Access
Provide the day, month, and year that you accessed the article online. End with a period.

CITATION

Rakower, Lauren H. "Blurred Line: Zooming in on Google Street View and the Global Right to Privacy." *Brooklyn Journal of International Law* 37.1 (2011): 317–47. *Academic Search Complete.* Web. 21 Feb. 2012.

MLA

25E

324

Key: Author. Title. Type of source. Publication information.
MLA DOCUMENTATION WITH CASE STUDY

Figure 25.4 Article from periodical on the Web.

1 AUTHOR INFORMATION
Write the author's last name, followed by a comma, the author's first name, and the middle initial (if given). End with a period.

2 TITLE INFORMATION
State the full title of the article, enclosed in quotation marks. Use a period before the closing quotation mark.

3 PUBLICATION INFORMATION

3a Name of the Web site, italicized.

3b Sponsor (owner) of the Web site.

3c Date of the original publication.

3d Date you accessed the article.

CITATION

McAuliffe, Kathleen. "How Your Cat Is Making You Crazy."
TheAtlantic.com. The Atlantic, Mar. 2012. Web. 21 Feb. 2012.

2. Article in Scholarly Journal with a Print Version: Database

Williams, Bronwyn T. "Seeking New Worlds: The Study of Writing beyond
Our Classrooms." *College Composition and Communication.* 62.1 (2010):
127–46. *Proquest.* Web. 24 Oct. 2011.

The final date (24 Oct. 2011) is the date you accessed the article on the Web.

3. Article in a Scholarly Journal with a Print Version: Direct Online Access

Hoge, Charles W., et al. "Mild Traumatic Brain Injury in U.S. Soldiers
Returning from Iraq." *New England Journal of Medicine* 358.5 (2008):
453–63. Web. 10 Sept. 2008.

4. Article in a Scholarly Journal Published Only Online: Direct Online Access

Rutz, Paul X. "What a Painter of 'Historical Narrative' Can Tell Us about War Photography." *Kairos* 14.3 (2010). Web. 11 Nov. 2010.

Some periodicals appear only online and publish no print version.

5. Article in a Weekly or Biweekly Magazine: Print

Foroohar, Rana. "Why the World Isn't Getting Smaller." *Time* 27 June 2011: 20. Print.

If there is no author given, begin with the title of the article.

"The Price Is Wrong." *Economist* 2 Aug. 2003: 58–59. Print.

6. Article in a Weekly or Biweekly Magazine: Database

Foroohar, Rana. "Why the World Isn't Getting Smaller." *Time* 19 June 2011. *Academic Search Complete.* Web. 28 Aug. 2011.

7. Article in a Weekly or Biweekly Magazine: Direct Online Access

Foroohar, Rana. "Why the World Isn't Getting Smaller." *Time.* Time, 19 June 2011. Web. 27 Aug. 2011.

The name of the Web site is italicized. The sponsor (owner) of the Web site precedes the date of publication.

8. Article in a Monthly or Bimonthly Magazine: Print

Goetz, Thomas. "The Feedback Loop." *Wired* July 2011: 126–33. Print.

9. Article in a Monthly or Bimonthly Magazine: Database

Goetz, Thomas. "The Feedback Loop." *Wired* July 2011: 126–33. *ProQuest.* Web. 16 Sept. 2011.

10. Article in a Monthly or Bimonthly Magazine: Direct Online Access

Goetz, Thomas. "The Feedback Loop." *Wired.* Conde Nast, 19 June 2011. Web. 16 Sept. 2011.

11. Article Published Only Online: Direct Online Access

Ramirez, Eddy. "Comparing American Students with Those in China and India." *U.S. News and World Report.* U.S. News and World Report, 30 Jan. 2008. Web. 4 Mar. 2008.

Many periodicals have "extra" online content that doesn't appear in print. The article in example 11 is only online.

12. Article in a Newspaper: Print

Hesse, Monica. "Love among the Ruins." *Washington Post* 24 Apr. 2011: F1+. Print.

MLA

25E

326

Key: Author. Title. Type of source. Publication information.

MLA DOCUMENTATION WITH CASE STUDY

Omit *A, An,* or *The* as the first word in a newspaper title. Give the day, month, and year of the issue (and the edition, if applicable). If sections are designated, give the section letter as well as the page number. If an article runs on nonconsecutive pages, give the starting page number followed by a plus sign (for example, 1+ for an article that starts on page 1 and continues on a later page).

If no author is listed, begin with the title of the article.

"Prepping for Uranium Work." *Denver Post* 18 June 2011: B2. Print.

If the city of publication is not part of the title, put it in square brackets after the title, not italicized.

13. Article in a Newspaper with Print Version: Database

Hesse, Monica. "Falling in Love with St. Andrews, Scotland." *Washington Post* 24 Apr. 2011. *LexisNexis Academic*. Web. 3 Oct. 2011.

14. Article in a Newspaper with Print Version: Direct Online Access

Hesse, Monica. "Falling in Love with St. Andrews, Scotland." *Washington Post*. Washington Post, 22 Apr. 2011. Web. 3 Oct. 2011.

15. Article from a News Site Published Only Online: Direct Online Access

Katz, David. "What to Do about Flu? Get Vaccinated." *Huffington Post*. Huffington Post, 28 Oct. 2010. Web. 25 May 2012.

16. Editorial: Print

"Primary Considerations." Editorial. *Washington Post* 27 Jan. 2008: B6. Print.

If an author is listed, include her or his name before the title, then provide the title and information about the type of publication.

17. Editorial: Database

"Primary Considerations." Editorial. *Washington Post* 27 Jan. 2008. *LexisNexis Academic*. Web. 14 Feb. 2008.

18. Editorial: Direct Online Access

"Garbage In, Garbage Out." Editorial. *Los Angeles Times*. Los Angeles Times, 2 Feb. 2008. Web. 22 Mar. 2008.

19. Letter to the Editor: Print

Goldstein, Lester. "Roach Coaches: The Upside." Letter. *Sierra* May/June 2011: 2. Print.

If the letter has a title, include it, then identify it as "Letter," as in example 19. If there is no title, include just the type, as in example 20.

20. Letter to the Editor: Direct Online Access

Ennis, Heather B. Letter. *U.S. News and World Report*. U.S. News and World
Report, 20 Dec. 2007. Web. 22 Dec. 2007.

21. Review: Print

Shenk, David. "Toolmaker, Brain Builder." Rev. of *Beyond Deep Blue: Building
the Computer That Defeated the World Chess Champion*, by Feng-Hsiung
Hsu. *American Scholar* 72 (2003): 150–52. Print.

The review in example 21 is of a book.

22. Review: Direct Online Access

Travers, Peter. Rev. of *Beginners*, dir. Mike Mills. *Rolling Stone*. Rolling Stone,
2 June 2011. Web. 25 Nov. 2011.

The review in example 22 is of a film.

23. Article in a Collection of Reprinted Articles: Print

Brumberg, Abraham. "Russia after Perestroika." *New York Review of Books* 27
June 1991: 53–62. Rpt. in *Russian and Soviet History*. Ed. Alexander Dallin.
Vol. 14. New York: Garland, 1992. 300–20. Print.

Textbooks used in college writing courses often collect previously printed
articles.

Wallace, David Foster. "Consider the Lobster." *Gourmet* Aug. 2004: 50–55.
Rpt. in *Creating Nonfiction: A Guide and Anthology*. Becky Bradway and
Doug Hesse. Boston: Bedford, 2009. 755–69. Print.

24. Article in a Looseleaf Collection of Reprinted Articles: Print

Hayden, Thomas. "The Age of Robots." *U.S. News and World Report* 23 Apr.
2001, 44+. Print. *Applied Science 2002*. Ed. Eleanor Goldstein. Boca Raton:
SIRS, 2002. Art. 66.

Give the citation for the original publication first, followed by the citation for
the collection.

25. Abstract in a Collection of Abstracts: Print

Marcus, Hazel R., and Shinobu Kitayamo. "Culture and the Self:
Implications for Cognition, Emotion, and Motivation." *Psychological
Review* 88 (1991): 224–53. Abstract. *Psychological Abstracts* 78 (1991):
item 23878. Print.

MLA

328 **25E**

Key: Author. Title. Type of source. Publication information.
MLA DOCUMENTATION WITH CASE STUDY

If a reader could not know that the cited material is an abstract, write the word *Abstract*, not italicized, followed by a period. Give publication information about the collection of abstracts. For abstracts identified by item numbers rather than page numbers, use the word *item* before the item number.

26. Abstract: Database

Marcus, Hazel R., and Shinobu Kitayamo. "Culture and the Self: Implications for Cognition, Emotion, and Motivation." Abstract. *Psychological Abstracts* 78 (1991): item 23878. *PsycINFO*. Web. 10 Apr. 2004.

This entry is for the same abstract shown in item 25, but here it is accessed from a database.

BOOKS

You can read books these days in four different formats.

1. **Print.**
2. **Digital version through an e-book.** E-Books are electronic versions of books for digital readers like the Kindle, Nook, iPad, or so on.
3. **Digital version from a database.** Some books are available through library databases; in a sense, you're "checking out the books" online.
4. **Digital version through direct online access.** Versions of some older books, whose copyrights have expired because their authors died more than 70 years ago, are available directly on the Web. Portions of several more recent books are also available directly on the Web, through sites like Google Books. However, the section you might need for your research is frequently not available.

Figure 25.5 shows how to cite a single-author print book. Figure 25.6 (page 330) shows how to cite a digital version of a book accessed through a database. We provide examples of all formats in examples 27–30. The same principles apply to all books. We also note that there are audio versions of some books: recordings of an actor (or sometimes, the author) reading the book. We explain how to cite audio books in example 67.

27. Book by One Author: Print

Turkle, Sherry. *Alone Together: Why We Expect More from Technology and Less from Each Other.* New York: Basic, 2011. Print.

28. Book by One Author: E-Book

Turkle, Sherry. *Alone Together: Why We Expect More from Technology and Less from Each Other.* New York: Basic, 2011. Kindle file.

Figure 25.5 Single-author print book.

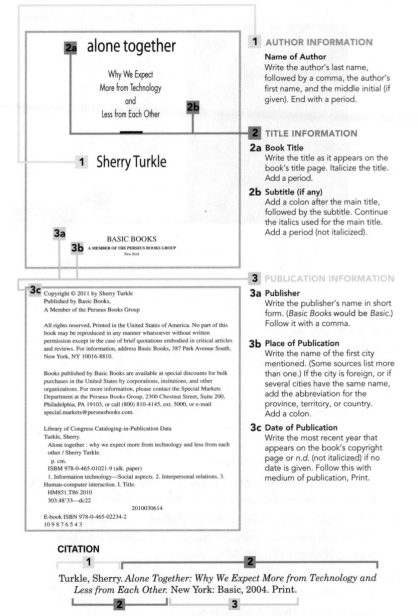

alone together (2a)

Why We Expect
More from Technology
and
Less from Each Other (2b)

Sherry Turkle (1)

(3a)
(3b)
BASIC BOOKS
A MEMBER OF THE PERSEUS BOOKS GROUP
New York

(3c) Copyright © 2011 by Sherry Turkle
Published by Basic Books,
A Member of the Perseus Books Group

All rights reserved. Printed in the United States of America. No part of this
book may be reproduced in any manner whatsoever without written
permission except in the case of brief quotations embodied in critical articles
and reviews. For information, address Basic Books, 387 Park Avenue South,
New York, NY 10016-8810.

Books published by Basic Books are available at special discounts for bulk
purchases in the United States by corporations, insitutions, and other
organizations. For more information, please contact the Special Markets
Department at the Perseus Books Group, 2300 Chestnut Street, Suite 200,
Philadelphia, PA 19103, or call (800) 810-4145, ext. 5000, or e-mail
special.markets@perseusbooks.com.

Library of Congress Cataloging-in-Publication Data
Turkle, Sherry.
  Alone together : why we expect more from technology and less from each
other / Sherry Turkle.
    p. cm.
  ISBM 978-0-465-01021-9 (alk. paper)
  1. Information technology—Social aspects. 2. Interpersonal relations. 3.
Human-computer interaction. I. Title.
  HM851.T86 2010
  303.48'33—dc22
                                              2010030614
E-book ISBN 978-0-465-02234-2
10 9 8 7 6 5 4 3

1 AUTHOR INFORMATION

Name of Author
Write the author's last name,
followed by a comma, the author's
first name, and the middle initial (if
given). End with a period.

2 TITLE INFORMATION

2a Book Title
Write the title as it appears on the
book's title page. Italicize the title.
Add a period.

2b Subtitle (if any)
Add a colon after the main title,
followed by the subtitle. Continue
the italics used for the main title.
Add a period (not italicized).

3 PUBLICATION INFORMATION

3a Publisher
Write the publisher's name in short
form. (*Basic Books* would be *Basic*.)
Follow it with a comma.

3b Place of Publication
Write the name of the first city
mentioned. (Some sources list more
than one.) If the city is foreign, or if
several cities have the same name,
add the abbreviation for the
province, territory, or country.
Add a colon.

3c Date of Publication
Write the most recent year that
appears on the book's copyright
page or *n.d.* (not italicized) if no
date is given. Follow this with
medium of publication, Print.

CITATION

1 | 2

Turkle, Sherry. *Alone Together: Why We Expect More from Technology and Less from Each Other.* New York: Basic, 2004. Print.

2 | 3

MLA

25E

330

Key: Author. Title. Type of source. Publication information.
MLA DOCUMENTATION WITH CASE STUDY

Figure 25.6 Digital version of a book accessed through a database.

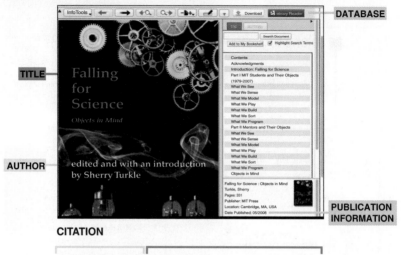

DATABASE

TITLE

AUTHOR

PUBLICATION INFORMATION

CITATION

Turkle, Sherry, ed. *Falling for Science: Objects in Mind.*

Cambridge, MA: MIT P, 2008. *Ebrary*. Web. 3 Aug. 2012.

29. Book by One Author: Database

Turkle, Sherry. *Evocative Objects: Things We Think With.* Cambridge: MIT P, 2007. *Ebrary*. Web. 3 May 2011.

30. Book by One Author: Direct Online Access

Turkle, Sherry. *Alone Together: Why We Expect More from Technology and Less from Each Other.* New York: Basic, 2011. *Google Books*. Google, 2011. Web. 25 July 2011.

31. Book by Two or Three Authors

Edin, Kathryn, and Maria Kefalas. *Promises I Can Keep: Why Poor Women Put Motherhood before Marriage.* Berkeley: U of California P, 2005. Print.

Lynam, John K., Cyrus G. Ndiritu, and Adiel N. Mbabu. *Transformation of Agricultural Research Systems in Africa: Lessons from Kenya.* East Lansing: Michigan State UP, 2004. Print.

For e-books, adapt this model to example 28. For a book in a database, see example 29. For a book accessed directly online, see example 30.

32. Book by More Than Three Authors

Saul, Wendy, et al. *Beyond the Science Fair: Creating a Kids' Inquiry Conference.* Portsmouth: Heinemann, 2005. Print.

Give only the first author's name, followed by a comma and the phrase *et al.* (abbreviated from the Latin *et alii*, meaning "and others"), or list all names in full in the order in which they appear on the title page.

For e-books, adapt this model to example 28. For a book in a database, see example 29. For a book accessed directly online, see example 30.

33. Two or More Works by the Same Author(s)

Jenkins, Henry. *Convergence Culture: Where Old and New Media Collide.* New York: New York UP, 2006. Print.

---. *Fans, Bloggers, and Gamers: Exploring Participatory Culture.* New York: New York UP, 2006. Print.

Give author name(s) in the first entry only. In the second and subsequent entries, use three hyphens and a period to stand for exactly the same name(s). If the person served as editor or translator, put a comma and the appropriate abbreviation (*ed.* or *trans.*) following the three hyphens. Arrange the works in alphabetical (not chronological) order according to book title, ignoring labels such as *ed.* or *trans.*

For e-books, adapt this model to example 28. For a book in a database, see example 29. For a book accessed directly online, see example 30.

34. Book by a Group or Corporate Author

American Psychological Association. *Publication Manual of the American Psychological Association.* 6th ed. Washington: APA, 2010. Print.

Cite the full name of the corporate author first, omitting the first articles *A, An,* or *The.* When a corporate author is also the publisher, use a shortened form of the corporate name at the publisher position.

For e-books, adapt this model to example 28. For a book in a database, see example 29. For a book accessed directly online, see example 30.

35. Book with No Author Named

The Chicago Manual of Style. 16th ed. Chicago: U of Chicago P, 2010. Print.

If there is no author's name on the title page, begin the citation with the title. Alphabetize the entry according to the first significant word of the title (ignore *A, An,* or *The*).

For e-books, adapt this model to example 28. For a book in a database, see example 29. For a book accessed directly online, see example 30.

36. Book with an Author and an Editor

Stowe, Harriet Beecher. *Uncle Tom's Cabin.* Ed. Elizabeth Ammons. New York: Norton, 2010. Print.

MLA

25E

332

Key: Author. Title. Type of source. Publication information.

MLA DOCUMENTATION WITH CASE STUDY

If your paper refers to the work of the book's author, put the author's name first. If your paper refers to the work of the editor, put the editor's name first.

Ammons, Elizabeth, ed. *Uncle Tom's Cabin*. By Harriet Beecher Stowe. New
York: Norton, 2010. Print.

For e-books, adapt this model to example 28. For a book in a database, see example 29. For a book accessed directly online, see example 30.

37. Translation

Nesbo, Jo. *The Leopard*. Trans. Don Bartlett. New York: Vintage, 2011.

For e-books, adapt this model to example 28. For a book in a database, see example 29. For a book accessed directly online, see example 30.

38. Work in Several Volumes or Parts

Chrisley, Ronald, ed. *Artificial Intelligence: Critical Concepts*. Vol. 1. London:
Routledge, 2000. Print. 4 vols.

If you are citing only one volume, put the volume number before the publication information. If you wish, you can give the total number of volumes at the end of the entry. MLA recommends using arabic numerals, even if the source uses roman numerals (*Vol. 6* rather than *Vol. VI*).

For e-books, adapt this model to example 28. For a book in a database, see example 29. For a book accessed directly online, see example 30.

39. Anthology or Edited Book

Purdy, John L., and James Ruppert, eds. *Nothing but the Truth: An
Anthology of Native American Literature*. Upper Saddle River:
Prentice, 2001. Print.

Use this model if you are citing an entire anthology. In the example above, *ed.* stands for "editor," so use *eds.* when more than one editor is named.

For e-books, adapt this model to example 28. For a book in a database, see example 29. For a book accessed directly online, see example 30.

40. One Selection from an Anthology or an Edited Book

Trujillo, Laura. "Balancing Act." *Border-Line Personalities: A New Generation
of Latinas Dish on Sex, Sass, and Cultural Shifting*. Ed. Robyn Moreno and
Michelle Herrera Mulligan. New York: Harper, 2004. 61–72. Print.

Teasdale, Sara. "Driftwood." *Flame and Shadow*. Ed. A. Light. N.p., 1920.
Project Gutenberg. 1 July 1996. Web. 18 Aug. 2008.

Give the author and title of the selection first and then the full title of the anthology. Information about the editor starts with *Ed.* (for "Edited by"), so don't use *Eds.* when there is more than one editor. Give the name(s) of the editor(s) in normal order rather than reversing first and last names. Give the page range of the selection at the end.

41. More Than One Selection from the Same Anthology or Edited Book

Bond, Ruskin. "The Night Train at Deoli." Chaudhuri 415–18.

Chaudhuri, Amit, ed. *The Vintage Book of Modern Indian Literature*. New York: Vintage, 2004. Print.

Vijayan, O.V. "The Rocks." Chaudhuri 291–96.

If you cite more than one selection from the same anthology, you can list the anthology as a separate entry with all of the publication information. Also list each selection from the anthology by author and title of the selection, but give only the name(s) of the editor(s) of the anthology and the page number(s) for each selection. Here, *ed.* stands for "editor," so it is correct to use *eds.* when more than one editor is named. List selections separately in alphabetical order by author's last name.

42. Article in a Reference Book

Burnbam, John C. "Freud, Sigmund." *The Encyclopedia of Psychiatry, Psychology, and Psychoanalysis*. Ed. Benjamin B. Wolman. New York: Holt, 1996. Print.

If the articles in the book are alphabetically arranged, you don't need to give volume and page numbers.

If no author is listed, begin with the title of the article.

"Ireland." *The New Encyclopaedia Britannica: Macropaedia*. 15th ed. 2002. Print.

If you're citing a widely used reference work, don't give full publication information. Instead, give only the edition and year of publication.

43. Article in a Reference Book: Database

"Lobster." *Encyclopaedia Britannica Online*. Encyclopaedia Britannica, 2011. Web. 29 June 2011.

44. Second or Later Edition

MLA Handbook for Writers of Research Papers. 7th ed. New York: MLA, 2009. Print.

If a book is not a first edition, the edition number is on the title page. Place the abbreviated information (*2nd ed.*, *3rd ed.*, etc.) between the title and the publication information. Give only the latest copyright date for the edition you are using.

For e-books, adapt this model to example 28. For a book in a database, see example 29. For a book accessed directly online, see example 30.

MLA

334 **25E**

Key: Author. Title. Type of source. Publication information.

MLA DOCUMENTATION WITH CASE STUDY

45. Introduction, Preface, Foreword, or Afterword

Hesse, Doug. Foreword. *The End of Composition Studies.* By David W. Smit.
Carbondale: Southern Illinois UP, 2004. ix–xiii. Print.

Give first the name of the writer of the part you're citing and then the name of
the cited part, capitalized but not underlined or in quotation marks. After the
book title, put *By* and the book author's full name, if different from the writer
of the cited material. If the writer of the cited material is the same as the book
author, use only the last name after *By*. After the publication information, give
inclusive page numbers for the cited part, using roman or arabic numerals as the
source does. When the introduction, preface, foreword, or afterword has a title,
include it in the citation before the section name, as in the following example:

Fox-Genovese, Elizabeth. "Mothers and Daughters: The Ties That Bind."
Foreword. *Southern Mothers.* Ed. Nagueyalti Warren and Sally Wolff.
Baton Rouge: Louisiana State UP, 1999. iv–xviii. Print.

For e-books, adapt this model to example 28. For a book in a database, see
example 29. For a book accessed directly online, see example 30.

46. Unpublished Dissertation or Essay

Stuart, Gina Anne. "Exploring the Harry Potter Book Series: A Study of
Adolescent Reading Motivation." Diss. Utah State U, 2006. Print.

Treat published dissertations as books.

For e-books, adapt this model to example 28. For a book in a database, see
example 29. For a book accessed directly online, see example 30.

47. Reprint of an Older Book

Coover, Robert. *A Night at the Movies, Or, You Must Remember This.* 1987.
Champaign: Dalkey Archive, 2007.

Republishing information can be found on the copyright page.

For e-books, adapt this model to example 28. For a book in a database, see
example 29. For a book accessed directly online, see example 30.

48. Book in a Series or Scholarly Project

Ardell, Jean Hastings. *Breaking into Baseball: Women and the National
Pastime.* Carbondale: Southern Illinois UP, 2005. Print. Writing
Baseball Series.

49. Book with a Title within a Title

Lumiansky, Robert M., and Herschel Baker, eds. *Critical Approaches to Six
Major English Works: Beowulf through Paradise Lost.* Philadelphia: U of
Pennsylvania P, 1968. Print.

MLA prefers the previous example, in which the embedded title is neither italicized nor set within quotation marks. However, MLA also accepts a second style for handling embedded titles. In this style, set the normally independent titles within quotation marks and italicize them, as follows:

Lumiansky, Robert M., and Herschel Baker, eds. *Critical Approaches to Six Major English Works: "Beowulf" through "Paradise Lost."* Philadelphia: U of Pennsylvania P, 1968. Print.

Use whichever style your instructor prefers.

For e-books, adapt this model to example 28. For a book in a database, see example 29. For a book accessed directly online, see example 30.

50. Bible or Sacred Text

Bhagavad Gita. Trans. Juan Mascaro. Rev. ed. New York: Penguin, 2003. Print.

The Holy Bible: New International Version. New York: Harper, 1983. Print.

The Qur'an. Trans. M.A.S. Abdel Haleem. New York: Oxford UP, 2004. Print.

For e-books, adapt this model to example 28. For a book in a database, see example 29. For a book accessed directly online, see example 30.

51. Government Publication with No Author

United States. Cong. Senate. Select Committee on Intelligence. *Report on the U.S. Intelligence Community's Prewar Intelligence Assessment of Iraq.* 108th Cong., 1st sess. Washington: GPO, 2004. Print.

For government publications that name no author, start with the name of the government or government body. Then name the government agency. (*GPO* is a standard abbreviation for *Government Printing Office,* the publisher of most US government publications.) Then include the title, any series information, the publication date, and the medium of publication.

For e-books, adapt this model to example 28. For a book in a database, see example 29. For a book accessed directly online, see example 30.

52. Government Publication with Named Author

Wallace, David Rains. *Yellowstone: A Natural and Human History, Yellowstone National Park, Idaho, Montana, and Wyoming.* U.S. Interior Dept. National Park Service. Official National Park Handbook 150. Washington: GPO, 2001. Print.

MLA also permits an alternative format, with the government body first, then the title, then "By" followed by the author's name.

MLA 25E

336

Key: Author. Title. Type of source. Publication information.
MLA DOCUMENTATION WITH CASE STUDY

United States. Interior Dept. National Park Service. *Yellowstone: A Natural and Human History, Yellowstone National Park, Idaho, Montana, and Wyoming*. By David Rains Wallace. Official National Park Handbook 150. Washington: GPO, 2001. Print.

For e-books, adapt this model to example 28. For a book in a database, see example 29. For a book accessed directly online, see example 30.

53. Government Publication: Direct Online Access

Huff, C. Ronald. *Comparing the Criminal Behavior of Youth Gangs and At-Risk Youths*. United States Dept. of Justice. Natl. Inst. of Justice. Oct. 1998. Web. 5 Aug. 2008.

54. Published Proceedings of a Conference

Rocha, Luis Mateus, et al., eds. *Artificial Life X: Proceedings of the Tenth International Conference on the Simulation and Synthesis of Living Systems*. 3–7 June 2006, Bloomington, IN. Cambridge: MIT P, 2006. Print.

For e-books, adapt this model to example 28. For a book in a database, see example 29. For a book accessed directly online, see example 30.

IMAGES, AUDIO, FILM, AND VIDEO

55. Photograph, Painting, Drawing, Illustration, etc. (Original)

Mydans, Carl. *General Douglas MacArthur Landing at Luzon, 1945*. Gelatin silver print. Soho Triad Fine Art Gallery, New York. 21 Oct.–28 Nov. 1999.

Give the name of the image's maker, if known, the title or caption of the image, the type of image, where you viewed the image, and when. If the image has no title, provide a brief description.

56. Photograph, Painting, Drawing, Illustration, etc. in a Periodical: Print

Greene, Herb. *Grace Slick*. Photograph. *Rolling Stone* 30 Sept. 2004: 102. Print.

Include maker, title, and type as in 55, but include publication information as for a print article.

57. Photograph, Painting, Drawing, Illustration, etc. in a Periodical: Direct Online Access

Morris, Christopher. *Man in Camouflage*. Photograph. *Atlantic*. The Atlantic Monthly Group, July/Aug. 2011. Web. 5 Aug. 2011.

58. Photograph, Painting, Drawing, Illustration, etc. in a Book: Print

The World's Most Populous Countries. Illustration. *Maps of the Imagination: The Writer as Cartographer*. By Peter Turchi. San Antonio: Trinity UP, 2004. 116–17. Print.

59. Photograph, Painting, Drawing, Illustration, etc.: Direct Online Access

Bourke-White, Margaret. *Fort Peck Dam, Montana.* 1936. Gelatin silver print. *Metropolitan Museum of Art.* Web. 5 Aug. 2008.

Give information about the Web site, the medium of publication, and the access date.

van Gogh, Vincent. *The Starry Night.* 1889. Oil on canvas. *MOMA.* Museum of Modern Art. Web. 5 Dec. 2011.

60. Comic or Cartoon: Print

Sutton, Ward. "Ryan's a Late Adopter." Cartoon. *New Yorker* 2 May 2011: 64. Print.

61. Comic or Cartoon: Direct Online Access

Harris, Sidney. "We have lots of information technology." Cartoon. *New Yorker.* Conde Nast, 27 May 2002. Web. 9 Feb. 2007.

62. Slide Show: Direct Online Access

Erickson, Britta, narr. *Visionaries from the New China. Atlantic.* Atlantic Monthly Group, 18 June 2007. Web. 11 Sept. 2008.

63. Photo Essay: Direct Online Access

Nachtwey, James. "Crime in Middle America." *Time.* Time, 2 Dec. 2006. Web. 5 May 2007.

64. Image from a Social Networking Site

Gristellar, Ferdinand. *The Gateway Arch.* Photograph. Ferdinand Gristellar. Facebook, 7 Aug. 2009. Web. 3 Sept. 2009.

65. Image from a Service or Distributor

World Perspectives. *Launching of the Space Shuttle* Columbia, *Florida, USA, 1998.* Photograph. Getty Images #AT3775-001. Web. 3 Mar. 2011.

In this example, the photographer was listed as "World Perspectives." Include the name of the service or distributor, and the item number or other identifier, if any.

66. Map, Chart, or Other Graphic: Direct Online Access

"Hurricane Rita." Graphic. *New York Times Online.* New York Times, 24 Sept. 2005. Web. 24 Sept. 2005.

67. Audio Book

Turkle, Sherry. *Alone Together: Why We Expect More from Technology and Less from Each Other.* Narr. Laural Merlington. Tantor Media, 2011. CD.

MLA

25E

338

Key: Author. Title. Type of source. Publication information.

MLA DOCUMENTATION WITH CASE STUDY

68. Sound Recording: CD, DVD

Verdi, Giuseppe. *Requiem.* Chicago Symphony Orchestra and Chorus. Cond.
Ricardo Muti. CSO Resound, 2010. CD.

Put first the name most relevant to what you discuss in your paper (performer, conductor, work performed). Include the recording's title, the medium for any recording other than a CD (*LP, Audiocassette*), the name of the issuer, and the year the work was issued.

69. Sound Recording: MP3

Radiohead. "Jigsaw Falling into Place." *In Rainbows.* Radiohead, 2007. MP3 file.

70. Sound Recording: Direct Online Access

Komunyakaa, Yusef. "My Father's Love Letters." *Poets.org Listening Booth.*
Academy of American Poets, 5 May 1993. Web. 19 Aug. 2008.

71. Podcast: Direct Online Access

Blumberg, Alex, and Adam Davidson. "The Giant Pool of Money." Podcast.
This American Life. 9 May 2008. Web. 19 Oct. 2009.

A podcast is an audio recording that is posted online. Thus, the publication medium is *Web.* Include as much of the following information as you can identify: author, title, sponsoring organization or Web site, date posted, and date accessed.

72. Film, Videotape, or DVD

It Happened One Night. Screenplay by Robert Riskin. Dir. and Prod. Frank
Capra. Perf. Clark Gable and Claudette Colbert. 1934. Sony Pictures,
1999. DVD.

Give the title first, and include the director, the distributor, and the year. For films that were subsequently released on tape or DVD, provide the original release date of the movie *before* the type of medium. Other information (writer, producer, major actors) is optional but helpful. Put first names first.

73. Video or Film: Direct Online Access

For video downloads, include the download date and the source.

It Happened One Night. Screenplay by Robert Riskin. Dir. and Prod. Frank
Capra. Perf. Clark Gable and Claudette Colbert. 1934. *Netflix.* Web. 15.
Dec. 2011.

CNN. *Challenger Disaster Live on CNN. YouTube.com.* YouTube, 27 Jan. 2011.
Web. 4 Mar. 2011.

Use this format for videos from YouTube and similar sites.

74. Broadcast Television or Radio Program

Include at least the title of the program (in italics), the network, the local station and its city, and the date of the broadcast.

Not for Ourselves Alone: The Story of Elizabeth Cady Stanton and Susan B. Anthony. By Ken Burns. Perf. Julie Harris, Ronnie Gilbert, and Sally Kellerman. Prod. Paul Barnes and Ken Burns. PBS. WNET, New York. 8 Nov. 1999. Television.

The Madeleine Brand Show. SCPR. KPCC, Pasadena. 20 June 2011. Radio.

For a series, also supply the title of the specific episode (in quotation marks) before the title of the program (italicized) and the title of the series (neither underlined nor in quotation marks).

"The Bruce-Partington Plans." *Sherlock Holmes.* RMPBS. KRMA, Denver. 30 June 2011. Television.

75. Television or Radio Program: Direct Online Access

"Bill Moyers." *The Daily Show.* Perf. Jon Stewart. Comedy Central. *Hulu.com.* Hulu, 1 June 2011. Web. 22 Sept. 2011.

"The Disappearing Incandescent Bulb." *The Madeleine Brand Show.* SCPR. KPCC, Pasadena. 20 June 2011. Web. 6 Oct. 2011. <http://www.scpr.org/programs/madeleine-brand/2011/06/20/the-disappearing-incandescent-bulb/>.

Because this source may be difficult to find, the URL is listed.

OTHER INTERNET SOURCES

This section shows models for other online sources. For such sources, provide as much of the following information as you can.

1. The author's name, if given.
2. In quotation marks, the title of a short work (Web page, brief document, essay, article, message, and so on); or italicized, the title of a book.
3. Publication information for any print version, if it exists.
4. The name of an editor, translator, or compiler, if any, with an abbreviation such as *Ed., Trans.,* or *Comp.* before the name.
5. Publication information for the Web:
   a. The italicized title of the Internet site (scholarly project, database, online periodical, professional or personal Web site). If the site has no title, describe it: for example, *Home page.*
   b. The date of electronic publication (including a version number, if any) or posting or the most recent update.

MLA

25E

340

Key: Author. Title. Type of source. Publication information.
MLA DOCUMENTATION WITH CASE STUDY

c. The name of a sponsoring organization, if any.
d. The medium of publication: Web.
e. The date you accessed the material.
f. The URL in angle brackets (< >), only when the reader probably could not locate the source without it. If you must break a URL at the end of a line, break only after a slash and do not use a hyphen.

Figure 25.7 shows how to cite a page from a Web site. Figure 25.8 (page 342) shows how to cite a posting on a blog.

76. Entire Web Site

WebdelSol.Com. Ed. Michael Neff. 2011. Web. 4 Aug. 2011.

77. Home Page (Organization or Company)

Association for the Advancement of Artificial Intelligence. AAAI, n.d. Web. 17
    Oct. 2011.

78. Personal Home Page

Hesse, Doug. Home page. Web. 1 Nov. 2011. <http://portfolio.du.edu/dhesse>.

Provide the URL if the page might be difficult to find.

79. Page from a Web Site

"Protecting Whales from Dangerous Sonar." *National Resources Defense
    Council.* NRDC, 9 Nov. 2005. Web. 12 Dec. 2005.

"Ethical and Social Implications of AI for Society." *Association for the
    Advancement of Artificial Intelligence.* AAAI, 3 May 2012. Web.
    19 May 2012.

Provide as much information as you can, starting with the author, if available, and the title of the page, followed by the site information.

80. Academic Department Home Page

Writing. Dept. home page. Grand Valley State U. Web. 26 Feb. 2010.

81. Course Home Page

St. Germain, Sheryl. Myths and Fairytales: From *Inanna* to *Edward
    Scissorhands.* Course home page. Summer 2003. Dept. of English,
    Iowa State U. Web. 20 Feb. 2005. <http://www.public.iastate.edu/
    sgermain/531.homepage.html>.

82. Government or Institutional Web Site

Home Education and Private Tutoring. Pennsylvania Department of Education,
    2005. Web. 5 Aug. 2008.

Figure 25.7 Page from a Web site.

1 TITLE

Title of the Work
State the full title of the work cited, enclosed in quotation marks. Use a period before the closing quotation mark.

2 PUBLICATION INFORMATION

2a Title of the Overall Web Site
Provide the title of the Web site (italicized), followed by a period.

2b Publisher or Sponsor of the Web Site
Leave one space after the title of the overall Web site and provide the publisher or sponsor of the Web site. If this information is not available, use *N.p.* End with a comma.

2c Date of Publication
Provide the available date (day, month, and year) of publication, followed by a period. If no date is available, use *n.d.*

2d Medium of Publication
Provide the medium of publication consulted (*Web*), followed by a period.

2e Date of Access
Provide the day, month, and year that you accessed the article online. End with a period.

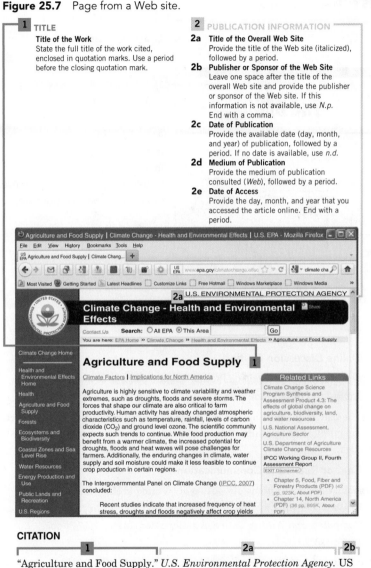

CITATION

"Agriculture and Food Supply." *U.S. Environmental Protection Agency.* US Environmental Protection Agency, 2012. Web. 5 Mar. 2012.

MLA

25E

342

Key: **Author. Title. Type of source. Publication information.**
MLA DOCUMENTATION WITH CASE STUDY

Figure 25.8 Posting on a blog.

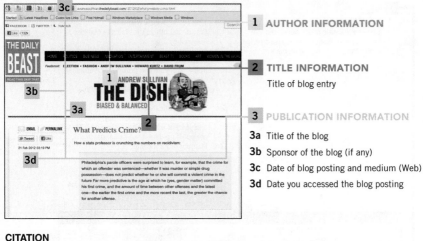

1 AUTHOR INFORMATION

2 TITLE INFORMATION
Title of blog entry

3 PUBLICATION INFORMATION

3a Title of the blog
3b Sponsor of the blog (if any)
3c Date of blog posting and medium (Web)
3d Date you accessed the blog posting

CITATION

Sullivan, Andrew. "What Predicts Crime?" *The Dish: Biased and Balanced.*
The Daily Beast, 21 Feb. 2012. Web. 18 Mar. 2012.

83. Online Discussion Posting

Firrantello, Larry. "Van Gogh on Prozac." Online posting. 23 May 2005. *Salon
Table Talk.* Web. 7 June 2005.

Give the date of the posting and the name of the bulletin board, if any. Then
give the publication medium, the access date and, in angle brackets, the URL
if needed.

84. Chat or Real-Time Communication

Berzsenyi, Christyne. Online discussion of "Writing to Meet Your Match:
Rhetoric, Perceptions, and Self-Presentation for Four Online Daters."
Computers and Writing Online. AcadianaMoo, 13 May 2007. Web.
13 May 2007.

Glenn, Maria. Chat. *Laurence Smith.* 9 Sept. 2010. Web. 9 Sept. 2010.

Give the name of the speaker or writer, a title for the event (if any), the forum,
date, publication medium, access date, and URL if needed.

85. E-Mail Message

Martin, Tara. "Visit to Los Alamos." Message to David Sanz. 25 July 2010.
E-mail.

Start with the name of the person who wrote the e-mail message. Give the title or subject line in quotation marks. Then describe the message, including the recipient's name. Add the date. Finally, write the medium of delivery (E-mail).

86. Posting on a Blog

Phillips, Matthew. "Need to Go to the ER? Not Until the Game's Over." *Freakonomics*. Freakonomics, LLC, 15 June 2011. Web. 14 Aug. 2011.

87. Wiki

"NASCAR Sprint Cup Series." *NASCAR Wiki*. Wikia, 11 Jan. 2011. Web. 6 Apr. 2011.

88. Posting on a Social Networking Site

Adler-Kassner, Linda. "Conversations toward Action." *Council of Writing Program Administrators*. Facebook, 5 Feb. 2010. Web. 6 May 2011.

OTHER PRINT, NONPRINT, AND ELECTRONIC SOURCES
89. Published or Unpublished Letter

Irvin, William. Letter to Lesley Osburn. 7 Dec. 2011. MS.

Williams, William Carlos. Letter to his son. 13 Mar. 1935. *Letters of the Century: America 1900–1999*. Ed. Lisa Grunwald and Stephen J. Adler. New York: Dial, 1999: 225–26. Print.

Begin the entry with the the author of the letter. Note the recipient, too. If the letter is published in a periodical, a book, or online, follow the appropriate citation format for these sources.

90. Microfiche Collection of Articles

Wenzell, Ron. "Businesses Prepare for a More Diverse Work Force." *St. Louis Post Dispatch* 3 Feb. 1990: 17. Microform. *NewsBank: Employment* 27 (1990): fiche 2, grid D12.

A microfiche is a transparent sheet of film (a *fiche*) with microscopic printing that needs to be read through a special magnifier. Each fiche holds several pages, with each page designated by a grid position. A long document may appear on more than one fiche.

91. Map or Chart

Colorado Front Range Mountain Bike Topo Map. Map. Nederland: Latitude 40, 2001. Print.

If you have accessed the map or chart online, follow example 66.

MLA

344 **25E**

Key: Author. Title. Type of source. Publication information.
MLA DOCUMENTATION WITH CASE STUDY

92. Report or Pamphlet

National Commission on Writing in America's Schools and Colleges. *The Neglected "R": The Need for a Writing Revolution.* New York: College Board, 2003. Print.

Use the format for books, to the extent possible, including whether you're citing a print or digital version.

93. Legal Source

Brown v. Board of Educ. 347 US 483-96. Supreme Court of the US. 1954. Print.

Include the name of the case, the number of the case (preceded by *No.*), the name of the court deciding the case, and the date of the decision. Legal sources can frequently be accessed through a database:

Brown v. Board of Educ. 347 US 483-96. Supreme Court of the US. 1954. *LexisNexis Academic.* Web. 25 Jan. 2010.

94. Interview

Friedman, Randi. Telephone interview. 30 Aug. 2008.

Winfrey, Oprah. "Ten Questions for Oprah Winfrey." By Richard Zoglin. *Time* 15 Dec. 2003: 8. Print.

Pope, Carl. Interview by Amy Standen. *Salon.com.* Salon Media Group, 29 Apr. 2002. Web. 27 Jan. 2005.

Note the type of interview, for example "Telephone" or "Personal" (face-to-face). For a published interview, give the name of the interviewed person first, identify the source as an interview, and then give details as for any published source: title; author (preceded by the word *By*); and publication details. Follow the citation format for a periodical, book, or Web source, as appropriate.

95. Lecture or Speech

Kennedy, John Fitzgerald. Greater Houston Ministerial Assn. Rice Hotel, Houston. 12 Sept. 1960. Speech.

Katz, Jennifer. "Spiral Galaxies." Astronomy 1000. University of Denver, Denver. 7 Feb. 2011. Lecture.

96. Live Performance (Play, Concert, Dance etc.)

All My Sons. By Arthur Miller. Dir. Calvin McLean. Center for the Performing Arts, Normal, IL. 27 Sept. 2005. Performance.

Nelson, Willie. Concert. Red Rocks Amphitheater, Denver. 22 June 2011. Performance.

97. Work of Art, Original

Cassatt, Mary. *La Toilette*. 1890. Oil on canvas. Art Institute of Chicago.

Fourquet, Léon. *The Man with the Broken Nose*. 1865. Marble. Musée Rodin, Paris.

98. Musical Score

Schubert, Franz. *Unfinished Symphony*. 1822. Print.

Italicize any musical work that has a title, such as an opera, a ballet, or a named symphony. Don't underline or put in quotation marks music identified only by form, number, and key, as follows.

Schubert, Franz. Symphony no. 8 in B minor. 1822. Print.

To cite a published score, use the following format.

Schubert, Franz. *Symphony in B Minor (Unfinished)*. 1822. Ed. Martin Cusid. New York: Norton, 1971. Print.

99. Advertisement

Southwest Airlines. Advertisement. ABC. 24 Aug. 2010. Television.

Canon Digital Cameras. Advertisement. *Time* 2 June 2003: 77. Print.

Samsung. Advertisement. *RollingStone*. Wenner Media, 8 Nov. 2005. Web. 11 Nov. 2005.

100. Video Game or Software

The Island: Castaway. N.p.: Awem Studio, 2010. Game.

"N.p." indicates that the place of publication is unknown.

101. Nonperiodical Publications on CD, DVD, or Magnetic Tape

Perl, Sondra. *Felt Sense: Guidelines for Composing*. Portsmouth: Boynton, 2004. CD.

Citations for publications on DVD, CD-ROM, or other recording formats follow guidelines for print publications, with two additions: list the publication medium (for example, *CD*), and give the vendor's name.

102. Materials on CD or DVD with a Print Version

"The Price Is Right." *Time* 20 Jan. 1992: 38. *Time Man of the Year*. CD-ROM. New York: Compact, 1993.

Information for the print version ends with the article's page number, 38. Following that comes the title of the CD-ROM (*Time Man of the Year*) and its publication information.

MLA

25F

346

Key: Author. Title. Type of source. Publication information.
MLA DOCUMENTATION WITH CASE STUDY

103. Materials on CD or DVD with No Print Version

"Artificial Intelligence." *Encarta 2003*. Redmond: Microsoft, 2003. CD-ROM.

Encarta 2003 is a CD-ROM encyclopedia with no print version.

104. PowerPoint or Similar Presentation

Delyser, Ariel. "Political Movements in the Philippines." University of Denver.
   7 Feb. 2010. PowerPoint.

105. Work in More Than One Publication Medium

Shamoon, Linda, et al., eds. *Coming of Age: The Advanced Writing Curriculum*.
   Coming of Age Course Descriptions. Portsmouth: Boynton, 2000. Print,
   CD-ROM.

This book and CD-ROM come together. Each has its own title, but the publication information—Portsmouth: Boynton, 2000—applies to both.

25F What are MLA format guidelines for your research papers?

👁 **Watch the Video**

Check whether your instructor has special instructions for the final draft of your research paper. If there are no special instructions, you can use the MLA STYLE guidelines here. The student paper in 25G was prepared according to these MLA guidelines.

25F.1 General formatting instructions—MLA

Use 8½-by-11-inch white paper. Double-space throughout. Use a one-inch margin on the left, right, top, and bottom. Don't justify the type.

Drop down ½ inch from the top edge of the paper to the name-and-page-number line described here. Then drop down another 1/2 inch to the first line, whether that is a heading, a title, or a line of the text of your paper. For an example, see page 351.

Paragraph indents in the body of the paper and indents in Notes and Works Cited are ½ inch, or about five characters. The indent in Microsoft Word is a hanging indent of 0.5 for "first line." The indent for a set-off quotation (see p. 352) is 1 inch, or about ten characters.

25F.2 Order of parts—MLA

Use this order for the parts of your paper: body of the paper; endnotes, if any (headed "Notes," without quotation marks); Works Cited list; attachments, if any (such as questionnaires, data sheets, or any other material your instructor tells you to include). Number all pages consecutively.

25F.3 Name-and-page-number header for all pages—MLA

Use a header consisting of a name-and-page-number line on every page of your paper, including the first, unless your instructor requires otherwise. Most word-processing programs have an "insert header" or "view header" function that automatically places a header ½ inch from the top edge of the page. In the header, type your last name (capitalize only the first letter), then leave a one-character space, and end with the page number. Align the header about an inch from the right edge of the paper; in most word-processing programs, this is a "flush right" setting.

25F.4 First page—MLA

MLA doesn't require a cover page but understands that some instructors do, in which case you should follow your instructor's prescribed format.

If your instructor does not require a cover page, use a four-line heading at the top of the first page. Drop down 1 inch from the top of the page. Start each line at the left margin, and include the following information.

Your name (first line)

Your instructor's name (second line)

Your course name and section (third line)

The date you hand in your paper (fourth line)

For the submission date, use either day-month-year form (26 Nov. 2012) or month-day-year style (Nov. 26, 2012).

On one double-spaced line below this heading, center the title of your paper. Don't underline the title or enclose it in quotation marks. On the line below the title, start your paper. As we noted earlier, double-space lines throughout your paper.

❶ Capitalization Alerts: (1) Use a capital letter for the first word of your title and the first word of a subtitle, if you include one. Start every NOUN, PRONOUN, VERB, ADVERB, ADJECTIVE, and SUBORDINATING CONJUNCTION with a capital letter. Capitalize the last word of your title, no matter what part of speech it is. In a hyphenated compound word (two or more words used together to express one idea), capitalize every word that you would normally capitalize: Father-in-Law.

(2) Don't capitalize an article (*a, an, the*) unless one of the preceding capitalization rules applies to it. Don't capitalize PREPOSITIONS, no matter how many letters they contain. Don't capitalize COORDINATING CONJUNCTIONS. Don't capitalize the word *to* used in an INFINITIVE. ●

25F.5 Notes—MLA

In MLA style, footnotes or endnotes serve two specific purposes: (1) for ideas and information that do not fit into your paper but are still worth relating; and (2) for bibliographic information that would intrude if you were to include it in your text.

TEXT OF PAPER

Eudora Welty's literary biography, *One Writer's Beginnings*, shows us how both the inner world of self and the outer world of family and place form a writer's imagination.[1]

CONTENT NOTE—MLA

1. Welty, who valued her privacy, resisted investigation of her life. However, at the age of seventy-four, she chose to present her own autobiographical reflections in a series of lectures at Harvard University.

TEXT OF PAPER

Barbara Randolph believes that enthusiasm is contagious (65).[1] Many psychologists have found that panic, fear, and rage spread more quickly in crowds than positive emotions do, however.

BIBLIOGRAPHIC NOTE—MLA

1. Others who agree with Randolph include Thurman 21, 84, 155; Kelley 421–25; and Brookes 65–76.

If you use a note in your paper (see p. 346), try to structure the sentence so that the note number falls at the end. The ideal place for a note number, which appears slightly raised above the line of words (called a "superscript number"), is after the sentence-ending punctuation. Don't leave a space before the number. Word processing programs have commands for inserting "references" such as notes, and you'll want to choose endnotes rather than footnotes. If you use the references feature to insert a note, the program will generally open a box in which you type the words of your note, the program then saves all your notes together, in order. If, instead, you use the "font" command, type the number on the line, highlight it, click on "superscript" in the font box, and then click "OK." Number the notes consecutively throughout the paper.

Place your notes on a separate page after the last page of the body of your paper and before the Works Cited list. Order them sequentially as they appear in the paper. Center the word *Notes* at the top of the page, using the same 1-inch margin; don't underline it or enclose it in quotation marks.

If you have notes that accompany tables or figures, treat them differently. Place table or figure notes below the table or illustration. Instead of note numbers, use raised lowercase letters: a, b, c.

25F.6 Works Cited list—MLA

The Works Cited list starts on a new page and has the same name-and-page-number heading as the previous pages. One inch below the top edge of the page, center the words "Works Cited." Don't underline them or put them in quotation marks.

Start the first entry in your list at the left margin one double space after the Works Cited heading. If an entry takes more than one line, indent each subsequent line after the first ½ inch. Double space all lines throughout.

25G A student's MLA-style research paper

MLA STYLE doesn't require an outline before a research paper. Nevertheless, many instructors want students to submit them. Most instructors prefer the standard traditional outline format that we discuss in section 5G. Unless you're told otherwise, use that format.

View the Model Document

Some instructors prefer what they consider a more contemporary outline format. Never use it unless it's explicitly assigned. It differs because it outlines the content of the INTRODUCTORY and CONCLUDING PARAGRAPHS, and full wording of the THESIS STATEMENT is placed in the outline of the introductory paragraph. We show an example of this type in the topic outline of Andrei Gurov's paper which appears next.

½″
Gurov i

Outline

I. Introduction

  A. The meaning of the term déjà vu

  B. Thesis statement: Although a few people today still prefer to believe that feelings of déjà vu have mysterious and supernatural origins, recent research in cognitive psychology and the neurosciences has shed much rational light on the phenomenon.

II. Percentage of people who report experiencing déjà vu

III. Misunderstandings of the phenomenon of déjà vu

  A. Precognition

  B. False memory

IV. New psychological and medical theories of déjà vu

  A. Human sight's two pathways

  B. Implanted memories

    1. Natural: from old memories long forgotten

    2. Manipulated: from subliminal stimulation

    3. Inattentional blindness

V. Conclusion

  A. Many years of paranormal explanations of déjà vu

  B. Scientific research after 1980

  C. Much promise for further research

1"

Andrei Gurov

Professor Ryan

English 101, Section A4

12 Dec. 2011

Déjà Vu: At Last a Subject for Serious Study

"Brain hiccup" might be another name for *déjà vu,*
French for "already seen." During a moment of déjà vu, a
person relives an event that in reality is happening for the first
time. The hiccup metaphor seems apt because each modern
scientific explanation of the déjà vu phenomenon involves a
doubled event, as this paper will demonstrate. However, such
modern scientific work was long in coming. In his article "The
Déjà Vu Illusion," today's leading researcher in the field, Alan
S. Brown at Southern Methodist University, states that "for over
170 years, this most puzzling of memory illusions has intrigued
scholars" but was hampered when "during the behaviorist
era . . . the plethora of parapsychological and psychodynamic
interpretations" multiplied rapidly (256). Thus, notions of the
supernatural and magic halted the scientific study of déjà vu
for almost two centuries. By the first quarter of the twentieth
century, it began again slowly. Although a few people today
still prefer to believe that feelings of déjà vu have mysterious or
supernatural origins, recent research in cognitive psychology
and the neurosciences has shed much rational light on the
phenomenon.

Student information appears top left, in four lines, double-spaced.

Center title one double space below information.

To capture interest, Andrei creates an unusual term and quotes a researcher.

Thesis statement presents the main idea.

continued >>

(Proportions shown in this paper are adjusted to fit space limitations of this book. Follow
actual dimensions discussed in this book and your instructor's directions.)

Gurov 2

Some people report never having experienced déjà vu, and the percentages vary for the number of people who report having lived through at least one episode of it. In 2004, Brown reports that of the subjects he has interviewed, an average of 66 percent say that they have had one or more déjà vu experiences during their lives (*Experience* 33). However, in early 2005 in "Strangely Familiar," Uwe Wolfradt reports that "various studies indicate that from 50 to 90 percent of the people [studied] can recall having had at least one such déjà vu incident in their lives."

Perhaps part of the reason for this variation in the range of percentages stems from a general misunderstanding of the phrase *déjà vu*, even by some of the earlier scientific researchers twenty or more years ago. Indeed, in today's society, people throw around the term *déjà vu* without much thought. For example, it is fairly common for someone to see or hear about an event and then say, "Wow. This is déjà vu. I had a dream that this exact same thing happened." However, dreaming about an event ahead of time is a different phenomenon known as *precognition*, which relates to the paranormal experience of extrasensory perception. To date, precognition has never been scientifically demonstrated. As Johnson explains about dreams, however,

> ... there is usually very little "data," evidence, or documentation to confirm that a Precognition has taken place. If a person learns about some disaster and THEN [author's emphasis] tells people that he/she has foreseen it the day before, that may or may not be true, because there is usually not corroborative confirmation of what the person claims.

Header includes student's last name and the page number.

Andrei summarizes one of three sources by Brown; a shortened title and page number show which.

Brackets mean Andrei inserted "studied" to make the sentence flow smoothly.

Andrei realizes instructor will know he wrote this sentence, which needs no documentation.

Block indent quotations of four lines or more. "[author's emphasis]" shows "THEN" was capitalized in original. Source had no pages.

continued >>

Gurov 3

Thus, precognition, a phenomenon talked about frequently but one that has never held up under scientific scrutiny, is definitely not the same as déjà vu.

False memory is another phenomenon mislabeled *déjà vu.* It happens when people are convinced that certain events took place in their lives, even though the events never happened. This occurs when people have strong memories of many unrelated occurrences that suddenly come together into a whole that's very close to the current experience. It seems like a déjà vu experience. This occurs from the

> converging elements of many different but related experiences. When this abstract representation, which has emerged strictly from the melding together of strongly associated elements, happens to correspond to the present experience, a déjà vu may be the outcome. (Brown, *Experience* 160)

To illustrate lab-induced false memory, Brown in *The Déjà Vu Experience* cites investigations in which subjects are shown lists of words related to sleep; however, the word *sleep* itself is not on the list. In recalling the list of words, most subjects insist that the word *sleep* was indeed on the list, which means that the memory of a word that was never there is false memory. This is exactly what happens when well-intentioned eyewitnesses believe they recall certain criminal acts even though, in fact, they never saw or experienced the events at all (159).

In the last twenty years especially, new theories have come to the fore as a result of rigorous work from psychological and medical points of view. In *Experience,* Brown surveys the literature and concludes that this relatively young field

Phrase introduces quotation.

All source information put in a parenthetical citation. Block quotation periods come before citation.

Only page number goes in parentheses when author named in text.

continued >>

Gurov 4

Transition paragraph introduces four new topics.

of investigation is dividing itself into four categories: (1) dual processing, (2) memory, (3) neurological, and (4) attentional. This paper briefly discusses the first and second as each relates to the third. Next, I discuss the fourth as it relates to the second.

Two related sources in one citation, separated by semicolon.

Brain-based studies of the human sense of sight are one heavily researched theory of déjà vu that has been partially explained in the last two decades. Such studies focus on the dual pathways by which the sight of an event reaches the brain (Glenn; Carey F1). For example, the left hemisphere processes information from the right eye and the right hemisphere processes information from the left eye. The brain is incapable of

Discusses first topic from previous paragraph.

storing data with respect to time and is only able to "see" events in relation to others. Each eye interprets data separately, at the same precise time. According to research, the human brain can perceive two visual stimuli at one instant as long as they are "seen" less than 25 milliseconds apart. Since the human brain

Citation shows paragraph summarizes several source pages.

is capable of interpreting both signals within this time, when events are perceived normally, they are seen and recognized by the brain as one single event (Weiten 69, 97–99, 211).

Occasionally, however, the neurological impulses that carry data from each eye to the brain are delayed. As Johnson explains, the person might be fatigued or have had his or her attention seriously distracted (as when crossing the street at a

To develop topic sentence, Andrei summarizes Johnson's explanation.

dangerous intersection). As a result, one signal may reach the brain in under 25 milliseconds, while the other signal is slowed and reaches the brain slightly more than 25 milliseconds later. Even a few milliseconds' delay makes the second incoming signal arrive late—and, without fail, the brain interprets the stimuli as two separate events rather than one event. The

continued >>

Gurov 5

person thus has the sensation of having seen the event before because the brain has recognized the milliseconds-later event as a memory.

Implanted memories are another well-researched explanation for the déjà vu phenomenon. Examples of implanted memories originate in both the natural and the lab-induced experiences of people. For instance, perhaps a person walks into the kitchen of a new friend for the first time and, although the person has never been there before, the person feels certain that he or she has. With hypnosis and other techniques, researchers could uncover that the cupboards are almost exactly like those that the person had forgotten were in the kitchen of the person's grandparents' house and that the scent of baking apple pie is identical to the smell the person loved when walking into the grandparents' home during holidays (Carey F1). Colorado State University Professor Anne Cleary and her colleagues conducted an experiment in which students studied images of simple scenes and then were shown a second set of images. Some of the second set were made to resemble the original study images. Students tended to "remember" those scenes that had elements in common, even if they were not identical (1083).

Thomas McHugh, a researcher at MIT, believes he has even discovered the specific neurological "memory circuit" in the brain that is the source of this kind of déjà vu (Lemonick). This circuit allows people to complete memories with just a single cue. For example, you can remember much about a football game you saw even if someone just mentions the two teams involved. Sometimes, however, the circuit "misfires," and it signals that a

Discusses second topic, memory, introduced above.

Specific example makes the point vividly.

Develops third topic with research on memory.

Specific example clarifies the point.

continued >>

Gurov 6

new memory is actually part of the pattern of an old one. Researchers Akira O'Connor, Colin Lever, and Chris Moulin claim that the false sensations of memory differ from those of familiarity. They call the former "déjà vécue," and note serious cases in which people live much of their life in this state. It remains to be seen whether their distinction will be confirmed.

Andrei illustrates concept by summarizing Wolfradt's account of Jacoby's work.

Wolfradt describes a lab-induced experiment in which psychologist Larry L. Jacoby in 1989 manipulated a group of subjects so that he could implant a memory that would lead to a déjà vu experience for each of them. He arranged for his subjects to assemble in a room equipped with a screen in front. He flashed on the screen one word so quickly that no one was consciously aware they had seen the word. Jacoby was certain, however, that the visual centers of the brain of each subject had indeed "seen" the word. Later, when he flashed the word leaving it on the screen long enough for the subjects to consciously see it, everyone indicated they had seen the word somewhere before. All the subjects were firmly convinced that the first time they had seen the word, it absolutely was not on the screen at the front of the room they were in. Some became annoyed at being asked over and over. Since Jacoby's work, lab-induced memory research has become very popular in psychology. In fact, it has been given its own name: *priming*. Alan Brown and Elizabeth Marsh confirmed Jacoby's findings in three follow-up studies (38–41).

Andrei begins fourth topic introduced earlier.

Inattention, or what some researchers call "inattentional blindness," is also an extensively researched explanation for the déjà vu experience. Sometimes people can see objects without any impediment right before them but still not process

continued >>

Gurov 7

the objects because they're paying attention to something else
(Brown, *Experience* 181). The distraction might be daydreaming,
a sudden lowering of energy, or simply being drawn to another
object in the environment. As David Glenn explains in "The
Tease of Memory":

> Imagine that you drive through an unfamiliar town
> but pay little attention because you're talking
> on a cellphone [sic]. If you then drive back down
> the same streets a few moments later, this time
> focusing on the landscape, you might be prone to
> experience déjà vu. During your second pass, the
> visual information is consciously processed in the
> hippocampus [of the brain] but feels falsely "old"
> because the images from your earlier drive still
> linger in your short term memory.

The busy lifestyle today would seem to lead to many
distractions of perception and thus to frequent experiences of
déjà vu; however, these are no more frequently reported than
any other causes reported concerning déjà vu.

One compelling laboratory experiment studying
inattention is described by Carey in "Déjà Vu: If It All Seems
Familiar, There May Be a Reason." He recounts a test with
many college students from Duke University in Durham, North
Carolina. The students were asked to look at a group of
photographs of the campus of Southern Methodist University in
Dallas, Texas, that were flashed before them at a very quick
speed. A small black or white cross was superimposed on each
photograph, and the students were instructed to find the cross
and focus on it (F6). Brown in *The Déjà Vu Experience* explains

The word
"sic," in
brackets,
shows the
source mis-
takenly made
"cell phone"
one word.

Andrei
anticipates
and answers
a reader's
possible
question.

In order to
explain "in-
attention,"
Andrei sum-
marizes an
experiment at
some length.

continued >>

Gurov 8

that the researchers assumed that the quick speed at which the photographs had been shown would result in no one's having noticed the background scenes. A week's time passed, and the same students were shown the pictures again, this time without the crosses. Almost all insisted that they had been to the college campus shown in the photos, which was physically impossible for that many students since they lived in Durham, North Carolina, and the college in the photographs was in Dallas, Texas (182–83). This means that the scenes in the photographs did indeed register in the visual memories of the students in spite of the quick speed and the distraction of looking only for the crosses.

The worlds of psychology and neurology have learned much since the age of paranormal interpretations of déjà vu experiences, starting around 1935. That is when rational science energetically began its disciplined investigations of brain-based origins of the déjà vu phenomenon. Concepts such as dual processing of sight, implanted memories, and inattentional blindness, among other theories, have gone far in opening the door to the possibilities of many more inventive theories to explain incidents of déjà vu. The leading researcher in the field today, Alan S. Brown, is among the strongest voices urging a vast expansion of investigations into this still relatively unexplored phenomenon. He is optimistic this will happen, given his whimsical remark to Carlin Flora of *Psychology Today*: "We are always fascinated when the brain goes haywire." Researchers conducting these studies might watch for the unsettling experiences of other investigators who "have had déjà vu about having déjà vu" (Phillips).

Parenthetical citation shows pages summarized in this sentence.

Concluding paragraph reviews theories that were presented in paper.

Two quotations, by Flora and Phillips, create a memorable ending.

continued >>

Gurov 9

Works Cited

Brown, Alan S. *The Déjà Vu Experience: Essays in Cognitive Psychology*. New York: Psychology, 2004. Print.

--- . "The Déjà Vu Illusion." *Current Directions in Psychological Science* 13.6 (2004): 256–59. Print.

--- and Elizabeth J. Marsh. "Digging into Deja Vu: Recent Research on Possible Mechanisms." *The Psychology of Learning and Motivation: Advances in Research and Theory*. Ed. Brian H. Ross. Burlington: Academic P, 2010, 33–62. Web. 20 Nov. 2011.

Carey, Benedict. "Déjà Vu: If It All Seems Familiar, There May Be a Reason." *New York Times* 14 Sept. 2004: F1+. *LexisNexis*. Web. 11 Nov. 2011.

Flora, Carlin. "Giving Déjà Vu Its Due." *Psychology Today* Mar.–Apr. 2005: 27. *Academic Search Premier*. Web. 7 Nov. 2011.

Glenn, David. "The Tease of Memory." *Chronicle of Higher Education* 23 July 2004: A12. Print.

Johnson, C. "A Theory on the Déjà Vu Phenomenon." 8 Dec. 2001. Web. 20 Nov. 2011.

Lemonick, Michael D. "Explaining Déjà Vu." *Time* 20 Aug. 2007. *Academic Search Premier*. Web. 5 Dec. 2011.

O'Connor, Akira R., Colin Lever, and Chris J. A. Moulin. "Novel Insights into False Recollection: A Model of Deja Vecu." *Cognitive Neuropsychiatry* 15.1–3 (2010): 118–44. Web. 14 Nov. 2011.

Phillips, Helen. "Looks Familiar." *New Scientist* 201.2701 (28 Mar. 2009): 28–31. Web. 20 Nov. 2011.

Works Cited, centered, begins on a new page. While Andrei's Working Bibliography had twice as many sources, his final draft includes only those related to his thesis.

Sources are listed in alphabetical order and double-spaced throughout, using hanging indentations.

Final Works Cited list has thirteen sources, five popular and the rest scholarly, proportions typical of a first-year college-level research paper.

continued >>

Thompson, Rebecca G., et al. "Persistent Déjà Vu: A Disorder
of Memory." *International Journal of Geriatric Psychiatry*
19.9 (2004): 906–07. Print.

Weiten, Wayne. *Psychology: Themes and Variations.* Belmont:
Wadsworth, 2005. Print.

Wolfradt, Uwe. "Strangely Familiar." *Scientific American Mind*
16.1 (2005): 32–37. *Academic Search Elite.* Web. 7 Nov. 2011.

APA Documentation with Case Study

26 ■ ■ ■ ■ ■ ■ ■ ■ ■ ■

Quick Points You will learn to

> ➤ Use APA in-text parenthetical documentation (see 26B and 26C).
> ➤ Use APA guidelines for a References list (see 26D and 26E).
> ➤ Format your paper according to APA guidelines (see 26I).

26A What is APA documentation style?

The American Psychological Association (APA) sponsors the **APA style**, a DOCUMENTATION* system widely used in the social sciences. APA style has two equally important features that need to appear in research papers.

1. Within the body of your paper, you need to use IN-TEXT CITATIONS, in parentheses, to acknowledge your SOURCES as described in sections 26B and 26C.

2. At the end of the paper, provide a list of the sources you used—and only those sources. Title this list, which contains complete bibliographic information about each source, "References," as explained in sections 26D and 26E.

See 26I for a sample student paper in APA style.

26B What are APA in-text parenthetical citations?

APA style requires parenthetical documentation (also called in-text citations) that identify a source by the author's name and the copyright year. If there is no author, use a shortened version of the title. In addition, APA style requires page numbers for DIRECT QUOTATIONS, but it recommends using them also for PARAPHRASES and SUMMARIES. Some instructors expect you to give page references for paraphrases and summaries and others don't, so find out your instructor's preference to avoid any problems. Put page numbers in parentheses, using the abbreviation *p.* before a single page number and *pp.* when the material you're citing falls on more than one page. Separate the parts of a parenthetical citation with commas. End punctuation always follows the citation unless it's a long quotation set in block style in which case the citation comes after the end punctuation.

If you refer to a work more than once in a paragraph, APA style recommends giving the author's name and the date at the first mention and then using only the name after that. However, if you're citing two or more works by the same author, include the date in each citation to identify which work you're citing. When two or more sources have the same last name, keep them clearly separate by using both first and last names in the text or first initial(s) and last names in parentheses.

---

*Words printed in SMALL CAPITAL LETTERS are discussed elsewhere in the Terms Glossary at the back of the book.

26C What are APA examples for in-text citations?

This section shows how to cite various kinds of sources in the body of your paper. The directory at the beginning of this tab corresponds to the numbered examples in this section.

1. Paraphrased or Summarized Source

> Modern technologies and social media tend to fragment individual identities (Conley, 2009).

Author name and date cited in parentheses.

> Dalton Conley (2009) contends that modern technologies and social media fragment individual identities.

Author name cited in text; date cited in parentheses.

2. Source of a Short Quotation

> Approaches adopted from business to treat students as consumers "do not necessarily yield improved outcomes in terms of student learning" (Arum & Roksa, 2011, p. 137).

Author names, date, and page reference cited in parentheses.

> Arum & Roksa (2011) find that approaches adopted from business to treat students as consumers "do not necessarily yield improved outcomes in terms of student learning" (p. 137).

Author names cited in text, followed by the date cited in parentheses incorporated into the words introducing the quotation; page number in parentheses immediately following the quotation.

3. Source of a Long Quotation

When you use a quotation of forty or more words, set it off in block style indented ½ inch from the left margin. Don't use quotation marks. Place the parenthetical reference one space after the end punctuation of the quotation's last sentence.

> Although some have called for regulating online games, others see such actions as unwarranted:
>
> > Any activity when taken to excess can cause problems in a person's life, but it is unlikely that there would be legislation against, for example, people excessively reading or exercising. There is no argument that online gaming should be treated any differently. (Griffiths, 2010, pp. 38–39)

Author name, date, and page reference cited in parentheses following the end punctuation.

4. One Author

> One of his questions is, "What binds together a Mormon banker in Utah with his brother or other coreligionists in Illinois or Massachusetts?" (Coles, 1993, p. 2).

In a parenthetical reference in APA style, a comma and a space separate a name from a year and a year from a page reference.

5. Two Authors

If a work has two authors, give both names in each citation.

> One report describes 2,123 occurrences (Krait & Cooper, 2003).

> The results that Krait and Cooper (2003) report would not support the conclusions Davis and Sherman (1999) draw in their review of the literature.

When you write a parenthetical in-text citation naming two (or more) authors, use an ampersand (&) between the final two names (as in the first example). However, write out the word *and* for references you include in your own sentence (as in the second example).

6. Three, Four, or Five Authors

For three, four, or five authors, use all of the authors' last names in the first reference. In all subsequent references, use only the first author's last name followed by *et al.* (meaning "and others"). No period follows *et*, but one always follows *al.*

FIRST REFERENCE

> In one study, only 30% of the survey population could name the most commonly spoken languages in five Middle Eastern countries (Ludwig, Rodriquez, Novak, & Ehlers, 2008).

SUBSEQUENT REFERENCE

> Ludwig et al. (2008) found that most Americans could identify the language spoken in Saudi Arabia.

7. Six or More Authors

For six or more authors, name the first author followed by *et al.* in all in-text references, including the first.

These injuries can lead to an inability to perform athletically, in addition to initiating degenerative changes at the joint level (Mandelbaum et al., 2005).

8. Author(s) with Two or More Works in the Same Year

If you use more than one source written in the same year by the same author(s), alphabetize the works by title for the REFERENCES list, and assign letters in alphabetical order to each work: (2007a), (2007b), (2007c). Use the year–letter combination in parenthetical references. Note that a citation of two or more such works lists the year extensions in alphabetical order.

Most recently, Torrevillas (2007c) draws new conclusions from the results of eight experiments conducted with experienced readers (Torrevillas, 2007a, 2007b).

9. Two or More Authors with the Same Last Name

Include first initials for every in-text citation of authors who share a last name. Be sure to use the same initials appearing in your References list at the end of your paper. (In the second example, a parenthetical citation, the name order is alphabetical, as explained in item 12.)

R. A. Smith (2008) and C. Smith (1999) both confirm these results.

These results have been confirmed independently (C. Smith, 1999; R. A. Smith, 2008).

10. Group or Corporate Author

If you use a source in which the "author" is a corporation, agency, or group, an in-text reference gives that name as author. Use the full name in each citation, unless an abbreviated version of the name is likely to be familiar to your audience. In that case, use the full name and give its abbreviation in brackets at the first citation; then, use the abbreviation for subsequent citations.

Although the space shuttle program has ended, other programs will continue to send Americans into space (National Aeronautics and Space Administration [NASA], 2011).

In subsequent citations, use the abbreviated form alone.

11. Work Listed by Title

If no author is named, use a shortened form of the title for in-text citations. Ignoring *A, An,* or *The,* make the first word the one by which you alphabetize the title in your References list at the end of your paper. The following example refers to an article fully titled "Are You a Day or Night Person?"

> Scientists group people as "larks" or "owls" on the basis of whether individuals are more efficient in the morning or at night ("Are You," 1989).

12. Two or More Sources in One Reference

If more than one source has contributed to an idea or opinion in your paper, cite the sources alphabetically by author in one set of parentheses; separate each source of information with a semicolon, as in the following example.

> Conceptions of personal space vary among cultures (Morris, 1977; Worchel & Cooper, 1983).

13. Personal Communication, Including E-Mail and Other Nonretrievable Sources

Telephone calls, personal letters, interviews, and e-mail messages are "personal communications" that your readers can't access or retrieve. Acknowledge personal communications in parenthetical references, but never include them in your References list at the end of your paper.

> Recalling his first summer at camp, one person said, "The proximity of 12 other kids made me—an only child with older, quiet parents—frantic for eight weeks" (A. Weiss, personal communication, January 12, 2011).

14. Retrievable Online Sources

When you quote, paraphrase, or summarize an online source that is available to others, cite the author (if any) or title and the date as you would for a print source, and include the work in your References list.

> It is possible that similarity in personality is important in having a happy marriage (Luo & Clonen, 2005, p. 324).

15. Sources with No Page Numbers

If an online or other source doesn't provide page numbers, use the paragraph number, if available, preceded by the abbreviation *para*. It is rare, however, to number paragraphs. If you can't find a page or paragraph number, cite a heading if possible.

(Daniels, 2010, para. 4)

(Sanz, 2009, Introduction)

(Herring, 2011)

16. Source Lines for Graphics and Table Data

If you use a graphic from another source or create a table using data from another source, provide a note at the bottom of the table or graphic, crediting the original author and the copyright holder. Here are examples of two source notes, one for a graphic using data from an article, the other for a graphic reprinted from a book.

GRAPHIC USING DATA FROM AN ARTICLE

Note. The data in columns 1 and 2 are from "Advance Organizers in Advisory Reports: Selective Reading, Recall, and Perception" by L. Lagerwerf et al., 2008, *Written Communication, 25*(1), p. 68. Copyright 2008 by Sage Publications.

GRAPHIC FROM A BOOK

Note. From *Academically Adrift: Limited Learning on College Campuses* (p. 97), by R. Arum and J. Roksa, 2011, Chicago: University of Chicago Press. Copyright 2011 by The University of Chicago.

26D What are APA guidelines for a References list?

Watch the Video

The **References** list at the end of your research paper provides complete bibliographic information for readers who may want to access the SOURCES you drew on to write your paper.

Include in the References list all the sources you quote, paraphrase, or summarize in your paper so that readers can find the same sources with reasonable effort. Never include in your References list any source that's not generally available to other people (see item 13 in 26C). Quick Box 26.1 provides general information about an APA References list, and section 26E gives many models for specific kinds of entries. See 26I for a sample of a student References list.

Quick Box 26.1

■ ■ ■ ■ ■ ■ ■ ■ ■ ■ ■

Guidelines for an APA-style References list

TITLE

The title is "References," centered, without quotation marks, italics, or underlining.

PLACEMENT OF LIST

Start a new page numbered sequentially with the rest of the paper, immediately after the body of the paper.

CONTENTS AND FORMAT

Include all quoted, paraphrased, or summarized sources in your paper that are not personal communications; however, if your instructor tells you also to include all the references you have simply consulted, please do so. Start each entry on a new line, and double-space all lines. Use a *hanging indent* style: The first line of each entry begins flush left at the margin, and all other lines are indented ½ inch.

Wolfe, C. R. (2011). Argumentation across the curriculum. *Written Communication, 28,* 193–218.

SPACING AFTER PUNCTUATION

APA calls for one space after commas, periods, question marks, and colons.

ARRANGEMENT OF ENTRIES

Alphabetize by the author's last name. If no author is named, alphabetize by the first significant word (ignore *A, An,* or *The*) in the title of the work.

AUTHORS' NAMES

Use last names, first initials, and middle initials, if any. Reverse the order for all authors' names, and use an ampersand (&) before the last author's name: Mills, J. F., & Holahan, R. H.

Give names in the order in which they appear on the work. Use a comma between each author's last name and first initial and after each complete name except the last. Use a period after the last author's name.

DATES

Date information follows the name information and is enclosed in parentheses. If date information falls at the end of your sentence, place a period followed by one space after the closing parenthesis.

For books, articles in journals that have volume numbers, and many other print and nonprint sources, the year of publication or production is

continued >>

Quick Box 26.1   (continued)

the date to use. For articles from most general-circulation magazines and newspapers, use the year followed by a comma and then the exact date that appears on the issue (month, month and day, or season, depending on the frequency of the publication). Capitalize any words in dates, and use no abbreviations.

CAPITALIZATION OF TITLES

For book, article, and chapter titles, capitalize the first word, the first word after a colon between a title and subtitle, and any proper nouns. For names of journals and proceedings of meetings, capitalize the first word; all NOUNS, VERBS, ADVERBS, and ADJECTIVES; and any other words four or more letters long.

FORMAT OF TITLES

Use no italics, quotation marks, or underlines for titles of shorter works (poems, short stories, essays, articles, Web pages). Italicize titles of longer works (books, newspapers, journals, or Web sites). If an italic typeface is unavailable, underline the title and the end punctuation using one unbroken line.

Do not drop any words (such as *A*, *An*, or *The*) from the titles of periodicals such as newspapers, magazines, and journals. See 26F for information on formatting the title of your own APA research paper.

ABBREVIATIONS OF MONTHS

Do not abbreviate the names of months in any context.

PAGE NUMBERS

Use all digits, omitting none. For references to books and newspapers only, use *p.* (for one page) and *pp.* (for more than one page) before page numbers. List all discontinuous pages, with numbers separated by commas: pp. 32, 44–45, 47–49, 53.

PUBLICATION INFORMATION

Publication information varies according to type of source. See 26E for how to cite articles from periodicals (both print or online), books (both print or digital), images and video, other Web sources, and miscellaneous sources.

26E   What are APA examples for sources in a References list?

The directory at the beginning of this tab corresponds to the numbered examples in this section. For quick help deciding which example you should follow, see the decision flowchart in Figure 26.1. You can find other examples in the *Publication Manual of the American Psychological Association* (6th edition) or at the APA Web site, http://www.apastyle.org.

Figure 26.1   Decision-making flowchart for APA References citations.

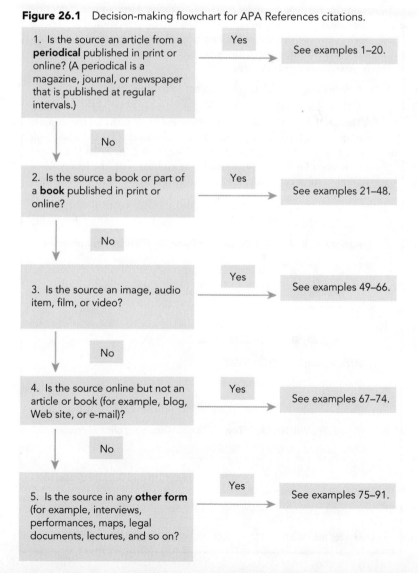

1. Is the source an article from a **periodical** published in print or online? (A periodical is a magazine, journal, or newspaper that is published at regular intervals.)
   — Yes → See examples 1–20.
   — No ↓

2. Is the source a book or part of a **book** published in print or online?
   — Yes → See examples 21–48.
   — No ↓

3. Is the source an image, audio item, film, or video?
   — Yes → See examples 49–66.
   — No ↓

4. Is the source online but not an article or book (for example, blog, Web site, or e-mail)?
   — Yes → See examples 67–74.
   — No ↓

5. Is the source in any **other form** (for example, interviews, performances, maps, legal documents, lectures, and so on?
   — Yes → See examples 75–91.

Quick Box 26.2 summarizes the basic entries for periodical entries. Variations on the basic entries follow the Quick Box.

Quick Box 26.2

Basic entries for periodical articles with and without DOIs—APA

Citations for periodical articles contain four major parts: author, date, title of article, and publication information (usually, the periodical title, volume number, page numbers, and sometimes a digital object identifier). Some citations also include information about the type of source in brackets; examples are reviews, motion pictures, and so on.

1. **Articles with a DOI (Digital Object Identifier): Print or online**

   A **DOI** is a numerical code sometimes assigned to journal articles. The DOI for an article will be the same even if the article appears in different versions including print and online. (To see where you can find an article's DOI, refer to Figure 26.2, p. 374.) If a source contains a DOI, simply conclude the citation with the letters "doi" followed by a colon, then the number. If a source has a DOI, always use this citation method.

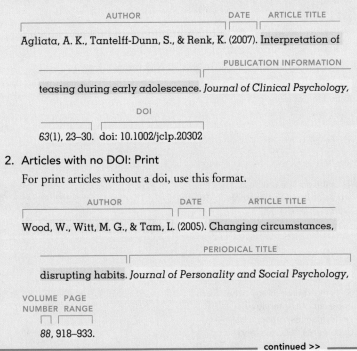

   AUTHOR · DATE · ARTICLE TITLE

   Agliata, A. K., Tantelff-Dunn, S., & Renk, K. (2007). Interpretation of

   PUBLICATION INFORMATION

   teasing during early adolescence. *Journal of Clinical Psychology,*

   DOI

   63(1), 23–30. doi: 10.1002/jclp.20302

2. **Articles with no DOI: Print**

   For print articles without a doi, use this format.

   AUTHOR · DATE · ARTICLE TITLE

   Wood, W., Witt, M. G., & Tam, L. (2005). Changing circumstances,

   PERIODICAL TITLE

   disrupting habits. *Journal of Personality and Social Psychology,*

   VOLUME PAGE
   NUMBER RANGE

   88, 918–933.

continued >>

Quick Box 26.2 (continued)

3. Articles with no DOI: Online

For online articles without a DOI, retrieval information begins with the words "Retrieved from," then the URL of the periodical's Web home page, and, occasionally, additional information. If you found the article through an online subscription database, do a Web search for the URL of the periodical's home page on the Web, and include the home page URL. If you can't find the periodical's Web home page, then name the database in your retrieval statement: for example, "Retrieved from Academic Search Premier database" (see example 20). If a URL must be divided on two or more lines, only break the address before slashes or punctuation marks.

Retrieval date: Include the date you retrieved the information only if the item does not have a publication date, is from an online reference book, or is likely to be changed in the future (such as a prepublication version of an article, a Web page, or a Wiki; see citation 72).

AUTHOR   DATE   ARTICLE TITLE

Eagleman, D. (2011, July/August). The brain on trial.

MAGAZINE TITLE   ONLINE RETRIEVAL INFORMATION

The Atlantic. Retrieved from http://www.theatlantic.com

Notice that the only punctuation in the URL is part of the address. Do not add a period after a URL.

PERIODICALS—APA REFERENCES

1. Article in a Journal with Continuous Pagination: Print

Williams, B. T. (2010). Seeking new worlds: The study of writing beyond our classrooms. *College Composition and Communication, 62,* 127–146.

Continuous pagination means that page numbers in each issue of a volume begin where the page numbers in the previous issue left off. So, for example, if issue one stopped at page 125, issue two would start at page 126. Just give the volume number, italicized after the journal title.

2. Article in a Journal with Continuous Pagination: Online, with DOI

Gurung, R., & Vespia, K. (2007). Looking good, teaching well? Linking liking, looks, and learning. *Teaching of Psychology, 34,* 5–10. doi: 10.1207/s15328023top3401_2

Figure 26.2 Journal article available in print and online, with a DOI.

A

EBSCO Research HOST Database

Sign In | Folder | Preferences | New Features! | Help

UNIV OF DENVER (Logout)

Basic Search | Advanced Search | Visual Search | Choose Databases

New Search | Keyword | Thesaurus | Cited References | Indexes | Language ▼

25 of 28 ▶ Result List | Refine Search | Print | E-mail | Save | Export | Add to folder

View: Citation | PDF Full Text | Cited References(17)

ARTICLE TITLE — Title: Interpretation of teasing during early adolescence. **Find More Like This**

AUTHORS — Author(s): Agliata, Allison Kanter, University of Central Florida, Orlando, FL, US. AKanter104@aol.com
Tantleff-Dunn, Stacey University of Central Florida, Orlando, FL, US.
Renk, Kimberly, University of Central Florida, Orlando, FL, US.

Address: Agliata, Allison Kanter, University of Central Florida, Department of Psychology, P.O. Box 161390, Orlando, FL. US. 32816. AKanter104@aol.com

PUBLICATION INFORMATION — Source: Journal of Clinical Psychology, Vol 63(I), Jan 2007 pp 23-30

DATE — Publisher: US: John Wiley & Sons

ISSN: 0021-9762 (Print)
1097-4679 (Electronic)

DOI — Digital Object Identifier: 10.1002/jclp.20302

Language: English

Keywords: *appearance*-related teasing, early adolescence, cognitive processes, memories, *physical appearance*, exposure, experience; body dissatisfaction

Abstract: Research has suggested that teasing, especially about *physical apperance*, is a common experience with

B

ARTICLE TITLE — **Interpretation of Teasing During Early Adolescence**

AUTHORS — Allison Kanter Agliata, Stacey Tantleff-Dunn, and Kimberly Renk
University of Central Florida

Research has suggested that teasing, especially about physical appearance, is a common experience with negative consequences for adolescents. This study aimed to examine the cognitive processes of adolescents exposed to teasing. Students from two middle schools were assigned randomly to view videotaped vignettes of appearance-related teasing, competency teasing, or a control situation and completed questionnaires to assess their cognitive reactions and memories of the teasing. Results indicated that adolescent girls recalled appearance-related teasing more readily than competency teasing, adolescent girls with high body dissatisfaction recalled fewer positive appearance words, and participants exposed to competency teasing were more likely to recall competency words. The findings indicated that cognitive processes may be important in the study of adolescents' interpretation of teasing and for clinical treatment of adolescents who are teased. © 2006 Wiley Periodicals, Inc. J Clin Psychol 63: 23–30, 2007.

Keywords: teasing; adolescents

Although adolescence has been identified as the time when individuals are most likely to experience hurtful teasing (Shapiro, Baumeister, & Kessler, 1991), surprisingly little empirical literature has emerged to further the understanding of how adolescents perceive teasing interactions or how clinicians can help adolescents cope more effectively with these difficult situations (Shapiro et al., 1991). Studies examining the content of teasing among young adolescents have reported that 66% of teasing consists of name-calling, the majority of which focuses on physical appearance, followed by competency teasing (Mooney, Creeser, & Blatchford, 1991; Scambler, Harris, & Milich, 1998; Shapiro et al., 1991). Depending on the personality of the child and his or her different interpretations of the teasing situation, teasing experiences may affect young adolescents in vastly different ways (Scambler et al., 1998).

DATE — This manuscript is based on a master's thesis completed by Allison Kanter Agliata under the supervision of Stacey Tantleff-Dunn.

PUBLICATION INFORMATION — Correspondence concerning this article should be addressed to: Allison Kanter Agliata, University of Central Florida, Department of Psychology, P.O. Box 161390, Orlando, FL 32816; e-mail: AKanter104@aol.com

JOURNAL OF CLINICAL PSYCHOLOGY, Vol. 63(1), 23–30 (2007) © 2007 Wiley Periodicals, Inc.

DOI — Published online in Wiley InterScience (www.interscience.wiley.com). DOI: 10.1002/jclp.20302

WILEY InterScience®

CITATION

Agliata, A.K., Tantleff-Dunn, S., & Renk, K. (2007). Interpretation of teasing

during early adolescence. *Journal of Clinical Psychology, 63*(1). 23–30.

doi: 10.1002/jcpl.2302

3. Article in a Journal with Continuous Pagination: Online, No DOI

Pollard, R. (2002). Evidence of a reduced home field advantage when a team moves to a new stadium. *Journal of Sports Sciences, 20*, 969–974. Retrieved from http://www.tandf.co.uk/journals/risp

No retrieval date is included because the final version of the article is being referenced.

4. Article in a Journal That Pages Each Issue Separately: Print

Peters, B. (2011). Lessons about writing to learn from a university–high school partnership. *WPA: Writing Program Administration, 34*(2), 59–88.

Give the volume number, italicized with the journal title, followed by the issue number in parentheses (not italicized), and the page number(s).

5. Article in a Journal That Pages Each Issue Separately: Online, with No DOI

Peters, B. (2011). Lessons about writing to learn from a university–high school partnership. *WPA: Writing Program Administration, 34*(2). Retrieved from http://wpacouncil.org/journal/index.html

6. In-press Article: Online

George, S. (in press). How accurately should we estimate the anatomical source of exhaled nitric oxide? *Journal of Applied Physiology.* doi:10.1152/japplphysiol.00111.2008. Retrieved February, 2008 from http://jap.physiology.org/papbyrecent.shtml

In press means that an article has been accepted for publication but has not yet been published in its final form. Therefore, there is no publication date, so although the article has a DOI, it also has a "retrieved from" statement that includes a date, in case anything changes.

7. Article in a Weekly or Biweekly Magazine: Print

Foroohar, R. (2011, June 27). Why the world isn't getting smaller. *Time*, 20.

Give the year, month, and date. If no author is listed, begin with the title of the article.

The price is wrong. (2003, August 2). *The Economist, 368*, 58–59.

8. Article in a Weekly or Biweekly Magazine: Online

Foroohar, R. (2011, June 27). Why the world isn't getting smaller. *Time.* Retrieved from http://www.time.com/time/

9. Article in a Monthly or Bimonthly Periodical: Print

Goetz, T. (2011, July). The feedback loop. *Wired, 19*(7), 126–133.

Give the year and month(s). Insert the volume number, italicized with the periodical title. Put the issue number in parentheses; do not italicize it.

10. Article in a Newspaper: Print

Hesse, M. (2011, April 24). Love among the ruins. *The Washington Post*, p. F1.

Use the abbreviation *p.* (or *pp.* for more than one page) for newspapers. If no author is listed, begin with the title of the article.

Prepping for uranium work. (2011, June 18). *The Denver Post*, p. B2.

11. Article in a Newspaper: Online

Hesse, M. (2011, April 22). Falling in love with St. Andrews, Scotland. *The Washington Post*. Retrieved from http://www.washingtonpost.com/

Give the URL from the newspaper's Web site. Some newspapers publish only online. Treat them the same way, as follows:

Katz, D. (2010, October 28). What to do about flu? Get vaccinated. *Huffington Post*. Retrieved from http://www.huffingtonpost.com

12. Editorial: Print

Primary considerations. (2008, January 27). [Editorial]. *The Washington Post*, p. B6.

Include the type of writing in brackets immediately after the date. For example [Editorial] or [Review] or [Letter].

13. Editorial: Online

Primary considerations. (2008, January 27). [Editorial]. *The Washington Post*. Retrieved from http://www.washingtonpost.com

14. Letter to the Editor: Print

Goldstein, L. (2011, May/June). [Letter to the editor]. Roach coaches: The upside. *Sierra*, 2.

15. Letter to the Editor: Online

Ennis, H. B. (2007, December 22). [Letter to the editor]. *U.S. News and World Report*. Retrieved from http://www.usnews.com

16. Book Review: Print

Shenk, D. (2003, Spring). Toolmaker, brain builder. [Review of the book *Beyond Deep Blue: Building the computer that defeated the world chess champion* by Feng-Hsiung Hsu]. *The American Scholar, 72*, 150–152.

17. Movie Review: Online

Travers, P. (2011, June 2). [Review of the motion picture *Beginners*, directed by Mike Mills]. *RollingStone*. Retrieved from http://www.rollingstone.com

18. Article in a Looseleaf Collection of Reprinted Articles

Hayden, T. (2002). The age of robots. In E. Goldstein (Ed.), *Applied Science 2002. SIRS 2002*, Article 66. (Reprinted from *U.S. News & World Report*, pp. 44–50, 2001, April 23).

19. Online Magazine Content Not Found in Print Version

Shulman, M. (2008, January 3). 12 diseases that altered history. [Supplemental material]. *U.S. News & World Report*. Retrieved from http://health.usnews .com/

The bracketed phrase [Supplemental material] indicates that content appears in the online version of this source that does not appear in the print version.

20. Abstract from a Secondary Source: Online

Walther, J. B., Van Der Heide, B., Kim, S., Westerman, D., & Tong, S. (2008). The role of friends' appearance and behavior on evaluations of individuals on Facebook: Are we known by the company we keep? *Human Communication Research 34*(1), 28–49. Abstract retrieved from PsycINFO database.

BOOKS—APA REFERENCES

Quick Box 26.3 summarizes the basic entry for books, both print and electronic. Variations on the basic entries follow. Where to locate a book's citation information is shown in Figure 26.3 (page 379).

Quick Box 26.3 ■ ■ ■ ■ ■ ■ ■ ■ ■ ■ ■

Basic entries for books—APA

All citations for books have four main parts: author, date, title, and publication information. For traditional print books, publication information includes place of publication and the name of the publisher. For electronic versions of books, publication information also includes retrieval information.

PLACE OF PUBLICATION

For U.S. publishers, give the city and state, using two-letter postal abbreviations listed in most dictionaries. For publishers in other countries, give

continued >>

> ### Quick Box 26.3 (continued)
>
> city and country spelled out. However, if the state or country is part of the publisher's name, omit it after the name of the city.
>
> #### PUBLISHERS
>
> Use a shortened version of the publisher's name except for an association, corporation, or university press. Drop *Co., Inc., Publishers*, and the like, but retain *Books* or *Press*.
>
>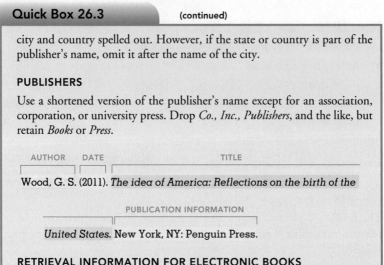
>
> AUTHOR   DATE   TITLE
>
> Wood, G. S. (2011). *The idea of America: Reflections on the birth of the*
>
> PUBLICATION INFORMATION
>
> *United States.* New York, NY: Penguin Press.
>
> #### RETRIEVAL INFORMATION FOR ELECTRONIC BOOKS
>
> If a book has a DOI (Document Object Identifier; see Quick Box 26.2 for an explanation), include that number after the title, preceded by doi and a colon. Most electronic books do not have a DOI. When there is no DOI, use "Retrieved from" followed by the URL where you accessed the book.

21. Book by One Author: Print

Turkle, S. (2011). *Alone together: Why we expect more from technology and less from each other.* New York, NY: Basic Books.

22. Book by One Author: Online

Turkle, S. (2007). *Evocative objects: Things we think with.* Retrieved from http://0-site.ebrary.com.bianca.penlib.du.edu/

Some books are increasingly available through library databases. APA does not include the name or location of the publisher in citations for online books.

23. Book by One Author: E-book or E-reader

Hertsgaard, M. (2011). *Hot: Living through the next fifty years on Earth.* [Kindle version]. Retrieved from http://amazon.com

The name of the version appears in brackets following the title, for example [Kindle version] or [Nook version]. "Retrieved from" precedes the URL of the site from which you downloaded the book.

24. Book by Two Authors

Edin, K., & Kefalas, M. (2005). *Promises I can keep: Why poor women put motherhood before marriage.* Berkeley, CA: University of California Press.

Figure 26.3 Citation information for a print book—APA.

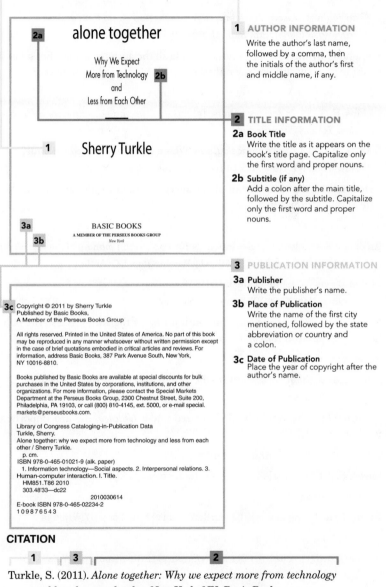

1 AUTHOR INFORMATION
Write the author's last name, followed by a comma, then the initials of the author's first and middle name, if any.

2 TITLE INFORMATION

2a Book Title
Write the title as it appears on the book's title page. Capitalize only the first word and proper nouns.

2b Subtitle (if any)
Add a colon after the main title, followed by the subtitle. Capitalize only the first word and proper nouns.

3 PUBLICATION INFORMATION

3a Publisher
Write the publisher's name.

3b Place of Publication
Write the name of the first city mentioned, followed by the state abbreviation or country and a colon.

3c Date of Publication
Place the year of copyright after the author's name.

CITATION

Turkle, S. (2011). *Alone together: Why we expect more from technology and less from each other.* New York, NY: Basic Books.

25. Book by Three or More Authors

Lynam, J. K., Ndiritu, C. G., & Mbabu, A. N. (2004). *Transformation of agricultural research systems in Africa: Lessons from Kenya.* East Lansing, MI: Michigan State University Press.

For a book by three to six authors, include all the authors' names. For a book by more than six authors, use only the first six names followed by *et al.*

26. Two or More Books by the Same Author(s)

Jenkins, H. (1992). *Textual poachers: Television fans and participatory culture.* New York, NY: Routledge.

Jenkins, H. (2006). *Convergence culture: Where old and new media collide.* New York, NY: New York University Press.

References by the same author are arranged chronologically, with the earlier date of publication listed first.

27. Book by a Group or Corporate Author

American Psychological Association. (2010). *Publication manual of the American Psychological Association* (6th ed.). Washington, DC: Author.

Boston Women's Health Collective. (1998). *Our bodies, ourselves for the new century.* New York, NY: Simon & Schuster.

Cite the full name of the corporate author first. If the author is also the publisher, use the word *Author* as the name of the publisher.

28. Book with No Author Named

The Chicago manual of style (16th ed.). (2010). Chicago, IL: University of Chicago Press.

Ignoring *The*, this would be alphabetized under *Chicago*, the first important word in the title.

29. Book with an Author and an Editor

Stowe, H. B. (2010). *Uncle Tom's cabin.* (E. Ammons, Ed.). New York, NY: Norton.

30. Translation

Nesbo, J. (2011). *The leopard.* (D. Bartlett, Trans.) New York, NY: Vintage.

31. Work in Several Volumes or Parts

Chrisley, R. (Ed.). (2000). *Artificial intelligence: Critical concepts* (Vols. 1–4). London, England: Routledge.

32. Anthology or Edited Book

Purdy, J. L., & Ruppert, J. (Eds.). (2001). *Nothing but the truth: An anthology of Native American literature.* Upper Saddle River, NJ: Prentice Hall.

33. One Selection in an Anthology or an Edited Book

Trujillo, L. (2004). Balancing act. In R. Moreno & M. H. Mulligan (Eds.),
*Borderline personalities: A new generation of Latinas dish on sex,
sass, and cultural shifting* (pp. 61–72). New York, NY: HarperCollins.

Give the author of the selection first. The word *In* introduces the larger work
from which the selection is taken. To refer to an anthology, see the Chaudhuri
citation in example 35.

34. Chapter from an Edited Book: Online

Gembris, H. (2006). The development of musical abilities. In R. Colwell (Ed).
MENC handbook of musical cognition and development. New York,
NY: Oxford University Press (pp.124–164). Retrieved from
http://books.google.com/books/

35. Selection in a Work Already Listed in References

Bond, R. (2004). The night train at Deoli. In A. Chaudhuri (Ed.), *The Vintage
book of modern Indian literature* (pp. 415–418). New York, NY: Vintage
Books.

Chaudhuri, A. (Ed.). (2004). *The Vintage book of modern Indian literature.* New
York, NY: Vintage Books.

Provide full information for the already cited anthology (first example), along
with information about the individual selection. Put entries in alphabetical
order.

36. Article in a Reference Book

Burnbam, J. C. (1996). Freud, Sigmund. In B. B. Wolman (Ed.), *The encyclopedia
of psychiatry, psychology, and psychoanalysis* (p. 220). New York, NY:
Holt.

If no author is listed, begin with the title of the article.

Ireland. (2002). In *The new encyclopaedia Britannica: Macropaedia* (15th ed.,
Vol. 21, pp. 997–1018). Chicago, IL: Encyclopaedia Britannica.

37. Second or Later Edition

Modern Language Association. (2009). *MLA handbook for writers of research
papers* (7th ed.). New York, NY: Author.

Any edition number appears on the title page. Place it in parentheses after
the title.

38. Introduction, Preface, Foreword, or Afterword

Hesse, D. (2004). Foreword. In D. Smit, *The end of composition studies*
(pp. ix–xiii). Carbondale, IL: Southern Illinois University Press.

If you're citing an introduction, preface, foreword, or afterword, give its author's name first. After the year, give the name of the part cited. If the writer of the material you're citing isn't the author of the book, use the word *In* and the author's name before the title of the book.

39. Reprint of an Older Book

Coover, R. (2007). *A night at the movies, or, you must remember this.*
   Champaign, IL: Dalkey Archive, 2007. (Original work published 1987)

You can find republishing information on the copyright page.

40. Book in a Series

Ardell, J. H. (2005). *Breaking into baseball: Women and the national pastime.*
   Carbondale, IL: Southern Illinois University Press.

Give the title of the book but not of the whole series.

41. Book with a Title within a Title

Lumiansky, R. M., & Baker, H. (Eds.). (1968). *Critical approaches to six major
   English works:* Beowulf *through* Paradise Lost. Philadelphia, PA:
   University of Pennsylvania Press.

42. Government Publication: Print

U.S. Congress. House Subcommittee on Health and Environment of the Committee
   on Commerce. (1999). *The nursing home resident protection amendments
   of 1999* (99-0266-P). Washington, DC: U.S. Government Printing Office.

U.S. Senate Special Committee on Aging. (1998). *The risk of malnutrition in nursing
   homes* (98-0150-P). Washington, DC: U.S. Government Printing Office.

Use the complete name of a government agency as author when no specific person is named.

43. Government Publication: Online

United States. Federal Reserve Board. (1998, July 22). *Conduct of monetary policy;
   report of the Federal Reserve Board pursuant to the Full Employment and
   Balanced Growth Act of 1978;* July 21, 1998 report. Retrieved 3 December 1998
   from the Federal Reserve Web site: http://www.federalreserve.gov
   /boarddocs/hh/1998/july/fullreport.htm

44. Published Proceedings of a Conference

Rocha, L., Yaeger, L., Bedau, M., Floreano, D., Goldstone, R., & Vespignani, A.
   (Eds.). (2006, June). *Artificial Life X: Proceedings of the Tenth International
   Conference on the Simulation and Synthesis of Living Systems.*
   Bloomington, IN. Cambridge, MA: MIT Press.

45. Thesis or Dissertation

Stuart, G. A. (2006). *Exploring the Harry Potter book series: A study of adolescent reading motivation.* Retrieved from ProQuest Digital Dissertations. (AAT 3246355)

The number in parentheses at the end is the accession number.

46. Entry from Encyclopedia: Online

Turing test. (2008). In *Encyclopaedia Britannica.* Retrieved February 9, 2008, from http://www.britannica.com/bps/topic/609757/Turing-test

Because the reference is to a work that may change, a retrieval date is included.

47. Entry from a Dictionary: Online

Asparagus. (n.d.). *Merriam-Webster's online dictionary.* Retrieved February 9, 2008, from http://dictionary.reference.com/

48. Entry from a Handbook: Online

Gembris, H. (2006). The development of musical abilities. In R. Colwell (Ed). *MENC handbook of musical cognition and development.* New York, NY: Oxford University Press (pp. 124–164). Retrieved from http://books.google.com/books/

IMAGES, AUDIO, FILM, AND VIDEO

49. Photograph, Painting, Drawing, Illustration, etc.: Original

Cassatt, Mary. (1890). *La toilette.* [Painting]. Art Institute of Chicago.

Fourquet, Léon. (1865). *The man with the broken nose.* [Sculpture]. Paris, France: Musée Rodin.

Mydans, C. (1999, October 21–November 28). *General Douglas MacArthur landing at Luzon, 1945* [Photograph]. New York, NY: Soho Triad Fine Art Gallery.

This form is for original works appearing in a gallery, museum, private collection, etc. The date in the third example shows that the work appeared only for a brief period, in this case at the Soho Triad Fine Art Gallery. Note that the medium of the work appears in brackets after its title.

50. Photograph, Painting, Drawing, Illustration, etc. in a Periodical: Print

Greene, H. *Grace Slick.* (2004, September 30). [Photograph]. *Rolling Stone,* 102.

51. Photograph, Painting, Drawing, Illustration, etc. in a Periodical: Online

Morris, C. (2011, July/August). *Man in camouflage.* [Photograph]. *The Atlantic.* Retrieved from http://theatlantic.com

52. Photograph, Painting, Drawing, Illustration, etc. in a Book: Print

The world's most populous countries. (2004). [Illustration]. In P. Turchi, *Maps of the imagination: The writer as cartographer* (pp. 116–117). San Antonio, TX: Trinity University Press.

Indicate the type of image in brackets following the title or, as in this example, the date.

53. Comic or Cartoon: Print

Sutton, W. (2011, May 2). Ryan's a Late Adopter. [Cartoon]. *The New Yorker*, *87*(11), 64.

54. Comic or Cartoon: Online

Harris, S. (2002, May 27). We have lots of information technology. [Cartoon]. *The New Yorker*. Retrieved from http://www.newyorker.com

55. Photo Essay: Online

Nachtwey, J. (2006, December 2). *Crime in middle America.* [Photo essay]. *Time*. Retrieved from http:/www.time.com

56. Image from a Social Networking Site

Gristellar, F. (2009, August 7). *The Gateway Arch.* [Photograph]. Retrieved from https://www.facebook.com/qzprofile.php?id=7716zf92444

57. Image from a Service or Distributor

World Perspectives. (1998). *Launching of the Space Shuttle Columbia, Florida, USA, 1998.* [Photograph]. Retrieved from http://gettyimages.com #AT3775-001.

In this example, the photographer was listed as "World Perspectives." Include the name of the service or distributor (in this case Getty Images), and the item number or other identifier, if any.

58. Map, Chart, or Other Graphic: Online

Hurricane Rita. (2005, September 24) [Graphic]. *New York Times Online.* Retrieved from http://www.nytimes.com/packages/html/national /20050923_RITA_GRAPHIC/index.html

59. Audio Book

Turkle, S. (2011). *Alone together: Why we expect more from technology and less from each other.* [MP3-CD]. Old Saybrook, CT: Tantor Media.

60. Sound Recording

Verdi, G. (1874). Requiem. [Recorded by R. Muti (Conductor) and the Chicago Symphony Orchestra and Chorus]. On *Requiem* [CD]. Chicago, IL: CSO Resound. (2010)

Winehouse, A. (2007). Rehab. On *Back to Black* [MP3]. Universal Republic Records. Retrieved from http://amazon.com

List the composer, date, title of the section, performer (if different from the composer), title of the album or compilation and then publication or retrieval information.

61. Audio Podcast

Blumberg, A., & Davidson, D. (Producers). (2008, May 9). *The giant pool of money*. [Audio podcast]. Retrieved from http://thisamericanlife.org

62. Film, Videotape, or DVD

Capra, F. (Director/Producer). (1934). *It happened one night* [Motion Picture]. United States: Columbia Pictures.

Madden, J. (Director), Parfitt, D., Gigliotti, D., Weinstein, H., Zwick, E., & Norman, M. (Producers). (2003). *Shakespeare in love* [DVD]. United States: Miramax. (Original motion picture released 1998)

For video downloads, include the download date and the source.

Capra, F. (Director/Producer). (2010). *It happened one night* [Motion Picture]. United States: Columbia Pictures. Retrieved from Netflix. (Original motion picture released 1934)

63. Video: Online

CNN. (2011, January 27). *Challenger disaster live on CNN* [Video file]. Retrieved from http://www.youtube.com/watch?v=AfnvFnzs9Is

Wesch, M. (2007, January 31). *Web 2.0 . . . the machine is us/ing us.* [Video file]. Retrieved from http://www.youtube.com/watch?v=6gmP4nk0EOE

Use this format for videos from YouTube and similar sites.

64. Broadcast Television or Radio Program, Single Event

Burns, K. (Writer/Producer), & Barnes, P. (Producer). (1999, November 8). *Not for ourselves alone: The story of Elizabeth Cady Stanton and Susan B. Anthony* [Television broadcast]. New York, NY: Public Broadcasting Service.

65. Episode from a Television or Radio Series

Doyle, A. C., & Hawkesworth, J. (Writers), & Gorrie, J. (Director). (2011, June 30). The Bruce-Partington plans. *Sherlock Holmes.* [Television broadcast]. KRMA, Denver, CO.

Brand, M. (Anchor). (2011, June 20). *The Madeleine Brand show* [Radio broadcast]. Pasadena, CA: KPCC.

66. Television or Radio Program: Online

Stewart, J. (Performer). (2011, June 1). Bill Moyers. *The Daily Show*. [Video file]. Retrieved from http://www.hulu.com

The disappearing incandescent bulb. (2011, June 20). *The Madeleine Brand Show*. [Radio recording]. KPCC, Pasadena, CA. Retrieved from http://www.scpr.org/programs/madeleine-brand/2011/06/20/the-disappearing-incandescent-bulb/

Give the name of the writer, director, or performer, if available; the date; the title of the episode; the title of the program or series; the type of recording; and retrieval information. Because the second source may be difficult to find, the URL is listed.

OTHER ONLINE SOURCES

If a Web source has a publication or posting date, the retrieval statement includes just the URL. If there is no publication date, include the date of retrieval.

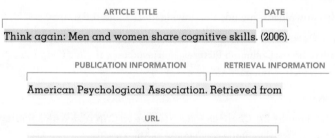

ARTICLE TITLE   DATE

Think again: Men and women share cognitive skills. (2006).

PUBLICATION INFORMATION   RETRIEVAL INFORMATION

American Psychological Association. Retrieved from

URL

http://www.psychologymatters.org/thinkagain.html

Nonretrievable sources: If others can't access a source you have used, APA style says not to include it in your References list. Examples are personal communications such as e-mail or text messages. Instead, cite them in the text with a parenthetical notation saying it's a personal communication (see example 70). If you have a scholarly reason to cite a message from a newsgroup, forum, social networking group, or electronic mailing list that is available in an electronic archive, then see examples 69, 71, 72, 73, and 74.

67. Entire Web Site

Association for the Advancement of Artificial Intelligence. (2008, March). Retrieved March 17, 2008, from http://www.aaai.org

Neff, M. (Ed.). (2011). WebdelSol. Retrieved August 4, 2011, from http://webdelsol.com

Because material on a Web site may change, use a "retrieved from" date.

68. Page from a Web Site

Think again: Men and women share cognitive skills. (2006). American
　　Psychological Association. Retrieved January 18, 2011, from
　　http://www.psychologymatters.org/thinkagain.html

Pennsylvania Department of Education. (n.d). Home education
　　and private tutoring. Retrieved March 4, 2011, from http://
　　www.education.state.pa.us/portal/server.pt/community
　　/home_education_and_private_tutoring/20311

In the second example, "n.d." indicates there was no date given. The retrieval
information, however, contains a date.

69. Real-Time Online Communication

Berzsenyi, C. (2007, May 13). Writing to meet your match: Rhetoric,
　　perceptions, and self-presentation for four online daters. *Computers
　　and Writing Online.* [Synchronous discussion]. Retrieved from
　　http://acadianamoo.org

If a chat, discussion, or synchronous (meaning available as it is happening)
online-presentation can be retrieved by others, include it in your References
list.

70. E-Mail Message

Because e-mails to individuals cannot be retrieved by others, they should not
appear on the References list. Cite them in the body of your paper, as in this
example:

> The wildfires threatened several of the laboratory facilities at Los Alamos
> (e-mail from T. Martin on June 20, 2011).

71. Posting on a Blog

Phillips, M. (2011, June 15). Need to go to the ER? Not until the game's over.
　　[Web log post]. Retrieved from http://www.freakonomics.com/2011/06/15
　　/need-to-go-to-the-er-not-until-the-games-over/

72. Wiki

NASCAR Sprint Cup series. (2011). [Wiki]. Retrieved April 6, 2011, from http://
　　nascarwiki.com

Machine learning. (n.d.) Retrieved January 5, 2008, from Artificial Intelligence
　　Wiki: http://www.ifi.unizh.ch/ailab/aiwiki/aiw.cgi

N.d. means "no date." Because a Wiki can change by its very nature, always
include a retrieval date.

73. Posting on a Social Networking Site

Adler-Kassner, L. (2011, May 6). Conversations toward action. [Facebook group]. Retrieved from Council of Writing Program Administrators at https://www.facebook.com/groups/106575940874

Include the citation in your References list only if it is retrievable by others. If it's not, cite it only in the body of your paper, as in example 70.

74. Message on an Online Forum, Discussion Group, or Electronic Mailing List

Firrantello, L. (2005, May 23). Van Gogh on Prozac. *Salon Table Talk*. [Online forum posting]. Retrieved February 15, 2009, from http://www.salon.com

Boyle, F. (2002, October 11). Psyche: Cemi field theory: The hard problem made easy [Discussion group posting]. Retrieved from news://sci.psychology.consciousness

Haswell, R. (2005, October 17). A new graphic/text interface. [Electronic mailing list message]. Retrieved May 20, 2011, from http://lists.asu.edu/archives /wpa-l.html

APA advises using *electronic mailing list*, as Listserv is the name of specific software.

OTHER SOURCES

75. Letters

Williams, W. C. (1935). [Letter to his son]. In L. Grunwald & S. J. Adler (Eds.), *Letters of the century: America 1900–1999* (pp. 225–226). New York, NY: Dial Press.

In the APA system, unpublished letters are considered personal communications inaccessible to general readers, so they do not appear in the References list. They are cited only in the body of the paper (see example 70). Letters that have been published or can be retrieved by others are cited as shown in this example.

76. Map or Chart

Colorado Front Range Mountain Bike Topo Map [Map]. (2001). Nederland, CO: Latitude 40.

77. Report, Pamphlet, or Brochure

National Commission on Writing in America's Schools and Colleges. (2003). *The neglected "R": The need for a writing revolution* (Report No. 2). New York, NY: College Board.

U.S. Department of Agriculture. (2007). *Organic foods and labels* [Brochure]. Retrieved December 8, 2008, from http://www.ams.usda.gov/nop /Consumers/brochure.html

78. Legal Source

Brown v. Board of Educ., 347 U.S. 483 (1954).

Include the name of the case, the number of the case, the name of the court deciding the case (if other than the US Supreme Court), and the year of the decision.

79. Abstract Submitted for Meeting or Poster Session

Wang, H. (2007). Dust storms originating in the northern hemisphere of Mars. [Abstract]. AGU 2007 Fall Meeting. Retrieved from http://www.agu.org /meetings/fm07/?content=program

80. Advertisement

Swim at home. (2005). [Advertisement]. *The American Scholar 74*(2), 2.

Nikon D7000. (2010, November). [Advertisement]. Retrieved December 12, 2010, from http://rollingstone.com

Southwest Airlines. (2010, August 24). [Advertisement]. ABC television.

81. Computer Software or Video Game

The Island: Castaway. (2010). [Video game]. N.p: Awem Studio.

"N.p." indicates that the place of publication is unknown.

Guitar hero III: Legends of rock. (2007). [Video game]. Santa Monica, CA: Activision.

Provide an author name, if available. Standard software (Microsoft Word) and program languages (C++) don't need to be given in the References list.

82. Policy Brief

Haskins, R., Paxson, C., & Donahue, E. (2006). *Fighting obesity in the public schools.* Retrieved from http://www.brookings.edu/media/Files/rc /papers/2006/spring_childrenfamilies_haskins/20060314foc.pdf

83. Presentation Slides or Images

Alaska Conservation Solutions. (2006). Montana global warming [PowerPoint slides]. Retrieved from http://www.alaskaconservationsolutions.com/acs /presentations.html

Delyser, A. (2010, February 7). Political movements in the Philippines. [Prezi slides]. University of Denver.

84. Interview

In APA style, a personal interview is not included in the References list. Cite the interview in the text as a personal communication, as in the following example.

> Randi Friedman (personal communication, June 30, 2010) endorses this view.

If the interview is published or can be retrieved by others, cite it as follows:

85. Lecture, Speech, or Address

Kennedy, J. F. (1960, September 12). Speech to the Greater Houston Ministerial Association, Rice Hotel, Houston, TX.

86. Live Performance

Miller, A. (Author), & McLean, C. (Director). (2005, September 27). *All my sons* [Theatrical performance]. Center for the Performing Arts, Normal, IL.

Nelson, W. (2011, June 22). *Country Throwdown Tour* [Concert]. Red Rocks Amphitheater, Denver, CO.

87. Microfiche Collection of Articles

Wenzell, R. (1990, February 3). Businesses prepare for a more diverse work force. [Microform]. *St. Louis Post Dispatch*, p. 17. *NewsBank: Employment* 27, fiche 2, grid D12.

A microfiche is a transparent sheet of film (a *fiche*) with microscopic printing that needs to be read through a special magnifier. Each fiche holds several pages, with each page designated by a grid position. A long document may appear on more than one fiche.

88. Musical Score

Schubert, F. (1971). *Symphony in B Minor (Unfinished)*. M. Cusid (Ed.). [Musical score]. New York, NY: Norton. (Original work composed 1822)

89. Nonperiodical Publications on CD, DVD, or Magnetic Tape

Perl, S. (2004). *Felt Sense: Guidelines for Composing*. [CD]. Portsmouth, NH: Boynton.

90. Materials on CD or DVD with a Print Version

The price is right. (1992, January 20). *Time*, 38. In *Time Man of the Year*. [CD]. New York, NY: Compact.

Information for the print version ends with the article's page number, 38. Following that comes the title of the CD-ROM (*Time Man of the Year*) and its publication information.

91. Materials on CD or DVD with No Print Version

Artificial intelligence. (2003). *Encarta 2003.* [CD]. Redmond, WA: Microsoft.

Encarta 2003 is a CD-ROM encyclopedia with no print version. "Artificial Intelligence" is the title of an article in *Encarta 2003*.

26F What are APA guidelines for writing an abstract?

As the APA *Publication Manual* (2010) explains, "an abstract is a brief, comprehensive summary" (p. 25) of a longer piece of writing. The APA estimates that an **abstract** should be no longer than about 120 words. Your instructor may require that you include an abstract at the start of a paper; if you're not sure, ask. Make the abstract accurate, objective, and exact. For an example of an abstract, see the student paper in 26I.

26G What are APA guidelines for content notes?

Content notes (usually called footnotes) in APA-style papers add relevant information that cannot be worked effectively into a text discussion. Use consecutive arabic numerals for note numbers. Try to arrange your sentence so that the note number falls at the end. Use a numeral raised slightly above the line of words and immediately after the final punctuation mark. Footnotes may either appear at the bottom of the page they appear on or all together on a separate page following the References. See page 393 for instructions on formatting the Footnotes page.

26H What are APA format guidelines for research papers?

Ask whether your instructor has instructions for preparing a final draft. If not, you can use the APA guidelines here. For an illustration of these guidelines, see the student paper in 26I.

👁 Watch the Video

26H.1 General instructions—APA

Print on 8½-by-11-inch white paper and double space. Set at least a 1-inch margin on the left, and leave no less than 1 inch on the right and at the bottom.

Leave ½ inch from the top edge of the paper to the title-and-page-number line (also known as a running head). Leave another ½ inch (or 1 inch from the top edge of the paper) before the next line on the page, whether that's a heading (such as "Abstract" or "Notes") or a line of your paper.

Indent the first line of all paragraphs ½ inch, except in your abstract, the first line of which isn't indented. Do not justify the right margin. Indent footnotes ½ inch.

26H.2 Order of parts—APA

Number all pages consecutively. Use this order for the parts of your paper:

1. Title page
2. Abstract (if required)
3. Body of the paper
4. References
5. Appendixes, if any
6. Footnotes, if any
7. Attachments, if any (questionnaires, data sheets, or other material your instructor asks you to include)

26H.3 Title-and-page-number line (running head) for all pages—APA

Use a title-and-page-number line on all pages of your paper. Place it ½ inch from the top edge of the paper, typing the title (use a shortened version if necessary) and leaving a five-character space before the page number. Use all capital letters in your running head. End the title-and-page-number line 1 inch from the right edge of the paper. Ask whether your instructor wants you to include your last name in the running head. The "header" tool on a word processing program will help you create the title-and-page-number line easily. See the sample student paper on page 396.

26H.4 Title page—APA

Use a separate title page. Include your running head. Center your complete title vertically and horizontally on the page. (Don't italicize, underline, or enclose your title it in quotation marks.) On the next line, center your name, and below that center the course title and section, your professor's name, and the date. See the sample student paper on page 396.

🛇 **Alerts:** (1) Use the guidelines here for capitalizing the title of your own paper and for capitalizing titles you mention in the body of your paper (but not in the REFERENCES list; see Quick Box 26.1).

(2) Use a capital letter for the first word of your title and for the first word of a subtitle, if any. Start every NOUN, PRONOUN, VERB, ADVERB, and ADJECTIVE

with a capital letter. Capitalize each main word in a hyphenated compound word (two or more words used together to express one idea): *Father-in-Law, Self-Consciousness.*

(3) Do not capitalize ARTICLES (*a, an, the*) unless one of the other capitalization rules applies to them. Do not capitalize PREPOSITIONS and CONJUNCTIONS unless they're four or more letters long. Do not capitalize the word *to* used in an INFINITIVE.

(4) In your running head, capitalize all letters. ●

26H.5 Abstract—APA

See 26F for advice about the abstract of your paper. Type the abstract on a separate page, using the numeral 2 in the title-and-page-number line. Center the word *Abstract* 1 inch from the top of the paper. Do not italicize or underline it or enclose it in quotation marks. Double-space below this title, and then start your abstract, double-spacing it. Do not indent the first line.

26H.6 Set-off quotations—APA

Set off (display in block style) quotations of forty words or more. See 26C for a detailed explanation and example.

26H.7 References list—APA

Start a new page for your References list immediately after the end of the body of your paper. One inch from the top of the paper center the word *References*. Don't italicize, underline, or put it in quotation marks. Double-space below it. Start the first line of each entry at the left margin, and indent any subsequent lines five spaces or ½ inch from the left margin. Use this hanging indent style unless your instructor prefers a different one. Double-space within each entry and between entries.

26H.8 Footnotes—APA

Put any notes on a separate page after the last page of your References list and any Appendixes. Center the word *Footnotes* one inch from the top of the paper. Do not italicize or underline it or put it in quotation marks.

On the next line, indent ½ inch and begin the note. Raise the note number slightly (you can use the superscript feature in your word processing program), and then start the words of your note, leaving no space after the number. If the note is more than one typed line, do not indent any line after the first. Double-space throughout.

261   A student's APA-style research paper

View
the Model
Document

Here is a student's research paper written according to APA STYLE. We first discuss the planning, researching, drafting, and revising that Leslie Palm did. We also include her final draft, including her title page, abstract, and References page.

Case Study

Leslie Palm was given this assignment for a research paper in an introductory sociology class: Write a research paper of 1,500 to 2,000 words about some aspect of contemporary gender roles. For guidance, refer to the *Simon and Schuster Handbook for Writers*, Chapters 21–24. Use APA documentation, explained in sections 26A–26E. Your topic, research question, and working bibliography are due in two weeks, and a draft of your paper is due two weeks later, both for peer review and instructor feedback. Your final draft is due one week after you receive comments on your first one.

When Leslie read her assignment, she was both pleased and intimidated by the amount of choice she had. She created a research checklist (Quick Box 21.3) and began a RESEARCH LOG, in which she listed several broad topics. These included women in sports, how men and women are portrayed in television shows, how boys and girls experience schooling, gender roles in the workplace, and many others. An avid video game player, Leslie had heard that women were attracted to different features of games than men, and she started pursing that topic. In the process, she started thinking about how other players, especially those multiple player online games, have responded to her. This eventually led to her RESEARCH QUESTION: "How are female characters in video games portrayed and treated?"

Leslie checked to see whether she could find enough credible sources to address this question. She accessed her college library's home page and searched the Academic Search Premier database, using combinations of KEYWORDS "gender," "video games," "female characters," "players," "physical characteristics," and so on. When the results turned up several dozen hits, she figured the topic and research question would work. She used NoodleBib software (21N) to gather the most promising sources into a WORKING BIBLIOGRAPHY, and she downloaded full-text versions of some of the articles and chapters. Leslie also did a general Internet search. Although this search yielded thousands of hits, many were off-topic, and still others, on evaluation, did not seem credible or sufficiently scholarly. However, she did find two sources that she added to her working bibliography.

She considered doing some field research, including e-mail interviews of several women gamers that she knew. Although she began that process, she realized that she didn't have enough time to do it well. She also checked with her professor, who preferred scholarly sources.

Leslie began reading her sources and taking CONTENT NOTES. She opened a document called "Women and Video Games Notes," inserted a heading for each source, and typed summaries or quotations from each source under its heading, along with her own thoughts about what the sources meant and how she might use them. Gradually, themes and issues began to emerge. Leslie opened a second document called "Women and Video Games Themes," in which she cut and pasted her content notes under topical headings. From this, she created a rough OUTLINE and began writing a draft. Her first rough draft allowed her to try out a thesis statement, check the logical arrangement of her material, and see whether she could synthesize her many sources.

That draft was almost 2,500 words. She asked a PEER RESPONSE GROUP which parts of the paper they found most interesting, and which topics she might cut. Leslie received helpful feedback, including that she was spending too much time describing individual games without analyzing them and that her topic about how young girls and boys learn to play, while interesting, was off-topic for this paper. Her instructor also pointed out these issues; in addition, she noted places where Leslie needed to do more research to back up some general claims.

Through a combination of cutting and adding, she produced a second draft. Using Chapter 26 of the *Simon and Schuster Handbook for Writers* as a guide, Leslie had to attend very closely to the details of correct PARENTHETICAL IN-TEXT CITATIONS (see 26B and 26C) within her paper and a correct REFERENCES list (see 26D and 26E) at the end. Because she'd used MLA DOCUMENTATION STYLE in other courses, she made sure not to confuse the two styles. Before doing her final editing and proofreading, Leslie wrote an abstract and made sure the format of the paper met APA standards.

Her final draft follows.

Running head
on all pages.
Shortened
title is flush
left; page
number flush
right.

Running head: WOMEN IN VIDEO GAMES   1

½″

1″

Title page
has title,
name, course,
instructor,
and date,
all centered
and double
spaced.

The Troubling Roles of Women in Video Games

Leslie Palm

Sociology 200

Professor K. Thetard

May 9, 2011

½″

WOMEN IN VIDEO GAMES   1″   2

1″

Abstract,
if required,
goes on
page 2.

Abstract

Despite the fact that 40% of video game players are
women, female characters and players are treated in ways
that are problematic. Video games often portray unrealistic
physical characteristics of female characters, exaggerating
certain body features. Many games portray women either as
vulnerable "damsels in distress" or as sexually aggressive.
Women game players often experience stereotyping or
harassment. Recent games are changing the way they
present female characters.

continued >>

WOMEN IN VIDEO GAMES   3

The Depiction of Women in Video Games

Lady Reagan Cousland the First jogs across a virtual pastoral landscape with a two-handed battleax strapped across her shoulders. She is the Player Character in a play through of *Dragon Age: Origins*, a 2009 single-player role-play game, and she is trying to progress through the main quest. However, other characters taunt her. "I have never seen a woman Grey Warden before," says one skeptically. Lady rolls her eyes before sharply answering, "That's because women are too smart to join."

"So what does that make you?" asks the interrupter.

"Insane," she replies.

This exchange exemplifies how women have frequently been portrayed and treated in video games for over two decades. Gaming has long been inaccurately considered an activity pursued almost solely by reclusive males caricatured as "pale loners crouched in the dark among Mountain Dew bottles and pizza boxes" (Wong, 2010). Game producers have mostly catered to this stereotypical player, with discouraging results. Despite evidence that large numbers of women play video games, and despite some important changes, women game characters continue to be physically objectified, represented either as passive or sexually aggressive, and even harassed.

According to data from the Entertainment Software Association (2011), 67% of American households own a video game console of some variety—and 40% of all players are women. In fact, "Women over 18 years of age are one of the

If you have an abstract, begin body of paper on page 3; if not, on page 2.

Introductory paragraphs create interest with a scene.

In-text citation has name and date; source had no pages.

Thesis statement.

continued >>

WOMEN IN VIDEO GAMES 4

Brackets show
writer added
language
to make
quotation fit
sentence.

Page number
in citation for
direct quote.

Paragraph
develops
first main
point, in topic
sentence.

With author
and date in
sentence, only
quoted page
numbers go
in citation.

industry's fastest growing demographics, [representing] a greater portion of the game-playing population (33 percent) than boys age 17 or younger (20 percent)" (Entertainment Software Association, 2011). And yet, studies show that both male and female gamers believe games to be a "particularly masculine pursuit" (Selwyn, 2007, p. 533).

Physical Characteristics of Female Characters

The most obvious gender stereotyping in many games comes from the nature of the characters' bodies or avatars. A 2007 content analysis of images of video game characters from top-selling American gaming magazines showed that male characters (83%) are more likely than female characters (62%) to be portrayed as aggressive; however, female characters are more likely to be sexualized (60 vs. 1%) and scantily clad (39 vs. 1%) (Dill & Thill, 2007, pp. 851–864). Even female characters that are considered strong or dominant in personality (such as Morgainn in *Dragon Age: Origins* or Sheva in *Resident Evil 5*) routinely dress in tops that are essentially strips of fabric and skin-tight leather pants. In fact, the reward for beating *Resident Evil 5* is that you get to dress the avatar Sheva in a leopard-print bikini.

In *Gender Inclusive Game Design*, Sherri Graner Ray (2003) outlined the physical traits seen between male and female avatars: females are characterized by "exaggerated sexual features such as large breasts set high on their torso, large buttocks, and a waist smaller than her head" (pp. 102–04). Dickerman, Christensen, and Kerl-McClain (2008) found similar qualities. Analyzing characters in 60 video games, Professors Edward Downs and Stacy Smith (2010) found that women were

continued >>

more likely to be "hypersexualized" then men, depicted with unrealistic body proportions, inappropriate clothing, and other qualities (p. 728).

Even nonhuman females receive this treatment. Game designer Andrea Rubenstein (2007) questions why females of nonhuman races in the popular game *World of Warcraft* are so much smaller and more feminine than their male counterparts. Of one species she notes, "The male is massive: tall with unnaturally large muscles and equally large hooves. . . . It would not be unreasonable to expect the female of the species to be similar." Apparently in *World of Warcraft's* earliest designs, the genders were far more similar; however, when screened to a pool of test gamers, complaints that the females were "ugly" resulted in their being changed to their current form. One scholar notes, "Since gamers and the like have been used to video representations of scantily-clad females and steroid-enhanced males," it is understandable that they would design nonhuman races in a similar way (Bates, 2005, p. 13).

Gender and Character Behavior

The personalities of the characters also demonstrate the gender bias in many games. Dietz's 1998 study of 33 games found that most did not portray women at all. Even ten years later, 86% of game characters were male (Downs & Smith, 2009). Only five of the games in Dietz's study portrayed women as heroes or action characters. The second most common portrayal in this study was as "victim or as the proverbial 'Damsel in Distress' " (Dietz, 1998, pp. 434–35). Examples of vulnerable women stretch from the 1980s to today, from Princess Peach (Nintendo's *Mario*) and Princess Zelda

"Even . . . treatment" is an effective transition that continues point from previous paragraph.

Direct quotation embedded in a sentence.

Second heading.

Topic sentence states second point.

continued >>

WOMEN IN VIDEO GAMES   6

(Nintendo's *The Legend of Zelda*) to Alice Wake (Remedy Entertainment's *Alan Wake*), Ashley Graham (Capcom's *Resident Evil 4*), and Alex Roivas (Nintendo's *Eternal Darkness: Sanity's Requiem*). The helpless woman, simply put, is a video game staple, as college students overwhelmingly recognized in one study (Ogletree & Drake, 2007).

A different staple role gaining popularity is that of the aggressive but sexy woman who will seduce you at night and then shoot you in the morning. Bayonetta, Jill Valentine (in *Resident Evil 3* and *Resident Evil 5*) and, of course, Lara Croft of the *Tomb Raider* series are all examples of this archetype. There is some debate as to whether these examples are evidence of new female power and liberation or simply a new form of exploitation. Dill and Thill (2007) argue that an aggressive female is not necessarily a liberated one, and that "many of these images of aggressive female video game characters glamorize and sexualize aggression." Eugene Provenzo agrees, pointing out that the contradiction between "the seeming empowerment of women, while at the same time . . . they're really being exploited in terms of how they're shown, graphically" (Huntermann, 2000).

Lara Croft is perhaps the epitome of the energetic, aggressive character as an over-exaggerated sexual object. Lead graphic artist Toby Gard went through five designs before arriving at her final appearance, and he began with the desire to counter stereotypical female characters, which he describes as "either a bimbo or a dominatrix" (Yang, 2007). Gard's inspirations included Swedish pop artist Neneh Cherry and comic book character Tank Girl, both feminist icons. Croft's original

Citation for source by 2 authors; no page number because not a direct quotation.

Paragraph introduces different aspect of second main point.

Ellipses show writer has cut language from quotation.

Specific example of female character.

continued >>

WOMEN IN VIDEO GAMES 7

incarnation was as the South American woman Lara Cruz. Gard disavows accusations of sexism in the design, and insists that the character's iconic breasts were a programming accident that the rest of the team fought to keep (McLaughlin & Rus, 2008).

The Treatment of Women Gamers

Video game culture reinforces negative gender roles for female players. Many multiplayer games encourage players to use headsets and microphones, a gender-revealing practice that is intended for easy strategizing. However, it often leads to sexual harassment and lewd commentary that also carries over to message boards, comments sections, and internet forums. Technology blogger Kathy Sierra was forced to abandon her website after multiple misogynistic comments and e-mails. Ailin Graef, who has made millions in the 3D chat-platform Second Life, was "swarmed by flying pink penises" during an interview in that virtual world (McCabe, 2008).

A study by psychologists at Nottingham Trent University in England determined that 70% of female players in massively-multiplayer online games chose to "construct male characters when given the option," presumably in an attempt to avoid such actions as female posters on gaming message boards being asked to post pictures of their breasts or "get the f*** off" (McCabe, 2008). Women gamers are considered so rare (which is surprising, given that they makes up 40% of players) that it's a common occurrence for male gamers to respond with a degree of shock any time a female shows up in game—even if that shock is complimentary or respectful. Sarah Rutledge, a 25-year-old female med student said of her gaming on *World of Warcraft*,

Heading followed by topic sentence that introduces third main point.

Two examples illustrate harassment.

Paragraph provides more examples of women players' treatment.

continued >>

WOMEN IN VIDEO GAMES   8

On the one hand, you get a lot of help and attention from guys playing the game, which can be helpful. You get invitations to join groups. But it's clear this has less to do with my ability than the fact I'm that curious creature: a woman. (personal communication, April 29, 2011)

One team of researchers found significant differences between men and women game players in gaining positive affects from gaming. They found males more likely than females to develop leadership, teamwork, and communicative skills, and they suggest this demonstrates games' biases toward males (Thirunarayanon, Vilchez, Abreau, Ledesma, & Lopez, 2010, p. 324).

Gradual Changes in Gender Roles and Gaming

In recent years gender roles have somewhat shifted. Often role-playing games permit the user to choose various characteristics of the Player Character, including making her female. Aside from appearance and responses from Non-Player Characters, the gender rarely affects a character's actual skills or attributes. More games have been released with females as the sole protagonists, including *Silent Hill 3* (Heather Mason), *No One Lives Forever* (Cate Archer), *Mirror's Edge* (Faith), and *Heavenly Sword* (Nariko). Jade, the protagonist of *Beyond Good and Evil* (released in 2003), has been praised for being strong and confident without being overtly sexualized. So have characters like Alyx Vance (co-protagonist of 2004's *Half-Life 2*) and Chell (protagonist of *Portal*, 2007, and *Portal 2*, 2011).

Chell in particular was heralded as a massive step forward in gender dynamics. People were surprised that "as the

Because source was a personal interview and not retrievable by others, Leslie cites it only in text, not in References.

Heading precedes a topic sentence that complicates paper's thesis.

Leslie includes characters' names in parentheses to provide more information.

continued >>

player, you're never even aware that you're a woman until you catch a glimpse of yourself in the third person" (*iVirtua*, 2007). In this way, Chell echoes the "original" feminist character Samus Aran of Nintendo's 1986 *Metroid;* one only discovers that Aran is female when she removes her bulky robot-armor during the ending scene, after twenty-plus hours of first-person gameplay. *Portal*, despite being an indie game produced by students as their thesis, became a hit, was wildly acclaimed by critics, and won multiple awards.

> Paragraph gives more detail for an example mentioned in previous sentence.

These developments don't satisfy all fans.. Some argue that a more all-inclusive focus actually threatens the quality of experience for stereotypically straight male gamers. Bioware, a Canada-based gaming company, came under fire during the releases of two major titles for featuring romance and dialogue options that cater not only to women, but to gays and lesbians. The release of *Dragon Age 2* in 2011 caused an uproar on its own message boards for allowing romantic options to be bisexual. One fan, "Bastal" (2011), protested that

> Complicating information gives paper a richer texture.

> the overwhelming majority of RPG gamers are indeed straight and male. . . . That's not to say there isn't a significant number of women who play Dragon Age and that BioWare should forego the option of playing as a women altogether, but there should have been much more focus in on making sure us male gamers were happy.

He and others then go on to propose a mode, which, if activated, would force male Companions to flirt only with female PCs, and vice versa. However, such views disturb game

> Quotation longer than 40 words set off block style, no quotation marks. Reference information appears in the part of the sentence introducing quote. Online source had no pages.

continued >>

WOMEN IN VIDEO GAMES   10

creators like David Gaider (2010), who argued that people
like Baltas are

> so used to being catered to that they see the lack of
> catering as an imbalance. . . . The person who says
> that the only way to please them is to restrict options
> for others is, if you ask me, the one who deserves it
> least.

Conclusion

"If we just continue to cater to existing (male) players,

Leslie includes the speaker's credentials, for emphasis.

we're never going to grow," says Beth Llewellyn, senior director
of corporate communications for Nintendow (Kerwick, 2007).
Video game companies have begun producing a new
generation of games that give women the opportunity to grab
a laser gun or broadsword and duke it out in billion-dollar

Sentence helps answer the "so what?" question.

franchises like *Halo*, *Fallout*, *Mass Effect*, *World of Warcraft* and
Guild Wars. However, depicting women more accurately and
favorably in games reaches a goal more important than mere
entertainment. "Video-simulated interfaces" are being used to

Because there are more than 6 authors, Leslie uses the first author and "et al."

train people for various professions (Terlecki et al., 2010, p. 30),
and it is crucial that these environments are suitable for all.
The promising news is that while there is still extensive gender
stereotyping (in both the gaming and the real world), game

Memorable final image.

makers are taking giant strides—in both boots and heels.

continued >>

WOMEN IN VIDEO GAMES   11

References

Bastal. (2011, March 22). Bioware neglected their main demographic: The straight male gamer. [Online discussion posting]. Retrieved from http://social.bioware.com/forum/1/topic/304/index/6661775&lf=8 (Topic 304, Msg. 1)

Bates, M. (2005). *Implicit identity theory in the rhetoric of the massively multiplayer online role-playing game (MMORPG).* (Doctoral Dissertation, Pennsylvania State University.) Available from ProQuest Dissertations and Theses database. (AAT 3172955)

Beasley, B., & Standley, T. C. (2002). Shirts vs. skirts: Clothing as an indicator of gender role stereotyping in video games. *Mass Communication & Society 5*, 279–93.

Dietz, T. L. (1998). An examination of violence and gender role portrayals in video games: Implications for gender socialization and aggressive behavior. *Sex Roles, 38*, 433–35.

Dickerman, C., Christensen, J., & Kerl-McClain, S. B. (2008). Big breasts and bad guys: Depictions of gender and race in video games. *Journal of Creativity in Mental Health, 3*(1), 20–29. doi: 10.1080/15401380801995076

Dill, K. E., & Thill, K. P. (2007, October 17). Video game characters and the socialization of gender roles: Young people's perceptions mirror sexist media depictions. *Sex Roles, 57*, 861–64.

Downs, E., & Smith, S. L. (2010): Keeping abreast of hypersexuality: A video game character content analysis. *Sex Roles, 62*, 721–733. doi: 10:1007/s11199-009-9637-1

Side notes: References begin on new page. "References" centered. Double-spaced and hanging indentations throughout. Journal article in print. Journal article online, with DOI.

continued >>

WOMEN IN VIDEO GAMES   12

Video game. *Dragon Age: Origins*. (2009). [Video Game]. Edmonton, Canada:
Bioware Studios.

Entertainment Software Association. (2011). *Essential facts
about the computer and video game industry 2010: Sales,
demographic and usage data*. Washington, DC: Author.
Retrieved from http://www.theesa.com/

**Comment
in an online
discussion.** Gaider, D. (2011, April 2). Response: Bioware neglected their
main demographic. [Online forum comment]. Retrieved
from http://social.bioware.com/forum/1/topic/304/index
/6661775&lf=8 (Topic 304, Msg. 2)

Huntemann, N. (Producer & Director). (2000). *Game over:
Gender, race & violence in video games*. [Video]. USA:
Media Education Foundation. Retrieved from
http://www.mediaed.org/

iVirtua Editorial Team. (2007, December 9). Portal is a feminist
masterpiece. London, England: iVirtua Media Group.
Retrieved from http://www.ivirtuaforums.com/portal-is-a
-feminist-masterpiece-great-read-media-studies-t14-61

Kerwick, M. (2007, May 13). Video games now starring strong
female characters. *The Record*. Retrieved from http://
www.popmatters.com/female-characters

**Newspaper
article avail-
able online.** McCabe, J. (2008, March 6). Sexual harassment is rife online. No
wonder women swap gender. *The Guardian*, p. G2.
Retrieved from http://www.guardian.co.uk/

Ogletree, S. M., & Drake, R. (2007). College students' video
game participation and perceptions: Gender differences
and implications. *Sex Roles, 56*, 537–542.
doi: 10.1007/s11199-007-9193-5

continued >>

WOMEN IN VIDEO GAMES   13

Ray, S. G. (2003). *Gender inclusive game design: Expanding the market.* Hingham, MA: Charles River Media.

Rubenstein, J. (2007, May 26). Idealizing fantasy bodies. *Iris Gaming Network.* Retrieved from http://theirisnetwork.org/

Terlecki, M., Brown, J., Harner-Steciw, L., Irvin-Hannum, J., Marchetto-Ryan, N., Ruhl, L., & Wiggins, J. (2011). Sex differences and similarities in video game experience, preferences, and self-efficacy: Implications for the gaming industry. *Current Psychology, 30,* 22–33. doi: 10.1007/s12144-010-9095-5

Thirunarayanon, M. O., Vilchez, M., Abreu, L., Ledesma, C., & Lopez, S. (2010). A survey of video game players in a public, urban research university. *Educational Media International, 47,* 311–327. doi: 10.1080/09523987-2010.535338

Wong, D. (2010, May 24). Five reasons it's still not cool to admit you're a gamer. *Cracked.* Retrieved from http://www.cracked.com/article_18571

Article from a Web site.

27

Chicago Manual (CM) and Council of Science Editors (CSE) Documentation

Quick Points   You will learn to

➤ Understand CM-style documentation (see 27A).
➤ Use CM-style documentation for Bibliographic notes (see 27B).
➤ Understand CSE-style documentation (see 27C).
➤ Use CSE-style documentation for a References list (see 27D).

27A   What is CM-style documentation?

Watch the Video

View the Model Document

The Chicago Manual of Style (CM) endorses two styles of documentation. One, **CM style**, is an author–date style, similar to the APA STYLE of IN-TEXT CITATIONS (see Ch. 26), that includes a list of SOURCES usually titled "Works Cited" or "References."

The other CM style uses a **bibliographic note system.** This system gives information about each source in two places: (1) in a *footnote* (at the bottom of a page) or an *endnote* (in a separate page following your paper) and, (2) if required, in a BIBLIOGRAPHY that begins on a separate page. We present this style here because it's often used in such humanities courses as art, music, history, philosophy, and sometimes English. Within the bibliographic note system, there are two substyles: "full" and "short."

27A.1   The full bibliographic note system in CM style

The CM full bibliographic note system requires you to give complete information, in a footnote or an endnote, the first time you cite a source. Because you're giving full information, you don't need to include a bibliography page. If you cite a source a second time, you provide shortened information that includes the last name(s) of the author(s) and the key words in the work's title. The following example uses the full bibliographic note system.

TEXT

Ulrich points out that both Europeans and Native Americans told war stories, but with different details and different emphases.[3]

FULL FOOTNOTE (SAME PAGE) OR ENDNOTE (SEPARATE PAGE FOLLOWING TEXT)

3. Laurel Thatcher Ulrich, *The Age of Homespun: Objects and Stories in the Creation of an American Myth* (New York: Knopf, 2001), 269.

SECOND CITATION OF THIS SOURCE

6. Ulrich, *Age of Homespun*, 285.

27A.2 The short bibliographic note system, plus bibliography, in CM style

In the abbreviated bibliographic note system, even your first endnote or foot-note provides only brief information about the source. You provide complete information in a bibliography, which appears as a separate page at the end of the paper. Following is an example of using the short bibliographic note system.

TEXT

Ulrich points out that both Europeans and Native Americans told war stories, but with different details and different emphases.[3]

ABBREVIATED FOOTNOTE (SAME PAGE) OR ENDNOTE (SEPARATE PAGE FOLLOWING TEXT)

3. Ulrich, *Age of Homespun*, 269.

BIBLIOGRAPHY (SEPARATE PAGE AT END OF THE PAPER)

Ulrich, Laurel Thatcher. *The Age of Homespun: Objects and Stories in the Creation of an American Myth.* New York: Knopf, 2001.

🛈 **Alert:** Ask your instructor which style he or she prefers. Remember that CM style requires a separate bibliography only when you use the short notes style, but your instructor may also prefer one with the full style. ●

Quick Box 27.1 provides guidelines for compiling CM-style bibliographic notes.

Quick Box 27.1 ■ ■ ■ ■ ■ ■ ■ ■ ■ ■ ■

Guidelines for compiling CM-style bibliographic notes

TITLE AND PLACEMENT OF NOTES

If you're using endnotes, place them all on a separate page, before your bibliography. Center the heading "Notes" an inch from the top of the page, without using italics, underlining, or quotation marks. If you're using foot-notes, place them at the bottom of the page on which the source needs to be credited. Never use a title above a note at the foot of the page. CM generally uses blank space (not a line) to divide the footnote(s) from the body text.

continued >>

Quick Box 27.1 (continued)

TITLE AND PLACEMENT OF BIBLIOGRAPHY

The abbreviated notes style requires a bibliography, which begins on a separate page at the end of the paper, following the endnotes page. An inch from the top of the page, center the heading "References" or "Works Cited" (either is acceptable in CM style). Don't underline or italicize the heading or put it in quotation marks.

FORMAT FOR ENDNOTES AND FOOTNOTES

Include an endnote or a footnote every time you use a source. Number notes sequentially throughout your paper whether you're using endnotes or footnotes. Use superscript (raised) arabic numerals for the footnote or endnote numbers in your paper. Position note numbers after any punctuation mark except the dash. The best position is at the end of a sentence, unless that position would be so far from the source material that it would be confusing. Don't use raised numbers in the endnote or footnote itself. Place the number, followed by a period, on the same line as the content of the note. Single-space both within each note and between notes. Indent each note's first line three-tenths of an inch (0.3" tab), which equals about three characters, but place subsequent lines flush left at the margin.

SPACING AFTER PUNCTUATION

A single space follows all punctuation, including the period.

AUTHORS' NAMES

In endnotes and footnotes, give the name in standard (first-name-first) order, with names and initials given in the original source. Use the word *and* before the last author's name if your source has more than one author.

In the bibliography, invert the name: last name, first name. If a work has two or more authors, invert only the first author's name. If your source has up to ten authors, give all the authors' names. If your source has eleven or more authors, list only the first seven and use *et al.* for the rest.

CAPITALIZATION OF SOURCE TITLES

Capitalize the first and last words and all major words.

SPECIAL TREATMENT OF TITLES

Use italics for titles of long works (such as books or periodicals), and use quotation marks around the titles of shorter works (such as articles or stories). Omit *A*, *An*, and *The* from the titles of newspapers and periodicals. For an unfamiliar newspaper title, list the city (and state, in parentheses, if the city isn't well known): *Newark (NJ) Star-Ledger*, for example. Use postal abbreviations for states.

continued >>

Quick Box 27.1   (continued)

PUBLICATION INFORMATION

Enclose publication information in parentheses. Use a colon and one space after the city of publication. Give complete publishers' names or abbreviate them according to standard abbreviations in *Books in Print.* Omit *Co., Inc.,* and so on. Spell out *University* or abbreviate to *Univ.* Never use *U* alone. Spell out *Press;* never use *P* alone. Don't abbreviate publication months.

PAGE NUMBERS

For inclusive page numbers, give the full second number for 2 through 99. For 100 and beyond, give the full second number only if a shortened version would be ambiguous: 243–47, 202–6, 300–304. List all discontinuous page numbers. (See "First Endnote or Footnote: Book" toward the end of this box.) Use a comma to separate parenthetical publication information from the page numbers that follow it. Use the abbreviations *p.* and *pp.* with page numbers only for material from newspapers, for material from journals that do not use volume numbers, and to avoid ambiguity.

CONTENT NOTES

Try to avoid using content notes, which differ from citation notes by providing information or ideas, not just references. If you must use them, use footnotes, not endnotes, with symbols rather than numbers: an asterisk (*) for the first note on that page and a dagger (†) for a second note on that page.

FIRST ENDNOTE OR FOOTNOTE: BOOK

For books, include the author, title, publication information, and page numbers when applicable. Some notes also include information about publication type (see example 12, below).

1. Becky Bradway, *Pink Houses and Family Taverns* (Bloomington: University of Indiana Press, 2002), 23.

FIRST ENDNOTE OR FOOTNOTE: ARTICLE

For articles, include the author, article title, journal title, volume number, year, and page numbers.

1. D. D. Cochran, W. Daniel Hale, and Christine P. Hissam, "Personal Space Requirements in Indoor versus Outdoor Locations," *Journal of Psychology* 117 (1984): 132–33.

SECOND MENTION IN ENDNOTES OR FOOTNOTES

Second (or later) citations of the same source can be brief. See 27B, example 1.

27B What are CM examples for bibliographic notes?

The following directory corresponds to the sample bibliographic note forms that follow it. In a few cases, we give sample Bibliography forms as well. If you need a model that isn't here, consult *The Chicago Manual of Style*, 16th ed. (Chicago: University of Chicago Press, 2010).

PERIODICALS

1. Article in a Scholarly Journal: Print

1. Bronwyn T. Williams. "Seeking New Worlds: The Study of Writing beyond Our Classrooms." *College Composition and Communication* 62, no. 1 (2010): 131. [full note]

2. Williams, "Seeking New Worlds," 131. [short note]

In a note, the author's name appears in regular order. Commas separate elements except for the page number, which follows a colon. In a full note, the volume number comes one space after the journal title. If there is an issue number, precede it with "no." (abbreviation of "number"). Provide both volume and issue number, if available.

Bibliography

Williams, Bronwyn T. "Seeking New Worlds: The Study of Writing beyond Our Classrooms," *College Composition and Communication* 62. no. 1 (2010): 127–46.

In the bibliography entry needed for the short note version, the author's name appears inverted, last name first. Periods separate the elements.

2. Article in Scholarly Journal: Online with a DOI

1. Regan Gurung and Kristin Vespia, "Looking Good, Teaching Well? Linking Liking, Looks, and Learning," *Teaching of Psychology* 34, no. 1 (2007): 7, doi: 10.1207/ s15328023top3401_2.   [full note]

2. Gurung and Vespia, "Looking Good," 7.   [short note]

Bibliography

Gurung, Regan, and Kristin Vespia. "Looking Good, Teaching Well? Linking Liking, Looks, and Learning." *Teaching of Psychology* 34, no. 1 (2007): 5–10. doi: 10.1207/ s15328023top3401_2.

For an explanation of Document Object Identifiers (DOI), see Quick Box 26.2.

3. Article in a Scholarly Journal: Online with a URL

1. Richard A. Bryant, "Disentangling Mild Traumatic Brain Injury and Stress Reactions," *New England Journal of Medicine* 358, no. 5 (2008): 527, http://www.nejm.org/doi/full/10.1056/NEJMe078235.

2. Bryant, "Disentangling," 527.

Bibliography

Bryant, Richard A. "Disentangling Mild Traumatic Brain Injury and Stress Reactions." *New England Journal of Medicine* 358, no. 5 (2008): 525–527. http://www.nejm.org/doi/full/10.1056/NEJMe078235

4. Article in a Scholarly Journal: From a Database

1. Bronwyn T. Williams, "Seeking New Worlds: The Study of Writing beyond Our Classrooms," *College Composition and Communication* 62, no.1 (2010): 143, Proquest.

Williams, "Seeking New Worlds," 143.

Bibliography

Williams, Bronwyn T. "Seeking New Worlds: The Study of Writing beyond Our Classrooms." *College Composition and Communication* 62, no. 1 (2010): 127–46. Proquest.

For articles from library or commercial databases, include as much information as possible about any print version. List the name of the database at the end of the entry (Proquest, in the preceding example). If the article has a stable URL (a unique URL that is permanently associated with it), provide it, as in the following example:

3. Michael Harker, "The Ethics of Argument: Rereading *Kairos* and Making Sense in a Timely Fashion," *College Composition and Communication* 59, no. 1 (2007): 77–97, http://www.jstor.org/stable/20456982.

5. Article in a Weekly or Biweekly Magazine: Print

1. Rana Foroohar, "Why the World Isn't Getting Smaller," *Time*, June 27, 2011, 20.

2. Foroohar, "Why the World," 20.

Bibliography

Foroohar, Rana. "Why the World Isn't Getting Smaller." *Time*. June 27, 2011, 20.

CM recommends citing magazine articles by the date only. If there is no author given, begin with the title of the article.

3. "The Price Is Wrong." *Economist*, August 2, 2008, 58–59.

6. Article in a Weekly or Biweekly Magazine: Online with a URL

1. Rana Foroohar, "Why the World Isn't Getting Smaller," *Time*, June 19, 2011, http://www.time.com/time/magazine/article/0,9171,2078119,00.html

2. Foroohar, "Why the World."

Bibliography

Foroohar, Rana. "Why the World Isn't Getting Smaller." *Time*, June 19, 2011.
http://www.time.com/time/magazine/article/0,9171,2078119,00.html.

The online version of this article did not list page numbers.

7. Article in a Monthly or Bimonthly Magazine: Print

1. Thomas Goetz, "The Feedback Loop," *Wired*, July 2011, 127.

See examples 1–6 for short note and bibliography forms.

8. Article in a Monthly or Bimonthly Magazine: Online

1. Thomas Goetz, "Harnessing the Power of Feedback Loops," *Wired*, July 2011, http://www.wired.com/magazine/2011/06/ff_feedbackloop/.

See examples 1–6 for short note and bibliography forms.

9. Article in a Newspaper: Print

1. Monica Hesse, "Love Among the Ruins," *Washington Post*, April 24, 2011, F1.

In CM style, page numbers for newspapers are optional and usually not included, but we've shown how to include one if your instructor requires. If no author is listed, begin with the title of the article:

2. "Prepping for Uranium Work," *Denver Post*, June 18, 2011.

If the city of publication is not part of the title, put it in square brackets after the title, not italicized:

3. "Goose Lake Council to Consider Study Proposal," *The Observer* [DeWitt, IA], July 30, 2011.

See examples 1–6 for short note and bibliography forms.

10. Article in a Newspaper: Online

1. Monica Hesse, "Falling in Love with St. Andrews, Scotland," *Washington Post*, April 24, 2011, http://www.washingtonpost.com/lifestyle /travel/falling-in-love-with-st-andrews-scotland/2011/04/18 /AFWZuoPE_story.html.

See examples 1–6 for short note and bibliography forms.

11. Editorials

1. "Primary Considerations," *Washington Post*, January 27, 2008: B6.

2. "Garbage In, Garbage Out," *Los Angeles Times*, February 2, 2008, http://www.latimes.com/news/printedition/la-ed-payroll2feb02,0,7684087.story.

Editorials are treated like any other newspaper article. If an author is listed, include her or his name before the title. See examples 1–6 for short note and bibliography forms.

12. Letter to the Editor: Print

1. Lester Goldstein, letter to the editor, *Sierra*, May/June 2011, 2.

CM style does not include any title that might be given for a letter to the editor. See examples 1–6 for short note and bibliography forms.

13. Letter to the Editor: Online

1. Heather B. Ennis, letter to the editor, *U.S. News and World Report*, 22 Dec. 2007, http://www.usnews.com/opinion/blogs/letters-to-the-editor /2007/12/20/sanctuaries-for-the-spirit.

See examples 1–6 for short note and bibliography forms.

14. Review

1. David Shenk, "Toolmaker, Brain Builder," review of *Beyond Deep Blue: Building the Computer That Defeated the World Chess Champion*, by Feng-Hsiung Hsu, *American Scholar* 72 (Spring 2003): 150–52.

2. Peter Travers, review of *Beginners*, directed by Mike Mills. *RollingStone*, June 2, 2011, http://www.rollingstone.com/movies/reviews /beginners-20110602.

Provide the name of the reviewer; title of the review, if any; the words "review of" followed by the name of the work reviewed; the name of the author, composer, director, etc.; then publication information. See examples 1–6 for short note and bibliography forms.

15. Article in a Looseleaf Collection of Reprinted Articles: Print

1. Thomas Hayden, "The Age of Robots," *US News and World Report*, April 23, 2001. Reprinted in *Applied Science 2002*, ed. Eleanor Goldstein (Boca Raton, FL: SIRS, 2002), art. 66.

Give the citation for the original publication first, followed by the citation for the collection. See examples 1–6 for short note and bibliography forms.

16. Abstract: Print

1. Hazel R. Marcus and Shinobu Kitayamo, "Culture and the Self: Implications for Cognition, Emotion, and Motivation," *Psychological Abstracts* 78 (1991), item 23878.

See examples 1–6 for short note and bibliography forms.

BOOKS

17. Book by One Author: Print

1. Sherry Turkle, *Alone Together: Why We Expect More from Technology and Less from Each Other* (New York: Basic Books, 2011), 43.   [full note]

2. Turkle, *Alone Together*, 43.   [short note]

Bibliography

Turkle, Sherry. *Alone Together: Why We Expect More from Technology and Less from Each Other*. New York: Basic Books, 2011.

18. Book by One Author: Downloaded from Library or Bookseller

1. Sherry Turkle, *Alone Together: Why We Expect More from Technology and Less from Each Other* (New York: Basic Books, 2011), Kindle edition, chap. 2.   [full note]

2. Turkle, *Alone Together*, chap. 2.   [short note]

Because books in electronic format often don't have stable page numbers, listing a chapter helps readers locate the citation.

Bibliography

Turkle, Sherry. *Alone Together: Why We Expect More from Technology and Less from Each Other*. New York: Basic Books, 2011. Kindle edition.

19. Book by One Author: Online

1. Sherry Turkle, *Alone Together: Why We Expect More from Technology and Less from Each Other* (New York: Basic Books, 2011), 43, http://books.google.com/.   [full note]

2. Turkle, *Alone Together*, 43.   [short note]

Bibliography

Turkle, Sherry. *Alone Together: Why We Expect More from Technology and Less from Each Other.* New York: Basic Books, 2011. http://books.google.com/.

20. Book by Two or Three Authors

1. Kathryn Edin and Maria Kefalas, *Promises I Can Keep: Why Poor Women Put Motherhood before Marriage* (Berkeley: University of California Press, 2005), 28.

2. Edin and Kefalas, *Promises*, 28.

Bibliography

Edin, Kathryn, and Maria Kefalas. *Promises I Can Keep: Why Poor Women Put Motherhood before Marriage.* Berkeley: University of California Press, 2005.

Include the names of two or three authors in notes. In the bibliography, invert the name of only the first author. For e-books, adapt this model to example 18. For a book accessed online, see example 19.

21. Book by More Than Three Authors

1. Wendy Saul et al., *Beyond the Science Fair: Creating a Kids' Inquiry Conference.* (Portsmouth: Heinemann, 2005), 74.   [full note]

2. Saul et al., *Beyond the Science Fair*, 74.   [short note]

Bibliography

Saul, Wendy, Donna Dieckman, Charles R. Pearce, and Donna Neutze. *Beyond the Science Fair: Creating a Kids' Inquiry Conference.* Portsmouth, NH: Heinemann, 2005.

In notes, give only the first author's name, followed by the phrase *et al.* (abbreviated from the Latin *et alii*, meaning "and others"). In the bibliography list all names in full in the order in which they appear on the title page. For e-books, adapt this model to example 18. For a book accessed online, see example 19.

22. Two or More Works by the Same Author(s)

Bibliography

Jenkins, Henry. *Convergence Culture: Where Old and New Media Collide.* New York: New York University Press, 2006.

---. *Fans, Bloggers, and Gamers: Exploring Participatory Culture.* New York: New York University Press, 2006.

Give author name(s) in the first entry only. In the second and subsequent entries, use three hyphens and a period to stand for exactly the same name(s). If the person served as editor or translator, put a comma and the appropriate abbreviation (*ed.* or *trans.*) following the three hyphens. Arrange the works in alphabetical (not chronological) order according to book title. For e-books, adapt this model to example 18. For a book accessed online, see example 19.

23. Book by a Group or Corporate Author

1. American Psychological Association, *Publication Manual of the American Psychological Association*, 6th ed. (Washington, DC: APA, 2010).

Cite the full name of the corporate author first, omitting the first articles *A, An,* or *The.* For e-books, adapt this model to example 18. For a book accessed online, see example 19. For short notes and bibliography forms, see examples 17–21.

24. Book with No Author Named

1. *The Chicago Manual of Style*, 16th ed. (Chicago: University of Chicago Press, 2010), 711.

If there is no author's name on the title page, begin the citation with the title. Alphabetize the entry according to the first significant word of the title (ignore *A, An,* or *The*).

For e-books, adapt this model to example 18. For a book accessed online, see example 19. For short notes and bibliography forms, see examples 17–21.

25. Book with an Author and an Editor

1. Harriet Beecher Stowe, *Uncle Tom's Cabin*, ed. Elizabeth Ammons (New York: Norton, 2010), 272.

2. Stowe, *Uncle Tom's Cabin*, 272.

Bibliography

Stowe, Harriet Beecher. *Uncle Tom's Cabin.* Edited by Elizabeth Ammons. New York: Norton, 2010.

If your paper refers to the work of the book's author, put the author's name first. If your paper refers to the work of the editor, put the editor's name first.

Ammons, Elizabeth, ed. *Uncle Tom's Cabin.* By Harriet Beecher Stowe. New
    York: Norton, 2010.

For e-books, adapt this model to example 18. For a book accessed directly online, see example 19.

26. Translation

1. Jo Nesbo, *The Leopard,* trans. Don Bartlett (New York: Vintage, 2011), 7.

For e-books, adapt this model to example 18. For a book accessed online, see example 19. For short notes and bibliography forms, see examples 17–21.

27. Work in Several Volumes or Parts

1. Ronald Chrisley, ed., *Artificial Intelligence: Critical Concepts* (London: Routledge, 2000), 4:25.

Bibliography

Chrisley, Ronald, ed. *Artificial Intelligence: Critical Concepts.* Vol. 4. London:
    Routledge, 2000.

If you are citing only one volume, put only that volume number before the publication information. For e-books, adapt this model to example 18. For a book accessed online, see example 19. For short notes and bibliography forms, see examples 17–21.

28. Anthology or Edited Book

1. John L. Purdy and James Ruppert, eds., *Nothing but the Truth: An Anthology of Native American Literature* (Upper Saddle River, NJ: Prentice, 2001), 12.

2. Purdy and Ruppert, *Nothing but the Truth,* 12.

Bibliography

Purdy, John L., and James Ruppert, eds. *Nothing but the Truth: An Anthology of Native American Literature.* Upper Saddle River, NJ: Prentice, 2001.

Use this model if you are citing an entire anthology. In the preceding example, *eds.* stands for "editors;" use *ed.* when only one editor is named. For e-books, adapt this model to example 18. For a book accessed directly online, see example 19.

29. One Selection from an Anthology or an Edited Book

1. Laura Trujillo, "Balancing Act," in *Border-Line Personalities: A New Generation of Latinas Dish on Sex, Sass, and Cultural Shifting*, ed. Robyn Moreno and Michelle Herrera Mulligan (New York: Harper, 2004), 62.

2. Trujillo, "Balancing Act," 62.

Bibliography

Trujillo, Laura. "Balancing Act." In *Border-Line Personalities: A New Generation of Latinas Dish on Sex, Sass, and Cultural Shifting*, edited by Robyn Moreno and Michelle Herrera Mulligan, 61–72. New York: Harper, 2004.

For e-books, adapt this model to example 18. For a book accessed directly online, see example 19.

30. More Than One Selection from the Same Anthology or Edited Book

Bibliography

Bond, Ruskin. "The Night Train at Deoli." In Chaudhuri, *Vintage Book*, 415–18.

Chaudhuri, Amit, ed. *The Vintage Book of Modern Indian Literature*. New York: Vintage, 2004.

Vijayan, O.V. "The Rocks." In Chaudhuri, *Vintage Book*, 291–96.

When you cite more than one selection from the same anthology, you can list the anthology as a separate entry with all of the publication information. Also list each selection from the anthology by author and title of the selection, but give only the name(s) of the editor(s) of the anthology, a short title, and the page number(s) for each selection. List selections separately in alphabetical order by author's last name. For e-books, adapt this model to example 18. For a book accessed online, see example 19. For short notes and bibliography forms, see examples 17–21.

31. Article in a Dictionary or Encyclopedia

1. *Encyclopaedia Britannica*, 15th ed., s.v. "Ireland."

If you're citing a widely used reference work, don't give full publication information. Instead, give only the edition and year of publication. In this case, *s.v.* means *sub vero* ("under the word"), which indicates looking up "Ireland" alphabetically in the source.

If the articles in the book are alphabetically arranged, you don't need to give volume and page numbers. If no author is listed, begin with the title of the article. For references with more substantial articles, cite them as you would chapters in a book:

1. Burnbam, John C. "Freud, Sigmund." *The Encyclopedia of Psychiatry, Psychology, and Psychoanalysis.* Ed. Benjamin B. Wolman. New York: Holt, 1996.

32. Article in a Reference Book: Database

1. Encyclopaedia Britannica Online, s.v. "Lobster," accessed June 29, 2011, http://www.britannica.com/EBchecked/topic/345506/lobster.

33. Second or Later Edition

1. *MLA Handbook for Writers of Research Papers*, 7th ed. (New York: MLA, 2009).

If a book is not a first edition, the edition number is on the title page. Place the abbreviated information (*2nd ed., 3rd ed.*, etc.) between the title and the publication information. Give only the latest copyright date for the edition you are using.

For e-books, adapt this model to example 18. For a book accessed online, see example 19. For short notes and bibliography forms, see examples 17–21.

34. Introduction, Preface, Foreword, or Afterword

1. Doug Hesse, foreword to *The End of Composition Studies*, by David W. Smit (Carbondale: Southern Illinois University Press, 2004), xi.

2. Hesse, foreword, xi.

Bibliography

Hesse, Doug. Foreword to *The End of Composition Studies*, by David W. Smit. ix–xiii. Carbondale: Southern Illinois UP, 2004.

Give first the name of the writer of the part you're citing and then the name of the cited part, without italics or quotation marks. When the introduction, preface, foreword, or afterword has a title, include it in the citation before the section name, as in the following example:

Fox-Genovese, Elizabeth. "Mothers and Daughters: The Ties That Bind." Foreword to *Southern Mothers*, iv–xviii. Edited by Nagueyalti Warren and Sally Wolff. Baton Rouge, LA: Louisiana State University Press, 1999.

For e-books, adapt this model to example 18. For a book accessed directly online, see example 19.

35. Unpublished Dissertation or Essay

1. Gina Anne Stuart, "Exploring the Harry Potter Book Series: A Study of Adolescent Reading Motivation," (PhD diss., Utah State University, 2006), ProQuest (AAT 3246355).

State the author's name first, then the title in quotation marks (not underlined), then a descriptive label (such as *Diss.* or *Unpublished essay*), followed by the degree-granting institution (for dissertations), and finally the date. Treat published dissertations as books. In the preceding example, "ProQuest" is the name of the database containing the dissertation, and the number in parentheses at the end is the accession number.

36. Reprint of an Older Book

1. Robert Coover, *A Night at the Movies, Or, You Must Remember This* (Champaign, IL: Dalkey Archive, 2007). First published 1987 by William Heinemann Ltd.

Republishing information can be found on the copyright page. For e-books, adapt this model to example 18. For a book accessed online, see example 19. For short notes and bibliography forms, see examples 17–21.

37. Book in a Series or Scholarly Project

1. Jean Hastings Ardell, *Breaking into Baseball: Women and the National Pastime*, Writing Baseball Series (Carbondale: Southern Illinois University Press, 2005).

For e-books, adapt this model to example 18. For a book accessed online, see example 19. For short notes and bibliography forms, see examples 17–21.

38. Book with a Title within a Title

1. Robert M. Lumiansky and Herschel Baker, eds, *Critical Approaches to Six Major English Works: "Beowulf" Through "Paradise Lost"* (Philadelphia: University of Pennsylvania Press, 1968).

Set the normally independent titles within quotation marks and italicize them. For e-books, adapt this model to example 18. For a book accessed online, see example 19. For short notes and bibliography forms, see examples 17–21.

39. Bible or Sacred Text

Bibliography

Bhagavad Gita. Translated by Juan Mascaro. Rev. ed. New York: Penguin, 2003.

The Holy Bible: New International Version. New York: Harper, 1983.

The Qur'an. Translated by M.A.S. Abdel Haleem. New York: Oxford University Press, 2004.

For e-books, adapt this model to example 18. For a book accessed online, see example 19. For short notes and bibliography forms, see examples 17–21.

40. Government Publication

Bibliography

US Senate. Select Committee on Intelligence. *Report on the U.S. Intelligence Community's Prewar Intelligence Assessment of Iraq.* 108th Cong., 1st sess. Washington, DC: Government Printing Office, 2004.

For government publications that name no author, start with the name of the government or government body. Then name the government agency. Then include the title, any series information, and publication information. If there is an author, begin with the author's name:

Wallace, David Rains. *Yellowstone: A Natural and Human History; Yellowstone National Park, Idaho, Montana, and Wyoming.* Interior Dept. National Park Service. Official National Park Handbook 150. Washington, DC: Government Printing Office, 2001.

41. Government Publication: Online

1. Ronald C. Huff, *Comparing the Criminal Behavior of Youth Gangs and At-Risk Youths* (United States. Dept. of Justice. Natl. Inst. of Justice. October, 1998), https://www.ncjrs.gov/txtfiles/172852.txt.

42. Published Proceedings of a Conference

1. Luis Mateus Rocha, ed., *Artificial Life X: Proceedings of the Tenth International Conference on the Simulation and Synthesis of Living Systems* (Cambridge, MA: MIT Press, 2006).

Treat published proceedings as you would chapters in a book.

IMAGES, AUDIO, FILM, AND VIDEO

The Chicago Manual of Style, 16th Edition, includes no examples of notes or bibliographic entries for photographs, illustrations, graphs or other images. When such materials are reproduced in a paper, CM recommends including a caption beneath the image, with source information included at the end of the caption. However, because student papers often refer to images as sources or discuss them as examples, we have provided some examples below, in CM style.

43. Photograph, Painting, Drawing, Illustration, etc. (Original)

1. Carl Mydans, *General Douglas MacArthur Landing at Luzon, 1945,* photograph displayed at Soho Triad Fine Art Gallery, New York (October 21–November 28, 1999).

2. Mydans, *General Douglas MacArthur.*

Bibliography

Mydans, Carl. *General Douglas MacArthur Landing at Luzon, 1945.* Photograph displayed at Soho Triad Fine Art Gallery, New York. October 21–November 28, 1999.

Give the name of the image's maker, if known, the title or caption of the image, the type of image, where you viewed the image, and when. If the image has no title, provide a brief description.

44. Photograph, Painting, Drawing, Illustration, etc. in a Periodical: Print

1. Herb Greene, *Grace Slick*, photograph, *Rolling Stone*, September 30, 2004: 102.

2. Greene, *Grace Slick*, 102.

Bibliography

Greene, Herb. *Grace Slick.* Photograph. *Rolling Stone* September 30, 2004: 102.

45. Photograph, Painting, Drawing, Illustration, etc. in a Periodical: Online

1. Christopher Morris, *Man in Camouflage*, photograph, *The Atlantic*, July/August 2011, http://www.theatlantic.com/magazine/archive/2011/07/invisible-inc/8523/

2. Morris, *Man in Camouflage.*

Bibliography

Morris, Christopher. *Man in Camouflage.* Photograph. *The Atlantic.* July/August 2011. http://www.theatlantic.com/magazine/archive/2011/07/invisible-inc/8523/.

46. Photograph, Painting, Drawing, Illustration, etc. in a Book: Print

Bibliography

"The World's Most Populous Countries." Illustration in *Maps of the Imagination: The Writer as Cartographer*, by Peter Turchi, 116–17. San Antonio, TX: Trinity University Press, 2004.

See 44 for example of notes.

47. Comic or Cartoon: Print

Bibliography

Sutton, Ward. "Ryan's a Late Adopter." Cartoon. *New Yorker*, May 2, 2011.

See 44 for example of notes.

48. Slide Show or Photo Essay: Online

Bibliography

Nachtwey, James. Crime in Middle America. *Time*, December 2, 2006.
    Accessed May 4, 2011, http://www.time.com/time/photogallery
    /0,29307,1947522,00.html.

See 44 for example of notes.

49. Image from a Service or Distributor

Bibliography

World Perspectives. *Launching of the Space Shuttle Columbia, Florida, USA,
    1998.* Photograph. Accessed March 3, 2011, from http://gettyimages.com.
    Getty Images (#AT3775-001).

In this example, the photographer was listed as "World Perspectives." Include
the name of the service or distributor, and the item number or other identifier,
if any. See 44 for example of notes.

50. Online Map, Chart, or Other Graphic: Online

Bibliography

"Hurricane Rita." Graphic from *New York Times Online*, September 24,
    2005. http://www.nytimes.com/packages/html/national
    /20050923_RITA_GRAPHIC/index.html.

See 44 for example of notes.

51. Audio Book

    1. Sherry Turkle, *Alone Together: Why We Expect More from
Technology and Less from Each Other,* read by Laural Merlington, Tantor
Media, 2011, CD.

52. Sound Recording

Verdi, Giuseppe. *Requiem.* Chicago Symphony Orchestra and Chorus. Ricardo
    Muti. CSO Resound B003WL7EJE, 2010. 2 compact discs.

Put first the name most relevant to what you discuss in your paper (performer, conductor, work performed). Include the recording's title, other
information (performer, composer, conductor), the name of the issuer,
the date the work was issued, the medium, and any additional recording
information.

Radiohead. "Jigsaw Falling into Place." From *In Rainbows*. Radiohead, 2007.
    MP3 file.

53. Sound Recording: Online

Komunyakaa, Yusef. "My Father's Love Letters." Performed by Yusef
Komunyakaa. Internet Poetry Archive, University of North Carolina
Press. http://www.ibiblio.org/ipa/audio/komunyakaa/my_father%27s_
love_letters.mp3.

54. Podcast

Blumberg, Alex and Adam Davidson. "The Giant Pool of Money." *This
American Life.* Podcast audio. May 9, 2008. http://www.thisamericanlife
.org/radio-archives/episode/355/the-giant-pool-of-money.

55. Film, Videotape, or DVD

It Happened One Night. Directed and produced by Frank Capra. 1934; Culver
City, CA: Sony Pictures, 1999. DVD.

Give the title first, and include the director, the distributor, and the year. For
films that were subsequently released on tape or DVD, provide the original
release date of the movie. Other information (writer, producer, major actors)
is optional but helpful. Put first names first.

For video downloads, include the download date and the source.

It Happened One Night. Directed and produced by Frank Capra. 1934;
Accessed December 15, 2010, from Netflix.

56. Video or Film: Online

"Challenger Disaster Live on CNN." YouTube video. Posted by CNN, January
27, 2011. http://www.youtube.com/watch?v=AfnvFnzs9ls.

57. Broadcast Television or Radio Program

Include at least the title of the program (in italics), the network, the local station and its city, and the date of the broadcast.

*Not for Ourselves Alone: The Story of Elizabeth Cady Stanton and Susan B.
Anthony.* By Ken Burns. Perf. Julie Harris, Ronnie Gilbert, and Sally
Kellerman. Prod. Paul Barnes and Ken Burns. PBS. WNET, New York.
8 Nov. 1999.

The Madeleine Brand Show. KPCC, Pasadena. 20 June 2011.

58. Television or Radio Program: Online

1. "Bill Moyers," *The Daily Show, with Jon Stewart,* Comedy Central, June
1, 2011, http://www.thedailyshow.com/watch/wed-june-22-2005/bill-moyers.

2. "The Disappearing Incandescent Bulb," *The Madeleine Brand Show,*
KPCC, June 20, 2011, http://www.scpr.org/programs/madeleine-brand/2011
/06/20/the-disappearing-incandescent-bulb/.

OTHER ONLINE SOURCES

59. Entire Web Site

WebdelSol.Com. Ed. Michael Neff. Accessed August 4, 2011.
http://www.webdelsol.com.

Association for the Advancement of Artificial Intelligence. Accessed October
17, 2011. http://www.aaai.org/home.html.

60. Page from a Web Site

American Psychological Association. "Think Again: Men and Women Share
Cognitive Skills." Last modified January 18, 2006. http://www.apa.org
/research/action/share.aspx.

Provide as much information as you can, starting with the author, if available,
and the title of the page, followed by the site information.

61. Online Discussion or Electronic Mailing List Posting

1. Richard Haswell to WPA-L mailing list, October 17, 2005, "A New
Graphic/Text Interface," http://lists.asu.edu/archives/wpa-l.html.

62. Chat or Real-Time Communication

Bibliography

Berzsenyi, Christyne. Online discussion of "Writing to Meet Your Match:
Rhetoric, Perceptions, and Self-Presentation for Four Online Daters."
Computers and Writing Online. AcadianaMoo. May 13, 2007. Accessed
March 3, 2012. http://acadianamoo.com.

Glenn, Maria. Chat. *Facebook*, September 9, 2010. Accessed September 9, 2010.

Give the name of the speaker or writer, a title for the event (if any), the forum,
date, publication medium, access date, and URL if needed.

63. E-Mail Message

1. Tara Martin, "Visit to Los Alamos," e-mail message to author, July 25, 2010.

Bibliography

Martin, Tara. "Visit to Los Alamos." E-mail message to author. July 25, 2010.

64. Posting on a Blog

1. Matthew Phillips, "Need to Go to the ER? Not Until the Game's Over."
Freakonomics.com (blog). June 15, 2011, http://www.freakonomics.com/2011/06
/15/need-to-go-to-the-er-not-until-the-games-over/.

Bibliography

Freakonomics.com (blog), http://www.freakonomics.com/.

65. Wiki

1. *NASCAR Wiki*, s.v. "NASCAR Sprint Cup Series," last modified January 11, 2011, http://nascarwiki.com.

OTHER SOURCES

66. Published or Unpublished Letter

Irvin, William. William Irvin to Lesley Osburn, December 8, 2011.

Williams, William Carlos. William Carlos Williams to his son, March 13, 1935. In *Letters of the Century: America 1900–1999*, edited by Lisa Grunwald and Stephen J. Adler, 225–26. New York: Dial, 1999.

67. Microfiche Collection of Articles

Wenzell, Ron. "Businesses Prepare for a More Diverse Work Force." *St. Louis Post Dispatch*, February 3, 1990: 17. Microform. *NewsBank: Employment* 27 (1990): fiche 2, grid D12.

68. Map or Chart

Colorado Front Range Mountain Bike Topo Map. Nederland, CO: Latitude 40, 2001.

If you have accessed the map or chart online, please follow example 49.

69. Report or Pamphlet

National Commission on Writing in America's Schools and Colleges. *The Neglected "R": The Need for a Writing Revolution*. New York: College Board, 2003.

Use the format for books, to the extent possible, including whether you're citing a print or online version.

70. Legal Source

1. Brown v. Bd. of Education, 347 U.S. 483 (1954).

Include the name of the case, the number of the case (preceded by *No.*), the name of the court deciding the case, and the date of the decision. Legal sources can frequently be accessed through a database:

2. Brown v. Bd. of Education, 347 U.S. 483 (1954). LexisNexis Academic.

71. Interview

1. Randi Friedman, telephone interview by author, August 30, 2011.

2. Carl Pope, interview by Amy Standen, *Salon.com*, April 29, 2002, http://www.salon.com/people/interview/2002/04/29/carlpope.

Note the type of interview, for example "telephone" or "personal" (face-to-face). For a published interview, give the name of the interviewed person first, identify the source as an interview, and then give details as for any published source. Follow the citation format for a periodical, book, or online source, as appropriate.

72. Lecture or Speech

1. Jennifer Katz, "Spiral Galaxies" (lecture in Astronomy 1000, University of Denver, Denver, CO, February 7, 2011).

Bibliography

Katz, Jennifer. "Spiral Galaxies." Lecture in Astronomy 1000, University of Denver, Denver, CO, February 7, 2011.

King, Martin Luther. "I Have a Dream." Speech presented at the Lincoln Memorial, Washington, DC, August 28, 1963. MP3 on American Rhetoric Top 100 Speeches. http://www.americanrhetoric.com/speeches /mlkihaveadream.htm.

If citing only the original, the entry would end after "1963." This entry goes on to cite an online version.

73. Live Performance (Play, Concert, Dance etc.)

Miller, Arthur. *All My Sons*. Directed by Calvin McLean. Performed at the Center for the Performing Arts, Normal, IL, September 27, 2005.

Nelson, Willie. *Country Throwdown Tour*. Performed at Red Rocks Amphitheater, Denver, CO, June 22, 2011.

74. Published Musical Score

1. Franz Schubert, *Symphony in B Minor (Unfinished)*, ed. Martin Cusid. New York: Norton, 1971.

75. Advertisement

1. Southwest Airlines, advertisement, ABC television, August 24, 2010.

2. Canon Digital Cameras, advertisement, *Time*, June 2, 2003, 77.

3. Budget Truck Rental, advertisement, *Huffington Post*, August 2, 2011, http://www.huffingtonpost.com.

76. Video Game or Software

The Island: Castaway. Computer game. N.p: Awem Studio, 2010.

"N.p." indicates that the place of publication is unknown.

27C What is CSE-style documentation?

The Council of Science Editors, or CSE, produces a manual called *Scientific Style and Format* to guide publications in mathematics, the life sciences, and the physical sciences. The information in this chapter adheres to the style **View** guidelines in the seventh edition of that manual. For up-to-date information, **the Model Document** go to the organization's Web site at http://www.councilscienceeditors.org.

CSE has two components: (1) citations within the text, called "in-text references," tied to (2) a bibliography, called "end references," at the end of the text. However, CSE offers three different options for in-text references: the citation-sequence system, the name-year system, and the citation-name system. In this chapter we explain the citation-name system, which the CSE most strongly endorses.

In the citation-name system, the in-text references use numbers to refer to end references that are arranged alphabetically. In other words, first complete the list of end references, arranging them alphabetically by author. Then, number each reference; for example, if you were documenting references by Schmidt, Gonzalez, Adams, and Zurowski, in your end references, you would arrange them:

1. Adams . . .

2. Gonzalez . . .

3. Schmidt . . .

4. Zurowski . . .

Finally, use superscript (raised) numbers for source citations in your sentences that correspond to the numbered author names in the end references. (Numbers in parentheses are also acceptable.)

IN-TEXT REFERENCES—CITATION-NAME

Sybesma[2] insists that this behavior occurs periodically, but Crowder[1] claims never to have observed it.

END REFERENCES—CITATION-NAME

1. Crowder W. Seashore life between the tides. New York: Dodd, Mead; 1931. New York: Dover Reprint; 1975. 372 p.

2. Sybesma C. An introduction to biophysics. New York: Academic; 1977. 648 p.

Quick Box 27.3 gives guidelines for compiling a References list. Especially pay attention to the arrangement of entries in a citation-name system.

When you're citing more than one reference at a time, list each source number in numeric order, followed by a comma with no space. Use a hyphen to show the range of numbers in a continuous sequence, and put all in superscript: [2,5–7,9]

Quick Box 27.3 ■ ■ ■ ■ ■ ■ ■ ■ ■ ■

Guidelines for compiling a CSE-style Cited References list

TITLE

Use "Cited References" or "References" as the title (no underlining, no italics, no quotation marks).

PLACEMENT OF LIST

Begin the list on a separate page at the end of the research paper. Number the page sequentially with the rest of the paper.

CONTENT AND FORMAT OF CITED REFERENCES

Include all sources that you quote, paraphrase, or summarize in your paper. Center the title one inch from the top of the page. Start each entry on a new line. Put the number, followed by a period and a space, at the regular left margin. If an entry takes more than one line, indent the second and all other lines under the first word, not the number. Single-space each entry and double-space between entries.

SPACING AFTER PUNCTUATION

CSE style specifies no space after date, issue number, or volume number of a periodical, as shown in the models in 27D.

ARRANGEMENT OF ENTRIES

Sequence the entries in alphabetical order by author, then title, etc. Number the entries. Put the number, followed by a period and a space, at the regular left margin.

AUTHORS' NAMES

Reverse the order of each author's name, giving the last name first. For book citations, you can give first names or use only the initials of first and (when available) middle names; for journal citations, use only initials. However, CSE style recommends you use only initials. Don't use a period or a space between first and middle initials. Use a comma to separate the names of multiple authors identified by initials; however, if you use full first names, use a semicolon. Don't use *and* or *&* with authors' names. Place a period after the last author's name.

continued >>

Quick Box 27.3   (continued)

TREATMENT OF TITLES

Never underline or italicize titles or enclose them in quotation marks. Capitalize a title's first word and any proper nouns. Don't capitalize the first word of a subtitle unless it's a proper noun. Capitalize the titles of academic journals. If the title of a periodical is one word, give it in full; otherwise, abbreviate the title according to recommendations established by the *American National Standard for Abbreviations of Titles of Periodicals*. Capitalize a newspaper title's major words, giving the full title but omitting *A, An*, or *The* at the beginning.

PLACE OF PUBLICATION

Use a colon after the city of publication. If the city name could be unfamiliar to readers, add in parentheses the postal abbreviation for the US state or Canadian province. If the location of a foreign city will be unfamiliar to readers, add in parentheses the country name, abbreviating it according to International Organization for Standardization (ISO) standards. Find ISO country codes at http://www.iso.org.

PUBLISHER

Give the name of the publisher, without periods after initials, and use a semicolon after the publisher's name. Omit *The* at the beginning or *Co., Inc., Ltd.,* or *Press* at the end. However, for a university press, abbreviate *University* and *Press* as *Univ* and *Pr*, respectively, without periods.

PUBLICATION MONTH

Abbreviate all month names longer than three letters to their first three letters, but do not add a period.

PAGE NUMBERS

For inclusive page numbers, shorten the second number as much as possible, making sure that the number isn't ambiguous. For example, use 233–4 for 233 to 234; 233–44 for 233 to 244; and 233–304, not 233–04, for 233 to 304. Give the numbers of all discontinuous pages, separating successive numbers or ranges with a comma: 54–7, 60–6.

TOTAL PAGE NUMBERS

When citing an entire book, the last information unit gives the total number of book pages, followed by the abbreviation *p* and a period.

continued >>

Quick Box 27.3 (continued)

FORMAT FOR CITED REFERENCES ENTRIES: BOOKS

Citations for books usually list author(s), title, publication information, and pages (either total pages when citing an entire work or inclusive pages when citing part of a book). Each unit of information ends with a period. Some entries have additional information.

1. Primrose SB, Twyman RM, Old RW. Principles of gene manipulation. London: Blackwell; 2002. 390 p.

FORMAT FOR CITED REFERENCES ENTRIES: ARTICLES

Citations for articles usually list author(s), article title, and journal name and publication information, each section followed by a period. Abbreviate a journal's name only if it's standard in your scientific discipline. For example, *Exp Neurol* is the abbreviated form for *Experimental Neurology*. In the following example, the volume number is 184, and the issue number, in parentheses, is 1. Notice the lack of a space after the semicolon, before the parentheses, and after the colon. Some entries have additional information.

1. Ginis I, Rao MS. Toward cell replacement therapy: promises and caveats. Exp Neurol. 2003;184(1):61–77.

27D What are CSE examples for sources in a list of references?

The directory that follows corresponds to the sample references that follow it. If you need a model not included in this book, consult *Scientific Style and Format*, 7th ed. (2006).

Directory: CSE Style for a Cited References List

■ BOOKS AND PARTS OF BOOKS 435

BOOKS AND PARTS OF BOOKS

1. Book by One Author

1. Hawking SW. Black holes and baby universes and other essays. New York: Bantam; 1993. 320 p.

Use one space but no punctuation between an author's last name and the initial of the first name. Don't put punctuation or a space between first and middle initials (*Hawking SW*). Do, however, use the hyphen in a hyphenated first and middle name (for example, *Gille J-C* represents *Jean-Charles Gille* in the next item).

2. Book by More Than One Author

1. Wegzyn S, Gille J-C, Vidal P. Developmental systems: at the crossroads of system theory, computer science, and genetic engineering. New York: Springer-Verlag; 1990. 595 p.

3. Book by a Group or Corporate Author

1. Chemical Rubber Company. Handbook of laboratory safety. 3rd ed. Boca Raton (FL): CRC; 1990. 1352 p.

4. Anthology or Edited Book

1. Heerrmann B, Hummel S, editors. Ancient DNA: recovery and analysis of genetic material from paleontological, archeological, museum, medical, and forensic specimens. New York: Springer-Verlag; 1994. 1020 p.

5. One Selection or Chapter in an Anthology or Edited Book

1. Basov NG, Feoktistov LP, Senatsky YV. Laser driver for inertial confinement fusion. In: Bureckner KA, editor. Research trends in physics: inertial confinement fusion. New York: American Institute of Physics; 1992. p. 24–37.

6. Translation

1. Magris C. A different sea. Spurr MS, translator. London: Harvill; 1993. 194 p. Translation of: Un mare differente.

7. Reprint of an Older Book

1. Carson R. *The sea around us.* New York: Oxford Univ Pr; 1951. New York: Oxford Univ Pr; 1991. 288 p.

8. All Volumes of a Multivolume Work

1. Crane FL, Moore DJ, Low HE, editors. *Oxidoreduction at the plasma membrane: relation to growth and transport.* Boca Raton (FL): CRC; 1991. 2 vol.

9. Unpublished Dissertation or Thesis

1. Baykul MC. *Using ballistic electron emission microscopy to investigate the metal-vacuum interface* [dissertation]. [Orem (UT)]: Polytechnic University; 1993. 111 p. Available from: UMI Dissertation Express, http://tls.il.proquest.com/hp/Products/DisExpress.html, Document 9332714.

10. Published Article from Conference Proceedings

1. Tsang CP, Bellgard MI. Sequence generation using a network of Boltzmann machines. In: Tsang CP, editor. *Proceedings of the 4th Australian Joint Conference on Artificial Intelligence;* 1990 Nov 8–11; Perth, AU. Singapore: World Scientific; 1990. p. 224–33.

PRINT ARTICLES FROM JOURNALS AND PERIODICALS

11. Article in a Journal

1. Ginis I, Rao MS. Toward cell replacement therapy: promises and caveats. Exp Neurol. 2003;184(1):61–77.

Give both the volume number and the issue number (here, *184* is the volume number and *1* is the issue number). Note that there is no space between the year and the volume, the volume and the issue, or the issue and the pages.

12. Journal Article on Discontinuous Pages

1. Richards FM. The protein folding problem. Sci Am. 1991;246(1):54–57, 60–66.

13. Article with No Identifiable Author

1. Cruelty to animals linked to murders of humans. AWIQ 1993 Aug;42(3):16.

14. Article with Author Affiliation

1. DeMoll E, Auffenberg T (Department of Microbiology, University of Kentucky). Purine metabolism in *Methanococcus vannielii.* J Bacteriol. 1993;175:5754–5761.

15. Entire Issue of a Journal

1. Whales in a modern world: a symposium held in London, November 1988. Mamm Rev. 1990 Jan;20(9).

The date of the symposium, November 1988, is part of the title of this issue.

16. Signed Newspaper Article

1. Kilborn PT. A health threat baffling for its lack of a pattern. New York Times (Final ed.). 2003 Jun 22;Sect. A:14 (col. 2).

Sect. stands for *section*. Note that there is no space between the date and the section.

17. Unsigned Newspaper Article

1. Supercomputing center to lead security effort. Pantagraph (Bloomington, IL) 2003 Jul 4; Sect. A:7.

18. Editorial or Review

CSE allows "notes" after the page number(s) that will help readers understand the nature of the reference.

1. Leshner AI. "Glocal" science advocacy [editorial]. Science. 2008;319(5865):877.

2. Myer A. Genomes evolve, but how? Nature. 2008;451(7180):771. Review of Lynch M, The Origins of Genome Architecture.

ELECTRONIC SOURCES ON THE INTERNET

In general, CSE style requires that you cite electronic sources by including the author's name, if available; the work's title; the type of medium, in brackets, such as [*Internet*] or [*electronic mail on the Internet*]; the title of the publication if there's a print version or, if not, the place of publication and the publishing organization; the date the original was published or placed on the Internet; the date you accessed the publication, preceded by the word *cited* enclosed in brackets; and the address of the source, if from the Internet or a database. Omit end punctuation after an Internet address.

19. Books on the Internet

1. Colwell R, editor. MENC handbook of musical cognition and development [Internet]. New York: Oxford University Press; c2006 [cited 2011 Feb 4]. Available from: http://books.google.com/books/

20. Articles with Print Versions on the Internet

1. Pollard R. Evidence of a reduced home field advantage when a team moves to a new stadium. J Sport Sci [Internet]. 2002 [cited 2010 Nov 5]; 20(12):969–974. Available from: http://0-find.galegroup.com.bianca.penlib.du.edu:80/itx /start.do?prodId=AONE

21. Articles Available Only on the Internet

1. Overbye D. Remembrance of things future: the mystery of time. The New York Times on the Web [Internet]. 2005 Jun 28 [cited 2009 Dec 11]. Available from: http://www.nytimes.com/2005/06/28/science/28time.html

22. Web Pages

Begin with author, if available; otherwise, begin with title.

1. Think again: men and women share cognitive skills [Internet]. Washington (DC): American Psychological Association; 2006 [cited 2011 Jan 17]. Available from: http://www.psychologymatters.org/thinkagain.html

2. Welcome to AAAI [Internet]. Menlo Park (CA): Association for the Advancement of Artificial Intelligence; c2008 [cited 2011 Mar 17]. Available from: http://www.aaai.org

23. Videos or Podcasts

1. Wesch M. Web 2.0 . . . the machine is us/ing us [Internet]. 2007 Jan 31 [cited 2010 Dec 14]. Available from: http://www.youtube.com/watch?v=6gmP4nk0EOE

OTHER SOURCES

24. Map

1. Russia and post-Soviet republics [political map]. Moscow: Mapping Production Association; 1992. Conical equidistant projection; 40 × 48 in., color, scale 1:8,000,000.

25. Unpublished Letter

1. Darwin C. [Letter to Mr. Clerke, 1861]. Located at: University of Iowa Library, Iowa City.

26. Video Recording

1. Nova—The elegant universe [DVD]. Boston: WGBH; 2004. 2 DVDs: 180 min., sound, color.

27. Slide Set

1. Human parasitology [slides]. Chicago: American Society of Clinical Pathologists; 1990. Color. Accompanied by: 1 guide.

28. Presentation Slides

1. Beaudoin E. Fruit fly larvae [PowerPoint slides]. Denver (CO): University of Denver; 2010 Oct 17. 49 slides.

PART

5

Understanding Grammar and Writing Correct Sentences

Parts of Speech and Sentence Structures

28

Quick Points   You will learn to

➤ Identify the parts of speech (see 28A–28J).
➤ Identify the parts of sentences (see 28K).

PARTS OF SPEECH

28A   Why learn the parts of speech?

Watch the Video

Learning the parts of speech helps you classify words according to their function in a sentence. To determine a word's part of speech, see how the word functions in a sentence. A word may have more than one function.

● We ate **fish**.

Fish is a noun. It names a thing.

● We **fish** on weekends.

Fish is a verb. It names an action.

28B   What is a noun?

Watch the Video

A **noun** names a person, place, thing, or idea: *student, college, textbook, education.* Quick Box 28.1 lists different kinds of nouns.

ESOL Tips: Here are some useful tips for working with NOUNS.*

• Nouns often appear with articles, other determiners, or limiting adjectives. See section 28F and Chapter 51.
• Words with these suffixes (word endings) are usually nouns: *-ness, -ence, -ance, -ty,* and *-ment.*

---

*Words printed in SMALL CAPITAL LETTERS are discussed elsewhere in the text and are defined in the Terms Glossary at the back of this book.

Quick Box 28.1

■■■■■■■■■■

Nouns

PROPER	names specific people, places, or things (first letter is always capitalized)	*Bruno Mars, Paris, Toyota*
COMMON	names general groups, places, people, or things	*singer, city, automobile*
CONCRETE	names things experienced through the senses: sight, hearing, taste, smell, or touch	*landscape, pizza, thunder*
ABSTRACT	names a quality, state, or idea	*freedom, shyness*
COLLECTIVE	names groups	*family, team*
NONCOUNT OR MASS	names "uncountable" things	*water, time*
COUNT	names countable items	*lake, minute*

28C What is a pronoun?

A **pronoun** takes the place of a NOUN. The words or word that a pronoun replaces is called the pronoun's ANTECEDENT. See Quick Box 28.2 for a list of different kinds of pronouns. For information on how to use pronouns correctly, see Chapters 30 and 31.

Watch the Video

- **David** is an accountant.

  The noun *David* names a person.

- **He** is an accountant.

  The pronoun *he* refers to its antecedent, *David*.

- The finance committee needs to consult **him**.

  The pronoun *him* refers to its antecedent, *David*.

Quick Box 28.2

■■■■■■■■■■

Pronouns

PERSONAL *I, you, its, her, they, ours*, etc.	refers to people or things	*I saw **her** take a book to **them**.*
RELATIVE *who, which, that, whom*	introduces certain NOUN CLAUSES and ADJECTIVE CLAUSES	*The book **that** I lost was valuable.*

continued >>

Quick Box 28.2 (continued)

INTERROGATIVE *which, who, whose,* and others	introduces a question	**Who** *called?*
DEMONSTRATIVE *this, that, these, those*	points out the antecedent	*Whose books are* **these?**
REFLEXIVE OR INTENSIVE *myself, themselves,* and other *-self* or *-selves* words	reflects back to the antecedent in the same sentence; intensifies the antecedent	*They claim to support* **themselves.** **I myself** *doubt it.*
RECIPROCAL *each other, one another*	refers to individual parts of a plural antecedent	*We respect* **each other.**
INDEFINITE *all, anyone, each,* and others	refers to nonspecific persons or things	**Everyone** *is welcome here.*

● **EXERCISE 28-1** Underline and label all nouns (N) and pronouns (P). Refer to 28A through 28C for help.

EXAMPLE

P N P N N P N
My mother celebrated her eightieth birthday this summer with her family and
N P N
friends; she greatly enjoyed the festivities.

1. More and more people live into their eighties and nineties because they get better health benefits and they take better care of themselves.
2. Many elderly people now live busy lives, continuing in businesses or volunteering at various agencies.
3. My mother, Elizabeth, for example, spends four hours each morning as a volunteer for the Red Cross, where she takes histories from blood donors.
4. My neighbors, George and Sandra, who are eighty-six years old, still own and run a card and candy shop.
5. Age has become no obstacle for active seniors as evidenced by the activities they pursue today. ●

28D What is a verb?

Main verbs express action, occurrence, or state of being. For information on how to use verbs correctly, see Chapter 29.

Watch the Video

- You **danced.** [action]
- The audience **became** silent. [occurrence]
- Your dancing **was** awesome! [state of being]

! **Alert:** If you're not sure whether a word is a verb, try substituting a different TENSE for the word. If the sentence still makes sense, the word is a verb.

NO   He is a **changed** man. He is a **will change** man.

YES   The man **changed** his mind. The man **will change** his mind. ●

● **EXERCISE 28-2**   Underline all main verbs. Refer to 28D for help.

EXAMPLE

The study of bats <u>produces</u> some surprising information.

1. Most bats developed many years ago from a shrewlike mammal.
2. One thousand different types of bats exist.
3. Bats comprise almost one quarter of all mammal species.
4. The smallest bat in the world measures only one inch long, while the biggest is sixteen inches long.
5. Bats survive in widely varied surroundings, from deserts to cities. ●

28E What is a verbal?

Verbals are verb forms functioning as NOUNS, ADJECTIVES, or ADVERBS. Quick Box 28.3 lists the three different kinds of verbals.

Quick Box 28.3 ■ ■ ■ ■ ■ ■ ■ ■ ■ ■

Verbals and their functions

INFINITIVE *to* + verb	1. noun	*To eat now is inconvenient.*
	2. adjective or adverb	*Still, we have far to go.*
PAST PARTICIPLE *-ed* form of REGULAR VERB or equivalent in IRREGULAR VERB	adjective	*Boiled, filtered water is safe.*
PRESENT PARTICIPLE *-ing* form of verb	1. noun (called a GERUND)	*Eating in diners on the road is an adventure.*
	2. adjective	*Running water may not be safe.*

● **ESOL Tip:** For information about correctly using the verbals called *infinitives* and *gerunds* as objects, see Chapter 55. ●

28F What is an adjective?

Watch the Video

Adjectives describe or limit NOUNS, PRONOUNS, and word groups that function as nouns. For information on how to use adjectives correctly, see Chapter 32.

- I saw a **green** tree.

  Green describes the noun *tree.*

- It was **leafy.**

  Leafy describes the pronoun *it.*

- The flowering trees were **beautiful.**

  Beautiful describes the noun phrase *the flowering trees.*

ESOL Tip: You can identify some adjectives by their endings. Often, words with the SUFFIXES *-ful, -ish, -less,* and *-like* are adjectives.

Determiners, frequently called *limiting adjectives,* tell whether a noun is general (*a* tree) or specific (*the* tree). Determiners also tell which one (*this* tree), how many (*twelve* trees), whose (*our* tree), and similar information.

The determiners *a, an,* and *the* are almost always called **articles.** *The* is a **definite article.** Before a noun, *the* conveys that the noun refers to a specific item (*the* plan). *A* and *an* are **indefinite articles.** They convey that a noun refers to an item in a nonspecific or general way (*a* plan).

Alert: Use *a* before a word that starts with a consonant: *a carrot, a broken egg, a hip.* Use *an* before a word that starts with a vowel sound: *an honor, an old bag, an egg.*

ESOL Tip: For information about using articles with COUNT and NON-COUNT NOUNS, PROPER NOUNS, and GERUNDS, see Chapter 52.

Quick Box 28.4 lists kinds of determiners. Notice, however, that some words in Quick Box 28.4 function also as pronouns. To identify a word's part of speech, check to see how it functions in each particular sentence.

- **That** car belongs to Harold.

  That is a limiting adjective.

- **That** is Harold's car.

  That is a demonstrative pronoun.

Quick Box 28.4

Determiners (or limiting adjectives)

ARTICLES
a, an, the

The news reporter used a cell phone to report an assignment.

DEMONSTRATIVE
this, these, that, those

Those students rent that house.

INDEFINITE
any, each, few, other, some, and others

Few films today have complex plots.

INTERROGATIVE
what, which, whose

What answer did you give?

NUMERICAL
one, first, two, second, and others

The fifth question was tricky.

POSSESSIVE
my, your, their, and others

My violin is older than your cello.

RELATIVE
what, which, whose, whatever, etc.

We do not know which road to take.

28G What is an adverb?

Adverbs describe or limit VERBS, ADJECTIVES, other adverbs, and CLAUSES. For information on how to use adverbs correctly, see Chapter 32.

👁 Watch the Video

- Chefs plan meals **carefully**.

  Carefully describes the verb *plan*.

- Fruits offer **very** crucial vitamins.

  Very describes the adjective *crucial*.

- Those french fries are **too** heavily salted.

  Too describes the adverb *heavily*.

- **Fortunately**, people are learning that overuse of salt is harmful.

  Fortunately describes the rest of the sentence, an independent clause.

Descriptive adverbs show levels of intensity, usually by adding *more* (or *less*) and *most* (or *least*): *more* happily, *least* clearly (32C). Many descriptive adverbs are formed by adding *-ly* to adjectives: *sadly, loudly, normally*. But many adverbs do not end in *-ly*: *very, always, not, yesterday,* and *well* are a few. Some adjectives look like adverbs but are not: *brotherly, lonely, lovely*.

Relative adverbs are words such as *where, why,* and *when*. They are used to introduce adjective or noun clauses.

Conjunctive adverbs describe by creating logical connections to other words. Conjunctive adverbs can appear anywhere in a sentence.

- **However**, we consider Isaac Newton an even more important scientist.
- We consider Isaac Newton, **however**, an even more important scientist.
- We consider Isaac Newton an even more important scientist, **however**.

Quick Box 28.5 lists the kinds of relationships that conjunctive adverbs can show.

Quick Box 28.5

Conjunctive adverbs and relationships they express

Relationship	Words
ADDITION	*also, furthermore, moreover, besides*
CONTRAST	*however, still, nevertheless, conversely, nonetheless, instead, otherwise*
COMPARISON	*similarly, likewise*
RESULT OR SUMMARY	*therefore, thus, consequently, accordingly, hence, then*
TIME	*next, then, meanwhile, finally, subsequently*
EMPHASIS	*indeed, certainly*

● **EXERCISE 28-3**   Underline and label all adjectives (ADJ) and adverbs (ADV). For help, consult 28E through 28G.

EXAMPLE

ADV   ADJ   ADJ
Young families carefully looking for a good pet should consider
     ADV
domesticated rats.

1. Rats are clean animals that easily bond to their human companions.
2. Two rats are better than one because they are gregarious animals who desperately need social interaction.
3. As intelligent animals, rats can be quickly trained to perform many tricks.
4. Humans consistently have been keeping rats as household pets for over 100 years.
5. Finally, they pose no more health risks than other pets. ●

28H What is a preposition?

Prepositions are words that convey relationships, usually of time or space. Common prepositions include *in, of, by, after, to, on, over,* and *since*. A preposition and the word or words it introduces form a PREPOSITIONAL PHRASE. For information about prepositions and commas, see 42K.2.

Watch the Video

- **In the fall**, we will hear a concert **by our favorite tenor**.
- **After the concert**, he will fly **to San Francisco**.

ESOL Tip: For a list of prepositions and their IDIOMS, see Chapter 54.

28I What is a conjunction?

A **conjunction** connects words, PHRASES, or CLAUSES. **Coordinating conjunctions** connect words, phrases, or clauses of equal rank. Quick Box 28.6 lists the coordinating conjunctions and the relationships they express.

- We hike **and** camp every summer.

  And joins two words.

- We hike along scenic trails **or** in the wilderness.

  Or joins two phrases.

- I love the outdoors, **but** my family does not.

  But joins two clauses.

Quick Box 28.6

Coordinating conjunctions and relationships they express

Relationship	Words	Relationship	Words
ADDITION	*and*	REASON OR CAUSE	*for*
CONTRAST	*but, yet*	CHOICE	*or*
RESULT OR EFFECT	*so*	NEGATIVE CHOICE	*nor*

Correlative conjunctions are two conjunctions used as pairs: *both . . . and; either . . . or; neither . . . nor; not only . . . but (also);* and *whether . . . or.*

- **Both** English **and** Spanish are spoken in many homes in the United States.
- **Not only** students **but also** businesspeople should study a second language.

Quick Box 28.7

Subordinating conjunctions and relationships they express

Relationship	Words
TIME	*after, before, once, since, until, when, whenever, while*
REASON OR CAUSE	*as, because, since*
RESULT OR EFFECT	*in order that, so, so that, that*
CONDITION	*if, even if, provided that, unless*
CONTRAST	*although, even though, though, whereas*
LOCATION	*where, wherever*
CHOICE	*than, whether*

Subordinating conjunctions introduce DEPENDENT CLAUSES, clauses of less importance than the INDEPENDENT CLAUSE in the sentence. Quick Box 28.7 lists the most common subordinating conjunctions. For information about how to use them correctly, see 38D through 38M.

- **Because** it snowed, school was canceled.
- Many people were happy **after** they heard the news.

28J What is an interjection?

Watch the Video

An **interjection** expresses strong or sudden emotion. Alone, an interjection is usually punctuated with an exclamation point (!). As part of a sentence, an interjection is usually set off by one or more commas.

- **Hooray!** I won the race.
- **Oh,** my friends missed seeing the finish.

● **EXERCISE 28-4** Identify the part of speech of each numbered and underlined word. Choose from noun, pronoun, verb, adjective, adverb, preposition, coordinating conjunction, correlative conjunction, and subordinating conjunction. For help, consult 28B through 28I.

The Mason-Dixon line primarily¹ marks the boundary² between Pennsylvania and Maryland. It was surveyed in the eighteenth³ century by Charles Mason and Jeremiah Dixon, who had previously⁴ worked together on a scientific⁵ expedition to South Africa.

In 1760, the Calverts of Maryland and the Penns of Pennsylvania hired [6] Mason and Dixon to settle a boundary [7] dispute between their parcels of [8] land. Mason and Dixon marked [9] their line every five [10] miles using stones [11] shipped from England, which are called crownstones. These markers were decorated with two coats-of-arms and can still be found scattered throughout [12] this part of the country.

Even though [13] Mason and [14] Dixon were British, they [15] had very different backgrounds. Mason was the son of a baker and trained in astronomy. Dixon was a Quaker, and he [16] specialized in surveying.

The line they drew in America eventually became [17] a symbolic [18] division between [19] free states and slave states until [20] the end of the Civil War. Because of [21] the line's importance, it [22] has been the focus of both [23] literature and music, such as the song [24] "Sailing to Philadelphia" by Mark Knopfler. ●

SENTENCE STRUCTURES

28K How is a sentence defined?

On a strictly mechanical level, a **sentence** starts with a capital letter and finishes with a period, question mark, or exclamation point. Grammatically, a sentence consists of an INDEPENDENT CLAUSE: *Boxing is dangerous.* From the perspective of its purpose, a sentence is defined as listed in Quick Box 28.8 on page 450.

28L What are a subject and a predicate in a sentence?

The **subject** and **predicate** of a sentence are its two essential parts. Without both, a group of words isn't a sentence. Quick Box 28.9 (page 450) shows the sentence pattern with both. Terms used in the Quick Box are defined after it.

Quick Box 28.8

Sentences and their purposes

- A **declarative sentence** makes a statement:
  - Boxing is dangerous.

- An **interrogative sentence** asks a question:
  - Is boxing dangerous?

- An **imperative sentence** gives a command:
  - Be careful when you box.

- An **exclamatory sentence** expresses strong feeling:
  - How I love boxing!

Quick Box 28.9

Sentence pattern I: Subjects and predicates

Complete Subject	+	Complete Predicate
• The red telephone		rang loudly.

SIMPLE SUBJECT · SIMPLE PREDICATE (VERB)

Complete Subject	+	Complete Predicate
• The telephone and the doorbell		rang loudly.

COMPOUND SUBJECT

Complete Subject	+	Complete Predicate
• The red telephone	rang and startled everyone in the room.	

COMPOUND PREDICATE

The **simple subject** is the word or group of words that acts, is described, or is acted on.

- The **telephone** rang.
- The **telephone** is red.
- The **telephone** was being connected.

The **complete subject** is the simple subject and its MODIFIERS.

- **The red telephone** rang.

A complete **compound subject** consists of two or more NOUNS or PRO-NOUNS and their modifiers.

- **The telephone and the doorbell** rang.

The **predicate** contains the VERB in the sentence. The predicate tells what the subject does, experiences, or what is being done to it.

- The telephone **rang**.
- The telephone **is** red.
- The telephone **was being connected**.

A **simple predicate** contains only the verb.

- The lawyer **listened**.

A **complete predicate** contains the verb and its modifiers.

- The lawyer **listened carefully**.

A **compound predicate** contains two or more verbs.

- The lawyer **listened and waited**.

 ESOL Tips: (1) The subject of a declarative sentence usually comes before the predicate, but there are exceptions (37O). In sentences that ask a question, part of the predicate usually comes before the subject. For more information about word order in English sentences, see Chapter 53. (2) In English, don't add a PERSONAL PRONOUN to repeat the stated noun.

NO	My **grandfather he** lived to be eighty-seven.
YES	My **grandfather** lived to be eighty-seven.
NO	**Winter storms** that bring ice, **they** cause traffic problems.
YES	**Winter storms** that bring ice cause traffic problems.

 EXERCISE 28-5 Use a slash to separate the complete subject from the complete predicate.

EXAMPLE

The Hollywood Sign is a famous American landmark.
The Hollywood Sign / is a famous American landmark.

1. The well-known sign was first built in 1923.
2. Originally, it spelled out the word "Hollywoodland."
3. The Hollywood Chamber of Commerce removed the word "land" from the sign in 1949.
4. The sign's caretaker, Albert Kothe, destroyed the letter "H" by crashing his car into it.
5. Excited visitors still flock to Mount Lee to see this cultural icon. ●

28M What are direct and indirect objects?

A **direct object** is a noun, pronoun, or group of words that completes the meaning of a TRANSITIVE VERB. To find a direct object, ask *whom?* or *what?* after the verb.

An **indirect object** tells *to whom* or *for whom* the action of a verb is directed. To find an indirect object, ask ***to whom? for whom? to what?*** or ***for what?*** after the verb.

Direct objects and indirect objects always fall in the PREDICATE of a sentence. Quick Box 28.10 shows how direct and indirect objects function.

Quick Box 28.10 ■ ■ ■ ■ ■ ■ ■ ■ ■ ■ ■

Sentence pattern II: Direct and indirect objects

Complete Subject	+	Complete Predicate

• The caller   offered   money.

                                 VERB   DIRECT OBJECT

Complete Subject	+	Complete Predicate

• The caller   offered the lawyer money.

                        VERB   INDIRECT   DIRECT
                                     OBJECT   OBJECT

Complete Subject	+	Complete Predicate

• The client   sent a retainer to the lawyer.

                      VERB   DIRECT   INDIRECT
                                 OBJECT   OBJECT

🌐 **ESOL Tips:** (1) In sentences with indirect objects that follow the word *to* or *for*, always put the direct object before the indirect object.

> **NO**   Will you please give **to John** this letter?
>
> **YES**   Will you please give this letter **to John?**

(2) When a PRONOUN is used as an indirect object, some verbs require *to* or *for* before the pronoun, and others do not. Consult the *Dictionary of American English* (Heinle and Heinle) about each verb when you're unsure.

> **NO**   Please explain **me** the rule.
>
>   The verb *explain* requires *to* before an indirect object.
>
> **YES**   Please explain the rule **to me.**
>
> **YES**   Please give **me** that book. Please give that book **to me.**
>
>   *Give* uses both patterns.

(3) When both the direct object and the indirect object are pronouns, put the direct object first and use *to* with the indirect object.

> **NO**   He gave **me it.**
>
> **YES**   He gave **it to me.**
>
> **YES**   Please give **me the letter.**

(4) Even if a verb does not require *to* before an indirect object, you may use *to* if you prefer. If you do use *to*, be sure to put the direct object before the indirect object.

> **YES**   Our daughter sent **our son** a gift.
>
> **YES**   Our daughter sent a gift **to our son.** 🌐

● **EXERCISE 28-6**   Draw a single line under all direct objects and a double line under all indirect objects. For help, consult 28M.

EXAMPLE

Toni Morrison's award-winning novels give <u>readers</u> the <u>gifts</u> of wisdom, inspiration, and pleasure.

1. Literary critics gave high praise to Toni Morrison for her first novel, *The Bluest Eye,* but the general public showed little interest.
2. *Song of Solomon* won Morrison the National Book Critics Circle Award in 1977, and *Beloved* won her the Pulitzer Prize in 1988.
3. A literary panel awarded Toni Morrison the 1993 Nobel Prize in Literature, the highest honor a writer can receive.

4. Her 1998 novel, *Paradise*, traces for readers the tragic lives of a rejected group of former slaves.
5. Twenty-five years after *The Bluest Eye* was published, Oprah Winfrey selected it for her reader's list, and it immediately became a bestseller. ●

28N What are complements, modifiers, and appositives?

COMPLEMENTS

A **complement** renames or describes a subject or an object in the predicate.

A **subject complement** is a NOUN, PRONOUN, or ADJECTIVE that follows a LINKING VERB. An **object complement** follows a DIRECT OBJECT and either describes or renames the direct object. Quick Box 28.11 shows how subject and object complements function in a sentence.

Quick Box 28.11 ■ ■ ■ ■ ■ ■ ■ ■ ■ ■ ■

Sentence pattern III: Complements

Complete Subject	+	Complete Predicate
• The caller		was a student.

LINKING VERB SUBJECT COMPLEMENT

Complete Subject	+	Complete Predicate
• The student		called himself a victim.

VERB DIRECT OBJECT OBJECT COMPLEMENT

● **EXERCISE 28-7**   Underline all complements, and identify each as a subject complement (SUB) or an object complement (OB).

1. Graphology is the study of handwriting.
2. Some scientists and psychologists call graphology a pseudoscience.
3. According to supporters of graphology, it is useful in law, business, and medicine.
4. Trained, professional graphologists are often consultants in legal cases.
5. For example, graphologists consider small letters evidence of shyness. ●

MODIFIERS

A **modifier** is a word or group of words that describes or limits other words. Modifiers appear in the subject or the predicate of a sentence.

- The **large red** telephone rang **loudly**.

  The adjectives *large* and *red* modify the noun *telephone*. The adverb *loudly* modifies the verb *rang*.

- The person **on the telephone** was **extremely** upset.

  The prepositional phrase *on the telephone* modifies the noun *person;* the adverb *extremely* modifies the adjective *upset*.

- **Because the lawyer's voice was calm**, the caller felt reassured.

  The adverb clause *because the lawyer's voice was calm* modifies the independent clause *the caller felt reassured*.

APPOSITIVES

An **appositive** renames the noun or pronoun preceding it.

- The student's story, **a tale of broken promises**, was complicated.

  The appositive *a tale of broken promises* renames the noun *story*.

- The lawyer consulted an expert, **her law professor**.

  The appositive *her law professor* renames the noun *expert*.

- The student, **Joe Jones**, asked to speak to his lawyer.

  The appositive *Joe Jones* renames the noun *student*.

Alert: For more about appositives and NONRESTRICTIVE ELEMENTS, see 42F. ●

28O What is a phrase?

A **phrase** is a group of words that does not contain both a SUBJECT and a PREDICATE and therefore cannot stand alone as an independent unit.

◉ Watch the Video

NOUN PHRASE

A **noun phrase** functions as a noun in a sentence.

- The **modern census** dates back to the seventeenth century.

VERB PHRASE

A **verb phrase** functions as a verb in a sentence.

- Two military censuses **are mentioned** in the Bible.

PREPOSITIONAL PHRASE

A **prepositional phrase** always starts with a preposition and functions as a modifier.

- William the Conqueror conducted a census **of landowners in 1086**.

  Two prepositional phrases come in a row, beginning with *of* and *in*.

ABSOLUTE PHRASE

An **absolute phrase** is a noun phrase that modifies the entire sentence.

- **Censuses being the fashion**, Quebec and Nova Scotia took sixteen counts between 1665 and 1754.

- Eighteenth-century Sweden and Denmark had complete records of their populations, **each adult and child having been counted**.

VERBAL PHRASE

A **verbal phrase** contains a verb form that functions as a noun or an adjective. They include INFINITIVES, present participles, past participles, and gerunds.

- In 1624, Virginia began **to count its citizens** in a census.

  To count its citizens is an infinitive phrase functioning as a direct object.

- **Amazed by some people's answers**, census takers always listen carefully.

  Amazed by some people's answers is a past participial phrase.

- **Going from door to door**, census takers interview millions of people.

  Going from door to door is a present participial phrase.

- **Going from door to door** takes many hours.

  The gerund phrase functions as the subject.

GERUND PHRASE

Although both **gerund phrases** and **present-tense participial phrases** use the *-ing* form of the verb, a gerund phrase functions only as a noun, whereas a participial phrase functions only as a modifier.

- **Including everyone in the census** mattered.

  This is a gerund phrase because it functions as a noun, the subject of the sentence.

- **Including everyone in the census**, Abby worked carefully.

  This is a present participial phrase because it functions as a modifier describing Abby.

● **EXERCISE 28-8** Combine each set of sentences into a single sentence by converting one sentence into a phrase—a noun phrase, a verb phrase, prepositional phrase, absolute phrase, verbal phrase, or gerund phrase. You can omit, add, or change words. Identify which type of phrase you created.

EXAMPLE

The key grip is an important person in the making of a film. The key grip is the chief rigging technician on the movie set.

Serving as the chief rigging technician on a movie set, the key grip is an important person in the making of a film. (verbal phrase)

1. They key grip is the head of the grip department. Grips provide support to the camera department.
2. Grips work with such camera equipment as tripods, dollies, and cranes. Grips have to set up this equipment in a variety of settings during the making of a feature film.
3. Grips are also responsible for safety on the movie set. They have to watch over potentially dangerous equipment like ladders, stands, and scaffolds.
4. The "best boy grip" is the assistant to the key grip. The "best boy electric" is the assistant to the gaffer, who is the head electrician.
5. Electricians handle all of the lights on a movie set. Grips are in charge of all of the nonelectrical equipment related to light.
6. Sometimes grips are needed to reduce sunlight. They can do this by installing black fabric over windows and other openings.
7. The use of grips dates back to circuses and vaudeville. Early grips held on to hand-cranked cameras to reduce movement. ●

28P What is a clause?

A **clause** is a group of words with both a SUBJECT and a PREDICATE. Clauses are either *independent (main) clauses,* or *dependent (subordinate) clauses.*

Watch
the Video

INDEPENDENT CLAUSES

An **independent clause** contains a subject and a predicate and can stand alone as a sentence. Quick Box 28.12 (page 458) shows the basic pattern.

DEPENDENT CLAUSES

A **dependent clause** contains a subject and a predicate but can't stand alone as a sentence. Dependent clauses are either adverb clauses or adjective clauses.

Quick Box 28.12 ■ ■ ■ ■ ■ ■ ■ ■ ■ ■ ■

Sentence pattern IV: Independent clauses

	Independent Clause	
Complete Subject	+	Complete Predicate
• The telephone		rang.

ADVERB CLAUSES

An **adverb clause** starts with a subordinating conjunction, such as *although*, *because*, *when*, or *until*. Adverb clauses usually answer some question about the independent clause: How? Why? When?

- **When the bond issue passes**, the city will install sewers.

  The adverb clause modifies the verb phrase *will install;* it explains when.

- They are drawing up plans **as quickly as they can**.

  The adverb clause modifies the verb phrase *drawing up;* it explains how.

- **Because homeowners know the flooding will end**, they feel relief.

  The adverb clause modifies the entire independent clause; it explains why.

🛈 **Alert:** When you write an adverb clause before an independent clause, separate the clauses with a comma; see 42C. ●

ADJECTIVE CLAUSES

An **adjective clause**, also called a *relative clause*, starts with a **relative pronoun**, such as *who, which*, or *that* or a RELATIVE ADVERB, such as *when* or *where*. An adjective clause modifies the noun or pronoun that it follows. Quick Box 28.13 shows how adverb and adjective clauses function in sentences.

- The car **that Jack bought** is practical.
- The day **when I can buy my own car** is getting closer.

Use *who, whom, whoever, whomever*, and *whose* when an adjective clause refers to a person or to an animal with a name.

- The Smythes, **who collect cars**, are wealthy.
- Their dog Bowser, **whom they spoil**, has his own car.

Quick Box 28.13

Sentence pattern V: Dependent clauses

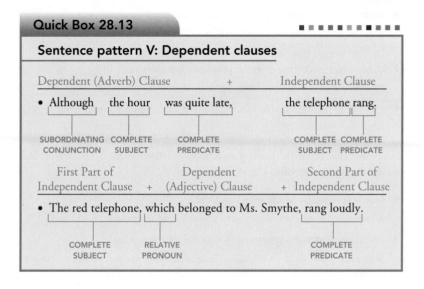

Dependent (Adverb) Clause   +   Independent Clause

• Although   the hour   was quite late,   the telephone rang.

| SUBORDINATING | COMPLETE | COMPLETE | COMPLETE | COMPLETE |
| CONJUNCTION | SUBJECT | PREDICATE | SUBJECT | PREDICATE |

First Part of   Dependent   Second Part of
Independent Clause   +   (Adjective) Clause   +   Independent Clause

• The red telephone, which belonged to Ms. Smythe, rang loudly.

| COMPLETE | RELATIVE | COMPLETE |
| SUBJECT | PRONOUN | PREDICATE |

Use *which* or *that* when an adjective clause refers to a thing or to an animal that isn't a pet. Sometimes, writers omit *that* from an adjective clause. For help in choosing between *that* or *which*, see Quick Box 30.4 in section 30S.

● **EXERCISE 28-9**   Underline the dependent clause in each sentence, and label it an adjectival (ADJ) or an adverbial (ADV) clause. For help, consult 28P.

EXAMPLE
ADV
The Stanley Hotel, which is located in Estes Park, Colorado, was built in 1909.

1. The Stanley Hotel is famous because it inspired Stephen King's novel *The Shining*.
2. Although based on King's book, the movie *The Shining* was filmed in England.
3. F. O. Stanley moved to Estes Park when he was diagnosed with tuberculosis.
4. He then built the hotel that now bears his name.
5. Visitors who believe the hotel is haunted claim to see Stanley's ghost in the lobby. ●

NOUN CLAUSES

Noun clauses function as nouns. Noun clauses can begin with many of the same words that begin adjective clauses: *that, who, which,* and their derivatives, as well as *when, where, whether, why,* and *how.*

- **What politicians promise** is not always dependable.

  What politicians promise is a noun clause functioning as the subject of the sentence.

- Voters often don't know **whether promises are serious**.

  Whether promises are serious is a noun clause functioning as the direct object.

- The electorate often cannot know **that the truth is being manipulated**.

Noun clauses and adjective clauses are sometimes confused with each other. Remember that the word starting an adjective clause has an ANTECEDENT, but the word starting a noun clause doesn't.

- Alert voters decide **whom they can trust**.

  Whom they can trust is a noun clause; *whom* has no antecedent.

- Politicians **who make promises** receive the attention of voters.

  Who make promises is an adjective clause describing *politicians*, the antecedent of *who*.

ESOL Tip: Noun clauses in INDIRECT QUESTIONS are phrased as statements, not questions: *Kara asked why we needed the purple dye*. Don't phrase a noun clause this way: *Kara asked why* did [or do] *we need the purple dye?*

ELLIPTICAL CLAUSES

An elliptical clause omits one or more words that are easily inferred from the context. To check for correctness, insert the word or words you omitted and look for grammatical accuracy.

- Engineering is one of the majors **[that] she considered**.
- She decided **[that] she would rather major in management**.
- **After [he takes] a refresher course**, he will be eligible for a raise.
- She is taller than I **[am]**.

EXERCISE 28-10   Use subordinate conjunctions and relative pronouns from the following list to combine each pair of sentences. You may use words more than once, but try to use as many different ones as possible. Some sentence pairs may be combined in several ways. Create at least one elliptical construction.

since	which	if	after	when	as
although	so that	unless	because	even though	that

EXAMPLE

Bluegrass music is associated with American South. It has roots in Irish and Scottish folk music.

Even though it has roots in Irish and Scottish folk music, bluegrass is associated with the American South.

1. Certain aspects of jazz seem to have influenced bluegrass. It involves players of an instrumental ensemble improvising around a standard melody.
2. However, the instruments used in jazz are very different than those played in bluegrass. This style of music usually uses a banjo, fiddle, mandolin, and dobro.
3. The singing in bluegrass involves tight harmonies and a tenor lead singer. People who listen closely to the vocal arrangements can hear this.
4. Bill Monroe, the founder of bluegrass, added banjo player Earl Scruggs to his band, the Blue Grass Boys. This allowed him to produce a fuller sound.
5. The Blue Grass Boys went into the studio in 1945 to record some songs for Columbia Records. They hit the charts with "Kentucky Waltz" and "Footprints in the Snow."
6. They began touring America with their own large circus tent. They then became one of the most popular acts in country music.
7. Lester Flatt and Earl Scruggs left Bill Monroe's band. They formed their own group called the Foggy Mountain Boys.
8. A famous Flatt & Scruggs song is considered one of the most popular and difficult to play on the banjo. This song is called "Foggy Mountain Breakdown."
9. Most banjo players cannot play "Foggy Mountain Breakdown" at the same speed that Earl Scruggs plays it. Very skilled players can.
10. Bluegrass must continue to attract new and young fans. Otherwise, it will fade into obscurity. ●

28Q What are the four sentence types?

English uses four SENTENCE types: simple, compound, complex, and compound complex. A **simple sentence** consists of one INDEPENDENT CLAUSE and no DEPENDENT CLAUSES.

Watch
the Video

- Charlie Chaplin was born in London on April 16, 1889.

A **compound sentence** consists of two or more independent clauses. These clauses may be connected by a COORDINATING CONJUNCTION, a semicolon alone, or a semicolon and a CONJUNCTIVE ADVERB.

- His father died early, **and** his mother spent time in mental hospitals.
- Many people enjoy Chaplin films; others do not.
- Many people enjoy Chaplin films; **however**, others do not.

A **complex sentence** is composed of one independent clause and one or more dependent clauses. (Dependent clauses are boldfaced.)

- **When times were bad**, Chaplin lived in the streets.
- **When Chaplin performed with a troupe that was touring the United States**, he was hired by Mack Sennett, **who owned the Keystone Company**.

A **compound-complex sentence** joins a compound sentence and a complex sentence. It contains two or more independent clauses and one or more dependent clauses. (Dependent clauses are boldfaced.)

- Chaplin's comedies were very successful, and he became rich **because he was enormously popular for playing the Little Tramp, who was loved for his tiny mustache, baggy trousers, big shoes, and trick derby**.
- **When studios could no longer afford him**, Chaplin co-founded United Artists, and then he produced and distributed his own films.

Alerts: (1) Use a comma before a coordinating conjunction connecting two independent clauses; see 42B.

EXERCISE 28-11 Decide whether each of the following sentences is simple, compound, complex, or compound-complex.

EXAMPLE

Air Force One is a term used to describe a technologically advanced aircraft used by the President of the United States. (simple)

1. Technically, Air Force One is the call name of any Air Force airplane carrying the President, but it usually refers to a specific airplane made by Boeing.
2. Because the aircraft is capable of being refueled in midair, Air Force One has unlimited range.
3. The onboard electronics are well protected, and they include the most advanced communications technology because the airplane often functions as a mobile command center.
4. The airplane provides 4,000 square feet of floor space and three levels, and it includes a large office and conference room.
5. Because the plane contains a fully operational medical center suite, Air Force One can provide essential medical care to the President.
6. The plane's two food galleys can feed up to 100 people at a time.

7. In order to accommodate the President's companions, the airplane includes rooms and services for advisors, Secret Service officers, members of the press, and other guests.
8. Even though Theodore Roosevelt was the first President to fly in an airplane in 1910, the call sign "Air Force One" was not created until 1953, when President Eisenhower flew in commercial air space.
9. The name "Marine One" usually refers to a helicopter carrying the U.S. President, and a helicopter carrying the Vice President is called "Marine Two."
10. Any aircraft of the United States Navy carrying the President is designated as "Navy One." ●

Complete the Chapter Exercises

---

29 Verbs

■ ■ ■ ■ ■ ■ ■ ■ ■

Quick Points   You will learn to

➤ Explain the functions and forms of verbs (see 29A–29F).
➤ Use verb tenses to express time (see 29G–29K).

29A What do verbs do?

A **verb** expresses an action, an occurrence, or a state of being.

Watch the Video

- Many people **overeat** on Thanksgiving.
- Mother's Day **fell** early this year.
- Memorial Day **is** tomorrow.

Verbs also reveal when something occurs—in the present, the past, or the future. See Quick Box 29.1 and Quick Box 29.2 (page 464).

LINKING VERBS

Linking verbs are main verbs that indicate a state of being or a condition. A linking verb is like an equal sign between a subject and its SUBJECT COMPLE-MENT. Quick Box 29.3 on page 465 shows how linking verbs function.

Quick Box 29.1

Information that verbs convey

PERSON   First person (the speaker: *I dance*), second person (the one spoken to: *you dance*), or third person (the one spoken about: *the man dances*).

NUMBER   Singular (*he **dances***) or plural (*they **dance***).

TENSE   Past (*we **danced***), present (*we **dance***), or future (*we **will dance***); see 29G through 29K.

MOOD   Moods are indicative (*we dance*), imperative (commands and polite requests: *dance*), or conditional (speculation, wishes: *if we were dancing . . .*); see 29L and 29M.

VOICE   Active voice or passive voice; see 29N through 29P.

Quick Box 29.2

Types of verbs

MAIN VERB   The word in a PREDICATE that says something about the SUBJECT: *She **danced** for the group.*

AUXILIARY VERB   A verb that helps a main verb convey information about TENSE, MOOD, or VOICE (29E). The verbs *be, do*, and *have* can be auxiliary verbs or main verbs. The verbs *can, could, may, might, should, would, must,* and others are MODAL AUXILIARY VERBS. They add shades of meaning such as ability or possibility to verbs: *She **might dance**.*

LINKING VERB   The verb that links a subject to a COMPLEMENT. *She **was** happy dancing.* *Be* is the most common linking verb; sometimes sense verbs (*smell, taste*) or verbs of perception (*seem, feel*) function as linking verbs. See also Quick Box 29.3.

TRANSITIVE VERB   The verb followed by a DIRECT OBJECT that completes the verb's message: *They **sent** her a fan letter.*

INTRANSITIVE VERB   A verb that requires no direct object: *Earlier she **danced**.*

Quick Box 29.3

Linking verbs

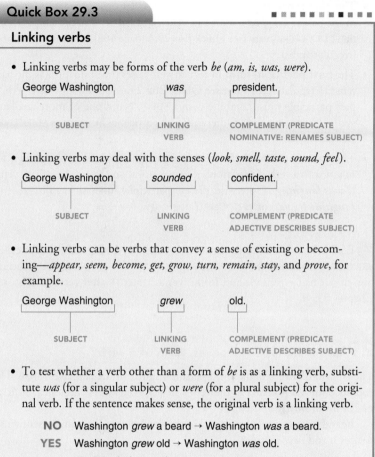

- Linking verbs may be forms of the verb *be* (*am, is, was, were*).

George Washington	*was*	president.
SUBJECT	LINKING VERB	COMPLEMENT (PREDICATE NOMINATIVE: RENAMES SUBJECT)

- Linking verbs may deal with the senses (*look, smell, taste, sound, feel*).

George Washington	*sounded*	confident.
SUBJECT	LINKING VERB	COMPLEMENT (PREDICATE ADJECTIVE DESCRIBES SUBJECT)

- Linking verbs can be verbs that convey a sense of existing or becoming—*appear, seem, become, get, grow, turn, remain, stay,* and *prove,* for example.

George Washington	*grew*	old.
SUBJECT	LINKING VERB	COMPLEMENT (PREDICATE ADJECTIVE DESCRIBES SUBJECT)

- To test whether a verb other than a form of *be* is as a linking verb, substitute *was* (for a singular subject) or *were* (for a plural subject) for the original verb. If the sentence makes sense, the original verb is a linking verb.

  NO Washington *grew* a beard → Washington *was* a beard.

  YES Washington *grew* old → Washington *was* old.

  Grew is a linking verb.

VERB FORMS

29B What are the forms of main verbs?

A MAIN VERB names an action (*People **dance***), an occurrence (*They **grow** tired*), or a state of being (*It **will be** hot later*). Main verbs have four forms.

Watch
the Video

- The **simple form** conveys an action, occurrence, or state of being taking place in the present (*I **laugh***) or, with an AUXILIARY VERB, in the future (*I **will laugh***).

- The **past-tense form** conveys an action, occurrence, or state completed in the past (*I laughed*). REGULAR VERBS add -*ed* or -*d* to the simple form. IRREGULAR VERBS vary (see Quick Box 29.4 [page 468] for a list of common irregular verbs).

- The **past participle form** in regular verbs uses the same form as the past tense. Irregular verbs vary; see Quick Box 29.4. To function as a verb, a past participle must combine with a SUBJECT and one or more auxiliary verbs (*I have laughed*). Otherwise, past participles function as ADJECTIVES (*crumbled cookies*).

- The **present participle form** adds -*ing* to the simple form (*laughing*). To function as a verb, a present participle requires one or more auxiliary verbs (*I was laughing*). Otherwise, present participles function as adjectives (*my laughing friends*) or as NOUNS (*Laughing is healthful*).

ESOL Tip: When verbs function as other parts of speech, they're called VERBALS. Verbals are INFINITIVES, PARTICIPLES, or GERUNDS. For information about using gerunds and infinitives as OBJECTS after certain verbs, see Chapter 55. ●

29C What is the -s, or -es, form of a verb?

The -*s* form of a verb is the third-person singular in the PRESENT TENSE. The ending -*s* (or -*es*) is added to the verb's SIMPLE FORM (*smell* becomes *smells*, as in *The bread smells delicious*).

Be and *have* are irregular verbs. For the third-person singular, present tense, *be* uses *is* and *have* uses *has*.

- The cheesecake **is** popular.
- The éclair **has** chocolate icing.

Even if you drop the -*s* ending in speech, always use it in writing.

- He **is** [not *be*] hungry.
- The bakery **has** [not *have*] fresh bread.

● **EXERCISE 29-1** Rewrite each sentence, changing the subjects to the word or words given in parentheses. Change the form of the verbs shown in italics to match the new subject. Keep all sentences in the present tense. For help, consult 29C.

EXAMPLE

The Oregon giant earthworm *escapes* all attempts at detection. (Oregon giant earthworms)

Oregon giant earthworms escape all attempts at detection.

1. Before declaring the Oregon giant earthworm a protected species, U.S. government agencies *require* concrete proof that it *is* not extinct. (a government agency) (they)
2. A scientist who *finds* one alive will demonstrate that Oregon giant earthworms *do* still exist, despite no one's having seen any for over twenty years. (Scientists) (the Oregon giant earthworm)
3. Last seen in the Willamette Valley near Portland, Oregon, the earthworms *are* white, and they *smell* like lilies. (the earthworm) (it)
4. Oregon giant earthworms *grow* up to three feet long. (The Oregon giant earthworm)
5. A clump of soil with a strange shape *indicates* that the giant creatures *continue* to live, but to demonstrate that they *are* not extinct, only a real specimen will do. (clumps of soil) (creature) (it) ●

29D What is the difference between regular and irregular verbs?

A **regular verb** forms its PAST TENSE and PAST PARTICIPLE by adding *-ed* or *-d* to the SIMPLE FORM: *type, typed; cook, cooked; work, worked; taste, tasted.*

In informal speech, some people skip over the *-ed* sound. In ACADEMIC WRITING, however, be sure to use it.

NO The cake was **suppose** to be ready.

YES The cake was **supposed** to be ready.

NO We **use** to bake.

YES We **used** to bake.

Irregular verbs don't consistently add *-d* or *-ed* endings to the simple verb to form the past tense and past participle. Unfortunately, a verb's simple form doesn't offer any indication whether the verb is regular or irregular. Quick Box 29.4 (page 468) lists the most frequently used irregular verbs.

⚠ **Alert:** For information about changing *y* to *i*, or doubling a final consonant before adding the *-ed* ending, see 49D. ●

Quick Box 29.4

Common irregular verbs

Simple Form	Past Tense	Past Participle
arise	arose	arisen
awake	awoke *or* awaked	awaked *or* awoken
be (is, am, are)	was, were	been
beat	beat	beaten
become	became	become
begin	began	begun
bend	bent	bent
bite	bit	bitten *or* bit
blow	blew	blown
break	broke	broken
bring	brought	brought
build	built	built
burst	burst	burst
buy	bought	bought
catch	caught	caught
choose	chose	chosen
cling	clung	clung
come	came	come
cost	cost	cost
cut	cut	cut
deal	dealt	dealt
dig	dug	dug
dive	dived *or* dove	dived
do	did	done
draw	drew	drawn
drink	drank	drunk
drive	drove	driven
eat	ate	eaten
fall	fell	fallen
fight	fought	fought
find	found	found
fly	flew	flown
forget	forgot	forgotten *or* forgot
freeze	froze	frozen

continued >>

Quick Box 29.4   (continued)   ■ ■ ■ ■ ■ ■ ■ ■ ■ ■

Simple Form	Past Tense	Past Participle
get	got	got *or* gotten
give	gave	given
go	went	gone
grow	grew	grown
hang ("to suspend")*	hung	hung
have	had	had
hear	heard	heard
hide	hid	hidden
hurt	hurt	hurt
keep	kept	kept
know	knew	known
lay	laid	laid
lead	led	led
lend	lent	lent
let	let	let
lie	lay	lain
light	lighted *or* lit	lighted *or* lit
lose	lost	lost
make	made	made
mean	meant	meant
prove	proved	proved *or* proven
read	read	read
ride	rode	ridden
ring	rang	rung
rise	rose	risen
run	ran	run
say	said	said
see	saw	seen
seek	sought	sought
send	sent	sent
set	set	set
shake	shook	shaken
shoot	shot	shot

*When it means "to execute by hanging," *hang* is a regular verb: *In wartime, some armies routinely **hanged** deserters.*

continued >>

Quick Box 29.4   (continued)   ■ ■ ■ ■ ■ ■ ■ ■ ■ ■

Simple Form	Past Tense	Past Participle
show	showed	shown *or* showed
shrink	shrank	shrunk
sing	sang	sung
sink	sank *or* sunk	sunk
sit	sat	sat
slay	slew	slain
sleep	slept	slept
speak	spoke	spoken
spin	spun	spun
spring	sprang *or* sprung	sprung
stand	stood	stood
steal	stole	stolen
sting	stung	stung
stink	stank *or* stunk	stunk
strike	struck	struck
swear	swore	sworn
swim	swam	swum
swing	swung	swung
take	took	taken
teach	taught	taught
throw	threw	thrown
wake	woke *or* waked	woken *or* waked
wear	wore	worn
wring	wrung	wrung
write	wrote	written

● **EXERCISE 29-2**   Write the correct past-tense form of the regular verbs given in parentheses. For help, consult 29D.

EXAMPLE

Native North Americans (invent) <u>invented</u> the game of lacrosse.

(1) Ancient lacrosse games (involve) _____ up to 1,000 men and (last) _____ the entire day. (2) Native Americans (play) _____ the game using balls they (create) _____ out of deerskin and wood.

(3) Lacrosse (serve) _____ many purposes in tribal life as warriors (train) _____ for battle and (resolve) _____ conflicts. (4) French missionaries eventually (name) _____ the game "la crosse," perhaps referring to the staffs Jesuit bishops (use) _____. (5) Lacrosse (resemble) _____ the Irish sport hurling, so when Irish immigrants (arrive) _____ in America in the 19th century, they (help) _____ to make the game more popular. ●

● **EXERCISE 29-3** Write the correct past-tense form of the irregular verbs given in parentheses. For help, consult Quick Box 29.4 in 29D.

EXAMPLE

In August 1969, the Woodstock music festival (begin) began as thousands of fans (drive) drove to upstate New York for three days of music.

(1) The official name of the festival (is) _____ the Woodstock Music and Art Fair. (2) It (draw) _____ nearly half a million people to Max Yasgur's farm, which (stand) _____ in the small town of Bethel, New York. (3) The concert (have) _____ to move to Bethel at the last minute after residents of the town of Woodstock (forbid) _____ organizers to hold the festival in their town. (4) Those who (come) _____ to hear music were not disappointed, since several well known artists (sing) _____ to the large crowd. (5) Performers such as Jimi Hendrix, Santana, and Janis Joplin (lend) _____ their talents to the festival. (6) Even though rain clouds occasionally (cast) _____ a shadow on the events, most people (stick) _____ it out the entire three days. (7) According to some reports, two women (give) _____ birth during the festival. (8) Because of the relatively peaceful atmosphere, many people (see) _____ the event as a symbol of countercultural ideals. (9) Filmmaker Michael Wadleigh (strive) _____ to capture that atmosphere in the film *Woodstock*, which he (shoot) _____ and edited with the help of a young Martin Scorsese. (10) The festival also (lead) _____ to a song written by Joni Mitchell called "Woodstock." (11) That song (become) _____ a hit for Crosby, Stills, Nash, and Young, which (make) _____ its debut as a group at Woodstock. (12) Although organizers (try) _____ to turn a profit with the event, they (lose) _____ money because many attendees did not purchase tickets. ●

29E What are auxiliary verbs?

((•
Listen
to the
Podcast

Auxiliary verbs, also called *helping verbs*, combine with MAIN VERBS to make VERB PHRASES. Quick Box 29.5 shows how auxiliary verbs work.

Quick Box 29.5 ■ ■ ■ ■ ■ ■ ■ ■ ■ ■ ■

Auxiliary verbs

VERB PHRASE

• I | am | | shopping | for new shoes.

  AUXILIARY   MAIN
  VERB   VERB

VERB PHRASE

• Clothing prices | have | | soared | recently.

  AUXILIARY   MAIN
  VERB   VERB

VERB PHRASE

• Leather shoes | might | | cost | hundreds of dollars.

  AUXILIARY   MAIN
  VERB   VERB

USING *BE, DO, HAVE*

The three most common auxiliary verbs, *be, do,* and *have,* can also be main verbs. Their forms vary widely, as Quick Boxes 29.6 and 29.7 show.

🌐 **ESOL Tip:** When *be, do,* and *have* function as auxiliary verbs for a third-person singular subject, don't add *-s* to the main verb.

> **NO**   **Does** the library **closes** at 6:00?
>
> **YES**   **Does** the library **close** at 6:00? •

MODAL AUXILIARY VERBS

Can, could, shall, should, will, would, may, might, and *must* are **modal auxiliary verbs,** which show the speaker's MOOD toward the VERB. They never change form.

- Exercise **can lengthen** lives.   [possibility]
- She **can jog** for five miles.   [ability]

Quick Box 29.6

Forms of the verb *be*

SIMPLE FORM	he
-s FORM	is
PAST TENSE	was, were
PRESENT PARTICIPLE	being
PAST PARTICIPLE	been

Person	Present Tense	Past Tense
I	am	was
you (singular)	are	were
he, she, it	is	was
we	are	were
you (plural)	are	were
they	are	were

Quick Box 29.7

Forms of the verbs *do* and *have*

SIMPLE FORM	do	have
-s FORM	does	has
PAST TENSE	did	had
PRESENT PARTICIPLE	doing	having
PAST PARTICIPLE	done	had

- You **must** jog regularly. [necessity, obligation]
- People **should protect** their bodies. [advisability]
- **May** I **exercise?** [permission]

🌐 **ESOL Tip:** For more about modal auxiliary verbs and the meanings they communicate, see Chapter 56. ●

● **EXERCISE 29-4**   Using the auxiliary verbs in the following list, fill in the blanks in the following passage. Use each auxiliary word only once, even if a listed word can fit into more than one blank. For help, consult 29E.

     are   have   may   will   might   can   has

EXAMPLE

Completing a marathon can be the highlight of a runner's life.

(1) The marathon _____ been a challenging and important athletic event since the 19th century. (2) Athletes who _____ training for a marathon _____ use one of the many online training guides. (3) Running with a partner or friend _____ boost confidence and motivation. (4) Beginning runners _____ find the first few weeks difficult but _____ soon see dramatic improvement in their performance. (5) Those who _____ successfully finished the race often want to repeat the experience. ●

29F What are intransitive and transitive verbs?

An **intransitive verb** requires no object to complete the verb's meaning: *I sing.* A **transitive verb** needs an object to complete the verb's meaning: *I need a guitar.* Many verbs can be transitive or intransitive, whereas others are only transitive: *need, have, like.* Only transitive verbs function in the PASSIVE VOICE.

The verbs *lie* and *lay* are often confused. *Lie* is intransitive and means "to recline, to rest." *Lay* is transitive and means "to put something down." In Quick Box 29.8, the word *lay* is both the past tense of *lie* and the present-tense simple form of *lay.* That makes things difficult, so our best advice is to memorize them.

Two other verb pairs tend to confuse people because of their intransitive and transitive forms: *raise* and *rise* and *set* and *sit. Raise* and *set* are transitive; they must be followed by an object. *Rise* and *sit* are intransitive; they cannot be followed by an object.

● **EXERCISE 29-5** Underline the correct word of each pair in parentheses. For help, consult 29F.

EXAMPLE

During the summer, Caroline enjoys (lying/laying) on the beach.

(1) One day, after (setting/sitting) her chair on the sand, Caroline (lay/laid) her blanket near her umbrella. (2) Worried about getting a sunburn, she (raised/rose) her umbrella and (lay/laid) under it. (3) After a brief nap, Caroline began (rising/raising) to her feet when she realized she had forgotten where she had (lain/laid) her cooler. (4) She soon found it (lying/laying) near her car, just where she had (sat/set) it earlier. (5) She decided to pick it up and (lie/lay) it down near where her blanket (lies/lays). ●

Quick Box 29.8

Using *lie* and *lay*

	lie	lay
SIMPLE FORM	lie	lay
-s FORM	lies	lays
PAST TENSE	lay	laid
PRESENT PARTICIPLE	lying	laying
PAST PARTICIPLE	lain	laid

INTRANSITIVE FORMS

PRESENT TENSE	The hikers **lie** down to rest.
PAST TENSE	The hikers **lay** down to rest.

TRANSITIVE FORMS

PRESENT TENSE	The hikers **lay** their backpacks on a rock.
	Backpacks is a direct object.
PAST TENSE	The hikers **laid** their backpacks on a rock.
	Backpacks is a direct object.

VERB TENSE

29G What is verb tense?

Verb **tense** conveys time by changing form. The three **simple tenses** in English divide time into present, past, and future. The simple **present tense** describes what happens regularly or what is consistently or generally true. The simple **past tense** indicates an action completed or a condition ended. The simple **future tense** indicates action to be taken or a condition not yet experienced.

- Rick **wants** to speak Spanish fluently. [simple present tense]
- Rick **wanted** to improve rapidly. [simple past tense]
- Rick **will want** to progress even further next year. [simple future tense]

The three PERFECT TENSES show more complex time relationships. For information on using the perfect tenses, see section 29I.

The three simple tenses and the three perfect tenses also have PROGRESSIVE FORMS. These forms indicate that the verb describes what is ongoing or continuing. For information on using progressive forms, see section 29J. Quick Box 29.9 (page 476) summarizes verb tenses and progressive forms.

Quick Box 29.9 ▪ ▪ ▪ ▪ ▪ ▪ ▪ ▪ ▪ ▪ ▪

Simple, perfect, and progressive tenses

SIMPLE TENSES

	Regular Verb	Irregular Verb	Progressive Form
PRESENT	I talk	I eat	I am talking; I am eating
PAST	I talked	I ate	I was talking; I was eating
FUTURE	I will talk	I will eat	I will be talking; I will be eating

PERFECT TENSES

	Regular Verb	Irregular Verb	Progressive Form
PRESENT PERFECT	I have talked	I have eaten	I have been talking; I have been eating
PAST PERFECT	I had talked	I had eaten	I had been talking; I had been eating
FUTURE PERFECT	I will have talked	I will have eaten	I will have been talking; I will have been eating

⊕ **ESOL Tip:** As Quick Box 29.9 shows, auxiliary verbs are necessary in the formation of most tenses, so never omit them.

NO I **talking** to you.

YES I **am talking** to you. ●

29H How do I use the simple present tense?

The **simple present tense** uses the SIMPLE FORM of the verb (see 29B). It describes what happens regularly, or what is generally or consistently true. Also, it can convey a specific future occurrence with verbs like *start, stop, begin, end, arrive,* and *graduate.*

- Calculus class **meets** every morning.   [regularly occurring action]
- Mastering calculus **takes** time.   [general truth]
- The course **ends** in eight weeks.   [specific future event]

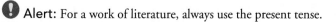

! **Alert:** For a work of literature, always use the present tense.

- In Shakespeare's *Othello*, Iago **manipulates** Othello, who **loves** his wife. **●**

29I How do I form and use the perfect tenses?

The **perfect tenses** describe actions or occurrences that affect the present or some other specified time. The perfect tenses are composed of an AUXILIARY VERB and a main verb's PAST PARTICIPLE (29B).

For the **present perfect tense** (see Quick Box 29.9), use *has* only for the third-person singular subjects and *have* for all other subjects. For the **past perfect**, use *had* with the past participle. For the **future perfect**, use *will have* with the past participle.

PRESENT PERFECT	America **has offered** help.
PRESENT PERFECT	The earthquake **has created** terrible hardship.
PAST PERFECT	After the tornado **had passed**, the heavy rain started.
	The tornado occurred before the rain, so the earlier event uses *had*.
FUTURE PERFECT	Our chickens' egg production **will have reached** five hundred per day by next year.
	The event will occur before a specified time.

29J How do I form and use progressive forms?

Progressive forms describe an ongoing event, action, or condition. They also express habitual or recurring actions or conditions. All progressive tenses use a form of the verb *be* plus the present participle of the main verb. The **present progressive** use a form of *be* to agree with its subject in person and number; the **present perfect progressive** uses a form of *be* to agree with its subject in number.

PRESENT PROGRESSIVE	The smog **is stinging** everyone's eyes.
PAST PROGRESSIVE	Eye drops **were selling** well last week.
FUTURE PROGRESSIVE	We **will be buying** more eye drops than usual this month.
	Recurring event that will take place in the future.
PRESENT PERFECT PROGRESSIVE	Scientists **have been warning** us about air pollution for years.
PAST PERFECT PROGRESSIVE	We **had been ordering** three cases of eye drops a month until the smog worsened.
FUTURE PERFECT PROGRESSIVE	By May, we **will have been selling** eye drops for eight months.

● **EXERCISE 29-6** Underline the correct verb in each pair of parentheses. If more than one answer is possible, be prepared to explain the differences in meaning between the two choices. For help, consult 29G through 29J.

EXAMPLE

According to an article in *National Geographic News*, weird plants (are taking root, would have taken root) in ordinary backyards.

1. Some, smelling like spoiled meat, (will have ruined, are ruining) people's appetites.
2. Stalks similar to male anatomy (typify, are typifying) other examples.
3. *Shockingly large, black, carnivorous,* and *volatile* (describe, is describing) additional unusual plants.
4. Indeed, many unusual plants (live, lived) in places the world over today.
5. Many people now (are planting, planted) these weird items in their backyards.
6. In 1999, in East Lothian, Scotland, Diane Halligan (founded, had founded) The Weird and Wonderful Plant Company because she (was, is) disappointed with the plant selection at her local garden centers.
7. Halligan (chose, is choosing) to open an extraordinary plant store because she (wanted, is wanting) to provide a source of unusual plants for others as well as herself.
8. Marty Harper in Staunton, Virginia, like Halligan in Scotland, (contends, are contending) that his company (fills, would have filled) a niche for himself and others.
9. Harper, after much study on the subject of strange plants, (is indicating, indicates) that Madagascar holds the record for the most weird plants on the planet.
10. Isolated from the rest of the world, Madagascar (has provided, will have provided) a haven for unusual plants to develop undisturbed.
11. *Rafflesia arnoldii* (is, are) the oddest plant Harper (has encountered, will have encountered).
12. Harper, in an interview with *National Geographic*'s John Roach, (reveals, is revealing) that *Rafflesia arnoldii*, a parasitic plant, (has, have) the world's largest bloom, stinks, and (held, holds) in its center six or seven quarts of water.
13. According to Harper, procreation (remains, has remained) the primary reason for the development of the ostensibly outlandish shapes, sizes, odors, and actions of these unusual plants the world over.

14. Douglas Justice, another weird-plant aficionado like Halligan and Harper, (says, is saying) he (wonders, is wondering) what (motivates, motivated) people to choose the odd plants.

15. Harper, however, (exclaims, is exclaiming), "Such plants (make, were making) me smile." ●

29K How do I use tense sequences accurately?

Verb **tense sequences** deliver messages about actions, occurrences, or states that occur at different times. Quick Box 29.10 shows how tenses in the same sentence can vary depending on the timing of actions (or occurrences or states).

Quick Box 29.10

Tense sequences

If your independent clause contains a simple-present-tense verb, then in your dependent clause you can

- use PRESENT TENSE to show same-time action:
  - I **avoid** shellfish because I **am** allergic to it.

- use PAST TENSE to show earlier action:
  - I **am** sure that I **deposited** the check.

- use the PRESENT PERFECT TENSE to show (1) a period of time extending from some point in the past to the present or (2) an indefinite past time:
  - They **claim** that they **have visited** the planet Venus.
  - I **believe** that I **have seen** that movie before.

- use the FUTURE TENSE for action to come:
  - The book **is** open because I **will be reading** it later.

  If your independent clause contains a past-tense verb, then in your dependent clause you can

- use the past tense to show another completed past action:
  - I **closed** the door when you **told** me to.

- use the PAST PERFECT TENSE to show earlier action:
  - The sprinter **knew** that she **had broken** the record.

- use the present tense to state a general truth:
  - Christopher Columbus **determined** that the world **is** round.

continued >>

Quick Box 29.10   (continued)

If your independent clause contains a present-perfect-tense or past-perfect-tense verb, then in your dependent clause you can

- use the past tense:
  - The bread **has become** moldy since I **purchased** it.
  - Sugar prices **had** fallen before artificial sweeteners first appeared.

If your independent clause contains a future-tense verb, then in your dependent clause you can

- use the present tense to show action happening at the same time:
  - You **will be** rich if you **win** the prize.

- use the past tense to show earlier action:
  - You **will win** the prize if you **remembered** to mail the entry form.

TENSE SEQUENCES

- use the present perfect tense to show future action earlier than the action of the independent-clause verb:
  - The river **will flood** again next year unless we **have built** a better dam by then.

If your independent clause contains a future-perfect-tense verb, then in your dependent clause you can

- use either the present tense or the present perfect tense:
  - Dr. Chu **will have delivered** five thousand babies before she **retires**.
  - Dr. Chu **will have delivered** five thousand babies before she **has retired**.

Alert: Never use a future-tense verb in a dependent clause when the verb in the independent clause is in the future tense. Instead, use a present-tense verb or present-perfect-tense verb in the dependent clause.

NO   The river **will flood** us unless we **will prepare** our defense.

YES   The river **will flood** us unless we **prepare** our defense.

YES   The river **will flood** us unless we **have prepared** our defense. ●

Tense sequences may include INFINITIVES and PARTICIPLES. To name or describe an activity or occurrence coming either at the same time as the time expressed in the MAIN VERB or after, use the **present infinitive**.

- I **hope to buy** a used car.

  To buy comes in the future. *Hope* is the main verb, and its action is now.

- I **hoped to buy** a used car.

  Hoped is the main verb, and its action is over.

- I **had hoped to buy** a used car.

  Had hoped is the main verb, and its action is over.

The PRESENT PARTICIPLE can show action happening at the same time.

- **Driving** his new car, the man **smiled**.

  The driving and the smiling happened at the same time.

To describe an action that occurs before the action in the main verb, use the perfect infinitive (*to have gone, to have smiled*), the PAST PARTICIPLE, or the present perfect participle (*having gone, having smiled*).

- Candida **claimed to have written** fifty short stories in college.

  Claimed is the main verb, and *to have written* happened first.

- **Pleased** with the short story, Candida **mailed** it to several magazines.

  Mailed is the main verb, and *pleased* happened first.

- **Having sold** one short story, Candida **invested** in a new computer.

  Invested is the main verb, and *having sold* happened first.

● **EXERCISE 29-7** Underline the correct verb in each pair of parentheses that best suits the sequence of tenses. Be ready to explain your choices. For help, consult 29K.

EXAMPLE

When he (is, <u>was</u>) seven years old, Yo-Yo Ma, possibly the world's greatest living cellist, (moves, <u>moved</u>) to the United States with his family.

1. Yo-Yo Ma, who (had been born, was born) in France to Chinese parents, (lived, lives) in Boston, Massachusetts, today and (toured, tours) as one of the world's greatest cellists.
2. Years from now, after Mr. Ma has given his last concert, music lovers still (treasure, will treasure) his many fine recordings.
3. Mr. Ma's older sister, Dr. Yeou-Cheng Ma, was nearly the person with the concert career. She had been training to become a concert violinist when her brother's musical genius (began, had begun) to be noticed.
4. Even though Dr. Ma eventually (becomes, became) a physician, she still (had been playing, plays) the violin.
5. The family interest in music (continues, was continuing), for Mr. Ma's children (take, had taken) piano lessons.

6. Although most people today (knew, know) Mr. Ma as a brilliant cellist, he (was making, has made) films as well.
7. One year, while he (had been traveling, was traveling) in the Kalahari Desert, he (films, filmed) dances of southern Africa's Bush people.
8. Mr. Ma first (becomes, became) interested in the Kalahari people when he (had studied, studied) anthropology as an undergraduate at Harvard University.
9. When he shows visitors around Boston now, Mr. Ma has been known to point out the Harvard University library where, he claims, he (fell asleep, was falling asleep) in the stacks when he (had been, was) a student.
10. Indicating another building, Mr. Ma admits that in one of its classrooms he almost (failed, had failed) German. ●

MOOD

29L What is "mood" in verbs?

Mood in verbs conveys an attitude toward the action. English has three moods: *indicative, imperative,* and *subjunctive.* Use the **indicative mood** to make statements about real things, about highly likely things, and for questions about fact.

INDICATIVE   The door to the tutoring center opened.   [real]

She seemed to be looking for someone.   [highly likely]

Do you want to see a tutor?   [question about a fact]

The **imperative mood** expresses commands and direct requests. Often, the subject is omitted in an imperative sentence but is nevertheless implied to be either *you* or one of the indefinite pronouns such as *anybody, somebody,* or *everybody.*

● **Alert:** Use an exclamation point after a strong command; use a period after a mild command or a request (see 41A, 41E). ●

IMPERATIVE   Please shut the door.

Watch out! That screw is loose.

The **subjunctive mood** expresses speculation, other unreal conditions, conjectures, wishes, recommendations, indirect requests, and demands. Often, the words that signal the subjunctive mood are *if, as if, as though,* and *unless.*

SUBJUNCTIVE   If I **were** you, I would ask for a tutor.

He requested that he **be** given a leave of absence.

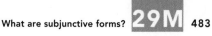

29M   What are subjunctive forms?

For the **present subjunctive**, always use the SIMPLE FORM of the verb for all PERSONS and NUMBERS.

- The prosecutor asks that she **testify** [not *testifies*] again.
- It is important that they **be** [not *are*] allowed to testify.

For the **past subjunctive**, use the simple past tense: *I wish that I **had** a car.* The one exception is for the past subjunctive of *be:* Use *were* for all forms.

- I wish that I **were** [not *was*] leaving on vacation today.
- They asked if she **were** [not *was*] leaving on vacation today.

USING THE SUBJUNCTIVE IN *IF, AS IF, AS THOUGH,* AND *UNLESS* CLAUSES

In dependent clauses introduced by *if, as if, as though,* and *unless,* the subjunctive describes speculations, conditions contrary to fact or highly unlikely.

- If it **were** [not *was*] to rain, attendance at the race would be disappointing.

  The subjunctive *were* indicates speculation.

- The runner looked as if he **were** [not *was*] winded, but he said he wasn't.

  The subjunctive *were* indicates a condition contrary to fact.

- Unless rain **were** [not *was*] to create floods, the race will be held this Sunday.

  Floods are highly unlikely.

Not every clause introduced by *if, unless, as if,* or *as though* requires the subjunctive. Use the subjunctive only when the dependent clause describes speculation or a condition contrary to fact.

INDICATIVE	If she **is** going to leave late, I **will** drive her to the race.
	Her leaving late is highly likely.
SUBJUNCTIVE	If she **were** going to leave late, I **would** drive her.
	Her leaving late is a speculation.

USING THE SUBJUNCTIVE IN *THAT* CLAUSES

The subjunctive conveys wishes, requests, demands, or recommendations in *that* clauses.

- I wish that this race **were** [not *was*] over.
- He wishes that he **had seen** [not *saw*] the race.
- The judges demand that the doctor **examine** [not *examines*] the runners.

Also, MODAL AUXILIARY VERBS *would, could, might,* and *should* can convey speculations and conditions contrary to fact.

- If the runner **were** [not *was*] faster, we **would** see a better race.

The issue here is that when an INDEPENDENT CLAUSE expresses a conditional statement using a modal auxiliary verb, you want to be sure that in the DEPENDENT CLAUSE you don't use another modal auxiliary verb.

NO   If I **would have trained** for the race, I **might have** won.

YES   If I **had trained** for the race, I **might have** won.

● **EXERCISE 29-8**   Fill in each blank with the correct form of the verb given in parentheses. For help, consult 29L and 29M.

EXAMPLE

Imagining the possibility of brain transplants requires that we (to be) <u>be</u> open-minded.

(1) If almost any organ other than the brain (to be) _____ the candidate for a swap, we would probably give our consent. (2) If the brain (to be) _____ to hold whatever impulses form our personalities, few people would want to risk a transplant. (3) Many popular movies have asked that we (to suspend) _____ disbelief and imagine the consequences should a personality actually (to be) _____ transferred to another body. (4) In real life, however, the complexities of a successful brain transplant require that not-yet-developed surgical techniques (to be) _____ used. (5) For example, it would be essential that during the actual transplant each one of the 500 trillion nerve connections within the brain (to continue) _____ to function as though the brain (to be) _____ lying undisturbed in a living human body. ●

VOICE

29N   What is "voice" in verbs?

Voice in a verb tells whether a subject acts or is acted on. A subject with an **active voice** verb performs the action.

- Most clams **live** in saltwater.
- They **burrow** into the sandy bottoms of shallow waters.

A subject with a **passive voice** verb receives the action indicated by the verb. Verbs in the passive voice use forms of *be, have,* and *will* as AUXILIARY VERBS with the PAST PARTICIPLE of the MAIN VERB.

- Clams **are considered** a delicacy by many people.
- Some types of clams **are** highly **valued** by seashell collectors.

29O How do I write in the active, not passive, voice?

Because the ACTIVE VOICE emphasizes the doer of an action, active constructions are more concise and dramatic (see 40C). Most sentences in the PASSIVE VOICE can be converted to active voice.

PASSIVE   African tribal masks are often imitated by Western sculptors.

ACTIVE   Western sculptors often imitate African tribal masks.

29P What are proper uses of the passive voice?

While the active voice is often better, sometimes you need to use the passive voice.

When the doer of an action is unknown or unimportant, writers use the passive voice.

- The lock **was broken** sometime after four o'clock.
- In 1899, the year I was born, a peace conference **was held** at The Hague.

—E. B. White, "Unity"

If you want to focus on events in a narrative, use the passive voice. Conversely, if you want to emphasize the people making the discoveries, use the active voice.

ACTIVE   Joseph Priestley **discovered** oxygen in 1774.

PASSIVE   Oxygen **was discovered** in 1774 by Joseph Priestley.

ACTIVE   The postal clerk **sent** the unsigned letter before I **could retrieve** it from the mailroom.

        The emphasis is on the doers of the action, *the postal clerk* and *I,* rather than on the events, *sent* and *could retrieve.*

PASSIVE   The unsigned letter **was sent** before it **could be retrieved** from the postal clerk.

        The emphasis is on the events, *was sent* and *could be retrieved,* not on the doers of the action.

● **EXERCISE 29-9** First, determine which sentences are in the active voice and which the passive voice. Second, rewrite each sentence in the other voice, and then decide which voice better suits the meaning. Be ready to explain your choice.

EXAMPLE

When Alfred Nobel wrote his last will in 1895, he created the Nobel Prizes. (*active; change to passive*)

The Nobel Prizes were created by Alfred Nobel, when he wrote his last will in 1895.

1. An enormous fortune was earned by Nobel when he invented dynamite in the 1860s. (*passive; change to active*)
2. An avid inventor, Nobel held over 300 patents. (*active; change to passive*)
3. *Nemesis*, a four-act play, was written by Nobel shortly before his death.
4. Beginning in 1901, the Nobel Prizes have honored people who work in physics, literature, chemistry, and world peace. (*active; change to passive*)
5. The list of categories for the Nobel Prize does not include mathematics. (*active; change to passive*) ●

Complete
the
Chapter
Exercises

Pronouns: Case and Reference

30
■ ■ ■ ■ ■ ■ ■ ■ ■ ■

Quick Points   You will learn to

➤ Use the proper pronoun case (see 30A–30K).
➤ Use pronouns with clear reference (see 30L–30S).

PRONOUN CASE

30A   What does "case" mean?

Watch
the Video

Case shows the relationship (subject, object, possession) of nouns and pronouns to other words in a sentence. Pronouns use different forms in different cases (**subjective, objective, possessive**). Nouns change form only in the possessive case. (For use of the apostrophe in the possessive, see Chapter 45.)

30B   What are personal pronouns?

Personal pronouns refer to persons or things. Quick Box 30.1 shows the case forms of personal pronouns in both the singular and the plural.

Quick Box 30.1

Case forms of personal pronouns

	Subjective	Objective	Possessive
SINGULAR	I, you, he, she, it	me, you, him, her, it	my, mine, your, yours, his, her, hers, its
PLURAL	we, you, they	us, you, them	our, ours, your, yours, their, theirs

Many difficult questions about pronoun case concern *who/whom* and *whoever/whomever*. For a discussion of how to choose between them, see 30G.

30C How do pronouns work in case?

In the subjective case, pronouns function as SUBJECTS.

Watch
the Video

- **He** proposed!
- **He** and **I** wanted an inexpensive wedding.
- **We** googled several wedding performers.
- John and **I** found an affordable one-woman band.

    I is part of the compound subject *John and I*.

In the objective case, pronouns function as OBJECTS.

- We saw **her** perform in a city park.
- She noticed John and **me** immediately.
- We showed **her** our budget.
- She enjoyed auditioning for **him** and **me**.

    Him and me is the compound object of the preposition *for*.

In the possessive case, nouns and pronouns usually indicate ownership or imply a relationship.

- The **musician's contract** was very fair.

    The possessive noun *musician's* implies a type of ownership.

- **Her contract** was very fair.

    The possessive pronoun *her* implies a type of ownership.

- The **musicians' problems** stem from playing cheap instruments.

    The possessive noun *musicians'* implies a type of relationship.

- **Their problems** stem from playing with cheap instruments.

    The possessive pronoun *their* implies a type of relationship.

Sometimes, however, the notion of "ownership" is stretched in possessive constructions. In such cases, use either the possessive with an apostrophe, or use an "of the" phrase.

- The **musician's arrival** was eagerly anticipated.
- The **arrival of the musician** was eagerly anticipated.
- The **musician's performance** was thrilling.
- The **performance of the musician** was thrilling.

🛑 **Alert:** Never use an apostrophe in personal pronouns: *ours, yours, its, his, hers, theirs* (45C). ●

30D Which case is correct when *and* connects pronouns?

When *and* connects pronouns, or nouns and pronouns, the result is a compound construction. Compounding, which means "putting parts together in a whole," has no effect on case. Always use pronouns in the subjective case when they serve as the subjects of a sentence; also, always use pronouns in the objective case when they serve as objects in a sentence. Never mix cases.

COMPOUND PRONOUN SUBJECT — **He and I** saw the solar eclipse.

COMPOUND PRONOUN OBJECT — That eclipse astonished **him and me**.

When you're unsure of the case of a pronoun, use the "Troyka test for case" in Quick Box 30.2. In this four-step test, you drop some of the words from your sentence so that you can tell which case sounds correct.

When pronouns are in a PREPOSITIONAL PHRASE, they are always in the objective case. (That is, a pronoun is always the OBJECT of the preposition.) This rule holds whether the pronouns are singular or plural.

NO   Ms. Lester gave an assignment *to* **Sam and I**.

YES   Ms. Lester gave an assignment *to* **Sam and me**.

Be especially careful when pronouns follow the preposition *between*.

NO   The dispute is *between* **Thomas and I**.
      The prepositional phrase, which starts with the preposition *between*, cannot use the subjective-case pronoun *I*.

YES   The dispute is *between* **Thomas and me**.
      The prepositional phrase, which starts with the preposition *between*, calls for the objective-case pronoun *me*.

Quick Box 30.2

Listen to the Podcast

Troyka test for case

SUBJECTIVE CASE

STEP 1: Write the sentence twice, once using the subjective case, and once using the objective case.

STEP 2: Cross out enough words to isolate the element you are questioning.

~~Janet and~~ **me**

~~Janet and~~ **I**

> learned about the moon.

STEP 3: Omit the crossed-out words and read each sentence aloud to determine which one sounds right.

    NO   **Me** learned about the moon.

    YES   **I** learned about the moon.

STEP 4: Select the correct version, and restore the words you crossed out.
Janet and I learned about the moon.

OBJECTIVE CASE

STEP 1: Write the sentence twice, once using the subjective case, and once using the objective case.

STEP 2: Cross out enough words to isolate the element you are questioning.

The astronomer taught ~~Janet and~~ **I**

The astronomer taught ~~Janet and~~ **me**

> about the moon.

STEP 3: Omit the crossed-out words and read each sentence aloud to determine which one sounds right.

    NO   The astronomer taught **I** about the moon.

    YES   The astronomer taught **me** about the moon.

STEP 4: Select the correct version, and restore the words you crossed out.
The astronomer taught **Janet and me** about the moon.

● **EXERCISE 30-1** Underline the correct pronoun of each pair in parentheses of each pair in parentheses. For help, consult 30C and 30D.

EXAMPLE

Bill and (I, me) noticed two young swimmers being pulled out to sea.

(1) The two teenagers caught in the rip current waved and hollered at Bill and (I, me). (2) The harder (they, them) both swam toward shore, the further away the undercurrent pulled them from the beach. (3) The yellow banners had warned Bill and (I, me) that a dangerous rip current ran beneath the water. (4) I yelled at Bill, "Between you and (I, me), (we, us) have to save them!" (5) (He and I, Him and me) both ran and dove into the crashing waves. (6) As former lifeguards, Bill and (I, me) knew what to do. (7) (We, Us) two remembered that the rule for surviving a rip current is to swim across the current. (8) Only when swimmers are safely away from the current should (they, them) swim toward shore. (9) I reached the teenage girl, who cried, "My boyfriend and (I, me) are drowning." (10) Bill rescued the frightened teenage boy, and when they were safely on shore, the boy looked at (he and I, him and me) and gasped, "Thanks. The two of (we, us) know you saved our lives." ●

30E How do I match cases with appositives?

Match an APPOSITIVE to the same case as the word or words it renames. Whenever you're unsure about case, use the "Troyka test for case" in Quick Box 30.2 to get your answer.

● **We** [not *Us*] tennis players practice hard.

The subjective pronoun *we* renames the subject *tennis players*.

● The winners **she and I** [not *her and me*] advanced to the finals.

The subjective pronouns *she and I* rename the subject *winners*.

● The coach trains **us** [not *we*] tennis players to practice hard.

The objective pronoun *us* renames the object *tennis players*.

● The crowd cheered the winners, **her and me** [not *she and I*].

The objective pronouns *her and me* rename the object *winners*.

30F How does case work after linking verbs?

A pronoun that follows a LINKING VERB either renames the SUBJECT or shows possession. When the pronoun following the linking verb renames, use the subjective case. When the pronoun shows possession, use the possessive case. If you're unsure, use the "Troyka test for case" in Quick Box 30.2.

- The contest winner was **she**.
- The contest winners were **she** and **I**.
- The prize is **hers**.
- The prize is **ours**.

● **EXERCISE 30-2** Underline the correct pronoun of each pair in parentheses.

EXAMPLE

Last summer, my dad and (I, me) decided to take a road trip across the United States, something (we, us) have wanted to do since I was young.

1. Since (we, us) lived in California, (we, us) decided that a cross-country trip to New York City would be the most fun for (we, us).
2. (We, Us), my father and (I, me), collected road maps and learned that (we, us) would be taking even-numbered highways since they usually travel east/west.
3. My cousins live in Arizona, so (we, us) stayed with (they, them), and (they, them) showed us the Grand Canyon.
4. I think the Grand Canyon was more fun for (we, us) because (they, them) had seen it many times before.
5. After a conversation between (me, I) and my dad, (us, we) decided that we would like to see the St. Louis Arch next.
6. The famous Gateway Arch is interesting to (him and me, he and I) because it was designed by Finnish-American architect Eero Saarinen, and my father and (me, I) have relatives in Finland.
7. The next adventure for (we, us) travelers was driving through the Great Smoky Mountains in Tennessee.
8. My father and (me, I) learned that the mountains are called "smoky" because (they, them) are often covered in a natural fog that makes (they, them) look smoky.
9. Our next stop was in Washington, DC, where my brother and his family live. It was nice for (we, us) brothers to have some time to visit because (we, us) had not seen each other in a long time.
10. My father and (me, I) then drove the rest of the way to New York City. We flipped a coin to see who would get to drive the car when we arrived in the city. The winner was (me, I). ●

30G When should I use *who, whoever, whom,* and *whomever?*

Who and *whoever* are in the SUBJECTIVE CASE and function as subjects. *Whom* and *whomever* are in the OBJECTIVE CASE and function as objects.

Listen
to the
Podcast

Whenever you're unsure of whether to use *who* or *whoever* or to use *whom* or *whomever*, apply the "Troyka test for case" in Quick Box 30.2. If you see *who* or *whoever*, test by temporarily substituting *he, she,* or *they*. If you see *whom* or *whomever*, test by temporarily substituting *him, her,* or *them*.

- **Who/Whom** is coming to your party?

  He/She is coming to your party, so *who* is correct.

- Will you let **whoever/whomever** into the house?

  You will let *him/her* into the house, so *whomever* is correct.

In sentences with more than one clause, isolate the clause with the pronoun (shown in **boldface**), and apply the test.

- Give the package to **whoever/whomever is at the door.**

  He is at the door, so *whoever* is correct.

- Invite those guests **who/whom you can trust.**

  You believe you can trust *them,* so *whom* is correct.

- I will invite **whoever/whomever I wish to come.**

  I wish *them* to come, so *whomever* is correct.

- I will invite **whoever/whomever pleases me.**

  He pleases me so *whoever* is correct.

- I will not invite strangers **who/whom show up at the house.**

  They show up at the house, so *who* is correct.

- Don't tweet people **who/whom I did not invite.**

  I did not invite *them,* so *whom* is correct.

- If uninvited guests arrive, I will tell the police **who/whom they are.**

  They are *they* (not *them*), so *who* is correct.

Remember that *who* and *whoever* can function only as subjects or subject complements in clauses. If the person(s) you refer to perform some action or are linked to a subject, *who/whoever* is correct.

● **EXERCISE 30-3** Underline the correct pronoun of each pair in parentheses. For help, consult 30G.

EXAMPLE

Women (<u>who</u>, whom) both hold jobs outside the home and are mothers serve a "double shift."

(1) Women (who, whom) raise families do as much work at home as at their jobs. (2) In North American society, it is still mainly women (who, whom) cook dinner, clean the house, check the children's homework, read to them, and put them to bed. (3) Nevertheless, self-esteem runs high, some researchers have found, in many women on (who, whom) families depend for both wage earning and child rearing. (4) Compared with women (who, whom) pursue careers but have no children, those (who, whom) handle a double shift experience less anxiety and depression, according to the research. (5) Perhaps the reason for this finding is that those for (who, whom) the extra paycheck helps pay the bills feel pride and accomplishment when they rise to the challenge. (6) However, other studies note that women (who, whom) have both jobs and children experience tremendous stress. (7) Those (who, whom) feel unable both to support and to nurture their children despite their maximum efforts are the women for (who, whom) the dual responsibility is an almost unbearable burden. ●

30H What pronoun case comes after *than* or *as*?

When *than* or *as* is part of a sentence of comparison, the sentence sometimes doesn't include words to complete the comparison outright. Rather, by omitting certain words, the sentence implies the comparison. For example, *My two-month-old Saint Bernard is larger **than** most full-grown dogs [are]* doesn't need the final word *are*.

When a pronoun follows *than* or *as*, the meaning of the sentence depends entirely on whether the pronoun is in the subjective case or the objective case. Here are two sentences that convey two very different messages, depending on whether the subjective case (*I*) or the objective case (*me*) is used.

1. My sister loved that dog more *than* **I**.

2. My sister loved that dog more *than* **me**.

In sentence 1, because *I* is in the subjective case, the sentence means *My sister loved that dog more than **I** [loved it]*. In sentence 2, because *me* is in the objective case, the sentence means *My sister loved that dog more than [she loved] **me**.* In both situations, you can check whether you're using the correct case by supplying the implied words to see if they make sense.

30I How do pronouns work before infinitives?

Most INFINITIVES consist of the SIMPLE FORMS of verbs that follow *to:* for example, *to laugh, to sing, to jump, to dance.* (A few exceptions occur when the *to* is optional: *My aunt helped the elderly man [to] cross the street;* and when the *to* is awkward: *My aunt watched the elderly man [to] get on the bus.*) For both the SUBJECTS of infinitives and the OBJECTS of infinitives, use the objective case.

- Our tennis coach expects **me** *to serve.*
- Our tennis coach expects **him** *to beat* me.
- Our tennis coach expects **us** *to beat* them.

30J How do pronouns work with *-ing* words?

When a verb's *-ing* form functions as a NOUN, it's called a GERUND: *Brisk **walking** is excellent exercise.* When a noun or PRONOUN comes before a gerund, the POSSESSIVE CASE is required: ***His** brisk **walking** built up his stamina.* In contrast, when a verb's *-ing* form functions as a MODIFIER, it requires the subjective case for the pronoun, not the possessive case: *He, **walking** briskly, caught up to me.*

Here are two sentences that convey different messages, depending entirely on whether a possessive comes before the *-ing* word.

1. The detective noticed the **man** *staggering.*
2. The detective noticed the **man's** *staggering.*

Sentence 1 means that the detective noticed the *man;* sentence 2 means that the detective noticed the *staggering.* The same distinction applies to pronouns: When *the man* is replaced by *him* or *the man's* by *his,* the meaning is the same as in sentences 1 and 2.

1. The detective noticed **him** *staggering.*
2. The detective noticed **his** *staggering.*

Use these distinctions in ACADEMIC WRITING even if you don't in speech.

● **EXERCISE 30-4** Underline the correct pronoun of each pair in parentheses. For help, consult 30H through 30J.

EXAMPLE

Ricky Jay holds the world's record for card throwing; no one can throw a playing card faster than (he/him).

(1) Many magicians agree that no one is better at sleight-of-hand magic than (he/him). (2) Younger magicians often say that Ricky Jay influenced (their/them) to become professional performers. (3) In addition to (him/his) being a respected sleight-of-hand artist, Jay is also a scholar and historian. (4) His interest in strange performers led (him/he) to write *Learned Pigs and Fireproof Women,* which discusses unusual acts and begins with (him/his) explaining their appeal to audiences. (5) Jay's acting career has involved (his/him) performing in several different movies

and TV shows. (6) In the James Bond film *Tomorrow Never Dies*, few could have played a villain as well as (he/him). (7) Other roles include (him/his) narrating the introduction to the movie *Magnolia*. (8) Overall, few performers have had such as varied and interesting career as (him/he). ●

30K What case should I use for *-self* pronouns?

Two types of pronouns end in *-self*: reflexive pronouns and intensive pronouns.

A **reflexive pronoun** is used as an object that refers to the same person or thing as the subject.

● The **detective** disguised ***himself***.

The reflexive pronoun *himself* refers to the subject *detective*.

● **We** purchased his disguise **ourselves**.

The reflexive pronoun *ourselves* refers to the subject *we*.

Never use a reflexive pronoun to replace a personal pronoun in the subjective case even if you believe it sounds "lofty."

NO   My teammates and **myself** will vote for a team captain.

YES   My teammates and **I** will vote for a team captain.

NO   That decision is up to my teammates and **myself**.

YES   That decision is up to my teammates and **me**.

Intensive pronouns are used to emphasize preceding nouns or pronouns.

● The detective felt that **his career *itself*** was at risk.

Itself emphasizes the previous noun *career*.

● He phoned his **attorney *himself***.

Himself emphasizes the previous noun *he*.

PRONOUN REFERENCE

30L What is pronoun reference?

The word or group of words that a pronoun refers to is called its **antecedent**. To be clear to your readers, be sure your pronouns refer clearly to their antecedents.

I knew a **woman**, lovely in **her** bones / When small **birds** sighed, **she** would sigh back at **them**.

—Theodore Roethke, "I Knew a Woman"

30M What makes pronoun reference clear?

Pronoun reference is clear when your readers know immediately to whom or what each pronoun refers. Quick Box 30.3 lists guidelines for using pronouns clearly, and the section in parentheses is where each is explained.

Quick Box 30.3 ■ ■ ■ ■ ■ ■ ■ ■ ■ ■ ■

Guidelines for clear pronoun reference

- Place pronouns close to their ANTECEDENTS (30N).
- Make a pronoun refer to a specific antecedent (30N).
- Do not overuse *it* (30Q).
- Reserve *you* only for DIRECT ADDRESS (30R).
- Use *that, which,* and *who* correctly (30S).

30N How can I avoid unclear pronoun reference?

Every pronoun needs to refer to a specific, nearby ANTECEDENT. If the same pronoun in your writing has to refer to more than one antecedent, replace some pronouns with their antecedents.

Watch the Video

NO   In 1911, **Roald Amundsen** reached the South Pole just thirty-five days before **Robert F. Scott** arrived. **He** [who? Amundsen or Scott?] had told people that **he** [who? Amundsen or Scott?] was going to sail for the Arctic, but **he** [who? Amundsen or Scott?] was concealing **his** [whose? Amundsen's or Scott's?] plan. Soon, **he** [who? Amundsen or Scott?] turned south for the Antarctic.

YES   In 1911, **Roald Amundsen** reached the South Pole just thirty-five days before **Robert F. Scott** arrived. **Amundsen** had told people that **he** was going to sail for the Arctic, but **he** was concealing **his** plan. Soon, **Amundsen** turned south for the Antarctic.

! Alert: Be careful with the VERBS *said* and *told* in sentences that contain pronoun reference. To maintain clarity, use quotation marks and slightly reword each sentence to make the meaning clear.

NO   **Her** mother told **her she** was going to visit **her** grandmother.

YES   **Her** mother told **her**, "**You** are going to visit your grandmother."

YES   **Her** mother told **her**, "**I** am going to visit your grandmother." ●

Further, if too much material comes between a pronoun and its antecedent, readers can lose track of the meaning.

- Alfred Wegener, a German meteorologist and professor of geophysics at the University of Graz in Austria, was the first to suggest that all the continents on earth were originally part of one large landmass. According to this theory, the supercontinent broke up long ago and the fragments drifted apart. ~~He~~ *Wegener* named this supercontinent Pangaea.

  Wegener, the antecedent of *he*, may be too distant for some readers. Remember to keep your pronouns and their antecedents close.

When you start a new paragraph, be cautious about beginning it with a pronoun whose antecedent is in a prior paragraph. You're better off repeating the word.

ESOL Tip: Many languages omit pronoun subjects because the verb contains subject information. In English, use the pronoun as a subject. For example, never omit *it* in the following: *Political science is an important academic subject. **It** is studied all over the world.*

● **EXERCISE 30-5** Revise so that each pronoun refers clearly to its antecedent. Either replace pronouns with nouns or restructure the material to clarify pronoun reference. For help, consult 30N.

EXAMPLE

People who return to work after years away from the corporate world often discover that business practices have changed. They may find fiercer competition in the workplace, but they may also discover that they are more flexible than before.

Here is one possible revision: *People who return to work after years away from the corporate world often discover that business practices have changed. Those people may find fiercer competition in the workplace, but they may also discover that business practices are more flexible than before.*

Most companies used to frown on employees who became involved in office romances. They often considered them to be using company time for their own enjoyment. Now, however, managers realize that happy employees are productive employees. With more women than ever before in the workforce and with people working longer hours, they have begun to see that male and female employees want and need to socialize. They are also dropping their opposition to having married couples on the payroll. They no longer automatically believe that they will bring family matters into the workplace or stick up for each other at the company's expense.

One departmental manager had doubts when a systems analyst for research named Laura announced that she had become engaged to Peter, who worked as a technician in the same department. She told her that either one or the other might have to transfer out of the research department. After listening to her plea that they be allowed to work together on a trial basis, the manager reconsidered. She decided to give Laura and Peter a chance to prove that their relationship would not affect their work. The decision paid off. They demonstrated that they could work as an effective research team, right through their engagement and subsequent marriage. Two years later, when Laura was promoted to assistant manager for product development and after he asked to move also, she enthusiastically recommended that Peter follow Laura to her new department. ●

30O How do pronouns work with *it, that, this,* and *which*?

Watch
the Video

When you use *it, that, this,* and *which*, be sure that your readers can easily and unmistakably understand each word refers to.

NO Comets usually fly by the earth at 100,000 mph, whereas asteroids sometimes collide with the earth. **This** interests scientists.

Does *this* refer to the speed of the comets, to comets flying by the earth, or to asteroids colliding with the earth?

YES Comets usually fly by the earth at 100,000 mph, whereas asteroids sometimes collide with the earth. **This difference** interests scientists.

Adding a noun after *this* or *that* clarifies the meaning.

NO I told my friends that I was going to major in geology, **which** made my parents happy.

Does *which* refer to telling your friends or to majoring in geology?

YES My parents were happy **because I discussed my major with my friends**.

YES My parents were happy **because I chose to major in geology**.

Also, the title of any piece of writing stands alone. Therefore, in your first paragraph, never refer to your title with *this* or *that*. For example, if an essay's title is "Geophysics as a Major," the following holds for the first sentence:

NO **This subject** unites the sciences of physics, biology, and paleontology.

YES **Geophysics** unites the sciences of physics, biology, and paleontology.

30P How do I use *they* and *it* precisely?

The expression *they say* forces your readers to infer precisely who is saying. Your credibility as a writer depends on your mentioning a source precisely.

NO   **They say** that earthquakes are becoming more frequent.

   They doesn't identify the authority who made the statement.

YES   **Seismologists** say that earthquakes are becoming more frequent.

The expressions *it said* and *it is said that* reflect imprecise thinking. Also, they're wordy. Revising such expressions improves your writing.

NO   **It said** in the newspaper that California has minor earthquakes almost daily.

YES   **The newspaper reported** that California has minor earthquakes almost daily.

30Q How do I use *it* to suit the situation?

The word *it* has three different uses in English. Here are examples of correct uses of *it*.

1. PERSONAL PRONOUN: Ryan wants to visit the 18-inch Schmidt telescope, but **it** is on Mount Palomar.

2. EXPLETIVE (sometimes called a *subject filler*, it delays the subject): **It** is interesting to observe the stars.

3. IDIOMATIC EXPRESSION (words that depart from normal use, such as using *it* as the sentence subject when writing about weather, time, distance, and environmental conditions): **It** is sunny. **It** is midnight. **It** is not far to the hotel. **It** is very hilly.

All three uses listed above are correct, but avoid combining them in the same sentence. The result can be an unclear and confusing sentence.

NO   Because our car was overheating, **it** came as no surprise that **it** broke down just as **it** began to rain.

   It is overused here, even though all three uses—2, 1, and 3 on the preceding list, respectively—are acceptable.

YES   **It** came as no surprise that our overheating car broke down just as the rain began.

◉ **ESOL Tip:** In some languages, *it* is not an expletive. In English, it is.

NO   Is a lovely day.

YES   **It** is a lovely day. ●

30R   When should I use *you* for direct address?

Reserve *you* for **direct address**, writing that addresses the reader directly. For example, we use *you* in this handbook to address you, the student. *You* is not a suitable substitute for specific words that refer to people, situations, or occurrences.

NO   Prison uprisings often happen **when you allow** overcrowding.

     The reader, *you*, did not allow the overcrowding.

YES   Prison uprisings often happen **when prisons are** overcrowded.

NO   In Russia, **you** often have to stand in long lines to buy groceries.

     Do *you*, the reader, plan to do your grocery shopping in Russia?

YES   **Russian shoppers** often stand in long lines to buy groceries.

● **EXERCISE 30-6**   Revise these sentences so that all pronoun references are clear. If a sentence is correct, circle its number. For help, consult 30O through 30R.

EXAMPLE

They say that reaching the summit of Mount Everest is easiest in the month of May.
Experienced climbers say that reaching the summit of Mount Everest is easiest in the month of May. [Revision eliminates imprecise use of *they*, see section 30P.]

1. Climbing Mount Everest is more expensive than you realize.
2. In addition to training, they need to raise as much as $60,000 for the expedition.
3. By contacting the Nepalese embassy in Washington, DC, you can secure the help of Sherpa guides.
4. The government of Nepal requires permits, copies of passports, and letters of recommendation for each climbing team.
5. Climbers will need to pack oxygen bottles, a first aid kit, medications, a satellite phone, walkie-talkies, and a laptop computer. This will ensure a climber's safety.
6. Climbers often use yaks because they are stronger than you and can carry more equipment.

7. They do not offer direct flights, so climbers from America usually need a couple of days to get to Katmandu, Nepal.
8. Once atop the mountain, you should prepare for the descent, which is just as dangerous as the ascent. ●

30S When should I use *that, which,* and *who?*

To use the pronouns *that* and *which* correctly, you want to check the context of the sentence you're writing. *Which* and *that* refer to animals and things. Only sometimes do they refer to anonymous or collective groups of people. Quick Box 30.4 shows how to choose between *that* and *which.* For information about the role of commas with *that* and *which,* see 42F.

Who refers to people and to animals mentioned by name.

● **John Polanyi, who** was awarded the Nobel Prize in Chemistry, speaks passionately in favor of nuclear disarmament.

● **Lassie, who** was known for her intelligence and courage, was actually played by a series of male collies.

Quick Box 30.4 ■ ■ ■ ■ ■ ■ ■ ■ ■ ■ ■

Choosing between *that* and *which*

Choice: Some instructors and style guides use either *that* or *which* to introduce a **restrictive clause** (a DEPENDENT CLAUSE that is essential to the meaning of the sentence). Others may advise you to use only *that* so that your writing distinguishes clearly between restrictive and **nonrestrictive clauses.** Whichever style you use, be consistent in each piece of writing:

● The zoos *that* (or *which*) **most children like** display newborn and baby animals.

The words *most children like* are essential for delivering the meaning that children prefer zoos with certain features and make up a restrictive clause.

No choice: You are required to use *which* to introduce a nonrestrictive clause (a dependent clause that isn't essential to the meaning of the sentence or part of the sentence).

● Zoos, **which most children like,** attract more visitors if they display newborn and baby animals.

The words *most children like* are not essential to the meaning of the sentence and make up a nonrestrictive clause.

Many professional writers reserve *which* for nonrestrictive clauses and *that* for restrictive clauses. Other writers use *that* and *which* interchangeably for restrictive clauses. For ACADEMIC WRITING, your instructor might expect you to maintain the distinction.

! Alert: Use commas before and after a nonrestrictive clause. Don't use commas before and after a restrictive clause; see 42K.4. ●

● **EXERCISE 30-7**   Fill in the blanks with *that, which*, or *who*. For help, consult 30S.

EXAMPLE

Antigua, which is an island in the West Indies, is a popular destination for European and American tourists.

1. Those _____ like to travel to Antigua may enjoy online gambling, _____ is legal on the island.
2. The sport _____ is most popular in Antigua is cricket.
3. Celebrities _____ own homes on the island include Oprah Winfrey, Eric Clapton, and Jamaica Kincaid.
4. The main airport, _____ is named after Prime Minister V. C. Bird, is located in the capital, St. John's.
5. The cruise ships _____ travel to Antigua often stop at St. John's, _____ became the seat of government in 1981. ●

Complete the Chapter Exercises

31 Agreement

■ ■ ■ ■ ■ ■ ■ ■ ■

Quick Points   You will learn to

➤ Match subjects and verbs in person and number (see 31A–31N).
➤ Match pronouns to the nouns to which they refer (see 31O–31T).

31A What is agreement?

Grammatical **agreement** links related grammatical forms. Specifically, you need to match subjects and verbs (see 31B through 31N) and pronouns and antecedents (see 31O through 31T).

SUBJECT–VERB AGREEMENT

31B What is subject–verb agreement?

Subject–verb agreement matches a SUBJECT to its VERB match in NUMBER (singular or plural) and PERSON (first, second, or third person). Quick Box 31.1 presents these major concepts in grammatical agreement.

Watch
the Video

- The **firefly glows**.

  Firefly, a singular subject in the third person, matches *glows*, a singular verb in the third person.

- **Fireflies glow**.

  Fireflies, a plural subject in the third person, matches *glow*, a plural verb in the third person.

Quick Box 31.1 ■ ■ ■ ■ ■ ■ ■ ■ ■

Grammatical agreement: first, second and third person

- **Number** refers to *singular* (one) and *plural* (more than one).

- The **first person** is the speaker or writer. *I* (singular) and *we* (plural) are the only subjects that occur in the first person.

  SINGULAR **I see** a field of fireflies.
  PLURAL **We see** a field of fireflies.

- The **second person** is the person spoken or written to. *You* (for both singular and plural) is the only subject that occurs in the second person.

  SINGULAR **You see** a shower of sparks.
  PLURAL **You see** a shower of sparks.

- The **third person** is the person or thing being spoken or written about. *He, she, it* (singular) and *they* (plural) are the third-person subject forms. Most rules for subject–verb agreement involve the third person.

  SINGULAR The **scientist sees** a cloud of cosmic dust.
  PLURAL The **scientists see** a cloud of cosmic dust.

31C Why is a final -s or -es in a subject or verb so important?

SUBJECT–VERB AGREEMENT often involves a final *s* (*or es* for words that end in *-s*). For verbs in the present tense, you form the SIMPLE FORM of third-person singular by adding *-s* or *-es: laugh, laughs; kiss, kisses*. Major exceptions are the verbs *be* (*is*), *have* (*has*), and *do* (*does*) (see 38C).

- That **student agrees** that **young teenagers watch** too much television.
- Those **young teenagers are** taking valuable time away from studying.
- That **student has** a part-time job for ten hours a week.
- Still, that **student does** well in college.

To make a subject plural, you add *-s* or *-es* to its end: *lip, lips; guess, guesses*. Exceptions include most pronouns (*they, it*) and a few nouns that for singular and plural either don't change (*deer, deer*) or change internally (*mouse, mice*). Quick Box 31.2 shows you the basic pattern for agreement using *-s* or *-es*.

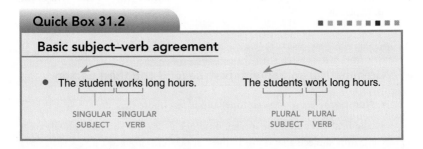

Quick Box 31.2

Basic subject–verb agreement

- The student works long hours.

  SINGULAR SUBJECT SINGULAR VERB

  The students work long hours.

  PLURAL SUBJECT PLURAL VERB

Alert: When you use an AUXILIARY VERB with a main verb, never add *-s* or *-es* to the main verb: *The coach **can walk** [not can walks] to campus. The coach **does like** [not does likes] his job.* ●

● **EXERCISE 31-1** Use the subject and verb in each set to write two complete sentences—one with a singular subject and one with a plural subject. Keep all verbs in the present tense. For help, consult 31C.

EXAMPLE

bird, sing

SINGULAR SUBJECT: When a *bird sings*, you will know spring is here.

PLURAL SUBJECT: When *birds sing*, you will know spring is here.

1. chair, rock
2. leaf, fall
3. river, flow
4. clock, tick

5. singer, sing
6. girl, laugh
7. hand, grab
8. loaf, rise ●

31D   Can I ignore words between a subject and its verb?

You can ignore all words between a subject and its verb. Focus strictly on the subject and its verb. Quick Box 31.3 shows you this pattern.

NO   **Winners** of the state contest **goes** to the national finals.

> *Winners* is the subject; the verb must agree with it. Ignore the words *of the state contest.*

YES   **Winners** of the state contest **go** to the national finals.

The subject *one of the . . .* requires a singular verb to agree with *one.* Ignore the plural noun that comes after *of the.* (For information on the phrase *one of the . . . who,* see 31L.)

NO   **One** of the problems **are** the funds needed for travel expenses.

YES   **One** of the problems **is** the funds needed for travel expenses.

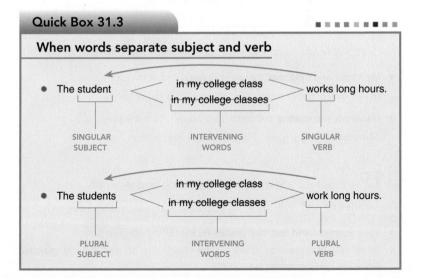

Quick Box 31.3

When words separate subject and verb

● The student < in my college class / in my college classes > works long hours.

SINGULAR SUBJECT — INTERVENING WORDS — SINGULAR VERB

● The students < in my college class / in my college classes > work long hours.

PLURAL SUBJECT — INTERVENING WORDS — PLURAL VERB

Similarly, eliminate all word groups between the subject and the verb, starting with *including, together with, along with, accompanied by, in addition to, except,* and *as well as.*

NO The **moon,** *as well as* the planet Venus, **are** visible in the night sky.

Moon is the subject. The verb must agree only with it.

YES The **moon,** as well as the planet Venus, **is** visible in the night sky.

31E How do verbs work when subjects are connected by *and*?

Watch the Video

Use a plural verb with a COMPOUND SUBJECT joined by *and*. Quick Box 31.4 shows you this pattern. (For related material on PRONOUNS and ANTECEDENTS, see 31P.)

* The **Cascade Diner** *and* **Joe's Diner** *have* [not *has*] salmon today.

These are two different diners.

Quick Box 31.4

When subjects are joined by *and*

* The student and the instructor work long hours.

COMPOUND SUBJECT (uses *and*)   PLURAL VERB

An exception occurs when *and* joins subjects that mean one thing or person.

* **My friend** *and* **neighbor** *makes* [not *make*] excellent chili.

In this sentence, the friend is the same person as the neighbor.

* **Macaroni** *and* **cheese** *contains* [not *contain*] many calories.

Macaroni and cheese is one dish so it takes a singular verb.

31F How do verbs work with *each* and *every*?

The words *each* and *every* are always singular and require a singular verb.

* *Each* **human hand and foot** *makes* [not *make*] a distinctive print.
* To identify lawbreakers, *every* **police chief, sheriff, and federal marshal** *depends* [not *depend*] on such prints.

⚠ **Alert:** Don't use *each* or *every* at the same time: ***Each*** [not *Each and every*] *robber has been caught.* (For more information about pronoun agreement for *each* and *every*, see 31I, 31P, and 31R.) ●

31G How do verbs work when subjects are connected by *or*?

When SUBJECTS are joined by *or*—or by the sets *either . . . or, neither . . . nor, not only . . . but (also)*—the verb agrees only with its closest subject. Quick Box 31.5 shows this pattern with *either . . . or.* (For related material on pronouns and antecedents, see 31Q.)

- ***Neither*** spiders ***nor* flies upset** *me.*
- ***Not only*** spiders ***but also*** all other **arachnids have** four pairs of legs.
- A meal of six clam fritters, two blue crabs, ***or*** a steamed **lobster sounds** good.

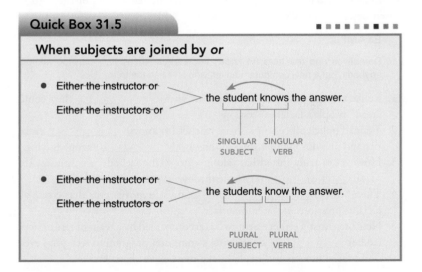

Quick Box 31.5

When subjects are joined by *or*

- Either the instructor or
- Either the instructors or

  the student knows the answer.

  SINGULAR SUBJECT   SINGULAR VERB

- Either the instructor or
- Either the instructors or

  the students know the answer.

  PLURAL SUBJECT   PLURAL VERB

31H How do verbs work with inverted word order?

In English sentences, the SUBJECT normally comes before its VERB: *Astronomy is interesting.* **Inverted word order** reverses the typical subject-verb pattern by putting the verb first. Most questions use inverted word order: *Is astronomy interesting?* In inverted word order, find the subject first and then check whether its verb agrees with it.

- Into deep space **shoot** probing **satellites**.

  The plural verb *shoot* agrees with the inverted plural subject *satellites*.

- On the television screen **is** an **image** of Saturn.

  The singular verb *is* agrees with the inverted singular subject *image*.

Alert: When *there* precedes the verb, see whether the subject is singular or plural, and then choose the form of *be* to agree with the subject. If *it* precedes the verb, use the singular form of *be* (*is, was*) whether the subject is singular or plural. ●

- **There** *are* nine **planets** in our solar system.
- **There** *is* probably no **life** on eight of them.
- **It** *is* astronomers who explore this theory daily.

  The verb *is* agrees with *it*, not with *astronomers*.

● **EXERCISE 31-2**   Supply the correct present-tense form of the verb in parentheses. For help, consult 31C through 31H.

EXAMPLE

Detectives and teachers (to know) know experienced liars can fool almost anybody, but a new computer can tell who is telling the truth.

1. Police officers and teachers often (to wish) _____ they could "read" people's facial expressions.
2. Trained police officers or a smart teacher (to know) _____ facial tics and nervous mannerisms (to show) _____ someone is lying.
3. However, a truly gifted liar, along with well-coached eyewitnesses, (to reveal) _____ very little through expressions or behavior.
4. There (to be) _____ forty-six muscle movements that create all facial expressions in the human face.
5. Neuroscientist Terrence Seinowski, accompanied by a team of researchers, (to be) _____ developing a computer program to recognize even slight facial movements made by the most expert liars. ●

31I   How do verbs work with indefinite pronouns?

Listen to the Podcast

Indefinite pronouns usually refer to nonspecific persons, things, quantities, or ideas. While most indefinite pronouns are singular, some are always plural, and a few can be singular *or* plural. Quick Box 31.6 lists indefinite pronouns according to what verb form they require. (For related material on pronouns and antecedents, see 31O–31R.)

Quick Box 31.6

Common indefinite pronouns

ALWAYS PLURAL

both	many

ALWAYS SINGULAR

another	every	no one
anybody	everybody	nothing
anyone	everyone	one
anything	everything	somebody
each	neither	someone
either	nobody	something

SINGULAR OR PLURAL, DEPENDING ON CONTEXT

all	more	none
any	most	Some

SINGULAR INDEFINITE PRONOUNS

- **Everything** about that intersection **is** dangerous.
- But whenever **anyone says** anything, **nothing is** done.
- **Each** of us **has** [not *have*] to shovel snow; **each is** [not *are*] expected to help.
- **Every** snowstorm of the past two years **has** [not *have*] been severe.
- **Every** one of them **has** [not *have*] caused massive traffic jams.

SINGULAR OR PLURAL INDEFINITE PRONOUNS (DEPENDING ON MEANING)

- **Some** of our streams **are** polluted.

  Some refers to the plural noun *streams*, so the plural verb *are* is correct.

- **Some** pollution **is** reversible, but **all** of it **threatens** the environment.

  Some and *all* refer to the singular noun *pollution*, so the singular verbs *is* and *threatens* are correct.

- **All** that environmentalists ask **is** to give nature a chance.

  All here means "the only thing," so the singular verb *is* is correct.

- Winter has driven the birds south; **all have** left.

  All refers to the plural noun *birds*, so the plural verb *have* is correct.

⚠ Alerts: (1) Use *this, that, these,* and *those* to agree with *kind* and *type. This* and *that* are singular, as are *kind* and *type; these* and *those* are plural, as are *kinds* and *types:* **This** [not *These*] **kind** of rainwear is waterproof. **These** [not *This*] **kinds** of sweaters keep me warm. (2) Rules for indefinite pronouns can conflict with methods of avoiding SEXIST LANGUAGE. For suggestions, see 31S. ●

31J How do verbs work with collective nouns?

((•
Listen
to the
Podcast

A **collective noun** names a group of people or things: *family, audience, class, number, committee, team, group,* and the like. When the group acts as one unit, use a singular verb. When members of the group act individually, use a plural verb.

- The senior **class** nervously *awaits* final exams.

   The *class* is acting as a single unit, so the verb is singular.

- The senior **class** *were fitted* for their graduation robes today

   The class members were fitted as individuals, so the verb is plural.

31K Does a linking verb agree with the subject complement?

Although a LINKING VERB joins a SUBJECT to its SUBJECT COMPLEMENT, the linking verb agrees with the subject, not with the subject complement.

   NO The worst **part** of owning a car *are* the bills.

   The subject is the singular *part,* so the plural verb *are* is wrong.

   YES The worst **part** of owning a car *is* the bills.

   The singular subject *part* agrees with the singular verb *is.*

31L What verbs agree with *who, which,* and *that?*

If the ANTECEDENT of *who, which,* or *that* is singular, use a singular verb. If the antecedent is plural, use a plural verb.

- The scientist will share the prize with the **researchers** *who* **work** with her.

   Who refers to *researchers,* so the plural verb *work* is used.

- George Jones is the **student** *who* **works** in the science lab.

   Who refers to *student,* so the singular verb *works* is used.

The phrases *one of the* and *the only one of the* immediately before *who*, *which*, or *that* require different verbs. *Who, which*, or *that* refers to the plural NOUN immediately following *one of the*, so the verb must be plural. Although *the only one of* is also followed by a plural word, *who, which*, or *that* must be singular to agree with the singular *one*.

- Tracy is **one of the** students **who talk** in class.

  Who refers to *students*, a plural antecedent, so the verb *talk* is plural.

- Jim is **the only one of the** students **who talks** in class.

  Who refers to *one*, a singular antecedent, so the verb *talks* is singular.

● **EXERCISE 31-3** Supply the correct present-tense form of the verb in parentheses.

EXAMPLE

Anyone who goes to the theme park Dollywood (to know) <u>knows</u> that it is located in Tennessee.

1. Each of the park's guests (to enjoy) thrill rides, music, and dinner theaters.
2. The cast of the Showtreet Palace Theater (to perform) shows for tourists.
3. Kidsfest is one of the festivals that (to attract) visitors each year.
4. For some people, the best reason for visiting Dollywood (to be) the rides.
5. All of the rides (to run) all day long, and no one (to seem) to mind waiting in line to ride them. ●

31M How do verbs work with amounts, fields of study, and other special nouns?

AMOUNTS

SUBJECTS that refer to time, sums of money, distance, or measurement are singular. They take singular verbs.

- **Two hours *is*** not enough time to finish. [time]
- **Three hundred dollars *is*** what we must pay. [sum of money]
- **Two miles *is*** a short sprint for some serious joggers. [distance]
- **Three-quarters of an inch *is*** needed for a perfect fit. [measurement]

FIELDS OF STUDY

The name for a field of study is singular even if it appears to be plural: *economics, mathematics, physics*, and *statistics*.

- ***Statistics* is** required of science majors.

  Statistics is a course of study, so the singular verb *is* is correct.

- *Statistics* **show** that a teacher shortage is coming.

  Statistics means *projections* here, so the plural verb *show* is correct.

SPECIAL NOUNS

Athletics, news, ethics, and *measles* are singular despite their plural appearance. Also, *United States of America* is singular: However, *politics* and *sports* take singular or plural verbs, depending on the meaning of the sentence.

- The *news* **gets** better each day.

  News is a singular noun, so the singular verb *gets* is correct.

- *Sports* **is** a good way to build physical stamina.

  Sports is one general activity, so the singular verb *is* is correct.

- Three *sports* **are** offered at the recreation center.

  Sports are separate activities, so the plural verb *are* is correct.

Jeans, pants, scissors, clippers, tweezers, eyeglasses, thanks, and *riches* are some words that require a plural verb, even though they refer to one thing. However, if you use *pair* with *jeans, pants, scissors, clippers, tweezers,* or *eyeglasses,* use a singular verb for agreement.

- These *slacks* **need** pressing.
- This *pair* of slacks **needs** pressing.

  Series and *means* can be singular or plural, according to their meaning.

- Two new TV *series* **are** big hits.

  Series refers to two individual items, so the plural verb *are* is correct.

- A *series* of disasters **is** plaguing our production.

  Series refers to a single group of disasters, so the singular verb *is* is correct.

31N How do verbs work with titles, company names, and words as themselves?

TITLES

A title itself refers to one work or entity, so a singular verb is correct.

- *Breathing Lessons* by Anne Tyler **is** a prize-winning novel.

COMPANY NAMES

A company should be treated as a singular unit, requiring a singular verb.

- *Cohn Brothers* **boxes** and **delivers** fine art.

WORDS AS THEMSELVES

Whenever you write about words as themselves to call attention to those words, use a singular verb, even if more than one word is involved.

- *We* **implies** that everyone is included.
- *Protective reaction strikes* **was** a euphemism for *bombing*.

● **EXERCISE 31-4** Supply the correct present-tense form of the verb in parentheses. For help, consult 31I through 31N.

EXAMPLE

The movie *Wordplay* is about those who (to enjoy) <u>enjoy</u> solving crossword puzzles.

1. When the movie plays at theaters, the audience often (to consist) _____ of different ages and types of people.
2. For fans of crossword puzzles, the major attraction (to be) _____ the challenges they present.
3. Every creator of puzzles (to know) _____ that in the most successful puzzles all of the clues (to be) _____ interesting.
4. *Setters* (to be) _____ is a term used by crossword puzzle fans to describe someone who creates puzzles.
5. These fans, which (to include) _____ celebrities like Jon Stewart, consider the Sunday puzzle in the *New York Times* one of the most difficult. ●

● **EXERCISE 31-5** This exercise covers all of subject-verb agreement (see 31B through 31N). Supply the correct form of the verb in parentheses.

EXAMPLE

Recent research suggests that high levels of social status (to bring) <u>bring</u> high levels of stress.

1. Most people (to believe) _____ that poor people obviously suffer considerably more from stress than do very wealthy people.
2. They understand that meeting basic needs like food and shelter (to generate) _____ huge amounts of stress.
3. A steady income and a large saving account clearly (to reduce) _____ stress levels and (to have) _____ mental and physical health benefits.
4. However, these benefits (to be) _____ true only to a certain point.
5. Research by sociologist Scott Schieman shows that people at the highest levels of society actually (to have) _____ high levels of stress.
6. There (to be) _____ many possible reasons for this effect.

7. One reason (to suggest) _____ that success makes people who are driven to succeed work even harder, creating a vicious cycle for them.

8. Another reason, which (to view) _____ an apparent perk of high status as an actual disadvantage, (to say) _____ that having authority over others (to result) _____ in people continually getting involved in conflict.

9. Statistics (to show) _____ that young professionals who (to be) _____ used to technological interruptions in demanding work settings may deal with stress better than older ones.

10. Even if it brings high stress, most of us (to prefer) _____ having high status over having low. ●

PRONOUN–ANTECEDENT AGREEMENT

31O What is pronoun–antecedent agreement?

Watch
the Video

Pronoun–antecedent agreement means that a PRONOUN matches its ANTE-CEDENT in NUMBER (singular or plural) and PERSON (first, second, or third person). Quick Box 31.7 shows you how to visualize this pattern of grammatical agreement. You might also want to consult Quick Box 31.1 in 31B for explanations and examples of the concepts *number* and *person*.

● The **firefly** glows when **it** emerges from **its** nest at night.

The singular pronouns *it* and *its* match their singular antecedent, *firefly*.

● **Fireflies** glow when **they** emerge from **their** nests at night.

The plural pronouns *they* and *their* match their plural antecedent, *fireflies*.

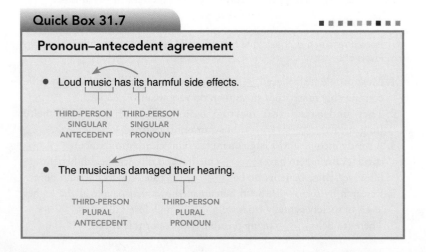

Quick Box 31.7

Pronoun–antecedent agreement

● Loud music has its harmful side effects.

THIRD-PERSON SINGULAR ANTECEDENT THIRD-PERSON SINGULAR PRONOUN

● The musicians damaged their hearing.

THIRD-PERSON PLURAL ANTECEDENT THIRD-PERSON PLURAL PRONOUN

31P How do pronouns work when *and* connects antecedents?

When *and* connects two or more ANTECEDENTS, they require a plural pronoun. This rule applies even if each separate antecedent is singular. (For related material on subjects and verbs, see 31E.)

● The **Cascade Diner** *and* **Joe's Diner** have closed **their** doors.

Two separate diners require a plural pronoun reference.

When *and* joins singular nouns that nevertheless refer to a single person or thing, use a singular pronoun.

● **My friend *and* neighbor** makes **his** [not *their*] excellent chili every Saturday.

The friend is the same person as the neighbor, so the singular *his* (or *her*) is correct. If these were two separate persons, *their* would be correct.

EACH, EVERY

The words *each* and *every* are singular, even when they refer to two or more antecedents joined by *and*. The same rule applies when *each* or *every* is used alone (see 31I). (For related material on subjects and verbs, see 31F.)

● *Each* **human hand** *and* **foot** leaves **its** [not *their*] distinctive print.

The rule still applies when the construction *one of the* follows *each* or *every*.

● *Each one of the* **robbers** left **her** [not *their*] fingerprints at the scene.

31Q How do pronouns work when *or* connects antecedents?

When *or*, *nor*, or *but* join ANTECEDENTS, the pronoun agrees only with the nearest antecedent, whether singular or plural. Quick Box 31.8 (page 516) shows you this pattern. (For related material on subjects and verbs, see 31G.)

● When a diner closes, either local mice or **the owner's cat** gets **itself** a meal.
● When a diner closes, either the owner's cat or **local mice** get **themselves** a meal.

31R How do pronouns work when antecedents are indefinite pronouns?

INDEFINITE PRONOUNS usually refer to nonspecific persons, things, quantities, or ideas. But in a sentence, context clarifies an indefinite pronoun's meaning, even if the pronoun has no specific antecedent. Most indefinite pronouns are

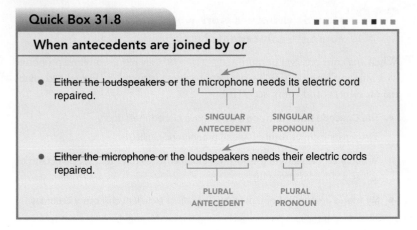

Quick Box 31.8

When antecedents are joined by *or*

- Either the loudspeakers or the microphone needs its electric cord repaired.

  SINGULAR ANTECEDENT   SINGULAR PRONOUN

- Either the microphone or the loudspeakers needs their electric cords repaired.

  PLURAL ANTECEDENT   PLURAL PRONOUN

singular. Two indefinite pronouns, *both* and *many*, are plural. A few indefinite pronouns can be singular or plural, depending on the meaning of the sentence.

For a list of indefinite pronouns, see Quick Box 31.6 in 31I. For more information about avoiding sexist language, especially with indefinite pronouns, see 31S. (For related material on subjects and verbs, see 31I.)

SINGULAR INDEFINITE PRONOUNS

- **Everyone** hopes to get **his or her** [not *their*] degree within a year.
- **Anybody** wanting to wear a cap and gown at graduation must have **his or her** [not *their*] measurements taken.
- **Each** of the students handed in **his or her** [not *their*] final term paper.

🛑 **Alert:** The use of *their* as a singular indefinite pronoun is becoming more common, even in many respectable publications. Although this usage may become standard in the future, we recommend that you avoid it. ●

SINGULAR *OR* PLURAL INDEFINITE PRONOUNS

- When winter break arrives for students, **most** leave **their** dormitories.

  Most refers to *students*, so the plural pronoun *their* is correct.

- As for the luggage, **most** is already on **its** way to the airport.

  Most refers to *luggage*, so the singular pronoun *its* is correct.

- **None** thinks that **he or she** will miss graduation.

  None is singular here, so the singular pronoun phrase *he or she* is correct.

- **None** of the students has paid **his or her** [not *their*] graduation fee yet.

  None is singular here, so the singular pronoun phrase *his or her* is correct.

- **None** are so proud as **they** who graduate.

  None is plural here, so the plural pronoun *they* is correct.

31S How do I use nonsexist pronouns?

A word is **nonsexist** when it carries neither male nor female gender. Each PRO-
NOUN in English carries one of three genders: male (*he, him, his*); female (*she,
her, hers*); or neutral (*you, your, yours, we, our, ours, them, they, their, theirs, it, its*).
Usage today favors nonsexist word choices. You therefore want to use gender-free
pronouns whenever possible. Quick Box 31.9 shows three ways to avoid using
masculine pronouns when referring to males and females together.

Questions often arise concerning the use of *he or she* and *his or her*. In
general, writers find these gender-free pronoun constructions awkward. To
avoid them, many writers make the antecedents plural. Doing this becomes
problematic when the subject is a SINGULAR INDEFINITE PRONOUN (see Quick
Box 31.6 in section 31I). In the popular press (such as newspapers and magazines), the use of the plural pronoun *they* or *them* with a singular antecedent has
been gaining favor. In ACADEMIC WRITING, however, it is better for you not to
follow the practice of the popular press. Language practice changes, however,
so what we say here is our best advice as we write this book.

Quick Box 31.9

■ ■ ■ ■ ■ ■ ■ ■ ■ ■

Avoiding the masculine pronoun when referring to males and females together

- **Solution 1:** Use a pair of pronouns—as in the phrase *he or she*. However,
  avoid using a pair more than once in a sentence or in many sentences
  in a row. A *he or she* construction acts as a singular pronoun.
  - **Everyone** hopes that **he or she** will win a scholarship.
  - A **doctor** usually has time to keep up to date only in **his or her** specialty.
- **Solution 2:** Revise into the plural.
  - **Many students** hope that **they** will win a scholarship.
  - **Most doctors** have time to keep up to date only in **their** specialties.
- **Solution 3:** Recast the sentence.
  - Everyone hopes to win a scholarship.
  - Few specialists have time for general reading.

31T How do pronouns work when antecedents are collective nouns?

A COLLECTIVE NOUN names a group of people or things, such as *family, group, audience, class, number, committee,* and *team.* When the group acts as one unit, use a singular pronoun to refer to it. When the group's members act individually, use a plural pronoun. If the sentence is awkward, substitute a plural noun for the collective noun. (For related material on subjects and verbs, see 31J.)

- The **audience** cheered as **it** stood to applaud the performers.

  The *audience* acted as one unit, so the singular pronoun *it* is correct.

- The **audience** put on **their** coats and walked out.

  The members of the audience acted as individuals, so all actions become plural; therefore, the plural pronoun *their* is correct.

- The **family** spends **its** vacation in Rockport, Maine.

  All the family members went to one place together.

If instead you wrote *The family spend their vacations in Maine, Hawaii, and Rome*, that might mean that each family member is going to a different place. You may prefer to revise that awkward sentence and use a plural noun phrase instead of a collective noun.

- The **family members** spend **their** vacations in Maine, Hawaii, and Rome.

● **EXERCISE 31-6** Underline the correct pronoun in parentheses. For help, consult 31O through 31T.

EXAMPLE

Many wonder where inventors like Benjamin Franklin get (his or her, their) creative energy.

1. Many so-called Founding Fathers are famous one or two of (his, his or her, their) accomplishments, but anyone who knows (his, her, his or her, their) history knows that Franklin is known for many things, including (his, her, his or her, their) inventions.
2. The armonica is not one of his well known inventions, but (its, their) design is ingenious.
3. Also called the glass harmonica, the armonica required a person to place (himself, herself, himself or herself) in front of the instrument and to rotate (its, their) glass bowls.
4. The lightning rod and the Franklin stove established his reputation as an inventor, but (it, they) remained in public domain because Franklin refused to secure patents for his inventions.

5. An inventor like Franklin does not limit (his, her, his or her, their) imagination to one field of science.

6. (He, She, He or she, They) can instead pursue many questions and the challenges (they, it) pose.

7. All scientists who study electricity should know that Ben Franklin provided the names (he, she, he or she, they) still use today for positive and negative electrons.

8. Franklin also named the Gulf Stream and mapped (their, its) current.

9. Franklin formed the first public lending library in America, which allowed people to borrow (its, their) books and read them at (his, her, his or her, their) leisure.

10. His public service record also includes the reform of the postal system and the establishment of The Academy and College of Philadelphia, which later merged (their, its) students with those of the State of Pennsylvania to become the University of Pennsylvania. ●

32 Adjectives and Adverbs

■ ■ ■ ■ ■ ■ ■ ■ ■ ■

Quick Points   You will learn to

➤ Distinguish between adjectives and adverbs (see 32A).
➤ Use adjectives and adverbs correctly (see 32B–32F).

32A What are the differences between adjectives and adverbs?

Although ADJECTIVES and ADVERBS both serve as modifiers—as words that describe other words—adjectives modify nouns and pronouns; adverbs modify verbs, adjectives, or other adverbs.

Watch the Video

ADJECTIVE	The **brisk** *wind* blew.
	The adjective *brisk* modifies the noun *wind*.
ADVERB	The wind *blew* **briskly**.
	The adverb *briskly* modifies the verb *blew*.

Many adverbs simply add *-ly* to an adjective (*eat swiftly, eat frequently, eat loudly*); others do not (*eat fast, eat often, eat well*). Not all words with an *-ly* ending are adverbs; some adjectives also end in *-ly* (*friendly dog*).

ESOL Tips: (1) In English, the adjective is always singular, even if its noun is plural: *The **hot** [not hots] drinks warmed us up.* (2) Word order in English restricts the placement of adjectives and adverbs: *Thomas closed* [don't place the adverb *carefully* here] *the window **carefully*** (see 54B and 54C).

● **EXERCISE 32-1**   Underline and label all adjectives (ADJ) and adverbs (ADV). Then, draw an arrow from each adjective and adverb to the word or words it modifies. Ignore *a, an,* and *the* as adjectives. For help, consult 32A.

EXAMPLE

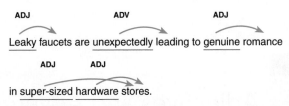

1. Today's singles carefully look for possible mates at discount home improvement stores across the country.
2. Understandably, many people find these stores a healthy alternative to dark bars and blind dates.
3. Recently, an employee in the flooring department quietly confided that the best nights for singles are Wednesdays and Thursdays, while weekends generally attract families.
4. A young single mom returns home excitedly because a quick trip to the lumber department for a new door resulted in a date for Saturday night.
5. A lonely widower in his fifties jokingly says he wishes he had developed earlier an interest in wallpapering and gardening.●

32B   When should I use adverbs—not adjectives— as modifiers?

Use only adverbs, not adjectives, to MODIFY verbs, adjectives, and other adverbs.

NO   The candidate inspired us **great**.

Adjective *great* cannot modify verb *inspired*.

YES The candidate inspired us **greatly**.

Adverb *greatly* can modify verb *inspired*.

NO The candidate felt **unusual** energetic.

Adjective *unusual* cannot modify adjective *energetic*.

YES The candidate felt **unusually** energetic.

Adverb *unusually* can modify adjective *energetic*.

NO The candidate spoke **exceptional** forcefully.

Adjective *exceptional* cannot modify adverb *forcefully*.

YES The candidate spoke **exceptionally** forcefully.

Adverb *exceptionally* modifies adverb *forcefully*.

32C What is wrong with double negatives?

A **double negative** uses two negative MODIFIERS when only one is clearly needed. Negative modifiers include *no, never, not, none, nothing, hardly, scarcely,* and *barely.*

Watch the Video

NO The factory workers will **never** vote for **no** strike.

YES The factory workers will **never** vote for **a** strike.

NO The union members did **not** have **no** money in reserve.

YES The union members did **not** have **any** money in reserve.

YES The union members had **no** money in reserve.

All verbs ending in *-n't* (*isn't, didn't, hasn't*) are also negatives (see 27D). When you use *-n't* contractions in sentences, don't add a second negative.

NO He **didn't** hear **nothing**.

YES He **didn't** hear **anything**.

NO They **haven't** had **no** meetings.

YES They **haven't** had **any** meetings.

Likewise, be careful to use the word *nor* only with *neither.*

NO Stewart **didn't** eat dinner **nor** watch television last night.

YES Stewart **didn't** eat dinner **or** watch television last night.

YES Stewart **neither** ate dinner **nor** watched television last night.

32D Do adjectives or adverbs come after linking verbs?

LINKING VERBS connect a SUBJECT to a COMPLEMENT. Always use an adjective, not an adverb, as the complement.

- The *guests looked* **happy**.

  The verb *looked* links subject *guests* to the adjective *happy*.

The words *look, feel, smell, taste, sound*, and *grow* may be linking verbs or action verbs. Use an adjective complement after a linking verb.

- Zora *looks* **happy**.

  Looks functions as a linking verb, so the adjective *happy* is correct.

- Zora *looks* **happily** at the sunset.

  Looks doesn't function as a linking verb, so the adverb *happily* is correct.

BAD, BADLY

((ᵗ●

Listen
to the
Podcast

Be alert to accepted academic usage of the words *bad* (adjective) and *badly* (adverb) after linking verbs.

> NO   The students felt **badly**.
>
> This means the students used their sense of touch badly.

> YES   The student felt **bad**.
>
> This means the student had a bad feeling about something.

> NO   The food smelled **badly**.
>
> This means the food had a bad ability to smell.

> YES   The food smelled **bad**.
>
> This means the food had a bad smell to it.

GOOD, WELL

The word *well* is used as adjective to refer only to health. Otherwise, *well* is an adverb.

- Evander seems **well**.

  The adjective *well* describes how Evander's health seems to be.

- Evander writes **well**.

  The adverb *well* describes the verb *writes*.

Use *good* as an adjective, except when you refer to health.

NO   She sings **good**.

The adjective *good* cannot describe the verb *sings*.

YES   She sings **well**.

The adverb *well* describes the verb *sings*.

● **EXERCISE 32-2** Underline the correct uses of negatives, adjectives, and adverbs by selecting between the choices in parentheses.

EXAMPLE

The Concert for Bangladesh (famous, <u>famously</u>) occurred on August 1st, 1971, and included two (<u>large</u>, largely) shows performed (energetic, <u>energetically</u>) at Madison Square Garden.

1. The concert did a (good, well) job raising awareness of the refugees who were treated (bad, badly) during the Bangladesh Liberation War and who also suffered (great, greatly) from a massive cyclone that hit the area in 1970.
2. The (high, highly) anticipated concert included several (famous, famously) musicians, who played (good, well) for the audience.
3. Members of the audience didn't (ever, never) expect to see George Harrison, who had not performed since the Beatles broke up, but he looked (happily, happy) as he played some of his (great, greatly) songs.
4. Another (notable, notably) important appearance was that of Bob Dylan, who appeared (rare, rarely) in public in the early 1970s, but he neither disappointed (nor, or) frustrated the crowd when he took the stage.
5. Many people consider this (massively, massive) show to be one of the first benefit concerts that are now more (common, commonly), and its roster of rock stars (easy, easily) makes it an important event. ●

32E What are comparative and superlative forms?

Comparison refers to a change in the form of modifiers (adjectives and adverbs) to indicate degrees of quality or intensity. When you compare two people or things, use the **comparative** form. When you compare three or more, use the **superlative** form.

Listen
to the
Podcast

REGULAR FORMS OF COMPARISON

Most adjectives and adverbs show comparison in one of two ways: either by adding *-er* or *-est* endings or by adding the words *more, most, less,* and *least* (see Quick Box 32.1 on page 524). The number of syllables in the modifier often determines which form to use.

Quick Box 32.1

Regular forms of comparison for adjectives and adverbs

POSITIVE	Use when nothing is being compared.
COMPARATIVE	Use when two things are being compared. Add the ending -er or the word more or less.
SUPERLATIVE	Use to compare three or more things. Add the ending -est or the word most or least.

Positive [1]	Comparative [2]	Superlative [3+]
green	greener	greenest
happy	happier	happiest
selfish	less selfish	least selfish
beautiful	more beautiful	most beautiful

- **One-syllable words** usually take -er and -est endings: *large, larger, largest* (adjectives); *far, farther, farthest* (adverbs).
- **Adjectives of two syllables** vary. If the word ends in -y, change the y to i and add -er, -est endings: *pretty, prettier, prettiest*. Otherwise, some two-syllable adjectives take -er, -est endings: *yellow, yellower, yellowest*. Others take *more, most* and *less, least: tangled, more tangled, most tangled; less tangled, least tangled*.
- **Adverbs of two syllables** use *more, most* and *less, least: quickly, more quickly, most quickly; less quickly, least quickly*.
- **Three-syllable words** use *more, most* and *less, least: exotic, more/most exotic, less/least exotic* (adjective); *busily, more/most busily, less/least busily* (adverb).

Alert: Be careful not to use a double comparative or double superlative. Use either the -er and -est endings or *more, most* or *less, least*.

- He was **younger** [not *more younger*] than his brother.
- Her music was the **loudest** [not *most loudest*] on the stereo. ●

IRREGULAR FORMS OF COMPARISON

Quick Box 32.2 lists *irregular* modifiers. We suggest that you memorize these for easy recall.

Quick Box 32.2

Irregular forms of comparison for adjectives and adverbs

Positive [1]	Comparative [2]	Superlative [3+]
good (*adjective*)	better	best
well (*adjective* and *adverb*)	better	best
bad (*adjective*)	worse	worst
badly (*adverb*)	worse	worst
many	more	most
much	more	most
some	more	most
little*	less	least

*When you're using *little* for items that can be counted (e.g., pickles), use the regular forms *little, littler, littlest.*

Alerts: (1) *Less* and *fewer* aren't interchangeable. Use *less* with NONCOUNT NOUNS, either items or values: *The sugar substitute has less **aftertaste**.* Use *fewer* with numbers or COUNT NOUNS: *The sugar substitute has fewer **calories**.* (2) Don't use *more, most* or *less, least* with absolute adjectives, adjectives that indicate a noncomparable quality or state, such as *unique* or *perfect*. Something either *is*, or *is not*, one of a kind. Degrees of intensity don't apply: *This teapot is **unique*** [not *the most unique*]; *The artisanship is **perfect*** [not *the most perfect*]. ●

● **EXERCISE 32-3**   Complete the chart that follows. Then, write a sentence for each word in the completed chart.

EXAMPLE

Tall, taller, tallest

The *tall* tree became *taller* over the years, but it was never the *tallest* in the forest.

Positive	Comparative	Superlative
_____	bigger	_____
slow	_____	_____
_____	more comfortable	_____
_____	_____	most attractive
lucky	_____	_____
_____	_____	happiest ●

32F Why avoid a long string of nouns as modifiers?

NOUNS sometimes MODIFY other nouns: *truck driver, train track, security system.* Usually, these combinations don't trouble readers. However, when you string together too many nouns in a row as modifiers, you challenge readers to distinguish the modifying nouns from the nouns being modified. You can revise such sentences in several ways.

REWRITE THE SENTENCE

NO   The traffic accident vehicle description form instructions are clear.

YES   The form for describing vehicles in traffic accidents has clear instructions.

CHANGE ONE NOUN TO A POSSESSIVE AND ANOTHER TO AN ADJECTIVE

NO   He will take the **United States Navy examination** for **navy engineer training**.

YES   He will take the *United States **Navy's** examination* for ***naval** engineer training*.

CHANGE ONE NOUN TO A PREPOSITIONAL PHRASE

NO   Our **student adviser training program** has won many awards.

YES   Our *training program **for student advisers*** has won many awards.

   This revision requires a change from singular *adviser* to plural *advisers*.

● **EXERCISE 32-4**   Underline the better choice in parentheses. For help, consult this entire chapter.

EXAMPLE

Alexis, a huge and powerful six-year-old Siberian tiger, (curious, <u>curiously</u>) explores her new zoo home together with five other tigers.

1. The new tiger home at the world-famous Bronx Zoo is a (special, specially) designed habitat, planted with (dense, denser) undergrowth so that it (close, closely) imitates the tigers' natural wilderness.

2. Like tigers in the wild, the six tigers in this habitat, which (more, many) experts consider the (more authentic, most authentic) of all artificial tiger environments in the world, will face some of the physical challenges and sensory experiences that keep them happy and (healthy, healthier).

3. Research shows that tigers feel (bad, badly) and fail to thrive in zoos without enrichment features placed in (good, well) locations to inspire tigers to stalk (stealthy, stealthily) through underbrush, loll (lazy, lazily) on heated rocks, or tug (vigorous, vigorously) on massive pull toys.

4. Wildlife zoologists think that the new Tiger Mountain exhibit will also serve zoo visitors (good, well) by allowing them to observe and admire the amazing strength, agility, and intelligence of a (rapid, rapidly) dwindling species.

5. Today, (fewer, less) than 5,000 Siberian tigers remain in the wild, which makes it imperative for zoos to raise people's awareness of the (great, greatest) need to prevent the extinction of these big cats that are considered among the (more, most) powerful, beautiful animals in the world. ●

Complete
the
Chapter
Exercises

33 Sentence Fragments

■ ■ ■ ■ ■ ■ ■ ■ ■

Quick Points   You will learn to

➤ Identify sentence fragments (see 33A–33B).
➤ Correct sentence fragments (see 33C–33G).
➤ Use intentional sentence fragments only when appropriate (see 33H).

33A   What is a sentence fragment?

A **sentence fragment** begins with a capital letter and ends with a period (or question mark or exclamation point), but it doesn't contain an INDEPENDENT CLAUSE. Fragments are merely unattached PHRASES or DEPENDENT CLAUSES.

Watch the Video

FRAGMENT	The rock star with many fans. [no verb]
CORRECT	The rock star with many fans toured on a special bus.
FRAGMENT	Traveled across the USA. [no subject]
CORRECT	The rock star's bus traveled across the USA.
FRAGMENT	Through the night. [a phrase without a verb or subject]
CORRECT	The rock star's bus traveled through the night.
FRAGMENT	Because the bus rolled along smoothly. [dependent clause starting with subordinating conjunction because]
CORRECT	Because the bus rolled along smoothly, the rock star slept soundly.

FRAGMENT Which allowed him to wake up refreshed. [dependent clause starting with relative pronoun *which*]

CORRECT The rock star slept soundly on the bus, which allowed him to wake up refreshed.

To learn to recognize sentence fragments, see 33B; to learn several ways to correct sentence fragments, see 33C through 33F.

The time for correcting fragments is not during DRAFTING. Instead, if you suspect you've written a sentence fragment, simply underline or highlight it and move on. Then during REVISING or EDITING, you can easily find it to check and correct.

33B How can I recognize a sentence fragment?

Quick Box 33.1 shows you how to recognize a sentence fragment. Following this Quick Box, we show how to correct each type of sentence fragment in 33C, 33D, and 33E.

Quick Box 33.1 ■ ■ ■ ■ ■ ■ ■ ■ ■

Watch
the Video

How to recognize four types of sentence fragments

1. If a word group starts with a SUBORDINATING CONJUNCTION, such as *when*, without being joined to a complete sentence, it's a sentence fragment (see 33C).

   FRAGMENT When winter comes early.

   CORRECT When winter comes early, ice often traps whales in the Arctic Ocean.

   CORRECT Winter comes early.

2. If a word group includes no VERB and ends with a period, it's a sentence fragment (see 33D).

   FRAGMENT Whales in the Arctic Ocean.

   CORRECT Whales **live** in the Arctic Ocean.

   Note that a VERBAL (the ones ending in *-ing* or *-ed*) is not a verb unless it teams up with an AUXILIARY VERB, such as *is* or *are* (see 33D). Verbals beginning with *to*, called INFINITIVES, remain as verbals. Auxiliary verbs have no effect on them.

——— continued >> ———

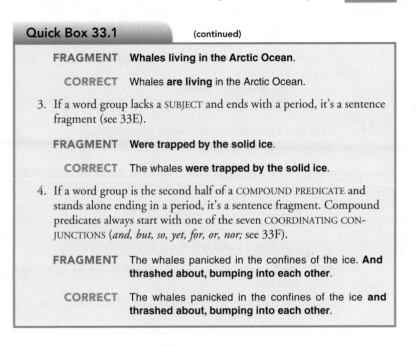

Quick Box 33.1 (continued)

> FRAGMENT **Whales living in the Arctic Ocean**.
>
> CORRECT Whales **are living** in the Arctic Ocean.
>
> 3. If a word group lacks a SUBJECT and ends with a period, it's a sentence fragment (see 33E).
>
> FRAGMENT **Were trapped by the solid ice.**
>
> CORRECT The whales **were trapped by the solid ice**.
>
> 4. If a word group is the second half of a COMPOUND PREDICATE and stands alone ending in a period, it's a sentence fragment. Compound predicates always start with one of the seven COORDINATING CONJUNCTIONS (*and, but, so, yet, for, or, nor;* see 33F).
>
> FRAGMENT The whales panicked in the confines of the ice. **And thrashed about, bumping into each other.**
>
> CORRECT The whales panicked in the confines of the ice **and thrashed about, bumping into each other**.

● **EXERCISE 33-1** Identify each word group as either a complete sentence or a fragment. If the word group is a sentence, circle its number. If it's a fragment, tell why it's incomplete. For help, see Quick Box 33.1.

EXAMPLE

Although having a five-year-old Twinkie might not seem desirable.

[Fragment. Starts with a subordinating conjunction (although) and lacks an independent clause to complete the thought.]

1. Because scientists are working on making foods "indestructible."
2. New preservation technologies responsible for bread puddings that can last four years.
3. Success with current experiments might mean people having to buy groceries only once a month.
4. That people on limited budgets won't have to throw away as much food.
5. Solves three challenges in making food last longer: controlling moisture, exposure to air, and bacteria and molds.
6. "Super sandwiches" packaged with chemicals that absorb oxygen can last three to five years.
7. To control bacteria, sterilizing food in a pouch subjected to pressures of 87,000 pounds per square inch.

8. Because of their tough protein fibers, meat products stand up particularly well to new preserving techniques.
9. Although victims of disasters like earthquakes, floods, and fires benefit from foods that can be stockpiled.
10. Stores with less need of refrigeration. ●

33C How can I correct a fragment that starts with a subordinating word?

First, you want to become entirely familiar with the list of SUBORDINATING CONJUNCTIONS (complete list appears in section 28I). If a word group starts with a subordinating conjunction without being joined to a complete sentence, it's a sentence fragment.

FRAGMENT	**Because the ship had to cut through the ice.**
CORRECT	**Because the ship had to cut through the ice**, the rescue effort took time.

The sentence fragment starts with the subordinating conjunction *because* and ends in a period, so it's a word group, not a complete sentence. Attaching the fragment to the start of an added complete sentence corrects the error.

CORRECT	The rescue effort took time **because the ship had to cut through the ice**.

Attaching the fragment to the end of an added complete sentence corrects the error.

CORRECT	**The ship had to cut through the ice.**

Dropping the subordinating conjunction *because* from the fragment corrects the error.

FRAGMENT	**Although the ice was twelve inches thick.**
CORRECT	**Although the ice was twelve inches thick**, the Russian icebreaker moved quickly.
CORRECT	The Russian icebreaker moved quickly, **although the ice was twelve inches thick**.

The fragment starts with the subordinating conjunction *although* and ends in a period, so it's just a word group. Attaching the fragment to a complete sentence corrects the error.

CORRECT	**The ice was twelve inches thick.**

Dropping the subordinating conjunction *although* eliminates the fragment.

Unless they start a question, the subordinating words *who* or *which* create a special type of sentence fragment.

> **FRAGMENT**   **Who thought the whales might panic from fear of the ship's noise.**
>
> **CORRECT**   The ship's loud motor worried the crew, **who thought the whales might panic from fear of the ship's noise**.
>
> Attaching the *who* fragment at the end of the complete sentence where it makes sense corrects the error.

> **FRAGMENT**   **Which sent booming sound waves through the water.**
>
> **CORRECT**   The ship's loud motor, **which sent booming sound waves through the water**, worried the crew.
>
> Placing the *which* fragment in the middle of the complete sentence where it makes sense corrects the error.

> **CORRECT**   The ship's loud motor, **which sent booming sound waves through the water**, worried the crew, **who thought the whales might panic from fear of the ship's noise**.
>
> Combining both the *who* and *which* sentence fragments with the complete sentence creates a richly textured message.

33D   How can I correct a fragment that lacks a verb?

If a word group includes no VERB and ends with a period, it's a sentence fragment. In looking for a verb, don't mistake a verbal for a complete verb. Verbals ending in *-ing* or *-ed* become verbs only when teamed up with an AUXILIARY VERB. Verbals beginning with *to*, called INFINITIVES, remain as verbals; auxiliary verbs have no effect on them.

> **FRAGMENT**   The sailors **debating** whether **to play** classical music over the ship's sound system.
>
> **CORRECT**   The sailors **were debating** whether **to play** classical music over the ship's sound system.
>
> Adding the auxiliary verb *were* to *debating* creates a complete verb, which corrects the error.

> **FRAGMENT**   The ship's crew **working** against time **to outrun** the hungry polar bears near the whales.
>
> **CORRECT**   The ship's crew **was working** against time **to outrun** the hungry polar bears near the whales.
>
> Adding the auxiliary verb *were* to *working* creates a complete verb, which corrects the error.

An APPOSITIVE is a descriptive word group that lacks a verb, so it can't stand alone as a sentence. An appositive needs to be placed within a sentence immediately next to what it describes.

FRAGMENT   **With their powerful sense of smell.** The polar bears ran toward nearby openings in the ice.

CORRECT   **With their powerful sense of smell,** the polar bears ran toward nearby openings in the ice.

CORRECT   The polar bears, **with their powerful sense of smell,** ran toward nearby openings in the ice.

The appositive placed immediately next to "the polar bears" within the sentence corrects the error.

FRAGMENT   **An enormously powerful icebreaker.** The ship arrived to free the whales.

CORRECT   **An enormously powerful icebreaker,** the ship arrived to free the whales.

CORRECT   The ship, **an enormously powerful icebreaker,** arrived to free the whales.

The appositive placed immediately next to "the ship" within the sentence corrects the error.

If a TRANSITIONAL EXPRESSION (complete list in 6G) starts a word group that lacks a verb, it's a sentence fragment.

FRAGMENT   **Therefore,** the hungry polar bears.

CORRECT   **Therefore, the polar bears were hungry.**

CORRECT   **Therefore, the hungry polar bears** knew they might soon have a feast.

The sentence fragment revised into a complete sentence or attached to a nearby sentence corrects the error.

FRAGMENT   **For example, Bach's sonatas for flute.**

CORRECT   The ship's crew chose **Bach's sonatas for flute.**

CORRECT   The crew wanted to play high-pitched music, **for example Bach's sonatas for flute.**

The sentence fragment revised into a complete sentence or attached to a nearby sentence corrects the error.

33E How can I correct a fragment that lacks a subject?

If a word group lacks a SUBJECT and ends with a period, it's a sentence fragment.

FRAGMENT **Had heard recordings of the high-pitched calls whales make.**

CORRECT Some crew members **had heard recordings of the high-pitched calls whales make**.

Inserting the subject *Some crew members* at the start of the fragment corrects the error.

FRAGMENT **Allowed some local inhabitants to take a few whales for much-needed food.**

CORRECT The icebreaker's captain **allowed some local inhabitants to take a few whales for much-needed food**.

Inserting the subject *The icebreaker's captain* at the start of the fragment corrects the error.

33F How can I correct a fragment that's a part of a compound predicate?

Many types of COMPOUND PREDICATES occur in sentences. One type contains two or more verbs connected by a COORDINATING CONJUNCTION (*and, but, for, or, nor, yet, so*). When a compound predicate isn't attached to the end of its companion sentence, it is a sentence fragment.

FRAGMENT With a flute concerto playing loudly on its speakers, the ship finally reached the whales. **And led them to freedom.**

CORRECT With a flute concerto playing loudly on its speakers, the ship finally reached the whales **and led them to freedom**.

Joining the compound predicate to the end of the complete sentence corrects the error.

CORRECT With a flute concerto playing loudly on its speakers, the ship finally reached the whales. **The ship led them to freedom.**

Dropping *and* and inserting a subject "the ship" corrects the error.

FRAGMENT The international media wrote about the amazing rescue of the trapped whales. **And the story spread throughout the world.**

CORRECT The international media wrote about the amazing rescue of the trapped whales, **and the story spread throughout the world.**

Joining the compound predicate to the end of the complete sentence corrects the error.

CORRECT   The international media wrote about the amazing rescue of the trapped whales. **The story spread throughout the world**.

Dropping *and* and inserting a subject "the story" corrects the error.

● **EXERCISE 33-2**   Find and correct any sentence fragments. If a sentence is correct, circle its number. For help, consult 33A through 33F.

EXAMPLE

Even though lice are a common problem for young children.
Correct: Lice are a common problem for young children.

1. Even though lice are not dangerous and do not spread disease, parents tend to worry about their children. Who have been infected with this parasite.
2. Although good hygiene is important, it does not prevent lice infestation. Which can occur on clean, healthy scalps.
3. Spread only through direct contact. Lice are unable to fly or jump.
4. Evidence of lice has been found on ancient Egyptian mummies, which suggests that lice have been annoying humans for a long time.
5. While lice can spread among humans who share combs or pillows or hats. Lice cannot be spread from pets to humans.
6. Doctors may prescribe special shampoos and soaps. To help get rid of the lice on a child's head.
7. Because lice do not like heat, experts recommend putting infected sheets and stuffed animals and pillows in a dryer for thirty minutes.
8. Just one is called a *louse*, and a louse egg is called a *nit*. Which is where we get the words *lousy* and *nit-pick*.
9. Using a hair dryer after applying a scalp treatment can be dangerous. Because some treatments contain flammable ingredients.
10. Although lice cannot live for more than twenty-four hours without human contact. ●

● **EXERCISE 33-3**   Go back to Exercise 33-1 and revise the sentence fragments into complete sentences. In some cases, you may be able to combine two fragments into one complete sentence. ●

33G How can I correct a list that is a fragment?

Two special fragment problems involve lists and examples. Lists and examples must be part of a complete sentence, unless they are formatted as a column.

You can correct a list fragment by attaching it to the preceding independent clause using a colon or a dash. You can correct an example fragment by attaching it to an independent clause (with or without punctuation, depending on the meaning) or by rewriting it as a complete sentence.

FRAGMENT   You have a choice of desserts. **Carrot cake, chocolate silk pie, apple pie, or peppermint ice cream.**

The list cannot stand on its own as a sentence.

CORRECT   You have a choice of desserts: carrot cake, chocolate silk pie, apple pie, or peppermint ice cream.

CORRECT   You have a choice of desserts—carrot cake, chocolate silk pie, apple pie, or peppermint ice cream.

FRAGMENT   Several good places offer brunch. **For example, the restaurants Sign of the Dove and Blue Yonder.**

Examples can't stand on their own as a sentence.

CORRECT   Several good places offer brunch—**for example**, the restaurants Sign of the Dove and Blue Yonder.

CORRECT   Several good places offer brunch. **Two examples are** the restaurants Sign of the Dove and Blue Yonder.

33H   How can I recognize intentional fragments?

Professional writers sometimes intentionally use fragments for emphasis and effect.

> But in the main, I feel like a brown bag of miscellany propped against a wall. Pour out the contents, and there is discovered a jumble of small things priceless and worthless. **A first-water diamond, an empty spool, bits of broken glass, lengths of string, a key to a door long since crumbled away, a rusty knife-blade, old shoes saved for a road that never was and never will be, a nail bent under the weight of things too heavy for any nail, a dried flower or two still a little fragrant.**
>
> —Zora Neale Hurston, *How It Feels to Be Colored Me*

Today, such fragments are also common in popular magazines and advertisements. A writer's ability to judge the difference between acceptable and unacceptable sentence fragments comes from much experience writing and from reading the works of skilled writers. Some instructors consider a sentence fragment an error; other teachers occasionally accept well-placed intentional fragments after a student has shown the consistent ability to write well-constructed complete sentences. Therefore, if you'd like to use a fragment for emphasis and effect, we advise that you either ask for your teacher's permission ahead of time or write a footnote to your essay that says you're using a sentence fragment intentionally and why.

● **EXERCISE 33-4** Revise this paragraph to eliminate all sentence fragments. In some cases, you can combine word groups to create complete sentences; in other cases, you must supply missing elements to rewrite. Some sentences may not require revision. In your final version, check not only the individual sentences but also the clarity of the whole paragraph. For help, consult 33B through 33F.

EXAMPLE

Although the subject of many amusing anecdotes. Diogenes remains an influential figure in Greek philosophy.

Correct: Although the subject of many amusing anecdotes, Diogenes remains an influential figure in Greek philosophy.

(1) Throughout his career as a philosopher and Cynic, Diogenes cultivated a following. That included the likes of Aristotle and Alexander the Great. (2) Diogenes was an important member of the Cynics, a group of people who rejected conventional life. The word *Cynic* comes from the Greek word for dog. (3) Diogenes lived like a beggar and slept in a tub. Which he carried around with him wherever he went. (4) He rejected the pursuit of wealth and once destroyed his wooden bowl. Because he saw a peasant boy drinking water with his hands. (5) Although none of his writings have survived, Diogenes produced dialogues and a play. That allegedly describes a social utopia in which people live unconventional lives. (6) Since he often walked around Athens in broad daylight with a lamp looking for an honest man. (7) When Plato defined *man* as a featherless biped, Diogenes plucked a chicken and said, "Here is Plato's man." (8) According to legend, Diogenes was once sunbathing when he was approached by Alexander the Great. Who was a fan of the eccentric Cynic. (9) Alexander asked if he could do anything for Diogenes. Which the philosopher answered by saying, "Don't block my sunlight." (10) Because Diogenes is a strange and interesting character. He has inspired works by such writers and artists as William Blake, Anton Chekhov, and Rabelais. ●

● **EXERCISE 33-5** Revise this paragraph to eliminate all sentence fragments. In some cases, you can combine word groups to create complete sentences; in other cases, you must supply missing elements to revise word groups. Some sentences may not require revision. In your final version, check not only the individual sentences but also the clarity of the whole paragraph. Refer to 33A through 33E for help.

(1) The English games cricket and rounders. (2) Are the forerunners of the American game baseball. (3) Which became popular in America in the nineteenth century. (4) According to the *New York Morning News*, in an article

from 1845. (5) Members of the New York Knickerbockers Club played the first reported baseball game. (6) Taking place at Elysian Fields in Hoboken, New Jersey. (7) Creating one of baseball's first teams, and writing "20 Original Rules of Baseball." (8) Alexander Cartwright is often called The Father of Baseball. (9) By scholars and historians of the game. (10) His new rules, which became known as Knickerbocker Rules. (11) Changed baseball in a number of ways. (12) Such as giving each batter three strikes and each inning three outs. (13) The first game, therefore. (14) That used the Knickerbocker Rules was played on June 19, 1846, in New Jersey. (15) Acting as umpire for this game. (16) Cartwright charged six-cent fines for swearing. (17) The Knicker-bockers lost this game by 22 points to a team. (18) That was known as "The New York Nine." ●

Complete
the
Chapter
Exercises

34 Comma Splices and Run-On Sentences

Quick Points   You will learn to

➤ Identify comma splices and run-on sentences (see 34A–34B).
➤ Correct comma splices and run-on sentences (see 34C–34G).

34A   What are comma splices and run-on sentences?

A **comma splice**, also called a *comma fault*, occurs when a comma, rather than a period, is used incorrectly between two or more complete sentences.

A **run-on sentence**, also called a *fused sentence* or a *run-together sentence*, occurs when two complete sentences run into each other without any punctuation. Comma splices and run-on sentences create confusion because readers can't tell where one thought ends and another begins.

COMMA SPLICE	The icebergs broke off from the **glacier, they** drifted into the sea.
RUN-ON SENTENCE	The icebergs broke off from the **glacier they** drifted into the sea.
CORRECT	The icebergs broke off from the **glacier. They** drifted into the sea.

There is one exception. A comma is correct between two independent clauses if the comma is followed by one of the seven coordinating conjunctions: *and, but, for, or, nor, yet, so*. See Chapter 42.

> **CORRECT** The icebergs broke off from the glacier, **and** they drifted into the sea.

! **Alert:** Occasionally, when your meaning suggests it, you can use a colon or a dash to join two independent clauses. ●

During DRAFTING, if you suspect that you've written a comma splice or a run-on sentence, simply underline or highlight it in boldface or italics, and move on. Later, you can easily find it to check and correct during REVISING and EDITING.

34B How can I recognize comma splices and run-on sentences?

When you know how to recognize an INDEPENDENT CLAUSE, you'll know how to recognize COMMA SPLICES and RUN-ON SENTENCES. An independent clause contains a SUBJECT and a PREDICATE and can stand alone as a complete sentence. Also, an independent clause doesn't begin with a SUBORDINATING CONJUNCTION or a RELATIVE PRONOUN, words that create dependence.

Interestingly, almost all comma splices and run-on sentences are caused by only four patterns. If you become familiar with these four patterns, listed in Quick Box 34.1, you'll more easily locate them in your writing.

! **Alert:** To proofread for comma splices, cover all words on one side of the comma and see if the words remaining form an independent clause. If they do, next cover all words you left uncovered, on the other side of the comma. If the second side of the comma is also an independent clause, you're looking at a comma splice. (This technique doesn't work for run-on sentences because a comma isn't present.) ●

Experienced writers sometimes use a comma to join very short independent clauses, especially if one independent clause is negative and the other is positive: *Mosquitoes don't bite, they stab*. In ACADEMIC WRITING, you'll be safe if you use a period or a semicolon, if the two independent clauses are closely related in meaning: *Mosquitoes don't bite; they stab*.

Quick Box 34.1

Detecting comma splices and run-on sentences

Watch
the Video

- Watch out for a PERSONAL PRONOUN starting the second independent clause.

  NO   The physicist Marie Curie discovered **radium, she** won two Nobel Prizes.

  YES   The physicist Marie Curie discovered **radium. She** won two Nobel Prizes.

- Watch out for a CONJUNCTIVE ADVERB (such as *furthermore, however, similarly, therefore*, and *then;* see Quick Box 28.5, section 28G, for a complete list) starting the second independent clause.

  NO   Marie Curie and her husband, Pierre, worked together at **first, however**, he died tragically at age forty-seven.

  YES   Marie Curie and her husband, Pierre, worked together at **first. However**, he died tragically at age forty-seven.

- Watch out for a TRANSITIONAL EXPRESSION (such as *in addition, for example, in contrast, of course*, and *meanwhile;* see Quick Box 6.4, section 6G.1, for a complete list) starting the second independent clause.

  NO   Marie Curie and her husband won a Nobel Prize for the discovery of **radium, in addition, Marie** herself won another Nobel Prize for her work on the atomic weight of radium.

  YES   Marie Curie and her husband won a Nobel Prize for the discovery of **radium; in addition, Marie** herself won another Nobel Prize for her work on the atomic weight of radium.

- Watch out for a second independent clause that explains, contrasts with, or gives an example of what's said in the first independent clause.

  NO   Marie Curie died of leukemia in **1934, exposure** to radioactivity killed her.

  YES   Marie Curie died of leukemia in **1934. Exposure** to radioactivity killed her.

34C How do I use a period to correct comma splices and run-on sentences?

You can use a period to correct comma splices and run-on sentences by placing the period between the two sentences.

COMMA SPLICE	A shark is all **cartilage, it** has no bones in its body.
RUN-ON SENTENCE	A shark is all **cartilage it** has no bones in its body.
CORRECT	A shark is all **cartilage. It** has no bones in its body.
COMMA SPLICE	Sharks can smell blood from a quarter mile **away, they** then swim toward the source like a guided missile.
RUN-ON SENTENCE	Sharks can smell blood from a quarter mile **away they** then swim toward the source like a guided missile.
CORRECT	Sharks can smell blood from a quarter mile **away. They** then swim toward the source like a guided missile.

34D How do I use a semicolon to correct comma splices and run-on sentences?

You can use a semicolon to correct comma splices and run-on sentences by placing the semicolon between the two sentences. Use a semicolon only when the separate sentences are closely related in meaning.

COMMA SPLICE	The great white shark supposedly eats **humans, research** shows that most white sharks spit them out after one bite.
RUN-ON SENTENCE	The great white shark supposedly eats **humans research** shows that most white sharks spit them out after one bite.
CORRECT	The great white shark supposedly eats **humans; research** shows that most white sharks spit them out after one bite.

34E How do I use a comma and a coordinating conjunction to correct comma splices and run-on sentences?

Watch the Video

You can correct a comma splice or a run-on sentence by inserting a comma followed by a coordinating conjunction (*and, but, for, or, nor, yet, so*) between the two independent clauses (42B).

When you use a coordinating conjunction, be sure that your choice fits the meaning of the material. *And* signals addition; *but* and *yet* signal contrast; *for* and *so* signal cause; and *or* and *nor* signal alternatives.

COMMA SPLICE	All living creatures send weak electrical charges in **water, a shark** skin can detect these signals.
RUN-ON SENTENCE	All living creatures send weak electrical charges in **water a shark** can detect these signals.
CORRECT	All living creatures send weak electrical charges in **water,** and **a shark** can detect these signals.

● **EXERCISE 34-1**   Revise the comma splices and run-on sentences by using a period, a semicolon, or a comma and coordinating conjunction.

EXAMPLE

Near the town of Bluffdale, Utah, in a desert valley by the Wasatch Range, is a massive building five times the size of the U.S. Capitol it will soon be filled with computers and intelligence experts.

Revised: Near the town of Bluffdale, Utah, in a desert valley by the Wasatch Range, is a massive building five times the size of the U.S. Capitol. It will soon be filled with computers and intelligence experts.

1. The Utah Data Center will store vast amounts of emails, cell phone calls, Internet searches, and other personal data, for example, agents will be able to track down everything from parking receipts to plane ticket information.
2. However, this $2 billion complex is designed to do more than serve as a warehouse of digital data breaking codes will be one of its major efforts.
3. The National Security agency is in charge of the Utah Data Center and will handle the data analysis, code breaking, and recommendations for action information gathered may prevent criminal or terrorist actions, increasing American security.
4. Some people worry that the center may exceed traditional security practices, it will have the capacity and even the mission to collect and analyze billions of messages from American citizens, storing trillions of pieces of data.
5. In an age where personal computers can routinely store as much as one or two terabytes of data, the capacity of the new data center is staggering, able to hold over a yottabyte equal to over 500 quintillion pages of text, a yottabyte is more than the total amount of human knowledge ever created. ●

34F   How do I use clauses to correct comma splices and run-on sentences?

You can correct a comma splice or run-on sentence by revising one of the two independent clauses into a dependent clause when one idea can logically be subordinated to the other. Also, be careful never to end the dependent clause with a period or semicolon. If you do, you've created a SENTENCE FRAGMENT.

CREATE DEPENDENT CLAUSES WITH SUBORDINATING CONJUNCTIONS

One way to create a dependent clause is to insert a SUBORDINATING CONJUNCTION (such as *because, although, when,* and *if*—see Quick Box 28.7, section 28I, for a complete list). Always choose a subordinating conjunction that fits the meaning of each particular sentence. Dependent clauses that begin with a subordinating conjunction are called ADVERB CLAUSES.

COMMA SPLICE	Homer and Langley Collyer had packed their house from top to bottom with **junk, police** could not open the front door to investigate a reported smell.
RUN-ON SENTENCE	Homer and Langley Collyer had packed their house from top to bottom with **junk police** could not open the front door to investigate a reported smell.
CORRECT	**Because** Homer and Langley Collyer had packed their house from top to bottom with **junk, police** could not open the front door to investigate a reported smell.

Because starts a dependent clause that is joined by a comma with the independent clause starting with *police*.

COMMA SPLICE	Old newspapers and car parts filled every room to the **ceiling, enough** space remained for fourteen pianos.
RUN-ON SENTENCE	Old newspapers and car parts filled every room to the **ceiling enough** space remained for fourteen pianos.
CORRECT	**Although** old newspapers and car parts filled every room to the **ceiling, enough** space remained for fourteen pianos.

The subordinating conjunction *although* starts a dependent clause that is joined by a comma with the independent clause starting with *enough*.

🅐 Alert: Place a comma between an introductory dependent clause and the independent clause that follows (see 42C). ●

CREATE DEPENDENT CLAUSES WITH RELATIVE PRONOUNS

You can create a dependent clause with a RELATIVE PRONOUN (*who, whom, whose, which, that*). Dependent clauses with a relative pronoun are called ADJECTIVE CLAUSES.

COMMA SPLICE	The Collyers had been crushed under a pile of **debris, the debris** had toppled onto the men.
RUN-ON SENTENCE	The Collyers had been crushed under a pile of **debris the debris** toppled onto the men.

CORRECT	The Collyers had been crushed under a pile of **debris *that* had toppled** onto the men.

The relative pronoun *that* starts a dependent clause and is joined with the independent clause starting with *The Collyers*, after deletion of *the debris*.

Alert: Sometimes you need commas to set off an adjective clause from the rest of the sentence. This happens only when the adjective is NONRESTRICTIVE (nonessential), so check carefully (see 42F). ●

● **EXERCISE 34-2** Working individually or with your peer-response group, identify and then revise the comma splices and run-on sentences. Circle the numbers of correct sentences.

Explore the Exercise

EXAMPLE

COMMA SPLICE	Basketball was invented in 1891, today, it is one of the world's most popular sports.
RUN-ON SENTENCE	Basketball was invented in 1891 today, it is one of the world's most popular sports.
CORRECT	Basketball was invented in 1891; today, it is one of the world's most popular sports.

1. James Naismith, a physical education professor at what is known today as Springfield College, needed an indoor sport for his students to play on rainy days, he invented basketball.
2. At first, he didn't use a net he used a peach basket.
3. Dribbling, the act of bouncing the ball between passes and shots, did not become common in basketball until much later, originally, players merely carried the ball.
4. Backboards were also not introduced until later, this kept fans from being able to interfere with the action.
5. Without balls made specifically for the sport, early basketball players had to use soccer balls in the 1950s, Tony Hinkle introduced the now famous orange balls that are easier for players and spectators to see.
6. The first official basketball game was played in 1892 in Albany, New York, only one point was scored.
7. Founded in 1946, the National Basketball Association (NBA) began with the help of owners of ice hockey arenas, many consider the game between the Toronto Huskies and the New York Knickerbockers in 1946 as the first official NBA game.
8. Although a three-point rule was first used in 1933, the NBA did not officially add the rule until 1979, the year that Larry Bird and Magic Johnson began playing professionally.

9. On March 2nd, 1962, in Hershey, Pennsylvania, Wilt Chamberlain, playing for the Philadelphia Warriors, scored a record 100 points in one game his average for the season was 50.4 points per game.

10. Now a worldwide sport, basketball debuted in the Olympics in 1936, the United States defeated Canada in a game played outdoors. ●

34G How do I use adverbs and transitions to correct comma splices and run-on sentences?

CONJUNCTIVE ADVERBS and other TRANSITIONAL EXPRESSIONS link ideas between sentences. When these words fall between sentences, a period or semicolon must immediately precede them, and a comma usually follows them.

Conjunctive adverbs include such words as *however, therefore, hence, next, then, thus, furthermore,* and *nevertheless* (see Quick Box 28.5, section 28G, for a complete list). Be careful to remember that conjunctive adverbs are not COORDINATING CONJUNCTIONS (*and, but,* and so on; see 34C.3).

COMMA SPLICE	Hannibal wanted to conquer Rome**, hence,** he crossed the Alps.
RUN-ON SENTENCE	Hannibal wanted to conquer Rome **hence,** he crossed the Alps.
CORRECT	Hannibal wanted to conquer Rome**. Hence,** he crossed the Alps.
CORRECT	Hannibal wanted to conquer Rome**; hence,** he crossed the Alps.

Transitional expressions include *for example, for instance, in addition, in fact, of course,* and *on the one hand/on the other hand* (see Quick Box 6.4, section 6G, for a complete list).

COMMA SPLICE	Hannibal enjoyed much public acclaim**, for** example, he achieved both military and political success.
RUN-ON SENTENCE	Hannibal enjoyed much public acclaim **for** example, he achieved both military and political success.
CORRECT	Hannibal enjoyed much public acclaim**. For** example, he achieved both military and political success.
CORRECT	Hannibal enjoyed much public acclaim**; for** example, he achieved both military and political success.

❶ **Alert:** A conjunctive adverb or a transitional expression is usually followed by a comma when it starts a sentence (see 42C). ●

● **EXERCISE 34-3** Revise comma splices or run-on sentences caused by incorrectly punctuated conjunctive adverbs or other transitional expressions. If a sentence is correct, circle its number.

however	therefore	also	next	then	thus
furthermore	nevertheless	indeed	for example		

EXAMPLE

Las Vegas is a large and popular city in Nevada known for entertainment and gambling, nevertheless, it was once a small, desert city.

Corrected: Las Vegas is a large and popular city in Nevada known for entertainment and gambling. Nevertheless, it was once a small, desert city.

1. When Las Vegas was first counted by the U.S. Census in 1910, it was a tiny town, indeed, the entire county only had 3,000 people.
2. Only a hundred years later, however, the population had ballooned to over half a million people.
3. Las Vegas remained a small railroad town for the first couple of decades of the twentieth century, then, when the nearby Hoover Dam was built in 1935, Las Vegas began to grow.
4. Other factors contributed to the growth of Las Vegas, for example, gambling was legalized in 1931 and many scientists moved there during World War II to work on the Manhattan Project.
5. Las Vegas is now famous for its gambling, therefore, it is sometimes known as "Sin City." ●

● **EXERCISE 34-4** Revise all comma splices and run-on sentences, using as many different methods of correction as you can.

(1) Energy psychology represents fairly new methods joining Eastern lines of thought to the mind and body and Western psychology and psychotherapy, according to an article by Leonard Holmes, PhD, proponents of energy psychology contend that striking acupuncture points and at the same time recalling an anxiety-producing incident can alleviate anxiety and phobias. (2) Holmes inquires whether this idea is true in fact, he goes on to question the connection the acupuncture points have to anxiety. (3) In the early 1980s, Roger Callahan, PhD, popularized procedures utilizing energy psychology, he called the procedures "The Callahan Technique" or "Thought Field Therapy." (4) In the beginning, Callahan's training programs were costly, generally hundreds of dollars, now, on the other hand, they are moderately priced. (5) Other therapists such as clinical psychologist David Feinstein, PhD, have joined the ranks promoting energy psychology, interestingly, Feinstein sells an interactive CD-ROM that presents guidance

in energy psychology/psychotherapy. (6) A qualified therapist can use the CD-ROM laypersons should not experiment with the contents of the CD-ROM. (7) Today, proponents of energy psychology contend it results in the successful handling of problems such as trauma, abuse, depression, and addictive cravings, other uses for energy psychology, or "Emotional Freedom Techniques" (EFT), as Gary Craig calls them on his Web site, include treatment for medical conditions such as headaches and breathing difficulties. (8) Craig, not a licensed health professional, contends the "missing piece to the healing puzzle" is EFT he quotes from supposedly scientific clinical trials indicating that patients have seen dramatic results in their conditions because of EFT. (9) Holmes thinks energy psychotherapy is still too early in its development to be widely applied he cautions the general public to avoid trying it on their own. (10) Holmes advises extreme caution for psychologists about continuing to use EFT more needs to be known from research. ●

Complete
the
Chapter
Exercises

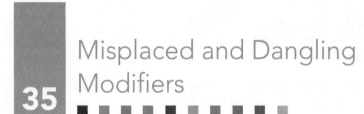

Misplaced and Dangling Modifiers

35

Quick Points   You will learn to

➤ Place modifiers carefully so that your intended meaning is clear (see 35A–35E).

MISPLACED MODIFIERS

35A   What is a misplaced modifier?

Watch
the Video

A MODIFIER is a word or group of words that describes or limits another word or group of words. A **misplaced modifier** is positioned incorrectly in a sentence, which means that it describes another word and changes the writer's meaning. Always place a modifier as close as possible to what it describes.

AVOIDING SQUINTING MODIFIERS

A misplaced **squinting modifier** can modify both the words before it and after it. Position your modifiers to communicate the meaning you intend.

NO   The speaker addressing us loudly condemned unions.

   Which happened loudly, addressing or condemning?

YES   Addressing us loudly, the speaker condemned unions.

YES   The speaker addressing us condemned unions loudly.

PLACING LIMITING WORDS CAREFULLY

Words such as *only, not only, just, not just, almost, hardly, nearly, even, exactly, merely, scarcely*, and *simply* can change the meaning of a sentence according to their placement. Note how placement of *only* changes the meaning of this sentence: *Professional coaches say that high salaries motivate players.*

- **Only** professional coaches say that high salaries motivate players.

  No one else says this.

- Professional coaches **only** say that high salaries motivate players.

  The coaches probably do not mean what they say.

- Professional coaches say **only** that high salaries motivate players.

  The coaches say nothing else.

- Professional coaches say that **only** high salaries motivate players.

  Nothing except high salaries motivates players.

- Professional coaches say that high salaries **only** motivate players.

  High salaries do nothing other than motivate players.

- Professional coaches say that high salaries motivate **only** players.

  High salaries motivate the players but no one else.

35B   How can I avoid split infinitives?

An INFINITIVE is a verb preceded by the word *to:* I want *to design* boldly. A **split infinitive** occurs when words are placed between *to* and its verb: I want *to boldly design.* Often, the effect is awkward.

NO   The student tried **to in some way pacify** his instructor.

   In some way is misplaced because it splits *to pacify.*

YES The student tried **to pacify** his instructor in some way.

YES In some way, the student tried **to pacify** his instructor.

Sometimes a split infinitive can actually achieve clarity or emphasis. Consider how the meaning changes in the sentence below, depending on whether the infinitive is split.

- She wanted *to more than double* her earnings.
- She wanted *to double more than* her earnings.

When you create clarity or achieve emphasis by splitting your infinitive, split freely.

35C How can I avoid other splits in my sentences?

Separation of closely related sentence elements, such as a subject and its verb or a verb and its object, causes your readers to lose meaningful connections between these words.

NO The announcer of Orson Wells's radio drama "War of the Worlds," because the script opened with a graphic descriptions of emergency broadcasts, convinced many people that the Earth was being invaded by Martians.

Readers lose the connection between the subject *announcer* and its verb *convinced*.

YES Because the script opened with graphic descriptions of emergency broadcasts, the announcer of Orson Wells's radio drama "War of the Worlds" convinced many people that the Earth was being invaded by Martians.

Readers easily grasp the connection between subject *announcer* and verb *convinced*.

NO Many churches **held** for their frightened communities **"end of the world" prayer services**.

Readers lose the connection between verb *held* and object *prayer services*.

YES Many churches **held "end of the world" prayer services** for their frightened communities.

Readers easily grasp the connection between verb *held* and object *prayer services*.

● **EXERCISE 35-1** Revise these ten sentences to correct misplaced modifiers, split infinitives, and other splits. If a sentence is correct, circle its number. For help, consult 35A through 35C.

EXAMPLE

The city of Deadwood is known for its many notorious residents made popular by a TV show including Wild Bill Hickok and Calamity Jane.

Made popular by a TV show, the city of Deadwood is known for its many notorious residents, including Wild Bill Hickok and Calamity Jane.

1. Deadwood, because of its location near the Deadwood Gulch and the Black Hills of South Dakota, was named for the dead trees found in that canyon.
2. The city's founding, during a gold rush that attracted a quarter of a million miners to the area, was in 1876.
3. The main source of revenue for the city was gambling, which was outlawed in 1905 but reinstated in 1989.
4. Today, tourists who visit Deadwood often gamble and enjoy the historical reenactments of the town's famous events.
5. Deadwood nearly was the home to a dozen of famous characters from the Old West.
6. Serving as the sheriff of Hays City and Abilene, Wild Bill Hickok worked to with an iron fist tame the lawless towns of the frontier.
7. Hickok moved to Deadwood after he without much success performed in a Wild West show.
8. During a poker game at Nuttall & Mann's saloon, Jack McCall shot for unknown reasons Will Bill.
9. The cards Hickok was holding included a pair of black aces, a pair of black eights, and an unknown fifth card now known as the dead man's hand.
10. The legends of Deadwood and Wild Bill in the stories of fiction writers and TV shows continue to grow. ●

● **EXERCISE 35-2** Using each list of words and phrases, create all the possible logical sentences. Insert commas as needed. Explain differences in meaning among the alternatives you create. For help, consult 35A through 35C.

> **EXAMPLE** exchange students
> learned to speak French
> while in Paris
> last summer

A. Last summer,/exchange students/learned to speak French/while in Paris.
B. While in Paris,/exchange students/learned to speak French/last summer.
C. Exchange students/learned to speak French/while in Paris/last summer.
D. Exchange students/learned to speak French/last summer/while in Paris.

1. chicken soup
   according to folklore
   helps
   cure colds
2. tadpoles
   instinctively
   swim
   toward
   their genetic relatives
3. the young driver
   while driving
   in the snow
   skidded carelessly
4. climbed
   the limber teenager
   a tall palm tree
   to pick a ripe coconut
   quickly
5. and cause mini-avalanches
   ski patrollers
   set explosives
   often
   to prevent
   big avalanches ●

DANGLING MODIFIERS

35D How can I avoid dangling modifiers?

A **dangling modifier** describes or limits a word or words that never actually appear in the sentence. To correct a dangling modifier, state clearly your intended SUBJECT in the sentence.

> **NO** **Approaching the island, a mountainous wall** was foreboding.
>
> This sentence suggests that the mountainous wall was approaching the island.

> **YES** Approaching the island, **we** saw a foreboding mountainous wall.

> **YES** As we approached the island, **we** saw a foreboding mountainous wall.
>
> Both revised sentences include the subject *we.*

> **NO** To allay our fears, our ship swerved around the island.
>
> This sentence suggests that our ship allayed our fears.

> **YES** To allay our fears, the pilot swerved our ship around the island.

A major cause of dangling and misplaced modifiers is the unnecessary use of the PASSIVE VOICE. Whenever possible, use the ACTIVE VOICE.

> **NO** **To earn money, tutoring services** are offered by Marlin.
>
> *Tutoring services* cannot earn money; *are offered* is passive voice.

> **YES** **To earn money, Marlin** offers tutoring services.

● **EXERCISE 35-3** Identify and correct any dangling modifiers in these sentences. If a sentence is correct, circle its number. For help, consult 35D.

EXAMPLE

To understand what happened to Krakatoa, the volcano and its history must be studied.

Corrected: To understand what happened to Krakatoa, one must study the volcano and its history.

1. In 1883, massive destruction was caused by the eruption of the volcano Krakatoa, an event recently examined in the book *Krakatoa: The Day the World Exploded.*
2. Exploding with a force 13,000 times stronger than the bomb dropped on Hiroshima, people thousands of miles away heard the eruption.
3. The loudest sound historically reported was generated by the explosion, with devastating tsunamis soon following.
4. Ejecting tons of debris into the air, the volcano destroyed or damaged hundreds of nearby villages.
5. Beginning to erupt around late July, larger eruptions didn't start until the middle of August.
6. Reaching over 100 feet in height and traveling at devastating speeds, major destruction was caused on the coastlines of Sumatra.
7. Lasting much longer than expected, people in nearby areas felt aftershocks until February of 1884.
8. To understand the magnitude of this volcanic eruption, changes in weather patterns were studied by scientists.
9. Darkening the sky for days afterwards and producing unusual sunsets, the ash and gases from the volcano temporarily lowered the average temperature of the earth.
10. Affecting the art of its time, the background of Edvard Munch's famous painting *The Scream* was inspired by Krakatoan sunsets. ●

Complete the Chapter Exercises

35E How can I proofread successfully for misplaced and dangling modifiers?

Sentence errors like MISPLACED MODIFIERS and DANGLING MODIFIERS are hard to spot because of the way the human brain works. Writers know what they mean to say when they write. When they PROOFREAD, however, they often misread what they've written for what they intended to write. The mind unconsciously adjusts for the error. In contrast, readers see only what's on the paper or screen. We suggest that you read your writing aloud, or have someone else read it to you, to proofread it for these kinds of problems.

Shifting and Mixed Sentences

36

Quick Points   You will learn to

➤ Write sentences that have consistent grammatical forms (see 36A–36J).

SHIFTING SENTENCES

36A   What is a shifting sentence?

Watch the Video

A **shift** within a sentence—or between sentences—is an unnecessary, often confusing, change in PERSON, NUMBER, SUBJECT, VOICE, TENSE, MOOD or DIRECT or INDIRECT DISCOURSE. When you begin writing in THIRD PERSON, for example, you challenge your readers if you switch to SECOND PERSON.

You can avoid writing shifting sentences and paragraphs by remaining consistent in your grammatical forms.

36B   How can I avoid shifts in person and number?

Watch the Video

Person indicates who or what performs or receives action. FIRST PERSON (*I, we*) is the writer or speaker; SECOND PERSON (*you*) is someone written or spoken to; THIRD PERSON (*he, she it, they*) is someone or something written or spoken about. Shifts in person often challenge your readers to clarify your meaning.

> **NO**   I enjoy reading financial forecasts, but **you** wonder which are accurate.
>
> First person *I* shifts unnecessarily to second person *you*.

> **YES**   I enjoy reading financial forecasts, but **I** wonder which are accurate.

NUMBER means *singular* (one) or *plural* (more than one). Be alert for needless shifts from one number to the other number.

> **NO**   Because **people** are living longer, **an employee** now retires later.
>
> The plural *people* needlessly shifts to the singular *employee*.

> **YES**   Because **people** are living longer, **employees** now retire later.

In ACADEMIC WRITING, reserve *you* for addressing the reader directly. Use the third person for general statements.

NO   I like my job in personnel because **you** get to interview job applicants.

The shift from first person *I* to second person *you* is misleading.

YES   I like my job in personnel because **I** get to interview job applicants.

NO   When **politicians** accept bribes, **you're** violating an oath of office.

The shift from third person *politicians* to second person *you* is misleading.

YES   When **politicians** accept bribes, **they're** violating an oath of office.

Be careful with singular words (often NOUNS) used in a general sense, such as *employee, student, consumer, neighbor, someone*. These third person singular words require third person singular pronoun references: *he, she,* and *it*. Because *they* is a plural pronoun, the word *they* cannot refer to a singular noun.

NO   When **an employee** is treated with respect, **they** are more motivated to do a good job.

The plural pronoun *they* cannot refer to the singular *an employee*.

YES   When **an employee** is treated with respect, **he or she** is more motivated to do a good job.

YES   When **employees** are treated with respect, **they** are more motivated to do a good job.

YES   **An employee** who is treated with respect is more motivated to do a good job.

YES   **Employees** who are treated with respect are more motivated to do a good job.

🛇 **Alert:** With INDEFINITE PRONOUNS (such as *someone, everyone,* or *anyone*), choose GENDER-NEUTRAL LANGUAGE. For advice, see 31S. ●

● **EXERCISE 36-1**   Eliminate shifts in person and number between, as well as within, sentences. Some sentences may not need revision. For help, consult 36B.

(1) First-time visitors to the Mall of America may be overwhelmed by its size, but you will also see its helpful design. (2) A shopper will notice that the mall is divided into architecturally distinct areas so they won't get lost. (3) The four sides of the mall have different themes and matching décor, so it is easy to navigate. (4) The architects named the four sides the North Garden, South Avenue, East Broadway, and West Market. (5) He or she also called the fourth floor's collection of nightclubs the Upper East Side to reflect an urban environment. (6) In spite of skeptics who thought the mall would never make money, it has been consistently successful in

renting its retail space and attracting shoppers. (7) The amusement park in the middle of the mall remains an important draw for families and children, and they have roller coasters and water rides. (8) Couples can enjoy fine dining and high-end shopping, and you can even get married in the mall's wedding chapel. ●

36C How can I avoid shifts in subject and voice?

A SHIFT in SUBJECT is rarely justified when it is accompanied by a shift in VOICE. The voice of a sentence is either *active (People expect changes)* or *passive (Changes are expected)*. Some subject shifts, however, are justified by the meaning of a passage: for example, *People look forward to the future, but the future holds many secrets.*

> **NO** Most **people expect** major improvements in the future, but some **hardships are** also **anticipated**.
>
> Both the subject (*people* to *hardships*) and the voice (active to passive) shift.

> **YES** Most **people expect** major improvements in the future, but **they** also **anticipate** some hardships.

> **YES** Most **people expect** major improvements in the future but also **anticipate** some hardships.

36D How can I avoid shifts in tense and mood?

TENSE refers to the time (past, present, future) in which the action of a VERB takes place. *We **will go** shopping after we **finish** lunch.* An unnecessary tense SHIFT within or between sentences can make the statement confusing or illogical.

> **NO** A campaign to clean up films in the United States **began** in the 1920s as various groups **try** to ban sex and violence from movies.
>
> The tense shifts from the past *began* to the present *try*.

> **YES** A campaign to clean up films in the United States **began** in the 1920s as various groups **tried** to ban sex and violence from movies.

> **NO** Film producers and distributors **created** the Production Code in the 1930s. Films that **fail** to get the board's seal of approval **do not receive** wide distribution.
>
> This shift occurs between sentences—the past tense *created* shifts to the present tense *fail* and *do not receive*.

> **YES** Film producers and distributors **created** the Production Code in the 1930s. Films that **failed** to get the board's seal of approval **did not receive** wide distribution.

MOOD indicates whether a sentence is a statement or a question (INDICATIVE MOOD), a command or request (IMPERATIVE MOOD), or a conditional or other-than-real statement (SUBJUNCTIVE MOOD). A shift in mood creates an awkward construction and can cause confusion.

NO The Production Code included guidelines on violence: **Do not show** details of brutal murders, and films **should not show** how to commit crimes.

The verbs shift from the imperative mood *do not show* to the indicative mood *films should not show*.

YES The Production Code included guidelines on violence: **Do not show** details of brutal murders, and **do not show** how to commit crimes.

This revision uses the imperative mood for both guidelines.

YES The Production Code included guidelines on violence: Films **were not to show** the details of brutal murders or ways to commit crimes.

NO The code's writers worried that **if a crime were** accurately **depicted** in a movie, **copycat crimes will follow**.

The sentence shifts from the subjunctive mood *if a crime were depicted* to the indicative mood *copycat crimes will follow*.

YES The code's writers worried that **if a crime were** accurately **depicted** in a movie, **copycat crimes would follow**.

36E How can I avoid shifts between indirect and direct discourse?

Indirect discourse is not enclosed in quotation marks because it reports, rather than quotes, something that someone said. In contrast, **direct discourse** is enclosed in quotation marks because it quotes exactly the words that someone said. Do not write sentences that mix indirect and direct discourse. Such SHIFTS confuse readers, who can't tell what was said and what is being merely reported.

NO She asked me **was I going out**.

This sentence shifts from indirect to direct discourse. Direct discourse requires quotation marks and changes in language.

YES She asked me **whether I was going out**.

This revision uses indirect discourse consistently.

YES She asked me **if I was going out**.

This revision uses indirect discourse consistently.

YES She asked me, **"Are you going out?"**

> This revision uses direct discourse with quotation marks. It makes the changes in language (such as INVERTED ORDER and verb TENSE) that accompany direct discourse.

Whenever you change from direct discourse to indirect discourse (when you decide to paraphrase rather than quote someone directly, for example), you need to make changes in TENSE and in other grammatical features for your writing to make sense. Simply removing quotation marks is not enough.

● **EXERCISE 36-2** Revise these sentences to eliminate incorrect shifts within sentences. Some sentences can be revised in several ways. For help, consult 36B through 36E.

EXAMPLE

In 1942, the U.S. government is faced with arresting five million people for not paying their federal income taxes.

In 1942, the U.S. government *was* faced with arresting five million people for not paying their federal income taxes.

1. Congress needed money to pay for U.S. participation in World War II, so a new tax system was proposed.
2. Tax payments were due on March 15, not April 15 as it is today.
3. For the first time, Congress taxed millions of lower-income citizens. Most people do not save enough to pay the amount of taxes due.
4. When a scientific poll showed lawmakers that only one in seven Americans had saved enough money, he became worried. ●

● **EXERCISE 36-3** Revise this paragraph to eliminate incorrect shifts between sentences and within sentences. For help, consult 36B through 36E.

(1) According to sociologists, people experience role conflict when we find ourselves trying to juggle too many different social roles. (2) When people reach overload, he or she decided, "to cut back somewhere." (3) For example, a well-known politician might decide not to run for reelection because family life would be interfered with by the demands of the campaign. (4) In other cases, you may delay having children so they can achieve early career success. (5) A person might say to themselves that I can't do this right now and focus instead on career goals. (6) In yet another example, a plant manager might enjoy social interaction with employees but consequently find themselves unable to evaluate him or her objectively. (7) In short, sociologists find that although not all role conflicts cause problems, great hardships are suffered by some individuals faced with handling difficult balancing acts. (8) People can minimize role conflicts, however, if we learn

to compartmentalize our lives. (9) A good example of this is people saying that I'm going to stop thinking about my job before I head home to my family. ●

MIXED SENTENCES

36F What is a mixed sentence?

A **mixed sentence** begins a sentence with one kind of construction (such as a PHRASE) and then switches to another (such as a PREDICATE). This scrambling of sentence parts dilutes your meaning. To avoid this error, match your opening (often your SUBJECT) to what follows both logically and grammatically.

NO   When we lost first prize motivated us to train harder.

      The PREDICATE of the sentence *motivated us to train harder* has no subject.

YES   When we lost first prize, we became motivated to train harder.

YES   Losing first prize motivated us to train harder.

NO   Because early television included news programs became popular with the public.

      The start of this sentence sets up a reason that doesn't match the rest of the sentence.

YES   Early television included news programs, which became popular with the public.

NO   Because of my damage to a library book is why they fined me heavily.

      A prepositional phrase such as *because of my damage* can't be the subject of a sentence.

YES   Because I damaged a book, the library fined me heavily.

YES   Because of the damage to my library book, I was fined heavily.

The phrase *the fact that* lacks CONCISENESS, and it also tends to cause a mixed sentence.

NO   The fact that quiz show scandals in the 1950s prompted the networks to produce even more news shows.

YES   The fact is that quiz show scandals in the 1950s prompted the networks to produce even more news shows.

      Adding *is* clarifies the meaning.

YES   Quiz show scandals in the 1950s prompted the networks to produce even more news shows.

      Dropping *the fact that* clarifies the meaning.

36G How can I correct a mixed sentence due to faulty predication?

Faulty predication, sometimes called *illogical predication*, occurs when a SUBJECT and its PREDICATE don't make sense together.

    NO   The purpose of television was invented to entertain people.

            A *purpose* cannot be *invented*.

    YES   The purpose of television was to entertain people.

    YES   Television was invented to entertain people.

Faulty predication often results from a lost connection between a subject and its SUBJECT COMPLEMENT.

    NO   Walter Cronkite's outstanding **characteristic** as a newscaster **was credible**.

            Cronkite may be credible but not his *characteristic*.

    YES   Walter Cronkite's outstanding **characteristic** as a newscaster **was credibility**.

            When *credibility* replaces *credible*, the sentence is correct.

    YES   Walter Cronkite was credible as a newscaster.

            Credible is correct when *Walter Cronkite* becomes the subject.

In ACADEMIC WRITING, avoid nonstandard constructions such as *is when* and *is where*. Often they lead to faulty predication.

    NO   A disaster **is when** TV news shows get some of their highest ratings.

    YES   TV news shows get some of their highest ratings during a disaster.

In academic writing, avoid constructions such as *the reason . . . is because*. Using both *reason* and *because* says the same thing twice.

    NO   One **reason** that TV news captured national attention in the 1960s **is because** it covered the Vietnam War thoroughly.

    YES   One **reason** TV news captured national attention in the 1960s **is that** it covered the Vietnam War thoroughly.

    YES   TV news captured national attention in the 1960s **because** it covered the Vietnam War thoroughly.

● **EXERCISE 36-4**   Revise the mixed sentences so that the beginning of each sentence fits logically with its end. If a sentence is correct, circle its number. For help, consult 36F and 36G.

EXAMPLE

The reason a newborn baby may stare at her hands or feet is because she can only focus on nearby objects.

A newborn baby may stare at her hands or feet because she can only focus on nearby objects.

1. By showing babies plain, black-and-white images will help them learn to recognize shapes and focus their vision.
2. Even though babies can see their parents' faces will not respond with a smile until they are a few weeks old.
3. Babies may gaze intently into a small, unbreakable mirror attached to the inside of their cribs.
4. While following an object with her eyes is when eye coordination develops.
5. Because of a newborn's limited ability to see color forces him to focus only on bright colors.
6. The reason babies occasionally cross their eyes is because they are perfecting their tracking skills.
7. Whether a light sleeper or a heavy sleeper, a typical baby does not need complete silence in order to rest well.
8. The fact that newborns can vary dramatically in their sensitivity to sounds and ability to sleep in noisy environments.
9. The reason that a two-month-old baby turns her head toward her parents' voice is because she is beginning to recognize familiar sounds.
10. Through changing his facial expression indicates he may find a particular sound soothing or comforting. ●

36H What are correct elliptical constructions?

An **elliptical construction** deliberately leaves out one or more words in a sentence for CONCISENESS.

- Victor has his book and Joan's.

  This means *Victor has his book and Joan's book.* The second *book* is left out deliberately.

Your elliptical constructions are correct when your discarded words are identical to words that are already in your sentence. The sample sentence above has an incorrect elliptical construction if the writer means that *Victor has his book, and Joan has her book.*

> **NO** During the 1920s, cornetist Manuel Perez **was leading** one jazz group, and Tommy and Jimmy Dorsey another.
>
> The words *was leading* cannot take the place of *were leading*, which is required after *Tommy and Jimmy Dorsey.*

> **YES** During the 1920s, cornetist Manuel Perez **was leading** one jazz group, and Tommy and Jimmy Dorsey **were leading** another.

> **YES** During the 1920s, cornetist Manuel Perez **led** one jazz group, and Tommy and Jimmy Dorsey another.
>
> *Led* is correct with both *Manuel Perez* and *Tommy and Jimmy Dorsey,* so *led* can be omitted after *Dorsey.*

361 What are correct comparisons?

When you write a sentence in which you want to compare two or more things, make sure that no important words are omitted.

> **NO** Individuals driven to achieve make **better** business executives.
>
> *Better* is a word of comparison (see 32E), but no comparison is stated.

> **YES** Individuals driven to achieve make **better** business executives **than do people not interested in personal accomplishments.**

> **NO** Most personnel officers value high achievers **more than risk takers**.
>
> *More* is a word of comparison, but it's unclear whether the sentence means that *personnel officers* or *risk takers* value achievers more.

> **YES** Most personnel officers value high achievers **more than they value** risk takers.

> **YES** Most personnel officers value high achievers **more than** risk takers **do**.

36J How can I proofread successfully for little words I forget to use?

If you unintentionally omit little words, such as articles, conjunctions, and prepositions, read your writing aloud or ask someone else to.

> **NO** On May 2, 1808, citizens Madrid rioted against French soldiers and were shot.

> **YES** On May 2, 1808, citizens **of** Madrid rioted against French soldiers and were shot.

> **NO** The Spanish painter Francisco Goya recorded both the riot the execution in a pair of pictures painted 1814.

> **YES** The Spanish painter Francisco Goya recorded both the riot **and** the execution in a pair of pictures painted **in** 1814.

● **EXERCISE 36-5** Revise these sentences to correct elliptical constructions, to complete comparisons, or to insert any missing words.

1. Champagne is a kind of sparkling wine grown in Champagne region France.
2. To be considered champagne, a sparkling wine must meet several conditions described French law.
3. The location of the vineyard is one requirement, and type of grapes another.
4. Most champagne producers agree that the Chardonnay and Pinot Noir grapes make champagne taste better.
5. When owners celebrate the launch of a new ship, they use bottles of champagne more often. ●

Complete
the
Chapter
Exercises

PART

6

Writing Effectively, Writing with Style

37 Style, Tone, and the Effects of Words

■ ■ ■ ■ ■ ■ ■ ■ ■ ■

Quick Points You will learn to

➤ Create an effective style and tone in writing (see 37A–37E).
➤ Use word choices that affect clarity, style, and tone (see 37F–37I).
➤ Avoid certain types of language (see 37J).

37A What are style and tone in writing?

Style and **tone** both refer to *how* you say something, in contrast with *what* you're saying. Consider the familiar instruction to airline passengers:

> "In preparation for landing, please return your seatbacks and tray tables to their fully upright and locked positions."

Flight attendants could provide the same directions in a different style:

> "Hey, we're landing. Put your seatbacks up, and while you're at it, put your tray tables up, too."

They could even say:

> "Our landing preparations oblige us to request your kind participation in the restoration of all seatbacks and tray tables to vertical modes."

The directions are the same, and all three examples are grammatically correct. However, you get a very different sense of the style and tone in each case. The first is polite and direct, the second is casual and chatty, and the third is pretentious and bureaucratic.

Neither style nor tone are rule bound, the way that grammar is. Writers have choices, and the kinds of words they choose and kinds of sentences they write affect style and tone. Of course, certain styles are appropriate for certain writing situations, and almost all situations require standard edited English.

37B What is standard edited English?

Watch
the Video

Standard edited English reflects the kind of written language expected in academic, business, and serious public writings. These standards apply in magazines such as *The Atlantic* and *Time;* in newspapers such as the *Washington*

Post and the *Wall Street Journal;* and in most nonfiction books. Standard edited English conforms to the widely established rules of grammar, sentence structure, punctuation, and spelling we cover in this handbook.

Although English has become the primary global language for business and other uses, it has many varieties. For example, American English differs from British English in terms of spellings ("color" v. "colour") or vocabulary ("truck" v. "lorry"). Even within the United States there are regional and cultural differences. Regional languages, also called **dialects**, are specific to certain geographical areas. For example, a *dragonfly* is a *snake feeder* in parts of Delaware, a *darning needle* in parts of Michigan, and a *snake doctor* or an *ear sewer* in parts of the southern United States. Depending on where you live, soft drinks are known as "soda," "pop," or "Coke."

It's important to realize that people who use regional or cultural variations communicate clearly to other members of their group. There's nothing essentially "wrong" with those dialects, then—except when their speakers and writers want to communicate with wider audiences. In academic, business, and civic situations, individuals clearly benefit from "code switching" to standard edited English, even if they continue using home languages in personal situations. It's no different from needing to switch from the casual language of Facebook to the more formal language of a job application letter. You need to use standard edited English for academic writing.

37C How can I write with style?

Writing with style comes with lots of practice and revision. It rarely shows up on most first drafts. Experimenting with different sentence structures and word choices, then thinking carefully about their effects, helps you create an effective style. Quick Box 37.1 gives several tips.

Quick Box 37.1

How to create a good writing style

- Use standard edited English (see 37B).
- Choose the right level of formality, personality and voice, and creativity for each writing situation (see 37D).
- Choose an appropriate tone (see 37E).
- Use exact diction and specific words (see 37F and 37G).

continued >>

Quick Box 37.1 (continued)

- Use figurative language (see 37H).
- Use gender-neutral language (see 37I).
- Avoid manipulative language, clichés, euphemisms, jargon, and bureaucratic language (see 37J).
- Try out different sentence types to maintain readers' interest (see 38A, 38N, 38R).
- Use sentence coordination and subordination to vary the pace (see 38D–38M).
- Vary sentence length to keep your readers' attention (see 38C).
- Employ the gracefulness of parallelism in sentences and larger sections for the pleasure of your readers (see Chapter 39).

37D What defines style and tone in writing?

Style and tone operate together through a combination of varying levels of formality, voice, and creativity, as we lay out in Quick Box 37.2.

Quick Box 37.2 ■ ■ ■ ■ ■ ■ ■ ■ ■ ■ ■

Elements and levels of style

Elements	Levels		
Formality	Informal	Semiformal	Formal
Voice	Intimate	Familiar/Polite	Impersonal
Surprise or creativity	Low (transparent)	Medium (translucent)	High (artistic)

The **level of formality** in writing can be roughly divided into three categories. Formal writing belongs in the structures and language of ceremonies, contracts, policies, or some literary writing. "Formal writing," by the way, doesn't mean dull and drab. **Informal writing** is casual, colloquial, and sometimes playful, usually found in text messages or social networks. Semiformal writing, which sits between these poles, is found in academic writing, as well as in much business and public writing. Its style is clear and efficient, and its tone is reasonable and evenhanded.

Generally, when you write for an audience about whom you know little, use a semiformal to formal style and tone. If informal writings are T-shirts and jeans, and formal writings are tuxedos and evening gowns, then semiformal writings are business-casual attire. Here are examples of writing in the three levels of formality.

INFORMAL   It's totally sweet how gas makes stars.

SEMIFORMAL   Gas clouds slowly transform into stars.

FORMAL   The condensations of gas spun their slow gravitational pirouettes, slowly transmogrifying gas cloud into star.

—Carl Sagan, "Starfolk: A Fable"

VOICE or **personality** refers to how much the writer calls attention to him- or herself, how much the writing conveys the presence of an individual person and, if so, what kind of person he or she seems to be. An intimate voice treats the reader as a close friend. A familiar or polite voice includes only experiences or personal thoughts that you might share in a professional relationship with an instructor, supervisor, or colleague. In such writing, the reader can glimpse the writer behind the language, but the emphasis is on content. An impersonal voice reveals nothing about the writer, so that the content is all that the reader notices.

Look at the following paragraph.

I would be willing to bet serious money that right now in your kitchen you have olive oil, garlic, pasta, parmesan cheese, and dried basil (maybe even fresh basil!). Nothing exotic there, right? They're ingredients we take for granted. But their appearance in our kitchens is a relatively recent phenomenon. Believe me, those big-flavor items did not come over on the Mayflower. It took generations, even centuries, for Americans to expand their culinary horizons to the point where just about everybody cooks Italian and orders Chinese take-out. Heck, the supermarket in my little Connecticut hometown even has a sushi bar.

—Thomas J. Craughwell, "If Only the Pilgrims Had Been Italian"

Several words and phrases in the passage create an intimate and informal voice, including "I would be willing to bet serious money," "believe me," and "heck." This is the voice of someone casual and confident enough to refer inclusively to "we" and use a chatty sentence fragment ("Nothing exotic there, right?") as if we're friends sitting in a coffee shop.

However, with a little revision, we can reduce the sound of the author's voice:

Most kitchens have olive oil, garlic, pasta, parmesan cheese, and dried or fresh basil. Although these are ingredients people take for granted, they appeared in kitchens relatively recently. They did not come over on the Mayflower. It took generations, even centuries, for Americans to expand their culinary horizons to the point where just about everybody cooks Italian and orders Chinese take-out. Even a small town supermarket may have a sushi bar.

Writers can get carried away with voice, creating one that is too friendly, self-important, or even annoying: A strong voice is inappropriate in some writing situations, including some academic writing and most business writing.

INTIMATE	Ever since I was a kid, TV shows with stupid characters bugged me. Do you maybe think it's because I've screwed up so much myself that I hate having my nose rubbed in it?
FAMILIAR/POLITE	I am frequently embarrassed by certain characters' actions on television shows.
IMPERSONAL	Characters' actions on television shows occasionally prove a source of embarrassment to certain viewers.

Creativity refers to the "surprise" element in writing, the degree to which readers notice the language itself rather than the content the language conveys. Consider, for example, the difference between "The room was red" and "The room was the color of a Daytona Beach sunburn." Figurative language (see 37C) creates surprise or calls attention to language. Writing that has a low level of surprises is *transparent*, like a clear window; readers scarcely notice its language. Writing with a medium level of surprises is *translucent*, like a lightly colored pane of glass; readers occasionally notice and appreciate the language, but content is primary. If a piece of writing is consistently surprising, it is *artistic*, like a stained glass window; the language frequently demands attention to itself.

TRANSPARENT	The acting in the film was unsuccessful, and the plot was dull.
TRANSLUCENT	The acting in the film was dismal, the plot a test of endurance.
ARTISTIC	Watching the acting and enduring the plot was like eating pizza that lacked a crust: frustrating, unsatisfying, and making you wish you hadn't taken a bite.

Of course, "artistic" does not necessarily mean better; extensive creativity is inappropriate in many writing situations. If you're writing instructions, science reports, or business projects, for example, you don't want language that calls attention to itself. A translucent or transparent style, however, will serve you well in most academic situations.

● **EXERCISE 37-1** Working individually or in a group, describe the style of each of the following paragraphs in terms of formality, voice, and surpise.

1.   Google has yet to hit upon a strategy that combines the innovation it is known for with an appeal to the self-interest that is the currency of the capital's power brokers. One reason AT&T and Microsoft have succeeded in stoking antitrust interest against Google—quite ironic, given that both companies

have been subject to large government antitrust actions—is that they're better versed in the fine points of lobbying. Both companies, for example, hold sway over many lawmakers by frequently reminding them how many employees live in their districts ("jobs" is a metric lawmakers respond to).

—Joshua Green, "Google's Tar Pit"

2.   Prices are rising for the black sludge that helps make the world's gears turn. If you think we're talking about oil, think again. Petroleum prices have tumbled from their record highs. No sooner was there relief at the pump, however, than came a squeeze at the pot. That jolt of coffee that a majority of American adults enjoy on a daily basis has gotten more expensive and could go even higher this year. . . .

—*New York Times*, "Joe Economics"

3.   In addition to participating in the promulgation of Treasury (Tax) Regulations, the IRS publishes a regular series of other forms of official tax guidance, including revenue rulings, revenue procedures, notices, and announcements. See Understanding IRS Guidance—A Brief Primer for more information about official IRS guidance versus non-precedential rulings or advice.

—Internal Revenue Service, "Tax Code, Regulations, and Official Guidance"

4.   Studies of home-based telework by women yield mixed results regarding the usefulness of telework in facilitating work–life balance. Most research on the social impacts of home-based telework focuses on workers—employees or self-employed—who deliberately choose that alternative work arrangement. Labour force analysts, however, predict an increase in employer-initiated teleworking. As a case study of the workforce of one large, financial-sector firm in Canada, this article considers the conditions of employment of involuntary teleworkers, those required by their employer to work full-time from a home office. In-depth interviews were conducted with a sample of 18 female teleworkers working for the case study firm in a professional occupation.

—Laura C. Johnson, Jean Andrey, and Susan M. Shaw, "Mr. Dithers Comes to Dinner"

5.   I remember vividly the moment that I entered the world of literacy, education, institutional "correctness," and, consequently, identity. I was demonstrating to my older sister how I wrote my name. The memory comes after I had been literally taught how to do it—which strokes of the pencil to use to create the symbols that equate to my name.

—Elise Geraghty, "In the Name of the Father" ●

● **EXERCISE 37-2**   Select one of the paragraphs in Exercise 37-1. Revise that paragraph to create a very different voice for it. ●

37E   What is tone in writing?

Tone in writing operates like tone of voice, except that you can't rely on facial expressions and voice intonations to communicate your message. Your choice of words determines how your readers "hear" you, and we list several different tones and examples in Quick Box 37.3.

Achieving the tone you want calls for experimenting with different words with similar meanings. If you consult a thesaurus, be sure to check the definition of any synonym that's new to you. Lynn once had an excellent student who used the word "profound" instead of "deep," without looking it up in a dictionary. The result was this sentence: "The trenches beneath some parts of that sea were dangerously profound." That misuse ruined an otherwise intelligent passage.

As with style, appropriate tone results from trying options. Quick Box 37.4 offers you some suggestions.

Quick Box 37.3

Some examples of desirable and undesirable tone

SERIOUS	It is important to respect the rights of all individuals participating in the meeting.
LIGHT OR BREEZY	Be nice to all the folks at the meeting, OK?
SARCASTIC	I suppose we'll all live happily ever after if we just smile and have tea and cupcakes.
MEAN	Respect others or suffer the consequences.
CONDESCENDING	Now, everyone, I know it's asking a lot of your little brains to understand, but please play nice with each other during our meeting today.
PRETENTIOUS	The degree of niceness displayed by meeting participants to one another, especially regarding each individual's rights, must be high in order to create optimal outcomes.
WHINING	It's so hard when we don't respect each other, so can't we please, for just this once and just for me, have a polite meeting?

Quick Box 37.4

■ ■ ■ ■ ■ ■ ■ ■ ■ ■ ■

How to use appropriate tone in writing

- Reserve a highly informal tone for conversational writing.
- Use a semiformal tone in your academic writing and when you write for supervisors, professionals, and other people you know only from a distance.
- Choose a tone that suits your topic and your readers.
- Whatever tone you choose, be consistent throughout a piece of writing.

● **EXERCISE 37-3**   Revise each of the sentences to create a very different tone. The sentences in Quick Box 37.3 provide some examples. For a further challenge, see how many different tones you can create.

1. Many Americans spend much of their leisure time watching professional sports.
2. If you want to waste your money buying organic foods, who am I to stop you?
3. When considering the purchase of clothing in order to possess a serviceable wardrobe, it is imperative to select items in which the color combinations are harmonious and pleasing. ●

37F   How can using exact diction enhance my writing?

Diction refers to your word choices. Your best chance of delivering your intended message is to choose words that fit your meaning exactly. To choose words exactly—that is, to have good diction—be alert to the concepts of DENOTATION and CONNOTATION.

37F.1   What is denotation in words?

The **denotation** of a word is its exact, literal meaning found in a reliable dictionary.

- An unabridged dictionary contains the most extensive, complete, and scholarly entries. *Unabridged* means "not shortened." The most comprehensive, authoritative unabridged dictionary of English is the *Oxford English Dictionary* (OED), which traces each word's history and gives quotations to illustrate changes in meaning and spelling over the life of the word.

- An abridged dictionary contains most commonly used words. *Abridged* means "shortened." Abridged dictionaries that serve the needs of most college students are "college editions." Typical of these are *Merriam-Webster's Collegiate Dictionary* (available online and in print) and *The New American Webster Handy College Dictionary*.

- A specialized dictionary focuses on a single area of language. You can find dictionaries of **slang** (for example, *Dictionary of Slang and Unconventional English*); word origins (for example, *Dictionary of Word and Phrase Origins*); synonyms (for example, *Roget's 21st Century Thesaurus*); **usage** (for example, *Garner's Modern American Usage*); idioms (for example, *A Dictionary of American Idioms*); regionalisms (for example, *Dictionary of American Regional English*); and many others.

ESOL Tip: *The Oxford Dictionary of American English* is particularly useful for students who speak English as a second (or third) language. ●

37F.2 What is connotation in words?

Connotation refers to ideas associated with a word. For example, *home* usually evokes more emotion than its denotation "a dwelling place" or its synonym *house*. *Home* carries the connotation, for some, of the pleasures of warmth, security, and love of family. For others, however, *home* may carry unpleasant connotations, such as abusive experiences.

USING A THESAURUS

In distinguishing among SYNONYMS—words close in meaning to each other— a thesaurus demonstrates connotation in operation. As you use a thesaurus, remain alert to the subtle differences of meaning. For instance, using *notorious* to describe a person famous for praiseworthy achievements is wrong. Although *notorious* means "well-known" and "publicly discussed"—which is true of famous people—the connotation of the word is "unfavorably known or talked about." George Washington is famous, not notorious. Adolf Hitler, by contrast, is notorious.

Alert: Most word-processing programs include a thesaurus. But be cautious in using it. Unless you know the exact meaning and part of speech of a synonym, you may choose a wrong word or create a grammatical error. For example, one thesaurus offers these synonyms for *deep* in the sense of "low (down, inside)": *low, below, beneath*, and *subterranean*. None of these could replace *deep* in a sentence such as *The crater is too deep* [not *too low, too below, too beneath*, or *too subterranean*] *to be filled with sand or rocks*. ●

● **EXERCISE 37-4** Working individually or with a group, look at each list of words and divide the words among three headings: "Positive" (good connotations); "Negative" (bad connotations); and "Neutral" (no connotations). If you think that a word belongs under more than one heading, you can assign it more than once, but be ready to explain your thinking. For help, consult a good dictionary.

EXAMPLE

assertive, pushy, firm, forceful, confident

Positive: assertive, confident; *Negative:* pushy, forceful; *Neutral:* firm

1. old, decrepit, elderly, mature, over the hill, venerable, veteran, antique, experienced
2. resting, inactive, unproductive, downtime, recess, quietude, standstill, vacation, interval
3. smart, know-it-all, brilliant, eggheaded, brainy, sharp, ingenious, keen, clever, intelligent
4. weird, unique, peculiar, strange, eccentric, inscrutable, peculiar, kooky, singular, one-of-a-kind, distinctive
5. smell, aroma, stench, fragrance, scent, whiff, bouquet, odor ●

37G How can using specific words enhance my writing?

Specific words identify individual items in a group (*snap peas, sweet corn*). General words relate to an overall group (*food*). Concrete words identify what can be perceived by the senses, by being seen, heard, tasted, felt, smelled (*warm, juicy cherry pie*), and convey specific images and details. Abstract words denote qualities (*nice*), concepts (*speed*), relationships (*friends*), acts (*cooking*), conditions (*bad weather*), and ideas (*justice*) and are more general.

Usually, specific and concrete words bring life to general and abstract words. Therefore, whenever you use general and abstract words, try to supply enough specific, concrete details and examples to illustrate them. Here are sentences with general words that come to life when revised with specific words.

GENERAL	His car gets good gas mileage.
SPECIFIC	His Miser gets about 35 mpg on the highway and 30 mpg in the city.
GENERAL	Her car is comfortable and easy to drive.
SPECIFIC	When she drives her new Cushia on a five-hour trip, she arrives refreshed and does not need a long nap to recover, as she did when she drove her ten-year-old Beater.

What separates most good writing from bad is the writer's ability to move back and forth between the general and the specific. Consider these sentences that effectively use a combination of general and specific words:

GENERAL   CONCRETE
• The carnival at night, a shimmering glow of blue, red, and neon lights,

ABSTRACT   SPECIFIC   CONCRETE
was amazing. The Pikes Peak Plummet, a hundred foot tower of black

                CONCRETE   GENERAL
metal and chrome, hurled twenty riders down a sixty-degree slope.

SPECIFIC   CONCRETE   GENERAL
The Whirlpool spun screaming teens in an open cylinder,

                    CONCRETE
bathing them in fluorescent strobe lights.

● **EXERCISE 37-5** Revise this paragraph by providing specific and concrete words and phrases to explain and enliven the ideas presented here in general and abstract language. You may revise the sentences to accommodate your changes.

A while ago, I visited a nice restaurant. It was located in a good neighborhood, and it was easy to find. The inside of the restaurant was pretty. There were a lot of decorations, which gave it character. The menu was creative and interesting. The food was delivered quickly, and the service was friendly. I enjoyed eating the meal. The appetizers were delicious and refreshing. The price of the meal was reasonable considering how much food I ordered. ●

37H What is figurative language?

Figurative language makes comparisons and connections that draw on one idea or image to enhance another. Quick Box 37.5 explains the different types of figurative language and describes one type you should avoid, the **mixed metaphor**.

Quick Box 37.5   ■ ■ ■ ■ ■ ■ ■ ■ ■ ■

Types of figurative language

- **Analogy:** Comparing similar traits shared by dissimilar things or ideas. Its length can vary from one sentence (which often takes the form of a simile or metaphor) to a paragraph.
  - A **cheetah sprinting across the dry plains** after its prey, the **base runner dashed** for home plate, cleats kicking up dust.

continued >>

Quick Box 37.5 (continued)

- **Irony:** Using words to suggest the opposite of their usual sense.
  - Told that a minor repair on her home would cost $2,000 and take two weeks, she said, **"Oh, how nice!"**
- **Metaphor:** Comparing otherwise dissimilar things. A metaphor doesn't use the word *like* or *as* to make a comparison. (See below about not using mixed metaphors.)
  - Rush-hour **traffic** in the city **bled out through major arteries** to the suburbs.
- **Personification:** Assigning a human trait to something not human.
  - The **book begged** to be read.
- **Overstatement** (also called *hyperbole*): Exaggerating deliberately for emphasis.
  - If this paper is late, the professor will **kill** me.
- **Simile:** Comparing dissimilar things. A simile uses the word *like* or *as*.
  - Langston Hughes observes that a deferred **dream dries up "like a raisin in the sun."**
- **Understatement:** Emphasizing by using deliberate restraint.
  - It feels **warm** when the temperature reaches **105 degrees**.
- **Mixed metaphor:** Combining two or more inconsistent images in one sentence or expression. Never use a mixed metaphor.

  > **NO** The violence of the hurricane reminded me of a train ride.
  >
  > A train ride is not violent, stormy, or destructive.

  > **YES** The violence of the hurricane reminded me of a train's crashing into a huge tractor trailer.

● **EXERCISE 37-6** Working individually or with a group, identify each type of figurative language or figure of speech. Also revise any mixed metaphors.

1. Exercise for the body is like education for the mind.
2. Waking up in the morning to exercise can be as hard as starting a car with a dead battery.
3. Exercise is the key ingredient in the recipe for a healthy life.
4. When I started my diet, I was dying of hunger!
5. When you exercise, pull out all the stops so you that you can put the pedal to the metal.
6. That last mile of my run punished me without mercy.
7. Exercising a muscle is like practicing an instrument.

8. "Oh, I feel absolutely great," she gasped after finishing a long run.
9. If the body is a temple, then regular exercise keeps the temple clean and strong.
10. Nothing good can happen in your life unless you exercise. ●

371 What is gender-neutral language?

Watch the Video

Gender-neutral language, also called *gender-free* or *nonsexist language*, uses terms that don't draw unnecessary attention to whether the person is male or female (for example, in replacing *policeman* with *police officer* or *doctors' wives* with *doctors' spouses*).

Sexist language assigns roles or characteristics to people based on their sex and discriminates against both men and women. For example, it assumes that nurses and homemakers are female by calling them "she," and that surgeons and stockbrokers are male by calling them "he." One common instance of sexist language occurs when writers us the pronoun *he* for anyone whose sex is unknown or irrelevant. Using masculine pronouns to represent all people distorts reality.

Nearly all businesses and professional organizations use gender-neutral language in written communications. This sound business practice promotes accuracy and fairness and includes all potential clients.

Gender-neutral language rejects demeaning **stereotypes** or outdated assumptions, such as "women are bad drivers" and "real men don't cry." In academic writing, treat both sexes equally. For example if you describe a woman by her looks, clothes, or age, do the same for a man in that context. Refer to names and titles in the same way for both men and women. Quick Box 37.6 offers you guidelines.

Quick Box 37.6

How to avoid sexist language

- Avoid using only the masculine pronoun to refer to males and females together. The *he or she* and *his or hers* phrases act as singular PRONOUNS that require singular VERBS. Avoid using *he or she* constructions more than once in a sentence or in consecutive sentences. Try switching to plural or omitting the gender-specific pronoun.

  NO   A **doctor** has little time to read outside **his** specialty.

  YES   A **doctor** has little time to read outside **his or her** specialty.

continued >>

Quick Box 37.6   (continued)

NO   A successful **stockbroker** knows **he** has to work long hours.

YES   Successful **stockbrokers** know **they** have to work long hours.

NO   **Everyone** hopes that **he or she** will win the scholarship.

YES   **Everyone** hopes to win the scholarship.

- Avoid using *man* when referring to both men and women.

NO   **Man** is a social animal.

YES   **People** are social animals.

NO   The history of **mankind** is predominately violent.

YES   **Human** history is predominately violent.

NO   Dogs are **men's** best friends.

YES   Dogs are **people's** best friends.

- Avoid stereotyping jobs and roles by **gender** when referring to both men and women.

NO	YES
chairman	chair, chairperson
policeman	police officer
businessman	businessperson, business executive
statesman	statesperson, diplomat
teacher . . . she	teachers . . . they
principal . . . he	principals . . . they

- Avoid expressions that seem to exclude one sex.

NO	YES
the common man	the average person
man-sized sandwich	huge sandwich
old wives' tale	superstition

- Avoid using demeaning and patronizing labels.

NO	YES
male nurse	nurse
gal Friday	assistant
coed	student
My girl can help.	My secretary can help. (*Or, better still:* Ida Morea can help.)

● **EXERCISE 37-7** Working individually or with a group, revise these sentences by changing sexist language to gender-neutral language. For help, consult 37I.

1. Dogs were one of the first animals to be domesticated by mankind.
2. Traditionally, certain breeds of dogs have helped men in their work.
3. On their long shifts, firemen often kept Dalmatians as mascots and companions, whereas policemen preferred highly intelligent and easily trained German shepherds.
4. Another breed, the Newfoundland, accompanied many fishermen on their ocean voyages, and the Newfoundland has been credited with rescuing many a man overboard.
5. Breeds known as hunting dogs have served as the helpers and companions of sportsmen.
6. Maids and cleaning women didn't need dogs, so no breed of dog is associated with women's work.
7. Another group that dogs have not helped is postmen.
8. Everyone who owns a dog should be sure to spend some time exercising his dog and making sure his dog is in good health.
9. No man-made inventions, such as televisions or computers, can take the place of having a dog.
10. Now even though most dogs do not work, they are still man's best friend. ●

🛈 **Alert:** Increasingly, you see "they" or "their" used as a singular pronoun, as in "Someone tripped and broke their nose." The English language continually changes, and perhaps in a few years this growing usage will become perfectly acceptable because it fills a need: English lacks a gender-neutral singular pronoun. However, such usage is still considered nonstandard in most academic and professional settings. ●

37J   What other types of language do I want to avoid?

In addition to avoiding sexist language, you need also to avoid several other kinds of language. We summarize this advice in Quick Box 37.7.

37J.1   Clichés

A **cliché** is an expression that has become worn out from overuse. Examples of clichés are *cheap as dirt, dead as a doornail,* and *straight as an arrow.* If you've heard certain expressions repeatedly, so has your reader. Try substituting your own fresh wording.

Quick Box 37.7

Language to avoid in academic writing

- Never use **slanted language**, also called *loaded language;* readers feel manipulated by the overly emotional TONE and DICTION.

  NO Our senator is a deceitful, crooked thug.

  YES Our senator lies to the public and demands bribes.

  NO Why do labs hire monsters to maim helpless kittens and puppies?

  YES Why do labs employ technicians who harm kittens and puppies?

- Never use pretentious language; readers realize you're showing off.

  NO As I alighted from my vehicle, my clothing became besmirched with filth.

  YES My coat got muddy as I got out of my car.

  NO He has a penchant for ostentatiously flaunting recently acquired haberdashery accoutrements.

  YES He tends to show off his new clothes shamelessly.

- Never use sarcastic language; readers realize you're being nasty.

  NO He was a regular Albert Einstein with my questions.

  This is sarcastic if you mean the opposite.

  YES He had trouble understanding my questions.

- Never use **colloquial language;** readers sense you're being overly casual and conversational.

  NO Christina tanked chemistry.

  YES Christina failed chemistry.

- Never use nonstandard English.

- Never use SEXIST LANGUAGE or STEREOTYPES (see 37I).

- Never use CLICHÉS (see 37J.1).

- Never use unnecessary JARGON (see 37J.2).

- Never use EUPHEMISMS, also called *doublespeak;* readers realize you're hiding the truth (more in 37J.3).

- Never use BUREAUCRATIC LANGUAGE (see 37J.4).

Interestingly, however, English is full of idioms that aren't clichés, phrases like *by and large* or and *from place to place.* You can use them freely. If you're not sure of how to tell the difference between a cliché and a common word group, remember that a cliché often—but not always—contains an image (*busy as a bee* and *strong as an ox*).

● **EXERCISE 37-8** Working individually or with a group, revise these clichés. Use the idea in each cliché to write a sentence of your own in plain, clear English.

1. The Raging Manatees softball players came to grips with the fact that their upcoming game would be a tough row to hoe.
2. The bottom line was that their worthy opponents, the Fierce Sunflowers, took no prisoners.
3. Still, the Manatees knew that they had to play like there was no tomorrow, because taking it one game at time would be the key to success.
4. Snatching victory from the jaws of defeat depended on remembering that their opponents still put on uniforms one leg at a time.
5. Although the effort would be Herculean, at the end of the day, the Manatees knew they could make the best of a bad situation. After all, the bigger they are, the harder they fall. ●

37J.2 Jargon

Jargon is the specialized vocabulary of a particular group, whether in academic disciplines, certain industries, hobbies, sports, and so on. Jargon uses words that people outside that group might not understand.

Reserve jargon for a specialist AUDIENCE. For example, a football fan easily understands a sportswriter's use of words such as *punt* and *safety*, but they are jargon words to people unfamiliar with American-style football. When you must use jargon for a nonspecialist audience, be sure to explain any special meanings.

The following example from a college textbook uses appropriate specialized language. The authors can assume that students know the meaning of *eutrophicates, terrestrial,* and *eutrophic.*

> As the lake eutrophicates, it gradually fills until the entire lake will be converted into a terrestrial community. Eutrophic changes (or eutrophication) are the nutritional enrichment of the water, promoting the growth of aquatic plants.
>
> —Davis and Solomon, *The World of Biology*

37J.3 Euphemisms

A **euphemism** is a more pleasing way of stating something that people find unpleasant. Sometimes, good manners dictate that we use euphemisms like *passed away* instead of *died.*

At other times, however, euphemisms drain truth from your writing. Unnecessary euphemisms might describe socially unacceptable behavior (for example, *Lee has an artfully vivid imagination* instead of *Lee lies*) or try to hide facts (for example, *He is between jobs* instead of *He's unemployed*). Avoid unnecessary euphemisms.

NO Our company will **downsize** to meet efficiency standards.

YES Our company has to cut jobs to maintain our profits.

NO We consider our hostages as **foreign guests** guarded by **hosts**.

YES We consider our hostages as enemies to be guarded closely.

37J.4 Bureaucratic language

Bureaucratic language uses words that are stuffy, overblown, and unnecessarily complex. This kind of language complicates the message and makes readers feel left out.

NO Given the certitude of deleterious outcomes from the implementation of pending policy changes, it shall be incumbent upon us to remedy negative consequences with positive alternatives as yet to be determined. In the event that said outcomes are to be derived and agreed upon by all constituencies having stake in their deployment, a directive shall be issued to each and every stakeholder for the purpose of responding to anticipated negative policy change outcome eventualities.

—from a corporate human resources manual

We would like to give a YES alternative for this example but regret that we can't understand enough of it to do so. If you, gentle reader, can, please contact us at doug.hesse@gmail.com or 2LTROYKA@gmail.com.

● **EXERCISE 37-9** Working individually or with a group, revise these examples of pretentious language, jargon, euphemisms, and bureaucratic language. For help, consult 37J.

1. Allow me to express my humble gratitude to you two benefactors for your generous pledge of indispensable support on behalf of the activities of our Bay City's youngsters.
2. No lateral transfer applications will be processed before an employee's six-month probation period terminates.
3. She gave up the ghost shortly after her husband kicked the bucket.
4. Creating nouns in positions meant for verbs is to utter ostentatious verbalizations that will lead inexorably to further obfuscations of meaning.
5. After his operation, he would list to port when he stood up and list to starboard when he sat down.

Complete
the
Chapter
Exercises

6. The precious youths were joy riding in a temporarily displaced vehicle.
7. The forwarding of all electronic communiqués must be approved by a staff member in the upper echelon.
8. Coming to a parting of the ways is not as easy as pie. ●

38 Sentence Variety and Style

Quick Points   You will learn to

➤ Use a variety of sentence patterns to give interest to your writing (see 38A, 38L–38P).

➤ Use variety and emphasis in your sentences (see 38B–38K).

38A How do sentences affect style?

Sentences affect style through their length (see 38C), structures like COORDINATION and SUBORDINATION (see 38K), and types. The main sentence types in English are SIMPLE, COMPOUND, COMPLEX, and COMPOUND-COMPLEX (see 28Q). A flurry of short, simple sentences creates a blunt style but loses readers' interest. A series of long compound, complex, or compound-complex sentences creates a lofty or stuffy style but sacrifices clarity. You can see the difference in the two versions of the same piece below.

1. Short, simple sentences

> The most worshipped and praised of all ancient sewers was Rome's Cloaca Maxima. It resided within the shrine of the goddess Cloacina. Warriors came here to purge themselves after battle. Young couples purified themselves here before marriage. The lovely Cloacina was an emanation of Venus. Her statue overlooked the imperial city's sewer pipes. The pipes transported 100,000 pounds of ancient *excrementum* [human waste] a day. It was built in the sixth century B.C. by the two Tarquins. It was hailed as one of the three marvels of Rome. The Cloaca became one of the city's great tourist traps. Agrippa rode a boat through it. Nero washed his hands in it.

2. Longer, compound and complex sentences

> The most worshipped and praised of all ancient sewers was Rome's Cloaca Maxima, whose spirit resided within the shrine of the goddess Cloacina, where warriors came to purge themselves after battle and young couples purified themselves before marriage. The lovely Cloacina was an emanation of Venus, and her statue overlooked the imperial city's sewer pipes as they transported 100,000 pounds of ancient *excrementum* [human waste] a day. Built in the sixth century B.C. by the two Tarquins, hailed as one of the three marvels of Rome, the Cloaca became one of the city's great tourist traps. Agrippa rode a boat through it. Nero washed his hands in it.
>
> —Frederick Kaufman, "Wasteland"

The second version was published in *Harper's Magazine*, which is aimed at a well-educated general AUDIENCE. Even that version ends with two simple sentences, a refreshing break after the longer ones. In fact, effective and stylistically interesting writing often contains a VARIETY of styles.

38B What are variety and emphasis in writing?

When you write sentences of different lengths and types, you create sentence variety. Along with sentence variety, emphasis adds weight to important ideas.

⊙ Watch the Video

Using techniques of variety and emphasis adds style and clarity to your writing. As you revise, apply the principles of variety and emphasis.

38C How do different sentence lengths create variety and emphasis?

To emphasize one idea among many others, you can express it in a sentence noticeably different in length from the sentences surrounding it. In the following example, a four-word sentence between two longer sentences carries the key message of the passage (**boldface** added).

> Today is one of those excellent January partly cloudies in which light chooses an unexpected landscape to trick out in gilt, and then shadow sweeps it away. **You know you're alive**. You take huge steps, trying to feel the planet's roundness arc between your feet.
>
> —Annie Dillard, *Pilgrim at Tinker Creek*

Sometimes a string of short sentences creates impact and emphasis. Yet, at other times, a string of short sentences can be dull to read.

● **EXERCISE 38-1** The following paragraph is dull because it has only short sentences. Combine some of the sentences to make a paragraph that has a variety of sentence lengths.

> There is a problem. It is widely known as sick-building syndrome. It comes from indoor air pollution. It causes office workers to suffer. They have trouble breathing. They have painful rashes. Their heads ache. Their eyes burn. ●

Similarly, a string of COMPOUND SENTENCES can be monotonous to read and may fail to communicate relationships among ideas.

● **EXERCISE 38-2** The following paragraph is dull because it has only compound sentences. Revise it to provide more variety.

> Science fiction writers are often thinkers, **and** they are often dreamers, **and** they let their imaginations wander. Jules Verne was such a writer, **and** he predicted spaceships, **and** he forecast atomic submarines, **but** most people did not believe airplanes were possible. ●

38D What are coordination and subordination?

👁 **Coordination** is an arrangement of ideas of approximately equal importance.
Watch
the Video **Subordination**, by contrast, arranges ideas of unequal importance. Using these arrangements effectively creates variety and emphasis in your writing. We explain these further in 38E and 38H, but here's an example.

TWO SENTENCES	The sky grew cloudy. The wind howled.
USING COORDINATION	The sky grew cloudy, and the wind howled.
USING SUBORDINATION 1	As the sky grew cloudy, the wind howled.
	Here, the *wind* receives the focus.
USING SUBORDINATION 2	As the wind howled, the sky grew cloudy.
	Here the *sky* receives the focus.

38E What is coordination of sentences?

COORDINATION of sentences is an arrangement of equivalent or balanced ideas in two or more INDEPENDENT CLAUSES. Coordination produces harmony by bringing related elements together. Whenever you use the device of coordination of sentences, be sure that it communicates the meaning you intend.

- The sky turned **brighter, and** people emerged happily from buildings.
- The sky turned **brighter;** people emerged happily from buildings.

38F What is the structure of a coordinate sentence?

A **coordinate sentence**, also called a *compound sentence* (28Q), consists of two or more INDEPENDENT CLAUSES joined either by a semicolon or by a comma and a COORDINATING CONJUNCTION. Here is the pattern for coordination of sentences.

Independent clause
$$\left\{ \begin{array}{l} \text{, and} \\ \text{, but} \\ \text{, for} \\ \text{, or} \\ \text{, nor} \\ \text{, yet} \\ \text{, so} \\ \text{;} \end{array} \right\}$$
independent clause.

38G What meaning does each coordinating conjunction convey?

When you use a **coordinating conjunction**, be sure that its meaning expresses the relationship between the equivalent ideas that you intend.

- **and** means addition
- **but** and **yet** mean contrast
- **for** means reason or choice
- **or** means choice
- **nor** means negative choice
- **so** means result or effect

⚠ **Alert:** Always use a comma before a coordinating conjunction that joins two INDEPENDENT CLAUSES (42B).●

38H How can I use coordination effectively?

COORDINATION is effective when each INDEPENDENT CLAUSE is related or equivalent. If they aren't, the result is an illogical pairing of unrelated ideas.

> **NO** Computers came into common use in the 1970s, and they sometimes make costly errors.
>
> The two ideas ideas are not related or equivalent.

> **YES** Computers came into common use in the 1970s, and now they are indispensable business tools.

Coordination also succeeds when it's not overused. Simply bundling sentences together with COORDINATING CONJUNCTIONS overburdens readers.

> **NO** Dinosaurs could have disappeared for many reasons, **and** one theory holds that a sudden shower of meteors and asteroids hit the earth, **so** the impact created a huge dust cloud that caused a false winter. The winter lasted for years, **and** the dinosaurs died.

> **YES** Dinosaurs could have disappeared for many reasons. One theory holds that a sudden shower of meteors and asteroids hit the earth. The impact created a huge dust cloud that caused a false winter. The winter lasted for years, killing the dinosaurs.

● **EXERCISE 38-3** Working individually or with a group, revise these sentences to eliminate illogical or overused coordination. If you think a sentence needs no revision, explain why.

EXAMPLE

The ratel is an animal often called a "honey badger," and it's actually more closely related to a weasel than a badger.

The ratel is an animal often called a "honey badger," **but** it's actually more closely related to a weasel than a badger.

1. The honey badger is a difficult opponent for predators, and it has thick, loose skin that protects it from injury, and it is able to fight fiercely with its strong claws.
2. Honey badgers are known to be fearless fighters, but they can often survive bites from venomous snakes.
3. They are skilled at digging their own burrows, but these holes usually only have one passage and are not very large.
4. Primarily carnivorous, honey badgers hunt rodents, snakes, and even tortoises, so at times they also eat vegetables, roots, and berries.
5. Honey badgers are difficult to kill and are expert burrowers, but they are a common nuisance to farmers and ranchers. ●

381 What is subordination in sentences?

SUBORDINATION is an arrangement of ideas of unequal importance within a sentence. Subordination is effective when you place the more important idea in an INDEPENDENT CLAUSE and the less important, subordinate idea in a DEPENDENT CLAUSE. Let your own judgment decide which of your ideas is most important, and subordinate other ideas to it.

INDEPENDENT CLAUSE   DEPENDENT

• Two cowboys fought a dangerous Colorado snowstorm **while they**

CLAUSE   DEPENDENT CLAUSE

were looking for cattle. When they came to a canyon,

INDEPENDENT CLAUSE

they saw outlines of buildings through the blizzard.

The passage below conveys the same message without subordination.

• Two cowboys fought a dangerous Colorado snowstorm. They were looking for cattle. They came to a canyon. They saw outlines of buildings through the blizzard.

38J What is the structure of a subordinate sentence?

A subordinate sentence starts the DEPENDENT CLAUSE with either a SUBOR-DINATING CONJUNCTION or a RELATIVE PRONOUN.

If they are very lucky, the passengers may glimpse dolphins near the ship.

—Elizabeth Gray, student

Pandas are solitary animals, **which** means they are difficult to protect from extinction.

—Jose Santos, student

For patterns of subordination, see Quick Box 38.1. Dependent clauses are either ADVERB CLAUSES or ADJECTIVE CLAUSES. An adverb clause starts with a subordinating conjunction. An adjective clause starts with a relative pronoun.

Quick Box 38.1   ■ ■ ■ ■ ■ ■ ■ ■ ■ ■

Subordination

SENTENCES WITH ADVERB CLAUSES

• **Adverb clause**, independent clause.
  • **After the sky grew dark**, the wind died suddenly.

• Independent clause, **adverb clause**.
  • Birds stopped singing, **as they do during an eclipse**.

• Independent clause **adverb clause**.
  • The stores closed **before the storm began**.

continued >>

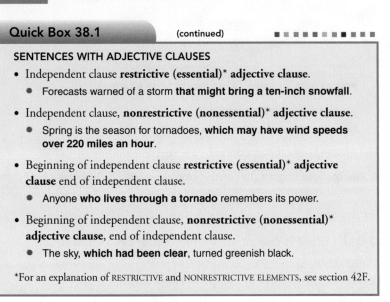

Quick Box 38.1   (continued)   ■ ■ ■ ■ ■ ■ ■ ■ ■ ■ ■

SENTENCES WITH ADJECTIVE CLAUSES

- Independent clause **restrictive (essential)* adjective clause.**
  - Forecasts warned of a storm **that might bring a ten-inch snowfall.**

- Independent clause, **nonrestrictive (nonessential)* adjective clause.**
  - Spring is the season for tornadoes, **which may have wind speeds over 220 miles an hour.**

- Beginning of independent clause **restrictive (essential)* adjective clause** end of independent clause.
  - Anyone **who lives through a tornado** remembers its power.

- Beginning of independent clause, **nonrestrictive (nonessential)* adjective clause,** end of independent clause.
  - The sky, **which had been clear,** turned greenish black.

*For an explanation of RESTRICTIVE and NONRESTRICTIVE ELEMENTS, see section 42F.

38K What meaning does each subordinating conjunction convey?

When you choose a SUBORDINATING CONJUNCTION, be sure that its meaning expresses the relationship between the ideas that you want to convey. Quick Box 38.2 lists subordinating conjunctions according to their different meanings.

Quick Box 38.2   ■ ■ ■ ■ ■ ■ ■ ■ ■ ■ ■

Subordinating conjunctions and their meanings

TIME
after, before, once, since, until, when, whenever, while
- **After** you have handed in your report, you cannot revise it.

REASON OR CAUSE
as, because, since
- **Because** you have handed in your report, you cannot revise it.

PURPOSE OR RESULT
in order that, so that, that
- I want to read your report **so that** I can evaluate it.

continued >>

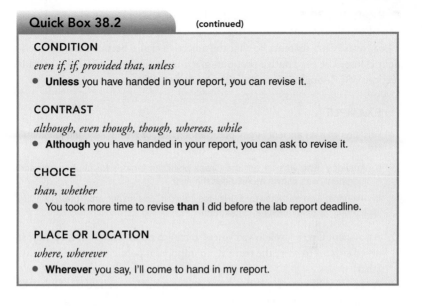

Quick Box 38.2   (continued)

CONDITION

even if, if, provided that, unless
- **Unless** you have handed in your report, you can revise it.

CONTRAST

although, even though, though, whereas, while
- **Although** you have handed in your report, you can ask to revise it.

CHOICE

than, whether
- You took more time to revise **than** I did before the lab report deadline.

PLACE OR LOCATION

where, wherever
- **Wherever** you say, I'll come to hand in my report.

● **EXERCISE 38-4** Working individually or with a group, combine each pair of sentences, using an adverb clause to subordinate one idea. Then, revise each sentence so that the adverb clause becomes the independent clause.

EXAMPLE

The U.S. Mint produces new coins. The U.S. Bureau of Engraving and Printing makes $1, $5, $10, $20, $50, and $100 bills.

a. While the U.S. Mint produces new coins, the U.S. Bureau of Engraving and Printing makes $1, $5, $10, $20, $50, and $100 bills.

b. While the U.S. Bureau of Engraving and Printing makes $1, $5, $10, $20, $50, and $100 bills, the U.S. Mint produces new coins.

1. The U.S. Mint can produce more than 50 million coins a day. The U.S. Bureau of Engraving and Printing can produce 20 million notes a day.
2. The Federal Reserve Banks are responsible for both destroying old money and ordering new coins and notes. They must keep the right amount of money in circulation.
3. Coins can stay in circulation for decades. People let them accumulate in jars and drawers in their homes.
4. A $1 bill lasts about fifteen to eighteen months. It reaches its average life span.
5. The U.S. Federal Reserve Banks destroy dirty, worn, and torn bills. The Federal Reserve Banks are destroying more than $40 billion worth of money a year. ●

● **EXERCISE 38-5** Working individually or with a group, combine each pair of sentences, using an adjective clause to subordinate one idea to the other. Then, revise each sentence so that the adjective clause becomes the independent clause. Use the relative pronoun given in parentheses. For help, consult sections 38I through 38K, especially Quick Box 38.1.

EXAMPLE

Aristides was an ancient Greek politician famous for his honesty and judgment. He was known as Aristides the Just. (who)

a. Aristides, *who* was an ancient Greek politician famous for his honesty and judgment, was known as Aristides the Just.

b. Aristides, *who* was known as Aristides the Just, was an ancient Greek politician famous for his honesty and judgment.

1. An ancient Greek law allowed voters to banish politicians from their city. It asked citizens to write the name of an unpopular politician on their ballots. (that)

2. A voter was filling out a ballot when Aristides the Just walked by. The voter needed help in spelling *Aristides*. (who)

3. Aristides knew the voter did not recognize him. He asked why the voter wanted to banish that particular politician. (who)

4. The voter said he resented hearing someone called "the Just" all the time. He handed Aristides his ballot. (who)

5. Aristides' reaction demonstrated that the nickname "the Just" was well deserved. His reaction was to write his own name on the voter's ballot even though that person's vote helped banish Aristides. (which) ●

38L   How can I use subordination effectively?

Effective SUBORDINATING CONJUNCTIONS communicate a logical relationship between the INDEPENDENT CLAUSE and the DEPENDENT CLAUSE. See Quick Box 38.2 for a list of subordinating conjunctions and their meanings.

> **NO**   **Because** he was injured in the sixth inning, he remained in the game.
>
> *Because* is illogical here; it says that his injury caused him to remain.

> **YES**   **Although** he was injured in the sixth inning, he remained in the game.
>
> *Although* is logical here; it says that he remained despite his injury.

Subordination is also effective when you avoid overusing it and crowding too many ideas together in one sentence. If you write a sentence with two or more dependent clauses, check that your message is clear.

NO A new technique for eye surgery, **which is supposed to correct nearsightedness, which previously could be corrected only by glasses**, has been developed, **although many eye doctors do not approve of the new technique because it can create unstable vision, which includes intense glare from headlights on cars and many other light sources**.

The base sentence *A new technique for eye surgery has been developed* is lost among five dependent clauses.

YES A new technique for eye surgery, **which is supposed to correct nearsightedness**, has been developed. Previously, only glasses could correct nearsightedness. Many doctors do not approve of the new technique **because it can create unstable vision**. The problems include intense glare from car headlights and many other sources of light.

This revision breaks one long sentence into four sentences, which clarifies the relationships among the ideas. Two dependent clauses remain, which balance well with the other sentence constructions. Some words have been moved to new positions.

 ESOL Tip: If readers advise that your sentences are too complex, limit the number of words in each sentence. Many ESOL instructors recommend that you revise any sentence that contains more than three clauses in any combination. ●

● **EXERCISE 38-6** Working individually or with a group, correct illogical or excessive subordination in this paragraph. As you revise according to the message you want to deliver, use some dependent clauses as well as some short sentences.

Although many people in the United States consider the hot dog an American invention, it actually originated in Germany in 1852 when butchers in Frankfurt, Germany, stuffed meat into a long casing, which, in honor of the town, they called a "frankfurter." Because one butcher noticed that the frankfurter resembled the shape of his dog, a dachshund, he decided to name the meat roll a "dachshund sausage," a name which caught on in Germany. When Germans brought dachshund sausages to the United States, peddlers sold them on the streets, although the dachshund sausages were so hot that people often burned their fingers because they had trouble holding the meat. When one clever peddler put the sausage in a bun, a *New York Times* cartoonist decided to draw a picture of hot dachshund sausages in buns, although he called them "hot dogs" because he didn't know how to spell *dachshund*. ●

38M How can I effectively use coordination and subordination together?

Your writing style improves when you combine a variety of sentence types, using COORDINATION and SUBORDINATION to improve the flow of ideas. This paragraph demonstrates a good balance of coordination and subordination.

> When I was growing up, I lived on a farm just across the field from my grandmother. My parents were busy trying to raise six children and to establish their struggling dairy farm. It was nice to have Grandma so close. While my parents were providing the necessities of life, my patient grandmother gave her time to her shy, young granddaughter. I always enjoyed going with Grandma and collecting the eggs that her chickens had just laid. Usually, she knew which chickens would peck, and she was careful to let me gather the eggs from the less hostile ones.

> —Patricia Mapes, student

When you use both coordination and subordination, never use both a COORDINATE CONJUNCTION and a SUBORDINATE CONJUNCTION to express one relationship in one sentence.

NO **Although** the story was well written, **but** it was too illogical.

Select either *although* or *but* to express the contrast, not both.

YES **Although** the story was well written, it was too illogical.

YES The story was well written, **but** it was too illogical.

● **EXERCISE 38-7** Working individually or in a group, use subordination and coordination to combine these sets of short, choppy sentences. For help, consult all sections of this chapter.

EXAMPLE
Owls cannot digest the bones and fur of the mice and birds they eat. They cough up a furry pellet every day.
Because owls cannot digest the bones and fur of the mice and birds they *eat, they* cough up a furry pellet every day.

1. Owl pellets are a rich teaching tool in biology classrooms around the country. The pellets provide an alternative to dissecting frogs and other animals.
2. Inside the pellet are the remains of the owl's nightly meal. They include beautifully cleaned hummingbird skulls, rat skeletons, and lots of bird feathers.
3. The owl-pellet market has been cornered by companies in New York, California, and Washington. These companies distribute pellets to thousands of biology classrooms all over the world.

4. Company workers scour barns and the ground under trees where owls nest to pick up the pellets. The pellets sell for $1 each.
5. The owl-pellet business may have a short future. The rural areas of the United States are vanishing. Old barns are being bulldozed. All the barns are torn down. The owls will be gone, too. ●

38N How do occasional questions, commands, or exclamations create variety and emphasis?

Most English sentences are DECLARATIVE—they make statements; they declare. For emphasis and variety, consider three other types of sentences you can choose.

An INTERROGATIVE sentence poses a question. Occasional questions, appropriately placed, tend to involve readers. An IMPERATIVE sentence issues a command. Occasional mild commands, appropriately used, gently urge readers to think along with you. An EXCLAMATORY sentence expresses strong or sudden emotion. Use exclamatory sentences sparingly in ACADEMIC WRITING.

● **Alert:** A declarative statement ends with a period (see Chapter 41)—or semicolon (see Chapter 43) or colon (see Chapter 44). A mild command ends with a period. A strong command and an exclamation end with an exclamation point (see Chapter 41). ●

Here's a paragraph with declarative, interrogative, and imperative sentences.

> Imagine what people ate during the winter as little as seventy-five years ago. They ate food that was local, long-lasting, and dull, like acorn squash, turnips, and cabbage. Walk into an American supermarket in February and the world lies before you: grapes, melons, artichokes, fennel, lettuce, peppers, pistachios, dates, even strawberries, to say nothing of ice cream. Have you ever considered what a triumph of civilization it is to be able to buy a pound of chicken livers? If you lived on a farm and had to kill a chicken when you wanted to eat one, you wouldn't ever accumulate a pound of chicken livers.

> —Phyllis Rose, "Shopping and Other Spiritual Adventures in America Today"

38O What are cumulative and periodic sentences?

In an **cumulative sentence**, the most common in English, information accumulates after an opening SUBJECT and VERB. To build suspense into your writing, you might occasionally use a **periodic sentence**. A periodic sentence reserves its main idea—its punch—until the end of the sentence. When you overuse them, however, periodic sentences lose their punch.

CUMULATIVE	A car hit a shoulder and turned over at midnight last night on the road from Las Vegas to Death Valley Junction.
PERIODIC	At midnight last night, on the road from Las Vegas to Death Valley Junction, a car hit a shoulder and turned over.

—Joan Didion, "On Morality"

You can build both cumulative and periodic sentences to dramatic—and sometimes excessive—lengths.

EXAMPLE: How cumulative sentences can grow

1. The downtown bustled with new construction.
2. **The downtown bustled with new construction**, as buildings shot up everywhere, transforming the skyline.
3. **The downtown bustled with new constructio**n, as buildings shot up everywhere, each a mixture of glass and steel, in colors from rust red to ice blue, transforming the skyline from a shy set of bumps to a bold display of mountains

EXAMPLE: How periodic sentences can grow

1. Marla accepted the job offer.
2. With some reservations about the salary offer and location, **Marla accepted the job offer**.
3. After a day of agonizing and a night without sleep, still having some reservations about the salary offer and location, especially with the company being in an unappealing city more than 400 miles from her fiancé, **Marla accepted the job offer.**

38P How can modifiers create variety and emphasis?

MODIFIERS can add richness to your writing and create a pleasing mixture of variety and emphasis. The longer cumulative and periodic sentence examples in section 38O illustrate the use of modifiers. Your choice of where to place modifiers depends on the focus you want each sentence to communicate, either on its own or in concert with its surrounding sentences. Place modifiers carefully to avoid the error known as a MISPLACED MODIFIER.

NO (MISPLACED MODIFIER)	A huge, hairy, grunting thing, I agreed that the bull was scary.
YES	A huge, hairy, grunting thing, the bull was scary, I agreed.

In the No example, it sounds like the writer, I, was huge, hairy, and grunting!

BASIC SENTENCE	The river rose.
ADJECTIVE	The **swollen** river rose.
ADVERB	The river rose **dangerously**.
PREPOSITIONAL PHRASE	The river rose **above its banks**.
PARTICIPIAL PHRASE	**Swelled by melting snow,** the river rose.
ABSOLUTE PHRASE	**Uprooted trees swirling away in the current,** the river rose.
ADVERB CLAUSE	**Because the snows had been heavy that winter,** the river rose.
ADJECTIVE CLAUSE	The river, **which runs through vital farmland,** rose.

● **EXERCISE 38-8** Working individually or with a group, expand each sentence by adding each kind of modifier illustrated in section 38P.

1. I bought a ball.
2. We found the park.
3. The children arrived.
4. The sun shone.
5. We played the game. ●

38Q How does repetition affect style?

You can repeat words that express a main idea to create a rhythm that draws attention to the main idea. PARALLELISM (Chapter 39), another kind of repetition, repeats grammatical structures as well as words. Here's an example that uses deliberate repetition along with a variety of sentence lengths to deliver its meaning.

> All traces of life, of natural expression, were gone from him. His face was like a human skull, a death's head, spouting **blood**. The eyes were filled with **blood**, the nose streamed with **blood**, the mouth gaped **blood**.

> —William Hazlitt, "The Fight"

At the same time, don't confuse deliberate repetition with a lack of vocabulary variety.

NO An insurance agent can be an excellent adviser when you want to buy a car. An insurance agent has complete records on most cars. An insurance agent knows which car models are prone to accidents. An insurance agent can tell you which car models are expensive to repair if they are in a collision. An insurance agent can tell you which models are most likely to be stolen.

Synonyms for *insurance agent, car,* and *model* should be used. Also, the sentence structure here lacks variety.

YES If you are thinking of buying a new car, an insurance agent, who usually has complete records on most cars, can be an excellent adviser. Any professional insurance broker knows which automobile models are prone to have accidents. Did you know that some cars suffer more damage than others in a collision? If you want to know which vehicles crumple more than others and which are the most expensive to repair, ask an insurance agent. Similarly, some car models are more likely to be stolen, so find out from the person who specializes in dealing with car insurance claims.

38R How else can I create variety and emphasis?

CHANGING WORD ORDER

Standard word order in English places the SUBJECT before the VERB.

- The **mayor** *walked* into the room.

  Mayor, the subject, comes before the verb *walked*.

Inverted order, which places the verb before the subject, creates emphasis.

- Into the room *walked* the **mayor**.

  Mayor, the subject, comes after the verb *walked*.

CHANGING A SENTENCE'S SUBJECT

The subject of a sentence establishes the focus for that sentence. To create the emphasis you want, you can vary each sentence's subject. Notice how the focus changes in each sentence below according to the subject (and its corresponding verb).

- **Our study showed** that 25 percent of college freshmen gain weight.

  Focus is on the study.

- **College freshmen gain weight** 25 percent of the time, our study shows.

  Focus is on the freshmen.

- **Weight gain hits** 25 percent of college freshmen, our study shows.

  Focus is on weight gain.

- **Twenty-five percent of college freshmen** gain weight, our study shows.

  Focus is on the percentage of students.

● **EXERCISE 38-9** Working individually or with a group, revise the sentences in each paragraph to change the passage's style. For help, consult the advice in all sections of this chapter.

1. Thirst is the body's way of surviving. Every cell in the body needs water. People can die by losing as little as 15 to 20 percent of their water requirements. Blood contains 83 percent water. Blood provides indispensable nutrients for the cells. Blood carries water to the cells. Blood carries waste away from the cells. Insufficient water means cells cannot be fueled or cleaned. The body becomes sluggish. The body can survive eleven days without water. Bodily functions are seriously disrupted by a lack of water for more than one day. The body loses water. The blood thickens. The heart must pump harder. Thickened blood is harder to pump through the heart. Some drinks replace the body's need for fluids. Alcohol or caffeine in drinks leads to dehydration. People know they should drink water often. They can become moderately dehydrated before they even begin to develop a thirst.

2. June is the wet season in Ghana. Here in Accra, the capital, the morning rain has ceased. The sun heats the humid air. Pillars of black smoke begin to rise above the vast Agbobgloshie Market. I follow one plume toward its source. I pass lettuce and plantain vendors. I pass stalls of used tires. I walk through a clanging scrap market. In the market hunched men bash on old alternators and engine blocks.

    —Based on a paragraph by Chris Carroll in "High Tech Trash"

3. Because of the development of new economies around the world, with resulting demands for new construction and goods, especially in places like China, there is a high demand for steel, and a new breed of American entrepreneurs is making money in meeting this opportunity. For much of industrial history, steel was made from iron ore and coke, a process that resulted in what might be called "new steel." However, it has now become even more profitable to make recycled steel, melting down junk and recasting it, a process made possible because steel, unlike paper and plastic, can be recycled indefinitely. Because the process saves energy and helps the environment by saving on the amount of ore that has to be mined, manufacturing recycled steel has benefits beyond profitability. ●

Complete the Chapter Exercises

39 Parallelism

■ ■ ■ ■ ■ ■ ■ ■ ■ ■

Quick Points   You will learn to

➤ Use parallel structures to give rhythm and grace to your writing (see 39A–39E).

39A   What is parallelism?

Watch the Video

When words, PHRASES, or CLAUSES within a sentence match in grammatical form, the result is **parallelism**. Parallelism can emphasize information or stress ideas in your writing.

● I came; I saw; I conquered

You gain several advantages in using parallel structures:

• You can express ideas of equal weight in your writing.
• You can emphasize important information or ideas.
• You can add rhythm and grace to your writing style.

Many writers attend to parallelism when they are REVISING. If you think while you're DRAFTING that your parallelism is faulty or that you can enhance your style by using parallelism, underline or highlight the material and keep moving forward. When you revise, you can return to the places you've marked.

Using COORDINATION, a **balanced sentence** delivers contrast, usually between two INDEPENDENT CLAUSES. Often, one clause is positive, the other negative.

> By night, the litter and desperation disappeared as the city's glittering lights came on; by day, the filth and despair reappeared as the sun rose.
>
> —Jennifer Kirk, student

🛈 **Alert:** In ACADEMIC WRITING, to avoid appearing to make the error of a COMMA SPLICE, use a semicolon (or revise in some other way), as in the following sentence.

● Mosquitoes don't bite; they stab. ●

39B How do words, phrases, and clauses work in parallel form?

When you put words, PHRASES, and CLAUSES into parallel form, you enhance your writing style with balance and grace.

PARALLEL WORDS	Recommended exercise includes running, swimming, and cycling.
PARALLEL PHRASES	Exercise helps people maintain healthy bodies and handle mental pressures.
PARALLEL CLAUSES	Many people exercise because they want to look healthy, because they need to increase stamina, and because they hope to live longer.

39C How does parallelism deliver impact?

Deliberate, rhythmic repetition of parallel forms creates balance, reinforcing the impact of a message.

> Go back to Mississippi, go back to Alabama, go back to South Carolina, go back to Georgia, go back to Louisiana, go back to the slums and ghettos of our northern cities, knowing that somehow this situation can and will be changed.

> —Martin Luther King Jr., "I Have a Dream"

If King had not used PARALLELISM, his message would have made less of an impact on his listeners. His structures reinforce the power of his message. A sentence without parallelism might have carried his message, but with far less effect: *Return to your homes in Mississippi, Alabama, South Carolina, Georgia, Louisiana, or the northern cities, and know that the situation will be changed.*

Here's a longer passage in which parallel structures, concepts, and rhythms operate. Together, they echo the intensity of the writer's message.

> The strongest reason why we ask for woman a voice in the government under which she lives; in the religion she is asked to believe; equality in social life, where she is the chief factor; a place in the trades and professions, where she may earn her bread, is **because** of her birthright to self-sovereignty; **because**, as an individual, she must rely on herself. No matter how much women prefer **to lean**, **to be** protected and supported, nor how much men desire **to have** them do so, they must make the voyage of life alone, and for safety in an emergency they must know something of the laws of navigation. To guide our own craft, we must be captain, pilot, engineer; with chart and compass to stand at the

wheel; to watch the wind and waves and know when to take in the sail, and to read the signs in the firmament over all.

—Elizabeth Cady Stanton, "Address for the Hearing of the Woman Suffrage Association"

● **EXERCISE 39-1** Working individually or with a group, highlight all parallel elements of the preceding Elizabeth Cady Stanton passage in addition to those shown in boldface. ●

39D How can I avoid faulty parallelism?

Faulty parallelism occurs when you join nonmatching grammatical forms.

PARALLELISM WITH COORDINATING CONJUNCTIONS

The coordinating conjunctions are *and, but, for, or, nor, yet*, and *so*. To avoid faulty parallelism, write the words that accompany coordinating conjunctions in matching grammatical forms.

> NO   **Love *and* being married** go together.
>
> YES   **Love *and* marriage** go together.
>
> YES   **Being in love *and* being married** go together.

PARALLELISM WITH CORRELATIVE CONJUNCTIONS

Correlative conjunctions are paired words such as *not only . . . but (also), either . . . or*, and *both . . . and*. To avoid faulty parallelism, write the words joined by correlative conjunctions in matching grammatical forms.

> NO   *Either* you must attend classes *or* will be failing the course.
>
> YES   *Either* you attend classes *or* fail the course.

PARALLELISM WITH *THAN* AND *AS*

To avoid faulty parallelism when you use *than* and *as* for comparisons, write the elements of comparison in matching grammatical forms.

> NO   **Having a solid marriage** can be more satisfying ***than* the acquisition of wealth.**
>
> YES   **Having a solid marriage** can be more satisfying ***than* acquiring wealth.**
>
> YES   **A solid marriage** can be more satisfying ***than* wealth.**

PARALLELISM WITH FUNCTION WORDS

Function words include ARTICLES (*the, a, an*); the *to* of the INFINITIVE (*to* love); PREPOSITIONS (for example, *of, in, about*); and sometimes RELATIVE PRONOUNS. When you use parallel structures, be consistent about either repeating or omitting a function word. Generally, repeat function words when the repetition clarifies your meaning or highlights the parallelism.

> NO **To assign** unanswered letters their proper weight, **free** us from the expectations of others, **to give** us back to ourselves—here lies the great, the singular power of self-respect.

> YES **To assign** unanswered letters their proper weight, **to free** us from the expectations of others, **to give** us back to ourselves—here lies the great, the singular power of self-respect.
>
> —Joan Didion, "On Self-Respect"

I have in my own life a precious friend, a woman of 65 **who has** lived very hard, **who is** wise, **who listens** well, **who has been** where I am and can help me understand it, and **who represents** not only an ultimate ideal mother to me but also the person I'd like to be when I grow up.

> —Judith Viorst, "Friends, Good Friends—and Such Good Friends"

We looked into the bus, which **was** painted blue with orange daisies, **had** picnic benches instead of seats, and **showed** yellow curtains billowing out its windows.

> —Kerrie Falk, student

● **EXERCISE 39-2** Working individually or with a group, revise these sentences by putting appropriate information in parallel structures. For help, consult sections 39A through 39E.

EXAMPLE

Difficult bosses affect not only their employees' performances but their private lives are affected as well.

Difficult bosses affect not only their employees' performances *but their private lives as well.*

1. According to the psychologist Harry Levinson, the five main types of bad boss are the workaholic, the kind of person you would describe as bullying, a person who communicates badly, the jellyfish type, and someone who insists on perfection.
2. As a way of getting ahead, to keep their self-respect, and for survival purposes, wise employees handle problem bosses with a variety of strategies.
3. To cope with a bad-tempered employer, workers can both stand up for themselves and reasoning with a bullying boss.

4. Often, bad bosses communicate poorly or fail to calculate the impact of their personality on others; being a careful listener and sensitivity to others' responses are qualities that good bosses possess.
5. Employees who take the trouble to understand what makes their bosses tick, engage in some self-analysis, and staying flexible are better prepared to cope with a difficult job environment than suffering in silence like some employees. ●

● **EXERCISE 39-3** Working individually or with a group, combine the sentences in each numbered item, using techniques of parallelism. For help, consult sections 39A through 39E.

EXAMPLE

College scholarships are awarded not only for academic and athletic ability, but there are also scholarships that recognize unusual talents. Other scholarships even award accidents of birth, like left-handedness.

College scholarships are awarded not only for academic and athletic ability *but also for unusual talents and even for accidents of birth, like left-handedness.*

1. A married couple met at Juniata College in Huntingdon, Pennsylvania. They are both left-handed, and they have set up a scholarship for needy left-handed students attending Juniata.
2. Writers who specialize in humor bankroll a student humor writer at the University of Southern California in Los Angeles. A horse-racing association sponsors a student sportswriter. The student must attend Vanderbilt University in Nashville, Tennessee.
3. The Rochester Institute of Technology in New York State chose 150 students born on June 12, 1979. Each one received a grant of $1,500 per year. These awards were given to select students to honor the school's 150th anniversary, which was celebrated on June 12, 1979.
4. The College of Wooster in Ohio grants generous scholarships to students if they play the bagpipes, a musical instrument native to Scotland. Students playing the traditional Scottish drums and those who excel in Scottish folk dancing also qualify.
5. In return for their scholarships, Wooster's bagpipers must pipe for the school's football team. The terms of the scholarships also require the drummers to drum for the team. The dancers have to cheer the athletes from the sidelines. ●

● **EXERCISE 39-4** Working individually or with a group, underline the parallel elements in these passages. Next, imitate the parallelism in the examples, using a different topic of your choice for each.

A. Even though large tracts of Europe and many old and famous States have fallen or may fall into the grip of the Gestapo and all the odious apparatus of Nazi rule, we shall not flag or fail. We shall go on to the end. We shall fight in France, we shall fight on the seas and oceans, we shall fight with growing confidence and growing strength in the air, we shall defend our island, whatever the cost may be. We shall fight on the beaches, we shall fight on the landing grounds, we shall fight in the fields and in the streets, we shall fight in the hills; we shall never surrender, and if, which I do not for a moment believe, this island or a large part of it were subjugated and starving, then our Empire beyond the seas, armed and guarded by the British Fleet, would carry on the struggle, until, in God's good time, the new world, with all its power and might, steps forth to the rescue and the liberation of the old.

—Winston Churchill

B. Our religion is the traditions of our ancestors—the dreams of our old men, given them in solemn hours of the night by the Great Spirit; and the visions of our sachems, and is written in the hearts of our people.

Our dead never forget this beautiful world that gave them being. They still love its verdant valleys, its murmuring rivers, its magnificent mountains, sequestered vales and verdant lined lakes and bays, and ever yearn in tender fond affection over the lonely hearted living, and often return from the happy hunting ground to visit, guide, console, and comfort them.

It matters little where we pass the remnant of our days. They will not be many. The Indian's night promises to be dark. Not a single star of hope hovers above his horizon. Sad-voiced winds moan in the distance. Grim fate seems to be on the Red Man's trail, and wherever he will hear the approaching footsteps of his fell destroyer and prepare stolidly to meet his doom, as does the wounded doe that hears the approaching footsteps of the hunter.

—Oration attributed to Chief Seattle ●

39E How does parallelism work in outlines and lists?

All items in formal OUTLINES and lists must be parallel in grammar and structure. (For more about outline format and outline development, see section 5G.)

OUTLINES

NO   Reducing Traffic Fatalities
    I. Stricter laws
       A. Top speed should be 55 mph on highways.
       B. Higher fines
       C. Requiring jail sentences for repeat offenders
    II. The use of safety devices should be mandated by law.

YES Reducing Traffic Fatalities
    I. Passing stricter speed laws
       A. Making 55 mph the top speed on highways
       B. Raising fines for speeding
       C. Requiring jail sentences for repeat offenders
    II. Mandating by law the use of safety devices

LISTS

NO Workaholics share these characteristics:
    1. They are intense and driven.
    2. Strong self-doubters
    3. Labor is preferred to leisure by workaholics.

YES Workaholics share these characteristics:
    1. They are intense and driven.
    2. They have strong self-doubts.
    3. They prefer labor to leisure.

● **EXERCISE 39-5** Working individually or with a group, revise this outline so that all lines are complete sentences in parallel form. For help, consult sections 5G and 39E.

IMPROVING HEALTH

  I. Exercise
    A. Aerobics
    B. Stretching and strength training
    C. Vary routine
  II. Better Eating Habits
    A. Healthy food
    B. Eat less
    C. Eat more often ●

Complete
the
Chapter
Exercises

40 Conciseness

■ ■ ■ ■ ■ ■ ■ ■ ■ ■

Quick Points   You will learn to

➤ Write concisely (40A–40E).

40A   What is conciseness?

Clear writing requires **conciseness**—sentences that are direct and to the point. By contrast, **wordiness** means you are padding sentences with words and phrases that increase the word count but contribute no meaning. As you're REVISING, look for ways to make your sentences more concise.

(margin: Watch the Video)

WORDY   ~~As a matter of fact,~~ the television station ~~which is in the local area~~
                                    T local
                 wins ~~a~~ ~~great~~ many awards ~~in the final analysis~~ because of its ~~type~~
                 ~~of~~ coverage of ~~all kinds of~~ controversial issues.

CONCISE   The local television station wins many awards for its coverage of
                 controversial issues.

40B   What common expressions are not concise?

Many common expressions we use in informal speech are not concise. Quick Box 40.1 lists some and shows you how to eliminate them.

Quick Box 40.1   ■ ■ ■ ■ ■ ■ ■ ■ ■ ■

Cutting unnecessary words and phrases

Empty Word or Phrase	Wordy Example Revised
as a matter of fact	Many marriages~~, as a matter of fact,~~ end in divorce.
at the present time	The revised proposal for outdoor lighting angers many villagers ~~at the present time~~.

(above "at the present time" struck-through: now)

continued >>

Quick Box 40.1 (continued)

Empty Word or Phrase	Wordy Example Revised
because of the fact that, in light of the fact that, due to the fact that	Because ~~of the fact that~~ the museum has a special exhibit, it stays open late.
by means of	We traveled by ~~means of a~~ car.
factor	The project's final cost was ~~the~~ essential ~~factor~~ to consider.
for the purpose of	Work crews arrived ~~for the purpose of~~ ^{to} fixing the potholes.
have a tendency to	The team ~~has a tendency~~ ^{tends} to lose home games.
in a very real sense	~~In a very real sense,~~ ^Aall firefighters are heroes.
in the case of	~~In the case of~~ ^Tthe election~~, it~~ will be close.
in the event that	~~In the event that~~ ^{If} you're late, I will buy our tickets.
in the final analysis	~~In the final analysis,~~ ^Nno two eyewitnesses agreed on what they saw.
in the process of	We are ~~in the process of~~ reviewing the proposal.
it seems that	~~It seems that~~ ^Tthe union went on strike over health benefits.
manner	The child spoke ~~in a reluctant manner.~~ ^{reluctantly.}
nature	The movie review was ~~of a~~ sarcastic ~~nature~~.
that exists	The crime rate ~~that exists~~ is unacceptable.
the point I am trying to make	~~The point I am trying to make is~~ ^Ttelevision reporters invade our privacy.
type of, kind of	Gordon took a relaxing ~~type of~~ vacation.
What I mean to say is	~~What I mean to say is~~ I love you.

● **EXERCISE 40-1** Working individually or with a group, revise this paragraph in two steps. First, underline all words that interfere with conciseness. Second, revise each sentence to make it more concise. (You'll need to drop words and replace or rearrange others.)

EXAMPLE

Because of the fact that a new building in Dubai was recently declared the "Tallest Building in the World," some people have a tendency to wonder how such a title is granted.

1. Because <u>of the fact that</u> a new building in Dubai was recently declared the "Tallest Building in the World," some people <u>have a tendency to</u> wonder who grants such a title.

2. Because a new building in Dubai was recently declared the "Tallest Building in the World," some wonder who grants such a title.

1. Tall buildings that exist are measured by a group known as The Council on Tall Buildings and Urban Habitat.

2. This group, as a matter of fact, was founded in 1969 and is responsible for determining which building is the tallest.

3. Due to the fact that buildings serve many purposes, it seems that there is debate on which buildings deserve consideration.

4. I am trying to make the point that The Council on Tall Buildings and Urban Habitat must distinguish between buildings and towers.

5. To be considered, a building has to be the kind of structure that has usable floor area.

6. In the event that a structure has no usable floor area, it is designated a tower.

7. Height is determined by means of measuring from the lowest pedestrian entrance to the highest point of the building.

8. There are debates that exist over the definitions used by the Council on Tall Buildings.

9. For example, in the event that a building has not opened yet, it cannot be considered.

10. Another debate and matter of controversy is whether a building's antenna is an essential factor in determining its height. ●

40C   What sentence structures usually work against conciseness?

Two sentence structures, although appropriate in some contexts, often work against CONCISENESS: EXPLETIVE constructions and the PASSIVE VOICE.

AVOIDING EXPLETIVE CONSTRUCTIONS

An **expletive construction** starts with *it* or *there* followed by a form of the VERB *be*. When you cut the expletive and revise, the sentence is more concise.

- ~~It is necessary for~~ students ~~to~~ fill in both questionnaires.

  (S ̦ must)

- ~~There are e~~ight instructors ~~who~~ teach in the Computer Science Department.

  (E)

🌐 **ESOL Tips:** (1) *It* in an expletive construction is not a PRONOUN referring to an ANTECEDENT. When expletive *it* occupies the subject position, the actual subject comes after the expletive: *It was the students who asked the question. Students* is the subject, not *it.* (2) *There* in an expletive construction does not indicate place. Although expletive *there* occupies the subject position, the actual subject comes after the expletive: *There were many students present. Students* is the subject, not *there.* ●

AVOIDING THE PASSIVE VOICE

In general, the passive voice is less concise and less lively than the ACTIVE VOICE. In the active voice, the subject performs the action named by the verb.

ACTIVE   Professor Higgins teaches public speaking.

    Professor Higgins, the subject, performs the action *teaches.*

In the passive voice, the subject receives the action named by the verb.

PASSIVE   Public speaking is taught by Professor Higgins.

    Public speaking, the subject, receives the action *taught.*

Unless your meaning justifies using the passive voice, choose the active voice. (For more information, see sections 29N through 29P.)

PASSIVE   Volunteer work was done by students for credit in sociology.

    The passive phrase *was done by students* is unnecessary for the intended meaning. *Students,* not *volunteer work,* are doing the action and should get the action of the verb.

ACTIVE   **The students did** volunteer work for credit in sociology.

ACTIVE   **Volunteer work earned** students credit in sociology.

    Since the verb has changed to *earned, volunteer work* performs the action of the verb.

The passive voice often creates wordy, overblown sentences, suggesting that a writer hasn't carefully revised.

> **NO** One very important quality that can be developed during a first job is self-reliance. This strength was gained by me when I was allowed by my supervisor to set up and conduct a survey project on my own.

> **YES** Many develop the important quality of self-reliance during their first job. I gained this strength when my supervisor allowed me to set up and conduct my own survey project.

> **YES** During their first job, many people develop self-reliance, as I did when my supervisor let me set up and conduct my own survey project.

If you're writing on a computer, you may find it helpful to use the word processing application's "Search" or "Find" feature to locate the words "was, is, be, were, and been" when you revise. This trick can help you find possible uses of passive voice and judge whether or not they need revision.

40D How else can I revise for conciseness?

Four other techniques can help you achieve CONCISENESS: eliminating unplanned repetition (40D.1); combining sentences (40D.2); shortening CLAUSES (40D.3); and shortening PHRASES and cutting words (40D.4).

40D.1 Eliminating unplanned repetition

Unplanned repetition delivers the same message more than once, usually in slightly different words. Unplanned repetition, or redundancy, unnecessarily burdens readers. The opposite—planned repetition—can create a powerful rhythmic effect (see 39E). As you revise, check that every word is necessary for delivering your message.

> **NO** Bringing **the project** to **final completion** three weeks early, the supervisor of **the project** earned our **respectful regard**.
>
> *Completion* implies *bringing to final; project* is used twice in one sentence; and *regard* implies *respect*.

> **YES** Completing the project three weeks early, the supervisor earned our respect.
>
> Eighteen words are reduced to eleven.

> **NO** **Astonished**, the architect **circled around** the building **in amazement**.
>
> *Circled* means "went around," and *astonished* and *in amazement* have the same meaning.

> **YES** **Astonished**, the architect **circled** the building.
>
> Nine words are reduced to six.

> **YES** The architect **circled** the building **in amazement**.
>
> Nine words are reduced to seven.

🌐 **ESOL Tip:** In all languages, words can carry an implied message. In English, some implied meanings can cause redundancy in writing. For example, *I wrote my blog by computer* is redundant. In English, *to write a blog* implies *by computer*. As you become more familiar with American English, you'll begin to notice such redundancies. ●

40D.2 Combining sentences

👁 Watch the Video

Sometimes you can fit information from several sentences into one sentence. (For more about combining sentences, see Chapter 38, particularly sections 38C, 38E, 38J, and 38M.)

TWO SENTENCES	The *Titanic* hit an iceberg and sank. Seventy-three years later, a team of French and American scientists located the ship's resting site.
SENTENCES COMBINED	Seventy-three years after the *Titanic* hit an iceberg and sank, a team of French and American scientists located the ship's resting site.
TWO SENTENCES	Cameras revealed that the stern of the ship was missing and showed external damage to the ship's hull. Otherwise, the *Titanic* was in excellent condition.
SENTENCES COMBINED	Aside from a missing stern and external damage to the ship's hull, the *Titanic* was in excellent condition.

40D.3 Shortening clauses

Look at clauses to see if you can more concisely convey the same information. For example, sometimes you can cut a RELATIVE PRONOUN and its verb.

WORDY	The *Titanic*, **which was** a huge ocean liner, sank in 1912.
CONCISE	The Titanic, a huge ocean liner, sank in 1912.

Sometimes you can reduce a clause to a word.

WORDY	The scientists held a memorial service for the passengers and crew **who had drowned**.
CONCISE	The scientists held a memorial service for the **drowned** passengers and crew.

An ELLIPTICAL CONSTRUCTION (see sections 28P and 36H) can shorten a clause. If you use this device, be sure that omitted words are implied clearly.

WORDY	**When they were** confronted with disaster, some passengers behaved heroically, **while** others **behaved** selfishly.
CONCISE	Confronted with disaster, some passengers behaved heroically, others selfishly.

40D.4 Shortening phrases and cutting words

Sometimes you can reduce a phrase or redundant word pair to a single word. Redundant word pairs and phrases include *each and every, one and only, forever and ever, final and conclusive, perfectly clear, few* (or *many*) *in number, consensus of opinion*, and *reason . . . is because.*

NO	**Each and every** person was hungry after the movie.
YES	**Every** person was hungry after the movie.
YES	**Each** person was hungry after the movie.
NO	The **consensus of opinion** was that the movie was dull.
YES	The **consensus** was that the movie was dull.
YES	**Everyone agreed** that the movie was dull.
WORDY	More than fifteen hundred **travelers on that voyage** died in the shipwreck.
CONCISE	More than fifteen hundred **passengers** died in the shipwreck.

Sometimes you can rearrange words so that others can be deleted.

WORDY	Objects **found** inside the ship included **unbroken** bottles of wine and expensive **undamaged** china.
CONCISE	**Undamaged** objects inside the ship included bottles of wine and expensive china.

40E How do verbs affect conciseness?

Action verbs are strong verbs. *Be* and *have* are verbs that can lead to wordy sentences. Action verbs can increase the impact of your writing and reduce the number of words in your sentences. You can often use strong verbs to reduce PHRASES and to replace NOUNS.

WEAK VERB	The plan before the city council **has to do with** tax rebates.
STRONG VERB	The plan before the city council **proposes** tax rebates.
WEAK VERBS	The board members **were of the opinion** that the changes in the rules **were changes they would not accept**.
STRONG VERBS	The board members **said** that **they would reject** the changes in the rules.

REPLACING A PHRASE WITH A VERB

Phrases such as *be aware of, be capable of, be supportive of* can often be replaced with one-word verbs.

- I **envy** [not *am envious of*] your mathematical ability.
- I **appreciate** [not *am appreciative of*] your modesty.
- Your skill **illustrates** [not *is illustrative of*] how hard you studied.

REVISING NOUNS INTO VERBS

Many nouns ending with *-ance, -ment,* and *-tion* (*tolerance, enforcement, narration*) are derived from verbs. Use of the vibrant verb will make your writing more concise.

> **NO** The **accumulation of** paper lasted thirty years.
>
> **YES** The paper **accumulated** for thirty years.
>
> **NO** We **arranged for the establishment of** a student advisory committee.
>
> **YES** We **established** a student advisory committee.
>
> **NO** The building **had the appearance of** having been neglected.
>
> **YES** The building **appeared** to have been neglected.

● **EXERCISE 40-2** Working individually or with a group, combine each set of sentences to eliminate wordy constructions.

EXAMPLE

Original: The Brooklyn Bridge was completed in 1883. It is one of the oldest suspension bridges in the United States

Revised: Completed in 1883, the Brooklyn Bridge is one of the oldest suspension bridges in the United States

1. The Brooklyn Bridge spans the East River. It connects Manhattan and Brooklyn. The span of the bridge is 1,595 feet.
2. When the Brooklyn Bridge opened, it was the longest suspension bridge in the world. It was the longest suspension bridge until 1903. In 1903, the Williamsburg Bridge became the longest suspension bridge in the world.
3. The original designer of the bridge was John Augustus Roebling. He was a German immigrant. He injured his foot then died from an infection. Before he died, he turned over control of construction to his son. His son's name was Washington Roebling.
4. Emily Warren Roebling supervised most of the building of the Brooklyn Bridge. Her husband, Washington Roebling, was unable to oversee construction. He had to stop working after suffering an illness.
5. Emily Warren Roebling spent fourteen years helping her husband oversee the building of the bridge. Her husband was sick. She had to learn

important things. She learned about stress analysis, cable construction, and catenary curves.

6. The bridge opened in May of 1883. Its opening was attended by several thousand people. The current president, Chester A. Arthur, attended the opening.

7. Some people were concerned about the bridge. They worried about the bridge's stability. P.T. Barnum was the founder of a famous circus. He led a parade of elephants over the bridge. There were 21 elephants in the parade.

8. The bridge celebrated its 100th anniversary in 1983. The president of the United States at that time was Ronald Reagan. He led a parade of cars across the bridge during the celebration.

9. Ken Burns is a filmmaker. In 1981, he made a documentary about the Brooklyn Bridge. Ken Burns has also directed documentaries about baseball and jazz and the Civil War.

10. The bridge has six lanes of automobile traffic. The bridge also allows for pedestrians to cross. Pedestrians can cross on a wide pedestrian walkway open to people who are walking. ●

Complete the Chapter Exercises

Using Punctuation
and Mechanics

41 Periods, Question Marks, and Exclamation Points

Quick Points   You will learn to

➤ Use periods, question marks, and exclamation points correctly (see 41A–41F).

Periods, question marks, and exclamation points are collectively called *end punctuation* because they occur at the ends of sentences.

- I love you. Do you love me? I love you!

PERIODS

41A   When does a period end a sentence?

A period ends a statement, a mild command, or an INDIRECT QUESTION.* Never use a period to end a DIRECT QUESTION, a strong command, or an emphatic declaration.

Watch the Video

END OF A STATEMENT

- A journey of a thousand miles must begin with a single step.

—Lao-tsu, *The Way of Lao-tsu*

MILD COMMAND

- Put a gram of boldness into everything you do.

—Baltasar Gracian

INDIRECT QUESTION

- I asked if they wanted to climb Mt. Ross.

If this statement were a direct question, it would end with a question mark: *I asked, "Do you want to climb Mt. Ross?"*

---

*Words printed in SMALL CAPITAL LETTERS are discussed elsewhere in the text and are defined in the Terms Glossary at the back of this book.

41B How do I use periods with abbreviations?

Most abbreviations (*Dr., Mr., Ms., Jr., Fri., St., a.m., p.m.*) call for periods; a few don't. (For more about abbreviations, see 48I through 48L.)

Alert: In ACADEMIC WRITING, spell out—don't abbreviate—the word *professor.*●

Abbreviations without periods include the postal codes for states (for example, IL, CO) and the names of some organizations and government agencies (for example, CBS and NASA).

- **Ms.** Yuan, who works at **NASA,** lectured to **Dr.** Garcia's physics class at 9:30 **a.m.**

Alert: At the end of a sentence, a single period marks both the abbreviation and the end of the sentence. However, a question mark or exclamation point follows an abbreviation period at the end of a sentence.

- The phone rang at 4:00 **a.m.**
- It's upsetting to answer a wrong-number call at 4:00 **a.m.!**
- Who would call at 4:00 **a.m.?** ●

QUESTION MARKS

41C When do I use a question mark?

A question mark ends a **direct question**, one that quotes exact words. (A period ends an **indirect question**, which tells of a question.)

- How many attempts have been made to climb Mt. Everest?

  An indirect question would end with a period: *She wants to know how many attempts have been made to climb Mt. Everest.*

Alert: Never use a question mark with a period, comma, semicolon, or colon.

NO   She asked, "How are you**?."**

YES   She asked, "How are you**?"** ●

Use a question mark after each question in a series whether or not you choose to capitalize the first word. (Do capitalize the first word when a question forms a complete sentence.)

- Whose rights does voter fraud violate**?** Mine**?** Yours**?** Or everyone's**?**

A polite command or request can be followed by either a period or a question mark. Choose consistently within each piece of your writing.

- Would you please send me a copy**.**

or

- Would you please send me a copy**?**

41D When can I use a question mark in parentheses?

Use a question mark within parentheses only when a preceding date or other numerical information is unknown.

- Chaucer was born in 1340 (?) in London.

The word *about* is often more graceful: *Chaucer was born **about** 1340.*
Also, use precise wording, not (?), to show IRONY or sarcasm.

NO   My algebra class is a pleasant **(?)** experience.

YES   My algebra class is as pleasant as a root canal.

EXCLAMATION POINTS

41E When do I use an exclamation point?

An exclamation point ends a strong command (*Look out behind you! Tell me the truth now!*) or an emphatic declaration (*There's been an accident! Hail to the Chief!*)

! **Alert:** Never combine an exclamation point with a period, comma, semicolon, or colon.

NO   "There's been an accident**!**," she shouted.

YES   "There's been an accident**!**" she shouted.

YES   "There's been an accident," she shouted.

Use this form if you prefer not to use an exclamation point. ●

41F What is considered overuse of exclamation points?

In ACADEMIC WRITING, use words, not exclamation points, to communicate the intensity of your message. Use this mark sparingly.

When we were in Nepal, we tried each day to see Mt. Everest. But each day we failed. **Clouds defeated us!** The summit never emerged from a heavy overcast.

Also, using exclamation points too frequently suggests an exaggerated sense of urgency.

NO   Mountain climbing can be dangerous. You must know correct procedures! You must have the proper equipment! Otherwise, you could die!

YES   Mountain climbing can be dangerous. You must know correct procedures. You must have the proper equipment. Otherwise, you could die!

Use precise wording, not (!), to show amazement or sarcasm.

NO   At 29,035 feet **(!)**, Mt. Everest is the world's highest mountain. Yet, Chris **(!)** wants to climb it.

YES   At **a majestic** 29,035 feet, Mt. Everest is the world's highest mountain. Yet, Chris, **amazingly,** wants to climb it.

● **EXERCISE 41-1**   Insert any needed periods, question marks, and exclamation points and delete any unneeded ones. For help, consult all sections of this chapter.

EXAMPLE

Dr Madan Kataria, who calls himself the Giggling Guru (!), established the world's first laughter club in 1995.

Dr. Madan Kataria, who calls himself the Giggling Guru, established the world's first laughter club in 1995.

1. More than 1,000 (?) laughter clubs exist throughout the world, each seeking to promote health by reducing stress and strengthening the immune system!
2. Dr Madan Kataria, a physician in Bombay, India, developed a yoga-like (!) strategy based on group (!) laughter and then set up laughter clubs.
3. Laughter clubs say, "Yes!" when asked, "Is laughter the best medicine."
4. The clubs' activities include breathing and stretching exercises and playful (?) behaviors, such as performing the opera laugh (!), the chicken laugh (!), and the "Ho-Ho, Ha-Ha" (?) exercise.
5. According to the German psychologist Dr Michael Titze, "In the 1950s people used to laugh eighteen minutes a day (!), but today we laugh not more than six (?) minutes per day, despite huge rises in the standard of living." ●

● **EXERCISE 41-2**   Insert needed periods, question marks, and exclamation points. For help, consult all sections of this chapter.

Complete the Chapter Exercises

Weather experts refer to a rise in surface temperature of the Pacific Ocean as El Niño, but La Niña refers to a drop in ocean temperature What effects can these changes cause In the spring of 1998, the cold water of La Niña surfaced quickly and produced chaotic and destructive weather In the American Northeast, rainfall amounts for June were three times above normal But no one expected the strangest consequence: snow in June Can you imagine waking up on an early summer morning in New England to snow Throughout the summer, most New England states failed to experience a single heat wave, which requires more than three days of 90 degree weather During that winter, the Great Lakes experienced record warmth, but California suffered from disastrously cold air A citrus freeze caused $600 million of damage That's more than half a billion dollars. ●

42 Commas

■ ■ ■ ■ ■ ■ ■ ■ ■ ■

Quick Points   You will learn to

➤ Use commas correctly (see 42A–42L).

42A   What is the role of the comma?

Watch the Video

The most frequently used mark of punctuation, a comma separates items of thought within a sentence. Quick Box 42.1 shows most uses of the comma. For a fuller explanation, check the sections indicated in parentheses.

Quick Box 42.1   ■ ■ ■ ■ ■ ■ ■ ■ ■ ■

Key uses of commas

COMMAS WITH COORDINATING CONJUNCTIONS LINKING INDEPENDENT CLAUSES (42B)

● Most people throw postcards out, **but** some are quite valuable.

COMMAS AFTER INTRODUCTORY ELEMENTS (42C)

● **Although most postcards cost only a quarter,** one recently sold for thousands of dollars.

● **On postcard racks,** several designs are usually available.

● **For example,** animals are timeless favorites.

● **However,** most cards show local landmarks.

continued >>

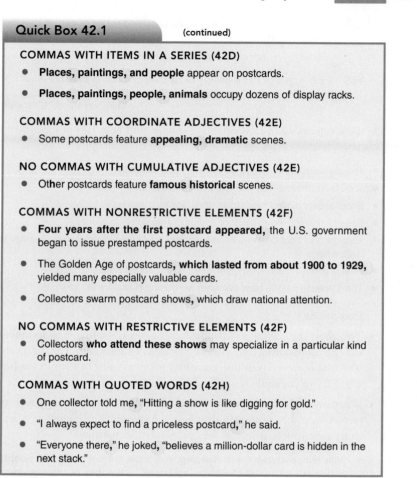

Quick Box 42.1 (continued)

COMMAS WITH ITEMS IN A SERIES (42D)

● **Places, paintings, and people** appear on postcards.

● **Places, paintings, people, animals** occupy dozens of display racks.

COMMAS WITH COORDINATE ADJECTIVES (42E)

● Some postcards feature **appealing, dramatic** scenes.

NO COMMAS WITH CUMULATIVE ADJECTIVES (42E)

● Other postcards feature **famous historical** scenes.

COMMAS WITH NONRESTRICTIVE ELEMENTS (42F)

● **Four years after the first postcard appeared,** the U.S. government began to issue prestamped postcards.

● The Golden Age of postcards, **which lasted from about 1900 to 1929,** yielded many especially valuable cards.

● Collectors swarm postcard shows, which draw national attention.

NO COMMAS WITH RESTRICTIVE ELEMENTS (42F)

● Collectors **who attend these shows** may specialize in a particular kind of postcard.

COMMAS WITH QUOTED WORDS (42H)

● One collector told me, "Hitting a show is like digging for gold."

● "I always expect to find a priceless postcard," he said.

● "Everyone there," he joked, "believes a million-dollar card is hidden in the next stack."

42B How do commas work with coordinating conjunctions?

Never use a comma when a coordinating conjunction links only two words, two PHRASES, or two DEPENDENT CLAUSES.

NO Habitat for Humanity depends on volunteers for **labor, and donations** to help with its construction projects.

Labor and *donations* are two words; the conjunction explains their relationship. No comma is needed.

YES Habitat for Humanity depends on volunteers for **labor and donations** to help with its construction projects.

NO   Each language has **a beauty of its own, and forms of expression** that are duplicated nowhere else.

A beauty of its own and *forms of expression* are only two phrases.

YES   Each language has **a beauty of its own and forms of expression** that are duplicated nowhere else.

—Margaret Mead, "Unispeak"

Do use a comma when a coordinating conjunction links two or more INDEPENDENT CLAUSES. Place the comma before the coordinating conjunction.

- The sky turned dark gray, **and** the wind died suddenly.
- The November morning had just begun, **but** it looked like dusk.
- Shopkeepers closed their stores early, **for** they wanted to get home.
- Soon high winds would start, **or** thick snow would begin silently.
- Farmers could not continue harvesting, **nor** could they round up their animals in distant fields.
- Drivers tried to reach safety, **yet** some unlucky ones were stranded.
- The firehouse whistle blew twice, **so** we knew a blizzard was closing in.

Exceptions

- Two short contrasting independent clauses are often linked by a comma with no coordinating conjunction: *Rex barks, he doesn't bite.* For ACADEMIC WRITING, however, your instructor may prefer a period or a semicolon (see Ch. 43) to a comma.

- When one or both independent clauses linked by a coordinating conjunction contain other commas, dropping the coordinating conjunction and using a semicolon instead of the comma clarifies meaning.

  - With temperatures below freezing, the snow did not melt; ~~and~~ **people** wondered, gazing at the white landscape, when they would see grass again.

🛈 Alerts: (1) Never put a comma *after* a coordinating conjunction that joins independent clauses.

NO   A house is renovated in two weeks **but,** a loft takes a week.

YES   A house is renovated in two weeks, **but** a loft takes a week.

(2) Never use a comma alone between independent clauses, or you'll create the error known as a COMMA SPLICE (see Chapter 34).

NO   Five inches of snow fell in two hours, driving was hazardous.

YES   Five inches of snow fell in two hours, **and** driving was hazardous. ●

● **EXERCISE 42-1**   Working individually or in a group, combine each pair of sentences using the coordinating conjunction shown in parentheses. Rearrange words when necessary.

EXAMPLE

Esperanto is a language invented by L. L. Zamenhof in 1887. It is now the most widely spoken artificial language. (and)

Esperanto is a language invented by L. L. Zamenhof in 1887, and it is now the most widely spoken artificial language.

for   and   nor   but   or   yet   so

1. Zamenhof believed that his invention would foster world peace. He believed that if people spoke a common language wars would cease. (for)
2. No country recognizes Esperanto as an official language. It is spoken by many people in at least 115 countries. (but)
3. Published in Warsaw, the first book of Esperanto grammar appeared in 1887. The first world congress of Esperanto speakers was held in France in 1905. (and)
4. Before World War II, Hitler denounced Esperanto. Its creator was Jewish. (for)
5. Stalin also attacked Esperanto and would not grant it official status. He would not allow its use in the Soviet Union. (nor)
6. The U.S. military has used Esperanto in training exercises. Soldiers can practice communicating in a foreign language. (so)
7. Similar to English, Esperanto uses 23 consonants and 5 vowels. It also uses 2 semivowels. (yet)
8. Most speakers of Esperanto have to learn the language through their own study. They learn in courses taught by volunteers. (or)
9. Esperanto has made its way into popular culture in movies, music, and literature. There is even a 1965 movie starring William Shatner in which all the dialogue is in Esperanto. (and)
10. If you want to learn Esperanto, it can be difficult to find support. There are Esperanto clubs in over 50 U.S. cities and many universities. (but) ●

42C   How do commas work with introductory clauses, phrases, and words?

A comma follows any introductory word, PHRASE, or CLAUSE that precedes an INDEPENDENT CLAUSE.

- **Predictably,** many dieters say sugar craving is their worst problem.
- **Before 1700,** sugar refineries appeared in London and New York.
- **Beginning in infancy,** we develop lifelong tastes for sweet foods.

- **Sweets being a temptation for many adults,** most parents avoid commercial baby foods that contain sugar.
- **Although fructose comes from fruit,** it's still sugar.
- **Nevertheless,** many people think fructose isn't harmful.
- **To satisfy a craving for ice cream,** even timid people sometimes brave midnight streets.

EXCEPTION

Some writers omit the comma after a short, unmistakably clear introductory element. In ACADEMIC WRITING, however, you'll never be wrong if you use the comma.

> YES   In 1992, the Americans with Disabilities Act was passed.

> YES   In 1992 the Americans with Disabilities Act was passed.

Place a comma after an introductory **interjection**, a word that conveys strong, sudden emotion: ***Oh***, *are you allergic to cats?* ***Well***, *you can't stop sneezing.*

⚠ **Alert:** Use a comma before and after a sentence MODIFIER in the middle of a sentence. When the sentence MODIFIER starts a sentence, follow it with a comma. When the sentence MODIFIER ends a sentence, put a comma before it.

- **By the way,** the parade begins at noon.
- The parade**, by the way,** begins at noon.
- The parade begins at noon**, by the way**.

- **However,** our float isn't finished.
- Our float**, however,** isn't finished.
- Our float isn't finished**, however**.

● **EXERCISE 42-2**   Working individually or with a group, combine each set of sentences into one sentence according to the direction in parentheses. Use a comma after the introductory element. You can add, delete, and rearrange words as needed. For help, consult 42C.

EXAMPLE

People have known that humor is good for them. They have known this for a long time. (Begin with *for a long time*.)

For a long time, people have known that humor is good for them.

1. People laugh. Scientists study them to find out what actually happens. (Begin with *when*.)
2. Scientists track our physiological reactions. They discover the chemicals we produce while we are laughing. (Begin with *in fact*.)

3. Our brains use dopamine when we laugh. Dopamine is a chemical we produce that makes us feel good. (Begin with *produced*.)

4. We sometimes activate our tear ducts by laughing. That reduces stress. (Begin with *interestingly*.)

5. Scientists tested people's saliva immediately after they laughed. Scientists concluded that immune systems may benefit from laughter. (Begin with *immediately*.)

6. Blood pressure and heart rates tend to go below baseline after we laugh. People should be happy about this effect because that's what happens after we exercise well. (Begin with *although*.)

7. Laughter causes the inner lining of our blood vessels to expand. This expansion produces good chemicals in our bodies. (Begin with *in addition*.)

8. One of these good chemicals is nitric oxide. It reduces inflammation and clotting. (Begin with *in the human body*.)

9. Laughter may even help with pain management. Laughter seems to have an analgesic effect. (Begin with *seeming*.)

10. Humor has so many physical benefits, and it makes us feel better. Try to enjoy a few laughs every day. (Begin with *because*.) ●

42D How do commas work with items in a series?

A series is a group of three or more elements—words, PHRASES, or CLAUSES—that match in grammatical form and are of equal importance in a sentence.

(((●
Listen
to the
Podcast

> Marriage requires **sexual, financial, and emotional** discipline.
>
> —Anne Roiphe, "Why Marriages Fail"

> Culture is a way of **thinking, feeling, believing**.
>
> —Clyde Kluckhohn, *Mirror for Man*

> My love of flying stems from my days of ice **skates, of swings, and of bicycles**.
>
> —Tresa Wiggins, student

> We have been taught **that children develop by ages and stages, that the steps are pretty much the same for everybody, and that to grow out of the limited behavior of childhood, we must climb them all**.
>
> —Gail Sheehy, *Passages*

Some publications omit the comma before *and* in a series. Check with your instructor about his or her preference.

NO The sweater comes in **blue, green, pink and black**.

Do the sweaters come in three or four colors?

YES The sweater comes in **blue, green, pink, and black**.

The comma before *and* indicates in four colors.

At all times, however, follow the "toast, juice, and ham and eggs" rule. That is, when one of the items in a series contains *and*, don't use a comma in that item.

When items in a series contain commas or other punctuation, separate them with SEMICOLONS instead of commas (see 43E).

If it's a bakery, they have to sell cake; if it's a photography shop, they have to develop film; and if it's a dry-goods store, they have to sell warm underwear.

—Art Buchwald, "Birth Control for Banks"

With three or more numbered or lettered items in a series, use commas (or semicolons if the items themselves contain commas) to separate them.

- To file your insurance claim, please enclose (1) a letter requesting payment, (2) a police report about the robbery, **and** (3) proof of purchase of the items you say are missing.

Alert: In a series, never use a comma before the first item or after the last item, unless a different rule makes it necessary.

NO **Artists, writers, and poets, have engaged** in daydreaming.

YES Artists, writers, and poets have engaged in daydreaming.

NO Such dreamers include, Miró, Debussy, Dostoevsky, and Dickinson.

YES Such dreamers include Miró, Debussy, Dostoevsky, and Dickinson.

YES Such dreamers include, **of course,** Miró, Debussy, Dostoevsky, and Dickinson.

As a sentence modifier, *of course* is set off from the rest of the sentence by commas before and after it (see 42C). ●

● **EXERCISE 42-3** Insert commas to separate the items in a series. If a sentence needs no commas, explain why.

EXAMPLE

Many punk and rock bands, such as Ramones The Talking Heads and Blondie, got their start in a famous club called CBGB.

Many punk and rock bands, such as Ramones, The Talking Heads, and Blondie, got their start in a famous club called CBGB.

1. Even though the club became famous for punk music, it was originally built for musicians who played country bluegrass and blues.

2. Founded in 1973 by Hilly Kristal, CBGB, located in the Bowery in New York City, is sometimes called "CBs" or "CBGBs."

3. Famous performances by singer Patti Smith the band Television and the British band The Police made CBGB an important place in the history of punk music.

4. The club has become part of popular American culture, making appearances in the TV show *The Simpsons* the Broadway show *Rent* and in the video game *Guitar Hero: Warriors of Rock.*

5. Legal battles financial troubles and political conflicts caused CBGB to close its doors in 2006, after a tribute concert featuring appearances by members of the Red Hot Chili Peppers and the band Television. ●

42E How do commas work with coordinate adjectives?

Coordinate adjectives are two or more ADJECTIVES of equal weight that describe—that is, modify—a NOUN. In contrast, **cumulative adjectives** build meaning from word to word, as they move toward the noun. The key to applying this rule is recognizing when adjectives are coordinate and when they aren't. Quick Box 42.2 tells you how.

((●
Listen
to the
Podcast

Quick Box 42.2

■ ■ ■ ■ ■ ■ ■ ■ ■ ■ ■

Tests for coordinate and cumulative adjectives

If either one of these tests works, the adjectives are coordinate and require a comma between them.

- Can the order of the adjectives be reversed without changing the meaning or creating nonsense? If yes, use a comma.

  NO   The concert featured **new several** bands.
  New several makes no sense.

  YES   The **huge, restless** crowd waited for the concert to begin.
  Restless, huge still carries the same meaning, so these are coordinate adjectives.

- Can *and* be sensibly inserted between the adjectives? If yes, use a comma.

  NO   The concert featured **several and new** bands.
  Several and new makes no sense.

  YES   The **huge and restless** crowd waited.
  Modifier *huge and restless* makes sense, so these are coordinate adjectives.

- Fans cheered as the **pulsating, rhythmic** music filled the stadium.

  Pulsating and *rhythmic* are coordinate adjectives.

- Each band had a **distinctive musical** style.

  Distinctive and *musical* aren't coordinate adjectives.

⓿ **Alert:** Don't put a comma after a final coordinate adjective.

  NO   Hundreds of **roaring, cheering, yelling, fans** filled the stadium.

  YES   Hundreds of **roaring, cheering, yelling fans** filled the stadium.

● **EXERCISE 42-4**   Insert commas to separate coordinate adjectives. If a sentence needs no commas, explain why. For help, consult 42E.

EXAMPLE

A scruffy beloved animal named Owney served as the unofficial mascot of the U.S. Railway Mail Service for nine years in the late 19th century.

A scruffy**,** beloved animal named Owney served as the unofficial mascot of the U.S. Railway Mail Service for nine years in the late 19th century.

1. Owney was a brown terrier-mix dog.
2. The myth was that he showed up as a skinny hungry stray one cold winter night in Albany, New York.
3. Owney began riding trains across the United States, where his fame earned him numerous shiny medals, so many that Postmaster General John Wanamaker gave him a harness to carry them all.
4. By 1897, the old sick dog had become somewhat mean, and he had to be put down after attacking a mail clerk.
5. Sad grateful postal workers raised money to have Owney's body preserved by taxidermy, and it still remains in the U.S. Postal museum. ●

42F How do commas work with nonrestrictive elements?

A **restrictive element** pinpoints, narrows, or restricts the meaning of its ANTECEDENT to a particular person or class: *Don't eat tomatoes **that are canned***. A **nonrestrictive element** describes but does not pinpoint, narrow, or restrict the meaning of its antecedent: *Berries, **which sweeten your breakfast**, are highly nutritious.*

Use commas to separate nonrestrictive elements from the rest of a sentence. Do not use commas to separate restrictive elements from their antecedents. Simply stated:

- Restrictive element—do not use commas.
- Nonrestrictive element—use commas.

NO Someone**, named Princess,** canceled the concert.

Named Princess narrows who *someone* is to Princess; it is restrictive. Commas are unnecessary.

YES Someone **named Princess** canceled the concert.

A restrictive, pinpointing element requires no comma.

NO Princess **who writes all her material** is suing her promoter.

Who writes all her material is descriptive and does not pinpoint Princess; it is nonrestrictive. Commas are required.

YES Princess**, who writes all her material,** is suing her promoter.

A nonrestrictive element needs to be set off by commas.

NO Princess started playing on a piano**, that was out of tune**.

That was out of tune is restrictive because it identifies the piano. No comma is necessary.

YES Princess started playing on a piano **that was out of tune**.

A restrictive, pinpointing clause requires no comma.

NO **A prolific artist** Princess is on her way to fame and fortune.

A prolific artist is a descriptive, nonrestrictive element, so it requires a comma.

YES **A prolific artist,** Princess is on her way to fame and fortune.

A nonrestrictive element requires a comma.

● **EXERCISE 42-5** Using your knowledge of restrictive and nonrestrictive elements, insert commas as needed. If a sentence is correct, explain why. For help, consult 42F.

EXAMPLE

During the summer when butterflies are most active gardeners can attract them by planting the right flowers.

During the summer, when butterflies are most active, gardeners can attract them by planting the right flowers.

1. In spring as birds and bees look for water and food certain plants and trees provide those needs and thus attract the greatest number of airborne visitors.
2. Gardeners who learn to attract birds may find they have fewer problems with insects and other unwelcome pests.
3. During suburban sprawl when cities eat up more and more land birds have to adapt by putting their nests in buildings.

4. Birds are attracted to pines and evergreens where they can find food and shelter.
5. Hungry birds who are not picky will enjoy a feeder stocked with black oil sunflower seeds.
6. Birds also need to eat insects which provide a higher protein content than seeds.
7. Some common plants such as butterfly weed and lantana are ideal for attracting butterflies.
8. Because they have the nectar that butterflies want these plants enhance any butterfly garden.
9. As butterflies pass by a garden looking for bright colors and strong fragrances they will notice flowers planted in large clumps.
10. Gardens that are favorable to birds and butterflies will also invite honeybees and other pollinators. ●

42G How do commas set off parenthetical expressions, contrasts, words of direct address, and tag sentences?

When you use parenthetical expressions, contrasts, direct address, or tag sentences, you insert information that is not essential to the principal message of your sentence. Set off such information with commas.

Parenthetical expressions are "asides."

- American farmers **(according to U.S. government figures)** export more wheat than they sell at home.
- A major drought, **sad to say,** wiped out this year's wheat crop.

Use commas to set off expressions of contrast, which state what is *not* the case.

- Feeding the world's population is a serious, **though not impossible,** problem.
- We must battle world hunger continuously, **not only as famine strikes**.

Use commas to set off words of direct address, which name the person or group being spoken to (addressed).

- Join me, **brothers and sisters,** to end hunger.
- Your contribution to the Relief Fund, **Steve,** will help us greatly.

A **tag sentence** ends with a "tag," an attached phrase or question. Set off a tag with a comma. When the tag is a question, the sentence ends with a question mark.

- People will give blood regularly, **I hope**.
- The response to the blood drive was impressive, **wasn't it?**
- The drought the ended, **hasn't it?**

● **EXERCISE 42-6** Add commas to set off any parenthetical or contrasting elements, words of direct address, and tag sentences. Adjust end punctuation as necessary. For help, consult 42G.

EXAMPLE

Writer's block it seems to me is a misunderstood phenomenon.

Writer's block, *it seems to me,* is a misunderstood phenomenon.

1. An inability to write some say stems from lack of discipline and a tendency to procrastinate.
2. In other words the only way to overcome writer's block is to exert more willpower.
3. But writer's block is a complex psychological event that happens to conscientious people not just procrastinators.
4. Such people strangely enough are often unconsciously rebelling against their own self-tyranny and rigid standards of perfection.
5. If I told you my fellow writer that all it takes to start writing again is to quit punishing yourself, you would think I was crazy wouldn't you? ●

42H How do commas work with quoted words?

Use commas to set off expressions (such as *he wrote* or *she proclaimed*) that accompany DIRECT DISCOURSE.

- Speaking of ideal love, the poet William Blake wrote, "Love seeketh not itself to please."
- "My love is a fever," said William Shakespeare about love's passion.
- "I love no love," proclaimed the poet Mary Coleridge, "but thee."

EXCEPTION

When the quoted words are blended into the grammatical structure of your sentence, don't use commas to set them off. These are instances of **indirect quotation** or INDIRECT DISCOURSE, usually occurring with *as* and *that*.

- The duke describes the duchess **as** "too soon made glad."
- The duchess insists **that** "appearing glad often is but a deception."

! **Alert:** When the quoted words end with an exclamation point or a question mark, retain that original punctuation, even if explanatory words follow.

QUOTED WORDS	*"O Romeo! Romeo!"*
NO	"O Romeo! Romeo**!,**" whispered Juliet from her window.
NO	"O Romeo! Romeo**,**" whispered Juliet from her window.
YES	"O Romeo! Romeo**!**" whispered Juliet from her window.
QUOTED WORDS	*"Wherefore art thou Romeo?"*
NO	"Wherefore art thou Romeo**?,**" Juliet urgently asked.
NO	"Wherefore art thou Romeo**,**" Juliet urgently asked.
YES	"Wherefore art thou Romeo**?**" Juliet urgently asked. ●

● **EXERCISE 42-7** Punctuate the following dialogue correctly. If a sentence is correct, explain why.

EXAMPLE

NO "I'm bored!," cried the little girl.

YES "I'm bored!" cried the little girl.

1. "Well, then" the girl's father replied "what would you like to do?"
2. The girl responded by saying that the park "sounds like a lot of fun."
3. "Have you finished your homework?," asked the father.
4. The little girl said "I don't have any homework to do. I finished it yesterday."
5. "Then let's go to the park!," announced the father. ●

421 How do commas work in dates, names, addresses, correspondence, and numbers?

When you write dates, names, addresses, correspondence, and numbers, use commas according to accepted practice. Quick Boxes 42.3 through 42.6 provide some guidelines.

Quick Box 42.3

■ ■ ■ ■ ■ ■ ■ ■ ■ ■ ■

Commas with dates

- Use a comma between the date and the year: *July 20, 1969.*
- Use a comma between the day and the date: *Sunday, July 20.*
- Within a sentence, use a comma on both sides of the year in a full date: *Americans sat near a TV set on July 20, 1969, to watch the lunar landing.*
- Never use a comma when only the month and year, or the month and day, are given. Also, never use a comma between the season and year.

  YES People knew that one day in **July 1969** would change the world.

  YES News coverage was especially heavy on **July 21**.

  YES In **summer 1969** a man walked on the moon.

- Never use a comma in an inverted date, a form used in the U.S. military and throughout the world except in the United States.

  YES People stayed near their televisions on **20 July 1969** to watch the lunar landing.

Quick Box 42.4

■ ■ ■ ■ ■ ■ ■ ■ ■ ■ ■

Commas with names, places, and addresses

- When an abbreviated academic degree (*MD, PhD*) comes after a person's name, use a comma between the name and the title (*Angie Eng, MD*), and also after the title if other words follow in the sentence: *The jury listened closely to the expert testimony of **Angie Eng, MD, last week**.*
- When an indicator of birth order or succession (*Jr., Sr., III, IV*) follows a name, never use a comma: *Martin Luther **King Jr**. or Henry **Ford II***
- When you invert a person's name, use a comma to separate the last name from the first: ***Troyka, David***
- When city and state names are written together, use a comma to separate them: ***Philadelphia, Pennsylvania***. If the city and state fall within a sentence, use a comma after the state as well: *My family settled in **Philadelphia, Pennsylvania**, before I was born.*
- When a complete address is part of a sentence, use a comma to separate all the items, except the state and ZIP code: *I wrote to **Shelly Kupperman, 1001 Rule Road, Upper Saddle River, NJ 07458**, for more information about the comma.*

Quick Box 42.5

■ ■ ■ ■ ■ ■ ■ ■ ■ ■

Commas in correspondence

- For the opening of an informal letter, use a comma: **Dear Betty,**
- For the opening of a business or formal letter, use a colon:

  Dear Ms. Kiviat:

- For the close of a letter, use a comma:

  Sincerely yours, **Best regards,** **Love,**

Quick Box 42.6

■ ■ ■ ■ ■ ■ ■ ■ ■ ■

Commas with numbers

- Counting from right to left, put a comma after every three digits in numbers with more than four digits.
  72,867 156,567,066

- A comma is optional in most four-digit numbers. Be consistent within each piece of writing.
  \$1776 \$1,776
  1776 miles 1,776 miles
  1776 potatoes 1,776 potatoes

- Never use a comma in a four-digit year: **1990** (*Note:* If the year has five digits or more, do use a comma: **25,000 BC**.)

- Never use a comma in an address of four digits or more: *12161 Dean Drive*

- Never use a comma in a page number of four digits or more: *see page 1338*

- Use a comma to separate related measurements written as words: *five feet, four inches*

- Use a comma to separate a scene from an act in a play: *act II, scene iv* (or *act 2, scene 4*)

- Use a comma to separate references to a page and a line: *page 10, line 6*

● **EXERCISE 42-8** Insert commas where they are needed. For help, consult 42I.

EXAMPLE

On June 1 1984 the small German-French production company released a feature film called *Paris Texas.*

On June 1, 1984, the small German-French production company released a feature film called *Paris, Texas.*

1. Made by the noted German director Wim Wenders, *Paris Texas* was set in an actual town in Lamar County Texas with a population of 24699.
2. The movie's title was clearly intended to play off the slightly more famous Paris in France.
3. The custom of naming little towns in the United States after cosmopolitan urban centers in the Old World has resulted in such places as Athens Georgia and St. Petersburg Florida.
4. As of December 1 2005 the American St. Petersburg was estimated to have nearly 250000 citizens and the American Athens nearly 109000.
5. By comparison, St. Petersburg Russia and Athens Greece were estimated to have populations of 4 million and 1 million, respectively. ●

42J How do commas clarify meaning?

A comma is sometimes needed to clarify the meaning of a sentence, even when no rule calls for one. You may prefer to revise your sentence to prevent misreading.

NO Of the gymnastic team's twenty five were injured.

YES Of the gymnastic team's **twenty, five** were injured.

YES Of **twenty on** the gymnastic team, five were injured. [preferred]

NO Those who can practice many hours a day.

YES **Those who can,** practice many hours a day.

YES **They** practice many hours a day **when they can.** [preferred]

NO George dressed and performed for the sellout crowd.

YES **George dressed,** and performed for the sellout crowd.

YES **After** George dressed, **he** performed for the sellout crowd. [preferred]

● **EXERCISE 42-9** Working individually or with a group, insert commas to prevent misreading.

EXAMPLE

> **NO** Of all the parts of the human body teeth tend to last the longest.
>
> **YES** Of all the parts of the human body, teeth tend to last the longest.

1. Humans like some other animals have two sets of teeth over a lifetime.
2. Sharks known for having deadly bites develop several sets of teeth throughout their lives.
3. Adult humans typically have 32 teeth 12 more than they had as children.
4. For children eruptions of teeth, also called teething, can be painful.
5. People who brush their teeth develop healthy gums and mouths. ●

42K How can I avoid misusing commas?

Most misuses of the comma are overuses—inserting unnecessary commas. This section summarizes the Alert notes in this chapter and lists other frequent misuses of the comma.

When advice against overusing a comma clashes with a rule requiring one, follow the rule that requires the comma.

● The town of Kitty Hawk, North Carolina, attracts thousands of tourists each year.

> While commas don't normally separate subject from verb, the comma is required here because of the rule that calls for a comma when the name of a state follows the name of a city within a sentence (see 42I).

42K.1 Commas with coordinating conjunctions

Never use a comma after a COORDINATING CONJUNCTION that joins two INDEPENDENT CLAUSES, unless another rule makes it necessary (see 42B). Also, don't use a comma to separate two items joined with a coordinating conjunction—there must be at least three (see 42D).

> **NO** The sky was dark gray **and,** it looked like dusk.
>
> **YES** The sky was dark gray**, and** it looked like dusk.

> **NO** **The moon, and the stars** were shining last night.
>
> **YES** **The moon and the stars** were shining last night.

42K.2 Commas with subordinating conjunctions and prepositions

Never put a comma after a SUBORDINATING CONJUNCTION or a PREPOSITION, unless another rule makes it necessary.

NO **Although,** the storm brought high winds, it did no damage.

YES **Although the storm brought high winds,** it did no damage.

> The comma follows the full introductory subordinate clause, not the subordinate conjunction that begins it.

NO The storm did no damage **although,** it brought high winds.

YES The storm did no damage **although it brought high winds.**

> No comma is required after a subordinating conjunction.

NO People expected worse **between,** the high winds and the heavy downpour.

YES People expected worse **between the high winds and the heavy downpour**.

> Don't separate prepositions from their objects with commas.

42K.3 Commas in a series

Never use a comma before the first, or after the last, item in a series, unless another rule makes it necessary (see 42D).

NO The gymnasium was decorated **with, red, white, and blue** ribbons for the Fourth of July.

NO The gymnasium was decorated with **red, white, and blue, ribbons** for the Fourth of July.

YES The gymnasium was decorated with **red, white, and blue** ribbons for the Fourth of July.

Never put a comma between a final COORDINATE ADJECTIVE and the NOUN that the adjectives modify. Also, don't use a comma between adjectives that are not coordinate (see 42E).

NO He wore an **old, baggy, sweater**.

YES He wore an **old, baggy sweater**.   [coordinate adjectives]

NO He has **several, new sweaters**.

YES He has **several new sweaters**.   [noncoordinate, or cumulative, adjectives]

42K.4 Commas with restrictive elements

Never use a comma to set off a RESTRICTIVE (limiting) element from the rest of a sentence (see 42F).

NO **Vegetables, stir-fried in a wok,** are crisp and flavorful.

Stir-fried in a wok is limiting, so commas aren't required.

YES **Vegetables stir-fried in a wok** are crisp and flavorful.

42K.5 Commas with quotations

Use commas only with DIRECT DISCOURSE, never with INDIRECT DISCOURSE.

NO Jon said **that, he likes** stir-fried vegetables.

YES Jon said **that he likes** stir-fried vegetables.

YES **Jon said, "I like** stir-fried vegetables."

42K.6 Commas that separate a subject from its verb or a verb from its object*

A comma is distracting between these elements, but in some cases another comma rule might supersede this guideline (as in the first example in section 42K).

NO **The brothers Wright, made** their first successful airplane flights on December 17, 1903.

As a rule, a comma doesn't separate a subject from its verb.

YES **The brothers Wright made** their first successful airplane flights on December 17, 1903.

NO These inventors enthusiastically **tackled, the problems** of powered flight and aerodynamics.

As a rule, a comma doesn't separate a verb from its object.

YES These inventors enthusiastically **tackled the problems** of powered flight and aerodynamics.

● **EXERCISE 42-10** Some commas have been deliberately misused in these sentences. Delete misused commas. If a sentence is correct, explain why.

EXAMPLE

NO Alchemy was an important philosophical and scientific tradition, that led to the development of chemistry and medicine.

---

*Preposition/object is covered in 42K.2.

YES Alchemy was an important philosophical and scientific tradition that led to the development of chemistry and medicine.

1. One of the goals of alchemy was the development, of the philosopher's stone.
2. In addition to turning base metals into the gold, the philosopher's stone, was supposed to grant immortality or eternal youth.
3. According to other legends, the philosopher's stone also, cured illnesses, revived dead plants, and created clones.
4. The fantastic claims about the philosopher's stone and mentions of it in historical writings, can be traced as far back as the fourth century.
5. Because, alchemists were attempting to turn metals into gold, they developed some laboratory techniques that are still used in chemistry.
6. Alchemy also helped develop important ideas, that are used in modern medicine, such as the dangers of heavy metal poisoning.
7. Robert Boyle, considered to be a founder of modern chemistry, began his work, as an alchemist.
8. The famous, important, scientist Isaac Newton wrote more about his work in alchemy than he did about optics or physics.
9. The origins of European alchemy, date back to ancient Greece and Egypt.
10. Unlike modern science, alchemy also relied upon, religion, mythology, ancient wisdom, and the occult.●

42L How can I avoid comma errors?

You can avoid most comma errors with these two bits of advice:

- As you write or reread what you've written, never insert a comma simply because you happen to pause to think or take a breath before moving on. Pausing isn't a reliable guide to comma usage. Throughout the United States and the world, people's breathing rhythms, accents, and thinking patterns vary greatly.

- As you're writing, if you're unsure about a comma, insert a circled comma. When you're EDITING, check this handbook for the rule that applies.

Complete the Chapter Exercises

43 Semicolons

Quick Points   You will learn to

➤ Use semicolons correctly (see 43A–43E).

43A   What are the uses of a semicolon?

A semicolon marks within a sentence a distinction that ranks stronger than a comma but less than a period. Quick Box 43.1 shows different patterns for using semicolons.

Quick Box 43.1

Semicolon patterns

- Independent clause; independent clause (see 43B).

- Independent clause; conjunctive adverb, independent clause (see 43C).

- Independent clause; transitional expression, independent clause (see 43C).

- Independent clause, one that contains a comma; coordinating conjunction followed by independent clause (see 43D).

- Independent clause; coordinating conjunction followed by independent clause, one that contains a comma (see 43D).

- Independent clause, one that contains a comma; coordinating conjunction followed by independent clause, one that contains a comma (see 43D).

- Independent clause containing a series of items, any of which contains a comma; another item in the series; and another item in the series (see 43E).

43B When can I use a semicolon, instead of a period, between independent clauses?

Decide whether a period (full separation) or a semicolon (partial separation) better distinguishes your closely related complete sentences (or INDEPENDENT CLAUSES). Be sure that a grammatically complete thought precedes your period or semicolon.

Watch the Video

- Ours is my spouse's second marriage. For me, it's the first, last, and only.

   The emphasis and contrast in the second sentence rate a period.

   This is my husband's second marriage; it's the first for me.

   —Ruth Sidel, "Marion Deluca"

🚫 **Alert:** Never use a comma alone between independent clauses; else, you'll create the error known as a COMMA SPLICE (Chapter 34). ●

43C When else can I use a semicolon between independent clauses?

When the second of a set of independent clauses closely related in meaning starts with a CONJUNCTIVE ADVERB or with a TRANSITIONAL EXPRESSION, you can choose to separate the clauses with a semicolon instead of a period. Also, insert a comma following a conjunctive adverb or transitional expression that starts an independent clause. Although some professional writers today omit the comma after short words (*then, next, soon*), the rule remains for most ACADEMIC WRITING.

- The average annual rainfall in Death Valley is about two inches**; nevertheless,** hundreds of plant and animal species survive and even thrive there.
- Photographers have spent years recording desert life cycles**; as a result,** we can watch bare sand flower after a spring storm.

🚫 **Alert:** Never use only a comma between independent clauses that are connected by a conjunctive adverb or word of transition—this rule will prevent you from creating the error known as a COMMA SPLICE. ●

43D How do semicolons work with coordinating conjunctions?

Typically, a comma separates two INDEPENDENT CLAUSES linked by a SUBORDINATING CONJUNCTION (see 42B). However, when one or more of the independent clauses already contain a comma, link the independent clauses with a semicolon. This can help your reader see the relationship between the ideas more clearly. Quick Box 43.1 shows the various combinations of this pattern.

When the peacock has presented his back, the spectator will usually begin to walk around him to get a front view**; but** the peacock will continue to turn so that no front view is possible.

—Flannery O'Connor, "The King of the Birds"

Our Constitution is in actual operation; everything appears to promise that it will last**; but** in this world, nothing is certain but death and taxes.

—Benjamin Franklin, in a 1789 letter

For anything worth having, one must pay the price**; and** the price is always work, patience, love, self-sacrifice.

—John Burroughs

43E When should I use semicolons between items in a series?

When a sentence contains a series of items that are long or that already contain one or more commas, separate the items with semicolons. Punctuating this way groups the elements so that your reader can see where one item ends and the next begins.

- The assistant chefs chopped onions, green peppers, and parsley**;** sliced chicken and duck breasts into strips**;** started a broth simmering**; and** filled a large, shallow copper pan with oil.

43F How do I avoid misusing the semicolon?

DON'T USE A SEMICOLON AFTER AN INTRODUCTORY PHRASE

If you use a semicolon after an introductory phrase, you create the error known as a sentence fragment (see Chapter 33).

NO   **Open until midnight;** the computer lab is well used.

The semicolon suggests that *open until midnight* is an independent clause.

YES   **Open until midnight,** the computer lab is well used.

DON'T USE A SEMICOLON WITH A DEPENDENT CLAUSE

If you use a semicolon with a DEPENDENT CLAUSE, you create a fragment.

NO   **Although the new dorms have computer facilities;** many students still prefer to go to the computer lab.

The semicolon suggests that an independent clause precedes it.

YES   **Although the new dorms have computer facilities,** many students still prefer to go to the computer lab.

USE A COLON, NOT A SEMICOLON TO INTRODUCE A LIST

When the words that introduce a list form an independent clause, use a colon, never a semicolon (44B).

NO **The newscast featured three major stories;** the latest pictures of Uranus, a speech by the president, and dangerous brush fires in Nevada.

The newscast featured three major stories is an independent clause, so the punctuation before the list should be a colon, not a semicolon.

YES **The newscast featured three major stories:** the latest pictures of Uranus, a speech by the president, and dangerous brush fires in Nevada.

● **EXERCISE 43-1** Insert semicolons as needed in these items. Also, fix any incorrectly used semicolons. If a sentence is correct, explain why. For help, consult all sections of this chapter.

EXAMPLE

Bicycle racing is as popular in Europe as baseball or basketball is in the United States, it is even more heavily commercialized.

Bicycle racing is as popular in Europe as baseball or basketball is in the United States; it is even more heavily commercialized.

1. The Tour de France is the world's best-known bicycle race, the 94-year-old Giro d'Italia runs a close second.
2. Both are grueling, three-week-long events that require cyclists to cover over 2,000 miles of difficult, mountainous terrain, and both are eagerly anticipated, draw enormous crowds along their routes, and receive extensive media coverage.
3. That media attention leads to marketing opportunities for the events' sponsors; which place ads along the race's route, in the nearby towns, and on the cyclists themselves.
4. Martin Hvastija, a participant in the 2003 Giro d'Italia, had no chance of winning the race, nevertheless, he drew extensive media attention for his sponsors.
5. His method was simple; he managed to ride out in front of the field for a few brief miles.
6. Although he had no chance of winning the race; newscasters beamed his image around the world during the short time he was a front-runner, during the same period; showing the world the brightly colored advertising logos on his jersey.
7. In addition to sponsoring individual athletes, corporations plaster ads all over the towns that the race goes through, they toss samples, coupons, and gadgets to spectators from promotional vehicles that ride the route an hour ahead of the cyclists, and they run ads during TV and radio coverage of the race.

8. In 2003, the organizers of the Giro took in over $8 million in fees from advertisers and $12 million in broadcast rights from the Italian state-owned TV network, RAI, however, these figures were down a bit from the previous year.

9. An additional source of revenues for race organizers is fees from the towns where the race starts and ends each day, as a result, organizers determine the actual course according to which cities are willing to pay the $120,000 charge.

10. Media watchers think the Giro d'Italia could become even more profitable and popular, especially among young adults, but only if it took a cue from the Tour de France by encouraging; more international press coverage, more star riders, and even heavier corporate sponsorship. ●

● **EXERCISE 43-2** Combine each set of sentences into one sentence so that it contains two independent clauses. Use a semicolon correctly between the two clauses. You may add, omit, revise, and rearrange words. Try to use all the patterns in this chapter, and explain the reasoning behind your decisions. More than one revision may be correct. For help, consult all sections of this chapter.

Complete
the
Chapter
Exercises

EXAMPLE

Although not as well known as Thomas Edison, the inventor Nikola Tesla was a revolutionary and important scientist. One biographer calls him "the man who invented the twentieth century."

Although not as well known as Thomas Edison, the inventor Nikola Tesla was a revolutionary scientist; one biographer calls him "the man who invented the twentieth century."

1. Tesla was born in what is now Croatia and studied at the Technical University at Graz, Austria. He excelled in physics, mechanical engineering, and electrical engineering.

2. Tesla's accomplishments include inventing alternating current. He also contributed to the fields of robotics, computer science, and wireless technology. And he helped increase knowledge of nuclear physics, ballistics, and electromagnetism.

3. The Italian inventor Guglielmo Marconi and Tesla both claimed to have invented the radio. However, the U.S. Supreme Court, in 1943, upheld Tesla's radio patent and officially credited him as the device's inventor.

4. In 1901, Tesla began construction of a tower that he claimed would create a global network of wireless communication and be able to control the weather. Unfortunately, Tesla soon lost funding and never finished the project.

5. At his lab in Colorado Springs, he was able to produce artificial lightning. This scene was vividly portrayed in the 2006 film *The Prestige*. ●

44 Colons

Quick Points   You will learn to

➤ Use colons correctly (see 44A–44E).

44A What are the uses of a colon?

A colon anticipates a list, an APPOSITIVE, or a QUOTATION after an INDEPEN-
DENT CLAUSE. Quick Box 44.1 shows different patterns for using a colon.

Quick Box 44.1

Colon patterns

- Independent clause: list (see 44B).
- Independent clause: appositive (see 44B).
- Independent clause: "Quoted words" (see 44B).
- Independent clause: Independent clause that explains or summarizes the
  prior independent clause (see 44B).

44B When can a colon introduce a list,
an appositive, or a quotation?

When a complete sentence—that is, an INDEPENDENT CLAUSE—introduces
a list, an APPOSITIVE, or a QUOTATION, place a colon before the words being
introduced. These words don't have to form an independent clause themselves,
but a complete sentence before the colon is essential.

Watch
the Video

INTRODUCING LISTED ITEMS

When a complete sentence introduces a list, a colon is required, as demonstrated in the following example.

- **If you really want to lose weight, you must do three things:** eat smaller
  portions, exercise, and drink lots of water.

  An independent clause precedes the list, so a colon is correct.

When the lead-in words at the end of an independent clause are *such as, including, like*, or *consists of*, never use a colon. If the lead-in words at the end of an independent clause are *the following* or *as follows*, do use a colon.

- **The students demanded improvements *such as* an expanded menu in the cafeteria, improved janitorial services, and more up-to-date textbooks.**

- **The students demanded *the following*: an expanded menu in the cafeteria, improved janitorial services, and more up-to-date textbooks.**

INTRODUCING APPOSITIVES

An APPOSITIVE is a word or words that rename a NOUN or PRONOUN. When an appositive is introduced by an independent clause, use a colon.

- **Only cats are likely to approve of one old-fashioned remedy for cuts:** a lotion of catnip, butter, and sugar.

  An independent clause comes before the appositive: *a lotion of catnip, butter, and sugar* renames *old-fashioned remedy*.

INTRODUCING QUOTATIONS

When an independent clause introduces a quotation, use a colon after it. (If the words introducing a quotation don't form an independent clause, use a comma.)

- **The little boy in *E.T.* did say something neat:** "How do you explain school to a higher intelligence?"

  The required independent clause comes before the quotation.

  —George F. Will, "Well, I Don't Love You, E.T."

44C When can I use a colon between two independent clauses?

Quick Box 44.1 shows the pattern for using a colon before a second INDEPENDENT CLAUSE that explains or summarizes a first independent clause. The first word after a colon may be capitalized for emphasis: *I'll say it once again: Snakes are lovable. I'll say it again: snakes are lovable.* Either option is correct.

44D What standard formats require a colon?

A variety of standard formats in American English require a colon. Also, colons are used in many DOCUMENTATION STYLES, as shown in Chapters 25, 26, and 27.

TITLE AND SUBTITLE

A Brief History of Time: From the Big Bang to Black Holes

HOURS, MINUTES, AND SECONDS

The plane took off at 7:15 p.m.

The runner passed the halfway point at 1:23:02.

🚫 **Alert:** In the military, hours and minutes are written without colons: *We meet at 0430, not at 0930.* ●

REFERENCES TO BIBLE CHAPTERS AND VERSES

Psalms 23:1–3

Luke 3:13

MEMOS

Date: January 9, 2012

To: Dean Kristen Olivero

From: Professor Daniel Black

Re: Student Work-Study Program

SALUTATION IN A BUSINESS LETTER

Dear Dr. Jewell:

44E   When is a colon wrong?

INDEPENDENT CLAUSES

A colon introduces a list, an APPOSITIVE, or a QUOTATION only after an INDEPENDENT CLAUSE. Similarly, a colon can be used between two independent clauses when the second summarizes or explains the first.

NO   The cook bought: eggs, milk, cheese, and bread.

   The cook bought isn't an independent clause.

YES   The cook bought eggs, milk, cheese, and bread.

A colon never follows a PHRASE or DEPENDENT CLAUSE. It follows an INDEPENDENT CLAUSE.

NO   Day after day: the drought dragged on.

   Day after day is a phrase, not an independent clause.

YES   Day after day, the drought dragged on.

NO   After the drought ended: the farmers celebrated.

   After the drought ended is a dependent clause, not an independent clause.

YES   After the drought ended, the farmers celebrated.

LEAD-IN WORDS

Never use a colon after the lead-in words *such as, including, like,* and *consists of.*

> **NO** The health board discussed many problems **such as:** poor water quality, aging sewage treatment systems, and the lack of alternative water supplies.

> **YES** The health board discussed poor water quality, aging sewage treatment systems, and the lack of alternative water supplies.
>
> This revision requires no colon.

> **YES** The health board discussed many problems**, such as** poor water quality, an aging sewage treatment system, and the lack of alternative water supplies.
>
> A comma, not a colon, is correct before *such as.*

> **YES** The health board discussed many problems**:** poor water quality, aging sewage treatment systems, and the lack of alternative water supplies.
>
> The colon after the independent clause introduces a list.

● **EXERCISE 44-1** Insert colons where needed and delete any not needed. If a sentence is correct, explain why.

EXAMPLE

> **NO** After months of work, Carlos was finally ready to mail his college applications to the following schools, Valley College, East California University, and Blakeville College.

> **YES** After months of work, Carlos was finally ready to mail his college applications to the following schools: Valley College, East California University, and Blakeville College.

1. To prepare for the application process, Carlos read the book *Expanding Your Options, A Guide to Writing a Successful College Application.*
2. Date   2 March 2012
   To   Office of Admissions
   To whom it may concern
3. Since the post office closed at 530, Carlos had to rush to meet the application deadline.
4. To represent himself effectively, Carlos wrote his application letter about his many successes, such as: his high grade point average, his work as the high school newspaper editor, and his community service.
5. After his application was completed and in the mail: he started to look forward to hearing back from the colleges.
6. He decided not to worry when he remembered the words of his favorite Bible quote from Matthew 6,34.

7. He also remembered the encouraging words from his guidance counselor: "Don't worry, Carlos. Something will work out for you."
8. He hoped that he would be accepted to his first choice, Valley College.
9. Valley College was his first choice because it offered: beautiful scenery, a diverse student body, and a small teacher-student ratio.
10. However: Valley College is very selective and admits only a small percentage of applicants. ●

Complete
the
Chapter
Exercises

45 Apostrophes

■ ■ ■ ■ ■ ■ ■ ■ ■ ■

Quick Points   You will learn to

➤ Use apostrophes correctly (see 45A–45G).

45A   What is the role of the apostrophe?

The apostrophe plays four roles: It creates the POSSESSIVE CASE of NOUNS (see 45B), forms the possessive case of INDEFINITE PRONOUNS (see 45E), stands for one or more omitted letters (a CONTRACTION; see 45D), and helps form plurals of letters and numerals (see 45F).

In contrast, here are two roles the apostrophe doesn't play: It doesn't form the plurals of nouns, and it doesn't form the plural of PERSONAL PRONOUNS in the possessive case.

45B   How do I use an apostrophe to show a possessive noun?

An apostrophe works with a NOUN to form the POSSESSIVE CASE, which shows ownership or a close relationship.

Watch
the Video

OWNERSHIP	The **writer's** pen ran out of ink.
CLOSE RELATIONSHIP	The **novel's** plot is complicated.

Possession in nouns can be communicated in two ways: by a PHRASE starting with *of* (*comments **of** the instructor; comments **of** Professor Furman*) or by an apostrophe and the letter *s* (*the instructor's comments; Professor Furman's comments*). Here's a list of specific rules governing the usage of *'s*.

- **Add *'s* to nouns not ending in -*s:***
  - She felt a **parent's** joy.

    Parent is a singular noun not ending in -*s*.
  - We care about our **children's** education.

    Children is a plural noun not ending in -*s*.

- **Add *'s* to singular nouns ending in -*s:*** You can add either *'s* or the apostrophe alone to show possession when a singular noun ends in -*s*. In this handbook, we use *'s* to clearly mark singular-noun possessives, no matter what letter ends the noun. Whichever choice you make, be consistent within each piece of writing.
  - The **bus's** (or **bus'**) air conditioning is out of order.
  - **Chris's** (or **Chris'**) ordeal ended.

  If you encounter a tongue-twisting pronunciation (*Moses's story*), you may decide not to add the additional -*s* (*Moses' story*). Do remember, however, to be consistent within each piece of writing.

- **Add only an apostrophe to a plural noun ending in -*s:***
  - The two **boys'** statements helped solve the crime.
  - The **workers'** contract permits three **months'** maternity leave.

- **Add *'s* to the last word in compound words and phrases:**
  - His **mother-in-law's** corporation has bought out a competitor.
  - The **attorney general's** investigation led to several arrests.

- **Add *'s* to each noun in individual possession:**
  - **Shirley's** and **Kayla's** houses are next to each other.

    Shirley and Kayla each own a house; they don't own the houses jointly.

- **Add *'s* to only the last noun in joint or group possession:**
  - **Kareem and Brina's** house has a screened porch.

    Kareem and Brina own one house.
  - **Pat and Justin's** houses always have nice lawns.

    Pat and Justin jointly own more than one house.

45C How do I use an apostrophe with possessive pronouns?

When a POSSESSIVE PRONOUN ends with -s (*hers, his, its, ours, yours*, and *theirs*), never add an apostrophe. Following is a list of PERSONAL PRONOUNS and their possessive forms. None of these possessive forms use *'s*.

Personal Pronouns	Possessive Forms	Personal Pronouns	Possessive Forms
I	my, mine	it	its
you	your, yours	we	our, ours
he	his	they	their, theirs
she	her, hers	who	whose

45D How do I use an apostrophe with contractions?

In a **contraction**, an apostrophe takes the place of one or more omitted letters. Be careful not to confuse a contraction with a POSSESSIVE PRONOUN. Doing so is a common spelling error, which many people—including employers—consider unprofessional. Whether or not that's fair, it's usually true.

((• Listen to the Podcast

it's (contraction for *it is*)   **its** (possessive pronoun)
they're (contraction for *they are*)   **their** (possessive pronoun)
who's (contraction for *who is*)   **whose** (possessive form of *who*)
you're (contraction for *you are*)   **your** (possessive pronoun)

> NO   The government has to balance **it's** budget.
> YES The government has to balance **its** budget.
>
> NO   The professor **who's** class was canceled is ill.
> YES The professor **whose** class was canceled is ill.

Remember that many instructors think contractions aren't appropriate in ACADEMIC WRITING. Nevertheless, the *MLA Handbook* accepts contractions, including *'90s* for *the 1990s*. In this handbook, we use contractions because we're addressing you, the student. We suggest, however, that before you use contractions in your academic writing, you check with your instructor. Here's a list of common contractions.

COMMON CONTRACTIONS

aren't = *are not*	isn't = *is not*	we're = *we are*
can't = *cannot*	it's = *it is*	weren't = *were not*
didn't = *did not*	let's = *let us*	we've = *we have*
don't = *do not*	she's = *she is*	who's = *who is*
he's = *he is*	there's = *there is*	won't = *will not*
I'd = *I would, I had*	they're = *they are*	you're = *you are*
I'm = *I am*	wasn't = *was not*	

Alert: One contraction required in all writing is *o'clock* (which means *of the clock*, an expression used long ago). ●

45E How do I use an apostrophe with possessive indefinite pronouns?

An apostrophe works with an INDEFINITE PRONOUN (see list in Quick Box 31.6 in 31I) to form the POSSESSIVE CASE, which shows ownership or a close relationship.

OWNERSHIP	**Everyone's** dinner is ready.
CLOSE RELATIONSHIP	**Something's** aroma is appealing.

Possession in indefinite pronouns can be communicated in two ways: by a PHRASE starting with *of* (*comments **of** everyone*) or by an apostrophe and the letter *s* (*everyone**'s** comments*).

45F How do I form the plural of miscellaneous elements?

Until recently, the plural of elements such as letters meant as letters, words meant as words, numerals, and symbols could be formed by adding either *'s* or *s*. Current MLA guidelines endorse the use of *s* only, with the exception of adding *'s* to letters meant as letters. MLA recommends using italics for letters meant as letters and words meant as words. The following examples reflect MLA practices.

PLURAL OF LETTERS MEANT AS LETTERS	Printing ***W's*** confuses young children.
PLURAL OF LETTERS MEANT AS WORDS	He earned all **Bs** in his courses.
PLURAL OF WORDS MEANT AS WORDS	Too many ***ifs*** in a contract make me suspicious.
PLURAL OF NUMBERS	Her e-mail address contains many **7s.**

PLURAL OF YEARS	I remember the **1990s** well.
PLURAL OF SYMBOLS	What do those **&s** mean?

45G When is an apostrophe wrong?

If you're a writer who makes apostrophe errors repeatedly, memorize the rules you need. Then you won't be annoyed by "that crooked little mark," a nickname popular with students who wish the apostrophe would go away. Quick Box 45.1 lists the major apostrophe errors.

Quick Box 45.1　　　　　　■ ■ ■ ■ ■ ■ ■ ■ ■ ■ ■

Leading apostrophe errors

((•●

Listen
to the
Podcast

- Never use an apostrophe with a PRESENT-TENSE verb.
  - Exercise **plays** [not **play's**] an important role in how long we live.
- Always use an apostrophe after the -s in a POSSESSIVE plural of a noun.
  - **Patients'** [not **Patients**] questions seek detailed answers.
- Never add an apostrophe at the end of a nonpossessive noun ending in -s.
  - Medical **studies** [not **studies'** or **study's**] show this to be true.
- Never use an apostrophe to form a nonpossessive plural.
  - **Teams** [not **Team's**] of doctors have studied the effects of cholesterol.

● **EXERCISE 45-1**   Rewrite these sentences to insert *'s* or an apostrophe alone to make the words in parentheses show possession. (Delete the parentheses.) For help, consult 45B and 45E.

EXAMPLE

All boxes, cans, and bottles on a (supermarket) shelves are designed to appeal to (people) emotions.

All boxes, cans, and bottles on a *supermarket's* shelves are designed to appeal to *people's* emotions.

1. A (product) manufacturer designs packaging to appeal to (consumers) emotions through color and design.
2. Marketing specialists know that (people) beliefs about a (product) quality are influenced by their emotional response to the design of its package.

3. Circles and ovals appearing on a (box) design supposedly increase a (product user) feelings of comfort, while bold patterns and colors attract a (shopper) attention.

4. Using circles and bold designs in (Arm & Hammer) and (Tide) packaging produces both effects in consumers.

5. (Heinz) ketchup bottle and (Coca-Cola) famous logo achieve the same effects by combining a bright color with an old-fashioned, "comfortable" design.

6. Often, a (company) marketing consultants will custom-design products to appeal to the supposedly "typical" (adult female) emotions or to (adult males), (children), or (teenagers) feelings.

7. One of the (marketing business) leading consultants, Stan Gross, tests (consumers) reactions to (companies) products and their packages by asking consumers to associate products with well-known personalities.

8. Thus, (test takers) responses to (Gross) questions might reveal that a particular brand of laundry detergent has (Russell Crowe) toughness, (Oprah Winfrey) determination, or (someone else) sparkling personality.

9. Manufacturing (companies) products are not the only ones relying on (Gross) and other corporate (image makers) advice.

10. (Sports teams) owners also use marketing specialists to design their (teams) images, as anyone who has seen the angry bull logo of the Chicago Bulls basketball team will agree. ●

● **EXERCISE 45-2** Rewrite these sentences so that each has a possessive noun. For help, consult 45B and 45E.

Complete
the
Chapter
Exercises

EXAMPLE

The light of a firefly gives off no heat.
A *firefly's* light gives off no heat.

1. The scientific name of a firefly is *lampyridae*, but nicknames of the bug include *glowworm* and *lightning bug*.

2. More than two thousand species of fireflies can be found throughout the temperate climates of the world.

3. The light of a firefly is caused by a chemical reaction in the organs of the abdomen.

4. Fireflies played a role in the mythology of ancient Mayans and were often compared to the light of a star.

5. Although it may be in the interest of nobody to know, fireflies are not flies at all; they are, according to the classifications of scientists, beetles. ●

46 Quotation Marks

■ ■ ■ ■ ■ ■ ■ ■ ■ ■

Quick Points   You will learn to

➤ Use quotation marks correctly (see 46A–46I).

46A   What is the role of quotation marks?

Quotation marks are most often used to enclose **direct quotations**—a speaker or writer's exact words. In addition, quotation marks enclose titles, and they alert readers to words you single out for consideration.

Double quotation marks open and close the entire quotation. Single quotation marks signal quotations within quotations: *Ray said, "I heard a man shout 'Help me,' but I couldn't respond."* Quotation marks operate only in pairs: to open and to close. Be sure to close all quotation marks you open.

Throughout this book, we use MLA STYLE to format examples. Other documentation styles require different formats. For MLA style, see Chapter 25; for APA STYLE, see Chapter 26.

46B   How do I use quotation marks with short direct quotations?

Use double quotation marks to start and finish a **short quotation**, which, in MLA STYLE, means a quotation fewer than four typed lines. Offer DOCUMENTATION information after a short quotation, before the sentence's period.

SHORT QUOTATIONS

Remarked director Fritz Lang of his masterpiece *Siegfried*, "Nothing in this film is accidental" (228).

A recent survey of leading employers found that almost all professional employees "are expected to write competently on the job" (11).

46C   Are quotation marks used with long quotations?

No. In MLA STYLE, a quotation is *long* if it occupies four or more typed lines. Instead of using quotation marks with a **long quotation**, indent all its lines as a block (that is, the quotation is "set off" or "displayed"). Give DOCUMENTATION information after the period that ends the quotation.

LONG QUOTATIONS

Gardner uses criteria by which to judge whether an ability deserves to be categorized as an "intelligence." Each must confer

> a set of skills of problem solving—enabling the individual <u>to resolve genuine problems or difficulties</u> [author's emphasis] that he or she encounters and laying the groundwork for the acquisition of new knowledge. (*Frames* 60–61)

In the Gardner example above, note that a capital letter is *not* used to start the quotation. The lead-in words (*Each must confer*) form an incomplete sentence, so they need the quotation to complete the sentence.

> Goleman also emphasizes a close interaction of the emotional and rational states with the other intelligences that Gardner has identified:

> These two minds, the emotional and the rational, operate in tight harmony for the most part, intertwining their very different ways of knowing to guide us through the world. Ordinarily there is a balance between emotional and rational minds, with emotion feeding into and informing the operations of the rational mind, and the rational mind refining and sometimes vetoing the inputs of the emotions. (9)

In the Goleman example above, note that a capital letter starts the quotation because the lead-in words are a complete sentence. (A colon can also end the lead-in sentence because it's preceded by an independent clause; see 44B.)

🛑 **Alert:** Whether a quotation is one word or occupies many lines, always document its SOURCE. Also, when you quote material, be very careful to record the words exactly as they appear in the original. ●

46D How do I use quotation marks for quotations within quotations?

👁 Watch the Video

MLA STYLE uses different formats for short and long quotations of prose that contain quotes within them. Quotes within short quotations take single quotation marks, while double quotes enclose the entire quotation. Give documentation information after the entire quotation, before the sentence's ending period. For other documentation styles, check each style's manual.

Quotes within longer quotations—four or more lines set off in a block—use double and single quotation marks exactly as the original source does. Give documentation information after the long quotation following the closing punctuation.

SHORT QUOTATIONS: USE SINGLE WITHIN DOUBLE QUOTATION MARKS (MLA STYLE)

With short quotations, the double quotation marks show the beginning and end of words taken from the source; the single quotation marks replace double marks used in the source.

ORIGINAL SOURCE

Most scientists concede that they don't really know what "intelligence" is. Whatever it might be, paper and pencil tests aren't the tenth of it.

—Brent Staples, "The IQ Cult," p. 293

STUDENT'S USE OF THE SOURCE

Brent Staples argues in his essay about IQ as an object of reverence: "Most scientists concede that they don't really know what 'intelligence' is. Whatever it might be, paper and pencil tests aren't the tenth of it" (293).

LONG QUOTATIONS: USE QUOTATION MARKS AS IN SOURCE

Since long quotations are set off (displayed) without being enclosed in quotation marks, show any double and single quotation marks exactly as the source does.

46E How do I use quotation marks for quotations of poetry and dialogue?

POETRY (MLA STYLE)

A *short* poetry quotation includes three lines or fewer of a poem. As with prose quotations (see 46D), double quotation marks enclose the material. If the poetry lines contain double quotation marks, change them to single quotation marks. To show a break between lines of poetry, use a slash (/) with one space on each side. Give DOCUMENTATION information after a short poetry quotation, before the period that ends the sentence (see also 47E).

- As Auden wittily defined personal space, "some thirty inches from my nose / The frontier of my person goes" (*Complete* 205).

A quotation of poetry is *long* if it includes more than three lines of a poem. As with prose quotations (see 46D), indent all lines as a block, without quotation marks. Start new lines exactly as your source does. Give documentation information after the quotation and after the period that ends the quotation.

🛇 **Alert:** When you quote poetry, follow the capitalization of your source. ●

DIALOGUE (MLA AND APA STYLES)

Dialogue, also called DIRECT DISCOURSE, presents a speaker's exact words. Enclose dialogue in quotation marks. In contrast, INDIRECT DISCOURSE reports what a speaker said and requires no quotation marks. Additionally, PRONOUN use and VERB TENSES also differ for these two types of discourse.

> DIRECT DISCOURSE   The mayor said, "I intend to veto that bill."
>
> INDIRECT DISCOURSE   The mayor said that he intended to veto that bill.

Use double quotation marks at the beginning and end of a speaker's words. This tells your reader which words are the speaker's. Also, start a new paragraph each time the speaker changes.

> "I don't know how you can see to drive," she said.
> "Maybe you should put on your glasses."
> "Putting on my glasses would help you to see?"
> "Not me; you," Macon said. "You're focused on the windshield instead of the road."
>
> —Anne Tyler, *The Accidental Tourist*

In American English, if two or more paragraphs present a single speaker's words, start each new paragraph with double quotation marks, but save the closing double quotation marks until the end of the last quoted paragraph.

● **EXERCISE 46-1** Working individually or with a group, decide whether each sentence that follows is direct or indirect discourse and then rewrite each sentence in the other form. Make any changes needed for grammatical correctness. With direct discourse, put the speaker's words wherever you think they belong in the sentence.

EXAMPLE

Dr. Sanchez explained to Mary that washing her hands in an important part of hygiene.

Dr. Sanchez explained, "Washing your hands is an important part of hygiene."

1. Mary asked, "If my hands aren't dirty, why is it so important to wash them?"
2. Dr. Sanchez replied that many diseases are spread because of inadequately washed and infected hands.
3. The Centers for Disease Control, explained Dr. Sanchez, argues that hand washing may seem trivial but it is a vital part of public health.

4. Mary asked, "Is it ok to use alcohol-based hand sanitizers instead of soap and water?"

5. Dr. Sanchez replied that soap and clean water are best, but a sanitizer with at least 60% alcohol is also very effective. ●

46F How do I use quotation marks with titles of short works?

Titles of certain short works are enclosed in quotation marks (other works, usually longer, need italics; see 48G). Short works include short stories, essays, poems, articles from periodicals, pamphlets, brochures, songs, and individual episodes of a series on television or radio.

- What is the rhyme scheme of Poe's poem "The Raven"?
- Have you read "The Lottery"? [short story]
- The best source I found is "The Myth of Political Consultants." [magazine article]
- Rand's essay "Apollo II" offers an eyewitness account of the launch.

Titles of some other works are neither enclosed in quotation marks nor written in italics. For guidelines, see Quick Box 48.1 in 48E and Quick Box 48.2 in 48G.

🛈 **Alert:** Unless the title of a paper you wrote quotes someone, don't enclose it in quotation marks. ●

● **EXERCISE 46-2** Working individually or with a group, correct any misuses of quotation marks. For help, consult 46F.

1. The song America the Beautiful by Katharine Lee Bates celebrates the natural beauty and the ideals that many people associate with the United States.

2. Ralph Waldo Emerson's essay The American Scholar praises the ideals of independence and self-reliance in American education and was first heard as an oration delivered to the "Phi Beta Kappa Society."

3. However, not only the ideals, but also the harsh realities of life in America for Filipino immigrants form the basis of Carlos Bulosan's autobiography, America Is in the Heart.

4. A film that honestly and poignantly reveals the realities facing a family of Irish immigrants in New York City and their hopes for a better life is In America.

5. The poet Langston Hughes in his poem Let America Be America Again is fierce in his criticism of the way poor people and minorities are often treated in the United States. ●

46G How do I use quotation marks for words used as words?

Choose consistently either quotation marks or italics to refer to a word as a word.

NO   Many people confuse affect and effect.

YES   Many people confuse "affect" and "effect."

YES   Many people confuse *affect* and *effect*.

Always put quotation marks around the English translation of a word or PHRASE. Also, use italics for the word or phrase in the other language.

- My grandfather usually ended arguments with *de gustibus non disputandum est* ("there is no disputing about tastes").

Many writers use quotation marks around words or phrases meant ironically or in other nonliteral ways.

- The proposed tax "reform" is actually a tax increase.

You can place quotation marks around technical terms—but only the first time they appear. Once you use and define the term, you no longer need quotation marks.

- "Plagiarism"—the undocumented use of another person's words or ideas—can result in expulsion. Plagiarism is a serious offense.

If you use a slang term in ACADEMIC WRITING, use quotation marks. However, when possible, revise your slang with language appropriate to academic writing.

- They "eat like birds" in public, but they "stuff their faces" in private.
- They **nibble** in public, but they **gorge themselves** in private.

A nickname doesn't call for quotation marks, unless you use the nickname along with the full name. When a person's nickname is widely known, you don't have to give both the nickname and the full name. For example, use *Representative Gabrielle Gifford* or *Representative Gabby Gifford*, whichever is appropriate in context. Because she's well known, don't use *Representative Gabrielle "Gabby" Gifford*.

● **EXERCISE 46-3** Working individually or with a group, correct any misuses of quotation marks. If you think a sentence is correct, explain why. For help, consult 46G.

EXAMPLE

The word asyndeton simply means that a conjunction has been omitted, as when Shakespeare writes, A woman mov'd is like a fountain troubled, / Muddy, ill seeming, thick, bereft of beauty.

The word "asyndeton" simply means that a conjunction has been omitted, as when Shakespeare writes, "A woman mov'd is like a fountain troubled, / Muddy, ill seeming, thick, bereft of beauty."

1. Shakespeare's phrases such as the sound and the fury from *Macbeth* and pale fire from *The Tempest* have been used by authors such as William Faulkner and Vladimir Nabokov as titles for their books.
2. Shakespeare's understanding of human nature was "profound" and helped him become a "prolific" writer.
3. Many words used commonly today, such as "addiction" and "alligator," were first used in print by Shakespeare.
4. To understand the difference between the words sanguinary and *sanguine* is important for a reader of Shakespeare because the former means bloody and the latter means optimistic.
5. In the play *Romeo and Juliet*, one of Shakespeare's most famous quotations is What's in a name? That which we call a rose / By any other name would smell as sweet. ●

46H How do I use quotation marks with other punctuation?

COMMAS AND PERIODS WITH QUOTATION MARKS

An appropriate comma or period is always placed *inside* the closing quotation mark.

Listen
to the
Podcast

- Jessica enjoyed F. Scott Fitzgerald's story "The Freshest Boy," so she was eager to read his novels.
- Max said, "Don't stand so far away from me."
- Edward T. Hall coined the word "proxemia."

SEMICOLONS AND COLONS WITH QUOTATION MARKS

A semicolon or colon is placed *outside* the closing quotation mark, unless it is part of the quotation.

- Computers offer businesses "opportunities that never existed before"; some workers disagree.   [semicolon after closing quotation mark]
- We have to know each culture's standard for "how close is close": No one wants to offend.   [colon after closing quotation mark]

QUESTION MARKS, EXCLAMATION POINTS, AND DASHES WITH QUOTATION MARKS

If the punctuation marks belong to the words enclosed in quotation marks, put them inside the quotation marks.

- "Did I Hear You Call My Name?" was the winning song.
- "I've won the lottery!" Arielle shouted.
- "Who's there? Why don't you ans—"

If a question mark, an exclamation point, or a dash doesn't belong to the material being quoted, put the punctuation outside the quotation marks.

- Have you read Nikki Giovanni's poem "Knoxville, Tennessee"?
- If only I could write a story like David Wallace's "Girl with Curious Hair"!
- Weak excuses—a classic is "My dog ate my homework"—never convince.

When you use quotation marks and want to know how they work with capital letters, see 48D; with brackets, 47C; with ellipsis points, 47D; and with the slash, 47E.

461 When are quotation marks wrong?

Never enclose a word in quotation marks simply for intensity or sarcasm.

NO   I'm "very" happy about the news.

YES   I'm very happy about the news.

Never enclose the title of your paper in quotation marks (or underline it). However, if the title of your paper contains another title that requires quotation marks, use those marks only for the included title.

NO   "The Elderly in Nursing Homes: A Case Study"

YES   The Elderly in Nursing Homes: A Case Study

NO   Character Development in Shirley Jackson's Story The Lottery

YES   Character Development in Shirley Jackson's Story "The Lottery"

● **EXERCISE 46-4** Correct any errors in the use of quotation marks and other punctuation with quotation marks. If you think a sentence is correct, explain why.

1. Mark Twain's observation "—Facts are stubborn things, but statistics are more pliable.—" is an interesting critique of news media.
2. Twain valued travel and said that it "liberates the vandal." He argues that you cannot become: "bigoted, opinionated, stubborn, narrow-minded"

if you travel. Someone who refuses to travel is, "stuck in one place" and thinks that" God made the world" for his "comfort and satisfaction."

3. In a poem called Genius, Mark Twain says that: Genius, like gold and precious stones / is chiefly prized because of its rarity.

4. Was it Shakespeare or Twain who wrote, "The course of true love never did run smooth?"

5. In a speech offering advice to young people, Twain said, "Be respectful to your superiors, if you have any". ●

Complete
the
Chapter
Exercises

47 Other Punctuation Marks

Quick Points   You will learn to

➤ Use dashes, parentheses, brackets, ellipses, and slashes correctly (see 47A–47I).

While dashes, parentheses, brackets, ellipsis points, slashes, and hyphens are not used frequently, each serves a purpose(s) and gives you further opportunities for writing precision and style.

DASH

47A When can I use a dash in my writing?

The dash, typed as two unspaced hyphens, interrupts a thought within a sentence—in the middle or at the end—for special emphasis or commentary. If you handwrite a dash, make it about twice as long as a hyphen.

USING DASHES FOR SPECIAL EMPHASIS

To emphasize an example, a definition, an appositive, or a contrast, you can use a dash or dashes. A dash tells your readers to take note, something special is coming. Use dashes sparingly so that you don't dilute their impact.

EXAMPLE

The caretakers—those who are helpers, nurturers, teachers, mothers—are still systematically devalued.

—Ellen Goodman, "Just Woman's Work?"

DEFINITION

Although the emphasis at the school was mainly language—speaking, reading, writing—the lessons always began with an exercise in politeness.

—Jade Snow Wong, *Fifth Chinese Daughter*

APPOSITIVE

Two of the strongest animals in the jungle are vegetarians—the elephant and the gorilla.

—Dick Gregory, *The Shadow That Scares Me*

CONTRAST

Fire cooks food—and burns down forests.

—Smokey the Bear

Place what you emphasize with dashes next to or nearby the material it refers to so that what you want to accomplish with your emphasis is not lost.

> NO   The current **argument is**—one that faculty, students, and coaches debate fiercely—whether to hold athletes to the same academic standards as others face.

> YES   The current **argument**—one that faculty, students, and coaches debate fiercely—**is** whether to hold athletes to the same academic standards as others face.

USING DASHES TO EMPHASIZE AN ASIDE

An aside, a writer's commentary often expressing personal views, is generally inappropriate for academic writing. Before you insert an aside, carefully consider both your writing purpose and your audience.

Television showed us the war. It showed us the war in a way that was—if you chose to watch television, at least—unavoidable.

—Nora Ephron, *Scribble Scribble*

🛈 **Alerts:** (1) If the words within a pair of dashes require a question mark or an exclamation point, place it before the second dash.

- A first date—do you remember?—stays in the memory forever.

(2) Never use commas, semicolons, or periods next to dashes. If such a need arises, revise your writing.

(3) Never enclose quotation marks in dashes except when the meaning requires them. These two examples show that, when required, the dash stops before or after the quotation marks; the two punctuation marks do not overlap.

- Many of George Orwell's essays—"A Hanging," for example—draw on his experiences as a civil servant.
- "Shooting an Elephant"—another Orwell essay—appears in many anthologies. ●

● **EXERCISE 47-1** Write a sentence about each topic, shown in italics. Use dashes to set off what is asked for, shown in roman, in each sentence. For help, consult 47A.

EXAMPLE

punctuation mark, an aside
Sometimes I get confused—but what's new?—about the difference between a colon and a semicolon.

1. *ice cream flavor*, an aside
2. *a shape*, a definition
3. *sport*, an appositive
4. *public transportation*, an example
5. *occupation*, a contrast
6. *musical instrument*, a definition
7. *TV show*, an aside
8. *American president*, an example
9. *country*, an appositive
10. *animal*, a contrast ●

PARENTHESES

47B When can I use parentheses in my writing?

Parentheses enclose material which (unlike dashes, 47A) connects the inserts they enclose loosely, not emphatically, to your sentence. Use parentheses sparingly. Overusing them causes your writing to lurch, not flow.

USING PARENTHESES TO ENCLOSE INTERRUPTING WORDS
EXPLANATION

After they've finished with the pantry, the medicine cabinet, and the attic, they will throw out the red geranium (too many leaves), sell the dog (too many fleas), and send the children off to boarding school (too many scuffmarks on the hardwood floors).

—Suzanne Britt, "Neat People vs. Sloppy People"

EXAMPLE

Though other cities (Dresden, for instance) had been utterly destroyed in World War II, never before had a single weapon been responsible for such destruction.

—Laurence Behrens and Leonard J. Rosen,
Writing and Reading Across the Curriculum

ASIDE

The older girls (non-graduates, of course) were assigned the task of making refreshments for the night's festivities.

—Maya Angelou, *I Know Why the Caged Bird Sings*

The sheer decibel level of the noise around us is not enough to make us cranky, irritable, or aggressive. (It can, however, affect our mental and physical health, which is another matter.)

—Carol Tavris, *Anger: The Misunderstood Emotion*

USING PARENTHESES FOR LISTED ITEMS AND ALTERNATIVE NUMBERS

Parentheses enclose the numbers (or letters) of listed items within a sentence. A displayed list uses periods, not parentheses, to enclose items.

- The topics to be discussed are *(1) membership, (2) fundraising, and (3) networking.*

❶ Alerts: For listed items that fall within a sentence, (1) use a colon before a list only if an INDEPENDENT CLAUSE comes before the list, and (2) use commas or semicolons to separate three or more items, but be consistent within a piece of writing. If, however, any item contains punctuation itself, use a semicolon to separate the items. ●

In legal writing and in some BUSINESS WRITING, you can use parentheses to enclose a numeral that repeats a spelled-out number.

- The monthly rent is three hundred fifty dollars ($350).
- Your order of fifteen (15) gross was shipped today.

In ACADEMIC WRITING, especially in subjects in which the use of figures or measurements is frequent, enclose alternative or comparative forms of the same number in parentheses: *2 mi (3.2 km).*

USING OTHER PUNCTUATION WITH PARENTHESES

A parenthetical complete sentence inserted within the body of another sentence does not start with a capital letter or end with a period. (It would, however, end with a question mark or exclamation point if one is required.) A complete parenthetical sentence standing alone follows regular rules of punctuation, as the previous sentence highlights.

NO If you decide to join us (We hope you do.), bring your dog also.

YES If you decide to join us (we hope you do), bring your dog also.

YES If you decide to join us, bring your dog also. (We hope you do.)

YES Your dog (isn't Rex his name?) will delight all my other guests.

As in the preceding examples, place a required comma outside your closing parenthesis unless you're using commas to set off a numbered list.

Place parentheses around quotation marks that come before or after any quoted words.

NO Alberta Hunter "(Down Hearted Blues)" is known for singing jazz.

YES Alberta Hunter ("Down Hearted Blues") is known for singing jazz.

BRACKETS

47C When do I need to use brackets in my writing?

Use brackets to feature an insert, such as an additional word or a brief definition, added by you to material which you are quoting.

ADJUSTING A QUOTATION WITH BRACKETS

When you use a quotation, you might need to change the form of a word (a verb's tense, for example), add a brief definition, or fit the quotation into the grammatical structure of your sentence. In such cases, enclose the material you have inserted into the quotation in brackets.

ORIGINAL SOURCE

Current research shows that successful learning takes place in an active environment.

—Deborah Moore, "Facilities and Learning Styles," p. 22

QUOTATION WITH BRACKETS

Deborah Moore supports a student-centered curriculum and agrees with "current research [that] shows that successful learning takes place in an active environment" (22).

ORIGINAL SOURCE

The logic of the mind is *associative;* it takes elements that symbolize a reality, or trigger a memory of it, to be the same as that reality.

—Daniel Goleman, *Emotional Intelligence*, p. 294

QUOTATION WITH BRACKETS

The kinds of intelligence are based in the way the mind functions: "The logic of the mind is *associative* [one idea connects with another]; it takes elements that symbolize a reality, or trigger a memory of it, to be the same as that reality" (Goleman 294).

USING BRACKETS TO POINT OUT AN ERROR IN A SOURCE OR TO ADD INFORMATION WITHIN PARENTHESES

In words you want to quote, sometimes page-makeup technicians or authors make a mistake without realizing it—a wrong date, a misspelled word, or an error of fact. You fix that mistake by putting your correction in brackets. This tells your readers that the error was in the original work and not made by you.

USING [SIC] TO SHOW A SOURCE'S ERROR

Insert *sic* (without italics), enclosed in brackets, in your MLA-style essays and research papers to show your readers that you've quoted an error accurately. *Sic* is a Latin word that means "so," or "thus," which says "It is so (or thus) in the original."

USE FOR ERROR

- A journalist wrote, "The judge accepted an [sic] plea of not guilty."

USE FOR MISSPELLING

- The building inspector condemned our structure in no uncertain terms: "There [sic] building is uninhabitable," he wrote.

USING BRACKETS WITHIN PARENTHESES

Use brackets to insert information within parentheses.

- That expression (first used in *A Fable for Critics* [1848] by James R. Lowell) was popularized in the early twentieth century by Ella Wheeler Wilcox.

ELLIPSIS POINTS

47D How do I use ellipsis points in my writing?

The word *ellipsis* means "omission." Ellipsis points in writing are a series of three spaced dots (use the period key on the keyboard). Use ellipsis points to indicate you've intentionally omitted words—even a sentence or more—from the source you're quoting. These rules apply to both prose and poetry.

47D.1 Using ellipsis points with prose

ORIGINAL SOURCE

These two minds, the emotional and the rational, operate in tight harmony for the most part, intertwining their very different ways of knowing to guide us through the world. Ordinarily, there is a balance between emotional and rational minds, with emotion feeding into and informing the operations of the rational mind, and the rational mind refining and sometimes vetoing the inputs of the emotions. Still, the emotional and rational minds are semi-independent faculties, each, as we shall see, reflecting the operation of distinct, but interconnected, circuitry in the brain.

—Daniel Goleman, *Emotional Intelligence*, p. 9

QUOTATION OF SELECTED WORDS, NO ELLIPSIS NEEDED

Goleman explains that the "two minds, the emotional and the rational" usually provide "a balance" in our daily observations and decision making (9).

QUOTATION WITH ELLIPSIS MID-SENTENCE

Goleman emphasizes the connections between parts of the mind: "Still, the emotional and rational minds are semi-independent faculties, each . . . reflecting the operation of distinct, but interconnected, circuitry in the brain" (9).

QUOTATION WITH ELLIPSIS AND PARENTHETICAL REFERENCE

Goleman emphasizes that the "two minds, the emotional and the rational, operate in tight harmony for the most part . . . " (9).

Note: In MLA style, place a sentence-ending period after the parenthetical reference.

QUOTATION WITH ELLIPSIS ENDING THE SENTENCE

On page 9, Goleman states: "These two minds, the emotional and the rational, operate in tight harmony for the most part. . . . "

Note: In MLA style, when all documentation information is written into a sentence—that is, not placed in parentheses at the end of the sentence—there's no space between the sentence-ending period and an ellipsis.

QUOTATION WITH SENTENCE OMITTED

Goleman explains: "These two minds, the emotional and the rational, operate in tight harmony for the most part, intertwining their very different ways of knowing to guide us through the world. . . . Still, the emotional and rational minds are semi-independent faculties" (9).

QUOTATION WITH WORDS OMITTED FROM THE MIDDLE OF ONE SENTENCE TO THE MIDDLE OF ANOTHER

Goleman states: "Ordinarily, there is a balance between emotional and rational minds . . . reflecting the operation of distinct, but interconnected, circuitry in the brain" (9).

QUOTATION WITH WORDS OMITTED FROM THE BEGINNING OF A SENTENCE AND FROM THE MIDDLE OF ONE SENTENCE TO A COMPLETE OTHER SENTENCE

Goleman explains: ". . . there is a balance between emotional and rational minds. . . . Still, the emotional and rational minds are semi-independent faculties, each, as we shall see, reflecting the operation of distinct, but interconnected, circuitry in the brain" (9).

When you omit words from a quotation, you also omit punctuation related to those words, unless it's needed for the sentence to be correct.

Goleman explains: "These two minds . . . operate in tight harmony" (9).

Comma in original source omitted after *minds*.

Goleman explains that the emotional and rational minds work together while, "still, ... each, as we shall see, [reflects] the operation of distinct, but interconnected, circuitry in the brain" (9).

Comma kept after *still* because it's an introductory word; *still* changed to begin with lowercase letter because it's now in the middle of the sentence; form of *reflecting* changed to improve the sense of sentence.

47D.2 Using ellipsis points with poetry

When you omit one or more words from a line of poetry, follow the rules stated above for prose. However, when you omit a full line or more from poetry, use a full line of spaced dots.

ORIGINAL SOURCE

LITTLE BOY BLUE
Little boy blue, come blow your horn,
The sheep's in the meadow, the cow's in the corn
Where is the little boy who looks after the sheep?
He's under the haystack, fast asleep.

QUOTATION WITH LINES OMITTED

LITTLE BOY BLUE
Little boy blue, come blow your horn,

. . . .

Where is the little boy who looks after the sheep?
He's under the haystack, fast asleep.

SLASH

47E When can I use a slash in my writing?

The slash (/), also called a *virgule* or *solidus*, is a diagonal line that separates or joins words in special circumstances.

USING A SLASH TO SEPARATE QUOTED LINES OF POETRY

To quote more than three lines of a poem, follow the rules in 46E. To quote three lines or fewer, enclose them in quotation marks and run them into your sentence—and use a slash to divide one line from the next. Leave a space on each side of the slash.

- One of my mottoes comes from the beginning of Anne Sexton's poem "Words": "Be careful of words, / even the miraculous ones."

Capitalize and punctuate each line of poetry as in the original—but even if the quoted line of poetry doesn't have a period, use one to end your sentence. If your quotation ends before the line of poetry ends, use ellipsis points (see 47D).

USING A SLASH FOR NUMERICAL FRACTIONS IN MANUSCRIPTS

To type numerical fractions, use a slash (with no space before or after the slash) to separate the numerator and denominator. In mixed numbers—that is, whole numbers with fractions—leave a space between the whole number and its fraction: 1 2/3, 3 7/8. Do not use a hyphen. (For information about using spelled-out and numerical forms of numbers, see 48M through 48O.)

USING A SLASH FOR *AND/OR*

When writing in the humanities, try not to signal alternatives with a slash, such as *and/or*. Where such combinations are acceptable, separate the words with a slash. Leave no space before or after the slash. In the humanities, listing both alternatives is usually better than separating choices with a slash.

NO   The best quality of reproduction comes from 35 mm slides/direct-positive films.

YES   The best quality of reproduction comes from 35 mm slides **or** direct-positive films.

NO   Each student must locate his/her own source material.

YES   Each student must locate his **or** her own source material.

● **EXERCISE 47-2** Supply needed dashes, parentheses, brackets, ellipsis points, and slashes. If a sentence is correct as written, circle its number. In some sentences, when you can use either dashes or parentheses, explain your choice.

EXAMPLE

There have been several famous entertainers Hedy Lamarr, Skunk Baxter, Brian May who are also accomplished scientists.

There have been several famous entertainers—Hedy Lamarr, Skunk Baxter, Brian May—who are also accomplished scientists.

1. Brian May is famous for being the guitar player for the rock band Queen one of my favorite bands of all time, but he also has a Ph.D. in astrophysics.
2. Besides being the guitarist, he also wrote one of Queen's biggest hits ("We Will Rock You" (1977)).
3. May wrote the lyrics for this famous rock anthem that includes the two lines, "Gonna take on the world some day, You got blood on your face."
4. After May earned his Ph.D. in astrophysics in 2008, another astronomer joked, "I don't know any scientists who look as much like Isaac Neuton (sic) as you do."
5. Of all the early Hollywood actresses, Lana Turner, Judy Garland, Ava Gardner, Hedy Lamarr may have been one of the most famous.

6. But Lamarr also invented a frequency-hopping system that is still used in the following modern devices: 1 wireless telephones 2 Bluetooth technology and 3 Wi-Fi networks.

7. Skunk Baxter is a guitar player known for his work with Steely Dan, "Rikki Don't Lose That Number" and "Reeling in the Years," and The Doobie Brothers, "Takin' It to the Street" and "What a Fool Believes."

8. In describing his decision to make a career change, Baxter said, "After we the band The Doobie Brothers had been together for so many years, many of the members diverged to their own musical directions."

9. Having some connections in the military, his next-door neighbor was a missile designer, Baxter began experimenting with new designs for data-compression algorithms.

10. This long-haired rock star—can you imagine?—was even granted high-level government security clearance by the U.S. Department of Defense. ●

● **EXERCISE 47-3** Follow the directions for each item. For help, consult all sections of this chapter.

EXAMPLE

Write a sentence that uses dashes and includes a definition.

I like to study Romance languages—languages derived from Latin.

1. Write a sentence that contains a numbered list.
2. Write a sentence that uses parentheses to set off a definition.
3. Quote a passage from the poem below that omits an entire line.
4. Write a sentence that quotes two lines from the poem below, and use a slash to separate the two lines.
5. Quote any part of the poem below and uses ellipsis points to omit word(s) from the poem.

> Little Lamb, who made thee?
>   Dost thou know who made thee?
> Gave thee life, and bid thee feed
> By the stream and o'er the mead;
> Gave thee clothing of delight,
> Softest clothing, woolly, bright;
> Gave thee such a tender voice,
> Making all the vales rejoice?
>   Little Lamb, who made thee?
>   Dost thou know who made thee?
>   —William Blake ●

HYPHEN

47F When do I need a hyphen in my writing?

A hyphen serves to divide words at the end of a line, to combine words into compounds, and to communicate numbers.

47G When do I use a hyphen at the end of a line?

((•
Listen
to the
Podcast
Set the default on your word processing program to avoid hyphenation. If you must divide a word, keep in mind the following procedures: (1) wherever possible, avoid dividing words with hyphens at the end of a line; (2) if a division is necessary, divide longer words by syllable and between consonants if possible (*omit-ting, ful-ness, sep-arate*); (3) never divide for one or two letters or for any one-syllable words (like *wealth* or *screamed*); (4) don't divide the last word on the first line of a paper, the last word in a paragraph, or the last word on a page.

47H How do I use a hyphen with prefixes and suffixes?

Prefixes are syllables in front of a **root**—a word's core, which carries the origin or meaning. Prefixes modify meanings. **Suffixes** also have modifying power, but they follow roots. Some prefixes and suffixes are attached to root words with hyphens, but others are not. Quick Box 47.1 shows you how to decide.

Quick Box 47.1 ■ ■ ■ ■ ■ ■ ■ ■ ■ ■ ■

Hyphens with prefixes and suffixes

- Use hyphens after the prefixes *all-, ex-, quasi-,* and *self-.*

YES	all-inclusive	self-reliant

- Never use a hyphen when *self* is a root word, not a prefix.

NO	self-ishness	self-less
YES	selfishness	selfless

- Use a hyphen to avoid a distracting string of letters.

NO	antiintellectual	belllike	prooutsourcing
YES	anti-intellectual	bell-like	pro-outsourcing

continued >>

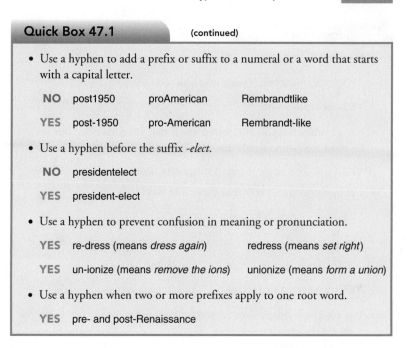

Quick Box 47.1 (continued)

- Use a hyphen to add a prefix or suffix to a numeral or a word that starts with a capital letter.

  NO   post1950   proAmerican   Rembrandtlike

  YES   post-1950   pro-American   Rembrandt-like

- Use a hyphen before the suffix *-elect*.

  NO   presidentelect

  YES   president-elect

- Use a hyphen to prevent confusion in meaning or pronunciation.

  YES   re-dress (means *dress again*)   redress (means *set right*)

  YES   un-ionize (means *remove the ions*)   unionize (means *form a union*)

- Use a hyphen when two or more prefixes apply to one root word.

  YES   pre- and post-Renaissance

471 How do I use hyphens with compound words?

A COMPOUND WORD puts two or more words together to express one concept. Compound words come in three forms: an open-compound word, as in *night shift;* hyphenated words, as in *tractor-trailer;* and a closed-compound word, as in *handbook.* Quick Box 47.2 lists basic guidelines for positioning hyphens in compound words.

Quick Box 47.2 ■ ■ ■ ■ ■ ■ ■ ■ ■ ■ ■

Hyphens with compound words

- Divide a compound word already containing a hyphen only after that hyphen, if possible. Also, divide a closed-compound word only between the two complete words, if possible.

  NO   self-con-scious   sis-ter-in-law   mas-terpiece

  YES   self-conscious   sister-in-law   master-piece

continued >>

Quick Box 47.2 (continued)

- Use a hyphen between a prefix and an open-compound word.

  NO antigun control [*gun control* is an open-compound word]

  YES anti-gun control

- Use a hyphen for most compound words that precede a noun but not for most compound words that follow a noun.

  YES well-researched report   report is well researched

- Use hyphens when a compound modifier includes a series.

  YES two-, three-, or four-year program

Complete the Chapter Exercises

- Never use a hyphen when a compound modifier starts with an *-ly* adverb.

  NO happily-married couple   loosely-tied package

  YES happily married couple   loosely tied package

- Use a hyphen with most COMPARATIVE (*-er*) and SUPERLATIVE (*-est*) compound forms, but not when the compound modifier includes *more/most* or *less/least*.

  NO better fitting shoe

  YES better-fitting shoe

  NO least-significant factors

  YES least significant factors

- Never use a hyphen when a compound modifier is a foreign phrase.

  YES *post hoc* fallacies

- Never use a hyphen with a possessive compound.

  NO a full-week's work   eight-hours' pay

  YES a full week's work   eight hours' pay

48 Capitals, Italics, Abbreviations, and Numbers

■ ■ ■ ■ ■ ■ ■ ■ ■

Quick Points You will learn to

➤ Use capital letters correctly (see 48A–48E).
➤ Use italics (underlining) correctly (see 48F–48H).
➤ Use abbreviations correctly (see 48I–48L).
➤ Use spelled out numbers and numerals correctly (see 48M–48N).

CAPITALS

48A When do I capitalize a "first" word?

FIRST WORD IN A SENTENCE

Always capitalize the first letter of the first word in a sentence.

Watch
the Video

● **F**our inches of snow fell last winter.

A SERIES OF QUESTIONS

If a series of questions imply, but are not themselves, complete sentences, you can choose capitals or not. Simply be consistent in each piece of writing.

● Whose rights does voter fraud deny? **M**ine? **Y**ours? **O**r everyone's?
● Whose rights does voter fraud deny? mine? yours? or everyone's?

SMALL WORDS IN TITLES OR HEADINGS

Capitalize the first word and all principal words of titles or headings. Do not capitalize ARTICLES, PREPOSITIONS, or CONJUNCTIONS in titles or headings unless one begins the title: *The Man without a Country*.

Capitalize the pronoun *I* and the interjection *O* (not *oh*) wherever these appear in a sentence: *Captain, O captain, I will follow you.*

AFTER A COLON

When a complete sentence follows a colon, choose consistently either a capital or lowercase letter in each piece of writing. If what follows your colon is not a complete sentence, don't capitalize the first word.

- The question remains: What will the jury decide?
- The question remains: what will the jury decide?
- The jury is considering all the evidence: motive, means, opportunity.

Alert: A colon can follow only a complete sentence (see 44A). ●

FORMAL OUTLINE

In a formal outline, start each item with a capital letter. Use a period only when the item is a complete sentence.

48B When do I use capitals with listed items?

A LIST WITHIN A SENTENCE

When a sentence itemizes other sentences, capitalize and punctuate the items as complete sentences: *The bank robbers made demands: (1) They want money. (2) They want hostages. (3) They want transportation.* When the items are not complete sentences, use commas between them unless the items contain commas. When they do, use semicolons between items. Use the word *and* before the last item if there are three or more nonsentence items.

> **YES** The reasons for the delay were (1) bad weather, (2) poor scheduling, **and** (3) equipment failure.

> **YES** The reasons for the delay were (1) bad weather, which had been predicted; (2) poor scheduling, which is the airline's responsibility; **and** (3) equipment failure, which no one can predict.

A DISPLAYED LIST

In a displayed list, each item starts on a new line. If the items are sentences, capitalize and punctuate the items as sentences. If the items are not sentences, choose a capital letter or not and punctuate appropriately. Simply be consistent in each piece of writing.

> **YES** We found three reasons for the delay:
> 1. Bad weather held up delivery of materials.
> 2. Poor scheduling created confusion.
> 3. Improper machine maintenance caused an equipment failure.

> **YES** The reasons for the delay were
> 1. bad weather,
> 2. poor scheduling, **and**
> 3. equipment failure.

⚠ **Alerts:** (1) If a complete sentence leads into a displayed list, you can end the sentence with a colon. However, if an incomplete sentence leads into a displayed list, use no punctuation. (2) Use PARALLELISM in a list. For example, if one item is a sentence, use sentences for all the items (see 39E); or if one item starts with a VERB, start all items with a verb in the same TENSE; and so on. ●

48C When do I use capitals with sentences in parentheses?

When you write a complete sentence within parentheses that falls within another sentence, don't start with a capital or end with a period—but do use a question mark or exclamation point, if needed. When you write a sentence within parentheses that doesn't fall within another sentence, capitalize and punctuate it as a complete sentence.

> I did not know . . . they called it the Cuban Missile Crisis. But I remember Castro. (We called him Castor Oil and were awed by his beard.) We might not have worried so much (what would the communists want with our small New Hampshire town?) except we lived 10 miles from a U.S. air base.
>
> —Joyce Maynard, "An 18-Year-Old Looks Back on Life"

48D When do I use capitals with quotations?

If a quotation within your sentence is itself not a complete sentence, never capitalize the first quoted word. If the quotation you have used in your sentence is itself a complete sentence always capitalize the first word.

- Mrs. Enriquez says that students who are learning a new language should visit that country and "absorb a good accent with the food."
- Talking about students who live in a new country Mrs. Enriquez says, "They'll absorb a good accent with the food."

In DIRECT DISCOURSE, introduced with verbs like *said, asked*, and others (see 18K) followed by a comma, capitalize the first letter of a quoted sentence. Don't capitalize partial quotes situated within a sentence, or the first word of a quoted sentence, which resumes after your commentary.

- Snooki said, "Italy was awesome! The pasta totally rocked."

  Quoted complete sentences always begin with capital letters.
- Snooki said that Italy was "awesome," and that its pasta "rocked."

  Partial quotations situated within a sentence need no capitals.
- "Italy and its pasta," snickered Snooki, "totally rocked."

  There is no need to capitalize *totally;* it simply continues the quote.

48E   When do I capitalize nouns and adjectives?

Capitalize **proper nouns** and ADJECTIVES formed from them to assign specificity: *We lease space in the building. We lease space in the Flatiron Building. He studies at a college in Boston. He studies at Boston College.*

Nouns and adjectives which are now COMMON lose capitals: *My in-laws purchased this china. I devour french fries daily.*

Should you notice capitalized words (like Company or Faculty) in professional writing which contradict our rules, remember that all writing is addressed to a specific AUDIENCE to achieve a specific PURPOSE. The context may favor capitalization of these words. Quick Box 48.1 models capitalization.

Quick Box 48.1   ■ ■ ■ ■ ■ ■ ■ ■ ■ ■ ■

Capitalization

	Capitals	Lowercase Letters
NAMES	Mother Teresa (*also, used as names:* Mother, Dad, Mom, Pa) Doc Holliday	my mother [relationship] the doctor [role]
TITLES	President Truman	the president
	Democrat [party member]	a democrat [believer in democracy]
	Representative Harold Ford	the congressional representative
	Senator Jon Kyl	a senator
	Queen Elizabeth II	the queen
GROUPS OF PEOPLE	Caucasian [race]	white, black [*also* White, Black]
	African American, Hispanic [ethnic group]	
	Irish, Korean, Canadian [nationality]	
	Jewish, Catholic, Protestant, Buddhist [religious affiliation]	
ORGANIZATIONS	Congress	the legislative branch of the U.S. government
	the Ohio State Supreme Court	the state supreme court
	the Republican Party	the party
	Wink Inc.	the company
	Chicago Cubs	a baseball team

continued >>

Quick Box 48.1 (continued)

	Capitals	Lowercase Letters
	American Medical Association	a professional group
	Sigma Chi	a fraternity
	Alcoholics Anonymous	a self-help group
PLACES	Los Angeles	the city
	the South [region]	turn south [direction]
	the West Coast	the U.S. states along the western seaboard
	Main Street	the street
	Atlantic Ocean	the ocean
	the Black Hills	the hills
BUILDINGS	the Capitol [in Washington, DC]	the state capitol
	Ace High School	a high school
	Front Road Café	a restaurant
	Highland Hospital	a hospital
SCIENTIFIC TERMS	Earth [as one of nine planets]	the earth [otherwise]
	the Milky Way, the Galaxy [as name]	our galaxy, the moon, the sun
	Streptococcus aureus	a streptococcal infection
	Gresham's law	the theory of relativity
LANGUAGES, SCHOOL COURSES	Spanish, Chinese	
	Chemistry 342	a chemistry course
	History 111	my history class
	Introduction to Photography	a photography course
NAMES OF SPECIFIC THINGS	Black Parrot tulip	a climbing rose
	Purdue University	the university
	Heinz ketchup	ketchup, sauce
	a Toyota Camry	a car
	Twelfth Dynasty	the dynasty
	the *Boston Globe*	a newspaper
TIMES, SEASONS, HOLIDAYS	Monday, Fri.	today
	September, February	a month
	the Roaring Twenties	the decade
	the Christmas season	spring, summer, autumn, winter, the fall semester

continued >>

Quick Box 48.1   (continued)

	Capitals	**Lowercase Letters**
	Kwanzaa, New Year's Day	a feast day, the holiday
	Passover, Ramadan	a religious holiday or observance
HISTORICAL EVENTS AND DOCUMENTS	World War II	the war
	Battle of the Bulge	the battle
	the Great Depression (of the 1930s)	the depression [any serious economic downturn]
	the Reformation	the eighteenth century
	Paleozoic	an era or age, prehistory
	the Bill of Rights	fifth-century manuscripts
RELIGIOUS TERMS	Athena, God	a goddess, a god
	Islam	a religion
	the Torah, the Koran (or Qur'an)	a holy book
	the Bible	biblical
LETTER PARTS	Dear Ms. Schultz:	
	Sincerely,	
	Yours truly,	
PUBLISHED AND RELEASED MATERIAL	"The Lottery"	[Capitalize first letter of first word and all other major words]
	A History of the United States to 1877	
	Jazz on Ice	the show, a performance
	Nixon Papers	the archives
	Mass in B Minor	the B minor mass
ACRONYMS AND INITIALISMS	NASA, NATO, UCLA, AFL-CIO, DNA	
COMPUTER TERMS	Gateway, Dell	a computer company
	Microsoft Word	computer software
	Firefox	a browser
	the Internet	a computer network
	World Wide Web, the Web	www
	Web site, Web page	a home page, a link
PROPER ADJECTIVES	Victorian	southern
	Midwestern	transatlantic
	Indo-European	alpine

● **EXERCISE 48-1** Individually or with a group, add capital letters as needed. See 48A through 48E for help.

1. The state of california is best known as the golden state, but other nick-names include the land of milk and honey, the el dorado state, and the grape state.
2. Most people think of san Francisco as northern california, but the city of Eureka, from the greek word meaning "I have found it," is 280 miles north of san Francisco, and the state line is another 90 miles north of eureka.
3. South of san Francisco on the california coast is santa Barbara, which hosts the annual Dickens Universe, a weeklong series of studies and celebrations of the famous writer charles dickens.
4. The highest point in the contiguous United States is mt. Whitney at 14,495 feet high, and the lowest place in the contiguous United States is bad Water in death valley at 282 feet below sea level, both located in california.
5. Having approximately 500,000 detectable seismic tremors per year, california rocks, literally.
6. Because the tehema county fairgrounds are located in red bluff, california hosts the largest three-day rodeo in the united States.
7. Numerous songs have been written about california, including "california girls" by the beach boys and the theme of the tv show *the beverly hillbillies*.
8. san Bernardino county with almost three million acres is the largest county in the united states.
9. Hollywood and movie stars are what many people associate california with, and well they might because two of California's governors, ronald reagan and arnold schwarzenegger, were actors before they became governors.
10. When told all these fantastic facts about california, a stereotypical valley girl would respond, "whatever." ●

ITALICS

48F What are italics?

Italic typeface slants to the right (*like this*); roman typeface does not (like this). MLA STYLE requires italics, not underlining, in all documents.

ROMAN   your writing
ITALICS   *your writing*

48G How do I choose between using italics and quotation marks?

As a rule, use italics for titles of long works (*Juno*, a movie) or for works that contain subsections (*Masterpiece Theater*, a television show). Generally, use quotation marks for titles of shorter works ("One and Only," a song) and for titles of subsections within longer works such as books (Chapter 1, "Loomings"). Quick Box 48.2 models usage in italics.

Quick Box 48.2

Italics, quotation marks, or nothing

Italics	Quotation Marks or Nothing
TITLES AND NAMES	
Sense and Sensibility [a novel]	title of student essay
Death of a Salesman [a play]	act 2 [part of a play]
A Beautiful Mind [a film]	the Epilogue [a part of a film or book]
Collected Works of O. Henry [a book]	"The Last Leaf" [a story in a book]
Simon & Schuster Handbook for Writers [a textbook]	"Agreement" [a chapter in a book]
The Prose Reader [a collection of essays]	"Putting in a Good Word for Guilt" [an essay]
Iliad [a book-length poem]	"Nothing Gold Can Stay" [a short poem]
Scientific American [a magazine]	"The Molecules of Life" [an article in a magazine]
Symphonie Fantastique [a long musical work]	Violin Concerto No. 2 in B-flat Minor [a musical work identified by form, number, and key—neither quotation marks nor italics]
U2 18 Singles [an album]	"With or Without You" [a song]
Lost [a television series]	"Something Nice Back Home" [an episode of a television series]
Kids Count [a Web site title]	Excel [a software program]

continued >>

Quick Box 48.2   (continued)

Italics	Quotation Marks or Nothing
the *Los Angeles Times* [a newspaper]*	

OTHER WORDS

Italics	Quotation Marks or Nothing
semper fidelis [words in a language other than English]	burrito, chutzpah [widely understood non-English words]
What does *our* imply? [a word meant as a word]	
the *abc*'s; the letter *x* [letters meant as letters]	6s and 7s; & [numerals and symbols]

*When *The* is part of a newspaper's title, don't capitalize or italicize it in MLA-style or CM-style documentation. In APA-style and CSE-style documentation, capitalize and italicize *The*.

48H   Can I use italics for special emphasis?

Some professional writers, especially writers of self-help material, occasionally use italics to clarify or stress points. In ACADEMIC WRITING, however, you're expected to convey special emphasis with your choice of words and sentence structure, not with italics (or underlining). If your message absolutely calls for it, use italics sparingly—when you're sure nothing else will do.

> Many people we *think* are powerful turn out on closer examination to be merely frightened and anxious.

> —Michael Korda, *Power!*

● **EXERCISE 48-2**   Edit these sentences for correct use of italics (or underlining), quotation marks, and capitals.

1. While waiting for my Dentist to call my name, I flipped through a copy of a magazine called "Entertainment Digest."
2. I enjoyed reading the Magazine because it included several interesting articles: Movie reviews, recipes, and tips for Spring cleaning.
3. I read a review of the movie "Night comes calling," which I learned is an adaptation of english writer Hugo Barrington's short story *Adventures in the Fog*.

4. I asked the Receptionist if I could keep the magazine because a few of the articles might help me in my Spanish and Economics classes.

5. For example, there was an article on a composer who wrote an Opera about *The Spanish Civil War.* ●

ABBREVIATIONS

481 What are standard practices for using abbreviations?

Watch the Video

Some abbreviations are standard in writing (*Mr.*, not *Mister*, in a name; *St.* Louis, the city, not *Saint* Louis). In some situations, you may have a choice whether to abbreviate or spell out a word. Choose what seems suited to your writing PURPOSE and your AUDIENCE, and be consistent within each piece of writing.

NO The great painter Vincent Van Gogh was **b**. in Holland in 1853, but he lived most of his life and died in **Fr.**

YES The great painter Vincent Van Gogh was **born** in Holland in 1853, but he lived most of his life and died in **France**.

NO Our field hockey team left after Casey's **psych** class on **Tues.**, **Oct.** 10, but the flight had to make an unexpected stop (in **Chi.**) before reaching **L.A.**

YES Our field hockey team left after Casey's **psychology** class on **Tuesday, October** 10, but the flight had to make an unexpected stop (in **Chicago**) before reaching **Los Angeles**.

NO Please confirm in writing your order for one **doz.** helmets in **lg** and **x-lg**.

YES Please confirm in writing your order for one **dozen** helmets in **large** and **extra large**.

Alerts: (1) Many abbreviations call for periods (*Mrs., Ms., Dr.*), but the practice is changing. The trend today is to drop the periods (*PS*, not *P.S.; MD*, not *M.D.; US*, not *U.S.*), yet firm rules are still evolving.

(2) Acronyms (pronounceable words formed from the initials of a name) generally have no periods: *NASA* (National Aeronautics and Space Administration) and *AIDS* (*a*cquired *i*mmune *d*eficiency *s*yndrome).

(3) Initialisms (names spoken as separate letters) usually have no periods (*IBM, ASPCA, UN*).

(4) U.S. Postal abbreviations for states have no periods (48K).

(5) When the final period of an abbreviation falls at the end of a sentence, that period serves also to end the sentence. ●

48J How do I use abbreviations with months, time, eras, and symbols?

MONTHS

According to MLA STYLE, abbreviations for months belong only in "Works Cited" lists, tables, charts, and the like. Write out the full spelling, never the abbreviation, in your ACADEMIC WRITING.

TIMES

Use the abbreviations *a.m.* and *p.m.* only with exact times: *7:15 a.m.; 3:47 p.m.* MLA style calls for the use of lowercase letters.

❶ Alert: Never use *a.m.* and *p.m.* in place of *morning, evening,* and *night.*

> **NO**   My hardest final exam is in the **a.m**. tomorrow, but by early **p.m.**, I'll be ready to study for the rest of my finals.

> **YES**   My hardest final exam is in the **morning** tomorrow, but by early **evening**, I'll be ready to study for the rest of my finals. ●

ERAS

In MLA style, use capital letters, without periods, in abbreviations for eras. Some writers prefer *CE* ("common era") to *AD* (Latin for *anno Domini,* "in the year of our Lord") as the more inclusive term. In addition, many writers prefer *BCE* ("before the common era") to *BC* ("before Christ").

When writing the abbreviations for eras, place *AD* before the year (*AD 476*) and all the others after the year (*29 BC; 165 BCE; 1100 CE*).

SYMBOLS

In MLA style, decide whether to use symbols or spelled-out words according to your topic and the focus of your document (see also 48M). However, only use a freestanding symbol, such as *$, %,* or *¢* with a numeral. With many exceptions, spell both the symbol and the numeral accompanying it (*twenty centimeters*), unless the number is more than one or two words (*345 centimeters,* not *three hundred forty-five centimeters*).

The exceptions include *$18; 7 lbs.; 24 KB; 6:34 a.m.; 5"; 32°;* and numbers in addresses, dates, page references, and decimal fractions (*8.3*). In writing about money, the form *$25 million* is an acceptable combination of symbol, numeral, and spelled-out word.

In confined spaces, such as charts and tables, use symbols with numerals (*2¢*). In documents that focus on technical matters, use numerals but spell out the unit of measurement (*2,500 pounds*)—in MLA style. Guidelines in other documentation styles differ, so you need to check each style's manual.

48K How do I use abbreviations for other elements?

TITLES

Use either a title of address before a name (**Dr.** *Daniel Klausner*) or an academic degree after a name (*Daniel Klausner,* **PhD**), not both. However, because *Jr., Sr., II, III,* and so forth are part of a name, you can use both titles of address and academic degrees: **Dr.** *Martin Luther King* **Jr.***; John Jay* **II, MD**.

Alerts: (1) Insert a comma both before and after an academic degree that follows a person's name, unless it falls at the end of a sentence: *Joshua Coleman,* **LLD***, is our guest speaker,* or *Our guest speaker is Joshua Coleman,* **LLD**. (2) Never put a comma before an abbreviation that is part of a given name: *Steven Elliott* **Sr.***, Douglas Young* **III**. ●

NAMES AND TERMS

If you use a term frequently in a piece of writing, follow these guidelines: The first time you use the term, spell it out completely and then put its abbreviation in parentheses immediately after. In later references, use the abbreviation alone.

- Spain voted to continue as a member of the **North Atlantic Treaty Organization** (**NATO**), to the surprise of other **NATO** members.

Use the abbreviation *U.S.* as a modifier before a noun (*the* **U.S.** *ski team*), but spell *United States* when you use it as a noun (*the ski team of the* **United States**).

ADDRESSES

If you include a full address in a piece of writing, use the two-letter postal abbreviation for the state name. For any other combination of a city and a state, or a state by itself, spell out the state name; never abbreviate it.

Alert: When you write the names of a U.S. city and state within a sentence, use a comma before and after the state.

NO   Portland, Oregon is much larger than Portland, Maine.

YES   Portland, Oregon, is much larger than Portland, Maine.

If you include a ZIP code, however, don't use a comma after the state. Do place the comma after the ZIP code. ●

SCHOLARLY WRITING (MLA STYLE)

MLA style permits abbreviations for the scholarly terms listed in Quick Box 48.3. Never use them in the body of your ACADEMIC WRITING. Reserve them for your "Works Cited" lists and for any notes you might write in a separate list at the end of your research paper.

usriIa

Quick Box 48.3

Major scholarly abbreviations—MLA style

anon.	anonymous	**i.e.**	that is
b.	born	**ms., mss.**	manuscript, manuscripts
c. *or* ©	copyright	**NB**	note well (*nota bene*)
c. *or* **ca.**	circa *or* about [with dates]	**n.d.**	no date (of publication)
cf.	compare	**p., pp.**	page, pages
col., cols.	column, columns	**par.**	paragraph
d.	died	**pref.**	preface, preface by
ed., eds.	edition, edited by, editor(s)	**rept.**	report, reported by
e.g.	for example	**rev.**	review, reviewed by; revised, revised by
esp.	especially	**sec., secs.**	section, sections
et al.	and others	**v.** *or* **vs.**	versus [*v.* in legal cases]
ff.	following pages, following lines, folios	**vol., vols.**	volume, volumes

48L When can I use *etc.*?

Avoid *etc.*, Latin for "and the rest," in ACADEMIC WRITING. Instead, use substitutes such as *and the like, and so on*—or better yet, use a more concrete description. If you do use *etc.*, use a *single period* after it even at the end of a sentence. Follow the single period with a comma if *etc.* comes before the end.

NO   For the picnic, we bought paper plates, plastic forks, **etc..**

YES   For the picnic, we bought paper plates, plastic forks, and **other disposable items**.

Alert: If you do write *etc.*, always put a comma after the period if the abbreviation falls in the middle of a sentence. ●

● **EXERCISE 48-3** Working individually or with a group, revise these sentences for correct use of abbreviations. For help, consult 48I through 48L.

1. Originally named the Geo. S. Parker Company, located in Salem, Mass., the toy co. changed its name to Parker Bros. when Chas. joined the business in 1888.

2. Sev. of their games have become quite famous, esp. Monopoly and Clue, both of which were released in the 20th cent.
3. The obj. of the game Monopoly (meaning "dominating the mkt.") is to get the most $ by purchasing, renting, & selling real est.
4. Clue, another pop. brd. game, is a murder mys. in which players move from 1 rm. to another, making accusations to reveal the i.d. of the murderer, the weapon used, and the room where the crime took place.
5. On a cold day in Jan., when the snow is 3 ft. deep and it's dark by early eve., passing the hrs. with your fam. and friends playing a board game is great fun. ●

NUMBERS

48M When do I use spelled-out numbers?

Watch the Video

Your decision to write a number as a word or as a figure depends on what you're referring to and how often numbers occur in your piece of writing. The guidelines we give in this handbook are for MLA STYLE, which focuses on writing in the humanities. For other disciplines, consult their style manuals.

When you use numbers to refer to more than one category, reserve figures for some categories of numbers and spelled-out words for other categories. Never mix spelled-out numbers and figures for a particular category.

NO   In **four** days, bids increased from **five** to **eight** to **17** to **233**.

YES   In **four** days, bids increased from **5** to **8** to **17** to **233**.

Numbers referring to bids are written as numerals, while *four* is spelled out because it refers to a different category: days.

🛑 **Alert:** For two-word numbers, use a hyphen between the spelled-out words, starting with *twenty-one* and continuing through *ninety-nine*. ●

If you use numbers infrequently in a document, spell out all numbers that call for no more than two words: *fifty-two cards, twelve hundred students*. If you use specific numbers often in a document (temperatures when writing about climate, percentages in an economics essay, or other specific measurements of time, distance, and other quantities), use figures: *36 inches, 11 nanoseconds*. In an approximation, spell out the numbers: *About twelve inches of snow fell*.

In the humanities, the names of centuries are always spelled out: *the eighteenth century*.

When you write for courses in the humanities, never start a sentence with a figure. Spell the number, or revise the sentence so that the number doesn't fall at the beginning. For practices in other disciplines, consult their manuals.

NO   **$375 dollars** for each credit is the tuition rate for nonresidents.

YES   **Three hundred seventy-five dollars** for each credit is the tuition rate for nonresidents.

YES   The tuition rate for nonresidents is **$375** for each credit.

48N   What are standard practices for writing numbers?

Quick Box 48.4 shows standard practices for writing numbers. Consider it a basic guide, and rely on the manual of each documentation style for answers to other questions you may have.

Quick Box 48.4   ■ ■ ■ ■ ■ ■ ■ ■ ■ ■ ■

Specific numbers in writing

DATES	August 6, 1941 1732–1845 from 34 BC TO AD 230 (*or* 34 BCE to 230 CE)
ADDRESSES	10 Downing Street 237 North 8th Street Export Falls, MN 92025
TIMES	8:09 a.m., 6:00 p.m. six o'clock (*not* 6 o'clock) four in the afternoon *or* 4 p.m. (*not* four p.m.)
DECIMALS AND FRACTIONS	0.01 98.6 3.1416 7/8 12 1/4 a sixth three-quarters (*not* 3-quarters) one-half
CHAPTERS AND PAGES	Chapter 27, page 2 p. 1023 *or* pp. 660–62 (MLA style)
SCORES AND STATISTICS	a 6–0 score 29% (or twenty-nine percent) a 5 to 1 ratio (*and* a ratio of 5:1) a one percent change (*and* at the 1 percent level)

continued >>

Quick Box 48.4	(continued)
IDENTIFICATION	94.4 on the FM dial
NUMBERS	please call (012) 345–6789
MEASUREMENTS	67.8 miles per hour
	2 level teaspoons
	a 700-word essay
	8-by-10-inch photograph
	2 feet
	1.5 gallons
	14 liters
ACT, SCENE,	act 2, scene 2 (*or* act II, scene ii)
AND LINE	lines 75–79
TEMPERATURES	40°F *or* –5°F
	20° Celsius
MONEY	$1.2 billion
	$3.41
	25¢ (*or* twenty-five cents)
	$10,000

● **EXERCISE 48-4** Revise these sentences so that the numbers are in correct form, either spelled out or as figures.

⚙️
Complete
the
Chapter
Exercises

1. The 102-story Empire State building, which is one thousand two hundred and fifty feet tall, is struck by lightning on an average of five hundred times a year.
2. If you have three quarters, four dimes, and 4 pennies, you have $1 and nineteen cents, but you still can't make even change for a dollar.
3. Lake Tahoe is the second deepest lake in the United States with a maximum depth of five hundred and one meters (1,645 ft).
4. 37 percent of Americans have passports, which means that nearly 2 out of 3 U.S. citizens cannot fly to Canada.
5. On March 2nd, nineteen sixty two, Wilt Chamberlain, playing basketball for the Philadelphia Warriors, scored 100 points.
6. Some people trace the origin of the knock-knock joke back to act two, scene three of Shakespeare's sixteen-eleven play *Macbeth*.
7. If you place a vertical stick in the ground on the Equator, it will cast no shadow at 12 o'clock p.m. on March twenty first.
8. Bamboo plants can grow up to one hundred centimeters every 24 hours, and they grow best in warm climates, but some species can survive in temperatures as low as twenty degrees below zero Fahrenheit.

9. The Boston Marathon, which began in 1897, is the world's oldest annual marathon and is held the 3rd Monday of every April.

10. 500,000 spectators watch the Boston Marathon every year as an average of twenty thousand runners each try to complete the twenty six point two mile run. ●

49 Spelling

Quick Points   You will learn to

➤ Use spelling rules to improve your spelling (see 49C–49E).
➤ Distinguish between homonyms and other easily confused words (see 49F).

49A   What makes a good speller?

You may be surprised to learn that many fine writers do not consider themselves good spellers. They do understand, however, two features of spelling, which may help you if you believe you struggle with precise spelling.

Watch the Video

First, precise spelling matters only in final drafts. The best time to check the spelling of words you doubt is as you're EDITING. Second, check the spelling of those words you doubt by consulting a dictionary. If you're unsure of the first few letters, then think of and find a synonym for your word in a thesaurus. Perhaps you'll see your word there—or an even sharper, clearer word.

Remember, a spell-check program in a word processor does not alert you to an error if you write another legitimate word. For example, if you write *affect* when you mean *effect*, or *from* when you mean *form*, spell-checks detect no error; alert readers do. To avoid noticeable spelling errors, rely on some helpful hints below.

49B   How can I proofread for errors in spelling and hyphen use?

Many spelling errors are the result of illegible handwriting, slips of the pen, or typographical mistakes. Catching these "typos" requires especially careful proofreading, using the techniques in Quick Box 49.1 (page 694).

Quick Box 49.1

Proofreading for errors in spelling

- Slow down your reading speed to allow yourself to concentrate on the individual letters of words rather than on the meaning of the words.

- Stay within your "visual span," the number of letters you can identify with a single glance (for most people, about six letters).

- Put a ruler or large index card under each line as you proofread, to focus your vision and concentration.

- Read each paragraph in reverse, from the last sentence to the first. This allows you to focus on spelling instead of meaning.

49C How are plurals spelled?

Watch the Video

The most common plural form adds *-s* or *-es* at the end of the word. The following list covers all variations of creating plurals.

- **Adding -s or -es:** Plurals of most words are formed by adding *-s: leg, legs; shoe, shoes; stomach, stomachs.* Words ending in *-s, -sh, -x, -z,* or "soft" *-ch* (as in *beach*) are formed by adding *-es* to the singular: *lens, lenses; tax, taxes; beach, beaches.*

- **Words ending in -o:** Add *-s* if the *-o* is preceded by a vowel: *radio, radios; cameo, cameos.* Add *-es* if the *-o* is preceded by a consonant: *potato, potatoes.* With a few words, you can choose the *-s* or *-es* plural form, but current practice generally supports adding *-es: cargo, cargoes; zero, zeros* or *zeroes.*

- **Words ending in -f or -fe:** Some words ending in *-f* and *-fe* are made plural by adding *-s: belief, beliefs.* Others require changing *-f* or *-fe* to *-ves: life, lives; leaf, leaves.* Words ending in *-ff* or *-ffe* simply add *-s: staff, staffs; giraffe, giraffes.*

- **Compound words:** For most compound words, add *-s* or *-es* at the end of the last word: *checkbooks, player-coaches.* In a few cases, the first word is made plural: *sister-in-law, sisters-in-law; miles per hour.* (For information about hyphens in compound words, see 49G.)

- **Internal changes and endings other than -s:** A few words change internally or add endings other than *-s* to become plural: *foot, feet; man, men; crisis, crises; child, children.*

- **Foreign words:** The best advice is to check your dictionary. Many Latin words ending in *-um* form the plural by changing *-um* to *-a: curriculum,*

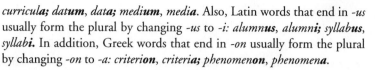

curricula; datum, data; medium, media. Also, Latin words that end in *-us* usually form the plural by changing *-us* to *-i: alumnus, alumni; syllabus, syllabi.* In addition, Greek words that end in *-on* usually form the plural by changing *-on* to *-a: criterion, criteria; phenomenon, phenomena.*

- **One-form words:** Some words have the same form in both the singular and the plural: nine *deer*, many *fish*, four *elk*.

● **EXERCISE 49-1**   Write the correct plural form of these words. For help, consult 49C.

1. yourself	6. millennium	11. echo
2. sheep	7. lamp	12. syllabus
3. photo	8. runner-up	13. wife
4. woman	9. criterion	14. get-together
5. appendix	10. lunch	15. crisis ●

49D How are suffixes spelled?

A SUFFIX is an ending added to a word that changes the word's meaning or its grammatical function. For example, adding the suffix *-able* to the VERB *depend* creates the ADJECTIVE *dependable*.

Watch the Video

- ***-y* words:** If the letter before a final *-y* is a consonant, change the *-y* to *-i* and add the suffix: *try, tries, tried.* Keep the *-y* when the suffix begins with *-i* (*apply, applying*). If the letter before the final *-y* is a vowel, keep the final *-y: employ, employed, employing.* These rules don't apply to IRREGULAR VERBS (see Quick Box 29.4 in section 29D).

- ***-e* words:** Drop a final *-e* when the suffix begins with a vowel, unless doing this would cause confusion: for example, *be + ing* can't be written *bing*, but *require* does become *requiring; like* does become *liking.* Keep the final *-e* when the suffix begins with a consonant: *require, requirement; like, likely.* Exceptions include *argue, argument; judge, judgment; true, truly.*

- **Words that double a final letter:** If the final letter is a consonant, double it *only* if it passes three tests: (1) Its last two letters are a vowel followed by a consonant; (2) it has one syllable or is accented on the last syllable; (3) the suffix begins with a vowel: *drop, dropped; begin, beginning; forget, forgettable.*

- ***-cede, -ceed, -sede* words:** Only one word in the English language ends in *-sede: supersede.* Only three words end in *-ceed: exceed, proceed, succeed.* All other words with endings that sound like "seed" end in *-cede: concede, intercede, precede.*

- **-ally and -ly words:** The suffixes *-ally* and *-ly* turn words into adverbs. For words ending in *-ic,* add *-ally: logically, statistically.* Otherwise, add *-ly: quickly, sharply.*
- **-ance, -ence**, and **-ible, -able:** No consistent rules govern words with these suffixes. When in doubt, look up the word.

49E What is the *ie, ei* rule?

The famous rhymed rule for using *ie* and *ei* is usually true:

I before *e* [bel**ie**ve, f**ie**ld, gr**ie**f],
Except after *c* [c**ei**ling, conc**ei**t],
Or when sounded like "ay"—
As in n**ei**ghbor and w**ei**gh [**ei**ght, v**ei**n].

You may want to memorize (sorry!) several exceptions to this rule.

- **ie:** consc**ie**nce, financ**ie**r, sc**ie**nce, spec**ie**s
- **ei:** **ei**ther, n**ei**ther, l**ei**sure, s**ei**ze, counterf**ei**t, for**ei**gn, forf**ei**t, sl**ei**ght (as in *sleight of hand*), w**ei**rd

● **EXERCISE 49-2** Follow the directions for each group of words. For help, consult 49D and 49E.

1. Add *-able* or *-ible:* (a) profit; (b) reproduce; (c) control; (d) coerce; (e) recognize.
2. Add *-ance* or *-ence:* (a) luxuri_____; (b) prud_____; (c) devi_____; (d) resist_____; (e) independ_____.
3. Drop the final *-e* as needed: (a) true + ly; (b) joke + ing; (c) fortunate + ly; (d) appease + ing; (e) appease + ment.
4. Change the final *-y* to *-i* as needed: (a) happy + ness; (b) pry + ed; (c) pry + ing; (d) dry + ly; (e) beautify + ing.
5. Double the final consonant as needed: (a) commit + ed; (b) commit + ment; (c) drop + ed; (d) occur + ed; (e) regret + ful.
6. Insert *ie* or *ei* correctly: (a) rel_____f; (b) ach_____ve; (c) w_____rd; (d) n_____ce; (e) dec_____ve. ●

49F Why are commonly confused words and homonyms misspelled?

English is rich with **homonyms**—words that sound alike but have different meanings and spellings: *hear, here; to, too, two; elicit, illicit; accept, except.*
In addition, "swallowed pronunciation," which occurs when speakers blur word endings, often causes misspellings and other errors: *use* and *used; prejudice*

and *prejudiced*. *Should of* is always incorrect, but it sounds like *should've*, a CONTRACTION for *should have*.

For more information about word usage that affects spelling, see the Usage Glossary in the back of the book. Quick Box 49.2 lists homonyms and other words that can be confused and lead to misspellings.

Quick Box 49.2

Homonyms and other frequently confused words

• ACCEPT	to receive
EXCEPT	with the exclusion of
• ADVICE	recommendation
ADVISE	to recommend
• AFFECT	to influence [VERB]; emotion [NOUN]
EFFECT	result [NOUN]; to bring about or cause [VERB]
• AISLE	space between rows
ISLE	island
• ALLUDE	to make indirect reference to
ELUDE	to avoid
• ALLUSION	indirect reference
ILLUSION	false idea, misleading appearance
• ALREADY	by this time
ALL READY	fully prepared
• ALTAR	sacred platform or place
ALTER	to change
• ALTOGETHER	thoroughly
ALL TOGETHER	everyone or everything in one place
• ARE	PLURAL form of *to be*
HOUR	sixty minutes
OUR	plural form of *my*
• ASCENT	the act of rising or climbing
ASSENT	consent [NOUN]; to consent [VERB]
• ASSISTANCE	help
ASSISTANTS	helpers
• BARE	nude, unadorned
BEAR	to carry; an animal

continued >>

Quick Box 49.2 (continued)

- BOARD — piece of wood
  BORED — uninterested

- BRAKE — device for stopping
  BREAK — to destroy, make into pieces

- BREATH — air taken in
  BREATHE — to take in air

- BUY — to purchase
  BY — next to, through the agency of

- CAPITAL — major city; money
  CAPITOL — government building

- CHOOSE — to pick
  CHOSE — PAST TENSE of *choose*

- CITE — to point out
  SIGHT — vision
  SITE — a place

- CLOTHES — garments
  CLOTHS — pieces of fabric

- COARSE — rough
  COURSE — path; series of lectures

- COMPLEMENT — something that completes
  COMPLIMENT — praise, flattery

- CONSCIENCE — sense of morality
  CONSCIOUS — awake, aware

- COUNCIL — governing body
  COUNSEL — advice [NOUN]; to advise [VERB]

- DAIRY — place associated with milk production
  DIARY — personal journal

- DESCENT — downward movement
  DISSENT — disagreement

- DESERT — to abandon [VERB]; dry, usually sandy area [NOUN]
  DESSERT — final, sweet course in a meal

- DEVICE — a plan; an implement
  DEVISE — to create

continued >>

Quick Box 49.2   (continued)

•	DIE	to lose life (dying) [VERB]; one of a pair of dice [NOUN]
	DYE	to change the color of something (dyeing)
•	DOMINANT	commanding, controlling
	DOMINATE	to control
•	ELICIT	to draw out
	ILLICIT	illegal
•	EMINENT	prominent
	IMMANENT	living within; inherent
	IMMINENT	about to happen
•	ENVELOP	to surround
	ENVELOPE	container for a letter or other papers
•	FAIR	light-skinned; just, honest
	FARE	money for transportation; food
•	FORMALLY	conventionally, with ceremony
	FORMERLY	previously
•	FORTH	forward
	FOURTH	number four in a series
•	GORILLA	animal in ape family
	GUERRILLA	fighter conducting surprise attacks
•	HEAR	to sense sound by ear
	HERE	in this place
•	HOLE	opening
	WHOLE	complete; an entire thing
•	HUMAN	relating to the species *Homo sapiens*
	HUMANE	compassionate
•	INSURE	to buy or give insurance
	ENSURE	to guarantee, protect
•	ITS	POSSESSIVE form of *it*
	IT'S	CONTRACTION for *it is*
•	KNOW	to comprehend
	NO	negative
•	LATER	after a time
	LATTER	second one of two things

continued >>

Quick Box 49.2   (continued)

• LEAD	a heavy metal [NOUN]; to guide [VERB]
LED	past tense of *lead*
• LIGHTNING	storm-related electricity
LIGHTENING	making lighter
• LOOSE	unbound, not tightly fastened
LOSE	to misplace
• MAYBE	perhaps [ADVERB]
MAY BE	might be [VERB]
• MEAT	animal flesh
MEET	to encounter
• MINER	a person who works in a mine
MINOR	underage; less important
• MORAL	distinguishing right from wrong; the lesson of a fable, story, or event
MORALE	attitude or outlook, usually of a group
• OF	PREPOSITION indicating origin
OFF	away from; not on
• PASSED	past tense of *pass*
PAST	at a previous time
• PATIENCE	forbearance
PATIENTS	people under medical care
• PEACE	absence of fighting
PIECE	part of a whole; musical arrangement
• PERSONAL	intimate
PERSONNEL	employees
• PLAIN	simple, unadorned
PLANE	to shave wood; aircraft
• PRECEDE	to come before
PROCEED	to continue
• PRESENCE	being at hand; attendance at a place or in something
PRESENTS	gifts
• PRINCIPAL	foremost [ADJECTIVE]; school head [NOUN]
PRINCIPLE	moral conviction, basic truth

continued >>

Quick Box 49.2   (continued)

- QUIET — silent, calm
  QUITE — very

- RAIN — water that falls to earth [NOUN]; to fall like rain [VERB]
  REIGN — to rule
  REIN — strap to guide or control an animal [NOUN];
  to guide or control [VERB]

- RAISE — to lift up
  RAZE — to tear down

- RESPECTFULLY — with respect
  RESPECTIVELY — in that order

- RIGHT — correct; opposite of *left*
  RITE — ritual
  WRITE — to put words on paper

- ROAD — path
  RODE — past tense of *ride*

- SCENE — place of an action; segment of a play
  SEEN — viewed

- SENSE — perception, understanding
  SINCE — measurement of past time; because

- STATIONARY — standing still
  STATIONERY — writing paper

- THAN — in comparison with; besides
  THEN — at that time; next; therefore

- THEIR — possessive form of *they*
  THERE — in that place
  THEY'RE — contraction of *they are*

- THROUGH — finished; into and out of
  THREW — past tense of *throw*
  THOROUGH — complete

- TO — toward
  TOO — also; indicates degree (*too much*)
  TWO — number following *one*

- WAIST — midsection of the body
  WASTE — discarded material [NOUN]; to squander,
  to fail to use up [VERB]

continued >>

Quick Box 49.2   (continued)

•	WEAK	not strong
	WEEK	seven days
•	WEATHER	climatic condition
	WHETHER	if, when alternatives are expressed or implied
•	WHERE	in which place
	WERE	past tense of *be*
•	WHICH	one of a group
	WITCH	female sorcerer
•	WHOSE	possessive form of *who*
	WHO'S	contraction for *who is*
•	YOUR	possessive form of *you*
	YOU'RE	contraction for *you are*
	YORE	long past

● **EXERCISE 49-3**   Circle the correct homonym or commonly confused word of each group in parentheses.

If (your, you're) an adult in 2012, (its, it's) three times more likely that you will live alone than you would (have, of) if you'd been an adult in 1950. (Know, No) longer is getting married (right, write, rite) out of high school or college considered a normal (right, write, rite) of passage. In the (passed, past), the (sight, cite, site) of a thirty-year-old living by him- or herself would have been (seen, scene) (by, buy, bye) many as (quite, quiet) disturbing. Even recently, the book *The Lonely American* (raised, razed) the concern that (maybe, may be) living alone would (lead, led) to (later, latter) depression. However, (to, two, too) (choose, chose) to live alone is no longer viewed as a (rode, road) to unhappiness. In fact, evidence shows that people who live alone tend to compensate by being socially active. (Weather, Whether) you feel lonely is less a matter of your circumstances (then, than) a matter of your activities. Sociologist Eric Klinenberg conveys the (sense, since) that (excepting, accepting) (whose, who's) happy simply on the basis of (their, there) living arrangements is (altogether, all together) a (waste, waist) of time. ●

49G   What are compound words?

A **compound word** puts together two or more words to express one concept.

Complete
the
Chapter
Exercises

Open compound words remain as separate words, such as *decision making*, *problem solving*, and *editor in chief*.

Hyphenated compound words use a hyphen between the words, such as *trade-in*, *fuel-efficient*, and *tax-sheltered*. For punctuation advice about hyphens, see 47I.

Closed compound words appear as one word, such as *proofread*, *citywide*, and *workweek*.

Single-word compounds usually start as open (two-word) compounds and then become hyphenated compounds before ending up as closed compounds. To check whether a compound term consists of closed, hyphenated, or open words, consult an up-to-date dictionary.

PART
8

Writing When English Is Not Your First Language

A Message to Multilingual Writers

Depending on how, when, and where you began learning English, you might feel very comfortable with spoken English but not written American English. Or you might understand English grammar quite well, but you might struggle with idioms, slang, and sentence structure. You might be an international student just learning the expectations of ACADEMIC WRITING* in American English, or you might be a bilingual student who went to high school in the United States. You might be an adult returning to school encountering academic writing for the first time, or you might be a student who received an advanced degree in another country but must now master written American English.

Learning to write American English is like learning to play a musical instrument. Few people can play fluently without first making many errors. If you become frustrated about the errors that you make in written English, we encourage you to realize that such mistakes show you're moving normally through the stages of second-language development. As with your progress in speaking, listening, and reading in a new language, absorbing the rules of American English grammar takes time.

What can help you advance as quickly as possible? If you attended school elsewhere before coming to the United States, we recommend that you recall how you were taught to present ideas in your written native language. Chances are you encountered quite a different system, especially when presenting information or making an argument. Compare your native system to how writing American English works. Becoming conscious of the similarities and differences can help you understand typical writing strategies in American English.

For example, most college essays and research papers in the United States use a direct tone and straightforward structure. Typically, the THESIS STATEMENT (the central message of the piece of writing) is expected at the end of the first paragraph; in a longer piece of writing, at the end of the second paragraph. Each paragraph that follows, known as a BODY PARAGRAPH, relates in content directly to the essay's thesis statement. Each body paragraph usually starts with a TOPIC SENTENCE that contains the main point of that paragraph. The rest of each body paragraph supports the main point made in the topic sentence. The final paragraph of an essay brings the content to a reasonable conclusion that grows from what has been written in the prior paragraphs.

We urge you always to honor your culture's writing traditions and structures. They reflect the richness of your heritage. We suggest that you look for possible interesting ways to blend the traditions and structures of writing in

---

* Words printed in SMALL CAPITAL LETTERS are discussed elsewhere in the text and are defined in the Terms Glossary at the back of this book.

your first language with the conventions of academic writing in the United States. We suggest, too, that you get to know *The American Heritage English as a Second Language Dictionary* because it includes many English idioms as well as sample sentences and phrases. If your college library doesn't own a few copies, ask your professor to request that the reference librarian purchase some for students like you to consult.

Our *Simon & Schuster Handbook* offers four special features we've designed specifically for you as a multilingual learner. Chapters 28 through 49 focus on the most challenging grammar issues that you face as you learn to write English. The chapters in the "ESOL" section that follow this letter address major grammar issues that often trouble multilingual writers. Also, in various chapters throughout the book, ESOL Tips offer you specific helpful hints about non-U.S. cultural references and grammar issues. As important, in Chapter 50 we've provided an "English Errors Transferred from Other Languages" chart in which you'll find information about trouble spots that commonly occur when speakers of selected non-English languages speak, read, or write English.

We greatly enjoy discovering the rich variations in the writing traditions of our students from many cultures of the world. As responsible U.S. writing teachers, however, we must explain what you need to do as writers in the United States. If you were in one of our classes, we would say "Welcome!" and ask you to teach us about writing in your native language. Using your knowledge of writing in your first language, we want to help you learn how to approach writing effectively in American English. You bring a richness of experience in communicating in more than one language that most U.S. students have never had, and we hope you're always proud of that experience.

Lynn Quitman Troyka
Doug Hesse

50 Multilingual Students Writing in U.S. Colleges and Universities

■ ■ ■ ■ ■ ■ ■ ■ ■

Quick Points   You will learn to

➤ Use the skills needed by multilingual writing students (see 50A–50E).

50A What do U.S. writing instructors expect in student writing?

Your past writing experiences influence the way you approach writing assignments. In the next passage, a bilingual student illustrates how her past experiences influenced her interpretation of writing assignments in the United States. (Note: The original draft has been edited to improve readability.)

> When I studied in the United States, I felt puzzled with different types of writing assignments. When I wrote my first term paper, I did not know what my professor did expect from me and how to construct my paper. My previous training in my first and second language writing taught me little about how to handle American English writing assignments. Because language teaching in my country is exam-oriented, I learned to write in Chinese and in English in the same way. I read a sample paper, analyzed its content and structure, and tried to apply its strengths to my own writing. Writing was not a creative process to express myself but something that was to be copied for the purpose of taking exams. As a result, when I didn't have a sample for my assignments, I really didn't know how to start.

If you're like this student, you may have difficulty understanding what your instructor expects you to do with a specific writing assignment. Your instructor might expect you to present a clear position on a topic; or to use examples from your personal experience to support your ideas; or to use quotations and comment on specific ideas from an assigned reading or an outside source; or all three. You can't expect yourself to guess what's needed, so never hesitate to ask your instructor questions about the assignment so that you understand exactly what he or she expects.

If your instructor asks students to write about a topic that relates to aspects of American culture with which you're not familiar, talk to him or her about the situation. Ask for guidance in how to find more information about the topic. Conversely, if you're writing about your own culture, keep in mind that your instructor and classmates may not know very much about it. This means you need to explain information and ideas for them in more detail than you would if you were writing for people who share your background. Here's how one student explains that experience.

> If I were writing in Chinese to Chinese readers and wanted to draw on a story in Chinese history as evidence, I would simply mention the name of the historic event or briefly introduce the story. However, when I am writing in American English to tell the readers the same story, I need to tell the story in detail. Otherwise, the U.S. readers would surely get lost.

50B What do U.S. instructors expect for analysis of readings?

When you write a paper based on a reading or on sources you have found for a research project, your teacher wants you to connect these sources to your own ideas after you read and analyze the material. Chapter 20 gives detailed advice about this type of writing. You need to refer to specific ideas and sentences in the material you are writing about, but you cannot rely too heavily on the author's wording and sentence structure; you need to use your own words and sentences by quoting, paraphrasing, or summarizing (see Ch. 18). In U.S. colleges and universities, if you use another author's words, sentence structure, or ideas, you must give the author credit. You do this by using DOCUMENTATION—and quotation marks when you use the exact words. If you don't, it's considered to be a serious offense called PLAGIARISM, which is the same as stealing something that belongs to someone else.

In contrast, using an author's wording in some cultures is not a problem. It may even be seen as a way of complimenting the author. Chapter 19 of this handbook provides detailed information about how to avoid getting into serious legal and academic trouble by engaging in plagiarism. Chapters 25–27 provide examples of four different documentation styles that you might use in your academic writing in the United States. Always ask your instructor if you're uncertain which style to follow.

Documenting sources helps your writing in two ways. By showing your honesty, documentation helps to develop your credibility as a writer. This improves your ethical stance, called *ethos* in Latin (see 3B). Also, giving credit to the original authors shows that you have done the necessary background work to find out what other people have said on a topic.

50C What kind of dictionary can help me the most?

As we suggest in our letter to ESOL students before this chapter, *The American Heritage English as a Second Language Dictionary* is an excellent resource. As important, we urge you to resist any dictionary that only translates words between your native language and English. Such a word-by-word system can't give you the ideas behind the English words. Instead, use an English-English dictionary (sometimes called a "Learner's Dictionary"), one written for non-native learners of English. Be careful of online translation programs such as GoogleTranslate because they often don't present the correct meaning.

50D How do I work with peer response groups, if required?

If your writing instructors expect you to participate in peer response groups (also called "peer review groups" or "peer editing"), refer to Chapter 9 in this handbook for explicit directions. Such activities might be new to you. Here are some strategies specifically for ESOL students to help make this experience more pleasant and useful.

- **If you need to comment on another's writing, word your statements or questions carefully:** For example, asking "How does this idea support your topic or relate back to your topic sentence or thesis statement?" sounds more polite and tactful than, "I don't see how this idea supports your topic."
- **Use modals auxiliary verbs to "hedge" your suggestions**. In English, modal auxiliary verbs often "soften" a statement. For example, "seem" in this statement makes it more polite: "This support does not seem to relate to your topic." It's nicer than "This support has no relation to your topic."
- If your writing instructors make comments on drafts of your essays, they expect to see suitable changes in your final essay based on their comments. Therefore, if you're unsure about what an instructor's comment means, never hesitate to ask for an interpretation—either from your instructor or from a tutor in the writing center.

50E What English errors come from other languages?

ENGLISH ERRORS TRANSFERRED FROM OTHER LANGUAGES

Languages	Error Topic	Sample Errors	Corrected Errors
	Singulars and Plurals (Ch. 52)		
Chinese, Japanese, Korean, Thai	no (or optional) plural forms of nouns, including numbers	**NO** She wrote many good **essay**. **NO** She typed two **paper**.	**YES** She wrote many good **essays**. **YES** She typed two **papers**.

continued >>

Languages	Error Topic	Sample Errors	Corrected Errors
Hebrew, Italian, Japanese, Spanish	use of plural with embedded plurals	**NO** We cared for five **childrens**.	**YES** We cared for five **children**.
Italian, Spanish	adjectives carry plural	**NO** They are **Americans** students.	**YES** They are **American** students.
Articles (Ch. 53)			
Chinese, Japanese, Hindi, Korean, Russian, Swahili, Thai, Turkish, Urdu	no article (*a, an, the*) but can depend on whether article is definite/indefinite	**NO** He ate sandwich.	**YES** He ate **a** sandwich.
Word Order (Ch. 54)			
Arabic, Hebrew, Russian, Spanish, Tagalog	verb before subject	**NO** **Questioned Avi** the teenagers.	**YES** **Avi questioned** the teenagers.
Chinese, Japanese, Hindi, Thai	inverted word order confused in questions	**NO** **The book was it** heavy?	**YES** **Was the book** heavy?
Chinese, Japanese, Russian, Thai	sentence adverb misplaced	**NO** We will go home **possibly** now.	**YES** **Possibly**, we will go home now.
Gerunds, Infinitives, and Participles (Ch. 56)			
French, German, Greek, Hindi, Russian, Urdu	no progressive forms or overuse of progressive forms with infinitive	**NO** They **talk** while she **talk**. **NO** They **are wanting** to talk now.	**YES:** They **are talking** while she **is talking**. **YES** They **want** to talk now.
Arabic, Chinese, Farsi, Russian	omit forms of *be*	**NO** She happy. **NO** She **talk** loudly.	**YES** She **is** happy. **YES** She **talks** loudly.
Chinese, Japanese, Korean, Russian, Thai	no verb ending changes for person & number	**NO** He **laugh** yesterday.	**YES** He **laughed** yesterday.
Arabic, Chinese, Farsi, French, Thai, Vietnamese	no or nonstandard verb-tense markers	**NO** They **has arrived** yesterday.	**YES** They **arrived** yesterday.
Japanese, Korean, Russian, Thai, Vietnamese	nonstandard passives	**NO** A car accident **was happened**.	**YES** A car accident **was caused by the icy roads**.

51 Handling Sentence-Level Issues in English

■ ■ ■ ■ ■ ■ ■ ■ ■

Quick Points   You will learn to

➤ Recognize sentence-level errors in English (see 51A–51K).

51A How can I improve the grammar and vocabulary in my writing?

The best way to improve your English-language writing, including your grammar and vocabulary, is by writing. Many students also find it helpful to read as much as they can in English to see how other authors organize their writing, use vocabulary, and structure their sentences. Improving your writing in a second language—or a first language, for that matter—takes time. You will probably find that your ability to communicate with readers improves dramatically if you work on the ideas outlined in the previous chapter. Sometimes, though, readers may find it hard to understand your ideas because of grammar or word choice problems. We have designed this chapter to help you improve in these areas.

51B How can I improve my sentence structure?

Sometimes students write sentences that are hard to understand because of problems with overall sentence structure or length. For example:

NO   When the school started, my first English class was English 1020 as a grammar class, I started learning the basics of grammar, and at the same time the basic of writing, I worked hard in that class, taking by the teacher advice, try to memorize a lot of grammar rules and at the same time memorize some words I could use them to make an essay point.

To correct the structural and length errors, the student needs to break the sentence into several shorter sentences (see Chapter 34), to revise her sentences so that they clearly connect to each other, and to work on her verb tenses. She might need to ask for extra help at the writing center or from her instructor.

> **YES** When school started, my first English class, English 1020, was a grammar class, where I started learning the basics of grammar. At the same time, I learned the basics of writing. I worked hard in that class, taking the teacher's advice and memorizing a lot of grammar rules. In addition, I memorized some words I could use in my essays to make my points.

● **EXERCISE 51-1** Many different revisions of the previous example of a student's uncorrected paragraph are possible. Write a different revision of that student's paragraph. ●

● **EXERCISE 51-2** A student wrote the following passage about his experiences learning English. Rewrite the passage, improving the student's sentence structure and punctuation. In your revision of this passage, correct any errors that you see in grammar or spelling. Afterward, compare your revision with a classmate's. Then examine a piece of your own writing to see if you need to revise any of your sentences because of problems with sentence structure. (While you are doing this, if you have any questions about correct word order in English, see Chapter 54.)

> I went to school in my country since I was three years old, I was in Arabic and French school, and that's was my dad choice because his second language is French. So my second language at that time was French. In my elementary school I started to learn how to make an essay in French and Arabic. I learned the rules and it is too deferent from English. But later on when I was in my high school I had two choices between English class and science class so I choose the science because that's was my major. After I graduate I went to American university and I start studying English and my first class was remedial English for people doesn't know anything about this language. I went to this class about two months and then I have moved to a new place and I start from the beginning as an ESL student. ●

51C How can I improve my word choice (vocabulary)?

An important aspect of writing in a second language is having enough vocabulary to express your ideas. Many students enjoy learning more and more words to be able to communicate precise meanings. Experiment in your writing with new words that you hear and read in other contexts. Keep lists of new words, and try to add a few new words each day.

51D How can I find and correct errors in my own writing?

Some multilingual writers find it easiest to find and correct their grammar errors by reading their writing aloud and listening for mistakes. This method is often preferred by students who feel their spoken English is better than their written English. Other writers like to ask a friend who is a native speaker of English to check their writing. Still other multilingual writers prefer to circle each place where they think they've made an error and then use their handbook to check themselves.

You might also keep a list of the types of grammar errors you make so that you can become especially sensitive to errors when proofreading. The best system is to make a master list of the errors in categories so that you can check efficiently. Section 51J provides an example of how to track your errors.

51E How can I correct verb errors in my writing?

51E.1 Verb Tense Errors

Many multilingual writers consider verb-form errors the most difficult to correct. They want to be sure that their verb forms express the appropriate time frame for the event or situation they're describing. For a detailed discussion of verb forms, see 29B–29F.

● **EXERCISE 51-3** Read the following passage in which a student describes his experiences as an international traveler. The student's instructor has underlined errors related to time frames expressed by the verbs. Correct the underlined verbs, changing them to the correct time frames.

My earliest memory of traveling was going to the Post Office with my dad to apply for a passport. I must have been eight or nine years old, and I flinched when the man <u>takes</u> my picture.

After I got my passport, we <u>plan</u> a trip to Europe. We visited France, Spain, and Portugal, then <u>cross</u> the Channel into Great Britain. I loved seeing the famous sights in England. I <u>am</u> excited to see Great Ben, and I even <u>have</u> a picture taken with me and a Royal Guard in front of Buckingham Palace. I <u>try</u> everything to make him smile, but he <u>keeps</u> his face cold as stone.

When I was a few years older, I <u>travel</u> to Germany as an exchange student. I had been studying the Reformation, so I <u>want</u> to see the famous Wittenberg church where Martin Luther <u>nails</u> his ninety-five theses to a door. During that trip, I also <u>enjoy</u> some leisure time at the very popular Oktoberfest, where I <u>drink</u> beer and <u>enjoy</u> the music. ●

If you struggle with errors in verb tense in your writing, try reading through your draft once and circling all the verbs. Then check each one in isolation.

51E.2 Verbal Errors

Some students are troubled by the distinction between a VERB and a VERBAL. A verbal is not a verb, but rather it's a verb form whose function has shifted to another part of speech. Three verbal forms are the participle (ADJECTIVE), the gerund (NOUN), and the infinitive (ADJECTIVE, NOUN, or ADVERB).

PARTICIPLE (ADJECTIVE):	Our **shedding** elms do not look healthy.
PARTICIPLE (ADJECTIVE)	Our **shedded** elms were cut down right away.
GERUND (NOUN):	A rapid **shedding** of leaves usually indicates elm disease.
INFINITIVE (NOUN):	Our elms were beginning **to shed** their leaves rapidly.
INFINITIVE (ADJECTIVE):	Our trees with Dutch elm disease gave us no time **to waste**.
INFINITIVE (ADVERB):	We cut our diseased trees **to maintain** the health of other trees.

Verbals used in sentences without AUXILIARY VERBS create SENTENCE FRAGMENTS.

NO   Our elm trees **to maintain** their health.

YES   Our elm trees have **to maintain** their health.
    The auxiliary verb *have* completes the sentence.

NO   Cutting down diseased elms **recommended**.

YES   Cutting down diseased elms *is* **recommended**.
    The auxiliary verb *is* completes the sentence.

NO   Urban landscapers **hired** to protect city parks.

NO   Urban landscapers **being hired** to protect city parks.

YES   Urban landscapers *are* **being hired** to protect city parks.
    The auxiliary verb *are* completes the sentence.

● **EXERCISE 51-4** Working individually or with a group, rewrite the following paragraph to eliminate the misuse of verbals as verbs. (Some sentences are correct.) You may add, change, or rearrange words.

Many embarrassing errors made by multinational corporations when translating U.S. brands or slogans abroad. For example, when Pepsi entered the Chinese market some years back, it translated the slogan, "Pepsi Brings You Back to Life," which means in Chinese, "Pepsi Brings Your Ancestors Back from the Grave." Braniff Airlines interested to tell passengers about the comfort of its seats by using the slogan "Fly in Leather." However, in Spanish, this slogan was translated into "Fly Naked." In Italy, a campaign by "Schweppes Tonic Water" aiming to quench customers' thirst. Understandably, Italians not rushing to buy what translate to "Schweppes Toilet Water." Advertisers outside the United States must remember that language, after all, is a primary tool that used to generate both customer interest and corporate profits. ●

51F How can I correct my errors in subject–verb agreement?

Subject–verb agreement means that a subject (a noun or a pronoun) and its verb must agree in number and in person. In the following two sentences, notice the difference in the way the subjects and the verbs that describe their actions agree: *Carolina runs charity marathons. They give her a sense of accomplishment.*

For more information about subject–verb agreement, review Chapter 31. To help you put subject-verb agreement rules into practice, try the next exercise.

● **EXERCISE 51-5** Examine the following student's description. The student's instructor has underlined verbs that do not agree with their subjects. Correct the underlined verb forms, changing them to agree with their subjects.

My goal <u>have</u> always been to learn how to enjoy travelling to different countries, which all <u>has</u> their own unique cultures. When I travel to unfamiliar places, I like to eat unusual dishes, even if they <u>appears</u> unusual at first. A tourist, even a seasoned one, <u>are</u> there to experience new things. And being willing to try new things <u>make</u> the journey more fulfilling. ●

51G How can I correct my singular/plural errors?

In English, if you're referring to more than one noun that is a count noun, you must make that noun plural, often by adding an *-s* ending. If you would like more information on this topic, see Chapter 52. To help you recognize when necessary plural forms are missing, try the next exercise.

● **EXERCISE 51-6** In the following passage, a student's instructor has underlined only the first two nouns that need to be plural. Read the passage, correct the two underlined nouns, and then find and correct the other nouns in the passage that need to be plural.

> Every country has its own <u>custom</u>. When traveling, it's important to remember that your way of doing <u>thing</u> may not be the same in other country. For example, in some places, it is common for customer to barter for a price on item for sale. Also, American generally shake hand when greeting one another, but in some places, it is common for friend to kiss. ●

Examine a piece of your own writing and make sure that you have used plural words correctly.

51H How can I correct my preposition errors?

Prepositions are words such as *in, on, for, over*, and *about*, which usually show where, how, or when. For example, in the sentence *She received flowers from her friend for her birthday*, the prepositions are *from* and *for*. Unlike some other languages, English has many prepositions, and knowing which one to use can be very difficult. You can find information about using prepositions in section 28H and in Chapter 55.

● **EXERCISE 51-7** In the following passage, the student's instructor has underlined problems with preposition use. Try to correct the preposition errors. In some cases, more than one answer may be correct. If you can't find the information you need from Chapter 55 or in a dictionary, you might ask a native English speaker for help.

> I've always wanted to learn languages other than my native language. I started taking English and French lessons <u>of</u> school and I liked the idea of becoming fluent <u>for</u> at least one language. I thought English would help me a lot <u>to</u> the future because it could help me communicate <u>to</u> people from all over the world. ●

If prepositions are something you struggle with in your own writing, ask an instructor or a native speaker of English to underline the errors in preposition usage in a piece of writing that you have done. Then go through your writing and correct the errors that have been underlined.

51I What other kinds of errors might I make?

Depending on your language background and your prior experience with writing in English (see 50E), you may make errors related to the use of articles (*a, an, the*), word order (where to place adjectives and adverbs in sentences), and various verb forms and noun forms (for example, problems with noncount nouns and helping verbs). For example, the next sentence has a problem with one article and the order of an adjective: *The New York City is a place exciting.* The corrected sentence is *New York City is an exciting place.* Chapters 52 through 57 address grammar errors that are often made by multilingual writers.

51J How can I keep track of my most common errors?

One way of becoming more aware of the types of errors you make is to keep track of the errors you often make in the papers you write. You can ask your instructor or a tutor to help you identify such errors, and you can make a list of them that you update regularly. Remember the passage from Exercise 51-3 about a student's travel experiences? After the student examined the teacher's comments on his paper, he made a list of his errors and included a correction and a note about the error type for each. Upon reviewing this list (see Figure 51.1), the student writer realized that many of his errors related to verb form.

Figure 51.1 A list of errors.

Specific Error	Correction	Type of Error
when the man takes	took	verb form
we plan a trip	planned	verb form
then cross the Channel	crossed	verb form
I am excited	was	verb form
I even have	had	verb form
I try everything	tried	verb form
he keeps his face	kept	verb form
I travel to Germany	traveled	verb form
I want to see	wanted	verb form
where Martin Luther nails	nailed	verb form
I also enjoy	enjoyed	verb form
where I drink beer	drank	verb form
and enjoy the music	enjoyed	verb form

● **EXERCISE 51-8**   Using one or more pieces of your writing, make an error list similar to the previous one. (You could make this list on a sheet of paper or in an electronic file.) Examine the list. What are the most common types of errors that you make? Once you have identified your common error types, refer to the relevant proofreading exercises in this chapter and to the relevant ones in Chapters 52 through 57. Also, remember to keep your common errors in mind when you proofread your future writing assignments. You might even keep a master checklist that you can return to when you proofread your writing. ●

51K   How can I improve my proofreading skills?

The most effective way to improve your proofreading skills is to practice frequently. Proofread your own writing and, after you have done so, ask your instructor, a tutor, or a friend who is a native English speaker to point out the location of errors that you did not see on your own. When you know which errors you've made, try to correct the errors without help. Finally, have your instructor or tutor check your corrections.

Another effective way to improve your proofreading skills is to exchange your writing with a partner. You can check for errors in his or her writing and he or she can check for errors in yours. You might find that, at first, it is easier to find errors if you look for one kind of error at a time. Try Exercises 51-9 and 51-10 for more proofreading practice.

● **EXERCISE 51-9**   After you read the following passage, rewrite it, correcting the linguistic errors you find.

I've always faced some problem in writing in English as it took me some time to get used to it. Facing these complexities encourage me to developed my skills in English writing. My first class in English was about grammar, spelling, and writing. I realize later that grammar is hard to learn, so I knew I have to put in a lot of effort to understand it perfectly and use it properly. I also had some difficulties for vocabulary, as it was hard to understand the meaning of some word.

Another thing that helped me with my English was when my mother enroll me in an English learning center that specialize in teach writing skills. After a month of taking classes, my teacher saw some improvement in my grammar and vocabulary. To test me, she asked me to write an essay on how to be successful. I was really excite of it and started write it immediately. After I finish my essay and my teacher check it, my teacher suggested that I take a few more classes for her. She taught me how to organized my ideas. After finishing these classes I realize that my writing was getting much better with time. ●

● **EXERCISE 51-10** In the following paragraph, a student describes the study of English at private schools in Japan. After you read the paragraph, rewrite it, correcting the errors that you find.

Recently, the number of private language schools are increased in Japan. These schools put special emphasize on oral communication skills. In them, student takes not only grammars and reading classes, which help them pass school examinations, but also speaking, listening classes. They can also study English for six year, which is same period as in public schools. Some of the teacher in these school are native speaker of English. Since these teachers do not use Japanese in the class, the students have to use the English to participate it. They have the opportunity to use the English in their class more than public school students. It is said that the students who took English in private schools can speak English better than those student who go to public schools. ●

⚙ Complete the Chapter Exercises

52 Singulars and Plurals

■ ■ ■ ■ ■ ■ ■ ■ ■ ■

Quick Points   You will learn to

➤ Distinguish between count and noncount nouns (see 52A).
➤ Use the proper determiners with singular and plural nouns (see 52B).

52A What are count and noncount nouns?

👁 Watch the Video

Count nouns name items that can be counted: *a radio* or *radios, a street* or *streets, an idea* or *ideas, a fingernail* or *fingernails.* Count nouns can be SINGULAR or PLURAL.

Noncount nouns name things that are thought of as a whole and not split into separate, countable parts: *rice, knowledge, traffic.* There are two important rules to remember about noncount nouns: (1) They're never preceded by *a* or *an*, and (2) they are never plural.

Here are several categories of noncount nouns, with examples in each category:

GROUPS OF SIMILAR ITEMS	clothing, equipment, furniture, jewelry, junk, luggage, mail, money, stuff, traffic, vocabulary
ABSTRACTIONS	advice, equality, fun, health, ignorance, information, knowledge, news, peace, pollution, respect
LIQUIDS	blood, coffee, gasoline, water
GASES	air, helium, oxygen, smog, smoke, steam
MATERIALS	aluminum, cloth, cotton, ice, wood
FOOD	beef, bread, butter, macaroni, meat, pork
PARTICLES OR GRAINS	dirt, dust, hair, rice, salt, wheat
SPORTS, GAMES, ACTIVITIES	chess, homework, housework, reading, sailing, soccer
LANGUAGES	Arabic, Chinese, Japanese, Spanish
FIELDS OF STUDY	biology, computer science, history, literature, math
EVENTS IN NATURE	electricity, heat, humidity, moonlight, rain, snow, sunshine, thunder, weather

Some nouns can be countable or uncountable, depending on their meaning in a sentence. Most of these nouns name things that can be meant either individually or as "wholes" made up of individual parts.

COUNT	You have **a hair** on your sleeve.
	In this sentence, *hair* is meant as an individual, countable item.
NONCOUNT	Kioko has black **hair**.
	In this sentence, all the strands of *hair* are referred to as a whole.
COUNT	**The rains** were late last year.
	In this sentence, *rains* is meant as individual, countable occurrences of rain.
NONCOUNT	**The rain** is soaking the garden.
	In this sentence, all the particles of *rain* are referred to as a whole.

When you are editing your writing (see 5K), be sure that you have not added a plural *-s* to any noncount nouns, for they are always singular in form.

🛈 **Alert:** Be sure to use a singular verb with any noncount noun that functions as a SUBJECT in a CLAUSE. ●

To check whether a noun is count or noncount, look it up in a dictionary such as the *Dictionary of American English* (Heinle and Heinle). In this dictionary, count nouns are indicated by [C], and noncount nouns are indicated by [U] (for "uncountable"). Nouns that have both count and noncount meanings are marked [C;U].

52B How do I use determiners with singular and plural nouns?

DETERMINERS, also called *expressions of quantity*, are used to tell how much or how many with reference to NOUNS. Other names for determiners include *limiting adjectives, noun markers*, and ARTICLES. (For information about articles—the words *a, an*, and *the*—see Chapter 53.)

Choosing the right determiner with a noun can depend on whether the noun is NONCOUNT or COUNT (see 52A). For count nouns, you must also decide whether the noun is singular or plural. Quick Box 52.1 lists many determiners and the kinds of nouns that they can accompany.

Quick Box 52.1

Determiners to use with count and noncount nouns

GROUP 1: DETERMINERS FOR SINGULAR COUNT NOUNS

With every singular count noun, always use one of the determiners listed in Group 1.

a, an, the	**a house**	**an egg**	**the car**
one, any, some, every, each, either, neither, another, the other	**any house**	**each egg**	**another car**
my, our, your, his, her, its, their, nouns with *'s* or *s'*	**your house**	**its egg**	**Connie's car**
this, that	**this house**	**that egg**	**this car**
one, no, the first, the second, etc.	**one house**	**no egg**	**the fifth car**

continued >>

Quick Box 52.1 (continued)

GROUP 2: DETERMINERS FOR PLURAL COUNT NOUNS

All the determiners listed in Group 2 can be used with plural count nouns. Plural count nouns can also be used without determiners, as discussed in section 52B.

the	**the bicycles**	**the rooms**	**the idea**
some, any, both, many, more, most, few, fewer, the fewest, a lot of, a number of, other, several, all, all the	**some bicycles**	**many rooms**	**all ideas**
my, our, your, his, her, its, their, nouns with *'s or s'*	**our bicycles**	**her rooms**	**student's ideas**
these, those	**these bicycles**	**those rooms**	**these ideas**
no, two, three, etc.; *the first, the second, the third*, etc.	**no bicycles**	**four rooms**	**the first ideas**

GROUP 3: DETERMINERS FOR NONCOUNT NOUNS

All the determiners listed in Group 3 can be used with noncount nouns (always singular). Noncount nouns can also be used without determiners.

the	**the rice**	**the rain**	**the pride**
some, any, much, more, most, other, the other, little, less, the least, enough, all, all the, a lot of	**enough rice**	**a lot of rain**	**more pride**
my, our, your, his, her, its, their, nouns with *'s or s'*	**their rice**	**India's rain**	**your pride**
this, that	**this rice**	**that rain**	**this pride**
no, the first, the second, the third, etc.	**no rice**	**the first rain**	**no pride**

🛑 **Alert:** The phrases *a few* and *a little* convey the meaning "some": *I have* **a few** *rare books* means "I have *some* rare books." *They are worth* **a little** *money* means "They are worth *some* money."

Without the word *a*, the words *few* and *little* convey the meaning "almost none": *I have* **few** [or *very few*] *books* means "I have *almost no* books." *They are worth* **little** *money* means "They are worth *almost no* money." ●

52C How do I use *one of*, nouns as adjectives, and *states* in names or titles?

ONE OF CONSTRUCTIONS

One of constructions include *one of the* and a NOUN or *one of* followed by a DETERMINER–noun combination (*one of my hats, one of those ideas*). Always use a plural noun as the OBJECT when you use *one of the* with a noun or *one of* with an adjective–noun combination.

> **NO** *One of the* **reason** to live here is the beach.

> **YES** *One of the* **reasons** to live here is the beach.

> **NO** *One of her best* **friend** has moved away.

> **YES** *One of her best* **friends** has moved away.

The VERB in these constructions is always singular because it agrees with the singular *one*, not with the plural noun: **One** *of the most important inventions of the twentieth century* **is** [not *are*] *television*.

For advice about verb forms that go with *one of the . . . who* constructions, see 31L.

NOUNS USED AS ADJECTIVES

ADJECTIVES in English do not have plural forms. When you use an adjective with a PLURAL NOUN, make the noun plural but not the adjective: *the* **green** [not *greens*] *leaves*. Be especially careful when you use a word as a MODIFIER that can also function as a noun.

● The bird's wingspan is ten inches.

Inches is functioning as a noun.

● The bird has a ten-inch wingspan.

Inch is functioning as a modifier.

Do not add *-s* (or *-es*) to the adjective even when it is modifying a plural noun or pronoun.

> **NO** Many **Americans** students are basketball fans.

> **YES** Many **American** students are basketball fans.

NAMES OR TITLES THAT INCLUDE THE WORD *STATES*

States is a plural word. However, names such as *United States* or *Organization of American States* refer to singular things—one country and one organization, even though made up of many states. When *states* is part of a name or title referring to one thing, the name is a SINGULAR NOUN and therefore requires a SINGULAR VERB.

> NO   The **United States have** a large entertainment industry.

> NO   The **United State has** a large entertainment industry.

> YES   The **United States has** a large entertainment industry.

52D   How do I use nouns with irregular plurals?

Some English nouns have irregularly spelled plurals. In addition to those discussed in section 49C, here are others that often cause difficulties.

PLURALS OF FOREIGN NOUNS AND OTHER IRREGULAR NOUNS

Whenever you are unsure whether a noun is plural, look it up in a dictionary. If no plural is given for a singular noun, add *-s* to form the plural.

Many nouns from other languages that are used unchanged in English have only one plural. If two plurals are listed in the dictionary, look carefully for differences in meaning. Some words, for example, keep the plural form from the original language for scientific usage and have another, English-form plural for nonscientific contexts: *formula, formulae, formulas; appendix, appendices, appendixes; index, indices, indexes; medium, media, mediums; cactus, cacti, cactuses; fungus, fungi, funguses.*

Words from Latin that end in *-is* in their singular form become plural by substituting *-es: parenthesis, parentheses; thesis, theses; oasis, oases.*

OTHER WORDS

Medical terms for diseases involving an inflammation end in *-itis: tonsillitis, appendicitis.* They are always singular.

The word *news*, although it ends in *s*, is always singular: *The **news is** encouraging.* The words *people, police,* and *clergy* are always plural even though they do not end in *s: The **police are** prepared.*

● **EXERCISE 52-1**   Consulting all sections of this chapter, select the correct choice from the words in parentheses and write it in the blank.

Complete the Chapter Exercises

EXAMPLE

It can be tricky to bake (bread, breads) <u>bread</u> in Denver, Colorado, because of that city's high (elevation, elevations) <u>elevation</u>.

1. Denver has an elevation of 5,280 (foot, feet) _____, and changes must therefore be made to baking (recipe, recipes) _____.
2. The 5,280-(foot, feet) _____ elevation lowers the boiling point of (water, waters) _____.
3. The leading (American, Americans) _____ expert in high-altitude baking recommends adding more (flour, flours) _____ to bread recipes.
4. If your recipe includes different kinds of (liquid, liquids) _____, the expert recommends adding additional (liquid, liquid) _____ to combat dryness.
5. One of the (effect, effects) _____ of the high altitude is that the crust of a loaf of (bread, breads) _____ will cook faster. ●

53 Articles

■ ■ ■ ■ ■ ■ ■ ■ ■

Quick Points   You will learn to

➤ Use articles correctly (see 53A–53C).

53A   How do I use *a*, *an*, or *the* with singular count nouns?

👁
Watch
the Video

The words *a* and *an* are called INDEFINITE ARTICLES. The word *the* is called the DEFINITE ARTICLE. Articles are one type of DETERMINER. (For more on determiners, see 28F; for other determiners, see Quick Box 52.1 in 52B.) Articles signal that a NOUN will follow and that any MODIFIERS between the article and the noun refer to that noun.

a chair	**the** computer
a brown chair	**the** teacher's computer
a cold, metal chair	**the** lightning-fast computer

Every time you use a singular count noun, a COMMON NOUN that names one countable item, the noun requires some kind of determiner; see Group 1 in Quick Box 52.1 (in 52B) for a list. To choose between *a* or *an* and *the*, you need to determine whether the noun is **specific** or nonspecific. A noun is considered *specific* when anyone who reads your writing can understand exactly and specifically to what item the noun is referring. If the noun refers to any of a number of identical items, it is *nonspecific.*

For nonspecific singular count nouns, use *a* (or *an*). When the singular noun is specific, use *the* or some other determiner. Quick Box 53.1 can help you decide when a singular count noun is specific and therefore requires *the.*

Quick Box 53.1

When a singular count noun is specific and requires *the*

- **Rule 1: A noun is specific and requires *the* when it names something unique or generally and unambiguously known.**
  - **The sun** has risen above **the horizon.**

    Because there is only one *sun* and only one *horizon*, these nouns are specific in the context of this sentence.

- **Rule 2: A noun is specific and requires *the* when it names something used in a representative or abstract sense.**
  - Benjamin Franklin favored **the turkey** as **the national bird** of the United States.

    Because *turkey* and *national bird* are representative references rather than references to a particular turkey or bird, they are specific nouns in the context of this sentence.

- **Rule 3: A noun is specific and requires *the* when it names something defined elsewhere in the same sentence or in an earlier sentence.**
  - **The ship *Savannah*** was the first steam vessel to cross the Atlantic Ocean.

    Savannah names a specific ship.
  - **The carpet in my bedroom** is new.

    In my bedroom defines exactly which carpet is meant, so *carpet* is a specific noun in this context.
  - I have **a computer** in my office. **The computer** is often broken.

    Computer is not specific in the first sentence, so it uses *a*. In the second sentence, *computer* has been made specific by the first sentence, so it uses *the*.

continued >>

Quick Box 53.1 (continued)

- **Rule 4: A noun is specific and requires *the* when it names something that can be inferred from the context.**
  - Monday, I had to call the technician to fix my computer again.

    A technician would be any of a number of individuals; *the technician* implies the same person has been called before, and so it is specific in this context.

Alert: Use *an* before words that begin with a vowel sound. Use *a* before words that begin with a consonant sound. Go by the sound, not the spelling. For example, words that begin with *h* or *u* can have either a vowel or a consonant sound. Make the choice based on the sound of the first word after the article, even if that word is not the noun.

an idea	**a g**ood idea
an umbrella	**a u**seless umbrella
an honor	**a h**istory book ●

One common exception affects Rule 3 in Quick Box 53.1. A noun may still require *a* (or *an*) after the first use if more information is added between the article and the noun: *I bought **a sweater** today. It was **a** (not the) **red sweater**.* (Your audience has been introduced to *a sweater* but not *a red sweater*, so *red sweater* is not yet specific in this context and cannot take *the*.) Other information may make the noun specific so that *the* is correct. For example, *It was **the red sweater that I saw in the store yesterday*** uses *the* because the *that* CLAUSE makes specific which red sweater the writer means.

53B How do I use articles with plural nouns and with noncount nouns?

With plural nouns and NONCOUNT NOUNS, you must decide whether to use *the* or to use no article at all. (For guidelines about using DETERMINERS other than articles with nouns, see Quick Box 52.1 in 52B.) What you learned in 53A about NONSPECIFIC and SPECIFIC NOUNS can help you choose between using *the* or using no article. Quick Box 53.1 in 53A explains when a singular count noun's meaning is specific and calls for *the*. Plural nouns and noncount nouns with specific meanings usually use *the* in the same circumstances. However, a plural noun or a noncount noun with a general or nonspecific meaning usually does not use *the*.

- Geraldo grows **flowers** but not **vegetables** in his garden. He is thinking about planting **corn** sometime.   [three nonspecific nouns]

PLURAL NOUNS

A plural noun's meaning may be specific because it is widely known.

- **The oceans** are being damaged by pollution.

  Because there is only one possible meaning for *oceans*—the oceans on the earth—it is correct to use *the*. This example is related to Rule 1 in Quick Box 53.1.

A plural noun's meaning may also be made specific by a word, PHRASE, or CLAUSE in the same sentence.

- Geraldo sold **the daisies from last year's garden** to the florist.

  Because the phrase *from last year's garden* makes *daisies* specific, *the* is correct. This example is related to Rule 3 in Quick Box 53.1.

A plural noun's meaning usually becomes specific by its use in an earlier sentence.

- Geraldo planted **tulips** this year. **The tulips** will bloom in April.

  Tulips is used in a general sense in the first sentence, without *the*. Because the first sentence makes *tulips* specific, *the tulips* is correct in the second sentence. This example is related to Rule 3 in Quick Box 53.1.

A plural noun's meaning may be made specific by the context.

- Geraldo fertilized **the bulbs** when he planted them last October.

  In the context of the sentences about tulips, *bulbs* is understood as a synonym for *tulips*, which makes it specific and calls for *the*. This example is related to Rule 4 in Quick Box 53.1.

NONCOUNT NOUNS

Noncount nouns are always singular in form (see 52A). Like plural nouns, noncount nouns use either *the* or no article. When a noncount noun's meaning is specific, use *the* before it. If its meaning is general or nonspecific, do not use *the*.

- Kalinda served us **rice**. She flavored **the rice** with curry.

  Rice is a noncount noun. By the second sentence, *rice* has become specific, so *the* is used. This example is related to Rule 3 in Quick Box 53.1.

- Kalinda served us **the rice that she had flavored with curry**.

  Rice is a noncount noun. *Rice* is made specific by the clause *that she had flavored with curry*, so *the* is used. This example is related to Rule 3 in Quick Box 53.1.

GENERALIZATIONS WITH PLURAL OR NONCOUNT NOUNS

Rule 2 in Quick Box 53.1 tells you to use *the* with singular count nouns that carry general meaning. With GENERALIZATIONS using plural or noncount nouns, omit *the*.

NO	**The tulips** are **the flowers** that grow from **the bulbs**.

YES	**Tulips** are **flowers** that grow from **bulbs**.

NO	**The dogs** require more care than **the cats** do.

YES	**Dogs** require more care than **cats** do.

53C How do I use *the* with proper nouns and with gerunds?

PROPER NOUNS

PROPER NOUNS name specific people, places, or things (see 28B). Most proper nouns do not require ARTICLES: *We visited **Lake Mead** with **Asha** and **Larry***. As shown in Quick Box 53.2, however, certain types of proper nouns do require *the*.

Quick Box 53.2 ■ ■ ■ ■ ■ ■ ■ ■ ■ ■

Proper nouns that use *the*

- **Nouns with the pattern *the . . . of . . .***
    the United States **of** America
    the Republic **of** Mexico
    the Fourth **of** July
    the University **of** Paris
- **Plural proper nouns**
    the United Arab Emirates
    the Johnsons
    the Rocky Mountains [*but* Mount Fuji]
    the Chicago Bulls
    the Falkland Islands [*but* Long Island]
    the Great Lakes [*but* Lake Superior]
- **Collective proper nouns (nouns that name a group)**
    the Modern Language Association
    the Society of Friends

continued >>

> ## Quick Box 53.2   (continued)
>
> - **Some (but not all) geographical features**
>   **the** Amazon   **the** Gobi Desert   **the** Indian Ocean
> - **Three countries**
>   **the** Congo   **the** Sudan   **the** Netherlands

GERUNDS

GERUNDS are PRESENT PARTICIPLES (the *-ing* form of VERBS) used as nouns: ***Skating** is challenging.* Gerunds are usually not preceded by *the*.

NO   **The constructing** new bridges is necessary to improve traffic flow.

YES   **Constructing** new bridges is necessary to improve traffic flow.

Use *the* before a gerund when two conditions are met: (1) The gerund is used in a specific sense (see 53A), and (2) the gerund does not have a DIRECT OBJECT.

NO   **The designing fabric** is a fine art.

   Fabric is a direct object of *designing*, so *the* should not be used.

YES   **Designing** fabric is a fine art.

   Designing is a gerund, so *the* is not used.

YES   **The designing of** fabric is a fine art.

   The is used because *fabric* is the object of the preposition *of* and *designing* is meant in a specific sense.

● **EXERCISE 53-1**   Consulting all sections of this chapter, decide which of the words in parentheses is correct and write it in the blank. If no article is needed, leave the blank empty.

Complete
the
Chapter
Exercises

EXAMPLE

In (a, an, the) _____ United States of America, (a, an, the) _____ highways are labeled with (a, an, the) _____ number that indicates (a, an, the) _____ highway's direction.

In (a, an, the) the United States of America, (a, an, the) [no article] highways are labeled with (a, an, the) a number that indicates the highway's direction.

1. If (a, an, the) _____ highway runs north and south, then it is designated with (a, an, the) _____ odd number, but (a, an, the) _____ highways that run east and west are given (a, an, the) _____ even number.

2. For example, (a, an, the) ＿＿ highway that runs north and south along (a, an, the) ＿＿ coast of California is called (a, an, the) ＿＿ Highway 1.
3. (A, An, The) ＿＿ interstate highway that runs east-to-west is given (a, an, the) ＿＿ low even number if it is in (a, an, the) ＿＿ southern U.S., such as (a, an, the) ＿＿ Interstate 10.
4. (A, An, The) ＿＿ three-digit freeway usually encircles (a, an, the) ＿＿ major city.
5. One of (a, an, the) ＿＿ America's most famous highways is (a, an, the) ＿＿ Route 66, which is (a, an, the) ＿＿ road that runs from Los Angeles to Chicago. ●

54 Word Order

■ ■ ■ ■ ■ ■ ■ ■ ■

Quick Points You will learn to

> Use appropriate English word order (see 54A).
> Place adjectives and adverbs in the proper places in sentences (see 54B–54C).

54A How do I understand standard and inverted word order in sentences?

In STANDARD WORD ORDER, the most common pattern for DECLARATIVE SENTENCES in English, the SUBJECT comes before the VERB. (To understand these concepts more fully, review 28L through 28P.)

SUBJECT   VERB
↓   ↓
● That book   was heavy.

With INVERTED WORD ORDER, the MAIN VERB or an AUXILIARY VERB comes before the subject. The most common use of inverted word order in English is in forming DIRECT QUESTIONS. Questions that can be answered with a yes or no begin with a form of *be* used as a main verb, with an auxiliary verb (*be, do, have*), or with a MODAL AUXILIARY (*can, should, will*, and others; see Chapter 57).

QUESTIONS THAT CAN BE ANSWERED WITH A YES OR NO

MAIN VERB   SUBJECT

- Was   that book heavy?

AUXILIARY
VERB   SUBJECT   MAIN VERB

- Have   you   heard the noise?

MODAL
AUXILIARY VERB   SUBJECT   MAIN VERB

- Can   you   lift the book?

To form a yes-or-no question with a verb other than *be* as the main verb and when there is no auxiliary or modal as part of a VERB PHRASE, use the appropriate form of the auxiliary verb *do*.

AUXILIARY
VERB   SUBJECT   MAIN VERB

- Do   you   want me to put the book away?

A question that begins with a question-forming word such as *why, when, where,* or *how* cannot be answered with a yes or no: ***Why*** *did the book fall?* Some kind of information must be provided to answer such a question; the answer cannot be simply yes or no because the question is not "*Did* the book fall?" Information on *why* it fell is needed: for example, *It was too heavy for me.*

INFORMATION QUESTIONS: INVERTED ORDER

Most information questions follow the same rules of inverted word order as yes-or-no questions.

QUESTION
WORD   MAIN VERB   SUBJECT

- Why   is   that book open?

QUESTION
WORD   AUXILIARY VERB   SUBJECT   MAIN VERB

- What   does   the book   discuss?

QUESTION
WORD   MODAL AUXILIARY   SUBJECT   MAIN VERB

- When   can   I   read the book?

INFORMATION QUESTIONS: STANDARD ORDER

When *who* or *what* functions as the subject in a question, use standard word order.

QUESTION WORD:
SUBJECT   MAIN VERB

- Who   dropped the book?

QUESTION WORD:
SUBJECT   MAIN VERB

- What   was the problem?

Alert: When a question has more than one auxiliary verb, put the subject after the first auxiliary verb.

FIRST   SECOND
AUXILIARY SUBJECT   AUXILIARY   MAIN VERB

- Would   you   have   replaced the book?

The same rules apply to emphatic exclamations: ***Was** that book heavy!* ***Did** she enjoy that book!* ●

NEGATIVES

When you use negatives such as *never, hardly ever, seldom, rarely, not only,* or *nor* to start a CLAUSE, use inverted order. These sentence pairs show the differences, first in standard order and then in inverted order.

- **I have never seen** a more exciting movie.   [standard order]

- **Never have I seen** a more exciting movie.   [inverted order]

- **She is not only** a talented artist **but also** an excellent musician.

- **Not only is she** a talented artist, **but she is also** an excellent musician.

- I didn't like the book, and **my husband didn't either**.

- I didn't like the book, and **neither did my husband**.

Alerts: (1) With INDIRECT QUESTIONS, use standard word order.

   NO She asked **how did I drop** the book.

   YES She asked **how I dropped** the book.

(2) Word order deliberately inverted can be effective, when used sparingly, to create emphasis in a sentence that is neither a question nor an exclamation (also see 38R). ●

54B How can I understand the placement of adjectives?

ADJECTIVES modify—describe or limit—NOUNS, PRONOUNS, and word groups that function as nouns (see 28F). In English, an adjective comes directly before the noun it describes. However, when more than one adjective describes the same noun, several sequences may be possible. Quick Box 54.1 shows the most common order for positioning several adjectives.

Quick Box 54.1

Word order: cumulative adjectives

1. **Determiners, if any:** *a, an, the, my, your, this, that, these, those,* and so on
2. **Expressions of order, including ordinal numbers, if any:** *first, second, third, next, last, final,* and so on
3. **Expressions of quantity, including cardinal (counting) numbers, if any:** *one, two, few, each, every, some,* and so on
4. **Adjectives of judgment or opinion, if any:** *pretty, happy, ugly, sad, interesting, boring,* and so on
5. **Adjectives of size or shape, if any:** *big, small, short, round, square,* and so on
6. **Adjectives of age or condition, if any:** *new, young, broken, dirty, shiny,* and so on
7. **Adjectives of color, if any:** *red, green, blue,* and so on
8. **Adjectives that can also be used as nouns, if any:** *French, Protestant, metal, cotton,* and so on
9. **The noun**

1	2	3	4	5	6	7	8	9
a		few		tiny		red		ants
the	last	six					Thai	carvings
my			fine		old		oak	table

54C How can I understand the placement of adverbs?

ADVERBS modify—describe or limit—VERBS, ADJECTIVES, other adverbs, or entire sentences (see 28G). Adverbs may be positioned first, in the middle, or last in CLAUSES. Quick Box 54.2 (page 736) summarizes adverb types, what they tell about the words they modify, and where each type can be placed.

Quick Box 54.2

■ ■ ■ ■ ■ ■ ■ ■ ■ ■

Word order: positioning adverbs

ADVERBS OF MANNER	• describe *how* something is done • are usually in middle or last position	Nick **carefully** groomed the dog. Nick groomed the dog **carefully**.
ADVERBS OF TIME	• describe *when* or *how long* about an event • are usually in first or last position • include *just, still, already,* and similar adverbs, which are usually in middle position	**First**, he shampooed the dog. He shampooed the dog **first**. He had **already** brushed the dog's coat.
ADVERBS OF FREQUENCY	• describe *how often* an event takes place • are usually in middle position • are in first position when they modify an entire sentence (see "Sentence Adverbs" below)	Nick has **never** been bitten by a dog. **Occasionally**, he is scratched while shampooing a cat.
ADVERBS OF DEGREE OR EMPHASIS	• describe *how much* or *to what extent* about other modifiers • are directly before the word they modify • include *only*, which is easy to misplace (see 35A)	Nick is **extremely** calm around animals. [*Extremely* modifies *calm*.]
SENTENCE ADVERBS	• modify the entire sentence rather than just one word or a few words • include transitional words and expressions (see 6G.1), as well as such expressions as *maybe, probably, possibly, fortunately, unfortunately,* and *incredibly* • are in first position	**Incredibly**, he was once asked to groom a rat.

🛑 **Alert:** Do not let an adverb separate a verb from its DIRECT OBJECT or INDIRECT OBJECT. ●

● **EXERCISE 54-1** Consulting all sections of this chapter, find and correct any errors in word order.

⚙️ Complete the Chapter Exercises

1. I was looking for a new interesting book, so I walked to the library.
2. Quietly, I asked the librarian where I could find biographies, and he pointed quickly his finger to a shelf.
3. I asked him, "You do have a biography of Emmy Noether?"
4. The librarian, who extremely was helpful, looked on a white old computer for me and said, "Yes."
5. "Where I can check it out?" I asked, excited to find finally a new book. ●

55 Prepositions

■ ■ ■ ■ ■ ■ ■ ■ ■

Quick Points   You will learn to

➤ Use *in*, *at*, and *on* to show time and place (see 55B).
➤ Use prepositions correctly (see 55C–55E).

PREPOSITIONS function with other words in PREPOSITIONAL PHRASES (28O). Prepositional phrases usually indicate *where* (direction or location), *how* (by what means or in what way), or *when* (at what time or how long) about the words they modify.

Watch the Video

  This chapter can help you with several uses of prepositions, which function in combination with other words in ways that are often idiomatic—that is, peculiar to the language. The meaning of an **idiom** differs from the literal meaning of each individual word. For example, the word *break* usually refers to shattering, but the sentence *Yao-Ming **broke into** a smile* means that a smile appeared on Yao-Ming's face. Knowing which preposition to use in a specific context takes much experience in reading, listening to, and speaking the language. A dictionary like the *Dictionary of American English* (Heinle and Heinle) can be especially helpful when you need to find the correct preposition to use in cases not covered by this chapter.

55A How can I recognize prepositions?

Quick Box 55.1 lists many common prepositions.

Quick Box 55.1

Common prepositions

about	below	in	opposite	toward
above	beside	in front of	out	under
across	between	inside	outside	underneath
after	beyond	instead of	over	unlike
against	but	into	past	until
along	by	like	plus	up
among	concerning	near	regarding	with
around	despite	next	round	within
as	down	of	since	without
at	during	off	through	
because of	except	on	throughout	
before	for	onto	till	
behind	from	on top of	to	

55B How do I use prepositions with expressions of time and place?

Quick Box 55.2 shows how to use the prepositions *in, at,* and *on* to deliver some common kinds of information about time and place. Quick Box 55.2, however, does not cover every preposition that indicates time or place, nor does it cover all uses of *in, at,* and *on.* Also, the Quick Box does not include expressions that operate outside the general rules. (Both these sentences are correct: *You ride **in** the car* and *You ride **on** the bus.*)

Quick Box 55.2

■ ■ ■ ■ ■ ■ ■ ■ ■ ■ ■

Using *in*, *at*, and *on* to show time and place

TIME

- ***in* a year or a month** (*during* is also correct but less common)
  in 1995   in May

- ***in* a period of time**
  in a few months (seconds, days, years)

- ***in* a period of the day**
  in the morning (afternoon, evening)
  in the daytime (morning, evening) *but* at night

- ***at* a specific time or period of time**
  at noon   at 2:00   at dawn   at nightfall
  at takeoff (the time a plane leaves)
  at breakfast (the time a specific meal takes place)

- ***on* a specific day**
  on Friday   on my birthday

PLACE

- ***in* a location surrounded by something else**
  in the province of Alberta   in the kitchen
  in Utah   in the apartment
  in downtown Bombay   in the bathtub

- ***at* a specific location**
  at your house   at the bank
  at the corner of Third Avenue and Main Street

- ***on* a surface**
  on page 20
  on the second floor *but* in the attic *or* in the basement
  on Washington Street
  on the mezzanine
  on the highway

55C How do I use prepositions in phrasal verbs?

Phrasal verbs, also called *two-word verbs* and *three-word verbs*, are VERBS that combine with PREPOSITIONS to deliver their meaning. In some phrasal verbs, the verb and the preposition should not be separated by other words: *Look at the moon* [not *Look the moon at*]. In separable phrasal verbs, other words in the sentence can separate the verb and the preposition without interfering with meaning: *I threw away my homework* is as correct as *I threw my homework away*.

Here is a list of some common phrasal verbs. The ones that cannot be separated are marked with an asterisk (*).

SELECTED PHRASAL VERBS

ask out	get along with*	look into
break down	get back	look out for*
bring about	get off	look over
call back	go over*	make up
drop off	hand in	run across*
figure out	keep up with*	speak to*
fill out	leave out	speak with*
fill up	look after*	throw away
find out	look around	throw out

Position a PRONOUN OBJECT between the words of a separable phrasal verb: *I threw it away.* Also, you can position an object PHRASE of several words between the parts of a separable phrasal verb: *I threw my research paper away.* However, when the object is a CLAUSE, do not let it separate the parts of the phrasal verb: *I threw away all the papers that I wrote last year.*

Many phrasal verbs are informal and are used more in speaking than in writing. For ACADEMIC WRITING, a more formal verb is usually more appropriate than a phrasal verb. In a research paper, for example, *propose* or *suggest* might be a better choice than *come up with*. For academic writing, acceptable phrasal verbs include *believe in, benefit from, concentrate on, consist of, depend on, dream of* (or *dream about*), *insist on, participate in, prepare for,* and *stare at.* None of these phrasal verbs can be separated.

● **EXERCISE 55-1** Consulting the preceding sections of this chapter and using the list of phrasal verbs in 55C, write a one- or two-paragraph description of a typical day at work or school in which you use at least five phrasal verbs. After checking a dictionary, revise your writing, substituting for the phrasal verbs any more formal verbs that might be more appropriate for academic writing. ●

55D How do I use prepositions with past participles?

PAST PARTICIPLES are verb forms that function as ADJECTIVES (56F). Past participles end in either *-ed* or *-d*, or in an equivalent irregular form (29D). When past participles follow the LINKING VERB *be*, it is easy to confuse them with PASSIVE verbs (29N), which have the same endings. Passive verbs describe actions. Past participles, because they act as adjectives, modify NOUNS and PRONOUNS and often describe situations and conditions. Passive verbs follow the pattern *be* + past participle + *by: The child **was frightened by** a snake.* An expression containing a past participle, however, can use either *be* or another linking verb, and it can be followed by either *by* or a different preposition.

- The child **seemed frightened by** snakes.

- The child **is frightened of** all snakes.

Here is a list of expressions containing past participles and the prepositions that often follow them. Look in a dictionary for others. (See 56B on using GERUNDS after some of these expressions.)

SELECTED PAST PARTICIPLE PHRASES + PREPOSITIONS

be accustomed to	be interested in
be acquainted with	be known for
be composed of	be located in
be concerned/worried about	be made of (*or* from)
be disappointed with (*or* in someone)	be married to
be discriminated against	be pleased/satisfied with
be divorced from	be prepared for
be excited about	be tired of (*or* from)
be finished/done with	

55E How do I use prepositions in expressions?

In many common expressions, different PREPOSITIONS convey great differences in meaning. For example, four prepositions can be used with the verb *agree* to create five different meanings.

> **agree to** means "to give consent": *I cannot **agree to** my buying you a new car.*

> **agree about** means "to arrive at a satisfactory understanding": *We certainly **agree about** your needing a car.*

agree on means "to concur": *You and the seller must **agree on** a price for the car.*

agree with means "to have the same opinion": *I **agree with** you that you need a car.*

agree with also means "to be suitable or healthful": *The idea of having such a major expense does not **agree with** me.*

You can find entire books filled with English expressions that include prepositions. The following list shows a few that you're likely to use often.

SELECTED EXPRESSIONS WITH PREPOSITIONS

ability in	different from	involved with *someone*
access to	faith in	knowledge of
accustomed to	familiar with	made of
afraid of	famous for	married to
angry with *or* at	frightened by	opposed to
authority on	happy with	patient with
aware of	in charge of	proud of
based on	independent of	reason for
capable of	in favor of	related to
certain of	influence on *or* over	suspicious of
confidence in	interested in	time for
dependent on	involved in [*something*]	tired of

Gerunds, Infinitives, and Participles

56

Quick Points   You will learn to

➤ Use gerunds and infinitives correctly (see 56A–56E).

PARTICIPLES are verb forms (see 29B). A verb's -*ing* form is its PRESENT PARTI-CIPLE. The -*ed* form of a regular verb is its PAST PARTICIPLE; IRREGULAR VERBS form their past participles in various ways (for example, *bend, bent; eat, eaten; think, thought*—for a complete list, see Quick Box 29.4 in 29D). Participles can function as ADJECTIVES (*a **smiling** face, a **closed** book*).

A verb's -*ing* form can also function as a NOUN (***Sneezing** spreads colds*), which is called a **gerund**. Another verb form, the **infinitive,** can also function as a noun. An infinitive is a verb's SIMPLE or base FORM, usually preceded by the word *to* (*We want everyone **to smile***). Verb forms—participles, gerunds, and infinitives—functioning as nouns or MODIFIERS are called VERBALS, as explained in 28E. This chapter can help you make the right choices among verbals.

56A How can I use gerunds and infinitives as subjects?

Gerunds are used more commonly than infinitives as subjects. Sometimes, however, either is acceptable.

- **Choosing** the right health club is important.

- **To choose** the right health club is important.

🔔 **Alert:** When a gerund or an infinitive is used alone as a subject, it is SIN-GULAR and requires a singular verb. When two or more gerunds or infinitives create a COMPOUND SUBJECT, they require a plural verb. (See 28L and 31E.)●

56B When do I use a gerund, not an infinitive, as an object?

Some VERBS must be followed by GERUNDS used as DIRECT OBJECTS. Other verbs must be followed by INFINITIVES. Still other verbs can be followed by either a gerund or an infinitive. (A few verbs can change meaning depending on whether they are followed by a gerund or an infinitive; see 56D.) Quick Box 56.1 (page 744) lists common verbs that must be followed by gerunds, not infinitives.

- Yuri **considered** *calling* [not *to call*] the mayor.

- He **was having trouble** *getting* [not *to get*] a work permit.

- Yuri's boss **recommended** *taking* [not *to take*] an interpreter to the permit agency.

Quick Box 56.1

Verbs and expressions that must be followed by gerunds

admit	dislike	object to
anticipate	enjoy	postpone
appreciate	escape	practice
avoid	finish	put off
consider	give up	quit
consist of	imagine	recall
contemplate	include	resist
delay	mention	risk
deny	mind	suggest
discuss	miss	tolerate

GERUND AFTER *GO*

The word *go* is usually followed by an infinitive: *We can **go to see*** [not *go seeing*] *a movie tonight.* Sometimes, however, *go* is followed by a gerund in phrases such as *go swimming, go fishing, go shopping*, and *go driving: I will **go shopping*** [not *go to shop*] *after work.*

GERUND AFTER *BE* + COMPLEMENT + PREPOSITION

Many common expressions use a form of the verb *be* plus a COMPLEMENT plus a PREPOSITION. In such expressions, use a gerund, not an infinitive, after the preposition. Here is a list of some of the most frequently used expressions in this pattern.

SELECTED EXPRESSIONS USING *BE* + COMPLEMENT + PREPOSITION

be (get) accustomed to	be interested in
be angry about	be prepared for
be bored with	be responsible for
be capable of	be tired of
be committed to	be (get) used to
be excited about	be worried about

- We **are excited about *voting*** [not *to vote*] in the next presidential election.

- Who **will be responsible for *locating*** [not *to locate*] our polling place?

! **Alert:** Always use a gerund, not an infinitive, as the object of a preposition. Be especially careful when the word *to* is functioning as a preposition in a PHRASAL VERB (see 55C): *We are committed **to changing*** [not *to change*] *the rules.*●

56C When do I use an infinitive, not a gerund, as an object?

Quick Box 56.2 lists selected common verbs and expressions that must be followed by INFINITIVES, not GERUNDS, as OBJECTS.

- She **wanted *to go*** [not *wanted going*] to the lecture.

- Only three people **decided *to question*** [not *decided questioning*] the speaker.

Quick Box 56.2			
Verbs and expressions that must be followed by infinitives			
agree	decline	like	promise
arrange	demand	manage	refuse
ask	deserve	mean	wait
attempt	expect	need	want
beg	hesitate	offer	
claim	hope	plan	
decide	learn	pretend	

INFINITIVE AFTER *BE* + COMPLEMENT

Gerunds are common in constructions that use a form of the verb *be* plus a COMPLEMENT and a PREPOSITION (see 56B). However, use an infinitive, not a gerund, when *be* plus a complement is not followed by a preposition.

- We **are eager *to go*** [not *going*] camping.

- I **am ready *to sleep*** [not *sleeping*] in a tent.

INFINITIVE TO INDICATE PURPOSE

Use an infinitive in expressions that indicate purpose: *I read a book **to learn** more about Mayan culture.* This sentence means "I read a book for the purpose of learning more about Mayan culture." *To learn* delivers the idea of purpose more concisely (see Chapter 40) than expressions such as *so that I can* or *in order to.*

INFINITIVE WITH *THE FIRST, THE LAST, THE ONE*

Use an infinitive after the expressions *the first, the last,* and *the one: Nina is the first* **to arrive** [not *arriving*] *and the last* **to leave** [not *leaving*] *every day. She's always the one* **to do** *the most.*

UNMARKED INFINITIVES

Infinitives used without the word *to* are called **unmarked infinitives**, or sometimes *bare infinitives.* An unmarked infinitive may be hard to recognize because it is not preceded by *to.* Some common verbs followed by unmarked infinitives are *feel, have, hear, let, listen to, look at, make* (meaning "compel"), *notice, see,* and *watch.*

- Please let me **take** [not *to take*] you to lunch.   [unmarked infinitive]

- I want **to take** you to lunch.   [marked infinitive]

- I can have Kara **drive** [not *to drive*] us.   [unmarked infinitive]

- I will ask Kara **to drive** us.   [marked infinitive]

The verb *help* can be followed by a marked or an unmarked infinitive. Either is correct: *Help me* **put** [or **to put**] *this box in the car.*

⚠ **Alert:** Be careful to use parallel structure (see Chapter 39) correctly when you use two or more gerunds or infinitives after verbs. If two or more verbal objects follow one verb, put the verbals into the same form.

    NO We went **sailing** and **to scuba dive**.

    YES We went **sailing** and **scuba diving**.

    NO We heard the wind **blow** and the waves **crashing**.

    YES We heard the wind **blow** and the waves **crash**.

    YES We heard the wind **blowing** and the waves **crashing**.

Conversely, if you are using verbal objects with COMPOUND PREDICATES, be sure to use the kind of verbal that each verb requires.

    NO We enjoyed **scuba diving** but do not plan **sailing** again.

        Enjoyed requires a gerund object, and *plan* requires an infinitive object; see Quick Boxes 56.1 and 56.2 in this chapter.

    YES We enjoyed **scuba diving** but do not plan **to sail** again. ●

56D How does meaning change when certain verbs are followed by a gerund or an infinitive?

WITH *STOP*

The VERB *stop* followed by a GERUND means "finish, quit." *Stop* followed by an INFINITIVE means "interrupt one activity to begin another."

- We **stopped** *eating*.

  We finished our meal.

- We **stopped** *to eat*.

  We stopped another activity, such as driving, to eat.

WITH *REMEMBER* AND *FORGET*

The verb *remember* followed by an infinitive means "not to forget to do something": *I must* **remember to talk** *with Isa. Remember* followed by a gerund means "recall a memory": *I* **remember talking** *in my sleep last night.*

The verb *forget* followed by an infinitive means "fail to do something": *If you* **forget to put** *a stamp on that letter, it will be returned. Forget* followed by a gerund means "do something and not recall it": *I* **forget having put** *the stamps in the refrigerator.*

WITH *TRY*

The verb *try* followed by an infinitive means "make an effort": *I* **tried to find** *your jacket.* Followed by a gerund, *try* means "experiment with": *I* **tried jogging** *but found it too difficult.*

56E Why is the meaning unchanged whether a gerund or an infinitive follows sense verbs?

Sense VERBS include words such as *see, notice, hear, observe, watch, feel, listen to,* and *look at.* The meaning of these verbs is usually not affected by whether a GERUND or an INFINITIVE follows as the OBJECT. *I* **saw** *the water* **rise** and *I* **saw** *the water* **rising** both have the same meaning in American English.

● **EXERCISE 56-1** Write the correct form of the verbal object (either a gerund or an infinitive) for each verb in parentheses.

EXAMPLE

(Build) _____ a campfire can be challenging.

Building a campfire can be challenging.

1. While camping outside, people often want (build) _____ a fire for warmth or for cooking food.
2. If you have ever attempted (light) _____ a fire, you know that you need a reliable ignition source, such as sturdy matches or a good lighter.
3. You will be capable of (create) _____ a decent campfire if you use dry wood.
4. For the sake of safety, do not let the fire (spread) _____ outside the fire pit.
5. When you are finished, you need (extinguish) _____ the fire completely. ●

56F How do I choose between *-ing* and *-ed* forms for adjectives?

Deciding whether to use the *-ing* form (PRESENT PARTICIPLE) or the *-ed* form (PAST PARTICIPLE of a regular VERB) as an ADJECTIVE in a specific sentence can be difficult. For example, *I am **amused*** and *I am **amusing*** are both correct in English, but their meanings are very different. To make the right choice, decide whether the modified NOUN or PRONOUN is *causing* or if it is *experiencing* what the participle describes.

Use a present participle (*-ing*) to modify a noun or pronoun that is the agent or the cause of the action.

● Micah described your **interesting** plan.

The noun *plan* causes what its modifier describes—interest; so *interesting* is correct.

● I find your plan **exciting**.

The noun *plan* causes what its modifier describes—excitement; so *exciting* is correct.

Use a past participle (*-ed* in regular verbs) to modify a noun or pronoun that experiences or receives whatever the modifier describes.

● An **interested** committee wants to hear your plan.

The noun *committee* experiences what its modifier describes—interest; so *interested* is correct.

● **Excited** by your plan, they called a board meeting.

The pronoun *they* experiences what its modifier describes—excitement; so *excited* is correct.

Here are frequently used participles that convey very different meanings, depending on whether the *-ed* or the *-ing* form is used.

amused, amusing
annoyed, annoying
appalled, appalling
bored, boring
confused, confusing
depressed, depressing
disgusted, disgusting
fascinated, fascinating

frightened, frightening
insulted, insulting
offended, offending
overwhelmed, overwhelming
pleased, pleasing
reassured, reassuring
satisfied, satisfying
shocked, shocking

● **EXERCISE 56-2**   Choose the correct participle from each pair in parentheses. For help, consult 56F.

Complete
the
Chapter
Exercises

EXAMPLE

It can be a (satisfied, satisfying) <u>satisfying</u> experience to learn about the lives of artists.

1. The artist Frida Kahlo led an (interested, interesting) _____ life.
2. When Kahlo was eighteen, (horrified, horrifying) _____ observers saw her (injured, injuring) _____ in a streetcar accident.
3. A (disappointed, disappointing) _____ Kahlo had to abandon her plan to study medicine.
4. Instead, she began to create paintings filled with (disturbed, disturbing) _____ images.
5. Some art critics consider Kahlo's paintings to be (fascinated, fascinating) _____ works of art, though many people find them (overwhelmed, overwhelming) _____.   ●

57 Modal Auxiliary Verbs

Quick Points   You will learn to

➤ Use modal auxiliary verbs to help main verbs convey information (see 57A–57C)

AUXILIARY VERBS are known as *helping verbs* because adding an auxiliary verb to a MAIN VERB helps the main verb convey additional information (see 29E). For example, the auxiliary verb *do* is important in turning sentences into questions. *You have to sleep* becomes a question when *do* is added: *Do you have to sleep?* The most common auxiliary verbs are forms of *be, have,* and *do.* Quick Boxes 29.6 and 29.7 in section 29E list the forms of these three verbs.

MODAL AUXILIARY VERBS are one type of auxiliary verb. They include *can, could, may, might, should, had better, must, will, would,* and others discussed in this chapter. Modals differ from *be, have,* and *do* used as auxiliary verbs in the specific ways discussed in Quick Box 57.1.

Quick Box 57.1 ■ ■ ■ ■ ■ ■ ■ ■ ■ ■ ■

Modals versus other auxiliary verbs

- Modals in the present future are always followed by the SIMPLE FORM of a main verb: *I **might go** tomorrow.*

- One-word modals have no *-s* ending in the THIRD-PERSON SINGULAR: *She **could** go with me; he **could** go with me; they **could** go with me.* (The two-word modal *have to* changes form to agree with its subject: *I **have to** leave; she **has to** leave.*) Auxiliary verbs other than modals usually change form for third-person singular: *I **do** want to go; he **does** want to go.*

- Some modals change form in the past. Others (*should, would, must,* which convey probability, and *ought to*) use *have* + a PAST PARTICIPLE. *I **can do** it* becomes *I **could do** it* in PAST-TENSE CLAUSES about ability. *I **could do** it* becomes *I **could have done** it* in clauses about possibility.

- Modals convey meaning about ability, necessity, advisability, possibility, and other conditions: For example, *I **can** go* means "I am able to go." Modals do not describe actual occurrences.

57A How do I convey ability, necessity, advisability, possibility, and probability with modals?

CONVEYING ABILITY

The modal *can* conveys ability now (in the present), and *could* conveys ability before (in the past). These words deliver the meaning "able to." For the future, use *will be able to.*

- We **can** work late tonight.

  Can conveys present ability.

- I **could** work late last night, too.

  Could conveys past ability.

- I **will be able to** work late next Monday.

  Will be able is the future tense; *will* here is not a modal.

Adding *not* between a modal and the MAIN VERB makes the CLAUSE negative: *We **cannot** work late tonight; I **could not** work late last night; I **will not be able to** work late next Monday.*

🛈 **Alert:** You will often see negative forms of modals turned into CONTRACTIONS: *can't, couldn't, won't, wouldn't,* and others. Because contractions are considered informal usage by some instructors, you will never be wrong if you avoid them in ACADEMIC WRITING, except when you are reproducing spoken words. ●

CONVEYING NECESSITY

The modals *must* and *have to* convey a need to do something. Both *must* and *have to* are followed by the simple form of the main verb. In the present tense, *have to* changes form to agree with its subject.

- You **must** leave before midnight.

- She **has to** leave when I leave.

In the past tense, *must* is never used to express necessity. Instead, use *had to*.

PRESENT TENSE We **must** study today. We **have to** study today.

PAST TENSE We **had to** [not *must*] take a test yesterday.

The negative forms of *must* and *have to* also have different meanings. *Must not* conveys that something is forbidden; *do not have to* conveys that something is not necessary.

- You **must not** sit there.

  Sitting there is forbidden.

- You **do not have to** sit there.

  Sitting there is not necessary.

CONVEYING ADVISABILITY OR THE NOTION OF A GOOD IDEA

The modals *should* and *ought to* express the idea that doing the action of the main verb is advisable or is a good idea.

- You **should** go to class tomorrow morning.

In the past tense, *should* and *ought to* convey regret or knowing something through hindsight. They mean that good advice was not taken.

- You **should have** gone to class yesterday.
- I **ought to have** called my sister yesterday.

The modal *had better* delivers the meaning of good advice or warning or threat. It does not change form for tense.

- You **had better** see the doctor before your cough gets worse.

Need to is often used to express strong advice, too. Its past-tense form is *needed to*.

- You **need to** take better care of yourself. You **needed to** listen.

CONVEYING POSSIBILITY

The modals *may, might*, and *could* can be used to convey an idea of possibility or likelihood.

- We **may** become hungry before long.
- We **could** eat lunch at the diner next door.

For the past-tense form, use *may, might*, and *could*, followed by *have* and the past participle of the main verb.

- I **could have studied** French in high school, but I studied Spanish instead.

CONVEYING PROBABILITY

Listen
to the
Podcast

In addition to conveying the idea of necessity, the modal *must* can also convey probability or likelihood. It means that a well-informed guess is being made.

- Marisa **must** be a talented actress. She has been chosen to play the lead role in the school play.

When *must* conveys probability, the past tense is *must have* plus the past participle of the main verb.

- I did not see Boris at the party; he **must have left** early.

● **EXERCISE 57-1** Fill in each blank with the past-tense modal auxiliary that expresses the meaning given in parentheses.

EXAMPLE

Last week, I (necessity) <u>had to</u> go on a business trip and leave my dog with my friend.

1. My friend said that he (ability) _____ watch my dog, Patches, for me while I was gone.
2. My friend (possibility) _____ said "No," but he generously agreed to help me.
3. He (probability) _____ taken good care of my dog because Patches seemed happy.
4. I (advisability) _____ packed more food for my dog because my friend had to buy some dog food with his own money.
5. When I returned from my trip, I (necessity) _____ send my friend a thank-you note. ●

57B How do I convey preferences, plans, and past habits with modals?

CONVEYING PREFERENCES

The modal *would rather* expresses a preference. *Would rather*, the PRESENT TENSE, is used with the SIMPLE FORM of the MAIN VERB, and *would rather have*, the PAST TENSE, is used with the PAST PARTICIPLE of the main verb.

● We **would rather see** a comedy than a mystery.

● Carlos **would rather have stayed** home last night.

CONVEYING PLAN OR OBLIGATION

A form of *be* followed by *supposed to* and the simple form of a main verb delivers a meaning of something planned or of an obligation.

● I **was supposed to meet** them at the bus stop.

CONVEYING PAST HABIT

The modals *used to* and *would* express the idea that something happened repeatedly in the past.

● I **used to** hate going to the dentist.

● I **would** dread every single visit.

⚠ **Alert:** Both *used to* and *would* can be used to express repeated actions in the past, but *would* cannot be used for a situation that lasted for a period of time in the past.

    NO I **would** live in Arizona.

    YES I **used to** live in Arizona.●

57C How can I recognize modals in the passive voice?

Modals use the ACTIVE VOICE, as shown in sections sections 57A and 57B. In the active voice, the subject does the action expressed in the MAIN VERB (see 29N and 29O).

    Modals can also use the PASSIVE VOICE (29P). In the passive voice, the doer of the main verb's action is either unexpressed or is expressed as an OBJECT in a PREPOSITIONAL PHRASE starting with the word *by*.

    PASSIVE   The waterfront **can be seen** from my window.
    ACTIVE   **I can see** the waterfront from my window.

    PASSIVE   The tax form **must be signed** by the person who fills it out.
    ACTIVE   The person who fills out the tax form **must sign** it.

● **EXERCISE 57-2**   Select the correct choice from the words in parentheses and write it in the blank. For help, consult 57A through 57C.

EXAMPLE

When I was younger, I (would, used to) <u>used to</u> love to go bicycle riding.

1. You (ought to have, ought have) _____ called yesterday as you had promised you would.
2. Judging by the size of the puddles in the street outside, it (must be rained, must have rained) _____ all night long.
3. Ingrid (must not have, might not have been) _____ as early for the interview as she claims she was.
4. After all the studying he did, Pedro (should have, should have been) _____ less frightened by the exam.
5. I have to go home early today, although I really (cannot, should not) _____ leave before the end of the day because of all the work I have to do. ●

● **EXERCISE 57-3** Select the correct choice from the words in parentheses and write it in the blank. For help, consult 57A through 57C.

Complete
the
Chapter
Exercises

EXAMPLE

We (must have, must) <u>must</u> study this afternoon.

1. Unfortunately, I (should not, cannot) _____ go to the movies with you because I have to take care of my brother tonight.
2. Juan (would have, would have been) _____ nominated class valedictorian if he had not moved to another city.
3. You (ought not have, ought not to have) _____ arrived while the meeting was still in progress.
4. Louise (must be, must have been) _____ sick to miss the party last week.
5. Had you not called in advance, you (may not have, may not have been) _____ aware of the traffic on the expressway. ●

Specific Writing Situations

58

An Overview of Writing Across the Curriculum

Quick Points   You will learn to

➤ Adapt your writing to various college courses (see 58A).
➤ Use cue words to tell what your college writing needs to accomplish (see 58B).

58A   What is writing across the curriculum?

Watch
the Video

Writing across the curriculum refers to the writing you do in college courses beyond first-year composition. (A related term is "writing in the disciplines," which usually refers to writing that is specific to individual majors.) Many features are common to good writing across disciplines, but there are also important differences. A chemistry lab report, for example, differs from a history paper. Quick Box 58.1 summarizes different types of writing across the curriculum.

Quick Box 58.1

Comparing the disciplines

Discipline	Types of Assignments	Primary sources	Secondary sources	Usual documentation styles
HUMANITIES history, languages, literature, philosophy, art, music, theater	essays, response statements, reviews, analyses, original works such as stories, poems, auto-biographies	literary works, manuscripts, paintings and sculptures, historical documents, films, plays, photographs, artifacts from popular culture	reviews, journal articles, research papers, books	MLA, CM
SOCIAL SCIENCES psychology, sociology, anthro-pology, education	research reports, case studies, reviews of the literature, analyses	surveys, interviews, observations, experiments, tests and measures	journal articles, scholarly books, literature reviews	APA

continued >>

Quick Box 58.1   (continued)

Discipline	Types of Assignments	Primary sources	Secondary sources	Usual documentation styles
NATURAL SCIENCES biology, chemistry, physics, mathematics	reports, research proposals and reports, science reviews	experiments, field notes, direct observations, measurements	journal articles, research papers, books	often CSE but varies by discipline

58B   What do I need to know about audience and purpose across the curriculum?

Unless an instructor or assignment tells you otherwise, the audience for academic writing consists of scholars, professors, and students in particular fields. As a result, you need to follow the conventions (including format and organization, types of evidence, tone and style, and documentation style) that are expected in each discipline. It's useful to study examples of the kinds of writing you've been asked to produce.

Purposes can vary widely. Some tasks mainly require explaining information, while others require making an argument. Most assignments contain **cue words** that tell what your writing needs to accomplish. Quick Box 58.2 presents some common cue words.

Quick Box 58.2   ■ ■ ■ ■ ■ ■ ■ ■ ■ ■ ■

Some common cue words

Cue Word	Meaning
ANALYZE	Separate into parts and discuss each, often including how it contributes to a meaning or implication.
CLASSIFY	Arrange in groups based on shared characteristics or functions.
CRITIQUE	Give your evaluation and support your reasons for it.
COMPARE	Show similarities and differences.

continued >>

Quick Box 58.2   (continued)

Cue Word	Meaning
DEFINE	Tell what something is to differentiate it from similar things.
DISCUSS	Explain and comment on, in an organized way, the various issues or elements involved.
EXPLAIN	Make clear a complex thing or process that needs to be illuminated or interpreted.
INTERPRET	Explain the meaning or significance of something.
REVIEW	Evaluate or summarize critically.
SUMMARIZE	Lay out the major points of something.
SUPPORT	Argue in favor of something.

59 Writing About the Humanities

Quick Points   You will learn to

➤ Understand the different types of humanities papers (see 59B).
➤ Understand different types of literature papers and identify major elements to analyze (see 59E–59F).

59A What are the humanities?

The humanities seek to represent and understand human experience, creativity, thought, and values. These disciplines usually include literature, languages, philosophy, and history; some colleges treat the fine arts (music, art, dance, theater, and creative writing) as part of the humanities.

59B What types of papers do I write in the humanities?

Writing in the humanities covers many types and purposes.

59B.1 Summaries

Occasionally your instructor will request an objective summary of a text; you might need to tell the plot of a novel or present the main points of an article (see 29B). Generally, however, a summary is a means to a greater end. For example, writing an interpretation often requires you to summarize parts of the source so that your points about it are clear.

59B.2 Syntheses

SYNTHESIS relates several texts, ideas, or pieces of information to one another (see 18F). For example, you might read several accounts of the events leading up to the Civil War and then write a synthesis that explains what caused that war.

59B.3 Responses

In a response, you give your personal reaction to a work, supported by explanations of your reasoning (see 20C). For example, do you think Hamlet's behavior makes sense? Do you agree with Peter Singer's philosophical arguments against using animals in scientific experiments? Clarify whether your instructor wants you to justify a response with references to a text.

59B.4 Interpretations

An interpretation explains the meaning or significance of a particular text, event, or work of art (Quick Box 59.1). For example, what does Plato's *Republic* suggest about the nature of a good society? What was the significance of the 9/11 tragedy for Americans' sense of security? Your reply isn't right or wrong; rather, you present your point of view and explain your reasoning. The quality of your reasoning determines how successfully you convey your point.

59B.5 Narratives

A narrative constructs a coherent story from separate facts or events. In a history class, for example, you might examine news events, laws, diaries and journals, and related materials to create a chronological version of what happened. You might interview people or others who knew them, read their letters or other writings, and consult related SOURCES, all to form a coherent story of their lives. Some writing assignments in the humanities may ask you to write about your memories or experiences. Chapter 10 provides detailed advice.

59B.6   Textual analyses

The humanities use a number of **analytical frameworks**, or systematic ways of investigating a work. Quick Box 59.1 summarizes several of them.

Quick Box 59.1

Selected analytical frameworks used in the humanities

RHETORICAL	Explores how and why people use LOGICAL, EMOTIONAL, and ETHICAL APPEALS to create desired effects on specific audiences, in specific situations (see 14C).
CULTURAL OR NEW HISTORICAL	Explores how social, economic, and cultural forces influence ideas, texts, art, laws, customs, and so on. Also explores how individual texts or events provide broader understandings of the past or present.
DECONSTRUCTIONIST	Assumes that the meaning of any given text is not stable or "in" the work. Rather, meaning always depends on contexts and the interests of the people in power. The goal of deconstruction is to produce multiple possible meanings of a work, often to undermine traditional interpretations.
FEMINIST	Focuses on how women are presented and treated, concentrating especially on power relationships between men and women.
FORMALIST	Centers on matters of structure, form, and traditional literary devices (plot, rhythm, imagery, symbolism, and others; see Quick Box 59.2).
MARXIST	Assumes that the most important forces in human experience are economic and material ones. Focuses on power differences between economic classes of people and the effects of those differences.
READER-RESPONSE	Emphasizes how the individual reader determines meaning. The reader's personal history, values, experiences, relationships, and previous reading all contribute to how he or she interprets a particular work or event.

Figure 59.1 Use analytic frameworks to interpret this photograph.

59C Which documentation style do I use in writing about the humanities?

Most fields in the humanities use the Modern Language Association (MLA) documentation style, which we explain and illustrate in Chapter 25. Some disciplines in the humanities use *Chicago Manual* (CM) style, as we explain in Chapter 27.

59D How do I write about literature?

Literature encompasses fiction (novels and stories), drama (plays, scripts, and some films), and poetry (poems and lyrics), as well as nonfiction with artistic qualities (memoirs, personal essays, and so on). Since ancient times, literature has represented human experience, entertained readers, and enlarged their perspectives about themselves, others, and different ways of living.

Writing effective papers about literature involves more than summarizing the plot. It involves CRITICAL THINKING and SYNTHESIS. In such papers, you state a CLAIM (an observation or a position about the work of literature) and convince your readers that your thesis is reasonable. For support, you make direct references to the work itself, by summarizing, paraphrasing, and quoting specific passages (see Ch. 18) and by explaining precisely *why* and *how* the selected passages support your interpretation.

59E How do I write different types of papers about literature?

When you read a literary work closely, look for details or passages that relate to your thesis. Mark up the text as you read by selectively underlining passages or by writing notes, comments, or questions in the margin.

59E.1 Writing a personal response

A personal response paper explains your reaction to a literary work or some aspect of it. You might write about why you did or did not enjoy reading a particular work, discuss whether situations in the work are similar to your personal experiences, explain why you agree or disagree with the author's point of view, or so on. For example, how do you react if a likable character breaks the law? As with all effective papers about literature, you need to explain your response by discussing specific elements of the text.

59E.2 Writing an interpretation

An interpretation explains the message or viewpoint that you think the work conveys. Most works of literature are open to more than one interpretation. Your task, then, is not to discover a single "right answer." Instead, your task is to determine a possible interpretation and provide an argument that supports it. The questions in Quick Box 59.2 (referring to the complete poem on pages 767–768) can help you write an effective interpretation paper.

Quick Box 59.2

■ ■ ■ ■ ■ ■ ■ ■ ■ ■ ■

Questions for an interpretation paper

1. What is a central theme of the work? For example, in the poem "Sympathy," a central theme might be despair. (The poem appears in 59H.)

2. How do particular parts of the work relate to the theme? In "Sympathy," the bird flying against the cage shows despair.

3. If patterns exist in the work, what might they mean? Patterns include repeated images, situations, and words. In "Sympathy," the phrase "I know why the caged bird . . ." forms a pattern.

4. What meaning does the author create through the elements listed in Quick Box 59.3?

5. Why might the work end as it does?

59E.3   Writing a formal analysis

A formal analysis explains how elements of a literary work function to create meaning or effect. Your instructor may ask you to concentrate on one element or to discuss how a writer develops a theme through several elements. The paper by student Sara Kho (see 59H) is an example of an interpretation based on a formal analysis. Quick Box 59.3 describes some of the major literary elements you might use in formal analyses.

Quick Box 59.3   ■ ■ ■ ■ ■ ■ ■ ■ ■ ■

Major elements to analyze in literary works

PLOT	Events and their sequence
THEME	Central idea or message
STRUCTURE	Organization and relationship of parts to each other and to the whole
CHARACTERIZATION	Traits, thoughts, and actions of the people in the work
SETTING	Time and place of the action
POINT OF VIEW	Perspective or position from which a narrator or a main character presents the material
STYLE	How words and sentence structure present the material
IMAGERY	Descriptive language that creates mental pictures for the reader
TONE	Author's attitude toward the subject of the work—and sometimes toward the reader—as expressed through choice of words, imagery, and point of view
FIGURES OF SPEECH	Unusual use or combination of words, such as META-PHOR or SIMILE, for enhanced vividness or effect
SYMBOLISM	The use of a specific object or event to represent a deeper, often abstract, meaning or idea
RHYTHM	Beat, meter
RHYME	Repetition of similar sounds for their auditory effect

59E.4 Writing a cultural analysis

A cultural analysis relates a literary work to broader historical, social, cultural, or political situations. Quick Box 59.4 lists some common topics for cultural analysis.

Quick Box 59.4 ■ ■ ■ ■ ■ ■ ■ ■ ■ ■ ■

Major topics for cultural analyses

GENDER	How does a work portray women or men and define or challenge their roles in society?
CLASS	How does a work portray relationships among the upper, middle, and lower classes? How do characters' actions or perspectives result from their wealth and power—or from their poverty and powerlessness?
RACE AND ETHNICITY	How does a work portray the influences of race and ethnicity on the characters' actions, status, and values?
HISTORY	How does a work reflect—or challenge—past events and values in a society?
AUTOBIOGRAPHY	How did the writer's life experiences influence his or her work?
GENRE	How is the work similar to or different from other works of its type (for example, plays, sonnets, mysteries, comic novels, memoirs)?

59F What special rules apply to writing about literature?

59F.1 Using correct verb tenses

👁 Watch the Video

Always use the PRESENT TENSE when you describe or discuss a literary work or any of its elements: *Walter* [a character] ***makes** a difficult decision when he **turns down** Linder's offer to buy the house.* In addition, always use the present tense for discussing what an author has done in a specific work: *Lorraine Hansberry, author of* A Raisin in the Sun, ***explores** not only powerful racial issues but also common family dynamics.* Always use a PAST-TENSE VERB to discuss historical events or biographical information: *Lorraine Hansberry's* A Raisin in the Sun ***was** the first play by an African American woman to be produced on Broadway.*

59F.2 Using your own ideas and using secondary sources

Some assignments call only for your own ideas about a literary work. Other assignments call for you to use SECONDARY SOURCES, in which experts discuss the literary text or other material related to your topic. You can locate secondary sources by using the research process explained in Chapter 22.

Watch the Video

59G How do I use documentation in writing about literature?

Documenting primary sources tells your readers exactly where to find the specific passages in the literary work you're quoting or summarizing. Documenting secondary sources credits the authors of those works and avoids PLAGIARISM. Unless your instructor requests another documentation style, use MLA STYLE (Ch. 25) for writing about literature.

59H A student's essay about literature

59H.1 Working on the assignment

Sara Kho, a student in first-year English, fulfilled an assignment to write an interpretation of Paul Laurence Dunbar's poem "Sympathy." In the process of drafting her paper, Sara realized that the images and the order in which they appeared are vital to understanding the poem.

59H.2 Learning about the poet, Paul Laurence Dunbar

Paul Laurence Dunbar was perhaps the first African American poet to receive wide critical acclaim. He was born in 1872, in Dayton, Ohio, to a mother who was a former slave and a father who had escaped slavery to fight in the Civil War. Supporters of his work included the Wright brothers (with whom he attended Dayton Central High) and the famous abolitionist Frederick Douglass. He worked briefly at the Library of Congress and read in various cities in the United States and in England. After producing twelve books of poetry, four books of short stories, a play, and five novels, he died in 1906, at the age of only 33.

View the Model Document

SYMPATHY

Paul Laurence Dunbar

> I know what the caged bird feels, alas!
> When the sun is bright on the upland slopes;
> When the wind stirs soft through the springing grass,
> And the river flows like a stream of glass;
> When the first bird sings and the first bud opes,

5

And the faint perfume from its chalice steals—
I know what the caged bird feels!

I know why the caged bird beats his wing
Till its blood is red on the cruel bars;
For he must fly back to his perch and cling   10
When he fain would be on the bough a-swing;
And a pain still throbs in the old, old scars
And they pulse again with a keener sting—
I know why he beats his wing!

I know why the caged bird sings, ah me,   15
When his wing is bruised and his bosom sore,—
When he beats his bars and he would be free;
It is not a carol of joy or glee,
But a prayer that he sends from his heart's deep core,
But a plea, that upward to Heaven he flings—   20
I know why the caged bird sings!

Student's essay about literature

Kho 1

Sara Kho

Professor Parrish

English 100

4 Mar. 2012

Images, Progression, and Meaning in "Sympathy"

How can a writer artfully convey the despair of not having

freedom? Paul Laurence Dunbar faces that challenge in his

poem "Sympathy," which uses the central image of a bird in

a cage. By choosing a creature that did nothing to deserve

its imprisonment, Dunbar invites readers to empathize with

anyone who has experienced a similar fate. The poem artfully

continued >>

builds its message through precise images and a meaningful procession of ideas.

"Sympathy" appears in three seven-line stanzas that closely match each other. The rhyme scheme in each is ABAABCC, and the first and seventh lines of each stanza begin with "I know what" or "I know why." Those lines, in fact, are nearly identical, and the result is a tightly compressed, even repetitive poem that makes readers pay close attention to any changes. Those changes create a dramatic progression in the poem.

The imagery in the first stanza focuses on the world beyond the cage. It's a world of strong visual senses, the sun "bright upon the upland slopes" (line 2) and the river flowing "like a stream of glass" (4). But Dunbar also invokes smell, with the flower's perfume, and he invokes sounds, including the wind softly stirring the grass (3) and a bird singing (5). (In the third stanza, that singing becomes a key idea—and a much different one.) References to the sun on the hills and to the "first bird" and "first bud" suggest dawn and possibilities, with potential that is almost holy. After all, the flower bud is a "chalice," a sacred vessel holding communion wine (6). However, the caged bird is removed from this world, and while the poet says, "I know what the caged bird feels" (7), he does not specifically name or describe that feeling. Instead, we are left to draw our own conclusions, comparing the limits of the cage to the possibilities of nature.

The imagery in the second stanza is much harsher and more concrete. Instead of the internal state of the bird's feeling, the poet describes an external, physical action, the bird's wings

continued >>

Kho 3

beating against the cage "Till its blood is red on the cruel bars" (9). Clearly this is a futile, painful, and ongoing action. The bird's "pain still throbs" (12), even "When his wing is bruised and his bosom sore" (16). Yet the bird persists, desperately longing to fly from branch to branch rather than to sit on a single artificial perch, in a cage that denies flight to a creature whose nature is to fly.

The brutal images of the second stanza give way to the surprising insights of the third one, which also have a physical action but of a different sort. We generally think of bird songs as pretty sounds, conveying happiness. However, "Sympathy" makes them "not a carol of joy or glee" (18) but, rather, something mournful and somber. The song is an extension of and accompaniment to the self-torture of wings beating against the cage. By calling that song a "prayer" and a "plea" (20), the poet transforms the bird from a mere animal behaving instinctively to a being with consciousness performing intentionally, calling to heaven. By separating one of heaven's creatures from nature, whoever has imprisoned the bird has violated not only its freedom but also the divine order. Further, it makes listening to and enjoying the bird's song almost a perverse act, since the bird sings out of torment. The poem's progression from feeling to beating to singing, then, traces a progression from instinct to action to hope.

Of course, the poem is about more than birds in cages. The key refrain is "I know why," which emphasizes the poet's clear identification with the bird. He can know why the bird feels, acts, and prays because he experiences the same loss of

continued >>

freedom; he feels, acts, and prays for similar reasons. Given Dunbar's autobiography, it's obvious to see this poem as commenting directly on the treatment of African Americans in the nineteenth century, even after the Civil War, as attitudes and events continued to restrict former slaves. The images powerfully support that interpretation.

However, Dunbar carefully doesn't restrict the poem only to people in one time and situation. By choosing the common image of a bird in a cage, he invites readers to identify with anyone, in any place and time, who has lost his or her freedom, for reasons beyond their control. Some of those people—and readers may be among them—may be physically separated from the world, but for others, the "imprisonment" may be more emotional or metaphorical. Dunbar, finally, was free to write and publish this poem, but that didn't diminish his sympathy with the caged bird—or our own sympathy with him.

Work Cited

Dunbar, Paul Laurence. "Sympathy." *The Collected Poetry of Paul Laurence Dunbar*. Ed. Joanne M. Braxton. Charlottesville: UP of Virginia, 1993. 102. Print.

60 Writing in the Social and Natural Sciences

■ ■ ■ ■ ■ ■ ■ ■ ■ ■

Quick Points   You will learn to

➤ Understand different types of papers in the social sciences (see 60B).
➤ Understand different types of papers in the natural sciences (see 60E).

60A   What are the social sciences?

The social sciences, which focus on people as individuals and in groups, include disciplines like economics, education, geography, political science, psychology, and sociology. In the social sciences, PRIMARY SOURCES include surveys and questionnaires, observations, interviews, and experiments. To prepare a questionnaire, use the guidelines in Quick Box 21.4 on page 262. For advice on collecting information through observation, see 21L, where we also explain interviewing strategies, especially in Quick Box 21.5.

The social sciences sometimes use data from experiments as a source. For example, if you want to learn how people react in a particular situation, you can set up that situation artificially and bring individuals (known as "subjects") into it to observe their behavior. With all methods of inquiry in the social sciences, you are required to treat subjects fairly and honestly, not in ways that could harm their body, mind, or reputation.

60B   What are different types of papers in the social sciences?

Watch
the Video

Instructors will sometimes assign the same kinds of writing in the social sciences as in the humanities (see 58C). Four additional types of papers are case studies, ethnographies, research reports, and research papers (or reviews of the literature).

60B.1   Case studies

A **case study** is an intensive study of one group or individual. Case studies are important in psychology, social work, education, medicine, and similar fields in which it's useful to form a comprehensive portrait of people. A case study is usually presented in a relatively fixed format, but the specific parts and their order vary. Most case studies contain the following components:

1. Basic identifying information about the individual or group
2. A history of the individual or group
3. Observations of the individual's or group's behavior
4. Conclusions and perhaps recommendations as a result of the observations

60B.2 Ethnographies

Ethnographies are comprehensive descriptions and interpretations of people interacting in a particular situation. Ethnographies commonly are written in education or the social sciences, with anthropology and sociology being prime examples. A sociologist might compose an ethnography of a classroom, for instance, to understand the interactions and relationships among students. The level of details needed in ethnographies has been described by anthropologist Clifford Geertz as "thick description." The more notes you take during observations, the better, because you can't be sure which ones will be important until you analyze and reflect on the information.

60B.3 Research reports

Research reports explain your own original research based on primary sources. Those sources may be interviews, questionnaires, observations, or experiments. Research reports in the social sciences often follow a prescribed format:

1. Statement of the problem
2. Background, sometimes including a review of the literature
3. Methodology
4. Results
5. Discussion of findings

60B.4 Research papers (or reviews of the literature)

More often for students, social science research requires you to summarize, analyze, and synthesize SECONDARY SOURCES. These sources are usually articles and books that report or discuss the findings of other people's primary research. To prepare a review of the literature, comprehensively gather and analyze the sources that have been published on a specific topic. *Literature* in this sense simply means "the body of work on a subject." Sometimes a review of the literature is a part of a longer paper, usually in the "background" section of a research report. Other times the entire paper might be an extensive review of the literature.

60C What documentation style do I use in the social sciences?

The most commonly used DOCUMENTATION STYLE in the social sciences is that of the American Psychological Association (APA). We describe APA documentation style and provide a sample student paper in Chapter 26. *Chicago Manual* (CM) documentation style is sometimes used in the social sciences (see Chapter 27).

60D What are the natural sciences?

The natural sciences include disciplines such as astronomy, biology, chemistry, geology, and physics. The sciences seek to describe and explain natural phenomena. The *scientific method*, commonly used in the sciences to make discoveries, is a procedure for gathering information related to a specific hypothesis. Quick Box 60.1 gives guidelines for using this method.

Quick Box 60.1   ■ ■ ■ ■ ■ ■ ■ ■ ■ ■ ■

Guidelines for using the scientific method

1. Formulate a tentative explanation (a *hypothesis*) for a scientific phenomenon.
2. Read and summarize previously published information related to your hypothesis.
3. Plan a method of investigation to test your hypothesis.
4. Experiment, following exactly the investigative procedures you have outlined.
5. Observe closely the results of the experiment, and write notes carefully.
6. Analyze the results. Do they confirm the hypothesis?
7. Write a report of your research. At the end, you can suggest additional hypotheses that might be investigated.

60E How do I write different types of papers in the natural sciences?

Two major types of papers in the sciences are reports and reviews.

60E.1 Science reports

Science reports tell about observations and experiments. When they describe laboratory experiments, they're usually called lab reports. Formal reports feature the eight elements identified in Quick Box 60.2. Less formal reports, which are sometimes assigned in introductory college courses, might not include an abstract or a review of the literature. Ask your instructor which sections to include in your report.

Quick Box 60.2

Parts of a science report

1. **Title.** Precisely describes your report's topic.

2. **Abstract.** Provides a short overview of the report to help readers decide whether or not your research is of interest to them.

3. **Introduction.** States the purpose behind your research and presents the hypothesis. Any needed background information and a review of the literature appear here.

4. **Methods and materials.** Describes the equipment, material, and procedures used.

5. **Results.** Provides the information obtained from your efforts. Charts, graphs, and tables help present the data in a way that is easy for readers to grasp.

6. **Discussion.** Presents your interpretation and evaluation of the results. Did your efforts support your hypothesis? If not, can you suggest why not? Use concrete evidence in discussing your results.

7. **Conclusion.** Lists conclusions about the hypothesis and the outcomes of your efforts, paying particular attention to any theoretical implications that can be drawn from your work. Be specific in suggesting further research.

8. **List of references.** Presents references cited in the review of the literature, if any. Its format conforms to the requirements of the DOCUMENTATION STYLE in the particular science that is your subject.

60E.2 Science reviews

A science review discusses published information on a scientific topic. The purpose of the review is to synthesize for readers all the current knowledge about the issue. Sometimes, science reviews go a step further to present a new interpretation of previously published material; in such a review, the writer presents EVIDENCE to persuade readers that the new interpretation is valid.

If you're required to write a science review, you want to

1. choose a very limited scientific issue;
2. use information that is current—the more recently published the articles, books, and journals you consult, the better;
3. accurately paraphrase and summarize material (see Ch. 18); and
4. document your sources.

If your review runs longer than two or three pages, you might want to use headings to help readers understand your paper's organization and idea progression.

60F Which documentation style do I use in the natural sciences?

Documentation styles differ among the various sciences. A common style is that of the Council of Science Editors (CSE), described in Chapter 27.

61 Writing Under Pressure

■ ■ ■ ■ ■ ■ ■ ■ ■ ■

Quick Points   You will learn to

➤ Identify skills that will help you write essay exams (see 61B).

61A When will I need to write under pressure?

All writers, student and professional, sometimes have to produce effective writing in a short time. Obvious examples are essay exams. Writers in the workplace frequently have to generate correspondence or reports in strict time limits.

61B How do I prepare for essay exams?

Begin preparing for exams well before the day of the test. Attend class diligently and take good notes. Be an active reader (see 3E).

Perhaps the best preparation comes from writing practice exams under time limits. Your instructors may offer questions from previous years or provide new questions to guide your studying. Alternatively, you may generate your own exam questions using cue words and key content words drawn from course material. Finally, ask your instructor whether an exam is "open book" so that you'll know if you can use books or notes during the test.

Because essay exams have firm time limits, you need to go through all of the steps in the WRITING PROCESS (see Ch. 5), but at high speed. Following are useful strategies.

- **Relax.** Never begin writing immediately. Instead, take a deep breath and let it out slowly to relax and focus your thoughts.

- **Read.** Read the test from beginning to end without skimming, so that you understand the questions completely. If you have a choice among topics, and equal credit is given to each, select the topics you know the most about.

- **Plan your time.** If the instructor indicates what percentage of your grade each question will affect, allot your time to your greatest advantage. Make sure to allow time for planning, DRAFTING, and proofreading.

- **Underline cue words.** These words tell you what you need to do in your essay. Quick Box 58.1, in section 58B, lists some common cue words with their meanings. Look for words such as *analyze, classify*, and *criticize*. An essay question might read like this:

  - **Analyze** Socrates' discussion of "good life" and "good death."

    Separate the concepts of "good life" and "good death" into parts and discuss each part.

- **Circle key content words.** Look for the keywords or major terms in a statement or question. An essay question might ask:

  - Review the effectiveness of **labor unions** in the **U.S. economy**.

    The key content words are *labor unions* and *U.S. economy*.

- **Use your time fully.** The best writers use every second available to write and polish. (Trust us, we've been in that spot often and have never regretted working right up to the time limit.)

62 Making Presentations

■ ■ ■ ■ ■ ■ ■ ■ ■ ■

Quick Points   You will learn to

➤ Adjust your presentation to fit your audience and purpose (see 62A–62C).
➤ Organize your presentation (see 62D).
➤ Use multimedia in your presentation (see 62E).

62A What are presentations?

Presentations—speeches often supported with multimedia tools—are common not only in college but also in work and public settings. Preparing a presentation and drafting a paper involve similar processes (see Ch. 5). This chapter provides additional advice.

62B How does my situation focus my presentation?

You need to adjust presentations to fit PURPOSES, AUDIENCES, roles, and any special considerations. Consider three different situations.

• You want to address a group of students to inform them about a film club you're starting.

• You need to persuade a management group at work to adopt a new set of procedures for making purchasing decisions.

• You plan to give a toast at a friend's wedding to express your feelings and to entertain the wedding guests.

Different approaches will be successful in each instance because your purpose and audience are different.

62C How do I adapt my message to my audience?

Adapting your presentation to your listeners means holding their interest and being responsive to their viewpoints. Consult the strategies for analyzing AUDIENCES in Quick Box 4.5 on page 54. Quick Box 62.1 suggests how to adapt your message to three types of audience.

> ### Quick Box 62.1 ■ ■ ■ ■ ■ ■ ■ ■ ■ ■
>
> **Adapting a presentation to your audience**
>
> | | |
> |---|---|
> | **UNINFORMED AUDIENCE** | Start with the basics and then move to a few new ideas. Define new terms and concepts and avoid unnecessary technical terms. Use visual aids and give examples. Repeat key ideas—but not too often. |
> | **INFORMED AUDIENCE** | Never give more than a quick overview of the basics. Devote most of your time to new ideas and concepts. |
> | **MIXED AUDIENCE** | In your introduction, acknowledge the more informed audience members who are present. Explain that you're going to review the basic concepts briefly so that everyone can build from the same knowledge base. Move as soon as possible toward more complex concepts. |

62D How do I organize my presentation?

A presentation has three parts: introduction, body, and conclusion.

62D.1 Introducing yourself and your topic

All audience members want to know three things about a speaker: Who are you? What are you going to talk about? Why should I listen? To respond effectively to these unasked questions, try these suggestions.

- Grab your audience's attention with an interesting question, quotation, or statistic; a bit of background information; a compliment; or an anecdote. If necessary to establish your credibility—even if someone has introduced you—briefly and humbly mention your qualifications as a speaker about your topic.

- Give your audience a road map of your talk: Tell where you're starting, where you're going, and how you intend to get there. Your listeners need to know that you won't waste their time.

62D.2 Following your road map

Listening to a presentation is very different from reading an essay. Audiences generally need help following the speaker's line of reasoning. Here are some strategies to keep your listeners' minds from wandering.

- Signal clearly where you are on your road map by using cue word transitions such as *first, second,* and *third; subsequently, therefore,* and *furthermore;* or *before, then,* and *next.*

- Define unfamiliar terms and concepts and follow up with strong, memorable examples.

- Occasionally tell the audience what you consider significant, memorable, or especially relevant and why. Do so sparingly, at key points.

- Provide occasional summaries at points of transition. Recap what you've covered and say how it relates to what's coming next.

62D.3 Wrapping up your presentation

Try ending with these suggestions.

- Never let your voice volume fall or your clarity of pronunciation falter because the end is in sight.

- Don't introduce new ideas at the last minute.

- Signal that you are wrapping up your presentation using verbal cues, such as "In conclusion" and "Finally." When you say "finally," mean it!

- Make a dramatic, decisive statement; cite a memorable quotation; or issue a challenge. Allow a few seconds of silence, and then say "thank you." Use body language, such as stepping slightly back from the podium, and then sit down.

62E How do I use multimedia in presentations?

Multimedia elements such as visual aids, sound, and video can reinforce key ideas in your presentation by providing illustrations or concrete images for the audience.

62E.1 Using traditional visual aids

Here are various types of visual aids and their uses. When using them, always make text or graphics large enough to be read easily at a distance.

- **Posters** can dramatize a point, often with color or images. Make sure a poster is large enough for everyone in your audience to see it.

- **Dry-erase boards** are preferable to chalkboards because colors on them are visually appealing. Use them to roughly sketch an illustration or to emphasize a technical word.

- **Handouts** are useful when the topic calls for a longer text or when you want to give your audience something to refer to later. Short, simple handouts work best during a presentation. Always include DOCUMENTATION information for any SOURCES you used. A strategic handout can be a useful backup just in case other technologies are missing or broken. Remember to wait until everyone has one before you begin speaking about it.

62E.2   Using presentation software

PowerPoint, the most widely used presentation software, can create digital slides. (A similar program, "Impress," is free from www.openoffice.org.) These slides can contain words, images, or combinations of both. To project your slides during a presentation, you need an LCD projector connected to your computer and a separate screen. See Figure 62.1.

View the Model Document

Never present so much information that your audience spends more time reading than to listening to you. Also, never simply read large amounts of text from your slides; your audience will quickly—and rightfully—become bored. People have coined the phrase "death by PowerPoint" in despair at presenters who simply repeat what's written on slides. For advice on designing presentation slides, see Quick Box 62.2 (page 782).

Figure 62.1   A sample PowerPoint slide.

Quick Box 62.2

■ ■ ■ ■ ■ ■ ■ ■ ■ ■ ■

Guidelines for designing PowerPoint or similar presentation slides

- **Keep slides simple.** Use only a few very short lines of text on each slide. An old rule is "six by six": no more than six lines, each with no more than six words.
- **Keep slides readable.** Make sure words and images are large enough to be read by everyone. Contrast is important. Use black text (or very dark colors) on a white background, or use white text on a very dark background.
- **Keep slides interesting.** A single well-chosen image can enhance a slide. Sometimes, in fact, a slide that consists only of an image (a photograph, a chart, or other graphic) can be quite effective.
- **Keep slides few.** It's far more effective to have 5 well-chosen and designed slides for a short talk than it is to have 20.

62E.3 Using sound or video clips

A brief sound file (for example, a few sentences from a speech) or a video clip (perhaps 20 to 30 seconds of footage) can occasionally help you illustrate a point. Keep them brief and be absolutely sure that your audience will recognize how they enhance your message and aren't just for show.

62E.4 Planning for multimedia in your presentation

Few things are more frustrating for you or annoying to your audience than technical problems during a presentation. Beforehand, make sure all your visual aids and multimedia will work well—and have a backup plan at hand in case they fail. Rehearse carefully with technology so that you can use it seamlessly during your presentation.

62F What presentation styles can I use?

Presentation style is the way you deliver what you have to say. You may memorize your talk, read it, speak without notes, or map it. Memorized talks often sound unnatural. Unless you've mastered the material well enough to recite it in a relaxed way, choose another presentation style. Reading your presentation aloud can bore your audience. If you have no choice but to read, avoid speaking in a monotone. Vary your pace and pitch. In general, avoid speaking without notes until you have considerable experience giving speeches, unless otherwise instructed by your professor or supervisor.

We recommend mapping your presentation. Mapping means creating a brief outline of your presentation's main points and examples, then using that outline to cue yourself.

Your body language can either add to or detract from your message. Eye contact is your most important nonverbal communication tool because it communicates confidence and shows respect for your listeners. Smile or nod at your audience as you begin. If you use a podium, stand squarely behind it before you begin speaking. When gestures aren't needed, rest your hands on the podium—don't scratch your head, dust your clothing, or fidget.

62G How do I make a collaborative presentation?

Group presentations are common in academic and business settings. Here are some guidelines to follow.

- Make sure, when choosing a topic or a position about an issue, that most members of the group are familiar with the subject.

- Lay out clearly each member's responsibilities for preparing the presentation.

- Agree on firm time limits for each person, if all members of the group are expected to speak for an equal amount of time. If there is no such requirement, people who enjoy public speaking can take more responsibility for delivery, and others can do more of the preparatory work or contribute in other ways.

- Allow enough time for practice. Plan at least two complete run-throughs of your presentation, using multimedia elements if you have them. Though each member can practice his or her own part alone, schedule practice sessions for the entire presentation as a group.

- As you practice your presentation, have different group members watch in order to make suggestions.

Writing for Digital Environments

63

Quick Points You will learn to

➤ Understand how to write for blogs and wikis (see 63B–63C).
➤ Understand how to create video and sound recordings and to produce Web sites (see 63D–63F).
➤ Understand good manners and privacy online (see 63G–63H).

63A What is writing for digital environments?

Writing for digital environments means producing texts that can best—or perhaps that can only—be read through computers, generally online. Examples include blogs, wikis, videos, podcasts, photo essays, Web pages, and social media. Digital composing (sometimes called "multimodal writing") opens possibilities that are difficult or impossible in traditional print papers. Digital environments

- Allow writers easily to incorporate images without the expense of printing.
- Allow writers to create or incorporate sound or visual recordings.
- Allow links to other sources available online.
- Allow instant publication to readers far and wide.
- Allow interactions, so that readers can share comments or writers can collaborate in different times and places.

Digital environments can also present challenges or complications by

- Requiring so much time and energy for design that they take attention away from writing.
- Raising copyright or ownership concerns by circulating found images without permission.
- Permitting people to post inappropriate comments on other peoples' work.
- Allowing work to be made public that isn't of the highest quality.

63B How do I write in a blog?

A Web log, or **blog**, is a Web site that displays a series of posts, or items. Posts are usually diary-like entries or observations but may also be images, videos, audio files, and links. Blogs generally focus on a particular topic.

Watch
the Video

Most have a similar design. The main content, a post about a particular topic, is in the center of the screen. The most recent post appears at the top of a page, followed by previous ones as a reader scrolls down. Many blogs contain a comment feature. Some blogs also have links to other blogs that focus on similar topics. Figure 63.1 shows a typical blog design.

Some instructors have students keep blogs as a course requirement. This follows the tradition of having students write journals as a regular way of writing about course content. The twist is that others can easily read and comment on each person's postings. If you're assigned to produce a course blog, your instructor will provide specific directions.

If you'd like to create your own blog, decide on a type and purpose, and imagine an AUDIENCE who cares about your perspective. You might participate in blogs and network with others, eventually gaining the attention of people who are interested in your ideas or experiences. Most important, have something interesting to say. Easily available software allows you to

Figure 63.1 Typical blog design.

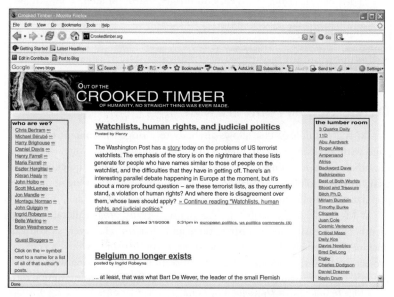

start blogging almost immediately with little worry or knowledge. For example, Blogger is a popular online community that gets you started with only a few mouse clicks. Quick Box 63.1 contains guidelines for writing in a blog.

Quick Box 63.1 ■ ■ ■ ■ ■ ■ ■ ■ ■ ■ ■

Guidelines for writing in a blog

- **Pick a unique title for your blog.** People and Internet search engines will recognize your blog if it has a good title.

- **Decide whether to use your own name or a made-up username.** You can protect your privacy to some degree if you have a pseudonym (literally, a "false name") or username. Especially if you're writing about controversial topics or taking controversial positions, you might not want employers, instructors, or even relatives to know your identity. Of course, an anonymous username doesn't give you license to be irresponsible or unethical. On the other hand, the advantage of your real name is that you get credit (and, we suppose, blame) for your writings. Think carefully about this decision.

- **Link, show, and share.** Include links in your posts to other, similar posts or items from the Web. Post images, videos, or audio files, but do respect copyrights. Share your posts and blog by participating on other blogs.

63C How do I write in a wiki?

A **wiki** is a technology that allows anybody to change the content of a Web page without using special Web writing or uploading software. *Wiki* is a Hawaiian word meaning "fast," and the name refers to how quickly people using this technology can collaborate and revise information. One of the more popular wiki applications is the online encyclopedia, Wikipedia.

Wikis can be useful tools for collaborative writing projects because group members can easily make contributions and changes. However, as you can imagine, this can also lead to complications. If you're using a wiki for a college project, you'll want to review strategies in section 9B for writing with others. If you want to create a new wiki, setting one up is fairly easy using simple software like Pbwiki (http://pbwiki.com/education.wiki). Quick Box 63.2 offers guidelines for writing in a wiki.

Quick Box 63.2

Guidelines for writing in a wiki

- **Revise with respect for others.** Consider ways to preserve what the person before you has written. Instead of deleting material, you might add qualifications, for example, words like "possibly" or phrases such as "in some cases" or "some have argued." You might add a section entitled "opposing arguments" (see 13G) that suggests an alternative viewpoint.

- **Cite your sources.** Whenever possible, cite your sources, and in some cases, find corroborating sources. Any addition to a wiki entry that contains references to reputable sources is less likely to be deleted or revised later, making your influence more lasting.

- **Post images, videos, and audio files.** Include links and references from other sources on the Web, but in every case, respect copyrights.

63D How do I use photographs?

Digital cameras and the Internet have made it cheap and easy to circulate pictures. Our culture has become visually oriented, and pictures can often enhance digital documents. We explain how to find, make, adjust, and place photographs in 7E.

63E How do I create video and sound recordings?

As you probably know from YouTube, online videos can be a great source of entertainment (or, depending on your point of view, a great waste of time). However, videos and sound recordings (such as radio essays or **podcasts**) can also be effective ways to deliver information or even make arguments. Videos often present complicated how-to directions more effectively than can words alone. Documentaries (think of versions of Ken Burns' famous series on the Civil War or jazz) vividly convey people and events.

Watch the Video

Despite their advantages, video and sound projects can take considerable time and expertise to do well. Just like written texts, they require planning, drafting, and revising, using technologies. Quick Box 63.3 (page 788) offers guidelines.

Figure 63.2 (page 789) shows the opening to a documentary video that student Siena Pinney created about a forest fire.

Quick Box 63.3

■ ■ ■ ■ ■ ■ ■ ■ ■ ■ ■

Guidelines for producing sound and video recordings

- **Plan your recording.** A good video or podcast has a beginning, middle, and end. Decide what elements you need to record for each.

- **Create and practice a script.** If your project has a narrator (and most projects do), write a script that contains what you plan to say, what will be on camera when you say it, and what music or sound effects you'll need. Practice the script before you record.

- **Create a storyboard for visual projects.** A storyboard is a series of rough sketches (you can use stick people, for example) that show the major scenes or elements in your video. It helps you plan the sequence and keep track of what shots you need to make.

- **Arrange to interview and record people** who will appear in your recording. Have anyone appearing in your work sign a release, a form that gives you permission to circulate their voice and images.

- **Find an appropriate place to record.** Unless you're trying to capture a real atmosphere (such as the crowd at a ball game or a protest), find a quiet place with good acoustics.

- **Use the best equipment available.** A dedicated video camera will generally produce better quality than a regular digital camera that has video capacity, for example. A dedicated microphone will work much better than a laptop's built-in microphone. Your college may have equipment for checking out.

- **Edit what you've recorded or shot.** The real work of producing an effective recording comes in editing the raw footage. You'll need to shorten some elements, move some around, and add transitions. You may even need to shoot new material in the middle of the process. Learn how to use free or cheap sound editing programs like Audacity (audacity.sourceforge.net/) or video editing programs like MovieMaker or iMovie.

Figure 63.2 Opening shot of documentary video.

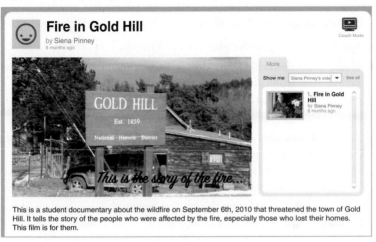

This is a student documentary about the wildfire on September 6th, 2010 that threatened the town of Gold Hill. It tells the story of the people who were affected by the fire, especially those who lost their homes. This film is for them.

63F How do I produce Web sites?

The Web writing process has five parts: (1) writing the content, (2) creating the structure of the content, (3) laying out the material on the screen, (4) checking whether the Web material is usable, and (5) loading the Web site on a **server**, a computer that is always online and available to Internet users.

63F.1 Creating a structure for a Web site

Almost all Web sites have a **home page**, a page that introduces the site and provides links to other pages. The home page functions like a table of contents or an entryway to a building. It needs to be appealing and give visitors clear directions for navigating. Here are some guidelines for creating a site's structure.

- Determine all the pages your site might contain and whether these pages need to be grouped into categories (groups of pages all on the same topic).
- Generate a list of categories.
- Plan **hyperlinks**, which are direct electronic connections between two pages.

63F.2 Choosing a template or designing a site

Unless you have considerable time, expertise, and the need for a unique Web site, we recommend using one of thousands of templates available online. A template (sometimes called a "theme") has predesigned places for titles, menus, texts, images, and so on. Once you selected a template, you paste your own materials into those places. Sites like Wordpress or Blogger provide free templates.

Here's some general advice about choosing and using a Web template.

- **Apply good design principles** (see Ch. 7).

- **Model after desirable Web sites**. Choose sites that have designs you admire. Find templates that have most of their qualities.

- **Choose an appropriate title**. Make sure your page tells readers exactly what they'll find there.

- **Keep backgrounds and texts simple**. Strive for a clean, uncluttered look. Dark text on a plain light background is easiest to read, with white being best. SANS SERIF fonts tend to be easiest to read on computer screens. Avoid multiple typefaces, sizes, colors, and busy backgrounds.

- **Use images to attract attention to important elements and to please the reader**. Readers will tend to look first at pictures and graphics.

- **Provide identifying information**. Generally, the bottom of a page includes the date the page is updated, along with your contact information.

63F.3 Incorporating photos into Web pages

Keep in mind that photographs can take a long time to download unless you reduce the size of the file through the picture editor in Microsoft Word or use a program like Photoshop.

63F.4 Editing and testing usability

Before you upload your Web page to a server, edit and proofread it as carefully as you would a print document. Use the checklist in Quick Box 63.4.

Quick Box 63.4 ■ ■ ■ ■ ■ ■ ■ ■ ■ ■ ■

Editing checklist for a Web site

- **Are any images broken?** Broken images show up as small icons instead of the pictures you want. The usual cause of broken images is mistyping the file name or failing to upload the image.

- **Do all the links work?** Missing, mistyped, or mislabeled files can cause broken links.

- **Is the Web site user-friendly?** Ask your friends, classmates, or colleagues to report anything unclear, inappropriate, or unattractive.

63F.5 Displaying a Web page

To display your finished Web page, you need space on a Web server, a centralized computer that is always online. Your college may offer Web space to its students, and services like WordPress and others offer free Web space. Your provider can explain how to upload content.

63G What is netiquette?

Netiquette, a word coined from *Net* and *etiquette*, demands that you use good manners as you write online or send e-mails. Unfortunately, blogs, discussion boards, and online comment sections are full of name-calling, personal attacks, and outlandish claims with no support, often unrelated to the topic at hand. Avoid being a troll (someone who posts irresponsibly), and avoid flaming (the sending of irresponsible messages). Avoid using ALL CAPS, which is both hard to read and taken as the equivalent of shouting, and also avoid writing in all lowercase letters, which can be taken as lazy or too cute.

When sending e-mails, use gender-neutral language. Always address business recipients or instructors by their full names, including any title such as *Ms.*, *Mr.*, or *Dr.* Also, use titles and last names, especially when you're communicating with people you've never met or corresponded with before. After you get to know people well, you might decide to lower your LEVEL OF FORMALITY. We suggest waiting until after those to whom you're writing begin to end their messages with their first names, especially when those people hold positions higher than yours.

63H What do I need to know about social networking?

Social networking platforms like Facebook or Twitter allow you to share material with others. Groups and organizations have set up social networking pages to publicize themselves, and some instructors have even developed pages for their courses.

As you use social networking, assume two things: (1) Nothing online is really private, and (2) Everything online is permanent. Even if you make everything private and visible only to approved friends, a stranger could easily end up viewing material you wouldn't want them to see. People have lost job opportunities because of what employers have found about them online. Only post things that you're confident represent you well, even to unforeseen readers. Don't be afraid to use and enjoy these powerful sites. We do! Just be sensible and aware.

Figure 63.3 Example of a social networking site.

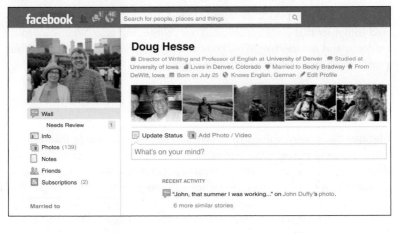

Writing for Work

64

Quick Points   You will learn to

- ➤ Identify features of types of workplace writing (see 64B–64G).
- ➤ Create résumés and application letters (see 64H–64I).

64A   Who writes in the workplace, and why?

If you're working, chances are good that you're writing. Writing infuses most workplaces, from corporate offices and health-care facilities to farms and factories. Even people who work independently (such as consultants, therapists, artists, and craftspeople) keep records, correspond with customers, and advertise their services. This chapter offers guidance for several common work-related writing tasks.

64B What are important features of work-related correspondence?

Correspondence is the general name for written communications, such as e-mails, memos, and letters, that you send to specific individuals. Your goal is to communicate plans, procedures, or purchases; share or ask for information; request specific actions; or influence decisions.

Work-related correspondence needs to appear professional, focused, and well informed. Avoid slang, abbreviations, informal words, or informal expressions. Use STANDARD EDITED ENGLISH grammar, spelling, and punctuation. Remember, too, that even casually written messages can have contractual significance or serve as evidence in court. Quick Box 64.1 provides general guidelines for writing work-related correspondence.

ESOL Tip: In some cultures, work-related correspondence is often sprinkled with elaborate language, many descriptive details, and even metaphors. Most American organizations, however, prefer correspondence that is clear and gets to the point quickly. ●

Quick Box 64.1 ■ ■ ■ ■ ■ ■ ■ ■ ■ ■ ■

Guidelines for work-related correspondence

- Address the recipient by name.
- Use GENDER-NEUTRAL LANGUAGE.
- Announce the PURPOSE of your communication at the outset.
- Be clear, concise, and specific.
- Be honest, positive, and natural, using a personal touch.
- Never spread gossip, personal opinion, put-downs, jokes, or chain letters.
- Edit ruthlessly for CONCISENESS and correctness.

64C How do I write work-related e-mail?

Business e-mail has formal purposes and AUDIENCES and should be free of slang or abbreviations like LOL (laughing out loud) or BTW (by the way).

The "cc" or "Copies" space is for the e-mail addresses of other people who need to see your message, even when they aren't expected to respond. When

View
the Model
Document

Figure 64.1 A professional e-mail.

To: sherrel. ampadu@jpltech.com
From: Chris Malinowitz <cmalinowitz@chateauby.com>
Subject: Confirming Meeting Arrangements
Cc: dmclusky@chateauby.com
Bcc:
Attached: C:\Documents and Settings\Desktop\Chateau Menus.doc

Dear Ms. Ampadu:

I am writing to confirm the final arrangements for your business meeting on June 17, 2012, at our conference center.

As you directed, we will set the room in ten round tables, each seating six. We will provide a podium and microphone, an LCD projector and screen, and a white board with markers. I understand that you will be bringing your own laptop. Our technician can help you set up.

You indicated that you would like to provide lunch and refreshments at two breaks. Attached please find our menus. You will need to make your lunch selections at least 48 hours in advance.

If you have any questions or wish to make any changes, I would be pleased to accommodate your needs. Thank you for choosing The Chateau at Brickyard.

Sincerely,

Chris Malinowitz
Catering Director, The Chateau at Brickyard

you use the "Bcc" (blind copy) space, you're sending a copy to someone without your primary recipients' knowing about it. Often, it's rude to send blind copies, but you might choose to blind-copy a long list of e-mail addresses so your recipients don't have to scroll through lots of names.

For the body of your e-mail, single-space the text, and double-space between paragraphs. Start paragraphs flush left at the margin. When you need to include a separate document with your e-mail, such as a report, compose it as a separate document in your word processing program, and attach it to your e-mail. Figure 64.1 is an example of a professional e-mail.

Know your workplace's policy covering issues such as use of business e-mail accounts for personal purposes and any legal responsibilities concerning your e-mail. Increasingly, businesses monitor their employees' e-mail.

Quick Box 64.2 summarizes some key points about writing business e-mail.

Quick Box 64.2

Guidelines for writing business e-mail

- Write a specific, not general, topic on the Subject line.
- Start your e-mail with a sentence that tells what your message is about.
- Put the details of your message in the second paragraph. Supply any background information that your recipients may need.
- Conclude your e-mail by asking for certain information or a specific action, if such is needed, or by restating your reason for writing.
- Follow netiquette (see 63G).
- Keep your message brief and your paragraphs short.
- Be cautious about what you say in a business e-mail, which could be forwarded to others without your permission.
- Forward an e-mail message only if you've asked the original sender for permission.
- At the end of your message, before your full name and position, use a commonly accepted complimentary closing, such as *Sincerely, Cordially,* or *Regards.*

64D How do I format and write memos?

Memos are usually exchanged internally (within an organization or business). Today e-mail takes the place of most memos, unless the correspondence requires a physical record or signature. The guidelines for writing e-mail (see 64C) also pertain to memos.

View the Model Document

The standard format of a memo includes two major parts: the headings and the body.

To:	[Name your audience—a specific person or group.]
From:	[Give your name and your title, if any.]
Date:	[Give the date on which you write the memo.]
Re:	[State your subject as specifically as possible in the "Subject" or "Re" line.]

Here are some guidelines for preparing a memo.

- **Introduction:** State your purpose for writing and why your memo is worth your reader's attention. Either here or at the conclusion, mention whether the recipient needs to take action.

- **Body:** Present the essential information on your topic. If you write more than three or four paragraphs, use headings to divide the information into subtopics (see 7D).

- **Conclusion:** End with a one- to two-sentence summary, a specific recommendation, or what action is needed and by when. Finish with a "thank you" line.

64E How do I format business letters?

View the Model Document

E-mail has generally taken the place of business letters; however, letters are sometimes still used for formal correspondence or when you want to establish a physical record of your communications. Cover letters (also called "letters of transmittal") accompany résumés, packages, reports, or other documents. Here are guidelines for the format and content of your business letters.

- **Paper:** Use 8½-by-11-inch paper. The most suitable color is white. Fold your business letters horizontally into thirds to fit into a standard number 10 business envelope (9½ by 4 inches).

- **Letterhead:** Use the official letterhead stationery (name, address, and logo, if any) of the business where you're employed. If no letterhead exists, center your full name, address, and phone number at the top of the page, and use a larger font than for the content of your letter. Keep it simple.

- **Format:** Without indents, use single spacing within paragraphs and double spacing between paragraphs, which is called **block style**. Figure 64.2 shows a job application letter in business format.

- **Recipient's name:** Use the full name of your recipient whenever possible. If you can't locate a name, either through a phone call to a central switchboard or on the Internet, use a specific category—for example, "Dear Billing Department," placing the key word "Billing" first (not "Department of Billing"). Always use gender-neutral language.

64F How do I write business reports?

Reports inform others inside or outside the workplace. Internal reports are designed to convey information to others in your workplace. They serve various purposes. For example, if you attend a professional meeting, you might provide a report of what you learned for your supervisor and colleagues who weren't there. If you have conducted extensive consumer research telephone interviews with potential customers, you might summarize and analyze your findings in a report. Being clear and concise are vital.

External reports inform audiences beyond the workplace. Generally, they have a secondary function of creating a good impression of the organization.

Figure 64.2   Sample job application letter.

Monica A. Schickel
1817 Drevin Avenue
Denver, CO 80208

Cell phone: (303) 555-7722
E-mail: mnsschl@wordnet.com
Professional portfolio: www.schickelgraphics.net

May 3, 2012

Jaime Cisneros
Publications Director
R.L. Smith Consulting
2000 Wabash Avenue
Chicago, IL 60601

Dear Mr. Cisneros:

Please consider my application for the graphic designer position currently being advertised on your company's Web site. I believe that my professional experiences, education, and skills prepare me well for this opportunity.

I am currently completing a paid internship at Westword, a weekly features and entertainment magazine in Denver, CO, where I have worked as an effective member of a creative team. My responsibilities have included designing advertisements, laying out sections, and editing photographs. Other related experience includes commissions as an illustrator and photographer. My professional portfolio demonstrates the range and quality of my work. As the enclosed résumé notes, I have additional experience in business environments.

Next month I will earn a BA in graphic design from The University of Denver, where my course of study has included extensive work in graphic design, photography, drawing, and illustration. Simultaneously, I will complete a minor in digital media studies that has included courses in Web design, video editing, and sound editing. I have expertise in all the standard software applications that would be relevant to your position.

I would be pleased to provide further information and to interview at your convenience. The opportunities at R.L. Smith closely match my background and goals, and the prospect of joining your team in Chicago is exciting. I look forward to discussing how I can contribute to your publications department.

Sincerely,

Monica A. Schickel
Monica A. Schickel

Common examples are annual reports, in which companies summarize their accomplishments during the previous year. However, other kinds of external reports are also common. For example, a school principal may write a report to parents that explain students' results on a statewide achievement test. Figure 64.3 (page 798) shows a section of one company's report. Document

Figure 64.3 A company's external report.

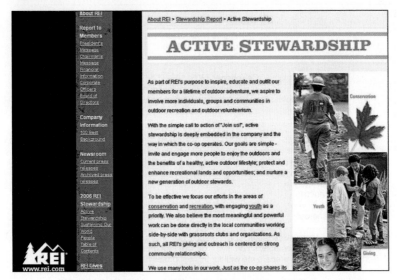

design, whether in print or on the computer screen, is important (see Ch. 7). Notice how the report in Figure 64.3 uses images and color.

64G How do I write business proposals?

We provide some detailed advice for writing proposals in Chapter 16. Business proposals are specialized versions of the larger category. They persuade readers to follow a plan, choose a product or service, or implement an idea. A marketing specialist might propose a new product line. A leader of a not-for-profit organization might propose a way to increase funding. Here are some specific guidelines for preparing a business proposal.

INTRODUCTION   Explain the project's purpose and scope. Describe the problem that the project seeks to solve, and lay out your solution. Include dates for beginning and completing the work. Project the outcomes and the costs. Be accurate and precise.

BODY   What is the product or service? What resources are needed? What are the phases of the project? Precisely how is each phase to be completed? What is the timeline? How will the project be evaluated?

CONCLUSION   Summarize the benefits of this proposal. Thank readers for their time. Offer to provide further information.

64H How do I write a résumé?

A résumé details your accomplishments and employment history. Its purpose is to help a potential employer determine whether you'll be a suitable candidate. To make a favorable impression, follow the guidelines for writing a résumé in Quick Box 64.3. Today, many employers have applicants upload their résumés to an employment Web site or send them as an e-mail attachment. Sometimes employers use software to scan electronic résumés, looking for keywords. Figure 64.4 (page 801) presents a sample résumé.

 View the Model Document

Quick Box 64.3

Guidelines for writing a traditional, scannable, or plain-text résumé

- At the beginning, include your name, address, e-mail address, and telephone number.

- Make the résumé easy to read. Label the sections clearly, and target the résumé to the position you want. Help employers see your most significant attributes quickly and easily.

- Adjust your résumé to fit your purpose. For example, if you're applying for a job as a computer programmer, you'll want to emphasize different facts than you would if you were applying for a job selling computers in an electronics store.

- Use headings to separate blocks of information. Include the following headings, as appropriate: "Position Desired" or "Career Objective"; "Education"; "Experience"; "Licenses and Certifications"; "Related Experience"; "Honors and Awards"; "Publications and Presentations"; "Activities and Interests"; and "Special Abilities, Skills, and Knowledge."

- When you list your work experience, place your most recent job first; when listing education, place your most recent degrees, certificates, or enrollments first.

- Write telegraphically. Start with verb phrases, not with the word *I*, and omit *a*, *an*, and *the*.

- Include only relevant information.

- Tell the truth. An employer who discovers you lied will likely fire you.

- Include references, or state that you can provide them on request.

- Try to fit all of the information on one page. If you need a second page, make sure the most important information is on the first page.

continued >>

Quick Box 64.3 (continued)

- Proofread carefully; even one spelling error or one formatting error can eliminate you from consideration.
- For print résumés, use high-quality paper that is white or off-white.
- Scannable résumés are designed to be scanned by machines that digitize their content. Sophisticated software then searches the database to match key terms to position requirements. As a result, scannable résumés need to be simpler: don't use columns, different fonts, lines or other graphics, or bold or italic fonts. Choose a clean sans serif font such as Arial or Geneva in a 10–12 point size. Include keywords that the computer can match to the job. Here is the keyword list Monica Schickel created for the scannable version of the resume in Figure 64.4:

KEYWORDS

Publications experience, graphic design, editing, photography, supervisor, editing, customer service, digital media, excellent Spanish, Adobe Creative Suite, Photoshop, InDesign, Quark, CSS, Dreamweaver, Web design, illustrator, proofread, Excel, Access, Publisher, newspaper, layout, sales, willing to relocate

- Plain-text résumés can be pasted directly into e-mails or into application databases. Use the same standards as for scannable resumes. Start every line of text at the left margin.

641 How do I write a job application letter?

View the Model Document

A job application letter always needs to accompany your résumé. Avoid repeating what's already on the résumé. Instead, connect the company's expectations to your experience by emphasizing how your background has prepared you for the position. Your job application letter, more than your résumé, reflects your energy and personality. Today, many employers have applicants upload letters to an application Web site, send them as e-mail attachments, or even send them as e-mails themselves. See Figure 64.2 for a sample letter and Quick Box 64.4 (page 802) for guidelines.

ESOL Tip: In some cultures, job applications may include personal information, such as an applicant's age, marital status, number of children, religion, or political beliefs. In North America, however, this is not standard practice. Such personal information does not help an employer determine how well you can perform a particular job, so avoid including it in your application. ●

Figure 64.4 A sample résumé.

MONICA A. SCHICKEL

1817 Drevin Avenue
Denver, CO 80208
Cell phone: (303) 555-7722
E-mail: mnsschl@wordnet.com
Professional portfolio: www.schickelgraphics.net

OBJECTIVE: Entry level position as a graphic designer or publications assistant

EXPERIENCE

9/12 – present	**Publications Intern** (half-time; paid), *Westword* (Denver, CO) • Design advertisements • Prepare photographs for publications • Lay out the "Tempo" section • Fact-check, edit, and proofread articles
6/10 - 8/12	**Customer Service Representative,** Wells Fargo Bank (Aurora CO). • Sold accounts to customers; made all sales goals • Created promotional posters
4/07 - 8/09	**Evening Assistant Manager,** McDonalds Restaurant (Longmont, CO). • Supervised 7 cooks and counter workers • Assured food and service quality

EDUCATION

8/11 – present	Bachelor of Arts, The University of Denver, expected June 2013 Major: Graphic Arts; Minor: Digital Media Studies
8/09 – 5/11	AA General Education, Front Range Community College, May 2011

SKILLS AND SELECTED EXPERIENCES

- Expert in complete Adobe Creative Suite
- Expert in complete Microsoft Office Suite
- Excellent Spanish language skills
- Illustrator and photographer; have completed several commissions (see portfolio, above)
- Vice President, Student Residence Halls Association
- Cartoonist and Designer, *The DU Clarion* (campus newspaper)
- Excellent customer service skills

REFERENCES: Available on request

Quick Box 64.4 ■ ■ ■ ■ ■ ■ ■ ■ ■ ■ ■

Guidelines for writing a job application letter

- Use one page only.

- Overall, think of your letter as a polite sales pitch about yourself and what benefits you can bring to the company. Don't be shy, but don't exaggerate.

- Use the same name, content, and format guidelines as for a business letter (see 64E).

- Address the letter to a specific person. If you can't discover a name, use a gender-neutral title such as "Dear Personnel Director."

  1. Telephone or send an e-mail to the company to which you're sending a letter or e-mail. State your reason for making contact, and ask for the name of the person to whom you need to address your letter.

  2. Address men as "Mr." and women as "Ms.," unless you're specifically told to use "Miss" or "Mrs." If your recipient goes by another title, such as "Dr." or "Professor," use it.

  3. If you can't identify a proper name and need to use a title alone, keep the title generic and gender-neutral.

     NO Dear Sir: [sexist]   Dear Sir or Madam: [sexist for both genders]

     YES Dear Human Resources Officer: Dear Sales Manager:

- Open your letter by identifying the position for which you're applying.

- Mention your qualifications and explain how your background will meet the job requirements.

- Make clear that you're familiar with the company or organization; your research will impress the employer.

- End by being specific about what you can do for the company. If the job will be your first, give your key attributes—but make sure they're relevant. For instance, you might state that you're punctual, self-disciplined, eager to learn, and hardworking.

- State when you're available for an interview and how the potential employer can reach you.

- Edit and proofread the letter carefully. If you have to hand-correct even one error, print the letter again.

USAGE GLOSSARY

This usage glossary explains the customary manner of using particular words and PHRASES. As used here, *informal* and *colloquial* indicate that words or phrases occur commonly in speech but should be avoided in ACADEMIC WRITING. *Nonstandard* indicates that words or phrases should not be used in either standard spoken English or writing.

All grammatical terms mentioned here are defined in the Terms Glossary at the back of the book. Also consult the commonly confused words listed in Quick Box 49.2.

a, an   Use *a* before words that begin with a consonant (*a dog, a grade, a hole*) or a consonant sound (*a one-day sale, a European*). Use *an* before words or acronyms that begin with a vowel sound or a silent *h* (*an owl, an hour, an MRI*). American English uses *a*, not *an*, before words starting with a pronounced *h*: *a* [*not* an] *historical event.*

accept, except   The verb *accept* means "agree to, receive." As a preposition, *except* means "leaving out." As a verb, *except* means "exclude, leave out."

> The workers were ready to **accept** [verb] management's offer **except** [preposition] for one detail: They wanted the no-smoking rule **excepted** [verb] from the contract.

advice, advise   *Advice*, a noun, means "recommendation." *Advise*, a verb, means "recommend, give advice."

> I **advise** [verb] you to follow your car mechanic's **advice** [noun].

affect, effect   As a verb, *affect* means "cause a change in, influence." (*Affect* also functions as a noun in the discipline of psychology.) As a noun, *effect* means "result or conclusion"; as a verb, it means "bring about."

> Loud music **affects** people's hearing for life, so some bands have **effected** changes to lower the volume. Many fans, however, don't care about the harmful **effects** of high decibel levels.

aggravate, irritate   *Aggravate* is used colloquially to mean "irritate." In formal writing, use *aggravate* to mean "intensify, make worse." Use *irritate* to mean "annoy, make impatient."

> The coach was **irritated** by her assistant's impatience, which **aggravated** the team's inability to concentrate.

ain't   *Ain't* is a nonstandard contraction. Use *am not, is not,* or *are not* instead.

all right   *All right* should be written as two words, never one (*not* alright).

allusion, illusion   An *allusion* is an indirect reference to something. An *illusion* is a false impression or idea.

> The applicant's casual **allusions** to many European tourist attractions created the **illusion** that he had seen them himself.

a lot *A lot* is informal for *a great deal* or *a great many;* avoid it in academic writing. Write it as two words (*not* alot) when you do use it.

a.m., p.m. These abbreviations may also be written as A.M., P.M. Use them only with numbers, not as substitutes for *morning, afternoon,* or *evening.*

> We will arrive **in the afternoon** [*not* in the p.m.], and we have to leave no later than **8:00 a.m.**

among, amongst, between Use *among* for three or more items and *between* for two items. American English prefers *among* to *amongst.*

> My three roommates discussed **among** [*not* between *or* amongst] themselves the choice **between** staying in school and getting full-time jobs.

amount, number Use *amount* for uncountable things (*wealth, work, corn, happiness*). Use *number* for countable items.

> The **amount** of rice to cook depends on the **number** of dinner guests.

an See *a, an.*

and/or This term is appropriate in business and legal writing when either or both of two items can apply: *The process is quicker if you have a wireless connection and/or a fax machine.* In the humanities, writers usually express the alternatives in words: *This process is quicker if you have a wireless connection, a fax machine, or both.*

anyplace *Anyplace* is informal. Use *any place* or *anywhere* instead.

anyways, anywheres *Anyways* and *anywheres* are nonstandard. Use *anyway* and *anywhere* instead.

apt, likely, liable *Apt* and *likely* are used interchangeably. Strictly, *apt* indicates a tendency or inclination. *Likely* indicates a reasonable expectation or greater certainty than *apt. Liable* denotes legal responsibility or implies unpleasant consequences.

> Alan is **apt** to leave early on Friday. I will **likely** go with him to the party. Maggy and Gabriel are **liable** to be angry if we do not show up.

as, as if, as though, like Use *as, as if,* or *as though,* but not *like,* to introduce clauses.

> This hamburger tastes good, **as** [*not* like] a hamburger should. It tastes **as if** [*or* as though *but not* like] it were barbequed over charcoal.

Both *as* and *like* can function as prepositions in comparisons. Use *as* to indicate equivalence between two nouns or pronouns. Use *like* to indicate similarity but not equivalence.

> Beryl acted **as** [*not* like] the moderator in our panel.

> Mexico, **like** [*not* as] Argentina, belongs to the United Nations.

assure, ensure, insure *Assure* means "promise, convince." *Ensure* and *insure* both mean "make certain or secure," but *insure* is reserved for financial or legal certainty, as in insurance.

> The agent **assured** me that he could **insure** my roller blades but that only I could **ensure** that my elbows and knees would outlast the skates.

as to *As to* is nonstandard. Use *about* instead.

awful, awfully Do not use *awful* or *awfully* in place of *terribly, extremely,* or *very.*

a while, awhile As two words, *a while* (an article and a noun) can function as a subject or object. As one word, *awhile* is an adverb; it modifies verbs. In a prepositional phrase, the correct form is *a while: for a while, in a while, after a while.*

> The seals basked **awhile** in the sun after they had played for **a while** in the sea.

backup, back up As a noun, *backup* is a copy of electronic data. *Backup* can also be used as an adjective to mean "alternative." *Back up* is a verb phrase.

> Many people recommend that you **back up** even your **backup** files.

bad, badly *Bad* is an adjective; use it after linking verbs. (Remember that verbs like *feel* and *smell* can function as either linking verbs or action verbs.) *Badly* is an adverb and is nonstandard after linking verbs (see 32D).

> Farmers feel **bad** because a **bad** drought has **badly** damaged the crops.

beside, besides *Beside* is a preposition meaning "next to, by the side of."

> She stood **beside** the new car, insisting that she would drive.

As a preposition, *besides* means "other than, in addition to."

> No one **besides** her had a driver's license.

As an adverb, *besides* means "also, moreover."

> **Besides**, she owned the car.

better, had better Used in place of *had better, better* is informal.

> We **had better** [*not* We better] be careful.

between See *among, amongst, between.*

bring, take Use *bring* to indicate movement from a distant place to a near place or to the speaker. Use *take* to indicate movement from a near place or from the speaker to a distant place.

> If you **bring** a leash to my house, you can **take** the dog to the vet.

but, however, yet Use *but, however,* or *yet* alone, not in combination with each other.

> The economy is strong, **but** [*not* but yet *or* but however] unemployment is high.

can, may *Can* signifies ability or capacity; *may* requests or grants permission. In negations, however, *can* is acceptable in place of *may.*

> When you **can** get here on time, you **may** be excused early.

can't hardly, can't scarcely These double negatives are nonstandard (see 32C).

censor, censure The verb *censor* means "delete objectionable material, judge." The verb *censure* means "condemn or reprimand officially."

> The town council **censured** the mayor for trying to **censor** a report.

chairman, chairperson, chair Many prefer the gender-neutral terms *chairperson* and *chair* to *chairman*; *chair* is more common than *chairperson*.

complement, compliment Each term functions as both a noun and a verb. As a noun, *complement* means "something that goes well with or completes." As a noun, *compliment* means "praise, flattery." As a verb, *complement* means "bring to perfection, go well with; complete." As a verb, *compliment* means "praise, flatter."

> The president's **compliment** was a fine **complement** to our celebration.
> When the president **complimented** us, her praise **complemented** our joy.

comprise, include See *include, comprise*.

conscience, conscious The noun *conscience* means "a sense of right and wrong." The adjective *conscious* means "aware or awake."

> To live happily, be **conscious** of what your **conscience** tells you.

continual(ly), continuous(ly) *Continual* means "occurring again and again." *Continuous* means "occurring without interruption."

> Intravenous fluids were given **continuously** for three days after surgery, so nurses were **continually** hooking up new bottles of saline solution.

could care less *Could care less* is nonstandard; use *couldn't care less* instead.

could of *Could of* is nonstandard; use *could have* instead.

couple, a couple of These terms are informal. Use *a few* or *several* instead.

> Rest for **a few** [*not* a couple *or* a couple of] minutes.

criteria, criterion A *criterion* is "a standard of judgment." *Criteria* is the plural form of *criterion*.

> Although charisma is an important **criterion** for political candidates to meet, voters must also consider other **criteria**.

data This is the plural of *datum*, a rarely used word. Informally, *data* is commonly used as a singular noun requiring a singular verb. In academic or professional writing, it is more acceptable to treat *data* as plural.

> The researchers' **data** suggest that some people become addicted to e-mail.

different from, different than *Different from* is preferred for formal writing, although *different than* is common in speech.

> Please advise the council if your research produces data **different from** past results.

don't *Don't* is a contraction for *do not* but not for *does not* (use *doesn't*).

> She **doesn't** [*not* She don't] like crowds.

effect See *affect, effect*.

elicit, illicit The verb *elicit* means "draw forth or bring out." The adjective *illicit* means "illegal."

> The government's **illicit** conduct **elicited** mass protest.

emigrate (from), immigrate (to) *Emigrate* means "leave one country to live in another." *Immigrate* means "enter a country to live there."

> My great-grandmother **emigrated** from the Ukraine in 1890. After a brief stay in Germany, she **immigrated** to Canada in 1892.

ensure See *assure, ensure, insure.*

etc. *Etc.* is the abbreviation for the Latin *et cetera*, meaning "and the rest." For writing in the humanities, avoid using *etc.* outside parentheses. Acceptable substitutes are *and the like, and so on*, and *and so forth.*

everyday, every day The adjective *everyday* means "daily." *Every day* is an adjective-noun combination that can function as a subject or an object.

> Being late for work has become an **everyday** occurrence. **Every day** that I am late brings me closer to being fired.

everywheres Nonstandard for *everywhere.*

except See *accept, except.*

explicit, implicit *Explicit* means "directly stated or expressed." *Implicit* means "implied, suggested."

> The warning on cigarette packs is **explicit:** "Smoking is dangerous to health." The **implicit** message is "Don't smoke."

fewer, less Use *fewer* for anything that can be counted (with count nouns): *fewer dollars, fewer fleas, fewer haircuts.* Use *less* with collective or other non-count nouns: *less money, less scratching, less hair.*

finalize Academic audiences prefer *complete* or *make final* instead of *finalize.*

> After intense negotiations, the two nations **completed** [*not* finalized] a treaty.

former, latter When two items are referred to, *former* signifies the first one and *latter* signifies the second. Avoid using *former* and *latter* in a context with more than two items.

> Brazil and Ecuador are South American countries. Portuguese is the most common language in the **former**, Spanish in the **latter**.

go, say *Go* is nonstandard when used for forms of *say.*

> After he stepped on my hand, he **said** [*not* he goes], "Your hand was in my way."

gone, went *Gone* is the past participle of *go; went* is the past tense of *go.*

> They **went** [*not* gone] to the concert after Ira **had gone** [*not* had went] home.

good and This phrase is an informal intensifier; omit it from writing.

> They were **exhausted** [*not* good and tired].

good, well *Good* is an adjective. Using it as an adverb is nonstandard. *Well* is the equivalent adverb.

> **Good** maintenance helps cars run **well**.

hardly See *can't hardly, can't scarcely.*

have, of Use *have*, not *of*, after such verbs as *could, should, would, might,* and *must.*

> You **should have** [*not* should of] called first.

have got, have to, have got to Avoid using *have got* when *have* alone delivers your meaning.

> I **have** [*not* have got] two more sources to read.

Avoid using *have to* or *have got to* for *must.*

> I **must** [*not* have got to] finish this assignment today.

he/she, s/he, his, her To avoid sexist language, use *he or she* or *his or her.* A less wordy solution is to use plural pronouns and antecedents.

> Every mourner bowed **his or her** head [*not* his head *or* their head].
>
> The **mourners** bowed **their** heads.

humanity, humankind, humans, mankind To avoid sexist language, use *humanity, humankind,* or *humans* instead of *mankind.*

> Some people think computers have influenced **humanity** more than any other twentieth-century invention.

i.e. This abbreviation refers to the Latin term *id est.* In formal writing, use the English translation *that is.*

if, whether At the start of a noun clause, use either *if* or *whether.*

> I don't know **if** [*or* whether] I want to dance with you.

In conditional clauses, use *whether* (*or* whether or not) when alternatives are expressed or implied.

> I will dance with you **whether or not** I like the music. I will dance with you **whether** the next song is fast or slow.

In a conditional clause that does not express or imply alternatives, use *if.*

> **If** you promise not to step on my feet, I will dance with you.

illicit See *elicit, illicit.*

illusion See *allusion, illusion.*

immigrate See *emigrate, immigrate.*

imply, infer *Imply* means "hint at or suggest." *Infer* means "draw a conclusion." A writer or speaker implies; a reader or listener infers.

> When the governor **implied** that she would not seek reelection, reporters **inferred** that she was planning to run for vice president.

include, comprise The verb *include* means "contain or regard as part of a whole." The verb *comprise* means "to be composed of."

inside of, outside of These phrases are nonstandard when used to mean *inside* or *outside.*

> She waited **outside** [*not* outside of] the dormitory.

In time references, avoid using *inside of* to mean "in less than."

I changed clothes **in less than** [*not* inside of] ten minutes.

insure   See *assure, ensure, insure.*

irregardless   *Irregardless* is nonstandard. Use *regardless* instead.

is when, is where   Avoid these constructions in giving definitions.

Defensive driving **requires that** [*not* is when] drivers stay alert.

its, it's   *Its* is a possessive pronoun. *It's* is a contraction of *it is.*

The dog buried **its** bone.

It's a hot day.

kind, sort   Use *this* or *that* with these singular nouns; use *these* or *those* with the plural nouns *kinds* and *sorts.* Also, do not use *a* or *an* after *kind of* or *sort of.*

Drink **these kinds of** fluids [*not* this kind of fluids] on **this sort of** [*not* this sort of a] day.

kind of, sort of   These phrases are colloquial adverbs. In formal writing, use *somewhat* instead.

The campers were **somewhat** [*not* kind of] dehydrated after the hike.

lay, lie   *Lay* (*laid, laid, laying*) means "place or put something, usually on something else" and needs a direct object. *Lie* (*lay, lain, lying*), meaning "recline," does not take a direct object (see 28M). Substituting *lay* for *lie* is nonstandard.

Lay [*not* Lie] the blanket down, and then **lay** the babies on it so they can **lie** [*not* lay] in the shade.

leave, let   *Leave* means "depart"; *let* means "allow, permit." *Leave* is nonstandard for *let.*

Let [*not* Leave] me use your car tonight.

less   See *fewer, less.*

lie   See *lay, lie.*

like   See *as, as if, as though, like.*

likely   See *apt, likely, liable.*

lots, lots of, a lot of   These are colloquial usages. Use *many, much,* or *a great deal* instead.

mankind   See *humanity, humankind, humans, mankind.*

may   See *can, may.*

maybe, may be   *Maybe* is an adverb; *may be* is a verb phrase.

Maybe [adverb] we can win, but our team **may be** [verb phrase] too tired.

may of, might of   *May of* and *might of* are nonstandard. Use *may have* and *might have* instead.

media This word is the plural of *medium*, yet colloquial usage now pairs it with a singular verb.

The **media** saturates us with information about every fire.

morale, moral *Morale* is a noun meaning "a mental state relating to courage, confidence, or enthusiasm." As a noun, *moral* means an "ethical lesson implied or taught by a story or event"; as an adjective, *moral* means "ethical."

One **moral** to draw from corporate downsizings is that overstressed employees suffer from low **morale**. Unhappy employees with otherwise high **moral** standards may steal from their employers.

most *Most* is nonstandard for *almost: Almost* [*not* Most] *all the dancers agree.* *Most* is correct as the superlative form of an adjective (*some, more, most*): *Most dancers agree.* It also makes the superlative form of adverbs and some adjectives: *most suddenly, most important.*

Ms. *Ms.* is a women's title free of reference to marital status, equivalent to *Mr.* for men. For a woman who does not use *Dr.* or another title, use *Ms.* unless she requests *Miss* or *Mrs.*

must of *Must of* is nonstandard. Use *must have* instead.

nowheres Nonstandard for *nowhere.*

number See *amount, number.*

of Use *have* instead of *of* after the following verbs: *could, may, might, must, should,* and *would.*

OK, O.K., okay All three forms are acceptable in informal writing. In academic writing, try to express meaning more specifically.

The weather was **suitable** [*not* OK] for the picnic.

outside of See *inside of, outside of.*

plus *Plus* is nonstandard as a substitute for *and, also, in addition,* or *moreover.*

The band will give three concerts in Hungary, **and** [*not* plus] it will tour Poland for a month. **Also** [*not* Plus], it may perform once in Vienna.

precede, proceed *Precede* means "go before." *Proceed* means "advance, go on; undertake; carry on."

Preceded by elephants and tigers, the clowns **proceeded** into the tent.

pretty *Pretty* is an informal qualifying word; in academic writing, use *rather, quite, somewhat,* or *very.*

The flu epidemic was **quite** [*not* pretty] severe.

principal, principle *Principle* means "a basic truth or rule." As a noun, *principal* means "chief person; main or original amount"; as an adjective, *principal* means "most important."

During the assembly, the **principal** said, "A **principal** value in this society is the **principle** of free speech."

proceed   See *precede, proceed.*

quotation, quote   *Quotation* is a noun; *quote* is a verb. Do not use *quote* as a noun.

> The newspaper **quoted** the attorney general, and the **quotations** [*not* quotes] quickly showed up in public health messages.

raise, rise   *Raise* (*raised, raised, raising*) means "lift" and needs a direct object. *Rise* (*rose, risen, rising*) means "go upward" and does not take a direct object (see 28M). Using these verbs interchangeably is nonstandard.

> If the citizens **rise** [*not* raise] up in protest, they may **raise** the flag of liberty.

real, really   *Real* is nonstandard as an intensifier, and *really* is almost always unnecessary; leave it out.

reason is because   This phrase is redundant; use *reason is that* instead.

> One **reason** we moved **is that** [*not* is because] we changed jobs.

regardless   See *irregardless.*

respective, respectively   The adjective *respective* relates the noun it modifies to two or more individual persons or things. The adverb *respectively* refers to a second set of items in a sequence established by a preceding set of items.

> After the fire drill, Dr. Pan and Dr. Moll returned to their **respective** offices [that is, each to his or her office] on the second and third floors, **respectively**. [Dr. Pan has an office on the second floor; Dr. Moll has an office on the third floor.]

right   *Right* is a colloquial intensifier; use *quite, very, extremely,* or a similar word for most purposes.

> You did **very** [*not* right] well on the quiz.

rise   See *raise, rise.*

scarcely   See *can't hardly, can't scarcely.*

seen   The past participle of *see* (*see, saw, seen, seeing*), *seen* is a nonstandard substitute for the past-tense form, *saw*. As a verb, *seen* must be used with an auxiliary verb.

> Last night, I **saw** [*not* seen] the show that you **had seen** in Florida.

set, sit   *Set* (*set, set, setting*) means "put in place, position, put down" and must have a direct object. *Sit* (*sat, sat, sitting*) means "be seated" and does not take a direct object (see 28M). Using these verbs interchangeably is nonstandard.

> Susan **set** [*not* sat] the sandwiches beside the salad, made Spot **sit** [*not* set] down, and then **sat** [*not* set] on the sofa.

should of   *Should of* is nonstandard. Use *should have* instead.

sit   See *set, sit.*

sometime, sometimes, some time The adverb *sometime* means "at an unspecified time." The adverb *sometimes* means "now and then." *Some time* is an adjective–noun combination meaning "an amount or span of time."

> **Sometime** next year we have to take qualifying exams. I **sometimes** worry about finding **some time** to study for them.

sort of See *kind of, sort of.*

such *Such* is an informal intensifier; avoid it in academic writing unless it precedes a noun introducing a *that* clause.

> The play got **terrible** [*not* such terrible] reviews. It was **such** a dull drama **that** it closed after one performance.

supposed to, used to The final *d* is essential in both phrases.

> We were **supposed to** [*not* suppose to] leave early. I **used to** [*not* use to] wake up as soon as the alarm rang.

sure *Sure* is nonstandard as a substitute for *surely* or *certainly.*

> I was **certainly** [*not* sure] surprised at the results.

sure and, try and Both phrases are nonstandard. Use *sure to* and *try to* instead.

than, then *Than* indicates comparison; *then* relates to time.

> Please put on your gloves, and **then** put on your hat. It is colder outside **than** inside.

that there, them there, this here, these here These phrases are nonstandard. Use *that, them, this,* and *these,* respectively.

that, which Use *that* with restrictive (essential) clauses only. *Which* can be used with both restrictive and nonrestrictive clauses; many writers, however, use *which* only for nonrestrictive clauses and *that* for all restrictive clauses (see 42F).

> The house **that** [*or* which] Jack built is on Beanstalk Street, **which** [*not* that] runs past the reservoir.

their, there, they're *Their* is a possessive. *There* means "in that place" or is part of an expletive construction (see 40C). *They're* is a contraction of *they are.*

> **They're** going to **their** accounting class in the building **there** behind the library. **There** are twelve sections of Accounting 101.

theirself, theirselves, themself These are nonstandard. Use *themselves* instead.

them Use *them* as an object pronoun only. Do not use *them* in place of the adjective *these* or *those.*

> Buy **those** [*not* them] strawberries.

then See *than, then.*

till, until Both are acceptable; except in expressive writing, avoid the contracted form *'til.*

to, too, two   *To* is a preposition. *Too* is an adverb meaning "also; more than enough." *Two* is the number.

> When you go **to** Chicago, visit the Art Institute. Go **to** Harry Caray's for dinner, **too**. It won't be **too** expensive because **two** people can share an entrée.

try and, sure and   See *sure and, try and*.

type   *Type* is nonstandard when used to mean *type of*.

> Use that **type of** [*not* type] glue on plastic.

unique   *Unique* is an absolute adjective; do not combine it with *more, most,* or other qualifiers.

> Solar heating is **uncommon** [*not* somewhat unique] in the Northeast. A **unique** [*not* very unique] heating system in one Vermont home uses hydrogen for fuel.

used to   See *supposed to, used to*.

utilize   Academic writers prefer *use* to *utilize*.

> The team **used** [*not* utilized] all its players to win the game.

way, ways   When referring to distance, use *way* rather than *ways*.

> He is a long **way** [*not* ways] from home.

well   See *good, well*.

where   *Where* is nonstandard when used for *that* as a subordinating conjunction.

> I read **that** [*not* where] Bill Gates is the richest man alive.
>
> **Where** is your house? [*not* Where is your house at?]

whether   See *if, whether*.

which   See *that, which*.

who, whom   Use *who* as a subject or a subject complement. Use *whom* as an object (see 28M).

who's, whose   *Who's* is a contraction of *who is*. *Whose* is a possessive pronoun.

> **Who's** willing to drive? **Whose** truck should we take?

would of   *Would of* is nonstandard. Use *would have* instead.

your, you're   *Your* is a possessive. *You're* is the contraction of *you are*.

> **You're** generous to volunteer **your** time at the elementary school.

TERMS GLOSSARY

Words printed in SMALL CAPITAL LETTERS in your *Simon & Schuster Handbook for Writers* indicate important terms that are defined in this glossary. The parenthetical references with each definition tell you the handbook sections where each term is most fully discussed. If you can't find a term's definition in this glossary, look for the term in the Index.

absolute phrase A phrase containing a subject and a participle that modifies an entire sentence: *The semester* [subject] *being* [present participle of *be*] *over, the campus looks deserted.* (28O)

abstract A very short summary that presents all the important ideas of a longer piece of writing. Sometimes appears before the main writing, as in APA style. (26F)

abstract noun A noun that names something not knowable through the five senses: *idea, respect.* (28B)

academic writing The writing people do for college courses and as scholarship published in print and online journals. (6D)

action verb A verb that describes an action or occurrence done by or to the subject. (40E)

active reading Annotating reading to make connections between your prior knowledge and the author's ideas. (3D)

active voice When a verb shows that its action or the condition expressed is done *by* the subject. The *active voice* stands in contrast with the *passive voice*, which conveys that the verb's action or condition is done *to* the subject. (29N)

adjective A word that describes or limits (modifies) a noun, a pronoun, or a word group functioning as a noun: *silly* joke, *three* trumpets. (28F, Ch. 32)

adjective clause A dependent clause, also known as a *relative clause*, that modifies a noun or pronoun that comes before it. An adjective clause begins with a relative word (such as *who, which, that,* or *where*). Also see *clause.* (28P)

advanced searches Also called *guided searches*. Allow you to search by entering information in a form online. (22D)

adverb A word that describes or limits (modifies) verbs, adjectives, other adverbs, phrases, or clauses: *loudly, very, nevertheless, there.* (28G, Ch. 32)

adverb clause A dependent clause beginning with a subordinating conjunction that establishes the relationship in meaning between itself and its independent clause. An adverb clause can modify an independent clause's verb or an entire independent clause. (28P)

agreement The concept of matching number and person of a subject and verb and of a pronoun and its antecedent. See also *antecedent.* (Ch. 31)

analogy An explanation of the unfamiliar in terms of the familiar, often comparing things not usually associated with each other. Analogy is a rhetorical strategy useful for developing a paragraph (6H). Unlike a simile, which uses *like* or *as* in making a comparison, an analogy does not use such words. (37H)

analysis A process of critical thinking, sometimes called *division*, that divides a whole into its component parts that shows how the parts interrelate. Analysis is a rhetorical strategy useful for developing paragraphs. (6H, Ch. 14)

analytical frameworks Systematic ways of investigating a work. (59B)

annotated bibliography Bibliography in which listed sources are accompanied by summaries of, or comments about, each source. (21O)

annotating Brief summaries or comments about a reading, perhaps in the margins, on a separate page, or in a computer file. (3D)

antecedent The noun or pronoun to which a pronoun refers. (30L)

APA style *APA* is the abbreviation for the American Psychological Association. APA style specifies the format and the form of citation and documentation used in source-based papers in many academic disciplines, especially psychology and most other social sciences. (Ch. 26)

appositive A word or group of words that renames the noun or noun phrase coming immediately before or after it: *my favorite month*, **October**. (28N)

argumentative writing Using rhetorical strategies to convince one's readers to agree with the writer's position about a topic open to debate. (Ch. 15)

articles Also called *determiners* or *noun markers*, the words *a, an,* and *the. A* and *an* are indefinite articles; *the* is a definite article. Also see *determiner.* (28F, Ch. 53)

assertion A statement that expresses a point of view about a topic. Often used by writers to develop a thesis statement. (5E)

assumption An idea or value that a writer takes for granted without proof. (3E)

audience The readers to whom a written document is primarily directed. (TIP 4, 5D)

auxiliary verb Also known as a *helping verb*, a form of *be, do, have,* or one of the modal verbs. Auxiliary verbs combine with main verbs to express tense, mood, and voice. Also see *modal auxiliary verbs.* (29E)

balanced sentences Sentences consisting of two short independent clauses that serve to compare or contrast. (39A)

bias Material that is slanted toward beliefs or attitudes and away from facts or evidence. (Ch. 43)

bibliographic note system Documentation system used by the *Chicago Manual of Style.* (27A)

bibliography A list of sources with their authorial and publication facts. (22H)

block style Style used in writing business letters. Block style uses no indents, single spacing within paragraphs and double spacing between paragraphs. All lines start flush left, which means at the left margin. (64E)

blog Shortened form of "Web log," an online journal usually updated on a fairly regular basis. (63B)

body paragraphs Paragraphs in an essay or other document that come between the introductory and concluding paragraphs. (6D)

book catalog Database that lists all books and bound volumes owned by a particular library. (Ch. 22)

Boolean expressions Words such as *AND, OR,* and *NOT* that researchers can use in a search engine to create keyword combinations that narrow and refine their searches. (22D)

brainstorming Listing all ideas that come to mind on a topic, and then grouping the ideas by whatever patterns emerge. (5E)

browser Software that allows people to connect to the Internet. Common examples are Microsoft Internet Explorer and Mozilla Firefox. (22C)

bureaucratic language Sometimes called *bureaucratese;* language that is overblown or overly complex. (37J)

call number Identification number, usually according to the Dewey Decimal System, used to store and retrieve an individual book or other library material. (22F)

case The form of a noun or pronoun that shows whether it's functioning as a subject, an object, or a possessive in a particular context. Nouns change form in the possessive case only (*city* can be a subject or object; *city's* is the possessive form). Also see *pronoun case.* (30A–30K, 45B)

case study Research that relies on the careful, detailed observation and analysis of one person or a small group of people. (60B)

catalog Also called a *card catalog*, often in digitized form an extensive and methodically organized list of all books and other bound volumes in a library. (22F)

cause and effect The relationship between outcomes (effects) and the reasons for them (causes), which is a rhetorical strategy for developing paragraphs. (6H, Ch. 13)

chronological order Also called *time order*, an arrangement of information according to time sequence; an organizing strategy for sentences, paragraphs, and longer pieces of writing. (6H)

citation Information that identifies a source referred to in a piece of writing. Also see *documentation*. (Chs. 25 and 26)

claim States an issue and then takes a position on a debatable topic related to the issue, supported with evidence and reasons. (5E)

classical argument An argument with a structure consisting of introduction, thesis statement, background, evidence and reasoning, response to opposing views, and conclusion. (15A)

classification A rhetorical strategy that organizes information by grouping items according to their underlying shared characteristics. (6H)

clause A group of words containing a subject and a predicate. A clause that delivers full meaning is called an *independent* (or *main*) *clause*. A clause that lacks full meaning by itself is called a *dependent* (or *subordinate*) *clause*. Also see *adjective clause, adverb clause, nonrestrictive element, noun clause, restrictive element*. (28P)

cliché An overused, worn-out phrase that has lost its capacity to communicate effectively: *soft as a kitten, lived to a ripe old age*. (37J)

close reading The practice of reading carefully, analytically, and critically. (3D)

clustering Also called *mapping*, it is an invention technique based on thinking visually about a topic and drawing attached balloons for its increasingly specific subdivisions. (5E)

CM style *CM*, the abbreviation for *Chicago Manual* style, is a form of citation and documentation used in many academic disciplines, including history and the arts. (27A–27B)

coherence The written or spoken progression from one idea to another using transitional expressions, pronouns, selective repetition, and/or parallelism to make connections between ideas explicit. (6G)

collaborative writing Students working together to write a paper. (Ch. 9)

collective noun A noun that names a group of people or things: *family, committee*. (31J)

colloquial language Casual or conversational language. (37J)

comma splice Sometimes called a *comma fault*, the error that occurs when a comma alone connects two independent clauses. (Ch. 34)

common noun A noun that names a general group, place, person, or thing: *dog, house*. (28B)

comparative The form of a descriptive adjective or adverb that expresses a different degree of intensity between two things: *bluer, less blue; more easily, less easily*. Also see *superlative*. (32E)

comparison and contrast A rhetorical strategy for organizing and developing paragraphs by discussing a subject's similarities (by comparing them) and differences (by contrasting them). (6H)

complement A grammatical element after a verb that completes the predicate, such as a direct object after an action verb or a noun or adjective after a linking verb. Also see *object complement* and *subject complement*. (28N, 29A)

complete predicate See *predicate*.

complete subject See *subject*.

complex sentence See *sentence.*

compound-complex sentence See *sentence.*

compound predicate See *predicate.*

compound sentence See *sentence.*

compound subject See *subject.*

compound word Two or more words placed together to express one concept, such as "fuel-efficient" or "proofread." (49G)

conciseness Writing that is direct and to the point. Its opposite, which is undesirable, is *wordiness.* (Ch. 40)

concluding paragraph Final paragraph of an essay, report, or other document. (6J)

concrete noun A noun naming something that can be seen, touched, heard, smelled, or tasted: *smoke, sidewalk.* (28B)

conjunction A word that connects or otherwise establishes a relationship between two or more words, phrases, or clauses. Also see *coordinating conjunction, correlative conjunction, subordinating conjunction.* (28I)

conjunctive adverb An adverb that expresses a relationship between words, such as addition, contrast, comparison, and the like. (28G)

connotation Ideas implied, not directly stated, by a word giving emotional overtones. (37F)

content notes Notes researchers write to record information about what each source they've found says—along with publication information so that the researcher can find the source again if needed. (21P)

context The circumstances that exist when a piece is written. (4F)

contraction A word in which an apostrophe takes the place of one or more omitted letters: *can't, don't, I'm, isn't, it's, let's, they're, we've, won't,* and others. (45D)

coordinate adjectives Two or more adjectives that carry equal weight in modifying a noun (***big, friendly*** *dog*).

The order of coordinating adjectives can be changed without changing the meaning. Also see *cumulative adjectives.* (42E)

coordinate sentences Two or more independent clauses joined by either a semicolon or a comma with coordinating conjunction showing their relationship; also called a *compound sentence.* Also see *coordination.* (38F)

coordinating conjunction A conjunction that joins two or more grammatically equivalent structures: *and, or, for, nor, but, so, yet.* (28I, 38G)

coordination The use of grammatically equivalent forms to show a balance in, or sequence of, ideas. (38D)

correlative conjunction A pair of words that joins equivalent grammatical structures: *both . . . and; either . . . or; not only . . . but also.* (28I)

count noun A noun that names items that can be counted: *radio, street, idea, fingernail.* (52A)

critical thinking A form of thinking in which you take control of your conscious thought processes by judging evidence, considering assumptions, making connections, and analyzing implications. (3A)

CSE style *CSE,* the abbreviation for the Council of Science Editors, is a form of citation and documentation used in the natural sciences. (27C–27D)

cue words Words that tell what an assignment suggests that students accomplish in their writing. (58B)

cumulative adjectives Adjectives that build up meaning from word to word as they get closer to the noun (***familiar rock*** *tunes*). The order of cumulative adjectives cannot be changed without destroying the meaning. Also see *coordinating adjectives.* (42E)

cumulative sentence The most common structure for a sentence, with the subject and a verb first, followed by modifiers adding details; also called a *loose sentence.* (38O)

dangling modifier A modifier that illogically attaches its meaning to the rest of its sentence, either because it is closer to another noun or pronoun than to its true subject or because its true subject is not expressed in the sentence. (Ch. 35)

database An electronic collection of citations and, frequently, articles or documents on a particular subject matter or field, or about a specific body of sources. (22C)

declarative sentence A sentence that makes a statement: *Sky diving is exciting.* Also see *exclamatory sentence, imperative sentence, interrogative sentence.* (28L)

deductive reasoning The process of reasoning from general claims to a specific instance. (3H)

definition A rhetorical strategy that defines or gives the meaning of terms or ideas. (6H)

deliberate repetition A writing technique that uses the conscious repetition of a word, phrase, or other element to emphasize a point or to achieve a specific effect on readers. (6G)

demonstrative pronoun A pronoun that points out the antecedent: *this, these; that, those.* (28C)

denotation The dictionary definition of a word. (37F)

dependent clause Also called *subordinate clause*, a subordinate clause can't stand alone as an independent grammatical unit. If it tries to, it is a sentence fragment. Also see *adjective clause, adverb clause, noun clause.* (28P)

description A statement that paints a picture in words. (6H)

descriptive adverb An adverb that describes the condition or properties of whatever it is modifying and has comparative and superlative forms: *happily, more happily, most happily.* (28G)

determiner A word or word group, traditionally identified as an *adjective*, that limits a noun by telling whether a

noun is general (**a** noun) or specific (**the** tree). (28F, 52B)

dialect Also called *regional language.* Language that is specific to a particular geographic area. (37B)

diction Word choice. (37F)

digital portfolio A collection of several texts in electronic format to represent the range of your skills and abilities. (8D)

direct address Words naming a person or group being spoken to: *"The solution, **my friends**, is in your hands."* (30R)

direct discourse Words that repeat speech or conversation exactly, always enclosed in quotation marks. Also see *indirect discourse.* (36E, 42G)

direct object A noun, pronoun, or group of words functioning as a noun that receives the action (completes the meaning) of a transitive verb. (28M)

direct question A sentence that asks a question and ends with a question mark: *Are you going to the concert?* (41C)

direct quotation See *quotation.*

direct title A title that tells exactly what the essay will be about. (5J)

documentation The acknowledgment of a source's words and ideas being used in any written document by giving full and accurate information about the source of the words used and about where those words can be found. Also see *documentation style.* (Chs. 25–27)

documentation style Any of various systems for providing information about the source of words, information, and ideas that a writer quotes, paraphrases, or summarizes from any source other than the writer. Documentation styles discussed in this handbook are MLA (Ch. 25), APA (Ch. 26), CM (27A–27B), and CSE (27C–27D).

document design The arrangement of words, images, graphics, and space on a page or screen. (Ch. 7)

double negative A nonstandard structure that uses two negative modifiers rather than one. (32C)

drafting The part of the writing process in which writers compose ideas in sentences and paragraphs, thereby creating *drafts*. A *discovery draft* is what some writers call an early, rough draft. (5G)

editing The part of the writing process in which writers check a document for the technical correctness in edited American English of its grammar, sentence structure, punctuation, spelling, and mechanics. (5J)

elliptical construction A sentence structure that deliberately omits words that can be filled in because they repeat words already in the sentence. (36H)

emotional appeal Rhetorical strategy intended to evoke empathy and compassion. Its Greek name is *pathos*. (3B, 15C)

ethical appeal Rhetorical strategy intended to evoke confidence in your credibility, reliability, and trustworthiness. Its Greek name is *ethos*. (3B, 15C)

ethnography A research method that involves careful observation of a group of people or a setting, often over a period of time. Ethnography also refers to the written work that results from this research. (60B)

euphemism Language that attempts to blunt certain realities by speaking of them in "nice" or "tactful" words. (37J)

evaluation Examining new ideas independently and fairly, avoiding biases and prejudices that you might have accepted without question before. (3G)

evidence Facts, data, and examples used to support a writer's assertions and conclusions. (24G)

example Specific incident or instance provided to illustrate a point. (6H)

exclamatory sentence A sentence beginning with *What* or *How* that expresses strong feeling: *What a ridiculous statement!* (28L)

expletive construction The phrase *there is (are), there was (were), it is (was)* at the beginning of a clause, which postpones the subject: *It is Mars that we hope to reach* (a better version would be *We hope to reach Mars*). (40C)

expressive writing Writing that reflects your personal thoughts and feelings. (4B)

fact Information or data widely accepted as true. (3E)

faulty parallelism Grammatically incorrect writing that results from nonmatching grammatical forms linked with coordinating conjunctions. (39D)

faulty predication A grammatically illogical combination of subject and predicate: *The purpose of television was invented to entertain.* (36G)

field research Primary research that involves going into, and taking notes on, real-life situations to observe, survey, interview, or be part of some activity. (21L)

figurative language Words that carry other meanings in addition to their literal meanings, sometimes by making unusual comparisons. Also see *analogy, irony, metaphor, personification, overstatement, simile, understatement.* (37H)

first person See *person.*

focused freewriting Freewriting that starts with a set topic or builds on one sentence taken from earlier freewriting. (5E)

formal outline An outline that lays out the topic levels of generalities or hierarchies and marks them with roman numerals, letters, and numbers indented in a carefully prescribed fashion. (5F)

frame Guides that suggest how to develop or structure an essay or assignment. (Part 2)

freewriting Writing nonstop for a period of time to generate ideas by free association of thoughts. (5E)

future perfect progressive tense The form of the future perfect tense that describes an action or condition ongoing until some specific future time: *I will have been talking when you arrive.* (29G)

future perfect tense The tense indicating that an action will have been completed or a condition will have ended by a specified point in the future: *I will have talked to him by the time you arrive.* (29I)

future progressive tense The form of the future tense showing that a future action will continue for some time: *I will be talking when you arrive.* (29G)

future tense The form of a verb, made with the simple form and either *shall* or *will,* expressing an action yet to be taken or a condition not yet experienced: *I will talk.* (29G)

gender The classification of words as masculine, feminine, or neuter. In English, a few pronouns show changes in gender in third-person singular: *he, him, his; she, her, hers; it, its, its;* also few nouns that define roles change form to show gender difference (*prince, princess*), but most no longer do (*actor, police officer, chairperson*). (37I)

gender-neutral language Nonsexist language. Also see *sexist language.* (37I)

general databases Include sources from a broad range of periodicals and books, both popular and scholarly. (22C)

generalization A broad statement without details. (Ch. 1)

general reference work The starting point for many college researchers that help identify keywords useful in searching for subject headings and catalogs— and for finding examples and verifying facts. (22H)

genre A category of writing characterized by certain features; for example, a short story or a research report. (4E)

gerund A present participle functioning as a noun: *Walking* is good exercise. Also see *verbal.* (28E, Ch. 56)

gerund phrase A gerund, along with its modifiers and/or object(s), which functions as a subject or an object: *Walking the dog can be good exercise.* See also *gerund.* (28O)

helping verb See *auxiliary verb.*

homonyms Words spelled differently that sound alike: *to, too, two.* (49F)

home page The opening main page of a Web site that provides access to other pages on the site categories. (63F)

hyperbole See *overstatement.*

hyperlink Connection from one digital document to another online. (63F)

idiom A word, phrase, or other construction that has a different meaning from its usual or literal meaning: *He lost his head. She hit the ceiling.* (Ch. 55)

illustration Provides support for the main idea of a paragraph by giving several examples, often ones that call on the five senses to picture them. (6H)

imperative mood The grammatical form that expresses commands and direct requests, using the simple form of the verb and almost always implying but not expressing the subject: *Watch out.* (29L)

imperative sentence A sentence that gives a command. *Go to the corner to buy me a newspaper.* (28L)

indefinite pronoun A pronoun, such as *all, anyone, each,* and others, that refers to a nonspecific person or thing. (31I, 31R)

independent clause A clause that can stand alone as an independent grammatical unit. (28P)

index List of main terms used in a text and the page(s) on which each term can be found. (22A)

indicative mood The grammatical form of verbs used for statements about real things or highly likely ones: *I think Grace will be arriving today.* (29L)

indirect discourse Reported speech or conversation that does not use the exact structure of the original and so is not enclosed in quotation marks. (36E, 42G)

indirect object A noun, pronoun, or group of words functioning as a noun that tells to whom, or for whom, the action expressed by a transitive verb was done. (28M)

indirect question A sentence that reports a question and ends with a period, not a question mark: *I asked if you are going.* (41C)

indirect quotation A quotation that reports a source's words without quotation marks, unless any words are repeated exactly from the source. It requires documentation of the source to avoid plagiarism. Also see *indirect discourse.* (42H)

indirect title Hints at an essay's topic; tries to catch the reader's interest by presenting a puzzle that can be solved by reading the essay. (5J)

inductive reasoning A form of reasoning that moves from particular facts or instances to general principles. (3H)

inference What is implied, not stated, by words. (3C)

infinitive A verbal made of the simple form of a verb and usually, but not always, preceded by the word *to.* It functions as a noun, an adjective, or an adverb. (Ch. 55)

infinitive phrase An infinitive, with its modifiers and/or object, which functions as a noun, an adjective, or an adverb. (28O)

informal outline Outline that doesn't follow the rules of a *formal outline.* (5F)

informal writing Word choice that creates a tone appropriate for casual writing or speaking. (37D)

intensive pronoun A pronoun that ends in *-self* and that intensifies its antecedent: *Vida **himself** argued against it.* Also see *reflexive pronoun.* (30K)

interjection An emotion-conveying word that is treated as a sentence, starting with a capital letter and ending with an exclamation point or a period: *Oh! Ouch.* (28J)

interrogative pronoun A pronoun, such as *whose* or *what,* that implies a question: *Who called?* (28C)

interrogative sentence A sentence that asks a direct question: *Did you see that?* (28L)

in-text citation Source information placed in parentheses within the body of a research paper. Also see *citation, parenthetical documentation.* (Chs. 25 and 26)

intransitive verb A verb that does not take a direct object. (29F)

introductory paragraph Opening paragraph of document that orients readers and generates interest in the topic or ideas that follow. (6C)

inverted word order In contrast to standard order, the main or auxiliary verb comes before the subject in a sentence: *In **walks** [verb] the president [subject].* Most questions and some exclamations use inverted word order: *Did [verb] you [subject] see the circus?* (31H, 38B)

irony Using words to imply the opposite of their usual meaning. (37H)

irregular verb A verb that forms the past tense and past participle other than by adding *-ed* or *-d.* (29D)

jargon Specialized vocabulary of a particular field or group that is not familiar to a general reader. (37J)

justify When used as a design term, it refers to aligning text evenly along both the left and right margins. (7C)

keywords Main words in a source's title, or that the author or an editor has identified as central to that source. Sometimes keywords are called *descriptors* or *identifiers.* (22D)

levels of formality The degrees of formality of language, reflected by word choice and sentence structure. A formal level is used for ceremonial and other occasions when stylistic flourishes are appropriate. A semiformal level, which is neither too formal nor too casual, is acceptable for most academic writing. (5J, 37D)

linking verb A main verb that links a subject with a subject complement that renames or describes the subject. Linking verbs convey a state of being, relate to the senses, or indicate a condition. (29A)

literal meaning What is stated "on the line" explicitly by words. (3C)

logical appeal Rhetorical strategy that intends to show readers that the argument depends on formal reasoning, including providing evidence and drawing conclusions from premises. Its Greek name is *logos*. (3B)

logical fallacies Flaws in reasoning that lead to illogical statements that need to be rejected in logical arguments. (3I)

long quotation A direct quotation that in an MLA-style source-based paper occupies, if it is prose, more than four lines of type, and if it is poetry, more than three lines of the poem. In an APA-style source-based paper, if it is more than forty words of prose. Long quotations are block indented on the page. Also see *short quotation*. (46C)

main clause See *independent clause*.

main verb A verb that expresses action, occurrence, or state of being and that shows mood, tense, voice, number, and person. (28D, 29B)

mechanics Conventions governing the use of capital letters, italics, abbreviations, and numbers. (Chs. 48–49)

memo Commonly shortened term for *memorandum*. A brief form of business correspondence with a format that is headed with lines for "To," "From," "Date," and "Subject" (or "Re") and uses the rest of its space for its message. (64D)

metaphor A comparison implying similarity between two things: *a mop of hair*. A metaphor does not use the words *like* or *as*, which are used in a simile to make a comparison explicit: *hair **like** a mop*. (37H)

misplaced modifier Describing or limiting words that are wrongly positioned in a sentence so that their message

either is illogical or relates to the wrong word(s). (Ch. 35)

mixed sentence A sentence that unintentionally changes from one grammatical structure to another incompatible grammatical structure, so that the result is garbled meaning. (36F)

mixed metaphor Inconsistent metaphors in a single expression: *You'll get into hot water skating on thin ice.* (37H)

MLA style *MLA*, the abbreviation for the Modern Language Association, specifies the format and the form of citation and documentation in source-based papers in English and some other humanities courses. (Ch. 25)

modal auxiliary verb A group of auxiliary verbs that communicate possibility, likelihood, obligation, permission, or ability: *can, might, would*. (29E)

modifier A word or group of words functioning as an adjective or adverb to describe or limit (modify) another word or word group. (28N)

mood The attribute of verbs showing a writer's orientation to an action by the way the verbs are used. English has three moods: imperative, indicative, and subjunctive. Also see *imperative mood, indicative mood, subjunctive mood*. (29L)

multimodal The use of a combination of words and images. (3L)

narrative writing Writing that tells a story. (6H)

netiquette Coined from the word *etiquette*, netiquette is good manners when using e-mail, the Internet, and online sites such as bulletin boards, chat rooms, etc. (63G)

noncount noun A noun that names "uncountable" things: *water, time*. (52A)

nonrestrictive clause A clause that is not essential to the sentence's meaning. (30S)

nonrestrictive element A descriptive word, phrase, or dependent clause that provides information not essential to understanding the basic message of the element it modifies; it is therefore set off by commas. Also see *restrictive element*. (42F)

nonsexist language See *sexist language*.

noun A word that names a person, place, thing, or idea. Nouns function as subjects, objects, or complements. (28B)

noun clause A dependent clause that functions as a subject, object, or complement. (28P)

noun phrase A noun along with its modifiers functioning as a subject, object, or complement. (28O)

number The attribute of some words indicating whether they refer to one (singular) or more than one (plural). (31B, 36B)

object A noun, pronoun, or group of words that receives the action of the verb (*direct object;* 28M); tells to whom or for whom something is done (*indirect object;* 28M); or completes the meaning of a preposition (*object of a preposition;* 28H).

object complement A noun or adjective renaming or describing a direct object after certain verbs, including *call, consider, name, elect,* and *think:* Some *call* daily **joggers** [object] **fanatics** [object complement]. (28N)

objective case The case of a noun or pronoun functioning as a direct object, an indirect object, an object of a preposition, or a verbal. A few pronouns change form to show the objective case (for example, *him, her, whom*). Also see *case*. (30A)

opinion A statement open to debate. (3E)

outline A technique for laying out ideas for writing in an orderly fashion that shows levels of generality. An outline can be formal or informal. (5F)

overstatement Deliberate exaggeration for emphasis; also called *hyperbole*. (37H)

paragraph A group of sentences that work together to develop a unit of thought. (6B)

paragraph development Rhetorical strategies for arranging and organizing paragraphs using specific, concrete details (RENNS) to support a generalization in the paragraph. (6B, 6D, 6F)

parallelism The use of equivalent grammatical forms or matching sentence structures to express equivalent ideas: *singing* and *dancing*. (6G, Ch. 39)

paraphrase A restatement of a source's ideas in language and sentence structure different from that of the original. (18C)

parenthetical documentation Citation of source information enclosed in parentheses that follows quoted, paraphrased, or summarized material from another source. Such citations alert readers that the material comes from a source other than the writer. Parenthetical documentation and a list of bibliographic information at the end of a source-based paper together document the writer's use of sources. (Chs. 25 and 26)

participial phrase A phrase that contains a present participle or a past participle and any modifiers and that functions as an adjective. Also see *verbal*. (28O, 38P)

participle A verb form that indicates the present tense (*-ing* ending) or the past tense (*-ed, -d, -n,* or *-t* ending). A participle can also function as an adjective or an adverb. Also see *present participle, past participle*. (Ch. 29)

parts of speech The names and definitions of types of words that give you a vocabulary for identifying words and understanding how language works to create meaning. (28A–28J)

passive voice The *passive voice* emphasizes the action, in contrast to the *active voice*, which emphasizes the doer of the action. If the subject is mentioned in the sentence, it usually appears as the object of the preposition *by: I was frightened by the thunder* (the active voice form is *The thunder frightened me*). (29N)

past participle The third principal part of a verb, the past participle is formed in regular verbs by adding *-d* or *-ed* to the simple form to create the past tense. In irregular verbs, past and past participle formation varies by adding a letter or two to the simple form: *break, broke, broken*. The past participle functions as a verb only with an auxiliary verb as its partner. (29B)

past perfect progressive tense The past-perfect-tense form that describes an ongoing condition in the past that has been ended by something stated in the sentence: *Before the curtains caught fire,* **I had been talking**. (29J)

past perfect tense The tense that describes a condition or action that started in the past, continued for a while, and then ended in the past: *I had talked to him before.* (29I)

past progressive tense The past-tense form that shows the continuing nature of a past action: *I was talking when you walked in.* (29J)

past subjunctive The simple past tense in the subjunctive mood. (29M)

past-tense verb The second principal part of a verb. In regular verbs, the past tense is formed by adding *-d* or *-ed* to the simple form. In irregular verbs, the formation of the past tense varies from merely adding a letter or two to the simple form: *break, broke; see, saw.* (29B)

peer-response group Groups of students in your class who gather together to read and constructively react to each other's writing. (9C)

perfect tenses The three tenses—the present perfect (*I have talked*), the past perfect (*I had talked*), and the future perfect (*I will have talked*)—that help to show complex time relationships between two clauses. (29I)

periodic sentence A sentence that begins with modifiers and ends with the independent clause, thus postponing the main idea—and the emphasis—for the end; also called a *climactic sentence.* (38O)

periodicals Magazines, newspapers, and journals published on a regular basis. (22G)

person The attribute of nouns and pronouns showing who or what acts or experiences an action. *First person* is the one speaking (*I, we*); *second person* is the one being spoken to (*you*); and *third person* is the person or thing spoken about (*he, she, it, they*). All nouns are third person. (31B, 36B)

personal pronoun A pronoun that refers to people or things: *I, you, them, it.* (30B)

personality The sense of the writer that comes through his or her writing; for example, friendly, bossy, shy, assertive, concerned, angry, and so on. (37D)

personification Assigning a human trait to something not human. (37H)

persuasive appeal Rhetorical strategies which appeal to the emotions, logic, or ethics of readers. (3B)

persuasive writing Writing that seeks to convince the reader about a matter of opinion. It is also known as *argumentative writing.* (Ch. 15)

phrasal verb A verb that combines with one or more prepositions to deliver its meaning: *ask **out**, look **into**.* (55C)

phrase A group of related words that does not contain a subject and predicate and thus cannot stand alone as an independent grammatical unit. A phrase can function as a noun, a verb, or a modifier. (28O)

plagiarism A writer's presenting another person's words or ideas without giving credit to that person. Writers use documentation systems to give proper credit to sources in standardized ways recognized by scholarly communities. Plagiarism is a serious offense, a form of intellectual dishonesty that can lead to course failure or expulsion from an institution. (Ch. 19)

planning Early part of the writing process in which writers gather ideas. (5A)

plural See *number*.

podcasts Brief sound files that are shared over the Internet, somewhat like online radio broadcasts. (63E)

point of view The perspective from which a piece is written. (3E)

possessive case The case of a noun or pronoun that shows ownership or possession. Also see *case*. (30A, 45A)

possessive pronoun A pronoun that shows ownership: *his, hers*, and so on. (45C)

predicate The part of a sentence that contains the verb and tells what the subject is doing or experiencing or what is being done to the subject. A *simple predicate* contains only the main verb and any auxiliary verb(s). A *complete predicate* contains the verb, its modifiers, objects, and other related words. A *compound predicate* contains two or more verbs, modifiers, objects, and other related words. (28L)

prediction A major activity of the *reading process*, in which the reader guesses what comes next. (3D)

premises In a deductive argument expressed as a syllogism, statements presenting the conditions of the argument from which the conclusion must follow. (3H)

prefix Letters added at the beginning of a root word to create a new word: *pretest*. (47H, 51C)

preposition A word that conveys a relationship, often of space or time, between the noun or pronoun following it and other words in the sentence: *under, over, in, out*. The noun or pronoun following a preposition is called the *object of the preposition*. (28H, Ch. 55)

prepositional phrase A group of words beginning with a preposition and including a noun or pronoun, which is called the *object of the preposition*. (28O)

presentation style The way you deliver what you have to say. Memorization, reading, mapping, and speaking with notes are different types of presentation styles. (62F)

present infinitive Names or describes an activity or occurrence coming together either at the same time or after the time expressed in the main verb. (29G)

present participle A verb's *-ing* form: *talking, singing*. Used with auxiliary verbs, present participles function as main verbs. Used without auxiliary verbs, present participles function as nouns or adjectives. (29B)

present perfect progressive tense The present-perfect-tense form that describes something ongoing in the past that is likely to continue into the future: *I have been talking for a while*. (29J)

present perfect tense The tense indicating that an action or its effects, begun or perhaps completed in the past, continue into the present: *I had talked to her before you arrived*. (29I)

present progressive tense The present-tense form of the verb that indicates something taking place at the time it is written or spoken about: *I am talking right now to her*. (29J)

present subjunctive The simple form of the verb for all persons and numbers in the subjunctive mood. (29M)

present tense The tense that describes what is happening, what is true at the moment, and/or what is consistently true. It uses the simple form (*I talk*) and the *-s* form in the third-person singular (*he talks, she talks, it talks*). (29G)

present-tense participial phrase A verbal phrase that uses the *-ing* form of a verb and functions only as a modifier (whereas a gerund phrase functions only as a noun). (28O)

primary sources Also called *primary evidence*, these sources are "firsthand" work such as written accounts of experiments and observations by the researchers who conducted them; taped accounts, interviews, and newspaper accounts by direct observers; autobiographies, diaries, and journals; and expressive works such as poems, plays, fiction, and essays. They stand in contrast to *secondary sources.* (21B)

process writing Presents instructions, lays out steps in a procedure, explains how objects work, or describes human behaviors. (6H, Ch. 12)

progressive forms Verb forms made, in all tenses, with the present participle and forms of the verb *be* as an auxiliary. Progressive forms show that an action, occurrence, or state of being is ongoing: *I am singing; he was dancing.* (29J)

pronoun A word that takes the place of a noun and functions in the same ways that nouns do. Types of pronouns are demonstrative, indefinite, intensive, interrogative, personal, reciprocal, reflexive, and relative. (28C)

pronoun–antecedent agreement The match required between a pronoun and its antecedent in number and person, including personal pronouns and their gender. (31O)

pronoun case The way a pronoun changes form to reflect its use as the agent of action (*subjective case*), the thing being acted upon (*objective case*), or the thing showing ownership (*possessive case*). (30A–30K)

pronoun reference The relationship between a pronoun and its antecedent. (30L–30S)

proofreading The act of reading a final draft to find and correct any spelling or mechanical mistakes, typing errors, or handwriting illegibility; the final step of the writing process. (5K)

proper noun A noun that names specific people, places, or things; it is always capitalized: *Tom Thumb, Buick.* (48E)

proposal or solution essays A piece of writing intended to persuade readers that a particular problem is best solved by the solution explained in that writing. (16A)

purpose Purposes for writing vary: to narrate, give information, analyze a text, argue or persuade, and evaluate. (4B)

quotation Repeating or reporting another person's words. *Direct quotation* repeats another's words exactly and encloses them in quotation marks. *Indirect quotation* reports another's words without quotation marks except around any words if they are repeated exactly from the source. Both direct and indirect quotation require documentation of the source to avoid plagiarism. (18B)

readers Readers are the audiences for writing; readers process material they read on the literal, inferential, and evaluative levels. (4C)

reciprocal pronoun The pronouns *each other* and *one another* referring to individual parts of a plural antecedent. (28C)

References The title of a list of sources at the end of a research paper or scholarly article or other written work used in many documentation styles, especially that of APA. (Ch. 26)

reflexive pronoun A pronoun that ends in *-self* and that reflects back to its antecedent: *They claim to support **themselves**.* (30K)

regular verb A verb that forms its past tense and past participle by adding *-ed* or *-d* to the simple form. Most English verbs are regular. (29D)

relative adverb An adverb that introduces an adjective clause: *The garage **where I usually park my car** was full.* (28G)

relative clause See *adjective clause.*

relative pronoun A pronoun—such as *who, which, that, whom, whoever,* and a few others—that introduces an adjective clause or sometimes a noun clause. (28P)

RENNS A memory aid for the specific, concrete details used to support a topic sentence in a paragraph: reasons, examples, names, numbers and the five sentences. (6F)

research A systematic process of gathering information to answer a question. (21A)

research log A diary of your research process; useful for keeping yourself organized and on track. (21G)

research or term paper A paper written using the results of research. (21C)

research question A question that provides a clear focus for your research and a goal for your writing process. (21F)

response essay Provides a summary of a source and gives your opinion—supported by reasons—about the source's ideas or quality. (20C)

restrictive clause A dependent clause that gives information necessary to distinguish whatever it modifies from others in the same category. In contrast to a nonrestrictive clause, a restrictive clause is not set off with commas. (30S)

restrictive element A word, phrase, or dependent clause that provides information essential to the understanding of the element it modifies. In contrast to a nonrestrictive element, a restrictive element is not set off with commas. Also see *nonrestrictive clause*. (42F)

revising A part of the writing process in which writers evaluate their rough drafts and, on the basis of their assessments, rewrite by adding, cutting, replacing, moving, and often totally recasting material. (5I)

rhetoric The art and skill of speaking and writing effectively. (6I)

rhetorical patterns Various techniques for presenting ideas to deliver a writer's intended message with clarity and impact, including logical, ethical, and emotional appeals. (3B) Rhetorical strategies involve stylistic techniques such as parallelism and planned repetition as well as patterns for organizing and developing writing such as illustration, description, and definition. (6H)

Rogerian argument An argument technique using principles developed by Carl Rogers in which writers strive to find common ground and thus assure readers who disagree with them that they understand others' perspectives. (15A)

role The position the writer is emphasizing for a given task; for example, student, client, taxpayer, parent, supervisor, helper, critic, or so on.

root The base part of a word; *useless*. (47H)

run-on sentence A sentence in which independent clauses run together without the required punctuation that marks them as complete units. Also known as a *fused sentence*. (Ch. 34)

sans serif Font types that do not have little "feet" or finishing lines at the top and bottom of each letter. (7C)

search engine An Internet-specific software program that can look through all files on Internet sites. (22C)

search strategy A systematic way of finding information on a certain topic. (21K)

secondary source A source that reports, analyzes, discusses, reviews, or otherwise deals with the work of someone else. It stands in contrast to a primary source, which is someone's original work or firsthand report. A reliable secondary source must be the work of a person with appropriate credentials, must appear in a respected publication or other medium, must be current or historically authentic, and must reflect logical reasoning. (21B)

second person See *person*.

sentence A group of words, beginning with a capitalized first word and ending with a final punctuation mark, that states, asks, commands, or exclaims something. A sentence must consist of at least one *independent clause*. A *simple sentence* consists of one independent clause. A *complex sentence* contains one independent clause and one or more dependent clauses. A *compound sentence* contains two or more independent clauses joined by a coordinating conjunction. A *compound-complex sentence* contains at least two independent clauses and one or more dependent clauses. (28K–28Q)

sentence fragment A portion of a sentence that is punctuated as though it were a complete sentence. (Ch. 33)

sentence outline A type of outline in which each element is a sentence. (5F)

sentence variety Writing sentences of various lengths and structures; see *coordinate sentence, cumulative sentence, periodic sentence, sentence.* (38B)

serif Font types that are characterized by little "feet" or finishing lines at the top and bottom of each letter. (7C)

server A computer that is always online and available to Internet users. (63F)

sexist language Language that unfairly or unnecessarily assigns roles or characteristics to people on the basis of gender. Language that avoids gender stereotyping is called *gender-neutral* or *nonsexist language.* (37I)

shift An unnecessary change within a sentence in person, number, voice, tense, or other grammatical framework that makes a sentence unclear. (36A–36E)

short quotation A direct quotation that occupies no more than four lines of type in an MLA-style source-based paper (for prose) or no more than three lines of poetry. In an APA-style source-based paper, a short quotation has no more than forty words of prose. Short quotations are enclosed in quotation marks. (46B)

simile A comparison, using *like* or *as,* of otherwise dissimilar things. (37H)

simple form Part of a verb, the simple form shows action, occurrence, or state of being taking place in the present. It is used in the singular for first and second person and in the plural for first, second, and third person. Simple forms divide time into past, present, and future. (29B, 29G)

simple predicate See *predicate.*

simple sentence See *sentence.*

simple subject See *subject.*

simple tenses The present, past, and future tenses, which divide time into present, past, and future. (29G)

singular See *number.*

slang Coined words and new meanings for existing words, which quickly pass in and out of use. Slang is inappropriate for most academic writing except when used intentionally as such. See *colloquial language.*

slanted language Language that tries to manipulate the reader with distorted facts. (37J)

source A print or online book, article, document, CD, other work, or person providing information in words, music, pictures, or other media. (21B)

specialized database A database of sources covering a specific discipline or topic. (22C)

specialized reference work A reference work (such as a dictionary, encyclopedia, biographical compendium) covering a specific discipline or topic. (22H)

specific noun A noun understood to be exactly and specifically referred to; uses the definite article *the.* (53A)

split infinitive One or more words coming between the two words of an infinitive. (35B)

squinting modifier A modifier that is considered misplaced because it isn't clear whether it describes the word that comes before it or the word that follows it. (35A)

standard edited English Written usage of the American English language, expected in academic writing, that conforms to mainstream rules of grammar, sentence structure, punctuation, spelling, and mechanics. Sometimes it is referred to as *standard English,* but given the diversity of dialects in the United States today, the term *standard* is less descriptive than it once was. (37B)

standard word order The most common sentence pattern in English, which places the subject before the verb. (38R, Ch. 54)

stereotype A kind of hasty generalization (a *logical fallacy*) in which a sweeping claim is made about all members of a particular ethnic, racial, religious, gender, age, or political group. (37I)

style The manner in which a writer expresses his or her ideas. (37A)

subject The word or group of words in a sentence that acts, is acted upon, or is described by the verb. A *simple subject* includes only the noun or pronoun. A *complete subject* includes the noun or pronoun and all its modifiers. A *compound subject* includes two or more nouns or pronouns and their modifiers. (28L)

subject complement A noun or adjective that follows a linking verb, renaming or describing the subject of the sentence. (28N)

subject directories Lists of topics or resources and services, with links to sources on those topics and resources. An alternative to keyword searches. (22E)

subjective case The case of the noun or pronoun functioning as a subject. Also see *case*. (30A)

subject–verb agreement The required match in number and person between a subject and a verb. (31B–31N)

subjunctive mood The verb orientation that expresses wishes, recommendations, indirect requests, speculations, and conditional statements: *I wish you were here.* (29L)

subordinate clause See *dependent clause*.

subordinating conjunction A conjunction that introduces a dependent clause and expresses a relationship between the word and the idea in the independent clause. (28I)

subordination The use of grammatical structures to reflect the relative importance of ideas in a sentence. The most important information falls in the independent clause, and less important information falls in the dependent clause or phrases. (38D)

suffix Letters added at the end of a root word to change function or meaning: *useless.* (47H, 51C)

summary A critical thinking activity to extract the main message or central point of a passage or other discourse. (18D)

superlative The form of an adjective or adverb that expresses the greatest degree of quality among three or more things: *bluest; most easily.* (32E)

syllogism The structure of a deductive argument expressed in two *premises* and a *conclusion*. The first premise is a general assumption or statement of fact. The second premise is a different assumption or statement of fact based on evidence. The conclusion is also a specific instance that follows logically from the premises. (3H)

synonym A word that is close in meaning to another word. (5J)

synthesis A component of critical thinking in which material that has been summarized, analyzed, and interpreted is connected to what one already knows (one's prior knowledge) (3F) from reading or experiences. (3F)

tag sentence An inverted verb–pronoun combination added to the end of a sentence that "asks" the audience to agree with the assertion in the first part of the sentence: *You know what a tag question is,* ***don't you?*** A tag is set off from the rest of the sentence with a comma. (42G)

tense The time at which the action of the verb occurs: in the present, the past, or the future. (29G)

tense sequence In sentences that have more than one clause, the sequencing of verb forms to reflect logical time relationships. (29K)

thesis statement A statement of an essay's central theme that makes clear the main idea, the writer's purpose, the focus of the topic, and perhaps the organizational pattern. (5E)

third person See *person*.

title The part of an essay that clarifies the overall point of the piece of writing. It can be *direct* or *indirect*. (5I)

tone The quality, feeling, or attitude that a writer expresses. (37A)

topic The subject of discourse. (5C)

topic outline An outline in which items are listed as words or phrases, not full sentences. (5F)

topic sentence The sentence that expresses the main idea of a paragraph. (6E)

Toulmin model A model that defines the essential parts of an argument as the *claim* (or *main point*), the *support* (or *evidence*), and the *warrants* (or *assumptions behind the main point*). (15B)

transition The word or group of words that connects one idea to another in discourse. Useful strategies for creating transitions include transitional expressions, conjunctive adverbs, parallelism, and planned repetition of key words and phrases. (6G)

transitional expressions Words and phrases that signal connections among ideas and create coherence. (6G)

transitive verb A verb that must be followed by a direct object. (29F)

understatement Figurative language in which the writer uses deliberate restraint for emphasis. (37H)

unity The clear and logical relationship between the main idea of a paragraph and the evidence supporting the main idea. As a design principle, the term refers to whether the elements (color, text, images) work together visually. (7B)

URL *URL* is the abbreviation for *Universal* (or *Uniform*) *Resource Locator.* It is the online address of a site or page on the Web. (22C)

unstated assumptions Premises that are implied but not stated. (3E)

usage A customary way of using language. (37F)

valid Correctly and rationally derived; applied to a deductive argument whose conclusion follows logically from the premises. Validity applies to the structure of an argument, not its truth. (3H)

verb A word that shows action or occurrence, or that describes a state of being. Verbs change form to show time (tense), attitude (mood), and role of the subject (voice). Verbs occur in the predicate of a clause. Verbs can be parts of verb phrases, which consist of a main verb, any auxiliary verbs, and any modifiers. Verbs can be described as transitive or intransitive, depending on whether they take a direct object. (28D, Ch. 29)

verb phrase A main verb, along with any auxiliary verb(s) and any modifiers. (28O)

verbal A verb form that functions as a noun, adjective, or adverb. (28E)

verbal phrase A group of words that contains a verbal (an infinitive, participle, or gerund) and its modifiers. (28O)

voice Attribute of verbs showing whether the subject acts (active voice) or is acted upon (passive voice). (29N)

warrants The writer's underlying assumptions, which are often implied rather than stated, that connect reasons to claims. (15B)

Web site A collection of related files online that may include documents, images, audio, and video. Web sites typically have a *home page* that provides links to this content. (22C, 63F)

wiki A Web site that allows multiple readers to change its content. (63C)

wordiness Writing that is full of words and phrases that don't contribute to meaning. The opposite of *conciseness.* (Ch. 40)

word order The order in which words fall in most English sentences. Usually, the subject comes before the predicate. Inverted word order can bring emphasis to an idea. Multilingual writers are often accustomed to word orders in sentences other than those used in English. (Ch. 54)

working bibliography A preliminary annotated list of useful sources in research writing with a brief summary of each source. (21M)

Works Cited In MLA documentation style, the list of standardized information about all sources drawn upon in a research paper or other scholarly written work. (Ch. 25)

writer's block The desire to start writing, but not being able to do so. (5I)

writing portfolio A collection of written works, often the final project of a writing course. (8A)

writing process Stages of writing in which a writer plans, drafts, revises, edits, and proofreads. The stages often overlap. (5A)

writing situation Elements for writers to consider at the beginning of the writing process: their writing topic, purpose, audience, context, role, and special requirements. (5C)

CREDITS

"Times of Our Lives" by Karen Wright from *Scientific American*, September 2002; **page 210:** From "Post-Teenage Wasteland?" by Ann Hulbert, © 2005, *The New York Times Magazine;* **pages 217–218:** From "Too Many Choices" from *Consumer Reports on Health* by Ronni Sandoff; **Figure 21.4:** Screenshot from NoodleTools. Copyright © NoodleTools, Inc., http:///www.NoodleTools.com. Permission is given to reproduce this as a handout for teaching or training purposes; **Figure 21.5:** Screenshot from Diigo.com. Reprinted by permission of Diigo.com; **Figure 22.1:** Home Page of Arapahoe Community College Library. Photo courtesy of Lisa Grabowski. Reprinted by permission of Arapahoe Community College; **Figure 22.2:** PsycINFO search, reprinted with permission of the American Psychological Association, publisher of the PsycINFO ® Database. Copyright © 2005. All rights reserved. For more information, contact PsycINFO@apa.org; **Figure 22.3:** EBSCO Research search engine, copyright © 2012 by EBSCO Publishing, Inc. All rights reserved; **Figures 22.6, 22.7, 22.8, and 22.9:** Reprinted by permission of the University of Denver; **Figures 22.10 and 23.1a and b:** Courtesy of Google; **Figures 23.1c and d:** EBSCO Research Engine, Copyright © 2005 by EBSCO Publishing, Inc. All rights reserved; **Figure 25.2:** From "In the Name of Citizenship: The Writing Classroom and the Promise of Citizenship," by Amy J.Wan from *College English*, Volume 74, Number 1, September 2011. Copyright © 2011 by the National Council of Teachers of English. Reprinted by permission of National Council of Teachers of English; **Figure 25.8:** Screenshot of "What Predicts Crime?" by Andrew Sullivan from "The Dish: Biased and Balanced" from *The Daily Beast*, February 21, 2012. Reprinted by permission of The Newsweek/Daily Beast Company LLC. All rights reserved; **page 567:** From "If Only the Pilgrims Had Been Italian" by Thomas J. Craughwell from *The American Spectator*, November 21, 2007. Reprinted by permission of *The American Spectator;* **pages 568–569:** From "Google's Tar Pit" by Joshua Green from *The Atlantic*, December 2007. Reprinted by permission of *The Atlantic*.

PHOTOS

Page 3: © ImageZoo/Alamy; **page 4:** StockbrokerXtra/AGE Fotostock America; **page 7:** © Arco Images GmbH/Alamy; **page 9, top:** © Ian Shaw/Alamy; **page 9, bottom:** Susan Montgomery/Shutterstock; **page 19:** Doctors Without Borders/ Medecins San Frontieres (MSF). South Sudan © Jean-Marc Jacobs; **page 40:** Douglas Hesse; **page 42:** Paul Conklin/Taxi/Getty Images; **page 43, top:** Peter Vadnai; **page 43, bottom:** James McConnachie/Rough Guides/DK Images; **page 44:** Ad Council; **page 45, top:** Ad Council; **page 45, bottom:** Ad Council; **page 48:** Douglas Hesse; **page 108:** Douglas Hesse; **page 112, top:** Douglas Hesse; **page 112, bottom:** Douglas Hesse; **page 113:** Douglas Hesse; **page 116:** Douglas Hesse; **page 120:** Douglas Hesse; **page 330:** MIT Press; **page 763:** AP Images; **page 781:** Douglas Hesse.

INDEX

PROOFREADING MARKS AND RESPONSE SYMBOLS

Your instructor might use response symbols to show where writing should be edited or revised. You can use proofreading marks on hard copy for editing or revision.

PROOFREADING MARKS

⌃⃮ **delete**
take ~~this~~this out

¶ **new paragraph**
This is the end. This is a new beginning.

↶ **transpose letters**
transpoes letters

⌐¬ **transpose words**
words transpose

∧ **insert**
A caret signals an addition

\# **add space**
addspace

◡ **close up space**
clo se up space

(SP) **spell out**
They live in (WI.) SP

rom **use roman type**
That sounds (silly) rom

ital **use italic type**
Washington Post ital

(cap) **use capital letters**
anne tyler cap

(lc) **use lowercase letters**
Drive North and then East. lc

RESPONSE SYMBOLS

ab	abbreviation error	686–690
ad	adjective or adverb error	519–527
ca	pronoun case error	486–495
cap	needs a capital letter	677–683
cl	revise a cliché	578–579
coh	needs coherence	92–97
coord	faulty coordination	585–586, 592–593
cs	comma splice	537–546
dev	needs development	85, 91–104
dm	dangling modifier	550–551
e	needs exact language	573–574
emph	needs emphasis	583, 593–597
frag	sentence fragment	527–537
hyph	hyphen needed	674–676, 693
inc	incomplete sentence	527–537
ital	italics error	683–686
k	awkward	546–551
lc	needs lowercase letter	677–683
mixed	mixed construction	557–561
mm	misplaced modifier	546–550
¶	new paragraph	85–104
no ¶	no new paragraph	85–104
//	faulty parallelism	598–604
pass	passive voice	485–486
pl	faulty plural	694–695
pro agr	pronoun agreement error	514–519
pro ref	pronoun reference error	495–502
p	punctuation error	616–676
,/	comma error	620–639
;/	semicolon error	640–644
:/	colon error	645–649
ᵛ	apostrophe error	649–654
"/"	quotation marks error	655–663
rep	too much repetition	609
shift	sentence shift	552–557
sl	revise slang	572
sp	spelling error	693–703
subord	subordination error	586–593
sxt	sexist language	517, 576–578
t, tense	verb tense error	475–482
trans	needs transition	93–95, 104
u	needs unity	92–97
us	usage error	UG-1–UG-11
v	verb form error	465–475
v agr	verb agreement error	503–514
var	needs sentence variety	582–597
w	wordy	605–613
wc	word choice error	571–574
ww	wrong word	564–582

Detailed Contents